TRADE IN THE
21ST CENTURY

TRADE IN THE 21ST CENTURY

BACK TO THE PAST?

Edited by
BERNARD HOEKMAN
ERNESTO ZEDILLO

BROOKINGS INSTITUTION PRESS
Washington, D.C.

The Brookings Institution is a private nonprofit organization devoted to research, education, and publication on important issues of domestic and foreign policy. Its principal purpose is to bring the highest quality independent research and analysis to bear on current and emerging policy problems. Interpretations or conclusions in Brookings publications should be understood to be solely those of the authors.

Library of Congress Control Number: 2020948922

ISBN 9780815729044 (pbk)
ISBN 9780815729051 (ebook)

9 8 7 6 5 4 3 2 1

Typeset in Avenir Next and Janson
Composition by Westchester Publishing Services

CONTENTS

PART III
ECONOMIC DEVELOPMENT AND THE TRADING SYSTEM

PREFACE

A TRIBUTE TO PATRICK MESSERLIN

This volume was conceived to honor Patrick Messerlin, a teacher, colleague, and friend to all the contributors. Patrick has spent much of his professional career doing highly insightful and policy-relevant applied economic research. In pointing out the economic costs of policies affecting trade in agricultural products, manufacturing, and services, he did not make many friends among the officials and politicians of his country, France, or in the European Commission. Patrick has always gone where the data and evidence took him, in the process making important contributions to both the economic literature and public policy debates.

The journey to publication of this book began in December 2011 when we organized a conference at the Yale Center for the Study of Globalization to celebrate Patrick's achievements and contributions as he prepared to retire from Sciences Po. Participants were invited to write papers related to the theme "Trade in the 21st Century: Back to the Past?" reflecting on the implications of the major changes that had occurred since the early to mid-1980s when many countries began engaging seriously in unilateral trade liberalization and pursuing a process of deregulation and privatization.

As we sought a motivational framework for the gathering, we raised several fundamental questions: What are implications for trade policy broadly defined, and more specifically for international cooperation in the trade area? Have the incentives to use the discriminatory policies that are subject to WTO rules really changed? Is there greater mileage in a return to a unilateral policy reform focus? Has the global focus on dealing with trade restrictions and distortions through a mercantilist process been a mistake, and do we need to go back to the past and make the case for unilateral reforms that will raise national welfare independent of what other countries do? Are we heading back to a balance-of-power world in economic relations (a la Bismarck's nineteenth century)—with major countries and blocs—North America, a China bloc, the European Union—focused on improving their terms of trade?

It was with this theme and these questions in mind that we issued our invitations. The response from Patrick's colleagues was overwhelmingly positive. An impressive range of scholars wanted to participate, some of whom Patrick had inspired and some of whom he had taught.

At the gathering, many began their remarks by paying personal tribute to Patrick and his influence on their work. Anne Krueger noted that he had been "a key contributor to our understanding of the costs of protectionist measures and the benefits of an integrated international economy. He's also been, in my judgment, more than most of us, exceptionally brave, taking on sacred cows in Europe and in France in a time when the opinion of policymakers is firmly set in other directions, and when the likelihood that opinion might change seemed discouragingly small." Simon Evenett commented, "What I took away from what Patrick had taught us is that, in some sense, the most important thing is to get to and understand the heart of the problem and to hell with whether or not it's convenient or makes you look good as a theorist or good as an econometrician." Alan Winters remarked, "We all owe Patrick a great debt for his companionship and intellectual leadership. Patrick once thanked me because he said just occasionally he was only the second most unpopular person in Brussels and that I had displaced him from the top spot. So, I'm very pleased to pay tribute to my comrade in arms."

Jagdish Bhagwati sent a message stating, "Patrick's contributions to our understanding of the cost of protection, and his relentless writings on it in the public policy space, have served the cause of enlightened trade policy, through thick and (often) thin. If we did not have Patrick in our midst, we would have had to invent him." This testimonial was particularly poignant to those of us who had heard Patrick explain that he essentially taught himself international trade theory by reading Professor Bhagwati's publications because Bhagwati's work—and that of other like-minded free trade economists—was not part of the curriculum at the time in France.

Patrick has been a leader in the analysis of the political economy of trade policy, with a special interest in the European case. His 2001 book on European trade policy is among his most cited publications and remains a standard text for anyone interested in understanding the EU's commercial policy. His early empirical studies of the political economy of antidumping were pathbreaking, and his insights regarding the incoherence that exists between trade and competition policy were particularly prescient and remain very relevant today. Patrick was among the first trade economists to think seriously about services trade policy, the links between trade and domestic regulatory policies, and the political economy drivers of subsidy programs. The latter led to an innovative project to determine and publicize the allocation of agricultural subsidies in France, in which he and several of his students helped to raise public awareness of the extent to which the benefits of EU agricultural support programs accrued to large and profitable farmers rather than to smallholders. A recurring feature of Patrick's professional contributions is his willingness—and ability—to document uncomfortable facts that those in authority would rather not confront. He has consistently addressed trade policy questions that have important practical implications rather than writing for a purely academic audience, pointing to the costs of protectionist policies, including in sectors given little attention by mainstream economists.

An example is his analysis of protectionist policies to promote or safeguard (French) culture, a subject of Patrick's research after retiring from Sciences Po. A visiting professorship in Korea led him to become interested in the drivers of the K-pop export phenomenon, which led to a large research project on trade in cultural products and related trade and industrial policies. At the time of this writing in 2020, the project has generated two edited volumes. Patrick remains very active and continues to cultivate fields that are neglected by others.

We have long been inspired by Patrick's example and have been privileged to work with and learn from him. As this book goes to press, it appears the world is regressing toward the types of discriminatory trade policies that he has done so much to analyze. The chapters in this volume by his friends and students illustrate that his example of undertaking careful empirical analysis of issues where multilateral solutions are called for is being emulated. And their contributions demonstrate that the need for such analysis and engagement is ever more urgent.

In closing, we would like to thank each of the accomplished contributors to this volume, who throughout the rather lengthy period from conference to publication obligingly updated their papers, in some cases twice. Their dedication to this project is indisputable proof of the breadth and depth of Patrick Messerlin's influence. We would also like to thank Haynie

Wheeler for her cheerful and expert management of the publication process and working closely with authors and Brookings to bring this project to fruition. We are also grateful to Matteo Fiorini for his help in updating data and generating some of the graphs and to Elena Cau and Jo Wielgo for their help in managing the financial and administrative side of this project at the Robert Schuman Centre for Advanced Studies. Finally, we wish to acknowledge the support provided to some of the authors by the European Union's Horizon 2020 research and innovation program under grant agreement No 770680 (RESPECT).

Bernard Hoekman
European University Institute

Ernesto Zedillo
Yale University

INTRODUCTION

THE INTERNATIONAL TRADING SYSTEM IN PROSTRATION, COURTESY OF THE UNITED STATES

BERNARD HOEKMAN AND ERNESTO ZEDILLO

Just as the WTO Doha Round reached its tenth anniversary in 2011, the Yale Center for the Study of Globalization convened a group of distinguished trade policy experts with a twofold purpose: one, to celebrate the admirable career of Patrick Messerlin as he was retiring from his long-held tenure as professor of international economics at Sciences Po in Paris; two, to undertake that celebration by deliberating about several critical issues and circumstances faced by the international trading system.

Notwithstanding our enthusiasm to acknowledge Patrick's numerous and valuable contributions to our common subject of interest, the mood prevailing throughout our discussions was rather somber.[1] After all, it was the tenth anniversary of the launching of the Doha Round of international trade talks whose successful conclusion was still nowhere in sight, despite many attempts, including the solemn commitment that the G-20 leaders had made at their September 2010 Pittsburgh summit, to get it done at the latest by the end of 2011, a promise clearly already broken when our group gathered at Yale in December.

We were equally concerned about the fragmentation of the trading system caused by the proliferation of regional trade agreements over the previous decade. We were also taking seriously the submission by one of our colleagues, Simon Evenett, that despite pledges made by the G-20 to reject

1

protectionism and boost world trade, the world was actually enduring "creeping protectionism," as evidenced in the regular reports on additional trade-restrictive actions across the globe produced by the admirable independent online monitor, the Global Trade Alert, that had been organized under his leadership in 2009.

Ironically, notwithstanding the rather grim prospects for international trade prevailing as our group met in New Haven in late 2011, in the early summer of 2020 it is tempting to look back with nostalgia at what were then our chief concerns about the rules-based trading system. Essentially, we were worried about the consequences—the lost economic opportunities of failing to reform and strengthen the system.

None of us could seriously entertain an imminent existential threat to the trading system. Indeed, some of our participants, despite the inauspicious circumstances, even envisioned a liberal international trading system that would continue to advance, as Michael Finger, a highly regarded trade expert, expressed in 2015 (and included as chapter 16 of this volume). Inspired by his study of the evolution of trade policy in Latin America, Mike was less worried about the lack of agreement within the WTO to further liberalize trade and update its governance rules than several other members of the group were at the time. His death in the summer of 2018 deprives us from knowing whether he would still hold an optimistic view about the likely evolution of the trading system considering recent events.

It was those recent events that motivated us to reactivate the group that had met back in 2011 and request updated versions of their original contributions to our 2011 discussion. As we began reading the new versions our colleagues sent in, our worry about the trading system being subject to stresses of a magnitude unprecedented since the 1930s was reaffirmed. Several of us, in the good company of many other trade scholars, are not shy to submit that the international trading system is under an existential threat. We argue here that this threat stems most directly and urgently from the protectionist US trade policies that have been piling up since early 2017. But as noted by Simon Evenett in chapter 6 of this volume, the trade policy trends have been negative since 2008. Pre-Trump there was already a steady buildup of trade discrimination, with many G-20 members putting in place both trade-restrictive and potentially competition-distorting export-promoting measures.

The Global Trade Alert data document that, notwithstanding the loose proclivity to use tariffs by some of the major trading countries, higher import tariffs are not yet the central feature of global trade policy dynamics. More than half of the measures that have been put in place are subsidies of some sort. This is not to say that tariffs and other traditional types of trade policies do not matter. As discussed by Chad Bown in chapter 2, emerging economies have been active users as well as targets of instruments such as antidumping actions—a policy tool used intensively by the European Union (EU), the United States, and other member nations of the Organization for Economic Cooperation and Development (OECD) in the 1980s to restrain import competition.[2]

Many of the chapters in this volume highlight both long-standing sources of international spillovers created by domestic policies such as agriculture (chapter 8 by Anne Krueger) and subsidies (chapter 9 by Bernard Hoekman and Douglas Nelson), and new challenges such as digital trade (chapter 10 by Erik van der Marel) and policy areas where global collective action is urgently needed, notably climate change and the role trade policy can play in greening economies (chapter 11 by Patrick Low). Moving forward on these important subjects calls for multilateral cooperation. It is pertinent to recall that in the 1980s, the complex web of import restrictions put in place to manage competition from East Asian countries and interest in expanding the trading system to include protection of intellectual property and trade in services resulted in the agreement to launch the Uruguay Round of multilateral trade negotiations.

Until recently, whether a similar dynamic would emerge or, instead, the world economy would splinter into regional arrangements centered on the United States, the EU, and countries in the Asia-Pacific, seemed to be the relevant concern. As noted by Alan Winters in chapter 4, the prospects for both multilateral cooperation in the World Trade Organization (WTO) and the implications of stronger regional bloc formation depend importantly on what China would do and the approach taken by the major OECD countries toward China. At present, however, the most relevant question is how deep and lasting the dramatic shift that has taken place in the trade policy of the United States will be, purportedly to better pursue its own national interest. The latter being a legitimate objective, it is essential to inquire whether the trade actions taken by the US government are truly consistent with the country's economic and geopolitical interests.

THE MYSTERY OF THE TPP WITHDRAWAL

On the third day of his administration in 2017, President Donald Trump signed an executive order to withdraw the United States from the successfully concluded Trans-Pacific Partnership (TPP) agreement. This action can be considered emblematic of the new administration's trade policy if only because it is impossible to find any economic or geopolitical justification for it or any meaningful domestic political reason that could override the benefits the country was bound to derive from its TPP membership.

It is not an exaggeration to say that the TPP was constructed to satisfy the interests and demands, as well as the standards and practices, of the United States to a much greater extent than any other previous trade agreement.[3] The American negotiators found the arguments and, perhaps more important, the leverage to make their TPP counterparts accept conditions that from the US perspective unquestionably improved upon previous regional and multilateral agreements. The US representatives pushed hard and got the most ambitious commitments to trade liberalization and related disciplines ever agreed in a trade deal. This is a highly significant fact because, among other reasons, the accord was made by a rather heterogenous group of countries—with significant variance in both the level of income (absolute and per capita) and the structure of gross domestic product (GDP).

The TPP required fast elimination of most tariffs with few exceptions, even in agriculture, a sector historically resistant to serious trade liberalization. Progress was also achieved in other areas traditionally excluded from trade agreements or subject to only weak disciplines, including subsidies and government procurement. One such area was state-owned enterprises (SOEs) where several key provisions were adopted to ensure a level playing field between SOEs and private enterprises (foreign and domestic).

The TPP covered investment as well as trade policies. It improved on existing bilateral investment agreements as it extended and reinforced obligations to provide nondiscriminatory treatment to foreign investors. These investment policy commitments were particularly important for services, where the market opening provided by the TPP was less ambitious. Investors in service activities, where foreign investment is allowed, were provided with both security and non-discriminatory treatment under the TPP, which also established an investor-state dispute settlement mechanism, an instrument aligned with the interests of US companies. The investment provisions were further complemented by disciplines on competition, which were more stringent than in previous preferential trade agreements (PTAs) signed by the United States.

The agreement went significantly beyond existing WTO and PTA provisions on the crucial issues of labor and environment, at least for political economy purposes. Less popular among some American constituencies was the clear win achieved by the US private sector in the protection of intellectual property rights, where the pharmaceutical industry got protections that considerably surpass those in the WTO.

Interestingly, the TPP prohibited signatories from having exchange rate misalignments and undertaking competitive devaluations—a demand put forward repeatedly by US officials. Furthermore, the agreement, for all practical purposes, got rid of the long-standing special and differential treatment in favor of developing countries, which although contained in other trade treaties including those of the WTO, is now much vilified by US officials.

Mysteriously, the TPP, patently crafted to accommodate US demands, proved to be too much of a good thing for the Trump administration, which proceeded to discard it and thus caused the United States to incur not only a meaningful economic cost but also a substantial loss in geopolitical influence in a critical part of the world.[4] After the US withdrawal, the eleven remaining TPP signatories slightly modified the agreement and signed it in Chile in March 2018 under the name Comprehensive and Progressive Agreement for Trans-Pacific Partnership (CPTPP). The decision to undertake this accord without the involvement of the United States may well prove to be a template for action in a world with American self-exclusion.

THE MYSTERY OF NEGLECTING ESSENTIAL ECONOMIC PRINCIPLES

Other than claiming that the withdrawal from the TPP was a great thing for the American worker because it was a terrible deal and a potential disaster for the country, the Trump administration never really provided any economic rationale for that action, which makes it practically impossible to inquire seriously into the validity of the decision. However, there is more information about the purported reasons for other trade policy actions by the Trump administration and therefore some grounds on which to check their soundness.

In a nutshell, the US administration has referred to four ideas that seem to provide the premises for its trade policy activism: one, to make trade fair and reciprocal; two, to induce the return of manufacturing jobs to the United States; three, to reduce bilateral trade imbalances; four, to fix the US overall trade and current account deficits.

American officials seem to imply that somehow the country's trading partners have managed to extract deals or simply get away with bad behavior conducive to trade surpluses that have drained manufacturing jobs from the US economy. The corollary of this view is that correcting, one by one, the existing bilateral trade imbalances—themselves the expression, in their opinion, of the unfairness and lack of reciprocity endured by the United States in its trade relations—not only would lead to gaining back lost manufacturing jobs but also to correcting the trade (and current account) deficit that for many years has been a feature of the American economy. Negotiating, one by one, new rules of engagement with trade partners has proven the preferred US approach to attempting such a correction.

The problem with this peculiar narrative is that it defies both reality and sound international economics. Take, for example, the concept of comparative advantage, which simply means that, with free trade, countries will tend to export goods that they produce relatively efficiently (with a low opportunity cost) and import goods that they produce relatively inefficiently (with a high opportunity cost). This implies that as firms and households in a country engage in international trade, an efficient outcome would entail a changing pattern of production—relatively more of some things and relatively less of others. This shift in production, which provides the opportunity to exchange goods and services in international markets, is what provides the gains in national income that countries derive from trade. It is not possible to have the latter without the former.

That an open economy like the United States—as it grew richer with increasing average productivity of its labor force—changed its productive structure, certainly to the detriment of traditional manufacturing sectors, should not come as a surprise. In fact, that structural shift is a robust measure of the country's great success. Had the United States still been producing the same products and with the same labor intensity that it did in the 1950s and 1960s, it would be a considerably less rich country than it is now, and its post-baby-boom labor force, by virtue of holding jobs like the ones their parents and grandparents had, would be a group of very unhappy (and poor) people.

The shift in countries like the United States toward employing relatively fewer people in traditional manufacturing has been heightened by fast technological progress, itself a very positive development but also a chief cause of phenomena such as labor force displacement, increasing skill premiums, and deepening wage inequality. These effects frequently are wrongly attributed purely to trade. Technological change, particularly in transportation and information technology has led to the fragmentation of production processes into complex global supply chains, a process in which US workers, as far as quality and compensation of jobs are concerned, have been clear beneficiaries. In modern manufacturing, most value is accrued in the preassembly and postassembly stages of production, thus rendering what is known as the smile curve (when value added is mapped against stages of production). It is in the higher-value-adding jobs of global manufacturing supply chains where US designers, technologists, entrepreneurs, engineers, financiers, and marketeers get employed (Baldwin 2013).

It is curious that some political leaders express so much longing for old-fashioned manufacturing jobs while not acknowledging the better jobs that open markets and technological progress bring. In short, those politicians are disregarding the benefits of production and trade specialization driven by comparative advantage, which is an old and sound economic principle. Almost as old, and equally sound, is the conceptual and empirical insight that free trade, simply by changing relative prices of both the products and the factors of production, is bound to change a country's income distribution and, depending on a host of factors, possibly in a regressive manner. This is why a conventional posture of the economics profession is that trade liberalization must be accompanied by other policy actions with a view to mitigating or even fully compensating those distributional effects that are deemed undesirable.

The mistaken picture of trade as a bellicose zero-sum game is completed by neglecting another basic economic principle: that the external balance of an economy is determined by the difference between gross domestic product and gross national expenditure. This is not high-powered economic theory but rather an expression of the elementary national income identity taught at the outset in elementary macroeconomics. Notwithstanding its simplicity, the identity is insightful, for it suggests that variables more directly influencing national income and expenditure can be more effective than trade instruments to balance a country's external accounts. It also suggests that focusing on bilateral imbalances is a totally idle exercise. If a country expends more than its national income it will have a deficit.

In short, ignoring the essential insights stemming both from the notion of comparative advantage and the basic national income identity of an open economy leads to using the wrong instrument—protectionism—to pursue two policy objectives: a change in the production and trade mix of the economy and a correction of its external imbalance. This undertaking is wrongheaded in its entirety for it causes harm to the US economy that is self-inflicted.

THE MYSTERY OF RENEGOTIATING NAFTA

Candidate Trump characterized the North American Free Trade Agreement (NAFTA) as "the worst trade deal maybe ever signed anywhere but certainly ever signed in this country" and committed to renegotiate it to make it "a great deal" or otherwise to "tear it up." It thus came as no surprise when, shortly after becoming president, his administration announced officially that it would initiate negotiations to update the agreement with Canada and Mexico.

The talks started off on the wrong foot, considering that in July 2017 the US Trade Representative (USTR), when formally explaining the objectives of the renegotiation, asserted that, because of NAFTA, the United States' "trade deficits have exploded, thousands of factories have closed, and millions of Americans have found themselves stranded" (Office of the United States Trade Representative 2017, 2).[5] There is not a single serious study anywhere that would support or give credence to this bizarre statement. It is therefore an enigma why the US officials included it along with other arguments that actually did make some sense, like the fact that NAFTA had been in place for almost a quarter of a century and therefore warranted certain updates in light of developments such as growth in electronic trade, and evolving views on matters such as intellectual property rights, protection of the environment, and labor and regulatory standards.

The rather awkward demands made by the American negotiators over practically the entire first year of talks made it hard to believe that the US government really wanted to modernize the old NAFTA. It looked rather as if their chief objective was to destroy trade and investment among the three North American partners to the point of making the agreement ineffective and even counterproductive. For too long the US representatives insisted on demands such as that trade in goods should be balanced—presumably by fiat, not by markets; a sunset clause that would terminate the agreement every five years unless the three governments agreed otherwise; a set of highly convoluted and discriminatory rules of origin (chiefly against Mexican exports) for the automotive industry; the freedom to impose seasonal antidumping tariffs on fruits and vegetables; nonreciprocal rules (favoring the United States) in government procurement; and making the NAFTA investor-state dispute settlement system optional, which would have allowed the United States to withdraw at any moment, thereby discouraging US firms from investing in Mexico and Canada.

Fortunately, the Mexican and Canadian governments did not cave to these peculiar demands and repeatedly submitted that they would rather take the unilateral termination of NAFTA as threatened by the American president than accept an agreement that would have the same practical consequence of killing the existing trade and investment opportunities among the three partners. To get a deal, the United States had to water down most of its positions. The most significant US demand accommodated by Mexico and Canada was in the automotive sector, where more restrictive and cumbersome rules of origin were accepted. It was agreed that 75 percent of any vehicle (as compared to the 85 percent that had been demanded by the United States) should contain components from North America to qualify for tariff-free imports, up from the NAFTA level of 62.5 percent; that 70 percent of the steel and aluminum used in the sector would also have to be from North America; and that 40 percent of a car or truck must be made by workers earning at least $16 per hour, a requirement clearly intended to dent Mexico's comparative advantage and establishing a delicate precedent of discriminatory rules of origin within a free trade agreement.

If effective, the new rules of origin would reduce both the regional and global competitiveness of the North American automotive industry and have bad consequences for its workers in the three countries. Fortunately, this adverse effect is limited in the case of cars because, if the rules fail to be met, cars could be exported by paying the most favored nation (MFN) tariff of 2.5 percent as long as total exports did not exceed an agreed number of vehicles; that number exceeded the existing level of exports, though only slightly in the case of Mexico. For trucks, however, the new rules of origin will almost certainly be binding since the MFN tariff is 25 percent.[6] On balance, there should be no doubt that the North American automotive industry as a whole will lose international competitiveness, a circumstance that makes it more likely that the United States will impose tariffs on cars from Europe, Japan, and Korea, a step that could give rise to retaliatory measures by those trade partners.

Although the original five-year sunset clause demand was dropped, the agreed provision instituting a revision of the instrument after six years and its extension after sixteen years only if affirmed by the partners, does introduce significant uncertainty about the stability of the pact, which obviously does not encourage investment. The same consequence is to be expected from the mutilations applied to the Investor-State Dispute Settlement, which practically disappeared for issues between Canada and the United States and was severely curtailed for cases between the United States and Mexico. In the new agreement, inequitably Mexico loses the protection from the arbitrary imposition of antidumping and countervailing duties that the NAFTA binational arbitration procedure provided, while Canada retains such protection.[7]

Curiously, the good parts of the renegotiated agreement are also somewhat redundant, at least for the United States. The CPTPP already contains most of the modernizing features of the United States-Mexico-Canada Agreement (USMCA) on intellectual property rights, e-commerce, and data. By signing the CPTPP, Mexico and Canada had already granted the United States the stronger disciplines on those aspects because of that instrument's commitment to nondiscrimination. In short, it is a total mystery what true advantages the United States will derive from launching a new agreement.

Disturbingly, the conclusion of the USMCA negotiations, while tempering US trade rhetoric against its North American partners, did not put an end to its hostile economic actions. For one thing, it took much longer than expected—until mid-May 2019—to exempt those neighbors from the tariffs that the United States imposed rather arbitrarily in early 2018 on steel and aluminum imports. By contrast, the Mexican and Canadian governments immediately fulfilled their commitment to suspend the retaliatory tariffs that they themselves had imposed on certain US exports.

Unfortunately, trade peace between the United States and Mexico did not last long. By the end of the same month, additional steel and aluminum tariffs were removed, President Trump was threatening to impose a 5 percent tariff on all imports from Mexico in June and to increase it by 5 percentage points every month until reaching 25 percent permanently by October if Mexico did not intensify its efforts to curb Central American migration at its southern border. Although the two governments were able to strike a deal that prevented the imposition of the announced tariffs, an extremely dangerous precedent of linking trade and migration issues in a very negative way was established. Consenting on more liberal migration policies as a sequel to significant trade openings has not been unusual; that is how single markets are born. But it is anomalous to impose on a country a specific migration policy under the threat of unilateral trade sanctions in circumvention of existing bilateral and multilateral agreements.[8]

THE MYSTERY OF THE TRADE WAR WITH CHINA

The unwarranted rough treatment of its North American trade partners pales in comparison with the trade aggressiveness displayed by the US government against China. Step by step, from initial moves that had not yet singled out China—first with tariffs on solar panels and washing machines and then on steel and aluminum products in early 2018—to the imposition of tariffs on imports specifically from China announced initially in March 2018 and extended repeatedly ever since, the Trump administration has set off an authentic trade war practically without precedent since the one that took place in the 1930s. To every US announcement of new tariffs, starting with the ones on steel and aluminum imports, China, not surprisingly, responded in kind, albeit in a measured and strategic way.

In chapter 4 of this volume, Alan Winters discusses the underlying economic dynamics that help us to understand the trade tensions that emerged following China's decision to reintegrate into the world economy in the 1980s. The speed and magnitude of China's growth and ability to leverage trade opportunities to support its economic development are historically unprecedented. China's rapid export growth led many countries to take measures to reduce import competition, as permitted by the WTO (Messerlin 2004),[9] as did concerns that some of the policies implemented in China are inadequately regulated by the WTO.[10] However, rather than using the WTO as a mechanism to agree on rules to manage the externalities that such policies may create, the United States has chosen to pursue an aggressive unilateral path.

The resulting tit-for-tat tariff exchange between the United States and China has transformed a formerly quite open trade relationship into one that threatens to set back the clock of their trade integration by forty years. Chad Bown, a meticulous observer of the American administration's trade actions, has calculated that if all the tariffs announced in 2018 and 2019 had materialized, the average US tariff on imports from China would have risen from 3.1 percent in 2017 to 24.3 percent by December 15, 2019, and would cover 96.8 percent of all products exported by China to the United States. Bown estimates that average US tariffs on Chinese products would be similar to the ones that the United States imposed with the infamous Smoot-Hawley Tariff Act of 1930 (Bown 2019).

In turn, China's announced retaliatory actions would have driven the average tariff on imports from the United States to 25.9 percent from 8 percent before the trade hostilities started. Yet, absent additional measures, 31 percent of US exports to China—including aircraft, semiconductors, and pharmaceuticals—would remain unaffected by the retaliatory tariffs, suggesting that China's reaction to the American trade hostilities was more restrained, particularly considering that China has taken no actions on US services exports and inward foreign direct investment (FDI) or played the card of disinvesting massively from US dollar-denominated financial assets. China, moreover, lowered its tariffs on imports from other countries, thus further reducing the competitiveness of US exports relative to third countries in the Chinese market.[11] The "phase 1" deal concluded by China and the United States in January 2020 retained the 25 percent tariffs imposed on $250 billion of Chinese exports but cut US tariffs on an additional $120 billion of Chinese exports imposed in September 2019 by 50 percent, to 7.5 percent, and suspended the US threat to impose punitive tariffs on those exports not already targeted by the United States. The main feature of the agreement was a promise by China to increase imports from the United States within two years by $200 billion more than the country had imported in 2017.[12] This explicitly mercantilist deal blatantly violates the fundamental rules of the WTO. It also makes no economic sense in that it is an exercise in trade diversion. The effect may be to put China into a position where it becomes a distributor of US goods for which there is global demand, importing and then re-exporting products to the rest of the world. This is a costly exercise that will increase trade transaction costs, but it will do nothing for US businesses.

Given how consequential the trade war against China could prove to be, inquiring about its rationale—or lack thereof—is even more important than in the case of other trade policy actions undertaken by the Trump administration. A logical place to start is with the formal arguments provided by the American government itself. The tariffs on imports of steel and aluminum announced on March 1, 2018—imposed not just against China but on imports from other trade partners and allies as well[13]—were purported to be necessary for reasons of US national security, allegedly in conformity internally with section 232 of the Trade Expansion of 1962 and externally with Article XXI of the General Agreement on Tariffs and Trade (GATT).[14]

Craig VanGrasstek, in chapter 3 of this volume, explains that presidents before Trump had used the national security provision only three times, and only against countries within the orbit of the Soviet Union. The European Union used the security invocation only twice during the GATT period, and like the United States, under conditions where the security reason was evident—restrictions against Argentina during the Falklands/Malvinas War and the withdrawal of preferential treatment to Yugoslavia right before its breakup. That the invocation of national security provisions was so infrequent over more than seven decades helps to explain why no country was asked to argue its security excuse before a dispute-settlement body.

Despite this antecedent, it is pertinent to determine whether the recent invocation by the United States is consistent with its WTO obligations. Of course, the US government would submit that it is. Interestingly, in its capacity as a third party in the WTO complaint by Ukraine against Russia regarding the latter's restrictions on traffic in transit from Ukraine through the Russian Federation,[15] the US government argued that the invocation of GATT Article XXI is self-judging and shall not be subject to review by a Dispute Settlement Understanding (DSU) Panel or the Appellate Body, in practice supporting Russia. Nevertheless, a WTO panel on the Ukrainian complaint was established and delivered its report in early April of 2019. It determined that WTO panels do have jurisdiction to review a government's invocation of the national security exception, thus rejecting the Russian and American assertion that the invocation of GATT Article XXI is wholly self-judging. However, the panel also determined that Russia's invocation of GATT Article XXI was justified given that the restrictive actions against Ukraine were taken during an emergency in international relations that has existed between the two countries since 2014.

The fact that the WTO panel found that it had jurisdiction to review whether a country had met the conditions for invoking national security as a justification for trade restrictions does not bode well for the US unilateral imposition of the steel and aluminum tariffs in effect since 2018—and others it has threatened on other products—on the basis of section 232 of the Trade Expansion Act of 1962. A WTO panel reviewing the WTO legality of the US steel and aluminum tariffs will find it difficult, if not impossible, to rely on the Russian case as a valid antecedent. Most US imports of steel and aluminum came from trade partners like Canada, Japan, Germany, Mexico, and other close allies. Very few of the imports came from countries the US government likes to see as adversarial, namely China and Russia.[16] Furthermore, over 70 percent of US steel demand is satisfied by domestic production.

It is bizarre that, on the eve of the third decade of the twenty-first century, trade in such basic metal commodities as steel and aluminum, or products like cars and trucks, can be posited as "strategic" from a national security perspective by any country. Such a claim could have been plausible a century ago, but not today. Not surprisingly, as reported by Bown and Irwin (2019), even the US Defense Department has been skeptical of the national security argument for imposing tariffs on steel and aluminum. VanGrasstek also argues that President Trump's reliance on the national security invocation is highly problematic, and characterizes it as an absurd, cynical, spurious, and abusive attempt to game the multilateral trading system, with the consequence of subjecting it to an existential threat.

The alleged reasons to impose tariffs on practically all Chinese exports to the United States are also questionable, to put it mildly. The "formal" justification started on August 14, 2017, with an instruction by President Trump to the USTR to investigate whether China "has implemented laws, policies, and practices and has taken actions related to intellectual property, innovation, and technology that may encourage or require the transfer of American technology and intellectual property to enterprises in China or that may otherwise negatively affect American economic interests."[17] The investigation, under section 301 of the Trade Act of 1974, was initiated a few days later and concluded with the report delivered by the USTR on March 22, 2018. On the same day, President Trump announced that tariffs on up to $60 billion on imports from China were forthcoming based on the section 301 investigation.

A brief discussion of the report that purportedly convinced the US government to launch the first great trade war of the twenty-first century is salient here. A first observation concerns the category of actions (acts, policies, and practices) that the USTR decided to inquire into and report about. Section 301 may be used to address trade agreement violations; actions that are inconsistent with US international legal rights; and actions that are unreasonable or discriminatory and that burden or restrict US commerce. Tellingly, the USTR did not build its case on either of the first two categories but, rather, on the third—action unreasonable or discriminatory, that "while not necessarily in violation of, or inconsistent with, the international legal rights of the United States, is otherwise unfair and inequitable" (US Congress, 1974, 3).[18]

One can only speculate why the USTR opted to go after the weaker, more ambiguous, and subjective violation contemplated in section 301. One plausible explanation is that USTR lawyers were aware that the actions they were mandated to investigate were hardly in violation of US rights stemming either from trade agreements or international law and therefore had to look for legally "softer" violations to report. Their inclination to do so perhaps was encouraged by the fact—as recognized at the outset in the USTR report—that the two other kinds of issues are justiciable in the WTO, an eventuality that most likely would have been profoundly distasteful to the Trump White House. By focusing on actions that are "unreasonable or discriminatory and that burden or restrict US commerce," the focus was put on something wherein the determination of violation (by China) would be purely unilateral while still being justified as legal under US statutes.

Key targets of the USTR are China's joint venture (JV) requirements and foreign equity limitations that, along with administrative approval processes, are allegedly used to extract commitments of transfer of technology from foreign investors. There is little hard evidence offered for this in the report. The report states that after WTO accession in 2001, to comply with its new obligations, China formally gave up its former practice of mandating technology transfers. However, it goes on to note that "since then, according to numerous sources, China's technology transfer policies and practices have become more implicit, often carried out through oral instructions and 'behind closed doors.'"[19] In fact, the report affirms that Chinese officials do not put their requirements in writing. We are asked to believe somehow that US companies, with a well-earned reputation for being law abiding, take improper verbal instructions from Chinese bureaucrats in secret and compromise the value of their businesses—by giving away proprietary technology—making sure that they do not leave any written trace of their bad behavior.

More plausible is the case, also put forward in the 301 report, that the pressure on foreign investors to be generous with their technology comes through their chosen local JV partners. If this were the case, it seems pertinent to believe that such JVs happen in sectors where Chinese law does not allow full foreign ownership—a circumstance that exists in varying degrees in practically all countries, including the United States—without violating any international legal obligation. When a foreign company nevertheless decides to do business in China, it is then expected that the economic value of the knowhow to be transferred is adequately accounted for in the corresponding cost-benefit analysis. Whether to enter into a JV becomes essentially a business decision. Of course, that company's home country may be entitled, by domestic and international law, to prohibit or place conditions on the transfer of certain technologies that company possesses and may proceed to exercise that right, as does happen from time to time, not least in the United States.

In sectors where there is no restriction on wholly foreign-owned enterprises (WFOEs) the Chinese government lacks legal capacity, but also has very limited practical capacity to force the feared technology transfer. It is not surprising, as the 301 report itself indicates, that in those unrestricted sectors, foreign companies prefer and do indeed have full ownership of their operations in China. Given the qualitative distinction between the case of JVs and WFOEs, it is extraordinary that the USTR report does not compare the quantitative importance of both vehicles to do business in China, at the very least to get an idea of the relative strength of the reputed arm twisting undertaken by China to forcefully acquire technology—granting, for the sake of argument, that such improper behavior has taken place.

The conspicuous omission of such a comparison is not due to lack of reliable information or research. For an excellent example of the latter, there is the work of Nicholas Lardy, who reports that, while in the early years of China's opening, practically none of the FDI into China was through fully owned foreign enterprises, in recent years as much as 70–80 percent of the total has been in that form (Lardy 2018). The claim that forced transfers of technology are pervasive in China, by means of use and abuse of JVs, simply cannot be objectively sustained. Nevertheless, that accusation is at the core of the formal justification of the US trade war with China.

That the core argument is at the very least questionable is something that must be considered in assessing the validity and severity of the actions undertaken by the Trump administration.

Admittedly, the USTR report deals with other alleged Chinese infractions. China is being accused of entertaining discriminatory licensing restrictions, encouraging certain outbound investments, committing cybercrimes to the detriment of American companies, supporting improperly and using inappropriately its state-owned enterprises, and even of having an industrial policy. The report concludes, as in the case of forced technology transfers through JVs, that China's acts, policies, and practices are unreasonable and burden or restrict US commerce. Granted—even in the face of weak supporting evidence offered in the 301 report—that there is some truth in those charges, there is the question of whether this warrants the massive trade hostilities initiated by the American government.

To answer that question, it is important first to distinguish among three kinds of actions imputed to the Chinese government: (1) actions that are legal and legitimate but are vilified as a result of unfairly applying a double standard or, even worse, that stem simply from enviousness and paranoia about China's economic successes over the last four decades; (2) actions that conform to the existing multilateral rules but create negative spillovers and should be the subject of a collective effort to update international standards consistent with the challenges of contemporary interdependence; and (3) actions that by any standard, present or conceivable for the future, are unacceptable—like outright theft of intellectual property (IP) or cybercriminality. Once such distinctions are accepted and the 301 report is analyzed in its entirety, it is impossible to find in it a sufficiently valid justification for the massive trade punitive measures taken against China by the Trump administration.

It is not a great stretch of imagination to infer that the authors of the report were also unconvinced that their findings could possibly be used to justify a massive trade war. Consider that, in addition to looking at the JVs, discriminatory licensing, cybercrimes, and misuse of SOEs, most of what it concluded were unreasonable practices burdening or restricting US commerce (reputedly a possible cause of sanctions) constituted "other acts, policies and practices of China." This heading comprised, among other things, inadequate protection of IP of American companies doing business in China and an alleged twisted use of China's cybersecurity, antimonopoly, and standardization laws. For these other alleged Chinese infractions, the report revealingly concludes:

> USTR acknowledges the importance of these issues and agrees with stakeholders that the matters warrant further investigation. . . . A range of tools may be appropriate to address these serious matters including more intensive bilateral engagement, WTO dispute settlement, and/or additional section 301 investigations.[20]

It is a mystery why this judicious consideration—that patently advises engagement in negotiations with China and reliance on the WTO—was not adopted for all the matters under investigation in the 301 report. The enigma grows when we consider that, as disclosed by former USTR Michael Froman, a US-China Bilateral Investment Treaty, launched toward the end of President George W. Bush's administration and effectively negotiated between 2014 and 2016, was 90 percent complete by the end of the Obama administration. The nearly agreed accord contained "binding and enforceable requirements on China to dramatically increase its intellectual property rights enforcement, prohibit forced technology transfer, adopt meaningful disciplines on state-owned enterprises and open vast portions of the Chinese economy to market competition, including from US firms" (Froman 2019).

If the arguments contained in the USTR section 301 report, which supposedly provide the strictly formal justification for the US trade war against China, do not really hold water, the question emerges whether there could be other economic arguments that may make sense from the perspective of the American national interest but were not made explicit by the Trump administration. Eddy Bekkers, Joseph Francois, Douglas Nelson, and Hugo Rojas-Romagosa attempt to answer that question in chapter 5 of this volume, relying on the insights provided by the theory of rational trade wars, defined as "an extended period during which a pair of countries, or groups of countries, apply instruments of trade policy with the intention of affecting a substantial share of the trade between those countries (or groups of countries) . . . to maximize national welfare by affecting the terms of trade."

Notwithstanding their open-minded search, Bekkers and coauthors end up declaring their failure to provide us with an economically rational explanation for the trade war. After a sincere try, laconically they conclude:

> So, as a practical matter, the theory of rational trade wars cannot tell us about actually existing trade wars. Perhaps more important, the

notion that it tells us anything about the trade policy of the Trump administration with say, China (or Europe, or its NAFTA partners) literally beggars belief. . . . In the case of the current trade policy of the Trump administration, the most difficult issue would seem to be figuring out what the president, and what for want of a better term we will call "advisers," are using for an objective function. Clearly not among them are: social welfare (however we might want to define that); reelection maximization as represented in standard political economy forces (to the extent that we can tell, the distribution of costs and benefits seems all wrong for that); and pursuit of geostrategic goals (the policies seem too collectively incoherent to reflect such goals). At this point, we seem to fall back on personal psychology, but this is an area in which, as economists, we are manifestly unqualified.

Other authors would question that "the pursuit of geostrategic goals" can be dismissed that easily as the raison d'être of the American administration's trade policy. VanGrasstek (chapter 3) suggests that "the evolution of American trade policy is best understood over the long run as a function of the international distribution of power and wealth, and especially the rise and fall of the country's leadership role." In this view, purportedly based on the idea of hegemonic stability, much of the Trump administration's trade actions can be seen as an attempt to rectify the policies favoring open markets—policies propelled and led by the United States itself in the past—that have allowed the ascendance of China.

This suggests the objective function is the preservation of US hegemony by preventing China from rising sufficiently to take the position the United States has enjoyed for a long time. Aaditya Mattoo and Robert W. Staiger argue that over the period of unchallenged dominance it is in the self-interest of the hegemon to support a rules-based system to preserve and enhance its own dominant condition, but when this condition begins to be threatened by the emergence of a meaningful competitor, the hegemon, the United States in our contemporary example, may turn against the rules-based system and fall back onto a power-based strategy to delay or even prevent the newly emerging power from taking over the dominant position—China in the present case. This strategy of seeking to delay the transition from one dominant power to the other only makes sense from a narrow and myopic perspective in which the challenging power or powers do not react. If they do, by raising their own tariffs and leveraging other policy instruments, the payoff to the hegemon is reduced. More important, it may be left exposed to suffer damages in the future caused by the rising powers acting in a system rendered undisciplined and weakened, ironically—as is happening now—by the hegemon itself (Mattoo and Staiger 2019).

Even in the most charitable interpretation of the current situation—that there is a certain logic for the United States to move from a rules-based to a power-based regime by means of trade policy—this misses the point that longer term it is better to count on a multilateral system capable of restraining other economic powers from actions that would damage the interests of the United States. There is nothing new in this proposition. It was dutifully applied by the United States when its GDP was the highest ever as a proportion of world GDP and there was little question about its military supremacy. That moment was right at the end of World War II. That was a time when the main multilateral institutions and other initiatives of international cooperation were launched under US leadership and over time supported the recovery and ascendancy anew of Europe and Japan. But more important—from the American perspective—these initiatives and institutions proved decisive in consolidating the economic and geopolitical supremacy of the United States, not least over the Soviet Union.

THE MYSTERY OF SEEKING TO CRIPPLE THE WTO

Among the institutions the United States endeavored to create and nourish, the one charged with establishing the rules for international trade (the GATT/WTO) has been by many measures extremely successful. Trade across borders has been key for countries that have achieved the most significant economic progress since the middle of the twentieth century, with China being exhibit number one, as discussed by L. Alan Winters in chapter 4. This performance would be unthinkable without the system that has allowed for increasingly open markets and rules to make them work more fluidly. The GATT/WTO has been the core of that system. Round after round, agreement after agreement, effort after effort by states, trade ministers, diplomats, and dedicated officials over several generations have delivered a governance mechanism that, despite its shortfalls, is considered one of the most singularly effective international institutions. By virtue of being endowed with a set of procedures to address disputes that uniquely constitutes an enforcement apparatus, the WTO is an aspirational model for other international arrangements that count on good rules yet lack levers to enforce them.

The WTO was provided at its birth (in 1994) with the Dispute Settlement Understanding mainly as a result of reasonable US insistence on the importance of implanting within the new institution a robust capacity to predictably secure the rights and enforce the obligations of the members, particularly as new sectors and issues were being brought under the disciplines of the GATT successor. Other countries overcame their original resistance as it became clear that the DSU would mitigate the risk of suffering from arbitrary and unilateral actions, particularly from the most powerful members.

In retrospect, the multilateral instrument for regulating international trade—the GATT followed by the WTO—has performed remarkably well, both in times of buoyancy such as during the Great Moderation, as well as in times of crisis such as the Great Recession, having usefully and beneficially served its members, the United States certainly among them. While the dispute settlement system has not always been successful in addressing trade conflicts, most disputes have been resolved. As noted by Jaime de Melo in chapter 15, even in very politically sensitive cases such as the long-running conflict between the United States and Latin American banana exporters and the EU, the system eventually delivered.

Notwithstanding the record, President Trump and his officials have not been hesitant about expressing their annoyance with the WTO. Curiously, after characterizing the WTO in exactly the same terms he had used before for the TPP and NAFTA as "the single worst trade deal ever made" (Micklethwait, Talev, and Jacobs 2018), he threatened to withdraw the United States from the organization, an action that by all accounts will carry a high cost for the world, including the United States itself, as Bown and Irwin have submitted in a careful analysis:

> A decision by President Trump to withdraw from the WTO—if deemed legal under US law—could deal a disastrous blow to America's foreign trade. The cost to consumers and import-reliant manufacturers . . . would be enormous. And the resulting foreign retaliation against American exporters—farmers and manufacturers alike—would severely damage the economy. (Bown and Irwin 2018, 8)

Having a country that represents almost one-fourth of world GDP and 15 percent of global exports leave the WTO clearly would enormously weaken the organization's mission and efficacy, causing serious damage to the prospects for global prosperity. Unfortunately, the United States does not even need to go outside the WTO to cause enormous damage, for it can do exactly that from inside simply by continuing to do what it has been doing for several years: blocking the appointment of any new members of the Appellate Body (AB) of the Dispute Settlement (DS) mechanism. The AB must have seven judges or members, and it needs a minimum of three to rule on an appeal. The term of two of the remaining three members expired in December 2019, as a result of which the AB became nonoperational. This could lead to a collapse of the DS capability the WTO has had since it was created. Significantly, the WTO's most distinctive and enviable characteristic would then be lost.

As in practically every multilateral institution, there is much in need of reform at the WTO, including its DSU. Practitioners, scholars, and a number of countries have put forward sensible ideas to improve the DS process that was negotiated almost three decades ago to address conditions very different from those prevailing now and the more complex circumstances that conceivably will arise in the future.[21] Yet the American grievances with the DSU do not seem to stem from the objective of making it a better multilateral instrument. As in other aspects of its trade policies, the Trump administration's undertaking against the AB is rooted in wrong or even false premises. President Trump has repeatedly said that the WTO was set up for the benefit of everybody but the United States, that his country loses almost all lawsuits, and that the system has been great for China and terrible for the United States.

All these views are unsubstantiated. No serious analysis has ever produced evidence of bias against the United States.[22] The United States is the most frequent user of the WTO DS system, having brought more cases than China and the EU combined. The United States has a higher proportion of wins (91 percent) than other complainants. It is also true that, as a defendant, the US proportion of losses is high (89 percent). These statistics reflect the fact that countries tend to bring cases where they estimate a high probability of winning, resulting in a pattern in which complainants tend to win. An exception is disputes involving China where the United States has done very well on both sides of the argument. Jeffrey J. Schott and Euijin Jung report that between 2002 and 2018, of the twenty-three cases brought by the United States challenging China's practices, its win-loss record was 19-0, with four cases pending. Conversely, in its fifteen complaints against the United States, China won only four, the United States won one and parts of three others, and six were pending (Schott and Jung 2019).

Closer scrutiny reveals that American officials are typically upset about losing cases brought against US trade remedy actions (antidumping and countervailing duties). On many occasions, the United States has been found in violation of the WTO Antidumping Agreement, a result that has ignited claims that US trade remedy laws were unfairly targeted by the WTO. To this accusation the first response must be that it is not the WTO that brings cases to the DS process. This prerogative belongs to the WTO member countries alone. Those crying foul at alleged targeting and bias should be made to confront the highly credible American analysts who agree that complaints against US trade remedy actions are caused by the United States' own aggressive use of such actions that plainly violate the rules agreed to by all signatories of the WTO, including the United States (see, e.g., Ikenson 2017).

Be that as it may, the objective of the Trump administration seems to go beyond merely winning cases against its trade remedy actions. By blocking new appointments to the AB the Trump administration has paralyzed the DS process and caused the WTO damage that may be irreparable for a long time. Without a functioning Appellate Body, the WTO may revert back to a one-stage DS process in which adoption of panel reports can be blocked. Professor Rachel Brewster puts it succinctly:

> The United States' block on Appellate Body nominations is a direct assault on the idea that disputes should be resolved through a neutral interpretation of trade law rather than more negotiated, economic-power-based solution. Without a dispute settlement system, international trade law would return to a GATT-era type system where panels would issue legal opinions but most significant trade disputes were resolved through negotiations, and where the meaning and operation of the law were largely determined through power politics. (Brewster 2018, 4)

A rationale for shutting down the AB, in addition to long-standing dissatisfaction with AB rulings against US antidumping measures, is that it closes the circle in the Trump administration's pursuit of aggressive unilateralism. If subject to WTO due process, many US trade policy actions would likely be found illegal, but such adjudication is undercut because the mechanism charged to decide cases is no longer operational. Thus, unilateral trade actions, like imposing tariffs on automotive imports from otherwise friendly trade partners on "national security" grounds, would not be contestable at the WTO. Bilateral negotiations would be the only expedient left. The VanGrasstek view of US behavior, described above, would be validated again, along with its obvious consequence: a multiplication of costly trade wars, as countries predictably would react to more US unilateralism with their own—as has happened already in response to the questionable US section 232 and section 301 tariffs.

As noted by Simon Evenett in chapter 6 of this volume, the EU has signaled that it can also "do stupid" in imposing retaliatory tariffs. Evenett argues that the classic "playbook" for dealing with American trade discrimination—targeted retaliation, bilateral negotiations to improve market access, and cooperation with the United States to pursue joint interests related to China through discussion of new rules of the game for subsidies, SOEs, and related matters—has major weaknesses. Retaliation appears to have limited salience in affecting US political dynamics and is costly, while negotiation of new PTAs runs into European sectoral sensitivities and resistance by major trading partners to consider acceptance of EU demands on nontrade issues. Finally, although the EU has been an active proponent of WTO reform and the pursuit of cooperation on a plurilateral basis, such efforts inevitably require time to bear fruit. Worryingly, Ursula von der Leyen, the president of the European Commission who took office in late 2019, has indicated the EU may be taking a more aggressive unilateral trade policy stance, implying a possible greater willingness to emulate the United States in putting aside multilateral disciplines (Vela 2019).

It is not hard to infer that a world economy under siege by a proliferation of trade barriers would be a feeble and unstable one, and not propitious for any country. Reconstituting the appeals function should be the highest priority for all the WTO members for their own national interest, including the United States. In 2017 the US government began blocking new appointments to the AB by invoking Article 2.4 of the DSU, which indicates that decisions by the DSB shall be made by consensus. In the view of the US representatives, this provision provides their government with veto power. This interpretation is not only arguable but outright wrong, in the opinion of reputable legal experts (see, e.g., Kuiper 2017; Hillman 2018). All WTO members have the collective responsibility to fill vacancies in the AB as they arise, given their precisely defined duty to administer the rules and procedures of the DSU. There is nothing preventing members from relying on a voting procedure to discharge their collective obligation to keep the DSU fully functional.

The WTO treaty provides that in the event of a conflict between a provision of the WTO Agreement and that of a subsidiary multilateral trade agreement (like the DSU), the provision in the WTO Agreement shall prevail. Article IX of the WTO permits voting and can be invoked if three-quarters of WTO members desire to do so.[23] Thus a vote to approve new appointments to the Appellate Body is possible. A vote is unlikely to be taken, however, for fear of setting a precedent and the further erosion of trust among members it may give rise to. A majority vote may also become the straw that breaks the camel's back, providing the United States with the excuse to leave the WTO, which would be a very unfortunate and costly decision for all purposes. Nevertheless, this regrettable scenario should be assessed not against a business-as-usual situation but against the prospect of a totally dysfunctional WTO dispossessed of its enforcement capacity. Preserving the existence and faculties of the WTO must be of the utmost priority.

Bernard Hoekman and Petros C. Mavroidis (chapter 7 in this volume), while not condoning the US decision to block appointment of new Appellate Body members, note that in principle many of the concerns expressed by the US government about the DSU are not particularly difficult to address. This is because, taken at face value—that is, assuming good faith, which is a questionable assumption at the time of this writing—the core of what the United States has been arguing is that WTO members should recommit to what was negotiated in the Uruguay Round. The elements of a possible solution along these lines began to emerge in late 2019. A group of WTO members tabled a proposal to reform the DSB's rules in order to address the concerns raised by the Trump administration.[24] An informal process during 2019 on the functioning of the Appellate Body led by Ambassador David Walker of New Zealand identified a series of measures that could be taken by decision of the WTO General Council that would address many of the matters raised by the United States. These included specific language addressing potential Appellate Body "overreach," a decision that panels and the AB will consider the provisions in the Antidumping Agreement that pertain to zeroing and to put in place a mechanism for regular dialogue between WTO members and the Appellate Body. A necessary condition for such a decision to be meaningful, as noted by Ambassador

Walker, is that there be an Appellate Body and thus that members agree to new appointments to the AB.[25]

At this writing in mid-2020, the United States has not considered any proposals sufficient to address its concerns. In the course of 2019, as it became more evident that efforts to induce the United States to cease blocking new appointments to the AB would not be successful, several WTO members, led by the European Union, began work on a "plan B" centered around putting in place a substitute mechanism that could be used on a voluntary basis by those WTO members who desire to be able to continue to appeal the findings of panels. This resulted in the establishment of a Multi-Party Interim Appeal Arbitration Arrangement (MPIA) in April 2020. The MPIA is intended to operate as an interim appeals board until the AB crisis is resolved. This permits signatories to appeal panel rulings and commits them to adopt and implement panel reports if they do not appeal. As of early summer 2020, twenty-one WTO members had signed the MPIA, including Brazil, Canada, China, the European Union, and Mexico.[26]

The MPIA reveals the strong commitment of many WTO members to retain an appeals mechanism. Whether this interim measure will evolve into a new DS system will depend on the ability of the WTO membership to agree on a broader effort to push for WTO reforms.

CAN WTO REFORM HELP RESUSCITATE MULTILATERAL COOPERATION?

The careful monitoring of trade policy trends by the Global Trade Alert (see chapter 1 by Evenett) makes clear there is a large agenda confronting WTO members. A basic purpose of the WTO is to provide a platform that allows countries to agree on rules to address trade-related policies that create adverse effects for trading partners and to support their implementation. The fact that it is not fulfilling this purpose matters for the global economy.

Several of the contributions to this volume discuss policy areas that call for multilateral cooperation and rulemaking to reduce potential international spillovers of national policies.[27] In chapter 8, Anne Krueger discusses agricultural policies; Bernard Hoekman and Douglas Nelson focus on the need to revisit existing rules of the road for subsidies and state-owned enterprises in chapter 9; Erik van der Marel analyzes issues associated with the rise of the digital economy in chapter 10; and in chapter 11 Patrick Low explores what can be done to blunt the potential conflict between actions to address climate change and WTO rules on the use of trade policies. All of these areas call for multilateral cooperation. Although some of these matters can be addressed partially in PTAs, the spillover effects of policies in these areas are often global in nature. Moreover, even where PTAs could in principle help to reduce the trade costs associated with national policies, in practice they may be of only limited utility. Thus Sébastien Miroudot and Ben Shepherd show in chapter 12 that to date PTAs have done little to reduce the costs of trading services. Similarly, it is unlikely that countries will be willing to consider disciplines on the use of industrial policies and subsidies in PTAs, as these would also benefit nonsignatories. A multilateral approach is required.

As noted in a 2018 report commissioned by the Bertelsmann Stiftung, a necessary condition for new rulemaking is a willingness to define a negotiating agenda.[28] Defining such an agenda requires dialogue and deliberation, something that has been in short supply (see, e.g., Odell 2015). Reasons for this include the consensus working practice and the outdated approach that is embedded in the WTO to recognize differences in levels of development and capacity across the membership (Hoekman 2019). Space constraints preclude a lengthy discussion of possible WTO reforms. Here we simply note that some initial positive steps have already been taken. One positive development is the breaking of the consensus constraint, with groups of WTO members deciding to launch plurilateral discussions and negotiations on new rules of the game or to agree on good regulatory practices in an area. Plurilateral discussions in the WTO are addressing liberalization of trade in environmental goods, approaches to assist micro-, small-, and medium-sized enterprises (MSMEs), rules of the game for e-commerce and digital trade, action to facilitate investment, and disciplines on domestic regulation of services. While not a panacea, plurilateral initiatives may lend themselves better to addressing specific policy cooperation challenges than PTAs or broader multilateral trade negotiation rounds that include all WTO members (Hoekman and Mavroidis 2015; Hoekman and Sabel 2019). As Hoekman and Nelson argue in chapter 9, this applies also to policies that are key areas of disagreement, such as subsidies and SOEs, in the sense that the major trading powers must agree on any rules in these areas.

Another positive step relates to the urgent challenge of dealing more effectively with development differences. In part the urgency is because the matter is a core demand of the United States (in this case supported by the EU and many other OECD nations). As important, a good case can be made that the approach that has historically been pursued is outdated and ineffective. The engagement of developing nations in the WTO is premised on the principle of "special and differential treatment" (SDT). This implies less than full reciprocity in trade negotiations and acceptance that developing nations should be less constrained in the use of trade policies than high-income countries. The constituent elements of SDT date back to the mid-1960s and were designed for a world economy that no longer exists. The challenge today is to identify and implement policies that promote economic development in a world of global value chain-based production, e-commerce, and digitization where small firms can become micro-multinationals by using electronic platforms and exploiting mobile information and communications technologies. Such policies will not revolve around trade policy but will rely on measures to enhance access to finance, adopt new technologies, ease cross-border payments, and develop efficient logistics.

A central feature of SDT is that it applies to all developing countries. The WTO, following precedent set under the GATT, does not define what constitutes a developing country, leaving it to members to self-determine their status. Outside the group of forty-seven (UN-defined) least-developed countries (LDCs), the only distinct group of developing countries identified in the WTO, there are no criteria that allow differentiation between developing countries. The United States has proposed that members agree to such criteria. This is very controversial and unlikely to be accepted. It has been proposed many times in the past to no avail. More important, it is not necessary. Rather than continuing to fight old battles, it would be more productive for WTO members to do more to identify good practices and policies to address market failures, complemented by provision of assistance where needed.

It is not sufficiently recognized that the WTO has made strides in revisiting the approach used to recognize economic development differences. Examples include the 2013 Agreement on Trade Facilitation and the launch of the Aid for Trade program at the WTO Ministerial conference in Hong Kong in 2005—an initiative that Patrick Messerlin helped to prepare the ground for in his role as co-chair of the UN Millennium Project Task Force on Trade and Finance in 2005 (see Millennium Project 2005)—and the associated Enhanced Integrated Framework for LDCs. Two chapters in this volume discuss these matters. In chapter 13, Olivier Cattaneo and Sébastien Miroudot spell out the implications of changes in the structure of the world economy and the need to update trade and development paradigms. In chapter 14, Jean-Jacques Hallaert provides a critical assessment of the WTO's Aid for Trade Initiative.

CONCLUDING REMARKS

It remains to be seen how deeply the Trump policies will damage the international trading system, and how long they will last. In only three years they have proven to be deleterious to the economic and geopolitical benefit of the United States. Irrespective of the duration of the "siege" endured by the rules-based mechanisms, it is clear that the system has suffered enormous harm caused by the US administration since 2017, but also from key governments' unwillingness to keep reforming it. As the work of several contributors to this volume shows, there is no lack of ideas for how to mend it and make it more effective. Political willingness to acknowledge that a better-functioning and stronger multilateral system is in the interest of all nations has been missing in the twenty-first century, with unmistakably tragic consequences. An enlightened reckoning, perhaps impelled by recent events, will be necessary to set in motion the reform and regeneration of the mechanisms of international cooperation and coordination—the trading system included. Such action will go far to propel both a recovery from the economic devastation caused by the great pandemic and a future of global prosperity, peace, and security.

NOTES

1. The appendix to this book provides a selected list of Patrick's publications.

2. Patrick Messerlin played a leading role in economic analysis of antidumping by the European Community (see in particular Messerlin 2001, 1989, and 1990).

3. For an excellent and succinct analysis of the TPP, see Schott (2018).

4. For a careful calculation of the economic cost, see Petri and others (2017).

5. Office of the United States Trade Representative, Executive Office of the President, Summary of the Objectives for NAFTA Renegotiation, July 17, 2017 (p. 2).

6. As in the case of the automotive sector, the textiles and apparel sector was also subject to more stringent rules of origin, which are also bound to impact the competitiveness of this industry in the regional and global market.

7. Another highly problematic precedent is the so-called China clause, by which a member could withdraw from the agreement if another of the partners enters into a trade accord with China that the member does not approve of. The China clause is clearly an economically redundant condition, given the stringent rules-of-origin and investment disciplines agreed to in the new deal. And it is certainly an unwarranted geopolitical overreach on the part of the United States.

8. In May 2019, Mexico was also hit with a tariff on its tomato exports to the United States, precipitating negotiations that led Mexico to accept nontariff barriers—in the form of additional inspections at the border—as well as higher reference prices for this product.

9. Patrick Messerlin was one of the first to analyze the use of contingent protection instruments against China; see Messerlin (2004).

10. Industrial subsidies and the significant role played by state-owned enterprises are examples. These are discussed in chapter 9 by Hoekman and Nelson.

11. Some of the decreases in tariffs were planned before the trade war, such as the adjustments to comply with the WTO Information Technology Agreement. Still, a substantial portion of the tariff reductions on imports from other countries are in reaction to the American trade hostilities.

12. See Economic and Trade Agreement between the Government of the United States and the Government of the People's Republic of China, January 15, 2020, https://ustr.gov/sites/default/files/files/agreements/phase%20 one%20agreement/Economic_And_Trade_Agreement_Between_The_United _States_And_China_Text.pdf.

13. Although imports by the United States of Chinese steel and aluminum are relatively small, US tariffs on these products marked the start of the trade war as the Chinese government responded with tariffs of 15 to 25 percent on $2.4 billion of imports from the United States.

14. General Agreement on Tariffs and Trade (GATT), Part II, Article XXI, "Security Exceptions," October 30, 1948, Geneva Final Act. Article XXI states that "Nothing in this Agreement shall be construed (a) to require any contracting party to furnish any information the disclosure of which it considers contrary to its essential security interests; or (b) to prevent any contracting party from taking any action which it considers necessary for the protection of its essential security interests (i) relating to fissionable materials or the materials from which they are derived; (ii) relating to the traffic in arms, ammunition and implements of war and to such traffic in other goods and materials as is carried on directly or indirectly for the purpose of supplying a military establishment; (iii) taken in time of war or other emergency in international rela-

tions; or (c) to prevent any contracting party from taking any action in pursuance of its obligations under the United Nations Charter for the maintenance of international peace and security.

15. Ukraine complained before the WTO in 2016, arguing that it would suffer a significant reduction in trade with Asia and the Caucasus region after the Russian government prohibited rail and road transport from Ukraine unless the route also went through Belarus.

16. The national security argument on the steel and aluminum tariffs is demolished in just one paragraph of Bown and Irwin (2019, p. 128).

17. Office of the United States Trade Representative (2017, 4n10).

18. Office of the United States Trade Representative (2018, 3).

19. Office of the United States Trade Representative (2018, 19).

20. Office of the United States Trade Representative (2018, 182).

21. See, for example, Payosova, Hufbauer, and Schott (2018). For government proposals, see e.g., the submission to the WTO General Council by the EU, China, Canada, India, Norway, New Zealand, Switzerland, Australia, Korea, Iceland, Singapore, Mexico, Costa Rica, and Montenegro on December 13, 2018. WTO, WT/GC/W/752/Rev.2.

22. It is worth noting that for most of the WTO's history one of the judges of the AB has been an American, a circumstance not enjoyed by any other country.

23. Art. IX WTO specifies that if voting occurs, unanimity is required for amendments relating to general principles such as nondiscrimination; a three-quarters majority for Interpretations of provisions of the WTO agreements and decisions on waivers; and a two-thirds majority for amendments relating to issues other than general principles. Where not otherwise specified and consensus cannot be reached, a simple majority vote suffices.

24. See note 21.

25. Informal Process on Matters related to the Functioning of the Appellate Body—Report by the Facilitator, H. E. Dr. David Walker (New Zealand), WTO JOB/GC/222, October 15, 2019.

26. Jointly the signatories represent 14 percent of the WTO membership, counting the EU as one. Disputes between MPIA signatories accounted for about a quarter of the total DSU caseload from 1995 to 2019. While substantial, many frequent users of the DSU, including India, Indonesia, Malaysia, and Russia, did not sign the MPIA.

27. For a comprehensive catalogue of such policy areas, see the papers compiled by the E-15 Initiative at https://e15initiative.org/publications/executive-summary-synthesis-report-full-report/.

28. Bertelsmann Stiftung, "Revitalizing Multilateral Governance at the World Trade Organization, 2018," https://www.bertelsmann-stiftung.de/en/publications/publication/did/revitalizing-multilateral-governance-at-the-world-trade-organization/.

REFERENCES

Baldwin, Richard. 2013. "Trade and Industrialization after Globalization's Second Unbundling: How Building and Joining a Supply Chain Are Different and Why It Matters." In *Globalization in an Age of Crisis: Multilateral Economic Cooperation in the Twenty-First Century*, edited by Robert Feenstra and Alan M. Taylor, 165–212. University of Chicago Press.

Bown, Chad. 2019. "US-China Trade War: The Guns of August." *Trade and Investment Policy Watch* (blog). Washington, D.C.: Peterson Institute for International Economics, September 20. https://www.piie.com/blogs /trade-and-investment-policy-watch/us-china-trade-war-guns-august.

Bown, Chad, and Douglas Irwin. 2018. "What Might a Trump Withdrawal from the World Trade Organization Mean for US Tariffs?" Policy Brief 18–23. Washington, D.C.: Peterson Institute for International Economics, November.

———. 2019. "Trump's Assault on the Global Trading System and Why Decoupling from China will Change Everything." *Foreign Affairs* 98 (5): 125–36.

Brewster, Rachel. 2018. "The Trump Administration and the Future of the WTO." *Yale Journal of International Law Online* 44.

Froman, Michael. 2019. "Trump Needs a Comprehensive Trade Deal with China. Luckily, He Has This to Build On." *Washington Post*, February 4.

Hillman, Jennifer. 2018. "Three Approaches to Fixing the World Trade Organization's Appellate Body: The Good, The Bad and The Ugly." Institute of International Economic Law, Georgetown University Law Center.

Hoekman, Bernard. 2019. "Urgent and Important: Improving WTO Performance by Revisiting Working Practices." *Journal of World Trade* 53 (3): 373–94.

Hoekman, Bernard, and Patrick Mavroidis. 2015. "Embracing Diversity: Plurilateral Agreements and the Trading System." *World Trade Review* 14 (1): 101–16.

Hoekman, Bernard, and Charles Sabel. 2019. "Open Plurilateral Agreements, International Regulatory Cooperation and the WTO." *Global Policy*. https://doi.org/10.1111/1758-5899.12694.

Ikenson, Dan. 2017. "US Trade Laws and the Sovereignty Canard." *Forbes*, March 9.

Kuiper, Peter Jan. 2017. "What to Do about the US Attack on the Appellate Body?" *International Economic Law and Policy* (blog). November 15. https://worldtradelaw.typepad.com/ielpblog/2017/11/guest-post-from

-pieter-jan-kuiper-professor-of-the-law-of-international-economic
-organizations-at-the-faculty-of-law-of-th.html.

Lardy, Nicholas R. 2018. "Does China Force Foreign Firms to Surrender Their Sensitive Technology?" *China Economic Watch* (blog). Washington, D.C.: Peterson Institute for International Economics, China Economic Watch, December.

Mattoo, Aaditya, and Robert W. Staiger. 2019. "Trade Wars: What Do They Mean? Why Are They Happening Now? What Are the Costs?" NBER Working Paper 25762. Cambridge, Mass.: National Bureau of Economic Research.

Messerlin, Patrick. 1989. "The EC Antidumping Regulations: A First Economic Appraisal, 1980–85. *Weltwirtschaftliches Archiv* 125 (3): 563–87.

———. 1990. "Antidumping Regulation or Pro-Cartel Law? The EC Chemical Cases." *World Economy* 13 (4): 462–92.

———. 2001. *Measuring the Costs of Protection in Europe: European Commercial Policy in the 2000s.* Washington, D.C.: Institution for International Economics.

———. 2004. "China in the World Trade Organization: Antidumping and Safeguards," *World Bank Economic Review* 18 (1): 105–30.

Micklethwait, John, Margaret Talev, and Jennifer Jacobs. 2018. "Trump Threatens to Pull US out of WTO If It Doesn't 'Shape Up.'" Bloomberg News, August 30.

Odell, John. 2015. "How Should the WTO Launch and Negotiate a Future Round? *World Trade Review* 14 (1): 117–33.

Office of the United States Trade Representative. 2017. "Addressing China's Laws, Policies, Practices, and Actions Related to Intellectual Property, Innovation, and Technology," 82 Fed. Reg. 39,007, August 17.

———. 2018. "Findings of the Investigation into China's Acts, Policies, and Practices Related to Technology Transfer, Intellectual Property, and Innovation Under Section 301 of the Trade Act of 1974," March 22.

Payosova, Tetyana, Gary Clyde Hufbauer, and Jeffrey Schott. 2018. "The Dispute Settlement Crisis in the World Trade Organization: Causes and Cures." Policy Brief 18-5. Washington, D.C.: Peterson Institute for International Economics, March.

Petri, Peter A., and others. 2017. "Going It Alone in the Asia Pacific: Regional Trade Agreements without the United States." Working Paper WP17–10. Washington, D.C.: Peterson Institute for International Economics.

Schott, Jeffrey J. 2018. "The TPP: Origins and Outcomes." In *Handbook of International Trade Agreements: Country, Regional and Global Approaches,* edited by Robert E. Looney, 401–11. London: Routledge.

Schott, Jeffrey J., and Euijin Jung. 2019. "In US-China Trade Disputes, the WTO Usually Sides with the United States." Washington, D.C.: Peterson Institute for International Economics, March.

United States Congress. 1974. "An Act to promote the development of an open, nondiscriminatory, and fair world economic system, to stimulate fair and free competition between the United States and foreign nations, to foster the economic growth of, and full employment in, the United States, and for other purposes." Public Law 93-618 (Trade Act of 1974).

UN Millennium Project. 2005. *Trade for Development.* Task Force on Trade. New York: UNDP.

Vela, Jakob Hanke. 2019. "EU Builds Anti-Trump Trade Bazooka." *Politico,* October 15.

PART I

TRADE POLICY TRENDS AND DEVELOPMENTS

1

THE PRE-TRUMP BUILDUP OF TRADE DISCRIMINATION

SCALE, DRIVERS, AND EFFECTS

SIMON EVENETT

The implementation of President Donald Trump's America First trade policy, which by mid-2020 had imposed import tariffs on approximately $300 billion of trade, was regarded by many analysts as a defining moment for the multilateral trading system. Some contrast brazen US unilateralism with policy choices in the years before, often crediting world trade rules with reining in protectionism. Paul Krugman, for example, has argued: "The world trading system is actually a quite remarkable construction—a framework that has consistently produced a high level of global cooperation. It has been pretty robust in the face of severe shocks—notably, the world did not see a resurgence of protectionism after the 2008 financial crisis" (Krugman 2018).

But is this true? Did governments refrain from discriminating against foreign commercial interests during and after the worst global economic crisis in three-quarters of a century? For those who only associate protectionism with tariff increases, the answer is clear: there was no resurgence in protectionism. But as every economics student who has taken an international trade class knows, tariffs are not the only policy instrument available to governments to discriminate against foreign commercial interests.

Much is at stake. There is the reputation of the World Trade Organization (WTO) to think of. Coming on top of the failure to conclude the Doha Development Agenda and the breakdown in the Appellate Body, a finding that WTO rules did not prevent widespread discrimination against foreign commercial interests during the crisis era would cast a darker cloud over the state of global cooperation on trade policy. An alternative perspective is that it may have been too much to expect an incomplete trade rulebook to rein in the behavior of desperate governments.

A finding that there has been widespread resort to trade discrimination might also call into question our understanding of both unilateral trade policy choice (in particular the literature relating business cycles to protectionism) (Rose 2013) and the theory of the WTO. Over the past twenty years the thrust of the latter has been to explain why cooperation between governments happens under the auspices of the WTO (Bagwell, Bown, and Staiger 2016). Where does that theory stand if the predominant feature of the past ten years has been unilateral, extensive resort to trade discrimination? Or, put differently, if the past decade has witnessed substantial resort to trade distortions, then how can this be reconciled with a body of theoretical work whose central finding is that governments forgo short-term advantage?

The evidential point of departure in this chapter from other assessments of the crisis-era protectionism that focus on tariff changes and trade defense actions (Bown 2011; Kee, Neagu, and Nicita 2013) is to employ a dataset that contains not only these policy instruments but other trade distortions as well. Those other trade distortions relate not only to measures that restrict imports but also to policies that stimulate exports. Once consideration is given to the gamut of public policies that can discriminate against foreign commercial interests, then the scale of commerce affected changes markedly from the low percentage points of trade affected that are reported, for example, in the WTO's monitoring reports on protectionism.

So as to be clear, I make no claim to have discovered nontariff measures or to be the first to study them. Baldwin (1970) serves as an important reminder that alert trade analysts have long been aware of the potential significance of policies other than tariffs and trade defense. Moreover Bhagwati (1988), among others, showed that resort to voluntary export restraints was the preferred discriminatory response following the sharp downturn of the early 1980s, not tariffs. Furthermore, agricultural trade economists have long been interested in the impact of state-provided export incentives, the importance of which in the contemporary era will soon become apparent.

Despite receiving a mandate from governments to document, measure, and assess nontariff measures in 1969, the United Nations has not been able to deliver reliable data on these state acts. Now that a database is available that contains lots of information of tariffs and nontariff measures, one goal of this chapter is to examine the amount of trade covered by different policy interventions that discriminate against foreign commercial interests. It is therefore possible to see whether focusing solely on tariffs and trade defense actions provides a misleading assessment of the scale of trade discrimination witnessed since the start of the global financial crisis in 2008.

Complicating the assessment of the impact of the WTO on government resort to trade discrimination is the fact that from November 2008 to December 2018 the leaders of the G-20 governments foreswore resort to certain trade policy instruments. The G-20 pledge to eschew protectionism was not a binding, enforceable obligation, unlike WTO commitments. For some, then, the G-20 pledge was cheap talk. However, for others—in particular, numerous political science, international relations, and international legal scholars—such "soft law" can alter behavior. This begs the question whether the pattern of discriminatory policy choice by the G-20 nations differed from those of other nations.

An exploratory empirical analysis of the determinants of G-20 and non-G-20 nations' resort to trade discrimination is conducted here. This analysis is far from definitive, but given the lack of research on the drivers of trade discrimination, it is a start that other analysts may wish to build upon. Since Eichengreen and Irwin (2010) demonstrated the importance of substitutability between tariff increases and devaluations of the national currency in the 1930s, consideration is given here to the possibility of substitution *or* complementarity between exchange rate changes as well as fiscal stimulus packages and the resort to trade discrimination.

An implication of the "embedded liberalism" perspective advanced by Ruggie (1982) is that international trade norms—such as nondiscrimination—can be suspended by governments if social or economic order is threatened by a crisis. Here I examine the extent to which the resort to trade discrimination correlates with the change in unemployment at the beginning of the global financial crisis.

I also examine the possibility that WTO obligations might have affected the form rather than the quantum of trade discrimination. Specifically, I present evidence on whether the extent of precrisis tariff binding overhang is correlated with measures of national trade policy once the global financial crisis hit. Taken together, the results of this exploratory empirical analysis shed light on whether G-20 government behavior differs from that of other nations and where it does not.

The emphasis throughout the chapter is on policy choice before President Trump was inaugurated. Given that his election was largely unanticipated, in particular before the second half of 2016, then the policy choices of other governments are unlikely to have been influenced by the expectation of his election and the America First trade policies that might follow.

In the remainder of the chapter I present evidence on the share of goods trade affected by crisis-era discrimination since November 2008. I compare the scale of pre-Trump trade discrimination worldwide with the amount of Chinese exports hit by US tariff increases in 2018, hence putting the first year of the Sino-US trade war in perspective. I present and analyze two sets of comparisons between the trade-related policy choices of the G-20 members and those of other nations.

DATA SOURCES EMPLOYED

The database on commercial policy intervention used in this study is the Global Trade Alert (GTA). Established in June 2009, it seeks to document *all* public policy *changes* that *alter the relative treatment* of domestic in relation to foreign firms around the *world*.[1] Country coverage, therefore, extends beyond the G-20. Identifying changes in public policy implies that the GTA database is best thought of as revealing the "delta" (the change) in public policy toward international business rather than the height or size of any trade distortion or liberalization.

The GTA does not confine itself to a predefined set of trade policy instruments or to those policy instruments covered by WTO agreements.[2] Nor does the GTA confine itself to measures that harm foreign commercial interests; liberalizing policy interventions are recorded too. Moreover, governments may discriminate against foreign commercial interests in markets abroad, not just in their home markets. Therefore, where relevant, the evidence includes changes in public policy toward exporters as well.

Wherever possible, official sources are used to document a public policy intervention; this has been the case in over 93 percent of the interventions documented. As of this writing, the Global Trade Alert database includes information on 20,477 different public policy interventions, over 14,000 of which harmed foreign commercial interests.[3]

The GTA database uses the classifications for nontariff measures developed by the United Nations (UN) Multi-Agency Support Team (MAST). Where possible, nontariff measures, including tariff rate quotas, are assigned to their respective MAST "chapter;" the next section refers to different MAST chapters.[4] Later I make a distinction between the more transparent commercial policy interventions and less transparent state actions and use the MAST classification to give a precise definition of the former.

Each entry in the GTA database contains information on the implementing jurisdiction; the dates a measure was announced, came into effect, or lapsed; the policy instrument used; the products or services affected; the sector affected; and a description of the measure.[5] From this information, it uses automated means to establish which trading partners are affected by the implementation of a measure. For example, if Switzerland raises the tariff on imported butter, then fine-grained UN trade data (from the UN COMTRADE database) are used to identify which trading partners exported butter to Switzerland in the year before the measure came into force. It assembles so-called support tables for international trade in goods, foreign direct investment, migration, and where possible services trade so that the identification of affected trading partners is subject to the least human intervention possible (thereby reducing the potential for human error).

To avoid including public policy interventions that are likely to have trivial effects on international commerce, the GTA team uses minimum thresholds. For example, trading partners for whom less than $1 million of trade is affected by a foreign state act are not included in reports of policy interventions contained in the GTA database. Moreover, state aid involving less than $10 million of state largesse or less than $10 million of commerce are excluded as well.

For each public policy intervention affecting goods trade in the GTA database, which includes information on the implementing jurisdiction, the product codes affected, and the affected trading partners, it is possible to calculate the total value of international trade that is "covered" or potentially affected by the implementation of that intervention. Given that the implementation of an intervention in a given year could affect the amount of trade in that year, estimates of the potential trade affected must come from prior years.

So as to avoid crisis-era intervention affecting any of the trade-affected calculations, the GTA team uses the global trade flows available at the six-digit level of the UN Harmonized Commodity Description and Coding System for 2005–2007, one to three years before the crisis began, to define the shares of world goods trade affected by each intervention. Data on the total value of global trade in the year before an intervention is implemented, as well as the calculated share of world trade, are then used to estimate the total amount of trade affected by the implementation of that intervention.[6]

The use of the GTA database in research, business analyses, media articles, and by governments is growing. At this writing in 2020, there are 1,690 entries in the Google Scholar database that mention the GTA and its findings. The GTA database is frequently downloaded from its website.[7] In 2016, the International Monetary Fund (IMF) noted that "the Global Trade Alert database has the most comprehensive coverage of all types of trade-discriminatory and trade-liberalizing measures, although it begins only in 2008" (IMF 2016). An independent comparison of available datasets on crisis-era trade policy found that the GTA had the largest country coverage of nontariff measures (Rau and Vogt 2019).

In the exploratory data analysis conducted here, I use three macroeconomic indicators. The data source for each is the World Bank's *World Development Indicators*. The first seeks to capture the scale of the fiscal stimulus that a government undertook and is measured by the logarithm of the ratio of final government consumption spending on goods and services at the end of a given period to that at the beginning of the time period in question. The second indicator relates to exchange rate depreciation. Here the specific measure used is the percentage depreciation in the value of a national currency against the US dollar during the period in question. The third indicator relates to the dislocation in a national labor market at the start of the global financial crisis. This is measured as the increase in percentage points of the unemployment rate from 2007 to 2009.

As part of the exploratory data analysis it was necessary to construct a measure of how constrained a WTO member's tariff policies were by its respective tariff bindings just before the global financial crisis began. Using the WTO publication *Tariff Profiles 2008* it was possible to calculate the difference between the mean bound tariff rate and the mean applied tariff rate for all goods for 2007 (or for the latest year available). Of the 123 jurisdictions for which these data were available, 96 had a tariff binding overhang of more than 7 percentage points.

The 7 percentage point threshold is important because it equals the size of the tariff increase undertaken by the United States when it implemented the Smoot-Hawley Tariff Act in 1930. Therefore, 78 percent of the WTO members for which data are available could have raised their tariffs by the same amount as Smoot-Hawley and not broken their WTO obligations at the beginning of the global financial crisis of 2008. Several large emerging markets (but not China) could have done so. Such evidence already casts doubt on the degree to which WTO obligations actually limited resort to trade discrimination at the start of the global financial crisis. Indeed, it would be better to argue that these 96 governments did not raise their tariffs significantly at the beginning of the crisis because they chose to, not because they were prevented from doing so by their WTO commitments.

The discussion now turns to an assessment of the amount of global trade affected by the buildup of discrimination against foreign suppliers of goods since November 2008, the month that the G-20 leaders declared for the first time that they would eschew protectionism.

THE BUILDUP OF CRISIS-ERA TRADE DISCRIMINATION WORLDWIDE

This section summarizes the principal implications of the GTA's data on the global goods trade that faces policy-induced discrimination. Although the focus of this chapter is on developments before President Trump was inaugurated, data for the years 2017–2019 are also presented for the sake of completeness.

In estimating the scale of world goods trade facing discrimination imposed by foreign governments, it is important to take these factors into account:

- a discriminatory measure may lapse or be removed,
- a measure may be implemented during a year and therefore require some adjustment for duration in force,

FIGURE 1-1. By 2016, more than two-thirds of global goods trade faced trade distortions implemented since the crisis began in 2008.

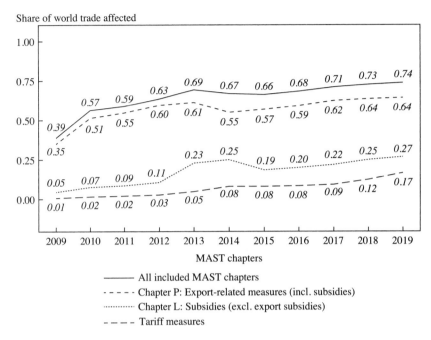

Source: Trade shares estimated using information on policy changes from the Global Trade Alert database and detailed international trade data from the UN COMTRADE database.

Note: MAST chapters = classifications for nontariff measures developed by the United Nations Multi-Agency Support Team (MAST).

- a particular trade flow may face multiple policy-induced trade distortions when competing at home or abroad, and
- state-provided export incentives by other governments may create trade distortions for a nation's exports to third markets.

Each of these factors has been accounted for in the estimates that follow.

Figure 1-1 presents, for each year from 2009 to 2019, estimates of the shares of world goods trade affected by every trade distortion in force in a given year (see the line "All included MAST chapters").[8] Given that the GTA started collecting data in November 2008, it should be noted that the shares presented would have been zero at the start. The reported shares therefore reveal how much of global goods trade was affected by the trade discrimination introduced since the beginning of the global financial year *and* that remained in force during each subsequent year. By 2016, before President Trump was inaugurated, more than two-thirds of global goods trade faced one or more trade distortions that were in effect that year.

The buildup over time in the shares of global goods trade affected by trade discrimination is shown clearly in figure 1-1. There was a huge jump at the start of the crisis era. In 2009, 39 percent of world goods trade competed against trade discrimination that had been implemented in the previous fourteen months (that is, since November 1, 2008). By 2010, the share had jumped to 57 percent, from which it rose more slowly to 69 percent in 2013. A plateau of sorts emerged during the period 2013–2016. After 2016, the share of world goods trade affected rose further, reaching 74 percent in June 2019.

Figure 1-1 also breaks down the total share of world goods trade affected by trade discrimination into three categories of policy instrument: import tariff increases, subsidies to import-competing firms (MAST chapter L), measures that affect exports including export incentives (MAST chapter P).[9] There are several pertinent findings.

First, in each year before and after President Trump was inaugurated, the share of world goods trade affected by measures to promote exports is larger than the shares affected by subsidies to local firms and by import tariff increases. From the global perspective, measures to expand exports and grab market share from foreign rivals are on a greater scale than measures to restrict imports.

Notice also that, in 2009, when many policymakers were worried about governments turning inward and succumbing to the import restrictions of the 1930s, in fact over one-third of world goods trade was affected by new export incentives. As policymakers pinched the protectionist balloon in one place, air was displaced, not eliminated.

It is, therefore, particularly unfortunate that so many trade analysts, journalists, and policymakers link trade discrimination or protectionism to import restrictions and falling world trade. Every agricultural trade economist is aware of the effects of export subsidies on global food trade. During the crisis years, that problem spread to manufactured goods trade, the WTO rules on export incentives for such goods notwithstanding.

Second, the fact that the share of global goods trade affected by export incentives fell in 2014 and the share affected by subsidies to local firms fell in 2015 implies that there is nothing inherent in the construction of the GTA dataset that implies these shares must rise over time.

Third, even though tariff increases in 2018 and 2019 received a lot of attention, in fact subsidies to import-competing firms still affect a larger share of world goods trade. Without in any way diminishing the potential resource misallocation and damage done by import tariff increases, taken together with the finding about export incentives, different types of subsidies dominate crisis-era trade discrimination. It may be that such subsidies are harder to detect—perhaps because they can be easier for governments to hide—but that does not deny their potential economic significance.

Fourth, underlying the statistics presented in figure 1-1 are thousands of discriminatory policy interventions documented by the GTA team. This serves as an important reminder that the world trading system can become thoroughly distorted by the accumulation of trade distortions. High-profile protectionist acts, such as Smoot-Hawley, are not necessary for a world trading system to become riddled with distortions.

Fifth, since figure 1-1 does report data on the shares of goods trade affected since President Trump was inaugurated, it is worth noting that the share of world trade affected by import tariff increases more than doubled from January 2016 to June 2019. Over the same timeframe the share of world goods trade affected by export incentives and subsidies to local firms also rose significantly. There is no suggestion that the United States is responsible for all of these changes.

Figure 1-1 can be thought of as revealing the share of world goods trade affected by the stock of trade distortions in force in each year. Another way of assessing the scale of world trade affected by government resort to trade discrimination is to compare the amounts of trade implicated by new trade distortions that are implemented each year. Figure 1-2 presents data on the latter.

Given the interest in the Sino-US bilateral tariff war, rather than report actual amounts of trade affected, each piece of data is benchmarked against the total value of Sino-US trade affected by tariff increases in 2018, indexing the latter at 100. Figure 1-2 presents data for each of the years 2009 to 2018 on the indexed value of trade affected by (a) US tariff increases that target only China and vice versa, (b) all tariff hikes that harm only one nation's exports, (c) all import distortions implemented in a given year, and (d) all export incentives implemented in a given year. Note also that the vertical axis of figure 1-2 uses a logarithmic scale.

The line at the bottom of figure 1-2 confirms that Sino-US targeting of each other's exports was unusually high in 2018, indeed at least ten times

FIGURE 1-2. Trade affected by the Sino-US bilateral tariff war pales in comparison with global totals for annual resort to new import distortions and new export incentives.

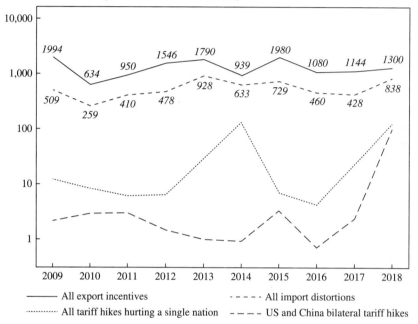

Total value of trade affected (indexed at 100 for the total value of trade affected by US-China tariff hikes in 2018)

——— All export incentives   - - - - - All import distortions
············ All tariff hikes hurting a single nation   – – – – US and China bilateral tariff hikes

Source: Trade shares estimated using information on policy changes from the Global Trade Alert database and detailed international trade data from the UN COMTRADE database.

higher than any year from 2009 to 2017. Targeting with tariff increases of any one nation's exports, which includes of course US targeting of Chinese exports and vice versa, spiked in 2014. This increase reflects the EU's withdrawal of trade preferences from Chinese goods, which came into force that year.[10] Not all tariff increases have the public profile of those imposed by the Trump administration.

A key finding in figure 1-2 is the extent to which the trade affected by new import distortions of any kind is, in every year, multiples of the tariff increases associated with the Sino-US tariff war in 2018. In fact, in 2018 the ratio of trade affected by new import distortions that year to trade affected by the tariff hikes between the United States and China was over eight, implying that plenty of other import restrictions were being imposed while attention focused on developments in Beijing and Washington. Another

FIGURE 1-3. The G-20 resorted to more trade discrimination and more subsidies than the next twenty largest trading nations.

Share of harmful measures (%)

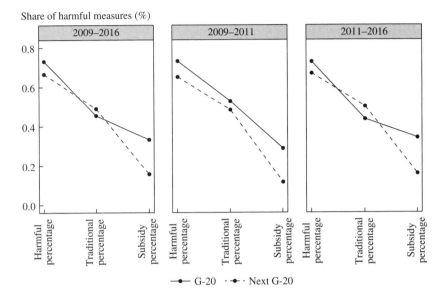

Source: Global Trade Alert database.

implication is that most policy interventions that restrict or limit imports do not target a single trading partner.

Another striking finding of figure 1-3 is that *in every year* the implementation of new export incentives has implicated more trade than that associated with new import distortions. The findings imply that in 2009 nearly twenty times as much trade was affected by new export incentives implemented that year than by the trade at risk from the bilateral Sino-US tariff war of 2018.

At least as far as the amount of trade affected is concerned, the findings in figure 1-2 call into question claims that US tariff hikes in 2018 and Chinese retaliation were a defining moment in the development of the world trading system.[11] In every year before the Sino-US trade war the amount of trade affected by import distortions and by export incentives was far greater. The prominence of an act of trade discrimination can be a misleading indicator of its global significance.

In sum, well before the Trump administration came into office governments around the world were engaging in trade discrimination. By 2016 over two-thirds of world goods trade was affected by trade discrimination that was in effect that year. Given that the GTA reporting started in November 2008, and allowing for the possibility that some discrimination may not have been documented, then the actual share of world goods trade affected is larger. Moreover, as shown in figure 4 of Evenett (2019), larger and larger proportions of world goods trade faced multiple policy-induced trade distortions. This is the consequence of the more than 11,000 instances of trade discrimination implemented worldwide between November 2008 and December 2016.

The absence of comparable information on the resort to trade discrimination before November 2008 might lead some to argue that it is unclear that the global financial crisis induced countries to increase trade discrimination. If this business-as-usual argument is correct, then it implies that there was sustained trade discrimination implicating significant scales of global commerce *before* the global financial crisis—in which case, it would be hard to argue that world trade rules reined in trade discrimination in that era as well.

Of course, it would be preferable to nail down the argument with data on commercial policy choice from before November 2008. Even without such data, logic dictates that one cannot simultaneously argue that the WTO was effective in deterring protectionism before the global financial crisis *and* that there was no fundamental change in trade discrimination after the crisis began.

The foregoing discussion makes clear that G-20 governments pursued an activist trade policy in the post-2008 period, continuing to do so well after the crisis had passed. One can legitimately ask how much the many measures distorted global trade flows, and what the net effect of trade activism has been on the volume of global trade.[12] Global trade bounced back relatively rapidly in the immediate postcrisis period, but stagnated thereafter, essentially growing at the pace of GDP. Many of the measures have the effect of stimulating national exports; others reduce the incentive to import. It is important to understand that there are good reasons why the policy response included less in the way of traditional trade-restricting instruments such as antidumping and safeguard actions, as these are less effective than government support in a world where firms increasingly are part of global value chains (see, for example, Gawande, Hoekman, and Cui 2015).

EXPLORATORY ANALYSIS OF THE DRIVERS OF NATIONAL
RESORT TO TRADE DISCRIMINATION

This section examines whether certain factors account for the cross-national variation in the relative treatment of domestic and foreign commercial interests. I pay particular attention to the share of a nation's entries in the GTA database whose implementation harmed foreign commercial interests, and often draw a distinction between policy measures implemented during the initial crisis response (November 2008 to December 2010) and afterward (but before the Trump administration took office—therefore, from January 2011 to December 2016). I do, however, occasionally present data for the entire period November 2008 to December 2016.

Moreover, this section often distinguishes between resort to traditional, more transparent policy instruments and resort to subsidies. The former are taken to include import tariff increases, trade defense measures, and safeguards (MAST chapter D), nonautomatic licensing procedures (MAST chapter E1), import quotas (MAST chapter E2), export restraints including voluntary export restraints (MAST chapter E5), tariff rate quotas (MAST chapter E6), and quantity controls not otherwise specified (MAST chapter E9). For the purposes of the analysis here, subsidies are taken to include subsidies to firms competing in home markets (MAST chapter L), export subsidies (MAST chapter P7), and export credits (MAST chapter P8). Recall that there are other forms of trade discrimination that fall outside these two groups; therefore observing, for example, an increased share of measures that are transparent does not automatically imply that the share of subsidies implemented by the same jurisdiction must be lower.

Recalling also the earlier discussion concerning the factors that may influence the behavior of G-20 governments, I often draw a distinction here between the variation in policy stance between G-20 members and other governments. Indeed, this provides a good starting point for the discussion in this section. First indicators of the resort to trade discrimination by the G-20 are contrasted with those of the next twenty largest trading nations (identified using precrisis trade data for 2007). In figure 1-3 the proportion of harmful measures implemented by the G-20 and the "next 20" is shown for all years and broken down into the initial crisis years and subsequent years.

In comparison with the next twenty largest trading nations, on average the policy mix of the G-20 nations was skewed more toward discrimination than liberalization and more toward the resort to subsidies, both for import-competing firms and for exporters. Resort to traditional instruments of trade discrimination was similar. Breaking out the policy responses between the initial crisis response and subsequent years is revealing. At the start of the crisis the G-20 nations tended to choose more traditional forms of discrimination and subsidies than the next twenty largest trading nations. After that, from 2011 to 2016, the G-20 resorted proportionally more to subsidies and less to transparent trade discrimination, such as tariff increases. Overall, the G-20 policy stance shifted away from more transparent trade discrimination as the crisis era lengthened.

I turn our attention now to other stylized facts concerning the crisis-era commercial policy response of the G-20 members in comparison with that of other nations. In what follows, rather than compute averages across the G-20 members, I treat each G-20 member as a separate observation, as well as all of the other customs territories (referred to collectively as non-G-20), not just the twenty next largest traders.

The first hypothesis considered is that governments that resort more to harmful measures also resort to more traditional forms of trade discrimination. For both the G-20 and non-G-20 countries during the entire period November 2008 to December 2016 (and for both subperiods) there is a strong negative and statistically significant relationship between resort to harmful measures and resort to transparent forms of trade discrimination, such as import tariffs (see figure 1-4). The negative relationship is stronger for the G-20 countries than for the non-G-20 countries. This finding is consistent with the claim that governments under more pressure to favor domestic commercial interests choose less transparent measures for doing so.

The second hypothesis is that governments that choose harmful measures also impose more subsidies. This hypothesis is not rejected by the data for the G-20 members and the non-G-20 members for the entire period and for the two subperiods. A positive correlation is found for the G-20 and non-G-20 countries in figure 1-5, suggesting that governments under more pressure to favor local firms did so through subsidies of different types.[13] That this is a global phenomenon is significant in light of the criticism that singles out China's system of subsidization.

The third hypothesis examined is that greater resort to trade discrimination correlates with a higher proportion of imports being affected by such

FIGURE 1-4. Governments that resorted more to trade discrimination resorted less to transparent trade restrictions, November 2008– December 2016.

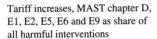

Tariff increases, MAST chapter D,
E1, E2, E5, E6 and E9 as share of
all harmful interventions

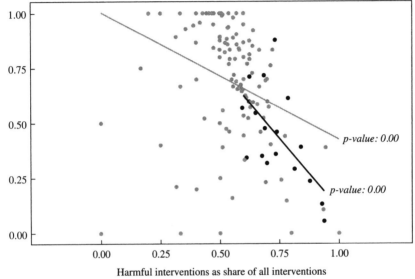

Harmful interventions as share of all interventions

● Non-G-20   ● G-20

Source: Global Trade Alert database.

Note: For each plot in figure 1-4 an ordinary-least-squares regression was performed on the relationship between the variables on the two axes for the G-20 sample and separately for the non-G-20 sample. The fitted lines are reproduced in each figure, as are the *p* values for the estimated coefficients.

discrimination. Figure 1-6 reveals no such correlation in the data for either the G-20 nations or the non-G-20 nations for the entire period (November 2008–December 2016). However, for the initial crisis phase a positive correlation was found for the non-G-20 nations, which might be related to the earlier finding that for these countries the resort to traditional forms of trade discrimination falls off slowly as the propensity to choose trade discrimination increases. Whatever the reason, figure 1-6 shows a clear difference in behavior between the G-20 and non-G-20 nations, at least as far as the initial crisis response is concerned.

The possibility that trade discrimination might substitute for exchange rate depreciation was noted at the beginning of the chapter. Here the dis-

FIGURE 1-5. Governments were more likely to use subsidies when they resorted to trade discrimination, November 2008–December 2016.

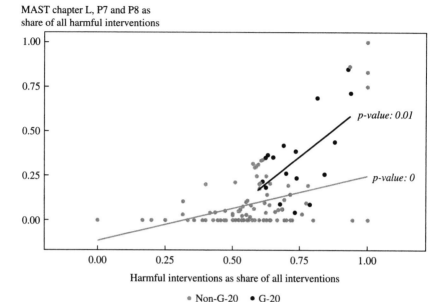

MAST chapter L, P7 and P8 as share of all harmful interventions

Harmful interventions as share of all interventions

• Non-G-20   • G-20

Source: Global Trade Alert database.

cussion is broadened to include fiscal policy stimulus, not least because many governments responded initially to the global financial crisis by increasing public expenditure on goods and services in a Keynesian manner. Later, of course, many governments embraced austerity programs, with the opposite implications for government spending (or at least for the growth of government spending).

Figure 1-7 plots the resort to trade discrimination (as measured by the share of measures implemented that were harmful to foreign commercial interests) against the logarithm of the ratio of government spending on final consumption goods between the respective end year and start year. For both the G-20 and non-G-20 there is a negative relationship between these two variables in the initial crisis response years, November 2008–December 2010, suggesting that fiscal stimulus acted as a substitute for tilting the commercial playing field in favor of national firms. However, the negative relationship is statistically significant only for the non-G20 nations. Moreover, the relationship breaks down for the later years (2011–2016). In sum, as far as

FIGURE 1-6. Only in the initial crisis response did greater resort to trade distortions result in a higher share of imports being affected, and then only for non-G-20 nations.

November 2008–December 2016

Share of imports affected by
harmful interventions implemented

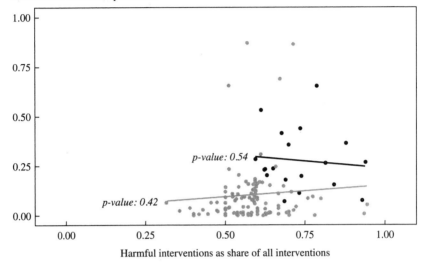

Harmful interventions as share of all interventions

Non-G-20   • G-20

November 2008–December 2010

Share of imports affected by
harmful interventions implemented

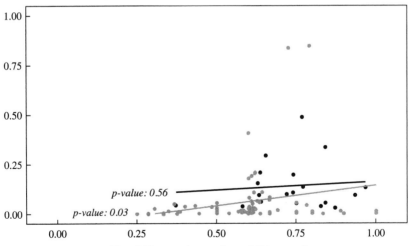

Harmful interventions as share of all interventions

Non-G-20   • G-20

FIGURE 1-7. **Non-G-20 governments that expanded government spending were less likely to resort to trade discrimination, but the relationship broke down after the initial crisis response.**

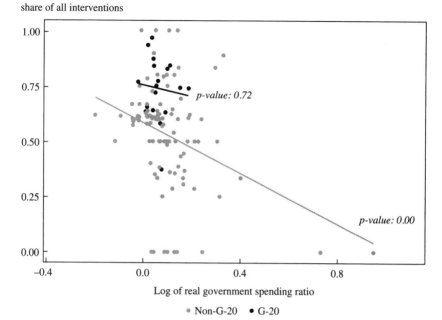

November 2008–December 2010

Harmful interventions as
share of all interventions

p-value: 0.72

p-value: 0.00

Log of real government spending ratio

● Non-G-20   ● G-20

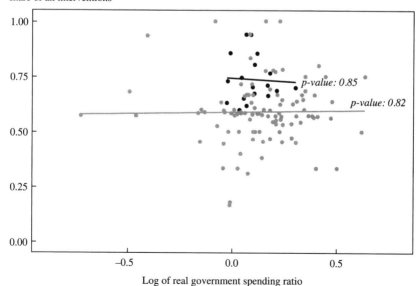

January 2011–December 2016

Harmful interventions as
share of all interventions

p-value: 0.85

p-value: 0.82

Log of real government spending ratio

● Non-G-20   ● G-20

Source: Global Trade Alert database.

fiscal policy is concerned, the substitutability hypothesis cannot be entirely rejected or entirely endorsed.

As far as the potential substitutability between exchange rate depreciation and resort to trade discrimination is concerned, if anything, these two policy interventions were complements for the non-G-20 nations during their initial crisis responses (see figure 1-8). Interestingly, no such relationship carries over to the period 2011–2016. Among the G-20 nations there is no strong relationship between these two policy choices during the initial crisis response (November 2008–December 2011) or subsequently (2011–2016). Once again, G-20 behavior appears to diverge from non-G-20 behavior.

To assess whether the initial dislocation in the labor market, as proxied by the increase in the rate of unemployment from 2007 to 2009, may have influenced the resort to trade discrimination, I plotted and analyzed the relationship between these variables (see figure 1-9). The "embedded liberalism" hypothesis of Ruggie suggests that accepted international norms, such as nondiscrimination toward trading partners, may be suspended if a crisis threatens social stability. The initial labor market impact of the global financial crisis differed from country to country, and so it is of interest to see if any clear relationship appears in the data.

The upper panel of figure 1-9 shows that, for the G-20 members, resort to trade discrimination was greater by governments whose economies experienced higher initial increases in unemployment. However, this positive relationship is not statistically significant. Interestingly, for the initial crisis years there is a mild negative relationship between the initial unemployment increase and trade discrimination for the non-G-20 countries, which is at odds with Ruggie's thesis. As the bottom panel of figure 1-9 shows, there is no apparent relationship between the initial increase in unemployment and the propensity to engage in trade discrimination from 2011 to 2016, suggesting that whatever initial shock there was to national labor markets did not have an enduring effect on commercial policy choice.

The tightness of a country's WTO obligations is the final conditioning factor considered here. Much is made of trade rules and their apparent power. Given the substantial differences in the tariff binding overhangs among WTO members before the global financial crisis hit, to what extent did governments with less room for maneuver choose different commercial policy mixes than others? Figure 1-10 plots the propensity to resort to discrimination against the tariff binding overhang in 2007 for the

FIGURE 1-8. For non-G-20 governments, resort to trade discrimination appears to complement exchange rate depreciation, but only in the initial crisis response.

November 2008–December 2010

Harmful interventions as share of all interventions

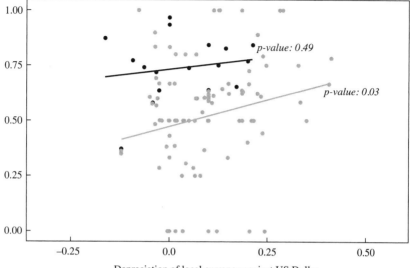

Depreciation of local currency against US Dollar, expressed as a long of the ratio

● Non-G-20   ● G-20

January 2011–December 2016

Harmful interventions as share of all interventions

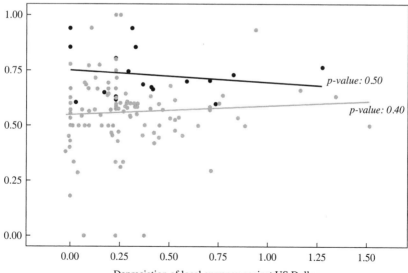

Depreciation of local currency against US Dollar, expressed as a long of the ratio

● Non-G-20   ● G-20

Source: Global Trade Alert database

FIGURE 1-9. Initial increases in unemployment may have affected resort to trade discrimination only in the early years of the crisis.

November 2008–December 2010

Harmful interventions as
share of all interventions

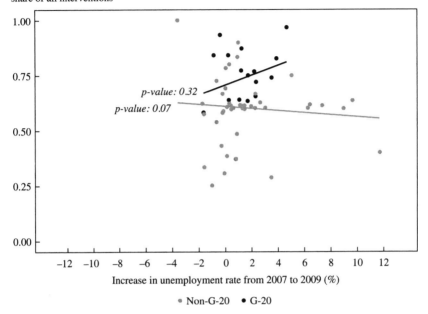

Increase in unemployment rate from 2007 to 2009 (%)

● Non-G-20   ● G-20

January 2011–December 2016

Harmful interventions as
share of all interventions

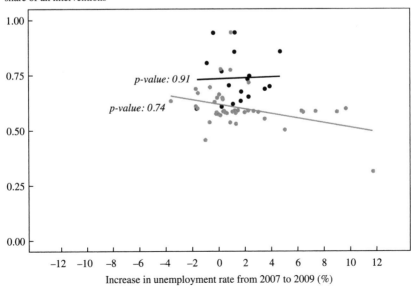

Increase in unemployment rate from 2007 to 2009 (%)

● Non-G-20   ● G-20

Source: Global Trade Alert database

FIGURE 1-10. G-20 members with smaller tariff binding overhangs tended to resort more to trade discrimination, but only after the initial crisis period was over.

November 2008–December 2010

Harmful interventions as
share of all interventions

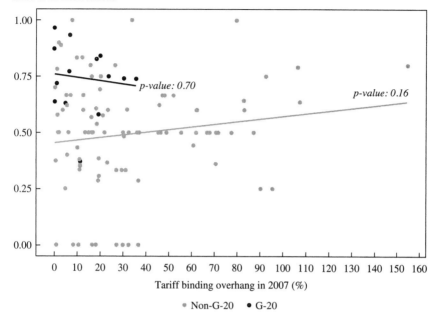

Tariff binding overhang in 2007 (%)

● Non-G-20   ● G-20

January 2011–December 2016

Harmful interventions as
share of all interventions

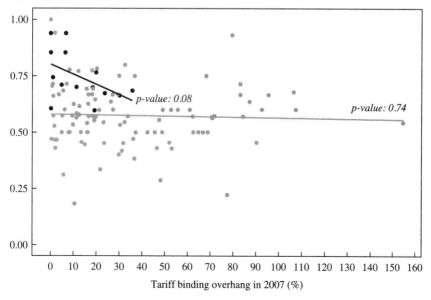

Tariff binding overhang in 2007 (%)

● Non-G-20   ● G-20

Source: Global Trade Alert database.

initial crisis years (November 2008–December 2010) and subsequently (January 2011–December 2016).

Reviewing both panels of Figure 1-10 for non-G-20 countries there is no evident relationship between their commercial policy responses and the tightness of their tariff bindings in either period. This may be because other factors matter or because there are better indicators of the strength of a nation's WTO disciplines. In contrast, for the G-20 members a negative relationship is found in both periods, implying that the smaller the tariff binding overhang the larger the resort to trade discrimination. However, it should be noted that that relationship is only statistically significant (and only at the 10 percent level) once the initial crisis era passed—that is, for the six years 2011–2016. It would appear that tighter tariff disciplines on G-20 members are associated with, if anything, a mix of more harmful policies toward foreign commercial interests.

Similar correlations were performed for the resort to transparent forms of trade discrimination (see figure 1-11). In both periods there is no apparent relationship between resort to transparent forms of trade discrimination and strictness of tariff bindings for the large group of non-G-20 countries. However, for the G-20 countries there is a statistically insignificant positive relationship, suggesting a weak tendency for G-20 members that have greater leeway to legally raise tariffs to resort to more transparent forms of trade discrimination (of which, tariff increases are one option.)

When it comes to subsidization, however, there is a stronger relationship between the tightness of tariff bindings and the propensity to intervene in this manner to harm foreign commercial interests (see figure 1-12). Although the statistical significance of the relationship is stronger for the years 2011–2016, in both periods those G-20 members that had less room to increase their import tariffs were more likely to subsidize local firms and exporters. Whatever one's assessment of the effect of WTO disciplines on the quantum of G-20 trade discrimination, this finding suggests that the latitude allowed governments in their precrisis tariff obligations at the WTO affected the form in which they discriminated against foreign commercial interests. Taking the findings of figures 1-11 and 1-12 together, G-20 governments appear to have substituted transparent trade restrictions for subsidies.

Overall, this exploratory data analysis reveals differences between G-20 and non-G-20 members in the use of trade discrimination and in the form of that discrimination. Monetary and fiscal policy choices appear to have

FIGURE 1-11. A weak positive correlation exists for the G-20 members between the size of tariff binding overhang and resort to more transparent trade discrimination.

November 2008–December 2010

Tariff increase, MAST chapter D, E1, E2, E5,
E6 and E9 as share of all harmful interventions

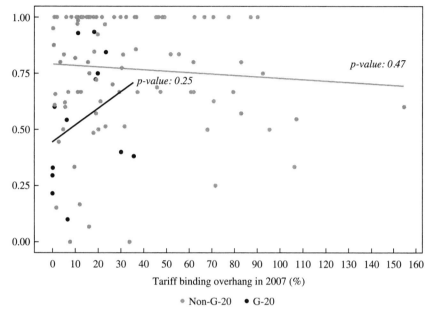

January 2011–December 2016

Tariff increase, MAST chapter D, E1, E2, E5,
E6 and E9 as share of all harmful interventions

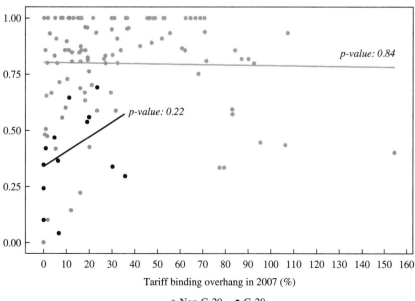

Source: Global Trade Alert database.

FIGURE 1-12. G-20 members with smaller tariff binding overhangs resorted more to subsidies, in particular after the initial crisis period was over.

November 2008–December 2010

MAST chapter L, P7 and P8 as
share of all harmful interventions

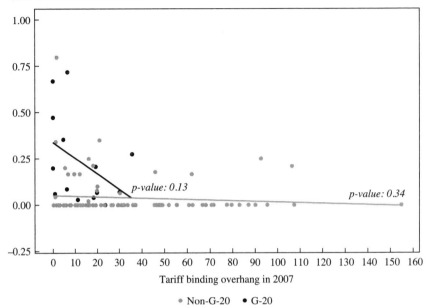

January 2011–December 2016

MAST chapter L, P7 and P8 as
share of all harmful interventions

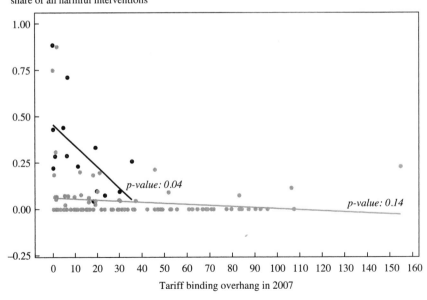

Source: Global Trade Alert database.

influenced the commercial policy decisions of the non-G-20 members more than the G-20 members, whereas the tightness of precrisis tariff bindings appears to have had more influence on the propensity and form of trade discrimination of the G-20 members than on the non-G-20 members.

CONCLUDING REMARKS

Given the attention that the Sino-US trade war has received, it is no wonder that analysts began examining the causes and consequences of this high-profile disruption to what many regarded as a well-functioning global trading system. Making use of a detailed dataset of public policy interventions collected over the past decade, the evidence presented here shows that the world trade in goods was thoroughly distorted, principally by trade-distorting subsidies, well before the election of Donald Trump seemed at all likely.

Since economic policy analyses require carefully specified initial conditions against which to judge a policy shock, such as imposing tariffs on several hundred billion dollars of Chinese imports, then taking account of how distorted trade was when the Trump administration took office could have material implications for the estimates of that shock. Put differently, modeling the impact of the Sino-US tariff war on the assumption that world goods markets are trading freely, or moderately freely, may be highly misleading.

Another important finding is that steps to stimulate national exports cover much more of world goods trade than steps to restrict imports. The trade policy response to the Great Depression of the 1930s involved significant resort to import restrictions and competitive devaluations. The trade policy response to the 2008 global financial crisis was dominated by measures to promote exports. Like generals, who are often accused of trying to refight the last war, many trade policy analysts appear to have looked for the 1930s policy response and, having found none, prematurely declared victory for the world trading system. There is no doubt that the economics and political economy of export incentives and import restrictions are different, but they are both trade distortions.

That nearly three-quarters of world trade currently faces one or more trade distortions imposed since the crisis began calls into question the effectiveness of current international trade rules.[14] Some may be tempted to argue that matters would have been worse in the absence of those trade rules. Surely the riposte is that if distortions to three-quarters of world trade constitute victory, then what constitutes defeat? Still, as the exploratory data analysis revealed, international trade rules may well have affected the form—if not necessarily the quantum—of trade discrimination implemented by the G-20 members.

One of the more interesting findings in the exploratory analysis is related to the differences in the factors that correlate with the commercial policy choices of the G-20 and non-G-20 countries. These differences are worth exploring further. Was G-20 policy choice different because these economies were larger, in absolute or relative terms? Or was there something about the dialogue among the G-20 members that altered their resort to trade discrimination? If so, what mechanism was at work and how did it add value to the dialogue under WTO auspices?

In sum, the travails of the world trading system predate the Trump administration. Stating that does not deny or diminish the harm being done to international trade and investment flows by the implementation of America First commercial policies. Those policies should be condemned on a number of grounds—economic, political, and geostrategic. The risk is that by concentrating attention on the high-profile tariff developments of the two years 2017–2019, other commercially significant forms of trade discrimination will be overlooked by analysts and policymakers. The consequences are likely to be poorly framed analysis and inadequate policy prescription.

NOTES

Thanks to Patrick Buess and Piotr Lukaszuk for their support in preparing the figures for this chapter. Any errors are mine. Comments are welcome and should be sent to simon.evenett@unisg.ch. The project to which this chapter contributes received funding from the European Union's Horizon 2020 research and innovation program under grant agreement no. 770680.

1. For a longer account of the methods used by the GTA team to document public policy see section four of Evenett (2019).

2. The pitfalls associated with confining data collection to a predefined set of trade policies are described in section three of Evenett (2019). The deeper question here is, given the many forms of cross-border commerce in existence in the twenty-first century, what definition of protectionism is fit for purpose? The GTA does not include information on technical barriers to trade, sani-

tary, and phytosanitary standards, and regional trade agreements, each of which some analysts contend can be a source of discrimination against foreign commercial interests. There exist other databases that document developments in each of the latter three areas of policy. Note also that the relative treatment test is not a test of WTO legality.

3. Statistics on global totals for policy interventions harming and benefiting foreign commercial interests can be obtained from Global Trade Alert, https://www.globaltradealert.org/global_dynamics.

4. For a list of sixteen MAST chapters of nontariff measures as well as other information about this UN initiative, see United Nations Conference on Trade and Development (UNCTAD), "International Classification of Non-Tariff Measures," https://unctad.org/en/PublicationsLibrary/ditctab20122 _en.pdf?user=46.

5. Products are classified using the six-digit level of disaggregation of the UN Harmonised System. This is the most disaggregated product classification for which international trade data is available worldwide. Services are assigned the relevant three-digit level of disaggregation of the UN Central Product Classification (CPC).

6. The GTA team has experimented with other ways to address the endogenity problem. For more information, kindly write to the author.

7. The data are available at Global Trade Alert, https://www.globaltrade alert.org/data_extraction.

8. The estimates for 2019 relate to the trade discrimination in effect in June 2019. Technically, import tariff increases do not have a place in the MAST classification, but since they are a form of trade discrimination they are included in the calculation for "all" trade distortions.

9. There are other forms of trade discrimination, such as government procurement measures to buy local products, that do not fit into these three categories. The purpose here is to show how much goods trade is affected by each of these three significant types of trade discrimination. Note also that any trade flow could be affected by more than one type of trade discrimination, so there is no reason to expect the sum of the trade affected in any year across these three classes of policy to equal or be less than the total for the "all" category.

10. For more details, see Legge, Lukaszuk, and Evenett (2018).

11. There may well be other grounds for arguing that the Sino-US trade war was a defining moment. Evenett and Fritz (2018) argue that the brazen nature of the US actions against China contrasts sharply with the creeping, hidden, or murky protectionism witnessed globally in prior years.

12. It is important, of course, to assess not just the number and types of measures used by governments but also how big the distorting effect has been on global trade. This is an important research question that is beyond the scope of

this chapter. It requires disentangling export-promoting from import-restricting policies and considering the associated changes in investment incentives for firms, which will be influenced by other factors, including technological changes and perceptions of policy uncertainty.

13. The correlation remains positive and the p values low if the observations where no subsidies were observed are dropped.

14. Even in the absence of export incentives, as of this writing some 40.9 percent of world goods trade faces other forms of trade discrimination. Containing protectionism to "just" two-fifths of global goods trade hardly seems a success either.

REFERENCES

Baldwin, R. E. 1970. *Nontariff Distortions of International Trade.* Washington, D.C.: Brookings.

Bagwell, K., C. Bown, and R. Staiger. 2016. "Is the WTO Passé?" *Journal of Economic Literature* 54 (4): 1125–31.

Bhagwati, J. 1988. *Protectionism.* MIT Press.

Bown, C. 2011. "Introduction." In *The Great Recession and Import Protection: The Role of Temporary Trade Barriers*, edited by Chad P. Bown, 1–51. London: CEPR and the World Bank, 2011.

Eichengreen, B., and D. Irwin. 2010. "The Slide to Protectionism in the Great Depression: Who Succumbed and Why?" *Journal of Economic History* 70 (4): 871–97.

Evenett, S. J. 2019. "Protectionism, State Discrimination, and International Business since the Onset of the Global Financial Crisis," *Journal of International Business Policy* 2 (1): 9–36.

Evenett, S. J., and J. Fritz. 2018. *Brazen Unilateralism: The US-China Tariff War in Perspective. The 23rd GTA Report.* London: CEPR Press.

Gawande, K., B. Hoekman, and Y. Cui. 2015. "Global Supply Chains and Trade Policy Responses to the 2008 Financial Crisis." *World Bank Economic Review* 29 (1): 102–28.

International Monetary Fund (IMF). 2016. *Subdued Demand: Symptoms and Remedies.* World Economic Outlook. Washington D.C. October. https://www.imf.org/en/Publications/WEO/Issues/2016/12/31/Subdued-Demand-Symptoms-and-Remedies.

Kee, H. L., C. Neagu, and A. Nicita. 2013. "Is Protectionism on the Rise? Assessing National Trade Policies during the Crisis of 2008." *Review of Economics and Statistics* 95 (1): 342–46.

Krugman, P. 2018. "A Trade War Primer." *New York Times*, June 3.

Legge, Stefan, Piotr Lukaszuk, and Simon Evenett. 2018. "Raising Tariffs on China without Grabbing Headlines." *Vox*, April 17. https://voxeu.org/article/raising-tariffs-china-without-grabbing-headlines.

Rau, M-L., and A. Vogt. 2019. "Data Concepts and Sources of Non-tariff Measures (NTMs)—an Exploratory Analysis." In *Behind-the-Border Policies: Assessing and Addressing Non-Tariff Measures*, edited by J. Francois and B. Hoekman. Cambridge University Press.

Rose, A. 2013. "The March of an Economic Idea? Protectionism Isn't Counter-cyclic (Anymore)." *Economic Policy* 28: 569–612.

Ruggie, J. 1992. "International Regimes, Transactions, and Change: Embedded Liberalism in the Postwar Economic Order." *International Organization* 36 (2): 379–415.

2

ANTIDUMPING AND MARKET COMPETITION

IMPLICATIONS FOR EMERGING ECONOMIES

CHAD P. BOWN

In the first fifteen years of the twenty-first century, antidumping use by the major emerging economies became a much more important feature of the World Trade Organization (WTO) system, rivaling its use by industrialized countries. By 2016, India, Turkey, Argentina, and Indonesia were each subjecting at least as large a share of the value of their imports to trade-distorting antidumping measures as the European Union, one of the largest "historical" users of the policy. Other emerging economies like Brazil and China were not far behind. Moreover, what had begun a century earlier as a policy mainly limiting North-North trade, and then later North-South trade, was rapidly emerging as a significant barrier to South-South trade.

Antidumping laws originated as the international counterpart of the domestic antitrust (competition) policies that industrialized countries began to enact in the late 1800s. Their initial purpose was to protect domestic consumers from predatory actions on the part of foreign suppliers (Viner

1923). However, antidumping remained an insignificant element of trade policy until the late 1970s. Tariffs on many products were still high enough to make competing imports only a minor threat to domestic producers. The criteria for antidumping protection were also difficult enough to satisfy that the United States, later the most important user of antidumping, did not impose any antidumping duties in the 1950s, and only about 10 percent of US cases in the 1960s resulted in duties (Irwin, 2005a). But by the 1980s, modifications to the General Agreement on Tariffs and Trade (GATT) made as a result of the 1979 completion of the Tokyo Round of GATT negotiations had "transformed this little used trade statute into the workhorse of international protection" (Prusa and Skeath 2002)—at least for the five users that initiated nearly all antidumping cases in the 1980s (the United States, Canada, the European Community, Australia, and New Zealand). The first change broadened the definition of "less than fair value" to include sales below cost as well as price discrimination between home and export markets. The second change weakened the injury requirement by reducing the emphasis on a causal link between dumped imports and material injury to the competing domestic industry. Over the next fifteen years, the antidumping activity of the historical users soared.

Along with the greatly increased use of antidumping came new concerns. Over the years, laws and procedures had evolved so as to weaken the original link between antidumping and threat of predation. Moreover, expanded use of antidumping especially, but also of countervailing duties and other forms of contingent protection, raised a different concern about the effect of these policies on conditions of market competition. Concern that injurious dumping might inhibit market competition over the long run gave way to a worry that antidumping laws were not designed to differentiate predatory dumping from ordinary lower-cost import competition and thus were being used purely as a protectionist device. That was followed by concern that existence and abuse of antidumping might actually lead to more collusive outcomes and less competitive markets than in the absence of antidumping laws. These fears spurred a sizable theoretical and empirical literature that peaked in the late 1990s.

I thus begin this chapter by reviewing and updating the normative case for antidumping. Antidumping started as an international extension of efforts via antitrust policy to prevent losses in overall economic well-being that result from the exercise of monopoly power in the domestic market. I then consider the literature on the US and European application of antidumping in the 1980s and 1990s, in which some analysts conclude that, rather than preventing foreign suppliers from gaining market power, antidumping measures may instead facilitate cartelization of the affected market. When this happens, domestic import-competing producers still gain, but overall economic well-being is reduced.

The examination continues with an analysis of important changes in the conditions of the world economy since the 1990s. I explore questions relating to the market-competition effects of antidumping in light of recent evidence that policies such as antidumping have proliferated globally and are now used much more by emerging market economies than by the industrialized economies. Has the case for, or against, antidumping changed for these as well as for the high-income economies, especially given the significant developments in world trade since the 1990s? These developments include the emergence of important new traders, most notably China; fragmentation of the value chain in many industries; and the increased role in world trade of multinational firms, including some based in countries that had little or no outward foreign direct investment until the twenty-first century.

The rest of the chapter proceeds with a brief review of the institutional evolution of antidumping laws from the perspective of competitiveness concerns; a description of the theoretical and empirical research from the 1980s and 1990s that analyzes and documents the market-segmenting consequences of contingent protection; and an investigation of the argument that the situation has changed somewhat in the 2000s. In particular, I explore the implications for emerging markets.

ANTIDUMPING PROVISIONS IN HISTORICAL CONTEXT

Why should trade arrangements like the GATT/WTO, whose stated purpose is to promote freer and more transparent conditions of trade, include provisions that allow members considerable freedom to protect domestic producers in a manner that is far from transparent?[1] The question is particularly relevant today, when a significant share of all trade is subject to protection via antidumping measures, along with other types of unilateral, nontransparent contingent protection, collectively known as temporary trade barriers (TTBs). During the recent global recession, domestic political pressure for protection rose around the world. Through use of antidumping and other WTO-legal TTBs, many members were able to increase the extent of protection for domestic industries while still complying with their WTO commitments (Bown 2011a, 2011b).[2]

Some economists justify antidumping as one of the important flexibilities that the GATT/WTO trade agreements provide to allow countries facing political or economic shocks to escape temporarily from their commitments to keep tariffs low. Antidumping also allows WTO members to undo some liberalization while maintaining overall cooperation with respect to trade policy—that is, without undermining the entirety of the agreements.[3] Indeed, evidence for the United States suggests that antidumping protection is more likely to be obtained in the face of economic shocks that put trade policy cooperation under additional stress (Bown and Crowley, 2013), while evidence from other countries indicates that antidumping may be used where overall tariff protection has recently been reduced (Bown and Tovar 2011).[4] Finger and Nogues (2005) present a number of case studies for Latin American economies suggesting that antidumping and other TTBs allowed governments to manage domestic political pressures for import protection while maintaining a generally liberal trade policy.[5] In other words, some controlled access to new protection may be the price of maintaining an open trading system. Implicit is the idea that overall gains from trade in a particular sector must sometimes be sacrificed in order to appease domestic groups that are harmed by competing imports. Vandenbussche and Zanardi (2010) quantify this implied sacrifice by estimating the effect of antidumping laws on *aggregate* trade flows between new adopters and their trading partners.[6]

But the early history of antidumping reflects a completely different rationale—one based on the possible use by foreign suppliers of temporarily low export prices to achieve market power. National antidumping laws in the United States and other industrialized countries predate the original GATT by several decades, and in their earliest versions were closely linked to antitrust policy. In 1904, Canada became the first country to impose an antidumping law, closely followed by New Zealand (1905) and Australia (1906). The first U.S antidumping statute (1916) was very narrow in its scope, requiring not only a low price of imports relative to some standard but also evidence of *intent* on the part of foreign suppliers to injure current or potential domestic producers and/or to achieve a monopoly position in the relevant domestic market—what came to be called *predatory dumping*. In terms of language, the original antidumping laws closely resemble antitrust statutes that address predatory pricing in domestic competition.

As with domestic antitrust laws, the original purpose of antidumping laws was to protect consumers by preventing abuse of market power. Similar to antitrust, the objective was to prevent losses of *overall* national well-being, rather than simply to prevent losses to import-competing producers, although the latter would be an inevitable result of applying the law. Under the original law, dumping was defined as setting an export price below that charged in the exporter's home market—that is, price discrimination, with no reference to cost of production. Moreover, rather than antidumping duties, the US law, similarly to antitrust statutes, called for importers of dumped goods to pay triple damages.

But despite the common roots of antidumping and antitrust laws, the criteria for intervention in the two bodies of laws soon diverged (Messerlin 1994). The US antidumping law was broadened in 1921 to allow antidumping action for any case in which the import price was below that in the home market, regardless of intent. Under the 1979 Trade Act, the scope was increased again by including dumping defined in terms of pricing below a constructed measure of average cost, including a required 8 percent profit margin (Shin 1998). Perhaps most important, while the goal of antitrust law was to protect overall national well-being by limiting the exercise of monopoly power, antidumping focused on protection of the domestic petitioners, without regard for effects on consumers.[7]

Did the original antidumping statutes address a real problem? Was predatory dumping an important policy concern at the time? Viner (1923, 61) refers to "writers hostile to Germany" who charged that "much of German dumping was actuated by predatory motives." However, Viner also notes the lack of conclusive evidence, pointing out that no such charges had been made against the powerful German *kartells* before the outbreak of war in 1914. But Sidak (1982) cites evidence from contemporary economic thought as well as legal commentary that prevention of monopolization, not simple deterrence of foreign competition, was the intent of the original 1916 US antidumping law. Sykes (1998) likewise finds evidence that concerns regarding predation motivated early Canadian and US antidumping statutes. Yet by the 1980s, the potential for protectionist *effect*, if not intent, of antidumping action had become clear. One important reason is that, in contrast to US antitrust law, application of antidumping does not require evidence that alleged foreign *intent* to achieve market power has a reasonable chance of success.

DUMPING, ANTIDUMPING, AND CONDITIONS
OF MARKET COMPETITION

This section reviews the theory and evidence through the 1990s on the relationship between dumping, antidumping trade policy, and the competitiveness of markets.

Theory: Dumping and Overall Economic Well-Being
in the Importing Country

Willig (1998) provides a theoretical survey of possible motivations for dumping and the associated effects on overall economic well-being in the importing country. He examines several types of dumping that have little or no relationship to creation of market power and distinguishes these from two categories of dumping that do aim at establishing market power. In the first group are simple price discrimination, cyclical dumping, and dumping by nonmarket economies. In all three cases, the likely effect on the importing country is to make the domestic market more, rather than less, competitive. Thus, as with other types of trade, overall economic well-being in the importing country is likely to be increased rather than reduced, with benefits to consuming households or industries outweighing losses to import-competing producers.

In contrast, dumping that does aim at establishing and exploiting market power can indeed impose losses on the importing country. The simpler form of potentially harmful dumping is predatory dumping, the international equivalent of predatory pricing: sellers accept losses in the short run in order to achieve monopoly profits further in the future. The foreign seller's low price is intended to force domestic competitors to exit the market, thereby allowing the foreign seller to secure market power and future monopoly profits. But the industrial organization literature suggests that the necessary conditions for successful predatory pricing are unlikely to be satisfied, and the same qualifications cast doubt on the importance of this behavior on the part of foreign producers. For the strategy to be successful, the foreign producer must be better able than the domestic incumbent firms to withstand the short-term losses associated with a low price and must have the production capacity necessary to serve a significant share of the importing country market at that low price. Moreover, the domestic industry must be characterized by barriers to entry and also to reentry by domestic firms once the foreign producer attempts to exploit its monopoly power by raising price. Likewise, actual and potential foreign supply must be highly concentrated; otherwise, competition among import suppliers would force the price of imports back toward the competitive level.

Strategic dumping is a more complicated form of dumping that is also potentially harmful to the importing country.[8] Dumping in this case exploits static or dynamic scale economies in the relevant industry, a condition inconsistent with perfect competition. US firms leveled allegations of strategic dumping in the 1980s after exporters in Europe and Japan began to challenge the US technological lead in research and development–intensive products. In strategic dumping, low-priced exports, possibly sold below full cost but almost always for less than the price in the exporter's home market, are used to increase the firm's or industry's size,[9] thereby achieving scale economies that result in lower costs or better products, and thus higher profits in the future. As domestic purchases shift toward imports, the market share of domestic suppliers is correspondingly reduced, with opposite effects on scale and profitability. Domestic import-competing suppliers may therefore be forced out of the market because they have higher costs or less advanced products. However, in contrast to predatory dumping, strategic dumping may be profitable for exporters even if it does not cause exit by domestic import-competing suppliers but merely raises the scale of exporter production while decreasing the scale of competing domestic firms.

As with predatory dumping, stringent conditions are required for this strategy to be profitable, and further conditions are required for strategic dumping to harm overall economic well-being in the importing country. First, the exporter's production must be large enough to achieve the relevant scale economies, while production by competing domestic firms must be small enough to prevent them from capturing similar benefits. Thus, if the strategic dumping story has any practical relevance, it would be for large exporters that are in competition with small domestic firms. Yet most antidumping cases during the 1980s and the early 1990s were brought by importing countries with large markets for the designated products and large domestic suppliers against exporting countries with smaller domestic markets and smaller producers, with the United States and the European Union serving as the "domestic" economies and thereby accounting for the largest number of antidumping initiations.[10]

A requirement for exporters to profit from strategic dumping is that the exporter's own market be protected—by trade policies, tastes, transportation costs, or more subtle barriers—from penetration by suppliers in the importing country, thus allowing producers to enjoy a profitable "sanctuary market." Countries appearing to provide this kind of sanctuary market for some products (such as autos, consumer electronics) included Japan in the 1970s and 1980s and South Korea in later decades. Profits on domestic sales then allow exporting at a price below average cost—that is, dumping. Some of the emerging economies that have been recent targets of antidumping do indeed protect their domestic markets for like products, but with the notable exception of China, these exporters' domestic markets are typically small relative to those of the importers. Thus it is hard to imagine that domestic producers in the import-competing country suffer any significant scale disadvantage caused by exclusion from these markets.[11]

A loss in overall economic well-being in the importing country due to strategic dumping also requires that foreign supply be highly concentrated or that the exporting country government control total export quantities. Otherwise, competition among exporters would force the price down toward average cost. In this case, consumers in the importing countries rather than the foreign suppliers would be the main beneficiaries of the scale economies captured by exporters. Of course, import-competing firms would lose, and the domestic industry might even disappear, though this could be true regardless of the reason why exporters' costs were lower. But the exporting countries most often alleged to be dumping (Japan in the 1980s, China today) have found effective ways to coordinate exporter behavior so as to limit total exports. The same potential for control might also exist when suppliers are subsidiaries in various exporting countries of the same multinational firm. Thus predation supported by the cost advantage of scale economies cannot be ruled out a priori. Nonetheless, for most of the relevant products, prices continued to fall even after domestic suppliers left the industry, rather than rising as exporters attempt to exploit their increased market power. Documented exceptions to this pattern have resulted more from trade measures (for example, the 1986 US-Japan semiconductor agreement discussed later) than from successful predation by exporters.

Evidence through the 1990s: Did Antidumping Target Predatory or Strategic Dumping?

Empirical evidence from the 1980s and 1990s suggests that antidumping law in its more recent expanded form was typically applied in cases where even the *necessary* conditions for successful predatory or strategic dumping were not satisfied. As Shin (1998) argues, dumping criteria based only on price or cost do not offer a practical method of distinguishing cases in which dumping is predatory from ones in which consumers are likely to benefit from increased competition. Accordingly, he searches for structural characteristics of markets in which predatory dumping is likely to be a profitable strategy in the long run. Such a market must be relatively concentrated, with significant barriers to new entry as well as to reentry by firms that have previously exited. Also, exporters to that market who are alleged to be dumping should be relatively concentrated, and import penetration into the market should be high or rapidly growing.

Shin examines US dumping cases for the period 1980 through 1989. For the industries in which dumping was found, he determines whether the structural characteristics necessary for successful predation were present— that is, whether damage to the United States from predatory dumping might plausibly be expected. He concludes that the domestic market-concentration criterion for successful predatory dumping was satisfied in only 39 of 282 cases with nonnegative outcomes—less than 14 percent of the cases. Moreover, this figure is an upper limit, since Shin does not, for example, go on to determine whether the concentrated markets were protected by barriers to entry or reentry, or whether foreign export supply was concentrated. Thus only rare cases among instances of confirmed dumping were likely to involve anticompetitive intent on the part of foreign firms. As a consequence, Shin concludes that, rather than protecting US consumers from predatory behavior, most applications of antidumping policy during the 1980s probably reduced US welfare by limiting beneficial import competition—though of course still increasing the profitability of domestic suppliers as well as those foreign exporters not subject to the antidumping actions.

In a similar study of dumping cases in the European Union during the period 1980–97, Bourgeois and Messerlin (1998) conclude that an even smaller share, around 2 percent, satisfied the conditions necessary for predatory behavior on the part of exporters alleged to be dumping. Like Shin (1998), they do not examine whether exporters had the capacity to exercise and maintain market power and thus to profit from earlier dumping, a second criterion that would have ruled out predatory behavior for at least some of these cases. As in the US cases, antidumping merely protected domestic import-competing industries from the effects of import competition, but at the expense of domestic users of the affected products.

While Bourgeois and Messerlin (1998) examine EU cases only to determine whether predatory behavior is plausible, Messerlin and Noguchi (1998) look specifically at electronic products such as television sets, compact disk players, microwave ovens, mobile phones, and photocopiers, where economic analysis of the 1980s highlighted the possibility of strategic behavior by exporters seeking to exploit static or dynamic scale economies. During this period, antidumping activity in the United States and Europe targeted mainly Japanese firms (about half of all cases) but also firms in Korea (one-quarter of all cases), and firms in Hong Kong, Taiwan, Singapore, and China (together about 20 percent of all cases). Messerlin and Noguchi found that about 80 percent of antidumping cases brought ended with "severe" antidumping measures—median tariffs or tariff equivalents around twice as high as the corresponding applied tariffs.

Messerlin and Noguchi examine the cases of color television sets and compact disk players to determine whether the three conditions required for profitable strategic dumping were satisfied. First, was the exporter's own market for the product protected? Second, was the exporter's own market large enough relative to the size of unprotected markets to put competing producers at a disadvantage? And third, were there static or dynamic scale economies in the relevant industry? For both products, a detailed examination reveals that even the necessary conditions for predatory or strategic dumping were not satisfied. With regard to strategic dumping, the evidence suggests that the European Union did much more than Japan to limit imports into its own domestic color television market and thus allow the domestic industry to capture possible benefits from scale economies. A US predatory dumping case brought by Zenith against twelve Japanese exporters of color televisions (the Matsushita case) made it to the US Supreme Court. The court concluded that if the firms' low export prices had indeed been motivated by predation, it would have taken more than forty years to recoup their initial losses in the US market (Mavroidis, Messerlin, and Wauters 2008, 13).

Irwin (1998) examines the experience of the US semiconductor industry, which brought dumping charges against Japanese producers in 1985. An important aspect of the case is that, unlike color television sets or compact disk players, semiconductors were an intermediate good, and the case thus affected not only the import-competing industry but also the downstream US computer industry. Irwin does not reach a firm conclusion regarding strategic dumping because of conflicting evidence as to whether

Japan's market for semiconductors was open to competing imports. However, he labels the case as one of "textbook cyclical dumping" in which world prices of semiconductors dropped sharply following a downturn in demand.[12] The case ended with a negotiated settlement in which Japan agreed to cost-based, company-specific price floors for their US sales as well as quantitative targets for their foreign market share; both measures *hindered* active competition among Japanese exporters. Some US computer companies responded to the price floors imposed on imports of critical semiconductor inputs by shifting assembly operations to other countries.[13] While the antidumping measures did not prevent US producers of semiconductors from exiting, they did encourage the entry of South Korean producers, but that was not enough to prevent prices to US buyers from rising sharply when demand rebounded.

Theory: How Antidumping Policy Can Worsen Conditions of Market Competition

I have noted that the original justification for antidumping laws was to prevent predation in the domestic market by foreign exporters—that is, to maintain competition among suppliers. But by the 1980s, broadening of the definition of dumping and the conditions under which affected domestic producers could obtain relief from competing imports had transformed antidumping into a particularly flexible, and therefore increasingly popular, means of increasing a domestic industry's protection without violating GATT commitments. The trade policy literature of the 1980s and 1990s went further, turning the original justification for antidumping—as a means to *prevent* monopolization of the domestic market—on its head by demonstrating that antidumping usually *increases* producers' market power and can even be used to *create and defend* cartels.

Effects of antidumping on market competition can come through several channels. First, as with other forms of protection, it is likely to reduce the total number of firms active in the domestic market and thereby to reduce the elasticity of demand facing each of them. Even if firms do not collude, the effect will be to raise the equilibrium markup of price over cost. Second, because antidumping can raise the cost of an imported input, it provides a means by which a more efficient competitor in the domestic market can force out a less competitive domestic rival.[14] Moreover, because antidumping cases target specific foreign exporters in specific locations, they provide a useful means of policing a tacit collusive arrangement. Finally, in the longer run even the threat of antidumping or other increases in protection can provide an inducement for foreign exporters to relocate their production via direct investment in the importing country.

A key insight underlying much of this literature is that antidumping measures are imposed (or not) as a response to market outcomes. Thus both domestic and foreign suppliers act strategically, taking into account effects on the behavior of other suppliers and the subsequent endogenous actions of trade authorities.[15] Blonigen and Prusa (2003) survey a range of theoretical findings. As in the literature on (domestic) imperfect competition, a wide range of outcomes can be obtained depending on whether firms set price or quantity and whether evidence of dumping or of injury is more important in the actions of trade authorities. They note that it is possible to obtain "just about any combination of distorted market effects, depending on the characteristics of the strategic game being played by the firms" (Blonigen and Prusa 2003, 241). Since the theoretical games begin from an equilibrium with distortions, antidumping can even result in a net increase in overall economic well-being in the importing country.

Mixed Evidence: Antidumping, Cartel Formation, and Other Competitiveness Concerns

As noted previously, empirical evidence established that the vast majority of antidumping cases filed during the 1980s and 1990s involved products whose predatory or strategic dumping would be highly unlikely to cause a downturn in overall economic well-being. Evidence in some of these cases suggests that antidumping actions may have had an effect opposite to its supposed goal—that is, by limiting efficient foreign competition, antidumping actually facilitated cartelization of the market. The likelihood of such an outcome is especially strong when nontariff antidumping measures such as voluntary export restraints or minimum price agreements are used.

For the European Union, Messerlin (1990) documents a link between antidumping and cartel formation with "twin" antidumping and antitrust cases—cases in which the same product was involved in an antidumping case and also an anticartel case. For the period of the 1980s, there were nearly thirty such anticartel cases, constituting about one-quarter of all anticartel cases during the decade. The one hundred related antidumping cases likewise constituted about one-quarter of all antidumping cases during the decade. Messerlin argues that termination of antidumping cases with a finding of "no dumping" may result when competing firms reach private collusive agreements. He provides detailed evidence for two chemical industry cartels—polyvinyl chloride (PVC) and low-density polyethylene (LdPE)—in which antidumping cases helped to enforce cartel arrangements. Although members of both cartels were later required to pay substantial fines as a result of antitrust actions, the strategy was nonetheless highly profitable overall for the firms involved.

For the United States, the evidence of the impact of antidumping on conditions of competition is mixed. Staiger and Wolak (1994) examine antidumping cases in the period 1980–85 and find that the mere filing of an antidumping investigation can have significant negative effects on trade, even without the imposition of a new tariff. Prusa (1992) notes that more than one-third of US antidumping petitions filed from 1980 through 1988 were withdrawn, which he interprets as possible evidence of a collusive agreement having been reached by domestic and foreign firms. This pattern continued into the 1990s, with about a quarter of all antidumping petitions from 1980 through 1998 being withdrawn (Blonigen and Prusa, 2003). Prusa argues that domestic firms involved in antidumping cases may be exempt from antitrust actions under the Noerr-Pennington doctrine. However, Taylor (2004) challenges this argument, as well as Prusa's assumption that withdrawn petitions are a signal of collusion. He points out that earlier research, notably by Prusa (1992), had aggregated withdrawn and settled cases. Taylor uses data only for antidumping cases filed from 1990 through 1997 that ended in a withdrawn petition *without a suspension agreement or a voluntary restraint agreement*. From an examination of monthly import data, Taylor finds no evidence of collusion in these cases. By design, Taylor's analysis omits cases settled through collusion-friendly measures such as price floors or quantitative restrictions (such as voluntary export agreements).[16]

Barfield's (2003) review of the effects of antidumping actions in several US high-technology industries is relevant here because these industries are precisely the kind where the necessary conditions for predatory or strategic dumping are most likely to be found. Yet Barfield concludes that "while the application of antidumping laws is problematic in any sector, it is particularly troublesome in high-technology sectors" (Barfield 2003, 5). The cases Barfield reviews are consistent with Messerlin's (1990) characterization of antidumping as a policy more likely to impede than to protect competition in the market of the importing country. As such, antidumping during this period was likely to benefit producers (in some cases including foreign producers) at the expense of consumers, the same result as with other types of protection. Barfield argues that antidumping is futile as a means to save uncompetitive companies and sectors, while it is damaging to market competition and impedes innovation—the lifeblood of high-technology industries.

Like Finger (1993, chap. 4), Barfield favors complete elimination of antidumping, with substitution of safeguard actions where domestic firms need more time to adjust to changing market conditions, while leaving evaluation of anticompetitive effects from possible predation to the antitrust authorities. Of course, both authors acknowledge that political opposition makes this "best" course of action unlikely. But Messerlin (1994) points to a variety of pitfalls related to simply replacing antidumping by competition rules. Messerlin's own preference—at least as a short-run solution until countries can agree on a common set of competition rules—is sequential enforcement, in which antitrust or competition authorities are explicitly mandated to evaluate potentially anticompetitive consequences of actions taken by antidumping authorities. Ideally, this ex post review process would discourage application of antidumping for anticompetitive ends.

One recent instance of antidumping used to protect domestic high-technology production was the US decision in May 2012 to apply antidumping duties on solar panels from China.[17] The president of SolarWorld USA, a US subsidiary of Germany's largest solar panel producer and the lead complainant in the case, called the US measure a "positive step" needed because "Chinese firms are seeking 'total dominance' of the sector that could lead to monopoly pricing in the long term" (Johnson and Sweet, 2012). In July 2012, SolarWorld USA's German parent led a group of manufacturers filing a similar complaint with the European Commission (Nicola and Roca 2012).[18]

Given the large number of producers in each market, as well as producers in many other countries, future predation by Chinese exporters seems a remote possibility.[19] Yet China has already demonstrated its ability to restrict exports ranging from apparel to raw materials and rare earths—a necessary condition for monopoly pricing. Even so, China's primary reason for supporting its solar firms is most likely similar to that of the United States—to maintain employment and promote the adoption of solar power. While US antidumping may indeed save some jobs in domestic solar panel factories at least in the short run, this will come at the cost of slowing US adoption of solar technology and thus reducing growth of employment in the downstream sector that installs solar panels. Moreover, China quickly retaliated against the US measure with its own investigation of US government support for clean-energy projects in five states (Areddy and Ma 2012), potentially affecting US hopes of increasing clean-energy exports to China. China also subsequently retaliated by imposing antidumping duties on imports of a key input—solar grade polysilicon—from both the United States and the European Union.

DUMPING, ANTIDUMPING, AND MARKET COMPETITION IN THE TWENTY-FIRST CENTURY

The broad consensus in the international trade literature of the 1980s and 1990s was that antidumping, whatever its original justification, had become nothing more than "ordinary protection, albeit with a good public relations program" (Finger 1993, chap. 2). Many economists went further, arguing that antidumping had become even worse than most ordinary protection because antidumping actions often ended in measures like voluntary export restrictions and price undertakings that restricted competition among suppliers. However, the subsequent evolution of world trade and trade policy justifies a fresh look at the classic concerns of dumping. Here I focus on three important changes: increased use of antidumping by emerging economies, increased fragmentation of production with a major role for multinational firms, and the rise of China as a major exporter. Under these new conditions, what are the likely consequences for competition in importing countries of dumping and antidumping?

Antidumping Use by Emerging Economies and Its Potential Impact in South-South Trade

Through the early 1990s, just five industrialized countries initiated almost all antidumping cases worldwide. But in recent years the use of antidumping and related temporary trade barriers by high-income countries has been leveling off, while some large emerging economies have become intensive users (Bown 2011a, 2011b). Figure 2-1 illustrates the changing share over the period 1997–2016 of all six-digit Harmonized System products imported by the G-20 economies collectively that were subject to antidumping or another temporary trade barrier (TTB) such as safeguards or countervailing duties.[20] As figure 2-1 indicates, by 2016 roughly 2.8 percent of all six-digit products imported by the major emerging economies were subject to some sort of TTB; this share rose steadily in the 2000s, roughly doubling between

FIGURE 2-1. G-20 Imports Subject to Formal Temporary Trade Barriers, 1997–2016

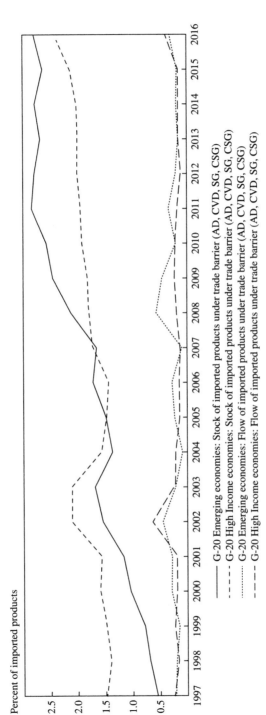

Percent of imported products

—— G-20 Emerging economies: Stock of imported products under trade barrier (AD, CVD, SG, CSG)
- - - - G-20 High Income economies: Stock of imported products under trade barrier (AD, CVD, SG, CSG)
· · · · · · · G-20 Emerging economies: Flow of imported products under trade barrier (AD, CVD, SG, CSG)
– – – G-20 High Income economies: Flow of imported products under trade barrier (AD, CVD, SG, CSG)

Source: Constructed with data from Bown (2018). Percentages based on counts of six-digit HS import products—that is, the number of product lines subject to any temporary trade barrier in that year relative to the total number of product lines with positive imports. (These percentages do not measure the share of trade value subject to temporary trade barriers.)

Notes: AD = antidumping; CVD = countervailing duty; SG = global safeguard; CSG = China-specific transitional safeguard. G-20 high-income economies include Australia, Canada, the European Union, Japan, South Korea, and the United States. G-20 emerging economies include Argentina, Brazil, China, India, Indonesia, South Africa, and Turkey, and exclude Mexico.

2004 and 2011. For the high-income economies, by 2016 roughly 2.4 percent of all six-digit imported products were subject to some TTB. This share had increased recently after holding relatively constant over the previous fifteen years and, perhaps surprisingly, did not rise substantially even during the Great Recession after 2007.

Figure 2-2 documents the changing incidence of these TTBs on exporting economies. Most striking is the impact on China's exports—by 2016, more than 9 percent of China's exports by value to other emerging economies were subject to a TTB, roughly 50 percent higher than the share in 2004. TTBs imposed by high-income economies show a trend in disproportionately targeting China, though the scale is less dramatic; by 2016, 5.8 percent of Chinese exports to high-income markets were subject to a TTB, up from 2.5 percent in 2004. Figure 2-2a documents that emerging economies have also frequently targeted exports from other emerging markets apart from China, though at a lower level. Over the period 2001–16, on average 1.3 percent of other (non-China) emerging economy exports to emerging economies were subject to a TTB in any given year.[21]

Three main points arise from the data. First, use of antidumping and other TTBs by emerging economies has been increasing, and these policies affect a significant range of imported products. Second, China has become the dominant target for both emerging-economy and high-income users of TTBs, with the rate of increase accelerating for emerging-economy users. Third, emerging economies have also frequently targeted imports from other (non-China) emerging-market exporters. These recent patterns in use of antidumping and other TTBs raise the question of how earlier research on antidumping and conditions of market competition may apply to emerging economies, both as users and as targets.[22] Table 2-1 summarizes G-20 economy specific statistics.

Fragmentation of Production and Multinational Activity

Fragmentation of the value chain in the production of many traded goods has been increasing over the last 40 years (Hummels, Ishii, and Yi 2001; Johnson and Noguera 2017), and the share of trade mediated by affiliates (and/or) parents of the same multinational firm rather than through arm's-length transactions is large. For example, nearly half of total US imports in 2000 were intra-firm transactions.[23] Increased fragmentation of production and trade between related parties complicate both the political economy of antidumping and its potential impact on conditions of market competition.

FIGURE 2-2. Export Sources Subject to G-20-Imposed Formal Temporary Trade Barriers, 1997–2016

a. Temporary Trade Barriers Imposed by G-20 Emerging Economies

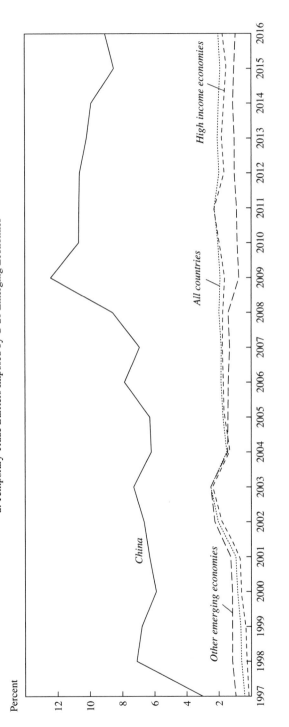

b. Temporary Trade Barriers Imposed by G-20 High-Income Economies

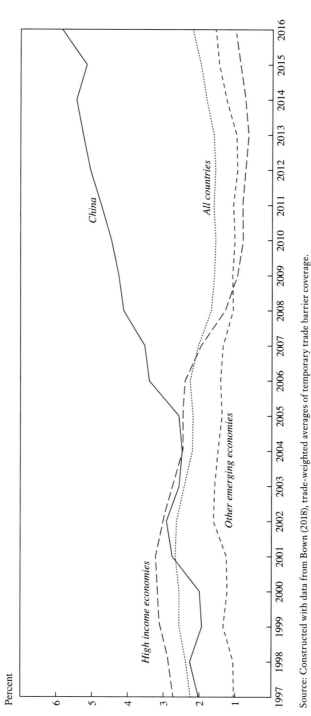

Source: Constructed with data from Bown (2018), trade-weighted averages of temporary trade barrier coverage.

Note: G-20 emerging economies include Argentina, Brazil, China, India, Indonesia, South Africa, and Turkey, and exclude Mexico. G-20 high-income economies include Australia, Canada, European Union, Japan, South Korea, and the United States.

TABLE 2-1. **G-20 Economies with Imports Subject to Antidumping or Related Temporary Trade Barriers in 2016**

Policy imposer	Share of value of imports subject to antidumping (%) (1)	Share of imported product lines subject to antidumping (%) (2)	Share of value of imports subject to any TTB (%) (3)	Share of imported product lines subject to any TTB (%) (4)
G-20 emerging economies	1.8	2.7	1.9	2.7
1. India	4.1	7.8	4.5	7.9
2. Argentina	2.6	4.6	2.8	4.7
3. Turkey	2.2	2.1	2.2	2.2
4. Brazil	1.2	0.6	2.0	0.8
5. Indonesia	1.9	2.6	1.9	2.6
6. China	1.4	1.1	1.4	1.1
7. Mexico	1.1	1.7	1.1	1.7
8. South Africa	0.4	0.4	0.4	0.4
G-20 high-income economies	2.1	2.3	2.2	2.4
1. United States	3.3	6.8	3.6	7.2
2. European Union	1.9	3.7	1.9	3.9
3. Australia	1.0	1.2	1.0	1.2
4. South Korea	0.7	1.3	0.7	1.3
5. Canada	0.5	0.6	0.5	0.6
6. Japan	0.0	0.1	0.0	0.1

Source: Bown (2018) and authors' calculations. Columns 1 and 3 are trade-weighted by HS-06 import values; columns 2 and 4 are based on simple counts of HS-06 product lines with positive imports. Countries are ranked from high to low according to data in column 3.

Note: TTB = temporary trade barrier, which includes antidumping (AD), countervailing duty, global safeguard, and China-specific transitional safeguard.

Antidumping measures affecting intermediate inputs raise the costs to firms further downstream in the supply chain, thereby hurting overall competitiveness relative to firms and production locations unencumbered by antidumping.[24] Thus, to the extent that international transactions occur between affiliates of the same multinational firm, exporters and importers have a shared incentive to keep markets free from new trade barriers.[25] Global supply chains and a significant role of multinationals might therefore be expected to reduce antidumping activity, at least for countries and industries particularly prominent in global supply chains.

But there are additional channels through which the changing nature of global trade could also influence antidumping activity and its consequences. Antidumping may provide an important incentive for multinationals to substitute local subsidiary production in a foreign market for exports—that is, "antidumping-jumping" foreign direct investment (FDI).[26] The important role of multinational firms in world trade also complicates the political economy of antidumping because it opens the door to new types of strategic behavior on the part of vertically integrated firms. Once a firm has established production in the former export market via FDI, its incentives with respect to antidumping or other trade barriers are likely to change. Trade barriers faced by other foreign suppliers can improve the firm's own position relative to competitors that rely on arm's-length transactions for imported inputs or that continue to serve the same market via exports. The firm may even increase its own exports from a foreign location in an attempt to trigger an antidumping investigation that will hamper competitors that lack local production capacity.[27]

The cases shown in table 2-2 illustrate the potential relevance of these issues for emerging markets. I conducted a search of the World Bank's Temporary Trade Barriers Database for cases in which the same six-digit Harmonized System (HS-06) products and firm names were involved in antidumping investigations initiated in different countries (Bown 2016). Table 2-2 reports examples in which subsidiaries of the same multinational corporations have been involved in antidumping investigations over similar or related products in multiple emerging-market jurisdictions.

In the first example, the major tire-making multinational corporations Michelin, Bridgestone, Goodyear, and Pirelli all have subsidiaries involved either as petitioners or as targeted firms in antidumping investigations in emerging markets such as Turkey, South Africa, India, Thailand, Brazil, and China.[28] In the second example, an Indian subsidiary of Osram (itself a subsidiary of the German multinational firm Siemens) was part of a petition for an Indian antidumping investigation of compact fluorescent lamps (CFLs) from China in which one of the targeted firms was Osram's own subsidiary in China. In cases involving Owens Corning, Continental Carbon, Monsanto, and Graftech, the emerging-market subsidiary of a US-headquartered multinational firm initiated an antidumping investigation against imports from another emerging market. Moreover, not all

TABLE 2-2. Examples of Multinational Firm Overlap in Emerging Market Antidumping (AD) Investigations, 2000–2016

Firms (headquarters)	Products (common HS code)	Explanation
Michelin (France); Bridgestone (Japan); Goodyear (United States); Pirelli (Italy)	Tires (401120)	1. 2004: Bridgestone and Pirelli subsidiaries in *Turkey* are among petitioners for AD on tires from *China* (measures imposed in 2005).
		2. 2005: Bridgestone and Goodyear subsidiaries in *South Africa* are among petitioners for AD on tires from *China* (no measures imposed).
		3. 2005, 2008: Several *Indian* tire manufacturers (no apparent multinational firm affiliation) are petitioners for AD on bus and truck tires from *China* and *Thailand* (measures imposed in 2007 and 2010, respectively). Goodyear subsidiary in India played an inactive role in one investigation, supplying information to the Indian authorities but not actively supporting the investigation. First investigation targeted Bridgestone subsidiary in Thailand. Second investigation targeted Michelin subsidiaries in China and Thailand.
		4. 2008: Bridgestone, Goodyear and Pirelli subsidiaries in *Brazil* are among petitioners for AD on truck tires from *China* (measures imposed in 2010).
		5. 2013: Bridgestone, Goodyear, Michelin, and Pirelli subsidiaries in *Brazil* are among petitioners for AD on truck tires from *Japan, Russia, South Africa, South Korea, Taiwan, and Thailand* (measures imposed in 2014).
Osram (Germany)	Compact fluorescent lamps (853931, 853990)	2007: Osram subsidiary in *India* is among petitioners for AD on compact fluorescent lamps from Osram subsidiary in *China* (measures imposed in 2009).

Owens Corning (United States)	Fiberglass (701912, 701931)	1. 2003: Owens Corning subsidiary in *South Africa* petitions for AD on glass fibers from *China* (petition ultimately withdrawn).
		2. 2006: Owens Corning subsidiary in *South Africa* petitions for AD on glass fibers from *Brazil* (petition ultimately withdrawn). One targeted firm in Brazil is the subsidiary of European glass fiber manufacturer Saint Gobain, which acquired the Owens Corning subsidiary in South Africa in 2007.
		3. 2009: Owens Corning subsidiary in *France* is among petitioners for AD on glass fiber from *China* (measures imposed in 2011).
		4. 2010: Owens Corning subsidiary in *India* is among petitioners for AD on glass fiber from *China* (measures imposed in 2011).
Continental Carbon (United States)	Carbon black (280300)	1. 2008: Continental Carbon subsidiary in *India* is among petitioners for AD on carbon black from six countries including *Australia*. The main target in Australia is Continental Carbon Australia, a licensee of Continental Carbon Technology, though not a subsidiary (measures imposed in 2010).
Monsanto (United States)	Glyphosate herbicide (293100, 380830)	1. 2001: Monsanto subsidiary in *Australia* petitions for AD on glyphosate from *China* (no measures imposed).
		2. 2001: Monsanto subsidiary in *Brazil* is among petitioners for AD on glyphosate from *China* (measures imposed in 2003).
		3. 2002: Monsanto subsidiary in *Argentina* petitions for AD on glyphosate from *China* (no measures imposed).

(continued)

TABLE 2-2. (continued)

Firms (headquarters)	Products (common HS code)	Explanation
Graftech (United States)	Graphite (854511)	1. 2003: Graftech subsidiary in *Italy* is among petitioners for AD on certain graphite from *India* (measures imposed in 2004).
		2. 2008: Graftech subsidiary in *Brazil* petitions for antidumping measures on certain graphite from *China* (measures imposed in 2009).
		3. 2010: Graftech subsidiary in *Mexico* petitions for AD on certain graphite from *China* (measures imposed in 2012).
		4. 2014: Graftech subsidiary in *South Africa* petitions for AD on certain graphite from *China* and *Pakistan* (measures imposed in 2015).
Indorama Synthetics (Indonesia)	Yarns, fibers	1. 2008: Yarn manufacturers in *Brazil* and *Turkey* are among petitioners for AD on yarn from Indorama Synthetics' headquarters in *Indonesia* (measures imposed in 2009).
		2. 2008: Indorama Synthetics subsidiary in *India* is among supporting petitioners for AD on yarn from *China* (targeting several firms not related to Indorama) and from an Indorama subsidiary in *Thailand* (measures imposed in 2009).
		3. 2009: Indorama Synthetics' headquarters in *Indonesia* is among petitioners for AD on polyester staple fiber from *China* (measures imposed in 2010).
		4. 2013: Indorama Synthetics' headquarters in *Indonesia* is among petitioners for AD on spin draw yarn, drawn textured yarn, and/or partially oriented yarn from *China, Malaysia, South Korea, Taiwan, India,* and *Thailand* (measures against Malaysia and Thailand imposed in 2015; no measures imposed against other exporters).

Source: Constructed with data from Bown (2016) and updates.

Note: HS = Harmonized System.

these examples are of multinationals headquartered in high-income economies. In the last case, subsidiaries in India and Thailand of Indorama Synthetics, an Indonesia-headquartered multinational firm, were among supporters of antidumping investigations of yarn and fiber imports.

Another reason to suspect that recent antidumping actions involving emerging economies may be enforcing rather than combating cartels is that some of these actions have targeted the same products that were identified in the links between antidumping use and cartel behavior in the 1980s and 1990s in high-income economies. Another search of the World Bank's Temporary Trade Barriers Database looked for cases involving polyvinyl chloride (PVC)—one of the products related to the in-depth examination by Messerlin (1990) in the European Community context—or another industrial chemical, polyethylene terephthalate (PET). As illustrated in tables 2-3 and 2-4, in more than fifty different instances over the period 1995–2016, one or more of twelve G-20 economies initiated antidumping investigations into either PVC or PET products (Bown 2016). Some economies initiated multiple, sequential investigations and imposed new import restrictions against many foreign suppliers, including each other. However, it is also notable that the PVC and PET antidumping petitions described in these tables involved dozens of firms. Other things equal, participation of many more firms in the global market should make the formation and subsequent enforcement of a cartel in any of these sectors more difficult than it was in the 1980s and 1990s.

These examples of multimarket contacts among multinational firms indicate the possibility of policies such as antidumping being used to segment markets in relatively concentrated industries. However, we have no direct evidence indicating collusive behavior by the firms involved in any of the cases, and there are other plausible explanations for the patterns displayed. For example, the same foreign firm could have been dumping simultaneously across multiple jurisdictions, thus triggering the related antidumping filings. More broadly, certain products or even industries may have characteristics inherent to their production process, such as high fixed costs, or a market structure that "fits" the evidentiary criteria required for a viable antidumping case. But even the potential for collusive action calls for research based on detailed information on multinational firm linkages across countries, and perhaps also careful monitoring by antidumping authorities to ensure that their actions do not inadvertently promote anticompetitive outcomes.

TABLE 2-3. Antidumping (AD) Activity in the Polyethylene Terephthalate (PET) Market, 1999–2016

---

1. Argentina (2004, 2012)
- Initiated AD in 2004 on Brazil, Korea, Taiwan (measures imposed on Brazil only in 2006)
- Initiated AD in 2012 on China, India, South Korea, Taiwan, and Thailand (measures imposed in 2013)
- Initiated AD in 2015 on Indonesia and USA (investigation on Indonesia ongoing; investigation on USA terminated in 2015)

2. Brazil (2002, 2004, 2007, 2010)
- Initiated AD in 2002 on India (no measures imposed)
- Initiated AD in 2004 on Argentina, South Korea, Taiwan, USA (measures imposed on Argentina and USA in 2005)
- Initiated AD in 2007 on India and Thailand (measures imposed in 2008)
- Initiated AD in 2010 on Mexico, Turkey, United Arab Emirates (measures imposed in 2012)
- Initiated AD in 2015 on China, India, and Indonesia (measures imposed in 2016)

3. China (1999, 2001)
- Initiated AD in 1999 on South Korea (measures imposed in 2000)
- Initiated AD in 2001 on South Korea (measures imposed in 2003)

4. EU (1999, 2000, 2003, 2009)
- Initiated AD in 1999 on India, Indonesia, South Korea, Malaysia, Taiwan, Thailand (measures imposed in 2000)
- Initiated AD in 2000 on India and South Korea (measures imposed in 2001)
- Initiated AD in 2003 on Australia, China, Pakistan (measures imposed in 2004)
- Initiated AD in 2009 on Iran, Pakistan, United Arab Emirates (measures imposed on Iran only in 2010)
- Initiated AD in 2011 on Oman and Saudi Arabia (investigation withdrawn in 2011)

5. South Korea (2007)
- Initiated AD in 2007 on China and India (measures imposed in 2008)

6. Turkey (2004)
- Initiated AD in 2004 on China, India, Indonesia, South Korea, Malaysia, Taiwan, Thailand (measures imposed in 2006)

7. USA (2001, 2003, 2004, 2007, 2015)
- Initiated AD in 2001 on India and Taiwan (measures imposed in 2002)
- Initiated AD in 2003 on EU, Japan, South Korea (no final measures imposed)

TABLE 2-3. (*continued*)

- Initiated AD in 2004 on India, Indonesia, Taiwan, Thailand (no final measures imposed)
- Initiated AD in 2007 on Brazil, China, Thailand, United Arab Emirates (measures imposed in 2008, except on Thailand)
- Initiated AD in 2015 on Canada, China, India, and Oman (measures imposed in 2016)

8. South Africa (2005)
- Initiated AD in 2005 on China, India, Indonesia, South Korea, Taiwan, Thailand (measures imposed on India, South Korea, and Taiwan in 2006)

9. Japan (2017)
- Initiated AD in 2016 on China (measures imposed in 2017)

10. Indonesia (2012, 2016)
- Initiated AD in 2012 on China, South Korea, Singapore, and Taiwan (investigation terminated in 2014)
- Initiated AD in 2016 on China, South Korea, and Malaysia (investigation ongoing)

Source: Constructed with data from Bown (2016) and updates.

The Rise of China and the Increasing Use of Export Restrictions

The importance of China as a dominant trader gives rise to additional issues relating to antidumping and how its use may be evolving in response to larger changes in the global economy. The first is associated with China's sheer size, the second with China's evident willingness and ability to use export restrictions in pursuit of its own policy objectives.

Even before its entry into the WTO in 2001, China had rapidly achieved a substantial share in the export markets of many industries, initially at the lower end of the technology spectrum (shoes and especially apparel) but increasingly in high-technology industries as well. In earlier decades, Japan's rapid export growth similarly disrupted established trading patterns, and Japan became a primary target of antidumping and other TTBs. But in sharp contrast to the case of Japan, many Chinese firms are integrated into international value chains, either as subsidiaries of multinational firms or as contractors exporting inputs (such as auto parts) or processing and assembling imported intermediate inputs for export (such as computers). In a new trade pattern, some goods once exported directly by Japan to the

TABLE 2-4. Antidumping (AD) Activity in the Polyvinyl Chloride (PVC) Market, 1995–2016

1. **Argentina (1999, 2012)**
- Initiated AD in 1999 on Mexico and USA (measures imposed in 2000)
- Initiated AD in 2011 on USA (no measures imposed)
- Initiated AD in 2012 on China and Germany (measures imposed in 2014)

2. **Australia (1996, 1997, 1999, 2001, 2012, 2014)**
- Initiated AD in 1996 on EU and South Korea (no final measures imposed)
- Initiated AD in 1997 on EU, India, Indonesia, Iran, Israel, United Arab Emirates (no measures imposed)
- Initiated AD in 1999 on EU, Indonesia, South Korea, Singapore (measures imposed in 2001, except on Indonesia)
- Initiated AD in 2001 on EU, Indonesia, Israel, Norway, Taiwan (measures imposed on Israel only in 2002)
- Initiated AD in 2012 on South Korea (measures imposed in 2012)
- Initiated AD in 2014 on China (no final measures imposed)

3. **Brazil (1997, 1998, 2000, 2001, 2007)**
- Initiated AD in 1997 on EU and USA (measures imposed on USA only in 1998)
- Initiated AD in 1998 on China and USA (measures imposed on China only in 1998)
- Initiated AD in 2000 on EU and USA (no measures imposed)
- Initiated AD in 2001 on Colombia, Japan, South Korea, North Korea, Thailand, Venezuela (no measures imposed)
- Initiated AD in 2007 on China and South Korea (measures imposed in 2008)

4. **China (2002)**
- Initiated AD in 2002 on Japan, South Korea, Russia, Taiwan, USA (measures imposed in 2003)
- Initiated AD in 2016 on Japan (preliminary measures imposed in 2017)

5. **India (2003, 2006, 2008, 2009, 2010, 2012)**
- Initiated AD in 2003 on EU, South Korea, Saudi Arabia (measures imposed on EU only in 2004)
- Initiated AD in 2006 on China, Indonesia, Japan, South Korea, Malaysia, Taiwan, Thailand, USA (measures imposed in 2008)
- Initiated AD in 2008 on China and Taiwan (measures imposed in 2009)
- Initiated AD in 2009 on China, Japan, South Korea, Malaysia, Russia, Taiwan, Thailand (measures imposed in 2011 (except on Japan)
- Initiated AD in 2010 on China (measures imposed in 2011)
- Initiated AD in 2012 on EU and Mexico (measures imposed in 2014)
- Initiated AD in 2014 on Mexico and Norway (measures imposed in 2015)

TABLE 2-4. (*continued*)

---

6. **South Korea (2004)**
- Initiated AD in 2004 on Japan (measures imposed in 2005)

7. **Turkey (2001, 2008)**
- Initiated AD in 2001 on EU, Israel, Russia, USA (measures imposed in 2003, except on Russia)
- Initiated AD in 2008 on China and Vietnam (measures imposed in 2008)

8. **USA (1995, 2002)**
- Initiated AD in 1995 on EU (no measures imposed)
- Initiated AD in 2002 on China (no final measures imposed)

9. **South Africa (1996, 2000, 2007)**
- Initiated AD in 1996 on Brazil, Canada, China, EU, Japan, North Korea, Taiwan, USA (measures imposed on Brazil, China, EU, and USA in 1997)
- Initiated AD in 2000 on EU, India, South Korea, Thailand (measures imposed in 2001)
- Initiated AD in 2007 on China and Taiwan (measures imposed in 2008)

Source: Constructed with data from Bown (2016) and updates.

United States and the European Union now arrive from China, but with much of their value in the form of inputs exported by Japan to China (Dean, Lovely, and Mora 2009). Because China plays such a large role in supply chains, aggressive trade policy measures on the part of the industrialized countries (still headquarters of most multinational firms) are less likely than in the earlier response to Japan's rise as a major exporter.

Another potential advantage China enjoys is the size of its economy. For industries where scale economies are important, China is far better positioned than earlier superexporters to bring down production costs by capturing these economies. As China becomes an important supplier of higher-technology goods and services, the large scale of its total production for both domestic sale and export offers an unprecedented opportunity to spread fixed costs, including the costs of research and development.[29]

The advantages due to China's size as a producer and exporter are complemented by China's status as a transition economy. Though the role of market forces in domestic resource allocation and trade has been increasing, the role of government at all levels remains important in many ways, ranging from terms on which firms are able to obtain capital to export incentives and restrictions. Although every country exercises industrial policy to some degree, it seems fair to say that top-down control over economic activity is still much more extensive in China than in most of the markets to which it exports. This is highly significant because of the possibility that dumping that can harm an importing country's overall economic well-being (that is, in situations in which gains to consumers do not outweigh losses to import-competing producers); the relative size and concentration of the export supply is important. To be profitable for exporters, both predatory and strategic dumping require the relevant exporters to have a substantial market share in the import-competing country and also that export supply is sufficiently concentrated to allow *coordinated* action by exporters once dumping has eliminated domestic import competition. Even in what would appear from the perspective of an outsider to be relatively competitive Chinese markets—with dozens or even hundreds of exporting firms—in diverse sectors including textiles and apparel and raw materials and rare earths, Chinese officials have demonstrated their ability to limit total exports to achieve policy objectives.[30] Although many other countries have also restricted their own exports for a variety of reasons, it is the unique combination of China's importance as an exporter and its willingness to curtail supply that makes the situation particularly conducive to predation in countries that import its products.

CONCLUSIONS

Over a century, antidumping has gradually evolved from an obscure and rarely used policy tool to one that now constitutes an important form of protection not subject to the same WTO controls as members' bound tariff rates. Rather, antidumping is one of several instruments that allow members to exceed their bound tariffs, albeit subject to very detailed WTO procedural disciplines.[31] Moreover, while the application of antidumping was until the WTO era mainly the province of a few traditional users, emerging markets have become some of the most active users of antidumping and related policies, as well as important targets of their application. And though these policies are known collectively as *temporary* trade barriers, WTO rules governing the duration of antidumping measures are much weaker than for safeguards.

As antidumping use has evolved and proliferated (about fifty countries now have antidumping statutes, although some are not active users), both its economic justification and the concerns raised by its possible abuse have also evolved. While the original justification of antidumping was to protect importing countries from predation by foreign suppliers, by the 1980s antidumping had come to be regarded as just another tool in the protectionist arsenal. Even more worrying, evidence began to mount that antidumping was being used in ways that actually enforced collusion and cartel arrangements rather than attacking anticompetitive behavior.

Today's world economy and international trading system are much different even from those of the early 1990s, when this concern reached its peak. Some changes, in particular the significant growth in the number of countries and firms actively engaged in international trade, tend to limit the possibility of predation by exporters. Moreover, antidumping has developed a political-economic justification as a tool that can help countries manage the internal stresses associated with openness. But other changes, especially the important role of multinational firms and intrafirm trade and the increased use by many countries of policies to limit exports, suggest that concerns about anticompetitive behavior by exporters cannot be entirely dismissed. Vigilance to ensure that antidumping is not abused by complainants to achieve and exploit market power thus remains appropriate today.

NOTES

I dedicate this paper to Rachel McCulloch—my longtime mentor, colleague, co-coauthor, and friend—who worked on an earlier draft before her passing in 2016. Thanks to Aksel Erbahar and Eva Zhang for outstanding research assistance and to Bernard Hoekman, Patrick Messerlin, Simon Evenett, Mike Finger, and participants at the conference "21st Century Trade Policy: Back to the Past?" conference at the Yale Center for the Study of Globalization for useful comments. Any remaining errors are my own.

1. The economic literature on antidumping is vast, and I have not attempted a comprehensive review. Nelson and Vandenbussche (2005) offer a two-volume selection of 47 significant contributions, including some of the classic references cited below. See also Blonigen and Prusa (2016).

2. Another WTO-legal means of increasing protection unilaterally is available to most emerging economies, whose bound tariff rates (the maximum rates to which a country has committed) typically exceed the currently applied tariff rates by a comfortable margin. It is still an open research question why many countries choose to use antidumping, safeguards, and other temporary trade barriers rather than simply raising applied tariffs when they have the legal right to do so. For example, an empirical study by Gawande, Hoekman, and

Cui (2015) examines determinants of the trade policy responses of seven large emerging market countries to the 2008–2009 global crisis. While all except China had average applied tariff rates well below their WTO bound rates, these countries made only limited use of the resulting "policy space" for unilateral tariff increases. The authors find support for several factors that might be expected to moderate pressure for increased protection, including participation of domestic firms in global supply chains.

3. Of course, WTO-legal safeguard protection was designed to address exactly this type of situation. However, antidumping enjoys several advantages from the viewpoint of an import-affected industry. Because dumping is considered an "unfair" trade practice, the injury requirement is less stringent than for a safeguards case. Furthermore, antidumping protection does not require compensation of foreign exporters and has no definite time limit on its application. Moreover, antidumping is inherently discriminatory, so restrictive measures can be applied only to some countries or even to some specific firms and not others. Often importers focus antidumping on new suppliers whose exports threaten the position of established foreign sources. Finally, unlike safeguards, antidumping is not typically subject to any final check from the head of state, who may decline new protection for a variety of reasons, including effects on consumers or relationships with trading partners.

4. For the United States in the period 1997–2006, Bown and Crowley (2013) find evidence consistent with the theory that antidumping and safeguards are used in response to the sorts of economic shocks and incentives modeled by Bagwell and Staiger's (1990) theory of cooperative trade agreements. Bown and Tovar (2011) find that India used antidumping and safeguard protection in the late 1990s and early 2000s to reverse much of the tariff reform carried out as part of its 1991–1992 International Monetary Fund program. This finding is consistent with the political-economy justification of antidumping—that is, the same domestic political pressures that led to higher ex ante tariffs in particular sectors were later accommodated through antidumping protection.

5. However, Moore and Zanardi (2009) reach a contrary conclusion. They use data for a sample of twenty-three developing countries, including some that have become aggressive users of antidumping, to examine whether use of antidumping has contributed to tariff reductions. Their results do not support the "safety valve" argument that the availability of antidumping encourages countries to liberalize. In fact, use of antidumping may have led to less rather than more liberalization, at least for countries in their sample.

6. Using a sample of forty-one countries that adopted antidumping laws after 1980, Vandenbussche and Zanardi find evidence of what they call a substantial "chilling effect" averaging 5.9 percent for five "tough new users" in their sample—a significant offset to the increased trade due to liberalization and a

figure much larger than the share of trade directly affected by temporary trade barriers (Bown 2011a). But Finger (2010) disputes the authors' characterization of the trade effects of antidumping as "too large to be dismissed as a 'small price to pay' for further liberalization" because Vandenbussche and Zanardi offer no evidence that the same overall liberalization could have been maintained at lower cost through alternate means. In fact, their own results indicate a high ratio of increased aggregate trade to trade lost through backsliding via antidumping—for example, six for Brazil and ten for Turkey. See also Egger and Nelson (2011).

7. National antidumping statutes vary, and some at least leave room for authorities to consider effects on consumers as well as producers. In practice, however, producers' interests are paramount in determining outcomes even where there is legal scope to do otherwise (Messerlin 1994).

8. For additional discussion of strategic dumping, see Messerlin 1994; Willig 1998; and Mavroidis, Messerlin, and Wauters 2008, 17–19.

9. Potential benefits from scale economies may be internal or external to the firm. Static internal scale economies may result from high fixed costs of production. Dynamic external scale economies may result from learning by doing, where one firm's improved production techniques may be quickly transmitted to other producers as workers move between firms. Even when improved technologies are protected by patents or trade secrets, competing firms usually benefit to some degree because innovating firms are not able to capture all the benefits.

10. Here country size offers a rough approximation to the domestic size of the relevant industry and thus the potential for gains through scale economies. However, industry size also depends on level of development, as measured, for example, by GDP per capita. Moreover, the industry may also serve other markets through exports or local subsidiary production. In particular, if scale economies are internal to the firm, as with a large fixed cost of research and development required by a particular product, a multinational firm will derive scale economies from its global production because the fixed costs can be spread over production in multiple locations.

11. Although supporters of aggressive antidumping enforcement often cite the sanctuary market hypothesis, preliminary empirical results reported by Moore (2015) cast some doubt on its practical relevance, at least for US firms facing antidumping actions abroad. Moore examines cases of US companies facing frequent antidumping actions and finds no evidence that their export success arose from a protected home market. Rather, antidumping actions typically target successful exporters and ones from capital-intensive industries like steel, chemicals, and plastics, where fixed costs are high. Steel products are also among the foreign exports most often targeted by US antidumping and other temporary trade barriers.

12. When demand falls, a competitive firm with fixed costs maximizes profits (that is, minimizes losses) at the output where market price is equal to marginal cost, as long as marginal cost is at least equal to the average *variable* cost of production. When the market price is too low to cover all costs of production, an exporting firm following this strategy is dumping. Irwin finds no evidence that the Japanese export price was less than marginal cost.

13. Similarly, soon after the United States imposed antidumping duties on flat-panel displays in 1991, Toshiba, Sharp, and Apple announced plans to shift assembly operations abroad (Irwin 2005b, 77–78).

14. Durling and Prusa (2003) note that raising rivals' costs is well known in the industrial organization literature as a strategy by which a dominant firm can limit supply from competitors. They make the case that import protection can be used in exactly this way. Although they focus on the effects of the US steel safeguard action of 2002, the same logic applies to any kind of protection that increases the cost of imported inputs. Also see Messerlin (1994).

15. "Strategic" behavior here refers to firms taking account of interactions between their own behavior and that of their rivals, as well as possible responses by trade authorities. See, for example, Staiger and Wolak (1989, 1992). In contrast, strategic dumping refers specifically to a firm's export sales at an artificially low price that are motivated by potential gains from increasing the scale of its production.

16. WTO rules restrict the use of voluntary export restraints, which were common before the Uruguay Round of multilateral trade negotiations. However, the WTO still permits use of price undertakings (price floors) to settle antidumping cases. As Moore (2005) shows, the two policies have identical effects under perfect competition, but the results differ when firms have market power.

17. Johnson and Sweet (2012); Sweet (2012). Duties ranged from 31 percent to nearly 250 percent. This antidumping duty was on top of a countervailing duty of 3 percent to 5 percent levied in March. The initial antidumping duties were followed by a second round of duties against China and Taiwan in 2014. When trade diversion continued from new third countries, the US industry then requested a global safeguard, which resulted in comprehensive import restrictions imposed in 2018.

18. Crowley, Meng, and Song (2019) provide an empirical assessment of the European Commission's antidumping case against Chinese solar panel producing firms and its impact on stock prices.

19. Japanese exports of color television sets and other consumer electronics in the 1980s provide an interesting parallel. Japan did create an export cartel that limited total sales to the United States at a price below that charged at home (classic dumping in the form of price discrimination). But while US production was indeed squeezed out by imports from Japan and other coun-

tries, prices of the imports continued to fall while quality continued to rise. Thus there is no evidence of successful predation, even if predation had been the original intent of Japan's Ministry of International Trade and Industry.

20. While most of the TTB use consists of antidumping measures, some countries (such as Turkey, India) have been increasing their use of relatively substitutable policies such as safeguards (Bown 2013).

21. Bown (2013, 2018) provides a detailed empirical assessment of use over time of antidumping and related TTBs to target exports of emerging economies.

22. Messerlin (2004) provides an early analysis of the emergence of China as a user of antidumping.

23. In their study of the determinants of intra-firm trade, Bernard and others (2010) report that 46 percent of total US imports in 2000 occurred between related parties. The importance of intrafirm transactions varied significantly by trading partner, ranging from close to zero to nearly 100 percent, and also by product.

24. Krupp and Skeath (2002) provide empirical evidence of a negative impact on production by downstream users of intermediate products subject to antidumping duties. The authors use a panel of thirteen upstream/downstream product pairs—such as methanol and formaldehyde—for the period 1977–92 to identify the effects of antidumping duties in the upstream industry on production and sales in the downstream industry. Antidumping duties upstream are confirmed to have a negative effect on downstream production. However, the authors do not find a significant negative effect on downstream value, perhaps because the direction of the effect on total revenue of lower quantity supplied depends on the elasticity of demand for the downstream product. A challenge for this type of research is finding upstream products tied significantly to specific downstream activities. Results are likely weaker to the extent that downstream producers have access to good substitutes for the input affected by antidumping.

25. Gawande, Hoekman, and Cui (2015) find evidence for seven large emerging market economies that participation in global supply chains helped to keep protectionism in check during the 2008–2009 global crisis.

26. An important early example of the relationship between administered protection and foreign direct investment came in the voluntary export restraint (VER) agreement negotiated between the United States and Japan in autos in 1981. In their support for protection, an explicit goal of the United Auto Workers was to encourage Japanese companies to establish factories in the United States. Likewise, although the gap left by European VERs on Japanese autos was initially filled by traditional European suppliers in Italy and Germany (De Melo and Messerlin 1988), VER-jumping Japanese FDI soon followed. On antidumping-jumping FDI, see Blonigen (2002). Washing

machines are a recent US example in which imports from South Korean firms (Samsung and LG) were hit first with antidumping, then with a global safeguard after the firms moved production to third countries. Each has also increased production in the United States that will allow them to avoid the tariffs (see Bown and Keynes 2018).

27. Blonigen and Ohno (1998) provide a theoretical model of "protection-building trade" in which foreign-headquartered firms locate production in the home country and then increase their own exports to the home country so as to *increase* protectionist pressures that would result in higher barriers against other foreign competitors in the future.

28. According to industry reports, Michelin, Bridgestone, Goodyear, and Continental together accounted for almost 55 percent of the world market in 2010 (Datamonitor 2011, 13). Michelin, Bridgestone, Goodyear, and Pirelli each have subsidiaries in many emerging markets, including China, the latter often through joint ventures. Not included in the table is the US 2009 China-specific safeguard tariff on tire imports, a case that was *not* brought by the US domestic tire producers—that is, US-headquartered firms or US affiliates of foreign-headquartered multinationals—but by the United Steelworkers on behalf of the industry's unionized labor force.

29. This may be one reason why constructed costs based on "similar" but much smaller countries produce such large dumping margins.

30. Shortly after the long-established Multi-Fibre Arrangement ended in 1995, China imposed restrictions on textile and apparel exports. This was done at the behest of the United States and the European Union. But the longer-run impact of this policy may have been to hasten upgrading of Chinese exports, consistent with China's own stated goals. On the other hand, the United States and the European Union opposed China's later restrictions on exports of raw materials and rare earths. They filed formal WTO dispute settlement proceedings in an attempt to have those export restrictions removed.

31. These include the right of affected exporters to file a dispute to challenge an antidumping action that violates the WTO rules, and such disputes have become increasingly common.

REFERENCES

Areddy, James T., and Wayne Ma. 2012. "Beijing Flares Up at US on Solar Tariff." *Wall Street Journal*, May 24.

Bagwell, Kyle, and Robert W. Staiger. 1990. "A Theory of Managed Trade." *American Economic Review* 80 (4): 779–95.

Barfield, Claude. 2003. *High-Tech Protectionism: The Irrationality of Antidumping Laws.* Washington, D.C.: AEI Press.

Bernard, Andrew B., and others. 2010. "Intra-Firm Trade and Product Contractibility" (long version). http://mba.tuck.dartmouth.edu/pages/faculty/andrew.bernard/iftlong.pdf.

Blonigen, Bruce A. 2002. "Tariff-Jumping Antidumping Duties." *Journal of International Economics* 57 (1): 31–49.

Blonigen, Bruce A., and Yuka Ohno. 1998. "Endogenous Protection, Foreign Direct Investment and Protection-Building Trade." *Journal of International Economics* 46 (2): 205–27.

Blonigen, Bruce A., and Thomas J. Prusa. 2003. "Antidumping." In *Handbook of International Economics*, edited by E. Kwan Choi and James Harrigan, 251–84. Malden, Mass: Blackwell.

———. 2016. "Dumping and Antidumping Duties." In *Handbook of Commercial Policy*. Vol. 1B, edited by Kyle W. Bagwell and Robert W. Staiger, 107–59. Amsterdam: Elsevier, North Holland.

Bourgeois, Jacques H. J., and Patrick A. Messerlin. 1998. "The European Community's Experience." *Brookings Trade Forum*: 127–45.

Bown, Chad P. 2011a. "Taking Stock of Antidumping, Safeguards and Countervailing Duties, 1990–2009." *World Economy* 34 (12): 1955–98.

———, ed. 2011b. *The Great Recession and Import Protection: The Role of Temporary Trade Barriers.* London: CEPR and World Bank.

———. 2013. "Emerging Economies and the Emergence of South-South Protectionism." *Journal of World Trade* 47 (1): 1–44.

———. 2016. "Temporary Trade Barriers Database." Washington, D.C.: World Bank. http://econ.worldbank.org/ttbd/.

———. 2018. "Trade Policy toward Supply Chains after the Great Recession." *IMF Economic Review* 66 (3): 602–16.

Bown, Chad P., and Meredith A. Crowley. 2013. "Self-Enforcing Trade Agreements: Evidence from Time-Varying Trade Policy." *American Economic Review* 103 (2): 1071–90.

Bown, Chad P., and Soumaya Keynes. 2018. "Tariff Time! Washing Machines and Dirty Trade Policy." *Trade Talks*, Episode 20, January 18.

Bown, Chad P., and Patricia Tovar. 2011. "Trade Liberalization, Antidumping and Safeguards: Evidence from India's Tariff Reform." *Journal of Development Economics* 96 (1): 115–25.

Crowley, Meredith A., Ning Meng, and Huasheng Song. 2019. "Policy Shocks and Stock Market Returns: Evidence from Chinese Solar Panels." *Journal of the Japanese and International Economies* 51: 148–69.

Datamonitor. 2011. "Industry Profile: Global Tires & Rubber." New York, June.

Dean, Judith M., Mary E. Lovely, and Jesse Mora. 2009. "Decomposing China-Japan-US Trade: Vertical Specialization, Ownership, and Organizational Form." *Journal of Asian Economics* 20 (6): 596–610.

De Melo, Jaime, and Patrick A. Messerlin. 1988. "Price, Quality and Welfare Effects of European VERs on Japanese Autos." *European Economic Review* 32 (7): 1527–46.

Durling, James P., and Thomas J. Prusa. 2003. "Using Safeguard Protection to Raise Domestic Rivals' Costs." *Japan and the World Economy* 15 (1): 47–68.

Egger, Peter, and Douglas Nelson. 2011. "How Bad Is Antidumping? Evidence from Panel Data." *Review of Economics and Statistics* 93 (4): 1374–90.

Finger, J. Michael, ed. 1993. *Antidumping: How It Works and Who Gets Hurt.* University of Michigan Press.

———. 2010. "WTO Flexibility Provisions." *Vox*, March 18. http://voxeu.org/index.php?q=node/4729.

Finger, J. Michael, and Julio Nogues, eds. 2005. *Safeguards and Antidumping in Latin American Trade Liberalization: Fighting Fire with Fire.* Washington, D.C.: World Bank.

Gawande, Kishore, Bernard Hoekman, and Yue Cui. 2015. "Global Supply Chains and Trade Policy Responses to the 2008 Crisis." *World Bank Economic Review* 29 (1): 102–28.

Hummels, David, Jun Ishii, and Kei-Mu Yi. 2001. "The Nature and Growth of Vertical Specialization in World Trade." *Journal of International Economics* 54 (1): 75–96.

Irwin, Douglas A. 1998. "The Semiconductor Industry." *Brookings Trade Forum*: 173–200.

———. 2005a. "The Rise of US Antidumping Activity in Historical Perspective." *World Economy* 28 (5): 651–68.

———. 2005b. *Free Trade under Fire.* 2nd edition. Princeton University Press.

Johnson, Keith, and Cassandra Sweet. 2012. "US Imposes Tariffs on China Solar Panels." *Wall Street Journal*, May 18.

Johnson, Robert C. and Guillermo Noguera. 2017. "A Portrait of Trade in Value Added over Four Decades." *Review of Economics and Statistics* 99 (5): 896-911.

Krupp, Corinne M., and Susan Skeath. 2002. "Evidence on the Upstream and Downstream Impacts of Antidumping Cases." *North American Journal of Economics and Finance* 13 (2): 163–78.

Mavroidis, Petros C., Patrick A. Messerlin, and Jasper-Martijn Wauters. 2008. *The Law and Economics of Contingent Protection.* Cheltenham, UK: Edward Elgar.

Messerlin, Patrick A. 1990. "Anti-Dumping Regulations or Pro-Cartel Law? The EC Chemical Cases." *The World Economy* 13 (4): 465–492.

———. 1994. "Should Antidumping Rules Be Replaced by National or International Competition Rules?" *World Competition* 18 (3): 37–54. Reprinted from *Assenwirtschaft (Swiss Review of International Economic Relations).* Special Issue, *International Competition Rules in the GATT/WTO System* (1994).

———. 2004. "China in the World Trade Organization: Antidumping and Safeguards." *World Bank Economic Review* 18 (1): 105–30.

Messerlin, Patrick A., and Yoshiyuki Noguchi. 1998. "Antidumping Policies in Electronic Products." *Brookings Trade Forum*: 147–71.

Moore, Michael O. 2005. "VERs vs. Price Undertakings under the WTO." *Review of International Economics* 13 (2): 298–310.

———. 2015. "Sanctuary Markets and Antidumping: An Empirical Analysis of US Exporters." *Weltwirtschaftliches Archiv/Review of World Economics* 151 (2): 309–28.

Moore, Michael O., and Maurizio Zanardi. 2009. "Does Antidumping Use Contribute to Trade Liberalization in Developing Countries?" *Canadian Journal of Economics* 42 (2): 469–95.

Nelson, Douglas R., and Hylke Vandenbussche, eds. 2005. *The WTO and Anti-Dumping.* Cheltenham, UK: Edward Elgar.

Nicola, Stefan, and Marc Roca. 2012. "Solarworld-Led Group Files China Anti-Dumping Case In Europe." Bloomberg, July 26. www.bloomberg .com/news/2012-07-26/solarworld-led-group-files-china-anti -dumping-case-in-europe.html.

Prusa, Thomas J. 1992. "Why Are So Many Antidumping Petitions Withdrawn?" *Journal of International Economics* 29 (1): 1–20.

Prusa, Thomas J., and Susan Skeath. 2002. "The Economic and Strategic Motives for Antidumping Filings." *Weltwirtschaftliches Archiv* 138 (3): 389–413.

Shin, Hyun Ja. 1998. "Possible Instances of Predatory Pricing in Recent US Antidumping Cases." *Brookings Trade Forum*: 81–97.

Sidak, Joseph Gregory. 1982. "A Framework for Administering the 1916 Antidumping Act: Lessons from Antitrust Economics." *Stanford Journal of International Law* 18 (2): 377–404.

Sweet, Cassandra. 2012. "US Solar-Panel Demand Expected to Double." *Wall Street Journal*, June 14.

Staiger, Robert W., and Frank A. Wolak. 1989. "Strategic Use of Antidumping Law to Enforce Tacit International Collusion." NBER Working Paper 3016. Cambridge, Mass.: National Bureau of Economic Research, June.

————. 1992. "The Effect of Domestic Antidumping Law in the Presence of Foreign Monopoly." *Journal of International Economics* 32 (3–4): 265–87.

————. 1994. "Measuring Industry-Specific Protection: Antidumping in the United States." *Brookings Papers on Economic Activity: Microeconomics*: 51–118.

Sykes, Alan O. 1998. "Antidumping and Antitrust: What Problems Does Each Address?" *Brookings Trade Forum*: 1–53.

Taylor, Christopher T. 2004. "The Economic Effects of Withdrawn Antidumping Investigations: Is There Evidence of Collusive Settlements?" *Journal of International Economics* 62 (2): 295–312.

Vandenbussche, Hylke, and Maurizio Zanardi. 2010. "The Chilling Trade Effects of Antidumping Proliferation." *European Economic Review* 54 (6): 760–77.

Viner, Jacob. 1923. *Dumping: A Problem in International Trade*. University of Chicago Press.

Willig, Robert D. 1998. "Effects of Antidumping Policy." *Brookings Trade Forum*: 57–79.

3

THE TRADE POLICY OF THE UNITED STATES UNDER THE TRUMP ADMINISTRATION

CRAIG VANGRASSTEK

Even the most casual observer will readily see that the international trading system is now in great turmoil, and that much of the uncertainty emanates from the United States. Less evident is the fact that we cannot lay all of the blame for the disorder on a single presidency. The country that had taken the lead after World War II, and whose economy helped to usher in a lengthy period of peace and prosperity, began to devote less attention to trade issues at least a full decade before Donald Trump took office in 2017. Even when the Obama administration took up major initiatives such as the Transatlantic Trade and Investment Partnership (TTIP) and a greatly expanded Trans-Pacific Partnership (TPP), it was reluctant to treat those negotiations with much urgency or to invest significant political capital in them. Trump's election nevertheless marked a critically significant inflection point, with the American posture toward the system rapidly turning from benevolent indifference to outright hostility. The trading partners of the United States, including erstwhile allies as well as potential adversaries, continue to puzzle over how we got to this juncture, how long we will be here, and where we may next be headed.

While only time and experience can fully answer the latter two questions, we can make a good start by focusing on the first. The principal purpose of this chapter is to place in context these upheavals in US policy so as to assess what might come next. I argue that the evolution of American trade policy is best understood over the long run as a function of the international distribution of power and wealth, and especially the rise and fall of the country's leadership role, but that in the short run policy is dominated by the exigencies of domestic politics. That latter point is especially relevant in these times, when the specific preferences of one man and his political base overwhelm all other considerations.

These twin internal and external processes coincide on a few critical points. Each is set in motion by the relative decline of the United States, which is in turn the consequence of two related economic processes. The first of these is the Law of Uneven Growth, that observed tendency of leading economies, especially the countries that vie for hegemony, to grow at different rates. That almost inescapable process of asynchronous growth is complemented at the domestic level by Creative Destruction, in which once-dominant industries are gradually displaced by competitors abroad and by new industries at home. These internal and external sources of disequilibrium require that leaders make periodic course corrections in their dealings with partners and rivals at home and abroad. While it is theoretically possible for the United States to navigate a steady course between these two hazards, making compensatory adjustments in its own policies and (if its partners consent) the structure of the international system, such accommodations require clear vision and a deft hand.

Relative decline may be all but inescapable, but still leaves wide scope for the responses of US policymakers. Had the American electorate made a more conventional choice in 2016, we would now be reviewing the continued attempts of orthodox statesmen to tweak the existing domestic and international system. The public instead opted for a man who promised to overturn that system altogether. Many outside observers hoped, and some may even have believed, that Trump's threats would prove to be mere campaign rhetoric that he would disavow once in office. Years of experience have put those comforting thoughts to rest.

Trade policy in the Trump administration began with a series of year-long phases by which the almost inchoate sentiments of a makeshift campaign were progressively transformed into ever more concrete policy. The first such phase lasted throughout 2016, which was dominated by the first presidential campaign in nearly a century to center on blatant appeals to protectionism, nationalism, and isolationism. The key slogans "Make America Great Again" and "America First" offered a glimpse of what Trump aimed to do in office. The principal theme of 2017 was the transliteration of these messages into somewhat more precise principles of governance. That started with an unapologetically protectionist inaugural address and continued through a series of executive orders espousing such principles as "Buy American and Hire American." It was not until 2018, however, that this disquieting ideology gave way to truly provocative action. That year began with the granting of protectionist petitions that had been filed months before by producers of solar panels and washing machines, and then turned to broader confrontations over intellectual property rights, steel, aluminum, and automobiles. By year's end, the United States had incited a full-fledged trade war in which China is the principal adversary but few countries can preserve their neutrality. That phase continued through 2019 and into 2020, which were dominated more by the continuation of established themes or initiatives than by the introduction of new ones.

The question now centers on what the years following 2020 will hold for US trade politics and the larger trading system. The answer will be determined above all else by whether the electorate ensures that the Trump administration was merely a four-year deviation; at the time of this writing, that decision is still four months in the future. Yet even if Donald Trump is denied a second term, the underlying causes of Trumpism may be with us as far as the eye can see. Whether that movement is in power or just waiting in the wings, policymakers in the United States and abroad can no longer take for granted that the United States is willing and able to exercise leadership in the trading system. And even if the country attempts a return to that earlier role, its foreign partners may be more leery than ever before.

THE CHALLENGE OF GLOBAL GOVERNANCE
AND THE RISE OF CHINA

China is the one element in US trade policy that matters even more than Trump. This is not the first time since World War II that the United States has faced a challenge to its leadership, nor the first time that a precipitous

American response seemed to put the multilateral trading system at risk. There are several respects in which the current dynamics replicate those of the 1980s, when US trade policy was dominated by a contest with Japan over industrial supremacy, but there are also some key differences. Chief among them is the conflation of international struggles. American policy-makers of a generation ago faced down one rival that was militarily strong but economically weak (the Soviet Union), and another challenger with just the opposite characteristics (Japan). By contrast, US concerns over both power and wealth are today combined in competition with China. The past and present melees are nonetheless alike in the collateral damage that they inflict on third parties. Just as the prior fight with Japan cast doubt on US support for the old General Agreement on Tariffs and Trade (GATT), so too has the current clash undermined the World Trade Organization (WTO). In fact, some of the most provocative measures imposed by the Trump administration have a more serious impact on neighbors and allies than they do on China.

The causes and consequences of Sino-American competition can best be understood by way of the theory of hegemonic stability, a paradigm that explains why global markets are often closed but sometimes open. It rests upon the assertion that an open world market is a public good from which every country benefits, but also acknowledges that it is in the nature of public goods to invite free-riding. Open markets therefore tend to be historically underprovided, with each country reserving the right to determine its own levels of protection, unless one especially influential country steps forward to lead. A hegemon will provide this public good both because open markets are in its economic interest and because it has the necessary power to persuade—or even to compel—others to cooperate. This paradigm suggests that markets would not have been open in the nineteenth century without British hegemony, that the global economic calamity of the 1930s was the inevitable consequence of a political vacuum, and that the peace and prosperity that followed World War II can be principally attributed to American leadership. It also implies that the actions of the hegemon are both self-serving and self-defeating: A leader must establish an open world market to reap the rewards of its own competitiveness, but the system that it fosters will create opportunities for its challengers. Just as the British-sponsored trade regime aided Germany, so too has China's growth been enabled by the current system.[1] Much of the Trump administration's policies may be seen as an attempt to correct for the policies of preceding administrations that, in the view of current officeholders, actively contributed to the challenger's ascendance.

We may reasonably expect the state of relations between the United States and China to influence—and perhaps to determine—the evolution of the global trading system for decades to come. Size alone makes this obvious: these two countries jointly account for 21 percent of world exports, 23 percent of its imports, 23 percent of the global population, and 39 percent of the global economy.[2] More to the point, they also comprise 100 percent of the contenders for hegemony. And while it cannot be taken for granted that China will continue to grow as fast as it has in recent decades, or that the relative position of the United States will steadily and irreversibly fall behind, the trends are undeniable. They prompt leaders in these two countries, and in all others, to anticipate a changing global environment in which Beijing's influence will rival or even surpass that of Washington.

The Impact of Relative US Decline on the Multilateral System

The last transfer of global leadership was deceptively easy. It was fortunate for the outgoing and incoming hegemons, and for the world, that London and Washington were on the same side in the most destructive war in history. The cousins worked closely during 1942–1947 to design the postwar global system, and devoted especially close attention to the trade component of that regime. It would be particularly ironic if it were the United States, and not China, that were to dismantle the remnants of that system— or at least require it to get on without the old leader. At the start of the Trump administration, it had appeared that there was a better-than-even chance that the United States would explicitly threaten to leave the WTO sometime in his tenure. That has not yet happened, but it is not difficult to imagine scenarios in which it may yet come to pass. One need look no further than the president's immediate disavowal of the TPP, followed by withdrawals from other agreements on such diverse topics as climate change and Iranian nuclear weapons, to see Trump's antipathy toward international cooperation. It should shock no one if the WTO were to join a list of jilted institutions that already includes the Human Rights Council, UNESCO, the Universal Postal Union, and the World Health Organization. And even while Trump has kept the United States in the WTO, he has rendered that membership virtually moot by pursuing policies that are antithetical to the spirit and the letter of this organization.

This is not to say that the abdication of US leadership is inevitable or permanent, or even that leadership by just one country is the only option. It is at least theoretically possible that the United States and China could become next Group of Two (G-2) that manages the multilateral trading system. The original G-2 of the immediate postwar era was strictly Anglo-American, but over the next few decades the European Union (and its predecessor bodies) took the British place. It long seemed that agreement between Washington and Brussels was both the necessary and sufficient condition for bringing any round of multilateral trade negotiations to a successful conclusion. Other countries frequently objected to a restricted, "green room" approach in which the major GATT decisions were made chiefly by the Quad (the G-2 plus Canada and Japan) plus a few other developed and developing countries, but the arrangement was undeniably productive. That all changed with the dawn of a new century, as became apparent at the failed WTO ministerial meetings of 1999 (which dissolved into chaos) and 2003 (where a transatlantic proposal epically failed to win over the rest of the WTO membership). Those episodes, especially the latter one, underlined the point that transatlantic concordance is no longer the sufficient condition for reaching multilateral deals. Some wonder if it will even be necessary in a new world order in which the post-Brexit European Union holds third place.

The decay of multilateralism may be traced in part to a diluted sense of a shared strategic purpose. WTO members are not divided by the old antagonisms of the Cold War, but neither are they united by them. The rising powers include some original GATT contracting parties that had already been influential in the old order, especially Brazil and India, as well as others that did not accede until after the WTO was established. In addition to China, the new entrants include Russia, Saudi Arabia, Taiwan, and Vietnam. Universality, diversity, and democracy come at a cost, as there is an inverse relationship between the number of decisionmakers in a system and the efficiency with which it can act. No objective observer could say that the nearly all-encompassing WTO has executed its legislative function as effectively as did the smaller, more cohesive GATT club. It did produce some results in the late 1990s, such as the Information Technology Agreement and several protocols on trade in services, but the launch of the new round in 2001 marked the start of an especially fruitless run. Modest accomplishments such as the Trade Facilitation Agreement are only a pale shadow of what the WTO members might achieve if they animated the Doha Round with as much ambition as its GATT-era predecessor.

How the Sino-American Rivalry Affects the Multilateral System

There are strong reasons to doubt that the same torch that London handed to Washington might be passed just as easily, and with the same effect, from Washington to Beijing. Even if the United States were willing to make the handoff, and China were prepared to exercise leadership in the multilateral system, the results might be quite different. The British and American versions of hegemony were at least rhetorically committed to the concept of a first among equals, and while both of the Anglo-American leaders were known to throw their weight around they typically favored persuasion over coercion. Future Chinese leaders may find inspiration in other, less inclusive and cooperative archetypes. The models in China's own past, whether one looks to the imperial period or the second half of the twentieth century, suggest a preference for hierarchical relations and a readiness to exert authority. Much depends on whether China is truly committed to a global economy in which markets matter more than states, or instead prefers a quasi-imperial system with more top-down direction. There is plenty of contradictory evidence in a country that is at once home to the world's largest Communist system, yet may soon host the world's largest market.

In the near term, the more pressing issue is how China's WTO membership alters the US perception of that institution and its willingness to make any new concessions—or even to respect the existing US commitments—on a most favored nation (MFN) basis. This situation is similar in one respect to how Congress approached MFN treatment early in the Cold War, when critics charged (however implausibly) that any tariff reductions made in the GATT might redound to the benefit of Moscow. That problem was easily solved in 1951, when legislators obliged the Truman administration to strip the Soviet bloc of its MFN privileges; this affected very little actual trade, and was uncomplicated by these countries' GATT status (apart from the special case of Czechoslovakia). Now that China is a WTO member, and eschews the Soviet-style autarky that it had once emulated, no such easy solutions are available. The only ways to ensure that China does not benefit from any agreements reached in the WTO are to negotiate them on a strictly plurilateral basis (which China opposes), or to abstain from multilateral negotiations altogether. The United States appears to have pursued the second option, albeit in a purely informal and unacknowledged manner, for the better part of a decade. Even after Trump leaves office, there may be considerable reluctance in Washington to negotiate new liberalization on a nondiscriminatory and multilateral basis.

Unless the United States and China settle on some modus vivendi that permits them to move ahead together in the WTO, they are more likely to let that institution go slack while each concentrates instead on free trade agreements (FTAs) or other bilateral approaches. To the extent that the United States freezes its current levels of MFN treatment, and liberalizes its tariffs and other trade barriers only on a discriminatory basis, it will treat China and other countries outside its FTA circle as the least favored nations.

THE CHALLENGE OF RESURGENT MERCANTILISM

The economic nationalism that underpins the Trump administration's policies is quite obvious, but should not be mistaken for mere protectionism. That narrow policy, which might most simply be defined as the imposition of border barriers to the entry of foreign goods and services so as to benefit domestic suppliers, can clearly be seen in both the rhetoric and the actions of this president. The true essence of this administration's approach to trade and foreign policy, however, is more properly characterized as mercantilism. This entails not merely a commercial objective, but a full-fledged doctrine of statecraft that is founded on a specific view of the relationship between power and wealth.

The Reversion to Mercantilism

While classical mercantilism encompassed a mixed bag of thinkers and practitioners, its adherents nevertheless shared some fundamental assumptions about the nature of conflict and the proper aim of economic governance. The doctrine's essentials can be reduced to a simple syllogism that is embraced just as enthusiastically in the new Washington of Donald Trump as it was in the old Versailles of Jean-Baptiste Colbert:

- **Major Premise**: All political and economic relations are hierarchical dealings in which one either dominates or is subordinate. The state is the dominant domestic institution, and the stronger, richer states dominate weaker, poorer states.

- **Minor Premise**: Power and wealth are inextricably linked, being both interchangeable and equal in importance. Each of these desiderata is zero-sum, such that any state's gains in power and wealth necessarily come at the expense of other states.

- **Conclusion**: Trade is an essential component in the power relations between states, and to that end the state should intervene to maximize exports (especially of finished goods), minimize imports (except for raw materials), and promote a positive trade balance.

The current reversion to mercantilism can be explained by both long-term international trends (especially the Law of Uneven Growth) and by the short-term political events within the United States. Where these two trends meet is in the process of Creative Destruction, a phenomenon that has been especially disruptive for labor-intensive US industries that face competitive challenges from lower-wage countries. Competition killed some of those firms, but the economy as a whole adjusted by becoming more services-intensive. The remaining manufacturers coped by outsourcing their inputs, moving operations off shore, or investing in labor-saving machinery. These adjustments worked well for many employers and policymakers, but not for all workers. Whatever job-shedding strategy management might favor, and politicians might facilitate, every option other than bankruptcy will always be more disruptive for labor than for capital. Some displaced hands can find work in more competitive industries, but many others suffer either declining wages or permanent joblessness. And while the rising trade deficit is not solely responsible for the secular decline in manufacturing, it is the cause most visible to the general public.

This economic transition was complemented by a political process in the 1980s and 1990s through which dying industries and displaced workers were temporarily placated by protectionist concessions, but by the turn of the century they had lost much of their influence in Washington. One reason why Donald Trump managed to secure the nomination of the supposedly protrade party, and then to win in the industrial states he needed to secure the presidency, was that he mobilized a reserve army of the formerly employed that other, more conventional politicians had long ago abandoned.[3]

One of the more notable aspects of the Trump administration's priorities is a sharp focus on manufactures. This is all the more remarkable when one considers that virtually all of the president's private successes have been in service sectors (especially real estate, entertainment, and the hospitality industry). That has not prevented Trump and others around him from treating steel, automobiles, and other heavy industries as somehow more "real" and masculine undertakings that are worthier of attention. The anomaly may be partly explained by political calculations, with policymakers always keeping an eye on the electoral map, but the administration also seems rooted in strongly nostalgic notions that find Creative Destruction easier to deny than to reverse. That sentiment takes concrete form in the revival of the trade-remedy and reciprocity laws.

The Revival of Trade-Remedy and Reciprocity Laws

When the administration turned in 2018 from rhetoric to action it did so primarily by resuscitating older trade laws that were largely forgotten but not yet gone. Trump began the year by resurrecting a long-dormant provision of the Trade Act of 1974 (section 201) when he granted global safeguards protection to producers of washing machines and solar panels. These cases represented the first US invocations of this statute, and its counterpart in international law, since the George W. Bush administration used it to protect steel in 2002. Trump followed up mid-year by reviving yet another disused provision of that 1974 law, invoking a "reciprocity" clause (section 301) that gives the president broad powers to define and enforce US rights. Trump used this law in a complaint against Chinese intellectual property policies, with the retaliatory measures that he imposed being the most precisely targeted shot in a spreading trade war. The Trump administration's preferred instrument for protecting the steel and aluminum industries is an even older and more obscure trade law that is based on claims of national security. The White House announced in March that it would use the president's authority under section 232 of the Trade Expansion Act of 1962 to restrict imports of these two metals from nearly all sources.

These were only the most high-profile manifestations of a broader trend in which the United States has returned to trade laws as a means of managing competition. The characteristics of these laws are summarized in table 3-1, and figure 3-1 shows their evolving use since 1975. Taking the long view, the frequency with which the Trump administration has used these instruments virtually matches what the United States did during the Uruguay Round (1986–1994). While there are some differences in the relative weight given to distinct laws, the overall rate of cases from 2017 through mid-2020

TABLE 3-1. **The Principal US Trade-Remedy Laws**

Listed in order of political discretion

Law	Purpose and process	How affected by Trump
Antidumping Duties (§731, Trade Act of 1930)	If the ITA finds that imports are dumped (i.e., sold at less than fair value), and the USITC finds that they cause or threaten material injury to US industries, the products are subject to duties equal to the dumping rate	In a potentially precedential action, the Department of Commerce self-initiated a case in 2017 against common alloy aluminum sheet imported from China.
Countervailing Duties (§701, Tariff Act of 1930)	If the ITA finds that imports benefit from prohibited subsidies, and the USITC finds that they cause or threaten material injury to a US industry, the products are subject to duties equal to the subsidy rate.	The Department of Commerce complemented the self-initiated antidumping case against Chinese aluminum with a countervailing duty case against the same product.
Global Safeguards (§201, Trade Act of 1974)	The USITC can recommend to the president that duties, quotas, or other remedies be granted to aid an industry that is found to suffer serious injury from increasing imports.	The administration revived this dormant law when in 2018 it granted petitioners' requests for protection against imports of washing machines and solar panels.
National Security Clause (§232, Trade Expansion Act of 1962)	The secretaries of commerce and defense can recommend that limits be imposed on imports that impair national security (e.g., by suppressing US production of strategic goods).	The administration invoked this rarely employed statute to impose restrictions on steel and aluminum, and threatens to do the same for automotive imports.
Unfair Trade Practices (§337, Tariff Act of 1930)	If the USITC finds that imports violate patents, trademarks, or copyrights, or are otherwise unfairly traded, it can issue a cease-and-desist order and/or exclude these products from the US market.	No change in policy; this is a technical statute administered entirely by the USITC.

(continued)

TABLE 3-1. *(continued)*

Listed in order of political discretion

Law	Purpose and process	How affected by Trump
Market Disruption by Communist Countries (§406, Trade Act of 1974)	The USITC can recommend to the president that duties, quotas, or other remedies be pursued to aid an industry that is found to suffer serious injury from increasing imports from a nonmarket economy.	No change in policy; this law has not been invoked since 1993.
Agricultural Imports (§22, Agricultural Adjustment Act of 1933)	The USITC can recommend that the president impose duties or quotas on imports that threaten to interfere with farm price-support programs.	No change in policy; this law has not been invoked since 1994.

Notes: ITA = International Trade Administration of the US Department of Commerce; USITC = US International Trade Commission.

has been, at forty-two per year, nearly identical to the forty-four per year achieved during those multilateral trade negotiations. No mere statistical fluke, that replication of the old trend instead demonstrates an implicit foundation of this administration's approach to trade policy: it is quite willing to accept the benefits that the United States garnered in those negotiations, but now balks at the costs. The principal benefits of the Uruguay Round, from the US perspective, were (1) the inclusion of new issues (especially intellectual property rights) within the scope of trade policy and (2) the adoption of new rules requiring that developing countries bear a bit more of the system's burdens. The principal cost, from a Trumpian worldview, came in the constraints that the revamped legal regime imposed on US unilateralism. An administration that is not willing even to accept the core GATT obligation that a country not raise its tariffs above their "bound" rates (i.e., the legal maxima) will be doubly reluctant to abide by WTO norms and rules that inhibit its conduct of trade warfare.

This point can best be appreciated by the aforementioned revival of trade laws that had once been prominent elements in US trade policy, but were subject to grand bargains in the Uruguay Round. That round did little to

FIGURE 3-1. Trade-Remedy and Reciprocity Cases Initiated in the United States, 1975–2020

Average annual number of cases initiated; data for 2020 are through June

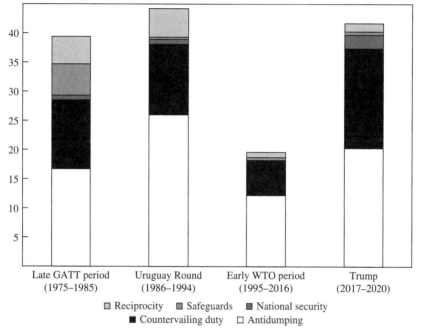

Late GATT period (1975–1985) · Uruguay Round (1986–1994) · Early WTO period (1995–2016) · Trump (2017–2020)

☐ Reciprocity   ▨ Safeguards   ■ National security
■ Countervailing duty   ☐ Antidumping

Sources: Compiled from US International Trade Commission documents, "Import Injury Investigations Case Statistics (FY1980–2008)," https://www.usitc.gov/trade_remedy/documents /historical_case_stats.pdf; "Import Injury Investigations," https://usitc.gov/trade_remedy/731_ad_701 _cvd/investigations.htm; USTR at https://ustr.gov/archive/assets/Trade_Agreements/Monitoring _Enforcement/asset_upload_file985_6885.pdf; and US Department of Commerce, https://www.bis.doc .gov/index.php/forms-documents/section-232-investigations/86-section-232-booklet/file.

Note: Antidumping and countervailing duty cases are based on products rather than partners (e.g., if petitions affecting the same product are simultaneously filed against three countries, that is counted as one petition rather than three).

constrain use of the antidumping (AD) and countervailing duty (CVD) statutes, which are arguably the most protectionist trade laws in practice but the least provocative in principle. By contrast, when the administration raised three other statutes from the dead it sparked serious concerns over America's commitment to the multilateral system. The Trump administration's readiness to employ the safeguard and reciprocity laws implies that it is not just prepared to ignore WTO norms and rules, but is actually eager to flout them; those concerns are even more severe in the case of section 232. Recent trends in the use of each law merit attention.

The AD statute is the oldest and most frequently used of the trade-remedy laws. Dumping is an unfair trade practice by which imported goods are sold at less than fair value, which may be below the cost of production, the price in the exporting country, or the price in third-country markets. The CVD law shares much in common with its AD counterpart, and cases under these twin laws are often prosecuted in tandem. The most important difference is that CVD investigations are based on allegations of government subsidies rather than the pricing practices of firms. Petitioners used to resort less frequently to the CVD law than to its AD counterpart, but that changed after nonmarket economies such as China lost their legal immunity to CVD cases in 2007.[4] The pace of AD/CVD filing picked up sharply in the first year of the Trump administration, which also saw the government's first self-initiation of cases since the Reagan administration. The pace of filings under these laws was somewhat slower in 2018–2019 than it had been in 2017, perhaps because prospective petitioners thought it might be less costly to rely on the administration's use of other statutes (especially section 232) than to foot the considerable expense of filing their own AD and CVD claims. It is also possible that protectionist industries hoped to see the Trump administration more aggressively use its authority to self-initiate AD/CVD cases. That did not happen, which may be one reason why the rate of filings in the first half of 2020 exceeded even the rapid pace set in 2017.

While the AD and CVD laws are treated as quasi-judicial statutes that are theoretically not subject to policymakers' whims, decisions to invoke the safeguards law are explicitly a matter of policy. The global safeguards law is a mechanism that allows domestic industries to petition for relief when import competition causes injury, even if those imports are fairly traded. The safeguard law requires that the US International Trade Commission (USITC) determine whether increasing imports are a substantial cause of serious injury to the domestic industry. If its injury determination is positive, the commission will recommend a remedy (e.g., quotas or tariffs). The president then has wide discretion to accept, reject, or modify the commission's recommendations. In actual practice, these tests are significant hurdles that many petitioners fail to clear. That is the chief reason why the number of petitions filed during 1986–1994 (far fewer than one per year) was so much lower than in the first decade after enactment of the Trade Act of 1974 (more than five per year). The action under this law dropped still further after the WTO came into effect. Although that institution's

Safeguard Agreement sought merely to reform this mechanism, and not to outlaw it, an unbroken series of dispute-settlement cases invariably found that the countries employing safeguards had violated their obligations. Ever since the Bush administration was required in 2003 to reverse the steel restrictions that it had imposed in 2002, Washington treated section 201 as a dead letter.

That all changed when producers of washing machines and solar panels filed safeguard petitions in 2017, leading the Trump administration to impose import restrictions in 2018. Both orders are now subject to challenges in the WTO's Dispute Settlement Body, and although the complaints have been slow-walked through the process—perhaps quite deliberately so—we may reliably anticipate that these safeguard actions will eventually be found to violate WTO obligations. Should this happen while Trump remains in office, it could set up a potentially hazardous confrontation. Past administrations have felt legally obliged to lift the restrictions they imposed under the safeguards law, but Trump seems far less intent on trimming his policies to meet the terms of international agreements and the rulings of dispute-settlement panels. In the event that the United States fails to remove protections that are found to contravene the rules of the Safeguard Agreement, it will only reinforce the already strong impression that US policymakers no longer respect their obligations in the WTO.

The revival of the reciprocity law raises that same concern. Generations of American policymakers have used the term "reciprocity" to mean a policy in which objectives are pursued by threatening or imposing sanctions unilaterally rather than either negotiating mutually beneficial agreements or bringing the disputes to a neutral court. Laws of this sort have been around since the first decades of independence, and have been of recurring importance throughout US history, but were rarely invoked in the first generation of hegemony. The principal exception to this rule was the Chicken War that the United States fought with the European Community in the 1960s. Following a revamping of the law in 1974, the section 301 authority became a major element in US trade policy. The Reagan administration was especially enamored of this law, using the threat of retaliation in order to advance its objectives on what were then called the "new issues" (i.e., services, intellectual property rights, and investment). Congress encouraged this move by enacting an entire family of related laws. Several of them were included in the Omnibus Trade and Competitiveness Act of 1988, such as one that focuses on countries' intellectual property practices (known as

"Special 301") and others dealing with such diverse subjects as government procurement, telecommunications trade, and foreign shipping practices.

The reciprocity laws returned to their former obscurity after the Uruguay Round. In the grandest of all that round's grand bargains, the United States tacitly agreed to sheath its reciprocity sword in exchange for other countries' agreement to accept disciplines on the new issues. Even if the US negotiators were not fully satisfied with the terms of the agreements on intellectual property rights and investment measures, and the General Agreement on Trade in Services did more to establish the architecture of liberalization than to reduce actual barriers, the United States had achieved its principal objective: the round enlarged the scope of trade disciplines to cover topics of high interest to an increasingly post-industrial economy. The agreements on these issues were to be adjudicated not unilaterally by the United States, but instead in a stronger dispute-settlement system that differed from its GATT predecessor in several respects. The new trade court does not allow any country to block a case by abusing the rule of consensus, it covers the full range of WTO agreements with a unified system, and was—at least until the United States began opposing new appointments—backed by an Appellate Body that provides greater consistency to the interpretation of the rules. For all of its shortcomings, the overall balance of concessions in the Uruguay Round leaned far more toward what the United States demanded than what many of its negotiating partners hoped to concede. That distinction seemed lost on the Trump administration when, as discussed later in this chapter, it decided to pursue its complaints against Chinese intellectual property rights violations through domestic rather than international law. It was as if the Uruguay Round never happened.

The Abuse of the GATT National Security Provision

The section 232 cases pose an even graver danger to the trading system than the Trump administration's revival of the safeguard and reciprocity laws. Beyond the direct presidential imprimatur that these national security cases bear, and the presumably greater implied resistance to an unfavorable ruling in the WTO dispute-settlement system, some of the products involved are inherently important. And even more than the aforementioned safeguard and reciprocity cases, Trump's invocation of national security for nakedly protectionist purposes meant deliberately violating a taboo. Before his time, American presidents were careful to ensure that they resorted to section 232 and its counterpart in international law (GATT Article XXI) only *in extremis*, employing the law almost exclusively as an instrument of energy security.[5]

That all ended in 2017, when one of the first acts of the Trump administration was to self-initiate section 232 investigations against steel and aluminum. That was only the beginning, with the administration also launching an investigation in 2018 against automobiles and automotive parts. That case has thus far remained more an instrument of leverage than protection, with the White House threatening to pull the trigger on car tariffs whenever it wants to step up pressure in any dispute with Canada, the European Union, or Japan. The Trump administration also received (but ultimately denied) petitions from producers of uranium and titanium sponge, and initiated cases in 2020 involving vanadium, electrical transformers, and mobile cranes. Having pursued eight cases in just three and a half years, this administration has resorted to section 232 five times more frequently than did the administrations of Ford through Obama (i.e., eighteen cases from 1975 through 2016).

As can be appreciated from the data in table 3-2, it was absurd for the administration to base its most protectionist actions to date on spurious claims of national security. More than two-thirds of US automotive imports, and well over half of steel and aluminum imports, come either from NATO countries or other partners that past presidents have formally designated as major non-NATO allies. Uranium was the only item subject to an early section 232 investigation for which a potential adversary (Russia) was a major supplier, and also the only one for which an appeal to national security seemed plausible, and yet it was the sole item in the section 232 docket of 2017–2018 for which the administration showed little enthusiasm.

This indiscriminate use of the national security law, and the implied willingness to abuse the corresponding exceptions clause in the WTO, may pose a greater threat to the multilateral trading system than any other aspect of Trump's trade policy. The danger arises in the administration's willingness to exploit WTO rules that are far more deferential toward claims of national security than they are toward other concerns that collide with trade. Any country that seeks to justify its otherwise trade-restricting measures under the general exceptions clause (GATT Article XX) faces a series of legal hurdles that very few manage to clear, but those same tests were not applied to invocations of GATT Article XXI. In the first seven decades of GATT and WTO history, no country invoking the national security

TABLE 3-2. Origins of US Imports Subject to National Security Investigations, 2017

Percentage shares of total US imports; bottom-line values based on imports for consumption

	Automobiles[a]	Iron and steel[a]	Aluminum[a]	Uranium[a]
NATO allies and related	43.2	38.3	45.9	70.3
Canada	20.8	15.5	40.2	32.6
European Union[b]	22.0	18.6	5.4	35.9
Norway	<0.1	0.5	<0.1	1.8
Turkey	0.4	3.7	0.3	. . .[d]
Major non-NATO allies (MNNAs)	27.8	19.8	10.7	0.7
Argentina	<0.1	0.7	3.2	. . .
Australia	<0.1	1.1	2.1	0.7
Japan	20.4	4.7	1.0	<0.1
Korea	7.4	8.3	0.6	<0.1
Taiwan	<0.1	3.7	0.2	<0.1
All other MNNAs[c]	<0.1	1.3	3.6	<0.1
Potential adversaries	0.8	10.5	19.0	25.4
China	0.8	2.6	9.6	0.6
Russia	<0.1	7.9	9.4	24.8
Rest of world	28.2	31.4	24.4	3.6
Mexico	27.1	7.1	1.5	. . .
All other	1.1	24.3	22.7	3.6
Value of total 2017 imports (billions of $)	212.6	33.7	16.9	2.6

Sources: Compiled from US International Trade Commission DataWeb, https://dataweb.usitc.gov/. Major Non-NATO Allies are listed at http://samm.dsca.mil/glossary/major-non-nato-allies.

[a] Automobiles are defined here as NAICS category 3361; iron and steel as NAICS category 3311; aluminum as NAICS category 3313; and uranium as HTS item 2844.

[b] The European Union per se is not a NATO ally, but the overlap of NATO and European Union membership is so large as to blur the distinction.

[c] "All other" MNNAs include Bahrain, Egypt, Israel, Jordan, Kuwait, Morocco, New Zealand, Pakistan, the Philippines, and Thailand.

[d] . . . = not applicable.

exception of GATT Article XXI had ever been obliged to justify its claim before a dispute-settlement panel. The near-automatic acceptance of invocations was correctly seen as a politically necessary norm, founded on the recognition that countries might prefer to leave the system altogether if the actions they take in pursuit of national security were subject to review by trade lawyers.

What is most remarkable about Article XXI is not the abuse that this virtual get-out-of-jail-free card might seem to invite, but the infrequency with which countries succumbed to the temptation—at least until now. Before the advent of Donald Trump, there were just three occasions in which the United States either explicitly invoked Article XXI or publicly implied that it was prepared to do so; all three involved countries that had affiliated with the Soviet Union only after joining the GATT.[6] Just a handful of other WTO members have availed themselves of the security exception. The European Union did so twice during the GATT period,[7] and developing countries repaired to this article a few times.[8] That leaves a single pre-2017 case in which a country's invocation was unambiguously abusive. This came in 1975, when Sweden imposed restrictions on footwear. Stockholm justified this measure by claiming that the country needed a viable industry to produce boots for its soldiers. The trade community shamed Sweden into removing the offending measures within two years, but did so without formally demanding a legal justification for its action.

This is just one of many ways in which the norms of the WTO are drifting away from those of the GATT. That may be a natural consequence of an expanding membership, with some of the newer entrants having less familiarity and commitment to the long-established traditions of this institution. That was apparent in two other sets of disputes that arose in 2017. Bahrain invoked Article XXI to justify actions that it took—together with Egypt, Saudi Arabia, and the United Arab Emirates—in a conflict with Qatar. Russia likewise invoked the article in one of a series of disputes with Ukraine.

Two aspects of that Russia-Ukraine dispute are especially significant. One was the full-throated support that Moscow received from Washington when it invoked this legal loophole, with both countries claiming that matters of national security should not be judiciable in a trade court.[9] The other was that the dispute-settlement panel disagreed with both countries on this matter of principle, even while determining that Russia's invocation was justified as a matter of practice. Tossing aside decades of reticence, with all earlier panels concluding that trade lawyers had no business judging national security decisions, this one opened a door that might eventually lead to places that no friend of the system should want to go. It is not difficult to imagine future cases in which panels may incur a member's wrath by second-guessing its sovereign right to define its own national security needs, even if that member abused the privilege in the first place. Hence the threat posed by the Trump administration's own resort to the national security argument: while it has clearly exploited the system by making security claims that do not come close to passing the smell test, the greater danger may lie in how panels respond. We may only speculate on the depth of the administration's motives. Its decision to pursue these cases may have been nothing but a cynical attempt to game the system by taking advantage of symmetrical weaknesses in domestic law (section 232 being the most discretionary of the trade-remedy laws) and the WTO (Article XXI being the most discretionary of the exceptions clauses). A more devious mind might perceive in this maneuver a deliberate incitement. Yet even if the Trump administration acted in these cases as an agent provocateur, daring the system to give it a plausible pretext for departing the WTO, it does not necessarily follow that a panel ought to take the bait.

In the normal course of events, we might expect the disputes over the steel and aluminum restrictions to have come to a head by the time of this writing (July 2020). The Trump administration imposed those section 232 measures in March 2018, and over the ensuing months many WTO members brought formal dispute-settlement complaints. It took several more months for the WTO to form a panel to hear these cases. If the dispute-settlement system operated as intended, we might anticipate the panel that was formed at the start of 2019 to have issued a ruling by early 2020. Like the panels in the safeguard cases, however, its work has already gone well past a year. It is clearly in the best interests of the system to run out the clock, and then some, insofar as the panel faces the true definition of a dilemma: a choice between two undesirable outcomes. If it were to side with the complainants, especially in the heat of a US presidential election, the panel would stage a made-for-television opportunity for Trump to storm out of an international organization that (he would claim) does not respect the national security of a sovereign state. If the panel were instead to allow the US restrictions to stand, it would not only ratify this gross abuse but invite other members to ape it. Given the choice, it may be the better part of valor for the system to exercise its discretion and postpone action until 2021.

Concentration on China and Collateral
Damage on Third Parties

The resurrection of the old reciprocity law is yet another area where the Trump administration revisited what seemed to have been a settled matter of law and policy. The United States appeared to have discontinued its use of section 301 in 1997, but exactly twenty years later the Office of the US Trade Representative (USTR) initiated an investigation under this law into Chinese acts, policies, and practices related to technology transfer, intellectual property, and innovation. The announcement of this section 301 case made no mention of the relevant WTO agreement or the rationale by which the USTR decided not to bring the matter to the multilateral system. It instead implied that, in a throwback to pre–Uruguay Round practices, the United States would define and enforce its rights via domestic law rather than international institutions. That was the clear implication of the sequence by which the retaliatory measures announced in 2018 preceded, rather than followed, the initiation of a formal US complaint in the WTO.

Predictably, retaliation against China was quickly followed by Chinese counterretaliation against US exports. There then ensued a lengthy series of tit-for-tat restrictions, together with numerous attempts by the Trump administration to limit the damage that the US import restrictions might wreak on domestic producers and consumers and that Chinese import restrictions might impose on US farmers. While the conflict remains a live issue as of this writing, Beijing has clearly demonstrated that it is just as capable as Washington of engaging in trade warfare and sustaining its economic costs. The most consequential outcome of the dispute may not be which side is ultimately deemed the winner or the loser, or how much damage they do to one another and to third parties in the interim, but the extent to which they are each prepared—and perhaps even eager—to reach a settlement that amounts to managed trade. The willingness that both presidents and their subordinates have shown to reach an out-of-court barter arrangement, with China pledging to purchase specified values of US goods, does not portend well for the trading system. If the Trump administration has its way, trade flows between the world's two largest economies may be determined as much by power politics as they are by market forces. That would be a retrogression of epic proportions.

The section 301 case is emblematic of a trend whereby the United States now has a two-speed approach to the conduct of trade disputes, reserving

FIGURE 3-2. The Concentration of US Trade Instruments on China, 1997–2020

Percentage share of totals in each presidential term; Trump data are through mid-2020

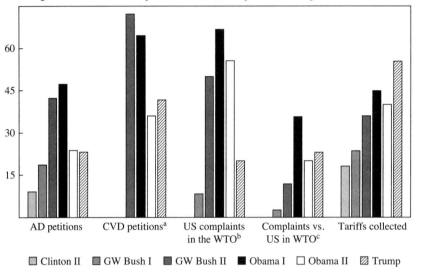

Sources: Antidumping and countervailing duty petitions calculated from World Bank data, http://data
.worldbank.org/data-catalog/temporary-trade-barriers-database and US International Trade
Commission data, http://www.usitc.gov/trade_remedy/731_ad_701_cvd/investigations/completed
/index.htm. WTO complaints calculated from WTO data, http://www.wto.org/english/tratop_e/dispu
_e/dispu_by_country_e.htm. Tariff data calculated from USITC DataWeb data at http://dataweb.usitc
.gov/scripts/INTRO.asp.

[a] Countervailing duty (CVD) petitions against China were not legally possible before a revised
interpretation of the law in 2007.
[b] Dispute settlement complaints in either direction were not legally possible before China's WTO
accession in 2001.
[c] Shares of antidumping (AD) and CVD petitions calculated on the basis of total countries and products
named in petitions. For example, if in a given year there is one AD petition filed against imports of
product X from China and one other country, plus another AD petition filed against imports of
product Y from only one other country, China accounts for 33.3 percent of all AD petitions.

the higher gear for China. This can be appreciated from the data in figure 3-2, which summarizes the shares of the main policy instruments that
are directed at China. The surge in AD cases can be attributed not just to
the rising share of US imports originating in China, but to special rules.
China is subject to the unique methodology employed for nonmarket economies (NMEs), in which price comparisons are made not against the exporting country but instead against a market-oriented "surrogate" country

(typically India). This makes it much easier for petitioners to show high rates of dumping. It is thus more attractive for petitioners to bring cases against China and Vietnam than any other country. The concentration of trade-remedy laws on China was further abetted by a decision in which the country lost its earlier exemption from CVD investigations. The Department of Commerce had previously read the law to mean that NMEs were immune from CVD investigations, based on the theory that it is impossible to isolate and assess the impact of subsidies in an economy that amounts to one big subsidy. The department reversed this doctrine in 2007, and in 2012 Congress approved legislation that reinforced this interpretation. This is one reason why, as previously seen in figure 3-1, the relative frequency of CVD cases has lately increased more rapidly than filings under the AD law.

It is interesting to note that while the concentration of trade instruments on China increased from the second Clinton through the first Obama term, it then tapered off in the second Obama term. That period saw a decline in the shares of AD and CVD cases that targeted China, as well as the percentage of WTO disputes brought by Washington against Beijing (and vice versa). The preliminary data suggest that this declining trend was only partially arrested under Trump, with the Chinese shares of AD and CVD cases in this administration closely resembling those of the second Obama term. Interpreting the data on disputes in the WTO is somewhat more complicated, as that depends on just how complex a game the Trump administration may be playing.

WTO dispute settlement is one area where the Trump administration has thus far shown little inclination to take full advantage of the opportunities to bring maximum pressure on China. This is a departure from the recent past. During the Obama administration, when the United States brought six cases against China, Beijing responded with just one complaint against the United States. Those numbers have been reversed in the Trump administration, with China bringing six complaints against the United States from 2017 through mid-2020 but being targeted by just two US complaints. The one trend that has continued almost unbroken across six presidential terms is the rising share of tariffs that are collected on imports from China. This rose from just 18 percent in the second Clinton term to 55 percent under Trump. That increase can be attributed not just to China's growing share of total imports, and the penalty tariffs that the Trump administration has imposed, but also to the spreading number of FTAs that give other partners duty-free access to the US market. It is to that discrimination that we now turn.

THE CHALLENGE OF DISCRIMINATION

One systemic challenge that predates the election of Donald Trump concerns the rise of discriminatory trade agreements. The creation of the WTO in 1995, which culminated a half-century of progress toward a comprehensive and multilateral trade regime, ironically came just when many of its most prominent members began negotiating discriminatory agreements in earnest. As an ideal, the trading system has long sought to achieve two seemingly complementary objectives: the reduction or elimination of trade barriers and an end to discrimination. The recent proliferation of FTAs implies that countries are willing to sacrifice nondiscrimination in pursuit of liberalization. The net results have been dubious, as the political capital that countries invest in FTAs might otherwise have been devoted to preserving and rebuilding the multilateral system.[10] By the time that Trump took office, many trade policymakers had already come to see FTAs not as a complement to but as a substitute for multilateralism. To that burden must also be added the rising proclivity of the United States and China to treat their FTAs with third parties as another front in their widening trade war.

As can be seen from the data in figure 3-3, the FTAs of the United States have come in three waves. The initial wave began when the United States struck its first FTA with Israel in 1985, followed by agreements with Canada and Mexico a few years later.[11] The pacts with the latter two partners mattered not just for the magnitude of the trade involved, but also (as discussed below) for the opportunity to set precedents on new issues. The second wave came from 2001 through 2012; while a few of the agreements during this period were initiated in the closing weeks of the Clinton administration, and others were not approved until early in the Obama administration, most of the action came during the administration of George W. Bush. This wave covered many more countries than had the first, but affected much less actual trade; several of these partners were chosen more for reasons of foreign policy than trade per se. The FTAs in this wave encompassed several countries in Latin America, as well as other partners in the Middle East and the Pacific Basin.

FIGURE 3-3. Shares of US Imports from Free Trade Agreement Partners and China

Shares of total US merchandise imports coming from each group

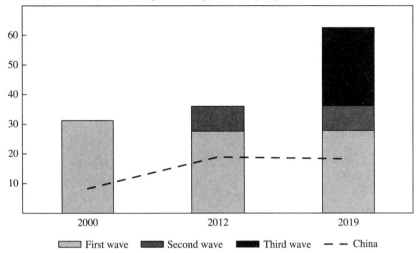

Source: Calculated from US International Trade Commission data at https://dataweb.usitc.gov/.

First Wave Partners: Canada, Israel, and Mexico

Second Wave Partners: Australia, Bahrain, Chile, Colombia, Costa Rica, Dominican Republic, El Salvador, Guatemala, Honduras, Jordan, Korea, Morocco, Nicaragua, Oman, Panama, Peru, and Singapore

Third Wave Partners: European Union, Japan, Kenya, and the United Kingdom

What is most notable about the first two waves is that they each honored an unspoken rule that long constrained the principal leaders in the multilateral system. That rule held that while the European Union, Japan, and the United States might negotiate agreements with small and mid-sized trading partners, they would deal with one another primarily in the GATT and (since 1995) the WTO. That rule has now been negated by a third wave of negotiations that began during the Obama administration, which initiated FTA negotiations with both the European Union and Japan (the latter as part of the TPP). As critical as Trump has been of his immediate predecessor, including withdrawal of the United States from the TPP, it did not take long for him to replicate those plans. His administration's FTA negotiations with major partners are nonetheless configured differently, being disaggregated in two ways: Brexit has led to separate negotiations with the European Union and the United Kingdom, and the Trump FTA negotiations with Japan are bilateral rather than megaregional.

The third wave of FTAs poses a much more serious challenge to the multilateral trading system than did either of its predecessors. This is partly due to a matter of size, as the new agreements push FTAs from being the exception to the rule. The data illustrated in figure 3-3 show that as of 2000, when only the first-wave FTAs were in effect, these agreements still covered less than one-third (31.3 percent) of all US goods imports. Those three partners' collective share of US imports declined slightly in the years that followed, and most of the FTA partners in the second wave (apart from Korea) were relatively small. The net effect was that by 2016, when all of the second-wave agreements were in force, FTA partners still accounted for just 35.5 percent of all imports. The new negotiations with major Atlantic and Pacific partners cover far larger shares. If all of the third-wave negotiations produce agreements, the FTAs will govern 62.5 percent of US imports (as measured in 2019). We may well wonder just how important future policymakers—whether they work for a president named Trump or Biden—will consider the WTO when well over half of their country's trade is conducted with FTA partners, and the combined value from all other countries (19.2 percent) is just a smidgen larger than what comes from China (18.2 percent).

The problem may only worsen if, as may well be expected, more partners ask to jump onto the bilateral bandwagon. There are just six countries other than China that (1) do not yet have FTAs with the United States, (2) are not currently negotiating such an agreement, and (3) account for more than 1 percent each of US imports. Three of them have already been parties to earlier US FTA negotiations that failed either bilaterally (i.e., Thailand) or regionally (i.e., Malaysia and Vietnam were in the TPP talks), and all of the rest are frequently mentioned as potential FTA candidates (i.e., India, Switzerland, and Taiwan). It would be entirely unsurprising if any or all of those countries, and perhaps a few others as well, were to engage in FTA negotiations with the United States in the years to come. That would not be good news either for the multilateral system as a whole or for the dozens of other, smaller partners who would be left behind. The dilemma for these smaller countries will only be exacerbated if, as is discussed in a later section, the United States maintains the implicit Trump policy of treating FTAs not merely as substitutes for multilateralism but indeed as exclusive blocs.

The latest wave of FTAs challenge the multilateral system not just in quantitative terms, but also in their qualitative intent. The first wave was explicitly intended to complement the multilateral system, with the Reagan administration using its North American negotiations as a means of advancing new issues both at the start of the Uruguay Round (which coincided with the launch of the US-Canada FTA negotiations) and at the conclusion (which followed shortly after the NAFTA negotiations ended). Even during the second wave, policymakers still denied that discrimination was incompatible with multilateralism. They instead subscribed to a theory of "competitive liberalization" by which bilateral negotiations were intended to promote greater ambition at the regional level, which was in turn expected to prod multilateral negotiations. Those hopes diminished as the new millennium progressed, however, when megaregional and multilateral negotiations proved less politically viable than bilateralism.

Even before the TPP and TTIP negotiations began, megaregionals had already proven to be fragile. The abortive Free Trade Area of the Americas (FTAA) and the pact planned in the Asia Pacific Economic Cooperation (APEC) forum were both launched in 1994 to establish free trade across wide geographic expanses, yet both were undone by internal disputes. The APEC initiative began to crumble when countries demanded that their "sacred cows" (e.g., fish in Japan) be isolated from liberalization, and the exceptions soon grew so large as to make the rule seem unworthy of pursuit. The FTAA negotiations were plagued from the start by the perennial rivalry between the United States and Brazil, and matters only got worse with the emergence of a trade-skeptical bloc led by Cuba on the outside and by Venezuela on the inside. Each of these megaregionals then fragmented into smaller initiatives, including numerous US FTAs reached during 2003–2006, several of which coalesced in the TPP. Every TPP country had previously been engaged in negotiating the FTAA, APEC, or both, and many of them reached bilateral agreements with one another between the collapse of those talks and the launch of the TPP. It all proved moot in the end.

While some megaregional negotiations collapse at the international level, others can fail to survive the domestic political process. Donald Trump proved that immediately after taking office, when he signed a memorandum directing the USTR to withdraw the United States from the TPP and to negotiate bilateral agreements instead. The eleven other TPP countries eventually decided to implement this agreement without its largest signatory. The new president also let the TTIP negotiations lapse, having inherited a draft that was far from complete.

The Trump Administration's Renegotiation of Existing Trade Agreements

The new administration spent the better part of 2017 and 2018 renegotiating a decades-old agreement with its Canadian and Mexican partners. These talks produced an agreement in principle at the end of September 2018, which Donald Trump dubbed the United States-Mexico-Canada Agreement (USMCA), and the neighbors signed the agreement three months later. The revised agreement entered into effect on July 1, 2020. Three aspects of the revised NAFTA merit attention. One of them, as reviewed in the next section, is a pledge that the United States extracted from Canada and Mexico concerning future negotiations with China. The conduct of these talks also marked a fundamental change in how the United States engages with its FTA partners, and its actual terms mark a subtler shift in the intended purpose of trade agreements.

The NAFTA renegotiation set a new pattern in the conduct of US commercial diplomacy, with the US side relying more than ever before on coercive tactics. While American negotiators in past generations were prepared to exploit obvious disparities in power and wealth, they typically approached these asymmetries with some tact. They would put forward tough demands, and make clear that they were prepared to walk if the other side did not bend, but the only way that they would threaten the imposition of new barriers in the midst of a negotiation was to suggest the willingness of Congress to go down that road. The Trump administration's negotiators sidestepped that usual ruse, preferring to act as both the good and the bad cop. They treated the North American partners no better than any others, were restricting steel and aluminum under the section 232 law, and repeatedly warned that similar restrictions on automobiles could be imminent. The Trump administration also threatened on numerous occasions to abrogate NAFTA unilaterally, or to reach a separate peace with one or the other neighbor. The Canadian and Mexican negotiators responded with counterretaliatory measures, at least for a time, but ultimately felt compelled to strike a bargain.

The more serious danger lies in the changing purpose of trade agreements, with the US aim having shifted from the creation of opportunities to the management of outcomes. Instead of setting the terms by which countries will reduce barriers to trade and investment, then allowing the market to sort it all out, the Trump administration explicitly adopted the mercantilist goal of seeking to run up a trade surplus. It hopes to achieve that end through such means as the manipulation of the agreement's rules of origin. The more restrictive automotive rules in the USMCA, for example, represent a reversion to the market-sharing principles that motivated the US-Canada Auto Pact of 1965. The Trump administration's efforts to determine outcomes can likewise be seen in the concessions it wrung from Canada on dairy products, and also in the way that it made the NAFTA renegotiation an instrument in its rivalry with China.

FTAs as Instruments of Sino-American Rivalry

Direct negotiations between Beijing and Washington have thus far been limited to truce talks in the trade war, with both sides being readier to steer the dispute into a collusive system of managed trade than to negotiate a truly liberalizing agreement. With a bona fide FTA being off the table, the United States and China have instead used trade agreements with third countries as an instrument of power. That point rests on two distinguishing characteristics: China and the United States typically account for large shares of any given partner's total trade, and yet each of them is less dependent on that exchange—globally and bilaterally—than are their partners. The United States is even less trade-dependent than China, with exports of goods and services being equal to just 12 percent of US GDP in 2018; exports then accounted for 19 percent of Chinese GDP.[12] Both were still below the world average of 30 percent. As for their relative weight in other countries' economies, China has been overtaking the United States in much of the world. Even among the many countries for which China has moved into the top spot, however, the United States often remains the second largest partner.

Trump initiated four FTA negotiations from 2018 to 2020, choosing many of the same partners that his predecessors had. The negotiations that his administration initiated with Japan in 2018 amounted to a second stab at the most important part of the TPP, just as the talks initiated that same year with the European Union and the United Kingdom sought to complete a piece of unfinished business from the Obama administration. The proposed agreement with Kenya is the only FTA negotiation of the Trump administration that does not reflect an effort to pick up where its immediate predecessor left off, but even this undertaking can be seen as the continuation of a well-established pattern in US trade relations with developing countries. As far back as the NAFTA negotiations with Mexico, followed by a series of later FTA negotiations in Central America and the Andes, the United States has often told the recipients of autonomous trade preferences that they ought to transform those special (and temporary) arrangements into permanent, reciprocal deals before the authorizations for these programs expire.

The most important difference between past and present FTA negotiations instead comes in Trump's insistence that they be exclusive. If his administration has its way, the world might well be headed towards a system where all commercially significant countries feel pressured to align themselves with one or another of the contenders for hegemony. As can be seen from the data in table 3-3, the Chinese and American FTA networks already encompass distinct sets of partners that nonetheless have similar collective sizes: The twenty FTA partners of the United States together account for 9.8 percent of global GDP, compared to the 9.6 percent controlled by China's twenty-four FTA partners. If both countries conclude and implement all of the agreements that are now being negotiated or contemplated, however, the United States will be well ahead of China. When one adds the share of global GDP controlled by the United States (24.2 percent) to the share held by its existing (first- and second-wave) partners, plus the 26.8 percent held by the countries with which it is now negotiating, the resulting bloc accounts for 60.8 percent of the world economy. While the FTAs that might ultimately comprise the Chinese bloc are larger in number, they will still account for a considerably smaller share of the global economy (37.4 percent).[13] From a multilateral perspective, the most important point here concerns just how little overlap one finds between these two blocs: The six countries that currently have FTAs with both the United States and China amount to just 4.5 percent of the world economy, although that share will grow to 13.7 percent if all of the negotiations that are now underway or under study come to fruition. This means that while Washington (and probably Beijing as well) may come to manage trade relations primarily through discriminatory channels, the rules thus established will affect only a slice of the world economy. This is precisely the sort of fragmentation that the architects of the GATT system sought to abolish.

Trump is not the first president to craft his FTA strategy with an eye to China, as this has been a mainstay of US policy for over a decade. The TPP was founded on two successive presidents' goal of strengthening ties with

TABLE 3-3. Free Trade Agreements of the United States and China

Aggregate figures show shares of global GDP held by all countries in each row or column; status of each initiative as of mid-2020

US FTA Partners	China's FTA partners			
	FTA in effect (9.6% of GDP)	FTA under negotiation (9.2% of GDP)	FTA under study (2.7% of GDP)	No plan or agreement
FTA in Effect (9.8% of GDP)	Australia Chile Costa Rica Korea Peru Singapore	Bahrain Israel Oman Panama	Canada Colombia	Dominican Republic El Salvador Guatemala Honduras Jordan Mexico Morocco Nicaragua
FTA under Negotiation (26.8% of GDP)	—	Japan[a]	—	European Union Kenya United Kingdom
No Plan or Agreement	Brunei[a] Maldives Cambodia Mauritius Indonesia Myanmar Laos New Zealand[a] Georgia Pakistan Hong Kong Philippines Iceland Switzerland Macau Thailand Malaysia[a] Vietnam[a]	Kuwait Qatar Moldova Saudi Arabia Norway Sri Lanka Palestine United Arab Emirates	Bangladesh Fiji Mongolia Nepal Papua New Guinea	*Group includes* inter alia — Algeria Iraq Argentina Kazakhstan Brazil Nigeria Ecuador Russia Egypt South Africa Ethiopia Turkey India[b] Ukraine Iran Venezuela

Sources: GDP data are for 2019, calculated from World Bank data https://data.worldbank.org/indicator/NY.GDP.MKTP.CD. FTAs from USTR at https://ustr.gov/trade-agreements/free-trade-agreements and MOFCOM at http://fta.mofcom.gov.cn/english/index.shtml.

[a] Denotes a country that would have been a US FTA partner if the United States had ratified the Trans-Pacific Partnership.

[b] India had participated in the China-led Regional Comprehensive Economic Partnership (RCEP) but then opted out of the talks in 2019.

partners in the Pacific Basin so as to compete effectively with China. There was no difference on this point between George W. Bush and Barack Obama, each of whom implicitly rejected the approach taken earlier by Bill Clinton. Whereas China had been a party to the ill-fated APEC negotiations launched on Clinton's watch in 1994, Beijing was quite deliberately excluded from the TPP that Bush began and Obama expanded. That did not prevent China from dealing with the other TPP countries one by one. By the time that those regional talks ended in 2015, the United States and its North American neighbors were the only TPP signatories that did not either have FTAs with China or were actively pursuing them.

The Trump administration does not seem content merely to compete with China for FTA partners, but actively discourages others from getting closer to Beijing. That was made evident in Article 32.10 of the revised NAFTA that it concluded in 2018. This provision requires that any party (read: Canada or Mexico) must inform the others (read: the United States) at least three months before commencing negotiations for an FTA with a nonmarket country (read: China). It further provides that if any party were to enter into such an agreement, that step would "allow the other Parties to terminate this Agreement on six-month notice and replace this Agreement with an agreement as between them (bilateral agreement)." The US negotiators thus obliged their Canadian and Mexican counterparts to choose sides. That principle bears a disquieting resemblance to the logic by which Vladimir Putin saw Ukraine's 2014 trade agreement with the European Union as a provocation, and insisted that this former Soviet republic renew its fealty to Moscow. That demand ultimately precipitated not just the (temporary) rejection of the EU-Ukraine agreement but also turmoil inside Ukraine and Russia's annexation of Crimea. This analogy should not be drawn too far; had Canada spurned the US demand for commercial monogamy, the United States would not have responded by seizing Canadian real estate. The provision nonetheless underlines the profound changes that the Trump administration hopes to have brought to the global trading system.

How Transatlantic Trade Agreements Affect the International System

Beyond the revision of existing FTAs, the Trump administration also aims to reach new bilateral agreements that conform more closely to its illiberal predilections. The first clean sheets of paper with which it will start—or the third wave, as described above—are agreements with the European

Union, Japan, and the United Kingdom. After announcing its plans for these FTA negotiations in late 2018, the United States also launched talks with Kenya in 2020 for a bilateral FTA. As of mid-2020, none of these negotiations appeared to be anywhere close to entering their end-games.

There are competing views on the implications that the planned pair of transatlantic FTAs may hold for the international trading system. One suggests that regional trade arrangements in general, and especially negotiations between the most influential countries, act to undermine the existing system. It could be argued that when the United States and the European Union launched the TTIP negotiations in 2013 they were walking away from multilateralism and nondiscrimination. An alternative view suggests that the proposed successors to the failed TTIP could instead contribute to the revitalization of the trading system by restoring lost momentum and setting precedents to be taken up in subsequent agreements, including those that the European Union and the United States may negotiate with third parties. These initiatives offer a chance not only to deepen the commitments made on the new issues, but to pick up where TTIP left off on other groundbreaking topics (e.g., state-owned enterprises).

There is considerable history to support that latter view, with FTAs having offered a means for the largest economies to deal with the topics that some WTO members resist. The sequence here can go either of two ways. In one variant, the *demandeur* on a new issue may use smaller agreements as a policy laboratory, demonstrating to other members how the issue might be handled if it were later taken up multilaterally. In another variation, the *demandeur* that has been rebuffed in its efforts to bring up an issue at the multilateral level may repair instead to bilateral and regional negotiations. The first of these sequences is best demonstrated by the approach that the United States took in the 1980s toward what were then called the "new issues" of services, investment, and intellectual property rights. The precedents set by the agreements that the United States reached with its immediate neighbors, first with Canada (1988) and then with both Canada and Mexico (1992), provided a demonstration effect for the new issues that were simultaneously under negotiation in the Uruguay Round. The second sequence is best illustrated by the approach that the European Union has taken to the four so-called Singapore issues of competition policy, government procurement, investment, and trade facilitation. Brussels pressed for WTO negotiations on these topics, but was forced by the strong opposition from developing countries to take all but trade facilitation off the table in the Doha Round. The EU negotiators then turned to FTA negotiations as their Plan B. Most of the agreements that the European Union and the United States have reached with developing country partners since the Uruguay Round cover not only the Singapore issues, but also other topics that never made it onto the table in Doha (e.g., labor rights and the environment).

The facts might more strongly argue for the optimistic than the pessimistic view of FTAs, were these normal times, but that conclusion may be too sanguine in the age of Trump. This administration's priorities look as much to the past as they do to the future; for all of its emphasis on innovation and intellectual property rights, it is at least equally interested in transforming a chronic merchandise trade deficit into a surplus. The same may be said for Trump's confrontational tactics, which bear a closer resemblance to the diplomacy of the early nineteenth than the late twentieth century.

THE CHALLENGE OF DOMESTIC POLITICS

No matter who occupies the White House, trade policymaking will remain perennially challenging for a system of government that is always divided by branch and frequently by party. This is a matter of constitutional design as well as public preference, and has grown even more problematic in recent decades. Whereas government was divided in just seven of the thirty-four Congresses (21 percent) from 1901 through 1968, the share grew to nineteen of the twenty-six Congresses (73 percent) from 1969 through 2020.

Donald Trump is only the latest president to discover just how much harder governance becomes when the opposition party controls at least one chamber of Congress. He was able to act in 2017–2018 with little restraint from the legislature because (1) he made full use of existing delegations of authority and (2) his party controlled both chambers. Some of the things that the administration planned to do in its second two years required the acquiescence of Congress, which became more challenging after Democrats recaptured control of the House of Representatives in the 2018 elections. That put the opposition party in a position not only to thwart Trump's plans, but also to keep him and his administration occupied by investigations and impeachment.

Trade is the only topic on which the Democrats as a whole are more closely aligned with Trump than are the Republicans in Congress, but there are some signs of change in both parties.[14] The shifts among Democrats can be seen both in the rising levels of protrade sentiment in that party's base and in a concurrent decline in the influence of the unions.[15] As for the Republicans, there is a chance that Trump's most lasting effect on domestic politics may be to return that party—or at least many of its votes and officeholders—to its protectionist roots. These are issues that may be at the forefront of US trade policy for the foreseeable future.

How a Domestic Role-Reversal Affects the Trading System

Divided government complicates all manner of policymaking, but is especially problematic for the approval of treaties. Even when the United States is the chief promoter of a new negotiation, the results may still be trashed at home. President Woodrow Wilson (a Democrat) set that pattern when he signed the Treaty of Versailles in 1919, only to see the Republican-controlled Senate gut it with amendments and then disown the mutilated corpse. Harry Truman was another Democrat who did no better when in 1947 he asked Congress—once more under Republican control—to approve the Havana Charter of the International Trade Organization. The only difference was that this time the rest of the world did not try to make a rump international institution function without the United States. As troublesome as this pattern may be for US negotiators, it also creates an opportunity. Following a good cop, bad cop pattern that is familiar to fans of police dramas, legislators can be made to play a usefully obstreperous role. Whenever members of Congress threaten to reject an agreement if it contains some undesirable concession, or to do the same if a key US demand is not met, they hope to strengthen the executive's leverage. The fact that the coordination between legislators and negotiators is imperfect is precisely what makes the tactic so effective. If foreign negotiators were to believe that Congress is really in the pocket of the executive, they would soon conclude that the act is nothing more than empty theatrics.

In the Trump administration the roles have been reversed, such that it is Congress that more often feels compelled to be the voice of reason. The US withdrawal from the TPP was unique only insofar as this time it was a president who undid a treaty, rather than letting Congress do the dirty work. Trump routinely taps into that part of the national character that is untroubled by the suggestion that it is acting in contravention of international law, sees multilateral organizations as cabals in which unscrupulous foreigners conspire to cheat Americans, and is prepared to respond not just

in kind but in advance. He is not the first politician to reiterate some variation on the outdated observation that the United States has never lost a war
or won a negotiation, but none of his predecessors placed so little stress on
the principle of *pacta sunt servanda* (agreements must be kept). His administration instead seems to treat any commitments made by prior presidents
as corrupt bargains or one-sided deals that it is free to violate, abrogate, or
renegotiate. Of all the areas where he leaves his mark, this may have the
most lasting impact on the US position in the world. A future president
could reverse almost any specific action that the current chief executive
might take, but that would merely reinforce the message that whatever the
United States promises (or threatens) today may hold only until the next
change of government. A bell cannot be unrung.

The Complications Brought on by New Issues

Even when presidents deal with members of their own party, they will run
into trouble whenever their initiatives impinge on the constitutional prerogatives of a co-equal branch or are contrary to the economic interests of
specific states and districts. Trade policymaking is made even more complicated by the introduction of new issues that are more divisive than those
of past generations. Traditional fights over free trade versus protection have
not disappeared altogether, but they sometimes have a lower profile than
disputes over such hot-button topics as labor rights, the environment, and
access to medicine. Some of these issues first arose in trade disputes that
other countries took to the GATT, complaining that the United States discriminated against imports when it enacted laws to protect the environment.
Other groups joined the fight after US negotiators brought new issues to
the table on behalf of domestic industries (for example, patent protection
for pharmaceuticals), and still others reflect the demands of social and
economic activists (such as labor rights). Whatever the economic or legal
cause, the political consequences of associating these issues with trade are
enormous. New issues mean new voices, and the diversity of participants
produces a clash of economic and social philosophies. This can amount to a
geometric rather than an arithmetic rise in the degree of difficulty.[16]

The old struggles over narrow, commercial issues such as tariffs and
quotas could typically be settled through some difference-splitting bargain
or by compensating the losing side. The newest issues are notable for involving not just producers with interests but also consumers and even socially conscious spectators. Groups that are more interested in political

causes than in their own economic interests are not easily placated by the usual instruments of cooption. These changes remade the tone and character of policy debates. While firms and labor unions act according to clearly identifiable economic interests in these matters, many of the new participants are ideologically inspired by political causes in which they have no financial stake. The newer entrants are interested in trade more for its political than its economic value, being less concerned by the effect of trade policy on sales and employment than on its utility to promote or retard some other end in domestic or foreign policy. These groups tend to put less faith in bargaining and compromise than do the traditional, typically more pragmatic interests. Both the tone and the outcome of a policy debate can be qualitatively different when participants are motivated by something other than narrow calculations of their own economic welfare. These new entrants are more likely to use the word "compromise" as a mark of opprobrium than approval, and cannot be easily bought off with exceptions or inducements.

Labor Rights as a Core Issue in
the Politics of Trade

Of all the issues that have come to be associated with trade policy, none is more politically divisive than labor rights. This may be attributed to an enduring fact of American political life: for the better part of a century, labor unions have been just as closely tied to the Democratic Party as business is associated with the Republican Party. The positions of these two groups have shifted markedly on trade, and in ways that may be surprising to anyone unfamiliar with the history of US policy. Before the 1940s, US manufacturers were more committed to protection than to free trade; before the 1960s, just the reverse was true for the most influential labor unions. Much of the dynamism in the partisan politics of trade can be attributed to the gradual reversal of these positions. Trade policy used to be the one issue on which the two parties were most clearly divided, with Republicans from Abraham Lincoln (in office 1861–1865) through Herbert Hoover (1929–1933) being firmly committed to protectionism, and most Democrats taking just the opposite position. The unions' position first began to waver in the 1960s, and just the opposite happened in the Republican Party. By the mid-1980s the two groups had completely reversed their polarities.

These shifting positions have had three impacts on US trade policy. The first is a sharp divide over trade adjustment assistance (TAA), a special program by which aid is extended to workers, firms, and communities that have been hurt by import competition. Whereas Democrats have strongly favored TAA ever since the Kennedy administration (1961–1963), Republicans usually oppose it. A second effect is in the partisan voting on trade agreements. From the late 1970s to the present, a majority of the Republicans in Congress could reliably be expected to approve most agreements that presidents submitted for their approval, but Democrats have been more difficult to persuade. The third difference concerns the terms on which Democrats might nonetheless be convinced to approve such agreements. As a general rule, their willingness to approve market-opening agreements has been greater whenever (1) the president concluding that agreement was a fellow Democrat, (2) the request was accompanied by an increase in TAA funding, and (3) the agreement in question included substantive provisions on labor rights.

That third point has been the most critical dividing line between the parties for years, especially for agreements in which most or all of the partners are developing countries. While there are many Democrats in Congress who will vote against almost any market-opening agreements, and some who take just the opposite view, the middle ground is held by those who insist that the United States use its leverage in trade negotiations as a means of promoting labor rights in the partner countries. The principal problem with this trade-labor link is not in the resistance that it provokes from the negotiating partners, but instead from the US business community and its Republican allies. Ever since 1991, when President George H. W. Bush had to bargain hard with Congress over the initiation of the NAFTA negotiations, the domestic politics of US trade policy have been repeatedly caught up in almost theological debates over this topic. Some outside observers assume that these fights are just new proxies for free trade versus protectionism, but that simplistic view of the issue does not survive a close examination.

Consider the bitter fight over the FTA with Colombia, which proved to be one of the most partisan and lengthy trade fights in US history. Unions and Democrats criticized Colombia's antilabor record, especially the murders of union organizers and officials, and in 2006 Democrats refused even to negotiate with the George W. Bush administration over the agreement's implementing legislation. The matter was not resolved until 2011, when President Barack Obama shepherded the FTAs with Colombia, Korea, and Panama through Congress. The severity of this fight cannot be explained solely by way of sectoral interests. Colombia was only the #23 source of US imports, and even less of what it provided was import-sensitive. By contrast, Korea supplied 2.5 times more imports than Colombia, and these imports were concentrated in such competitive sectors as automobiles and steel. And while Korea was the target of seventeen antidumping petitions filed during 2000–2011, Colombia was subject to just one. In short, if unions and Democrats calibrated their opposition solely according to narrow calculations of protectionist interest, they should have concentrated their fire on Korea. Throughout the maneuvering over these two agreements, it was widely expected in Washington that the Korean FTA would be passed as long as Seoul made a few more concessions to US demands on market access for automobiles and meat, but that Democrats would prefer to kill the Colombian agreement outright. The Korean agreement ultimately won support from only a minority among Democrats in the House (31 percent), but that was nearly twice what the US-Colombia FTA received (16 percent).

Compared to these past confrontations, the debate in the 116th Congress (2019–2020) over approving the USMCA (i.e., the revised NAFTA) was far less partisan. Notwithstanding the fact that it took many months for Democrats and Republicans to settle on the terms of the agreement's implementing legislation, with labor issues once more being the most significant sticking point, this trade agreement was among the few issues for which internecine conflict in this congress proved relatively low. While it would be a great exaggeration to suggest that the two parties held their differences entirely in abeyance, the fact that they ultimately "got to yes" is remarkable. That distinguishes trade from the many other topics on which Capitol Hill generated much sound and fury for two years, all of which ultimately signified nothing. Beyond a failed impeachment effort, Congress proved incapable of enacting new legislation on such diverse yet important subjects as immigration, health care, and taxes. The other notable fact is that when Congress approved the NAFTA-revision bill it did so on votes that were, by comparison with the struggles summarized above, very nearly nonpartisan. When the House of Representatives approved the bill in December 2019 by a vote of 385 to 41, the number of votes that it won from Democrats (193) was nearly identical to the number it won from Republicans (192). Much the same thing happened when the Senate took up the bill: while

Democrats cast all but one of the ten "nay" votes, they also provided thirty-eight of the "aye" votes. That January 16, 2020 vote was all the more remarkable for its timing, coming just a week before the Senate began debating the preliminary motions in the president's impeachment trial. The question now is whether that one incident was unique and transitory, or if it presages a new alignment in partisan positions. The answer depends above all on whether the Republican experience with Trumpism proves to be a temporary flirtation or a lasting repolarization.

CONCLUDING OBSERVATIONS

The trends and events reviewed here underline the peril in which the international trading system now finds itself. For good or for ill, the health of that system has long depended on the capacity and willingness of the United States to provide leadership. The focus of this analysis has been on just how far the Trump administration has gone in reversing the policies pursued by Franklin Roosevelt through Barack Obama, all of whom started from the premise that both the United States and the world are better off if markets are generally open. This is not to say that the Trump administration broke radically from established US positions on all trade issues. There are some matters on which its policies show real continuity, in substance if not in style, with those of past presidents—it is negotiating FTAs with largely the same partners with which the Obama administration dealt, for example, and its use of trade-remedy and reciprocity laws is reminiscent of what the Reagan administration did. Taken as a whole, however, the principal themes of trade policy in this administration represent a negation of American leadership. Its action poses an existential threat to a multilateral system in which the United States has invested considerable political capital over several generations.

Some speculation is in order on whether and how this deviation might be corrected. This chapter is written at a time (July 2020) when it remains uncertain whether Trump's remaining time in office may be measured in months or years, but either way we can be certain that while his administration will be finite, the environment in which it emerged will not fundamentally change. Those observations beg the question of whether the United States will attempt once again to exercise responsible leadership in the global trading system.

The answer does not depend solely on personalities, as there are structural issues at stake. No matter who occupies the White House, and contrary to the intentions of the Trump administration, neither the Law of Uneven Growth nor the process of Creative Destruction are easily reversed. The long-term trends have been evident for decades, with successive presidents seeking to manage a relative US decline even as they dealt with shifts in the composition of the domestic economy. Trump's predecessors tried to do so by making incremental adjustments to US policies and the trading system; he has instead tried to overturn that system altogether. The extent of the damage will depend first on whether the current experiment with Trumpism is held to just four years, and second on how his successor tries to pick up the pieces.

This is partly a matter of which party controls government. The events of the last several years have reinforced the old lesson that trade is not the core issue dividing Democrats from Republicans. As noted above, the parties have already switched their polarities on this issue twice. With Republicans having been rock-ribbed protectionists during the century that followed Lincoln's 1860 election, and Trump yanking the party back to that position in 2016, their free-trade tenure lasted little more than a generation. It may be possible for Republicans to regain that position, depending on the course of Trumpism within the party, but in the near term the internal debates in the Democratic Party may be more consequential for US trade policy. That may come down to a struggle between the party's internationalist and labor wings.

For over a century, the postures that each party has taken on trade issues have been the product of two perennial divides: internationalism versus isolationism, and capital versus labor. Democrats have consistently been more devoted than Republicans to the notion that the interests of the United States are best secured through international cooperation, whether that took the form of functional organizations or military alliances, and the party's political base has always depended far more on labor than on capital. Trade politics were relatively simple when these two divides were in alignment. From the 1930s through the mid-1960s, both the internationalist and the labor wings of the Democratic Party favored open markets. It was only with the emergence of chronic trade deficits, especially in labor-intensive manufactures, that tensions arose between the party's factions. Democrats have sought ever since to reconcile their internal differences, such as by making labor rights a key objective in trade negotiations, but these initiatives have had only limited success. From Kennedy through Obama, every Democratic president has been an internationalist whose ability to move trade initiatives through Congress has been complicated by the tricky politics of intraparty conflict and interparty rivalry. That is the position in which Joe Biden will find himself, should he be elected the forty-sixth president of the United States. He is more associated with the internationalist wing of his party than were most other contenders for the Democratic nomination, but his ability to act on those instincts will be bounded by the same constraints that his predecessors have faced.

Compared to trade policy under the Trump administration, the policies of a Biden administration might be distinguished more by what the president declines to do than by what he affirmatively seeks. Assuming that a Biden administration maintains the Democratic preference for cooperation with allies and respect for the rule of law, we may expect it to avoid unnecessary provocations and outright violations of the trading system's rules and norms. That may well mean returning to the shelves those trade laws that had fallen into disuse after the Uruguay Round, including the reciprocity, safeguards, and national security statutes; to the extent that the United States resorts to protectionism, it may depend once more on the private sector's resort to the AD and CVD laws. We might also anticipate a moratorium on the US withdrawals from international organizations, and perhaps a return to those from which the Trump administration removed the United States.

While a post-Trump United States may end its retreat from global institutions, that is a far cry from a true revival of multilateralism. Assuming that a Biden administration were to complete any FTA negotiations that it inherits, the United States will soon trade more with the partners in these discriminatory agreements than it does with the rest of the WTO membership. And to the extent that the WTO comes to be seen primarily as the place where the United States deals with China, the members of that institution may continue the established trend whereby they devote more time to adjudicating their existing agreements than to negotiating new ones. It is questionable just how sustainable that may be over the long term. Trade liberalization may also have to compete with purely domestic policies that are disquieting to free-traders. No rational politician in any party can unsee what they all saw in 2016, when economic nationalism had wide appeal, and even office seekers who reject the more extreme elements of Trumpism see real value in "Buy American" themes. In short, we should not expect the departure of Donald Trump—whenever and however that happens—to mean an end to Trumpism.

EPILOGUE: FROM TRUMP TO BIDEN

There are three reasons why we should not expect the results of the 2020 presidential and congressional elections, which came between this chapter's writing and the book's publication, to create the domestic political foundations needed for the full restoration of US leadership in the trading system. First, while the final Senate results were still pending as of this writing, it appears that Joe Biden will be the first president in 32 years (and the first Democratic president in 136 years) to face divided government from the day he took office. Second, neither of the parties will have clear positions on trade as long as Democrats are divided between the progressives and the internationalists, and Republicans have yet to decide whether theirs is merely the opposition party, a party of principle, or a cult of personality. Third, the pandemic muddled the message by ensuring that the election would not be a referendum on Trump's economic policies. So while the next four years may be less turbulent, and the United States may show greater fidelity to alliances and the rule of law, the domestic and international trends that already bedeviled US trade policy before Donald Trump took office will not disappear after he leaves.

NOTES

The project to which this chapter contributes has received funding from the European Union's Horizon 2020 research and innovation program under grant agreement no. 770680.

1. For an elaboration on this argument, see VanGrasstek (2019).

2. All shares calculated from World Bank data at https://data.worldbank.org/.

3. The author explores the domestic political economy of protectionism at greater length in chapter 6 of VanGrasstek (2019).

4. This point is discussed in a later section.

5. Past presidents used this law and its predecessor statute to impose restrictions on oil imports five times, but invoked it only twice on behalf of other industries. President Reagan resorted to Section 232 in a 1981 ferroalloys case, and again in a 1986 machine tools case.

6. The United States invoked Article XXI in 1949 in order to apply the newly enacted embargo on exports of strategic goods against Czechoslovakia,

and did the same in 1985 when Nicaragua objected to an embargo imposed by President Reagan. The Kennedy administration was prepared to cite this article in defense of its embargo on Cuba, but that was rendered moot by Cuba's failure to lodge a formal complaint.

7. The first EU invocation came in a 1982 defense of the import restrictions that it (together with Australia and Canada) imposed on Argentina during the Falklands/Malvinas war. Brussels also invoked Article XXI in 1991 to justify its withdrawal of preferential treatment from Yugoslavia; the breakup of that country made a panel moot.

8. On the accession of Portugal in 1961, for example, Ghana stated that its boycott of Portuguese goods was justified under Article XXI because Angola posed a constant threat to peace on the African continent. Honduras and Colombia settled a dispute in 1999 over their maritime boundaries, but Nicaragua objected and imposed a 35 percent tariff on all imports from Honduras and Colombia. Nicaragua then invoked Article XXI when those countries sought a panel. The parties eventually agreed to take the issue up in the International Court of Justice, and no WTO panel was formed.

9. See the November 7, 2017, statement of the United States in support of Russia as posted by the Office of the US Trade Representative at https://ustr .gov/sites/default/files/enforcement/DS/US.3d.Pty.Sub.Re.GATT.XXI.fin .percent28public percent29.pdf.

10. For a more thorough examination of preferences in US trade policy, see chapters 13–15 of VanGrasstek (2019).

11. The negotiations for the original (bilateral) FTA with Canada concluded in 1988, followed by the trilateral NAFTA that was initially concluded in 1992 (then modified and approved in 1993).

12. Calculated from World Bank data at https://data.worldbank.org /indicator/NE.EXP.GNFS.ZS.

13. The 37.4 percent is the sum of China (16.3 percent) plus its current FTA partners (9.6 percent) and the partners that are either still negotiating (9.2 percent) or under study (2.3 percent).

14. For a fuller review of this issue see VanGrasstek (2018).

15. The share of American workers represented by unions rose from 5 percent in 1933 to 22 percent in 1945, plateaued for a time, and then fell from 23 percent in 1983 to 12 percent in 2015. Calculated from US Department of Commerce, *Historical Statistics of the United States, Colonial Times to 1970* (1975), p. 178; and Bureau of Labor Statistics data at https://data.bls.gov/pdq/Survey OutputServlet.

16. The author examines the political economy of new issues in VanGrasstek (2019, chap. 5).

4

CHINA AND THE WORLD TRADING SYSTEM

WILL "IN AND UP" BE REPLACED BY "DOWN AND OUT"?

L. ALAN WINTERS

This chapter examines the integration of China into the world trading system. It discusses the size and nature of the shocks that it administered to the world economy and some of the reactions to those shocks proposed by policymakers and academics. From its awakening in 1978, China was welcomed into the global economy and generated a huge boost in output and incomes—the "in and up" referred to in the title. More recently, however, concerns have been expressed about the health of the Chinese economy, and steps have also been taken to curtail its trade, both by excluding it from the major trade initiatives that we have come to term the "megaregionals" and through the direct imposition of trade sanctions by the United States—the "down and out." It is too early to predict the outcome of the latter phenomenon, but it is important to understand some of the history and causes of China's integration in order to reduce the chances of policy running into disaster down a blind alley.

It is a great pleasure to honor Patrick Messerlin in this chapter. Patrick has been one of the foremost exponents of applied trade policy analysis and advice over several decades, with an unfailing focus on the key issues of the day. I argue that integrating China into the global economy in a way that benefits nearly all presents perhaps the most important international trade and trade policy issue of our present era, and so it is no surprise that it is one that Patrick has also addressed.

This chapter argues that the shock that the emergence of China is administering to the world economy is larger than any seen previously—and by a large margin. The shock has many manifestations, but here, in line with Patrick's great expertise, I focus on its effects on and through the world trading system. I suggest that, although the huge increase in global production that the success of China brings has produced widespread benefits, there will inevitably be some stresses and indeed possibly some losers. Some of these stresses are essentially microeconomic—competitive pressure on firms elsewhere in the world—while another set arises from the macroeconomic imbalances that China's rapid growth has induced globally. Part of China's integration into the global economy entailed joining the World Trade Organization (WTO) in 2001, and it has become a forum in which many of the stresses just noted have been debated: I note that China has adapted almost completely to the standard forms of behavior within the WTO despite suffering from a number of asymmetries in treatment by other members. One potential asymmetry that has mercifully been put on the backburner for now is to bring exchange rates within the purview of the WTO with a view to punishing China's alleged undervaluation of its currency. But it was followed by another in the form of the megaregional trade deals—notably the Trans-Pacific Partnership (TPP)—that I argue were designed to exclude China; and as that receded, a third emerged in the form of the Trump administration's hostile trade (and other) policies toward China.

Possibly the most important role of economists in policymaking—and one that characterizes significant parts of Patrick Messerlin's career—is to discourage policymakers' instincts to react to challenges inappropriately. At least until recently, most of the challenges that China has posed within the trading system have eventually been dealt with constructively, which is something both Chinese and Western governments can take some credit for. However, it is not a given that this pattern will persist.

THE MACROECONOMIC SHOCK

In the three decades following the Communist Revolution in 1949, China displayed a respectable but by no means spectacular rate of economic growth. Maddison (2007, table 2.2b) suggests that, after an initial fall, the growth in Chinese gross domestic product (GDP) was 4.4 percent per year over the period 1952–1978, with growth in GDP per capita at 2.3 percent; this growth was associated with a strong reorientation from agriculture to industry. Over this period, China increased its share of world GDP from 4.6 percent to 4.9 percent. Arguably more important from our point of view, however, is that over the preceding two hundred years China had played little role in the world economy and that the decades of Communism did nothing to redress this. In 1950, China exported goods worth $11.6 per capita of population at 1990 prices (compared with war-torn Japan's $42.21) and by 1973 this had grown to $13.26 (compared to Japan's $874.87) (Maddison 2007, table 2.4). So far as international economics was concerned, China barely existed.

In 1978, China took the first tentative steps toward opening up, first internally, with the household responsibility system, and then gradually externally. The outlines of the rest of the story are well known: China's GDP and exports, and even its imports, grew phenomenally. Table 4-1 summarizes the situation starting from 1981, the approximate point at which it had discernible effects on the rest of the world.

Rows 2 and 3 of the table show China maintaining aggregate growth of 10 percent per year for nearly four decades, whether in (constant) market prices or international prices (purchasing power parity). Moreover, China managed more successfully than other developing countries to control population growth (see row 1) with the result that income per head increased by 9 percent annually. Such strong growth is not wholly unprecedented; Korea, Taiwan, and Japan all showed similar trends for at least two decades (see Winters and Yusuf 2007). But two features *are* unprecedented: first, the differential between the supergrower's growth rates and that of the world economy during their growth phases (Winters and Yusuf 2007, table 1.2), and second, the combination of rapid growth and huge size. Table 4-2, which is partly inspired by a slide from McKinsey, makes the point powerfully. While it took Britain, as the only industrial country in the eighteenth century, 155 years to double income per head from the boundary of extreme

TABLE 4-1. China's Growth, 1981–2017

	1981	2017	Growth per year (%)
Population (billions)	0.994	1.386	1.0
GDP (billions of constant 2005 US$)[a]	228	5.274	10.0
GDP, PPP[b] (billions of constant 2011 international $)	746	21,224	10.7
GDP per capita, PPP (constant 2011 international $)	750	15,309	9.6

Source: World Development Indicators Online, March 7, 2019.

[a] GDP in constant prices was collected directly until 2014 and extrapolated using data in 2010 dollars from there.

[b] PPP = purchasing power parity. The PPP data for 1981 were estimated from data on a 2005 price basis and the conversion factors implied between the 2011 and 2005 bases. Both were collected from WDI Online in June 2011.

TABLE 4-2. Chinese Growth in Long-Run Context

Country	Doubling period[a]		Initial population	
	Years	Duration (in years)	Millions	Percent of world
Britain	1700–1855	155	9	1.4
United States	1820–1873	53	10	0.9
Germany	1830–1894	64	28	2.4
Japan	1906–1939	33	47	2.6
China	1983–1995	12	1,023	21.8

Sources: Maddison (2006). World population data interpolated from Goldewijk (2005), except for 1983, which comes from World Development Indicators Online.

[a] Period for the doubling of GDP per capita from $1,300 in purchasing power parity to $2,600.

poverty to well into middle-income territory, it took the United States and Germany about sixty years in the nineteenth century, Japan thirty-three years in the early twentieth century, and China twelve years in the later twentieth century. And while the first four countries represented no more than 2.6 percent of the world's population at the start of their growth spurts, China had more than 20 percent of the population.

Growth of the magnitude that China has generated affects global equilibriums in many areas such as the UN Security Council and the International Court of Justice, as well as simple economic ones. However, so far as other countries are concerned, those pertaining to the world trading system are the most immediate, direct, and visible and quite possibly the most important. For example, exploding levels of international trade were a key contributor to China's successful growth model, and also to the aggregate levels of international trade, growth, and prosperity elsewhere. And booming trade has also underpinned other aspects of China's international economic relations that have also proved contentious—for example, its aid policies and its massive levels of reserves and consequent role in international finance.

China's enormous appetite for natural resources, including food and energy, affects prices and availability elsewhere and raises incentives for production and investment in these international industries, regardless of whether they are used to produce goods for China's own consumption or that of others. All international trade has distributional effects—which is why it is so contentious—but the introduction of a huge supplier at the labor-intensive end of the spectrum of comparative advantage has had profound competitive effects on other labor-abundant countries, and these effects are gradually starting to spread to other countries as China develops other skills and comparative advantages. Moreover, the large production that China has made available has driven down prices for consumers, especially the poorer ones who purchase less sophisticated varieties (Broda and Weinstein 2009).

The trade link also has institutional form in the shape of the WTO. While accession to the WTO must have boosted China's growth and integration, it correspondingly means that if anything did go wrong, the WTO would be damaged with a consequent loss of the other functions it plays in the world economy such as settling disputes, transmitting information, and smoothing relations between other pairs of countries.

The changes in China's international trade are proportionately even larger than those in aggregate income shown in table 4-2. Table 4-3 shows that the growth of Chinese exports and imports averaged over 15 percent for nearly four decades and that of foreign exchange reserves over 17 percent. These reserves covered eight months of imports in 1981, at which point Chinese trade was more or less balanced; by 2014 the reserves had increased to cover nearly two years' worth of imports, and exports exceeded imports

TABLE 4-3. China's Changing International Trade, 1981–2017

	1981	2017	Growth per year (%)
Exports (billions of $)	14.6	2,418	15.3
Imports (billions of $)	14.6	2,208	15.0
Fuels and ores as a percentage of:			
Imports	6.0[a]	25.9	
Exports	25.2[a]	2.7	
Reserves (billions of $)	10.1	3,236	17.4
as a percentage of annual imports	69	147	

Source: World Development Indicators Online, March 7, 2019.

[a] Refers to 1984, not 1981.

by about 20 percent. Moreover, China has shifted from being a net exporter of industrial raw materials to being a massive net importer. Since 2014, China's trade imbalance and accumulation of reserves have declined somewhat.

THE MICROECONOMIC SHOCK
FOR MANUFACTURERS

Given the size of the macroeconomic turnaround just outlined, it is not surprising that some sectors faced significant pressure and adjustment as a result of the emergence of China as a major manufacturer. I illustrate this pressure from three separate perspectives. First, Wood and Mayer (2009) consider the effect of China's arrival on global factor endowments and on the resulting changes in other countries' comparative advantage. While the emergence of China obviously contributed some land, capital, and skilled labor to the world's endowments of factors of production, its principal and disproportionately large contribution was in unskilled labor. Wood and Mayer estimate that it raised the global ratio of labor with basic education to all labor by 7 to 9 percent and reduced the ratio of land + natural resources to all labor by 10 to 17 percent.[1] The authors say that neither of these impacts was either vast or trivial. I doubt if any such shock had been experienced over a period as short as two decades.

The consequence of these changes in the global aggregates was that many countries that had previously been able to trade as unskilled labor-abundant countries now found themselves outside that class and having to behave instead as abundant in (middle-level) skills or in natural resources.

The resulting adjustments, compressed into so short a period, were potentially quite dramatic. Applying a Heckscher-Ohlin model of world trade in which capital flows freely and hence may be ignored, Wood and Mayer calculate that these changes in endowments meant that *on average* other countries reduced the ratio of labor-intensive manufactures to primary production by 7 to 10 percent for output and 10 to 15 percent for exports. In East Asia, which had long appeared to be the most labor-abundant region, these developments caused significant deindustrialization. Elsewhere, Wood and Mayer argue, they were quantitatively less significant, although they did still have an effect.

The second and third exercises to identify competitive pressure concern competition between Mexican and Chinese producers, most of which, I argue, takes place in the US market. As a middle-income producer of relatively labor-intensive manufactures, Mexico might be thought to be particularly vulnerable to competition from China, especially given that within the North American preferential trade bloc, Mexico has a specific comparative advantage in such sectors. Moreover the focus on third-country markets as the locus of competition provides an important policy perspective, for even if Mexico chose to protect its own market from Chinese competition, it cannot unilaterally do so in the third markets in which the two suppliers meet.

In the second exercise, reported fully by Iacovone, Rauch, and Winters (2013), we look at the effect of Chinese competition on the survival chances and sales of Mexican firms both at home and in the United States. The sample comprises plant-level data for nearly all Mexican manufacturers (data on some small firms are missing) over the period 1994–2004. Over six thousand plants are covered and nearly three thousand individual products. As well as considering competition in a third market, the other innovation of this work is to allow the effects of competition to vary by firms with plant size and product—with the importance of a product in its plant's total output.

The results are consistent and stark. While competition from China (measured as China's share of Mexican or US imports of the product concerned) seems to hit smaller plants and minor products quite hard, it has relatively little impact on plants' main products or on the largest plants. In line with other literature on firms, one can take size as a good proxy for productivity, so the conclusion is that competition tends to drive weaker plants and products either out of business or to contract, while leaving stronger ones either unaffected or even able to expand.

FIGURE 4-1. The Effect of Chinese Competition on Product Sales and Exit, 1994–2004

Marginal impact of competition, product level

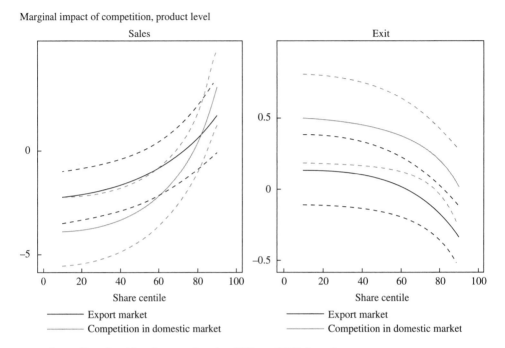

Source: Reproduced from Iacovone, Rausch and Winters (2013), figure 3.

Figure 4-1 summarizes Iacovone, Rauch, and Winters's (2013) results for products. Similar patterns are uncovered at the level of the plant. The horizontal axis reports product size (position in the ranking of plants— centiles) and the vertical axis the marginal effect of an increase in Chinese competition on plant sales in Mexico (domestic) and the United States (exports) in the left-hand block and the marginal effect on the probability of the products being withdrawn from sale completely (exit) in the right-hand block. For small products (where, say, they account for 10 percent of a plant's total sales) the effect on sales is strongly negative—a 1 percent increase in competition leading to a 0.4 percent decline in Mexican sales, whereas for products at the 90th centile, the effect on sales is positive—approximately 0.1 percent for export sales and approximately 0.3 percent for domestic sales. The broken lines are 95 percent confidence intervals and so one can see that the latter effect is significantly positive. Turning to exit on the right, the story is the same. For small products (10th centile) the effect of a 1 percent increase in Chinese competition is to increase the probability of exit from the export market by about 0.1 percent and from the home market by about 0.5 percent. For large plants, competition reduces the probability of exit— that is, it is associated with an increase in the chances of survival. We cannot identify the precise mechanism at work here, but it may well be that as Chinese competition eliminates weaker firms, sector-specific factors of production are released for stronger firms to take on.[2]

The stress is plain here. While Chinese competition may be a constructive force for the long-run growth of productivity and incomes—it helps to eliminate the weak and boost the strong—it is a political nightmare in distributional terms in most countries and is likely to raise serious calls for the management or even curtailment of trade. Giving in to this will mean benefits forgone in both China and its trading partners.

The final evidence of competitive pressure shows how Chinese competition constrains the export prices of Mexican producers in the US market. Pang and Winters (2012) use data at the six-digit level of the Harmonized System classification between 1992 and 2008 to show that *on average* changes in Chinese prices on the US market induce changes in Mexican prices in the same direction and of a little under half the size.[3] Chinese pricing has been very competitive over this period driven by China's strongly increasing productivity: for example, Hsieh and Ossa (2016) suggest that productivity growth in Chinese manufacturing sectors ranged from 7.4 percent to 24.3 percent and averaged 13.8 percent over the period 1995–2007. Thus while Chinese producers have been able keep prices down because their costs are falling, Mexican producers have felt obliged to follow suit partially; but with weaker productivity growth, they have seen their margins squeezed. These results are consistent with the previous ones of exit and declining sales, but may also be partly additional to them. Iacovone, Rauch, and Winters did not have data on margins, and so it is perfectly possible that even though Mexican firms stayed in business, they did so with weaker margins and hence lower value added.

These last results also cast light on a further cause of concern that has been expressed about China—"exporting deflation." Much of this argument is of a macro nature, which I will deal with later, but if it is to be taken literally as placing downward pressure on prices, the mechanism must be as I have described here. A number of scholars have tried to identify the effect of Chinese growth on aggregate prices by relating prices in the United States or other developed countries to the quantity of Chinese exports (see, e.g., Kamin, Marazzi and Schindler 2006). Such attempts have largely failed and led to the conclusion that China is not exporting deflation (Broda and Weinstein 2010). Part of the problem is that despite China's large size and openness, goods from China still account for only around 3 percent of US expenditure, and hence can have only a tiny direct influence on US aggregate price indices. If China is to have a discernible effect on such indices, it *has to be* by influencing the prices at which other producers sell, and this is the issue that Pang and Winters (2012) tackle directly.

More recently there has been an influential literature on the effects of Chinese trade on local economies in the United States—see, for example, Autor and others (2014) and related works. These have argued that imports from China have had a persistent negative effect on employment and welfare in the localities that produced goods in most direct competition with China, and also some aggregate employment effects as well. While the hardships that Autor and colleagues identify are real enough and clearly pose a challenge to the neoclassical view of smoothly adjusting economies, it is important to remember that they do not undertake a full welfare evaluation. For that one needs to consider the advantages of lower prices for consumers (Broda and Weinstein 2010) and the collateral benefits that accrue to US exporters (Feenstra and Sasahara 2018).

These results do indeed suggest that China contributed to the "Great Moderation" whereby Western economies seemed more or less to have abolished inflation, despite operating at high levels of capacity utilization and stoking up a huge credit boom. They are also, however, eminently reversible, and although current preoccupations with China are more to do with China exporting deflation via declining demand and output (see next section), when these cyclical phenomena have worked themselves out I would expect China to exercise very much less downward pressure on Western prices.

CHINA AND THE WTO

The World Trade Organization has rightly sought a global membership, and welcoming China in late 2001 was perhaps the biggest and most natural recent step toward that goal. China's accession has been analyzed extensively—including by Patrick Messerlin himself—and I shall consider only three aspects of it: China's behavior as an active member of the WTO, the criticisms of China's role in the ongoing Doha Round, and the recent escalation of tariff hostilities between the United States and China.

There was some interest—and concern in some quarters—as to how China would settle into the WTO institutionally. China has not had a great enthusiasm for joining organizations in which it played no formative role, and the question arose whether China would behave as "regular club member," be disruptive, or just remain aloof. After eighteen years we can say with confidence that China has become a "regular member," pursuing, like other members, what it perceives as its own interests within the context of existing WTO rules and practices. Of course, other members have not always been comfortable with China's actions, and some have accused China of violating the spirit if not the letter of WTO rules. However, while there are clearly issues to be addressed and a strong case for extending and making WTO rules more explicit, it does not seem to me that China has behaved fundamentally differently from other large members.

For example, China has played an active role in the achievement of transparency within the WTO. As Collins-Williams and Wolfe (2010) have observed, over the period to 2006–2008, China made over 500 notifications on product standards to the WTO Committee on Technical Barriers to Trade (TBT), was active in the Subsidies and Countervailing Measures Committee, and even participated in the Agriculture Committee. China has also been heavily involved in the WTO's dispute settlement procedures. It has more often been respondent than plaintiff, but the surprising figure is the frequency with which it has taken third-party status—observing and making minor contributions to cases primarily involving other members. Most commentators see this last phenomenon as a conscious learning strategy by which China sought to develop the skills and experience necessary to handle its own cases successfully.

Hsieh (2010) argues that China's lack of legal capacity has been a major constraint on its ability to pursue WTO disputes independently and may have led it to fare less well in the cases it has been involved in. As with so many issues that it identifies, China has set about redressing the lack of skills vigorously. WTO Centers were set up in several universities, and Chinese scholars are increasingly active in academic and policy debate around trade policy and the trading system. Patrick Messerlin has greatly aided this learning process himself, by fostering links and forums in which Chinese and other commentators can meet.

Kennedy (2012) offers a detailed account of China's engagement in WTO disputes. He concludes that China has been playing the role of a "system maintainer" by conforming to the practices of WTO dispute settlement, even as those practices develop. China has mainly used the system to challenge the differentiated treatment of its exports meted out by its two largest trading partners, the United States and the European Union, at least some of which stems from what the Chinese consider to be an asymmetric and unfair Protocol of Accession. Kennedy argues that the cases that China has initiated arise largely in retaliation to occasions in which it felt that a particular partner was initiating "too many" cases against China; that they were, perhaps, "warning shots" about the problems that an uncooperative China could cause. Such retaliation is by no means unique to China. Moreover, China has never initiated a case against a developing country, even those that have participated in cases against China. Hence, overall, fears that China would disrupt the WTO's enforcement function have not materialized.

Two specific asymmetries irked the Chinese in particular: nonmarket treatment and export restraints. On the former, the EU and the United States denied China market economy status in antidumping cases, which increased both the frequency and the severity with which they claimed to find dumping. Nonmarket treatment was due to cease in 2016 according to the Protocol of Accession, but in the EU case the cessation was substantially nullified by modifications to the general rules for the application of antidumping duties and an official handbook helping EU firms to identify and bring cases against alleged dumping. Critically, however, on its face this development eliminated the discrimination felt by China.

The second asymmetry that caused upset was that China is more constrained from imposing export restrictions than are other WTO members. Within the mercantilist mindset that conditions the structure and practice of the WTO, consciously restraining exports is almost inconceivable and faces very few constraints in the WTO agreements: quantitative export restrictions are generally discouraged, but export taxes remain entirely unconstrained for all but a few recently acceded countries. China is among these, having been required to commit to using export taxes on only eighty-four products that were listed in its Protocol of Accession.

Every past GATT/WTO dispute concerning export restrictions has revolved around the accusation that a member has been reducing the price of an input to downstream producers and so enhancing its competitiveness unfairly (a mercantilist argument). And, at least in some cases, there has been a subtheme that the policy involved has increased prices abroad. China has now been involved in two such cases—a dispute brought in 2009 over export taxes and quantitative restrictions on exports of bauxite, coke, fluorspar, magnesium, manganese, phosphate (yellow phosphorus), silicon (metal and carbide), and zinc, and one brought in 2012 on exports of so-called rare earths, tungsten and molybdenum. Both concluded with rulings that rejected nearly every argument put forth by the Chinese, and in particular rejected claims that the export restrictions were necessary in order to prevent environmental damage and conserve resources (GATT Article XX (paragraphs (b) and (g) respectively). The problem for the Chinese in both cases was that domestic use of the minerals in question was increasing and domestic prices were lower at the same time that exports were being curtailed, although in the rare earths case these conditions largely disappeared soon after the case commenced.[4]

Chinese irritation was redoubled in the rare earths case by the dispute panel and the Appellate Body of the WTO finding that even if export restrictions were necessary to conserve rare earth resources, the Chinese did not have access to Article XX of the GATT, which recognizes this as a potentially legitimate reason to control exports. This is because the article in the Protocol of Accession that deals with export restraints did not explicitly specify that it was subject to Article XX of the GATT. Thus although the Protocol of Accession and the rest of the WTO treaty are to be read as a whole in defining China's rights and obligations, it was successfully argued that this did not amount to permitting later documents (the Protocol) to appeal to earlier ones (Article XX) except where this had been explicitly negotiated. Since the Protocol of Accession negotiated access to Article XX on some issues but not for export restraints, the Appellate Body interpreted its absence in the latter as conscious and binding. There is no evidence that the members of WTO would have resisted such a direct appeal to Article XX, and so it seems to me that the Chinese might reasonably ask the lawyers handling their accession process whether or not they had let their clients down!

Export restraints are just as disruptive to a liberal trading regime as import restraints, and so I would place high priority on disciplining their use. Maybe, as a country that has already largely submitted to such disciplines, China could lead such a negotiation.

A second alleged challenge to Chinese integration into the WTO is the Doha Round, which some, particularly in the United States, held to be stalled because China offered too little. That China should offer a good deal of liberalization was accepted by everyone, including the Chinese, but here I think other countries were making a mountain out of a molehill.

China's accession process was long-lived and entailed a huge amount of reform and liberalization. The Doha Round was initiated as the accession process drew to a close, and was billed both to last only three to four years and to be substantially about continuing the business of the Uruguay Round. In 2001, when it started, no one expected China to play an active role. Over the Doha Round's extended life, China more than trebled the size of its economy, and it recognized that it had to contribute something. However, the demands made of China for deep cuts in tariffs on manufactured products from the levels agreed at accession seemed quite unreasonable. Certainly China could not stand aside from the general liberalization that a successful conclusion to the Doha Round would have entailed, but to blame China for the demise of the round by not offering more, seems ill-informed.

A further complaint that China might have leveled against the WTO in 2019 is that it offered scant protection against trade barriers that lie at the very edge of or beyond WTO consistency. The United States' use of the national security argument for restricting imports of steel and aluminum (section 232 of the US code and Article XXI of the GATT) is barely sustainable given many of such imports come from Canada and Mexico with which the USA has virtually impregnable land borders; and the threat of applying similar treatment to imports of motor vehicles is plainly not appropriate. In neither case are China's exports affected to any great extent, but in terms of undermining the system of which China is a major member (and beneficiary) they are still serious threats.[5]

Much more directly threatening are the United States' section 301 actions against imports from China. Justified on grounds of China's unfair practices in technology transfer, intellectual property, and innovation, the United States imposed tariffs of 25 percent on 818 products worth $34 billion in July 2018, 25 percent on 279 products worth $16 billion in August 2018, and 10 percent on 5,745 products worth $200 billion in September 2018, with the threat to raise them to 25 percent in December unless China desisted. (The latter step is in abeyance in March 2019 while trade talks continue.)

These are unilateral policies that China has little prospect of overturning without signing an asymmetric trade agreement with the United States, and they thus represent the very antithesis of the WTO's multilateral rules-based system. They are part of a consistent policy of hostility toward China that spreads beyond mere trade—and, indeed, while trade concessions may buy off President Trump, who obsesses about the trade balance, they may well not work on US Trade Representative Robert Lighthizer, who seeks to bring manufacturing back to the United States, or on the US high-tech industry, which wishes to use trade policies to cripple or destroy China's efforts to achieve technological parity with the United States.[6] By mid-2020, after a brief pause, commercial strife had resurfaced at increased levels of intensity with sanctions against a leading Chinese company (Huawei), diplomatic spats, and very hostile rhetoric, especially around human rights. Coupled with the aggressive instincts of the White House, it manifestly threatens the very fabric of the WTO and makes the restoration of the latter's standing more important than at any time in its short history.

GLOBAL IMBALANCES AND CHINESE GROWTH

The major complaint against China until recently was its huge current account surpluses over the period 2005–2011 and the resulting massive stock of international reserves. The corresponding deficits elsewhere were held to drain demand out of partner countries (exporting deflation from a different perspective), and the imbalances are frequently named as a major cause of the financial crisis of 2007 and onward. There is little truth in either statement, but it is important to keep them in perspective. Moreover, ten-plus years on from the crisis, after the Chinese surplus has substantially eroded, one might even discern a certain (misplaced) nostalgia for the "old" way of running the world economy with booming demand in China.

Macroeconomically the imbalances of the early 2000s reflected, but also permitted, the boom from 2002 to 2007, with the surplus countries able to increase their output and employment strongly and the deficit countries to maintain high levels of consumption and demand. Of course, we can now see that such growth was unsustainable and that adjustment had to occur, but absent the financial crisis (which was not caused by the Chinese, even if it was facilitated by them), it is not clear that overheating per se created particularly large problems. In the event, however, massive adjustment was required of the world economy; both private and government sectors retrenched to try to restore their balance sheets, hence cutting demand on a very broad front; the financial sector nearly collapsed and subsequently cut back lending vigorously, further curtailing demand. The Chinese government played a very constructive role in addressing the immediate crisis, by supporting Chinese and world demand through a huge investment boom funded by extensive borrowing. This helped to support aggregate demand and also substantially reduced the Chinese trade imbalance. As discussed below, however, in the longer run, this response arguably stored up problems for later.

China did not cause the financial crisis, which rather arose from the combination of light regulation and macroeconomic stress in the new millennium. Rajan (2009) argues that, partly because competitive pressures from China and other low-cost producers constrained real wages among less skilled workers, American policymakers looked to private credit markets to boost their spending power; this, in turn, caused the real estate boom and the stock of toxic mortgages that so burdened the financial system and private portfolios. On the supply side of the credit market, the low returns associated with the loose monetary policy behind this distributional policy and the Great Moderation led banks to incur far too many risks in the search for profits. One should not blame any of this on China, but it is the case that the high level of Chinese reserves and the absence of local instruments with which to absorb high savings in China granted these mistakes huge space in which to work their mischief. The fact that China deposited its surplus dollars in New York kept the merry-go-round running far longer than it would have in other circumstances.

An important question is what lay behind the surpluses? Macroeconomics is basically the process of unpicking the relationships between several endogenous variables. While clearly booming exports and stagnating imports were the proximate causes of the Chinese current account surplus, they were not the underlying causes. Export growth accelerated from about 2001 partly because China's accession to the WTO encouraged foreign direct investment (FDI) from Japan, Taiwan, and Korea. There was also a significant slowdown in import growth after 2004 mainly as net imports of heavy industrial products fell. This partly reflected a buildup of the stock of equipment over the preceding few years, but also the shift in Chinese capabilities so that domestic supplies increased strongly. These changes are partly exogenous and partly symptoms of more fundamental forces.

One frequently proposed causal candidate for the surplus is China's exchange rate policy, which since around 2004 has been associated with moderate undervaluation. Identifying over- or undervaluation is not straightforward, and while some undervaluation of the renminbi is clear, claims of major undervaluation seem misplaced. For example, between 2005 and 2010, unit labor costs in China increased by about one-third, and the nominal effective exchange rate appreciated by 14 percent; and between 2010 and 2013 the figures were over 50 percent and 11 percent respectively.[7] That China chose to keep its real exchange rate relatively low stems from three strong policy imperatives. The first was to sustain employment growth in its export industries with the twin related objectives of maintaining its high rate of export-led growth and of preserving "social harmony." Chinese policymakers were conscious of a trade-off between political reforms and economic returns: crudely characterized, as long as employment and real wages keep growing rapidly, the population will tolerate the constraints on political freedoms and not seek to disturb the Communist Party's hold on power. Many commentators spoke of a 7 percent per year threshold below which social unrest will occur, but as far as I am aware, this was based on no formal analysis.

Chinese policymakers, who in my experience are extremely hard-headed and well informed, undoubtedly recognized that a slowdown in growth was inevitable at some stage, but their political masters have found it much more comfortable to postpone the difficult adjustment a bit longer. The period from 2016 to 2019 illustrates this well: each effort to curtail credit expansion is followed by a relaxation as growth begins to falter. And all of this has been accompanied by increasing intolerance of political dissent.

The second imperative was to self-insure against a repeat of the 1997–1998 crisis in which many Asian countries felt abused by the international system and specifically by the International Monetary Fund in return for emergency borrowing. Quite consciously and at times explicitly, they said never again would they risk falling under the influence of the "Washington consensus." The result was a massive accumulation of reserves throughout most of Asia, and I believe that China was part of that movement based on its observation of its neighbors rather than its own direct experience. In both of these objectives, past exchange rate policy had been extraordinarily successful, and we should appreciate the difficulties that policymakers face in shifting to a different strategy at the behest of other countries.

The third imperative was that a large and rapid exchange rate appreciation would have created large paper losses in renminbi for the holders of dollar assets. To the extent that these were the commercial banks, there could easily have been a messy banking crisis, for received wisdom is that the banks are already burdened by very high levels of nonperforming loans. While the Chinese government has the resources to support and recapitalize the banks if necessary, it is very nervous about processes that it cannot fully control and dislikes acting under duress. Of course, the reserves held by the Bank of China (over \$3 trillion at their peak) would also show large paper losses when appreciation occurred, but these would have been easier to gloss over than those in the commercial sector.[8]

The true cause of China's large current account surplus was macro-economic imbalance—high net savings by the household, corporate, and government sectors. Chinese households have high savings relative to those in many developing countries, but, at about 20 percent of GDP, not unprecedentedly so.[9] Moreover, given the very rapid rate at which China's population is aging, the one-child policy, and the relative lack of government-provided services and pensions, high savings seem rational and likely to persist. Much more unusual are enterprise savings, which accounted for about 20 percent of GDP in the mid-2000s. Lane and Schmukler (2007) argue that these reflect the low (zero) dividends paid by private (state) firms coupled with policies that boost enterprise profits strongly—subsidies to inputs such as land and borrowing and low wages supported by rural-urban migration. Until these distortions are addressed and ways found to switch corporate profits into consumption (possibly via the government account with taxes and social expenditure), the imbalances will not be per-manently cured.

As noted above, China leaned into the wind as world demand collapsed in 2008–2009 by stimulating official borrowing and investment and was praised for doing so. However, as was argued at the time and has subse-quently proved correct, the investment exacerbated Chinese excess capac-ity in manufacturing and significantly increased the stock of bad debt. Hence this policy made the inevitable cyclical downturn as these positions were unwound deeper and longer, and made the climb toward a long-run sustainable growth path even steeper. As was already clear in 2007, this path requires the Chinese economy to switch from investment and exports as drivers to domestic consumption and innovation. The combination of a steep cyclical retrenchment with a dramatic change in growth strategy and the inevitable slowing as the economy gets closer to the technological frontier and the population ages poses a significant policy challenge for the Chi-nese government. Growth fell from around 10 percent per year in 2010–2011 to around 7 percent in 2013–2014 to 6 percent in 2018. At least some com-mentators now fear that it is not a Chinese boom but a Chinese bust that will pose the greatest macroeconomic challenge.

EXCLUDING AND CONSTRAINING CHINA

China's formidable growth has provided a series of challenges for the current high-income countries and the international institutions that they tend to dominate. These range from the serious competitive threat that China has posed to Western industry (and hence, perhaps, incomes) through the challenge to the Western liberal economic model to the strategic challenge as China starts to seek influence in its region and in the world commensurate with its economic power. Thus the Western attitude toward China evolved from welcoming in the 1980s to a much more defensive posture in the first half of the 2010s, which sought, inter alia, to curb China's export expansion and oblige it to liberalize its policies, especially toward state-owned enterprises. As already noted, after 2016 the United States became much more overtly hostile toward China, if more random in its policymaking. In this section, I consider two past examples and one current example of such exclusionary behavior. These are the "out" in the chapter's title.

The first example goes back to global imbalances. Some commentators—such as Rodrik (2010)—appealed to something like figure 4-2 to argue that trade and trade policy lay behind China's massive current account surplus: crudely the argument was that because the surplus boomed as a percentage of GDP shortly after China's accession to the WTO, the latter must have been responsible for it.[10] I deal with this at some length for two reasons: first Patrick Messerlin and I have both argued over the years that the interventionist conclusions derived from this view were wrong; second, the problem has now largely dissipated on its own, which suggests that the rush to change institutions to solve it was as unnecessary as it was dangerous to the world trading system.

Rodrik's argument starts with the assertion that economic growth (and certainly China's growth strategy) requires a rapidly growing tradable manufactures sector, because this is typically where the highest productivity activities are found. An intense focus on this sector does not occur with market forces alone because of a variety of market failures—poor property rights protection, unrequited spillovers between firms, coordination failures, and others, which impinge disproportionately on this sector. Hence activist polices are required and have, says Rodrik, been used in virtually every case of successful growth. Countries have variously used polices such as directed credit, production subsidies, export subsidies, and protection to

FIGURE 4-2. China's Trade Balance and Current Account, 1966–2016 (percent of GDP)

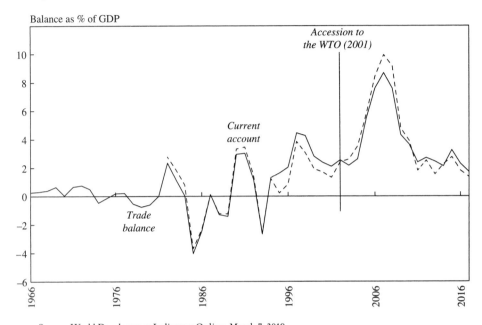

Source: World Development Indicators Online, March 7, 2019.

Note: Trade balance is the difference between exports of goods and services and imports of goods and services, both as a percentage of GDP; WDI Online does not report the Chinese current account on a balance of payments basis before 1982.

achieve tradables growth. Exchange rate undervaluation can also be used and is historically associated with rapid growth, and its use as a growth policy is attractive because it does not require sector-specific interventions, which are both difficult to design and subject to capture.[11]

One of Rodrik's innovations is to stress that growth is related to the production of tradables, rather than to their export. This means that if a country can simultaneously increase the demand for tradables along with their supply, it can grow rapidly without a large trade surplus. Subsidies, possibly bolstered by protection to prevent demand seeping abroad, are the obvious route to do this, and this is the way in which industrial policy works. Rodrik argues that optimal intervention would see all countries using subsidies to cure their local market failures and that in this case the spillovers between countries would become irrelevant because each country would be at its optimum. According to Rodrik, the problem until 2011 was that WTO membership prevented China (and other countries) from using subsidies, so the government had to turn to exchange rate undervaluation as a second-best tool to boost tradables. But undervaluation must inevitably lead to surpluses, he argues, and that is why the WTO is responsible for the global imbalances. The "obvious" solution to this, about which Rodrik (2011) is explicit, is to restore the legitimacy of unilateral trade and industrial policy, specifically subsidies, and to manage exchange rates multilaterally.

Rodrik's writing is seductive, but his analysis is wrong in several respects. First, there are many ways to boost tradables output that are WTO-consistent—for example, improving logistics, labor training and education, and consumption subsidies. They are arguably less immediate and direct than straight production subsidies, but they are not ineffective. Second, subsidies and protection are just as dangerous to the world economy as trade surpluses. Consider, for example, the intense reactions of partners' industries to subsidies elsewhere, which can easily set off subsidy wars of the sort that we saw in the 1930s (which also saw competitive devaluations, by the way). The idea that the optimal intervention offers a stable solution to the global policy game is a chimera—almost certainly this situation is characterized by a prisoner's dilemma in which country A wants to subsidize and to prevent country B from doing so. There is no guarantee that a subsidy-permissive regime would not degenerate into a subsidy free-for-all with massive intervention. The current clamor against China's state-owned enterprises is evidence enough of how unpalatable partners find a major player's subsidies, actual or merely suspected. And we find greater propensity to subsidize industry in nearly every government in the world.

Third, it is also hard to manage exchange rates. The global community has many times called for exchange rates to be managed by the IMF and has always failed; efforts through other groups such as the G-7 have only rarely succeeded. The United States has no intention of surrendering its exchange rate sovereignty to the IMF or an equivalent body, so no WTO-like enforcement mechanism for exchange rates is imminent. There is just no evidence that countries that compete in subsidy space as Rodrik would allow would willingly surrender their policy space in exchange rates. I am not arguing that some coordination over exchange rates is not desirable, just that it is hardly feasible.

If Rodrik's idea to ditch the subsidies disciplines of the WTO and replace them with an exchange rate code seems dangerous, the pressure from some commentators to take exchange rates into the WTO, and hence to make them subject to the WTO Dispute Settlement Mechanism, seems equally so. Mattoo and Subramanian (2009) make the case and it has been taken up by several US representatives and European politicians. Because the complexity of measuring undervaluation is great, the whole basis of a dispute will be contentious, and still more so will be the identification of the government manipulation that is alleged to cause it. Mattoo and Subramanian say these calculations should be done by the IMF and that their doing it on behalf of the WTO will somehow make it politically less contentious than the WTO's doing it on its own behalf, but I do not see why. One reason WTO's codification of trade interventions is effective is because it replaces political pressures with technical definitions with a very narrow focus. The process is not perfect, but it tends to draw the political poison. There seems little chance that with something as complicated as macroeconomic management, the same trick will work—see, for example, Staiger and Sykes (2010) on the difficulties of even defining exchange rate undervaluation in WTO terms.

It is difficult to see how trade sanctions will address exchange rate frictions effectively: trade sanctions will not cure macroeconomic distortions, at least not without massive cost. Moreover, because they would be aimed against the whole tradables sector, they would largely lack the ability that "regular" sanctions have to switch the cost of one tradable sector's protection to another exporting one. But that is not the big worry. The big worry is that trying to use sanctions in this way will inflict major damage on the WTO as an institution, and that by giving it an impossible brief we will destroy the value that we currently reap form the WTO and take for granted. The WTO has neither the structure (all decisions are made by committees of members; none by the secretariat, which might be better able to maintain a technical view) nor the institutional robustness to be able survive the sort of contentious and high-stakes decisions that dispute panels and the Appellate Body would have to take in exchange rate cases. Having failed in such cases, the magic that currently leads to high degrees of compliance with WTO decisions would be destroyed, and we would be left with little leverage against "regular" violations. Once this happened the chances of other cooperation—for example, that in committees on other business— would also disappear. In other words, I fear that hanging the exchange rate millstone round the WTO's neck would bring it down. Of course, given the United States' policy of blocking the appointment of Appellate Body members has emasculated half of the dispute settlement process, the WTO as an effective organization might not last long enough for any of this to matter.

The second example of 'out' was the so-called megaregional trade deals—the Trans-Pacific Partnership (TPP) and the Transatlantic Trade and Investment Partnership (TTIP).[12] The former was a trade agreement concluded between twelve Pacific countries—Australia, Brunei Darussalam, Canada, Chile, Japan, Malaysia, Mexico, New Zealand, Peru, Singapore, the United States, and Vietnam. They had a combined GDP of $27.8 trillion (37 percent of the global total), total trade of $11.6 trillion (26 percent) and a combined population of about 802 million (11 percent).[13] There were several possible motives for the US proposal to enlarge the pre-existing Pacific-4 Agreement into the TPP in 2008. For example, it may have been an attempt to revive the flagging Doha Round in the WTO; or an attempt to reinterest US business in international trade policy, which was necessary because it had expressed next to no interest in the Doha Round; and to some, it was a way for President George W. Bush to embarrass the Democratic Party because they would have to choose between a probusiness position (supporting TPP) or a prolabor one (opposing it). Virtually all Americans agreed, however, that it was a chance to bind a significant number of partners to the American conception of economic policy, and most believed that in doing so they would counter China's growing influence on East Asian countries.

Modeled substantially in the US image, the TPP provided for liberalization of agriculture, government procurement and e-commerce, significant labor clauses, significant restraints on state-owned enterprises, and much stronger intellectual property protections. Most of these would involve China in huge reforms that would clearly stretch its political consensus severely, possibly to the breaking point. Moreover, whereas Vietnam was to be permitted long adjustment periods and a degree of latitude in enforcement, any realistic reading of Sino-US relations suggests that China would have received no such concessions.

Once the members of the TPP had accepted these norms, they would naturally press, along with the United States, for other countries to adopt them. Thus there would suddenly have been a coalition accounting for nearly 40 percent of world GDP proposing a specific set of rules within the world trading system, which would have been very hard for other countries to resist. The TPP was essentially an attempt to define trading standards not merely for its members but for the world. I argued this in Winters (2014), and it was made explicit in October 2015 by President Barack Obama in his weekly radio address, stating that "without this agreement, competitors that don't share our values, like China, will write the rules of the global economy."[14] If China, India, or Brazil felt that these disciplines were too arduous or just did not fit their needs, the world trading system would effectively be sundered. Moreover, given that the TPP would be attractive to smaller economies and that the latter would probably be offered quite accommodating terms, the split would tend to deepen over time rather than the opposite.

The second brick in the wall to exclude China was the Trans-Atlantic Trade and Investment Partnership. The TTIP had many parallels with the TPP and sought to go further with deeper agreement on regulatory issues. An avowed aim was to "strengthen the multilateral trading system" and "to enshrine Europe and America's role as the world's standard-setters" (European President Van Rompuy).[15] This reads very much like an agreement to cooperate to make sure that outcomes in the trading system are as the US and EU wanted them—and with around half of world GDP between them and a further 15 percent in the rest of TPP, the choice facing the others would have been capitulation or exclusion.

In 2014, Patrick Messerlin and Jinghui Wang suggested that the EU and China should reach a trade accord of their own. Although I do not like discriminatory arrangements in principle, it would at least have offered an alternative locus of rule writing to the TPP. But in fact, the Europeans became wholly focused on negotiating the TTIP, which consciously or otherwise provided the United States with the perfect lever to preclude EU-China collaboration. Any such effort that got close to a conclusion could be stopped by a US hint that it might drop out of the TTIP.

Although the United States failed to exclude China from effective membership in the world trading system by introducing exchange rate manipulation as a cause for trade remedies, its indirect approach of building a rule-making coalition that could more or less impose rules on the rest of the world seemed close to fruition. China was, indeed, potentially "out" of the system for a decade, and I, for one, could not rid my mind of Cordell Hull's strictures about discrimination: "You could not separate the idea of commerce from the idea of war and peace. . . . Wars were often largely caused by economic rivalry conducted unfairly" (Hull 1948, 84).

But then Donald Trump seemed to ride to the rescue. The TTIP was already making slow progress and received no encouragement from Trump.

Immediately on taking office in January 2017, President Trump withdrew the United States from the TTP. The carefully constructed wall crumbled. It is true that, rather surprisingly, the other eleven members transformed the TPP into a new agreement—the Comprehensive and Progressive Agreement on Trans-Pacific Partnership (CPTPP), maintaining most of the characteristics that the former inherited from its parent, America. But without the world's largest economy, the CPTPP is unlikely to have a serious impact on world regulatory standards. The TTIP, meanwhile, just faded away.

The demise of the TPP did not, however, presage a period of stability. Soon into his administration, Trump's mercantilist instincts and his fiercely anti-China trade team combined to renew the effort to exclude China, but this time not through a subtle and sophisticated process of building coalitions, but by brute force. As I briefly described earlier, the United States initiated a hostile trade policy and a rhetorical campaign against China free of any subtlety at all. Eventually China will have to liberalize further if it is to prosper, and it is at present moving in the opposite direction. It is possible that Trump's overt hostility will have the desired effect, but the descent into bilateralism and power politics means that the cost to the world trading system and all those who rely on it could be very large.

CONCLUDING THOUGHTS

China's economic rise has been remarkable—faster and far larger than we have ever seen before or could even have dreamed of four decades ago. The benefits in terms of increased global output and income are large, and, at least to the extent that these are manifest in rising commodity prices, they are shared with some of the poorest countries in the world. Adjustment to such a shock is inevitably painful at times and in places, and I have identified several such instances in this chapter. However, while the first twenty-five years of adjustment to China's emergence were characterized by strong Chinese growth and mostly accommodating policies among established powers, the period since 2005 has been characterized by increasing angst on the part of other countries. This in turn has led them to move from a position that was generally accepting and welcoming (with some exceptions, of course) to one in which the prevailing sentiment, especially in the United States, appears to be one of fear and exclusion.

The events discussed here certainly do not suggest that the advanced nations face no costs in adjusting to China, or that we do not need to reform the WTO, especially in the area of state-owned enterprises. However, I would argue that other countries have been large beneficiaries of Chinese growth and that some of the issues that have concerned them have cured themselves in the natural course of events. Thus I do not believe that we would be well advised to make fundamental changes to the world trading system rules in order ease the stresses perceived to be emanating from China. Rather we should seek to preserve the multilateral system that is the pinnacle of the postwar settlement and seek to engage China as an equal in a cooperative fashion.

NOTES

1. The differences reflect different ways of aggregating across countries. The smaller estimates weight countries' endowments together by their shares of world trade, the larger ones by shares of world labor force.

2. In additional tests we show that skill-intensive firms fare better than less skill-intensive ones and that larger firms and products appear to be better placed to take advantage of the improved and cheaper flow of intermediate inputs that Chinese expansion entails.

3. The model is based loosely on a Bertrand model of duopolistic interaction with differentiated products, whereby producers compete via prices, as used, for example, by Chang and Winters (2002).

4. Karapinar (2011) offers a good discussion of the raw materials case. Bond and Trachtman (2016) cover the rare earths one. In the interests of transparency I note that I advised the European Commission in the latter case.

5. The "solution" to these tariffs for several partners has been to agree to voluntary export restraints (gray area measures), which undermines one of the principal achievements of the Uruguay Round.

6. The depth of American angst about China can be gauged by a speech by Vice President Mike Pence at the Hudson Institute on October 4, 2018, which bordered on the hysterical. See "Remarks by Vice President Pence on the Administration's Policy Toward China," https://www.whitehouse.gov /briefings-statements/remarks-vice-president-pence-administrations-policy -toward-china/.

7. Unit labor costs are from US Department of Commerce, "Labor costs" (https://acetool.commerce.gov/cost-risk-topic/labor-costs); exchange rate data are from the IMF's International Financial Statistics, via the eLibrary (https:// data.imf.org/regular.aspx?key=61545850).

8. The losses are just as real, however, and as Larry Summers has observed, China is very far from maximizing its economic returns by building up such reserves of inevitably depreciating assets.

9. See Vincelette and others (2010, fig 2) for the data.

10. Figure 4-2 reports the trade balance over a long period but the current account only since 2005, because these are the only data now in World Development Indicators Online (https://databank.worldbank.org/reports.aspx?source=world-development-indicators). In an earlier version of this chapter I used current account data over the period 1980–2011, and they told exactly the same story.

11. Undervaluation's disadvantage of taxing the consumption of tradables appears to count for rather little with governments focused on growth.

12. More detail on the arguments in the next few paragraphs can be found in Winters (2017).

13. All statistics come from WDI online and refer to 2013.

14. "Obama Jabs at China as He Defends TPP Trade Deal," October 10, 2015, http://news.yahoo.com/obama-jabs-china-defends-tpp-trade-deal-131620791.html.

15. "Remarks by President Obama, UK Prime Minister Cameron, European Commission President Barroso, and European Council President Van Rompuy on the Transatlantic Trade and Investment Partnership," June 17, 2013, www.whitehouse.gov/the-press-office/2013/06/17/remarks-president-obama-uk-prime-minister-cameron-european-commission-pr.

REFERENCES

Autor, D. H., and others. 2014. Trade Adjustment: Worker-Level Evidence. *Quarterly Journal of Economics* 129 (4): 1799–1860.

Bond, E., and J. Trachtman. 2016. "China-Rare Earths: Export Restrictions and the Limits of Textual Interpretation." *World Trade Review* 15 (2): 189–209.

Broda, C., and J. Romalis. 2009. "The Welfare Implications of Rising Price Dispersion." Working Paper. Clemson University. http://economics.clemson.edu/files/priceinequality-july18.pdf.

Broda, C., and D. Weinstein. 2010. "Exporting Deflation? Chinese Exports and Japanese Prices." In *China's Growing Role in World Trade*, edited by R. Feenstra and S. Wei, 203–27. University of Chicago Press.

Chang, W., and L. A. Winters. 2002. "How Regional Blocs Affect Excluded Countries: The Price Effects of MERCOSUR." *American Economic Review* 92 (4): 889–904.

Collins-Williams, T., and R. Wolfe. 2010. "Transparency as a Trade Policy Tool: The WTO's Cloudy Windows." *World Trade Review* 9 (4): 551–81.

Feenstra, R. C., and A. Sasahara. 2018. The "China Shock," Exports and US Employment: A Global Input–Output Analysis. *Review of International Economics* 26 (5): 1053–83.

Hsieh, C., and R. Ossa. 2016. "A Global View of Productivity Growth in China." *Journal of International Economics* 102: 209–24.

Hull, C. 1948. *The Memoirs of Cordell Hull.* 2 vols. New York: Macmillan.

Iacovone, L., F. Rauch, and L. A. Winters. 2013. "Trade as an Engine of Creative Destruction: Mexican Experience with Chinese Competition." *Journal of International Economics* 89 (2): 379–92.

Kamin, S., M. Marazzi, and J. Schindler. 2006. "The Impact of Chinese Exports on Global Import Prices." *Review of International Economics* 14 (2): 179–201.

Karapinar, B. 2011. "China's Export Restriction Policies: Complying with 'WTO Plus' or Undermining Multilateralism," *World Trade Review* 10 (3): 389–408.

Kennedy, M. 2012. "China's Role in WTO Dispute Settlement." *World Trade Review* 11 (4): 555–89.

Lane, P., and J. Schmukler. 2007. "International Financial Integration of China and India." In *Dancing with Giants: China, India, and the Global Economy,* edited by L. A. Winters and S. Yusuf, chap. 3. Washington, D.C.: World Bank.

Maddison, A. 2007. *The World Economy.* Vol. 2: *A Millennial Perspective*; Vol. 2: *Historical Statistics.* Paris: Organization for Economic Cooperation and Development.

Martin, W. J., and K. Anderson. 2011. "Export Restrictions and Price Insulation during Commodity Price Booms." *American Journal of Agricultural Economics* 94 (2): 422–27.

Mattoo, A., and A. Subramanian. 2009. "Currency Undervaluation and Sovereign Wealth Funds: A New Role for the World Trade Organization." *World Economy* 32 (8): 1135–64.

Pang, W. L., and L. A. Winters. 2012. "Exporting Deflation? The Effect of Chinese Competition on Mexican Export Prices. Mimeo, University of Sussex.

Petri, P., M. Plummer, and F. Zhai. 2011. "The Trans-Pacific Partnership and Asia-Pacific Integration: A Quantitative Assessment." Working Paper, Economics Series 119. Honolulu: East-West Center. http://hdl.handle.net/10125/22298.

Rajan, R. 2009. *How Hidden Fractures Still Threaten the Global Economy.* Princeton University Press.

Rodrik, D. 2010. "Making Room for China in the World Economy." *American Economic Review* 100 (2): 89–93.

———. 2011. *The Globalization Paradox: Democracy and the Future of the World Economy.* New York: W. W. Norton. Sharma, R. 2011. "Food Export Restrictions: Review of the 2007–2010 Experience and Considerations for Disciplining Restrictive Measures." Commodity and Trade Policy Research Working Paper 32. Rome: Food and Agriculture Organization.

Staiger, R., and A. Sykes. 2010. "Currency Manipulation and World Trade." *World Trade Review* 9 (4): 583–627.

Vincelette, G., and others. 2010. "China Global Crisis Avoided, Robust Economic Growth Sustained." Policy Research Working Paper 5435. Washington, D.C.: World Bank.

Winters, L. A. 2014. "The Problem with T-TIP." *VoxEU*, May 22, 2014. www.voxeu.org/article/problem-ttip.

———. 2017. "The WTO and Regional Trading Agreements: Is It All Over for Multilateralism?" In *Assessing the World Trade Organisation: Fit for Purpose*, edited by M. Elsig, B. Hoekman, and J. Pauwelyn, 344–75. Cambridge University Press.

Winters, L. A., and S. Yusuf, eds. 2007. *Dancing with Giants: China, India, and the Global Economy*. Washington, D.C.: World Bank.

Wood, A., and J. Mayer. 2009. "Has China De-industrialised Other Developing Countries? *Review of World Economics* 147 (2): 325–50.

5

TRADE WARS

NOBODY EXPECTS THE SPANISH INQUISITION

**EDDY BEKKERS, JOSEPH FRANCOIS, DOUGLAS NELSON,
AND HUGO ROJAS-ROMAGOSA**

Trade wars, like heart attacks, earthquakes, and financial crises are un-predictable events, as was the Spanish Inquisition (at least according to Monty Python). There are risk factors that increase the likelihood of an event, but point predictions are not possible. Perhaps more important, once one of these events has occurred, there is a body of scientific knowledge based on which the relevant experts can predict consequences of the event and prescribe courses of action to control those consequences. That statement is supported by our experience with heart attacks, earthquakes, and financial crises, but the case of trade wars seems much less certain. Without prejudice to the Spanish Inquisition, in this paper we argue that economic theory of rational trade wars provides very little explanatory leverage. The short version of the argument is that, where heart attacks are physiological events whose causes and consequences are physiological, earthquakes are geological events whose causes and consequences are geological, and financial crises (at least in a first-order kind of way) are economic events whose causes and consequences are economic, trade wars are fundamentally political events whose causes are almost completely political and whose consequences are to a significant degree also political.

Contemporary economic theory (loosely since the end of World War II) happens to have developed during a uniquely peaceful and liberal period in world history. This fact has had a marked effect on how economists have thought about trade wars. In a world without trade wars, we are free to understand trade wars as being about terms of trade. Similarly, we can convince ourselves that the collective effort at trade liberalization has primarily been about internalization of a terms-of-trade externality, when the success of trade liberalization has rested firmly on convincing domestic politicians that "trade policy is foreign policy" (Cooper 1972; Nelson 1989); and in a world in which international trade is not a domestic political issue, we are free to treat the politics of trade as being about the effect of trade policy on household factor incomes. The result is that in an environment in which trade policy is very much public politics and trade wars are a very real possibility, we are unprepared to provide serious analysis or advice.

In this chapter, we focus specifically on trade wars, leaving the politics of antitrade populism for another time and place. We begin with a brief overview of the theory of rational trade wars. From there we look back to the historical experience of trade wars and the current attempts to calculate the levels of protection implied by the theory of rational trade wars. We conclude that neither the history nor the calculations provide much in the way of evidence in favor of the applicability of the theory.[1] We then look more closely at the assumption structure of the theory, focusing in particular on what would have to be true of the government's objective function for the theory of rational trade wars to be informative with respect to the behavior of actual governments. We conclude with a discussion about the likely content of those objective functions.

ON RATIONAL TRADE WARS

Before proceeding to a description of the modern and contemporary theory of rational trade wars, it is necessary to say what we mean by a trade war.[2] We mean an extended period during which a pair of countries, or groups of countries, apply instruments of trade policy with the intention of affecting a substantial share of the trade between those countries (or groups of countries). This is generally instrumental behavior, but there need be no implication that the ultimate, or unique, goal of the policy is to determine the structure of trade. However, in the theory of rational trade wars proper, as we discuss later, the assumed unique goal of trade policy is to maximize national welfare by affecting the terms of trade. This literature focuses on tariffs, and to some extent on quantitative restrictions, but without prejudice to the wide range of instruments that have been used in historical trade wars (e.g., quantitative restrictions of various sorts, navigation acts, colonial structures, embargoes, staple laws, and others).

The modern and contemporary theory of rational trade wars is based fundamentally on the theory of the optimal tariff. In its most basic form, two countries and two goods, which is the form the great majority of the literature on rational trade wars applies, optimal tariff theory is quite simple. The policy-active country acts as a monopsonist, restricting access to the market for its importable good, resulting in a fall in the price of the importable on the inframarginal (i.e., still imported) units. That is, the policy results in an improvement in the terms of trade for the policy-active country. The optimal tariff just balances, at the margin, this terms-of-trade gain against the loss in welfare from the distortions in consumer and producer choices caused by that policy. The size of the optimal tariff is a function of the elasticity of the foreign country's export supply curve. Specifically, $t^{opt} = 1/\varepsilon^*$, where ε^* is the elasticity of export supply by the foreign country. Even in this textbook case, the result is deceptively simple. As Murray Kemp (1969, 300) pointed out years ago:

> Much attention has been lavished on this formula. But it provides scant guidance in the search for an optimal t since it involves two, not one, unknowns. The value of ε^* depends on the position of the foreign demand curve at which it is evaluated; the point on the foreign demand curve depends on the import demand by the tariff-imposing country; that in turn depends on the internal distribution of income; but, finally, the post-tariff distribution of income depends on the arbitrary pattern of lump-sum taxes and subsidies. There is, then, not a single optimal τ but an infinity.

We will return to these issues shortly, but first we need to turn from the case of one policy-active country to two. That is, we consider the analysis of rational trade wars. The modern theory of rational trade wars proceeds from a critique of the optimal tariff analysis that a large economy targeted by an optimal tariff would likely retaliate. This retaliation would take the form of a rational response—that is, the adoption of an optimal tariff defined relative to the first country's tariff-distorted offer curve. In the modern theory, countries will continue to retaliate in this tit-for-tat fashion until neither country can gain by changing its tariff. At that point, the trade war is over. As Scitovsky (1942) noted, there were two conjectures about this end point: first, that it would occur before autarky was reached; and second, that both countries would lose relative to free trade. In what has become the standard reference in the modern literature, Johnson (1953–1954) showed that the first conjecture was correct, but that it was completely possible for one country to "win" a rational trade war (i.e., have higher national welfare after the trade war than under free trade).[3]

The contemporary theory of rational trade wars cuts through the details of the tit-for-tat retaliation process by applying standard game theoretic analysis to focus on the Nash equilibrium. Thus the end point (the Nash equilibrium) becomes the trade war, and the analyst can, in principle, calculate the Nash optimal tariffs for each country. Furthermore, assuming that the Nash equilibrium is unique and both countries lose, both of which became components of the conventional baseline for rational trade war analysis, it was easy to see that a trade war was a prisoners' dilemma (Riezman 1982). Not only did this provide expository clarity, but, faced with very low tariffs among the major trading nations of the world, trade economists were able to take advantage of the extensive body of work on how repetition, under a variety of assumptions, permits players to support cooperation (Osborne 2004, chap. 14). From this insight grew a whole body of work on trade cooperation and, in particular, the role of the WTO (Bagwell and Staiger 2002).

At a minimum, the theory of rational trade wars clearly illustrates one fundamental problem with optimal tariff theory and thus contributes to pedagogy in an important way. For the purposes of this chapter, however, we are interested in whether it contributes to our understanding of trade wars as they exist in the wild. To be clear, we do not expect the theory to predict the outbreak of a trade war (though we might hope it would point to risk factors), but we would like it to help us understand the appropriate response. In the next section, we briefly discuss some empirics of trade wars. We begin with historical trade wars.

TRADE WARS IN HISTORY

For most of human history, long-distance trade was simply too expensive to constitute a major part of any community's consumption. There was robbery and brigandage, but there is no way to think about trade wars between communities. Eventually, political leaders come to see control over trade as an essential instrument in the conflict between national powers. We tend to associate the link between power and plenty with the mercantilist era (roughly the seventeenth and eighteenth centuries), but the common understanding of that link emerged from a longer process of state building and international political struggle between the emerging European powers. Spain, Portugal, Great Britain, the Netherlands, and France struggled to establish centralized political orders domestically and dominant positions with the emerging international political system. This project required the development of a more centralized state apparatus and significant increases in government revenue to cover the costs of expensive new technologies of war (Mann 1986; Parker 1996; Hoffman, 2015). Control over international trade was widely understood to be an essential part of this struggle (Mann 1986; Ormrod 2003; Findlay and O'Rourke 2007). The control of foreign trade, including the attempt to extract fiscal resources from that trade, involved tariffs, colonies, the chartering of companies of "merchant adventurers," navigation acts, and staple laws. For our purposes, the essential fact, as clearly recognized by the writers in the mercantilist tradition, was that policies had as goals both power and plenty (Viner 1948). There is no obvious way to incorporate trade wars of the mercantilist era into the framework of rational trade wars. This is not to say that we cannot represent revenue maximization as a central part of the objective of these centralizing states; but it was only one component, and often not the most important component, of their "trade policy."[4] Unlike these policies, where trade restrictions were an essential part of a broader geostrategic conflict, we might see the Hawley-Smoot tariffs as a trade war (Kindleberger 1986), but again it is far from clear that rational trade war theory captures much that is essential about this case. By virtually all accounts, these tariffs were a response to macroeconomic conditions in a pre-Keynesian environment where governments lacked instruments for responding to economic downturns (and where they had very little effect; see, e.g., Eichengreen 1992).

Embargoes on all trade, or a substantial share of it, are closely related to these trade policies. Heckscher's (1922) study of the continental system (Napoleon's blockade of continental trade with Great Britain 1806–1814) is a classic. The early United States tried embargoes a number of times during the early Republic (Irwin 2017). Restrictions on trade were an essential part of the Nazi strategy for constructing a continental political economy (Hirschman 1945), and wartime trade was tightly controlled by embargoes (Milward 1977).[5] Embargoes, and other forms of restriction, on trade between East and West were widely practiced during the Cold War (Milward 1984; Hogan 1987; Nelson 1989; Gaddis 2005). Perhaps even more than for the trade wars, embargo policies were driven by military and geostrategic concerns to the exclusion of the sorts of terms-of-trade considerations that underlie the theory of rational trade wars. Embargoes have also been extensively used as instruments of policy between quite asymmetric powers. The archetypal case is embargoes against South Africa, but we see demands for similar policies today in the use of embargoes against Iran and the movement to boycott Israel over its policies toward Palestinians. Most of the sizable literature on these embargoes focuses on the economic effects of the policies, but there is virtually no attempt to analyze optimal policies, in part because the goals are primarily noneconomic.

TRUMP ADMINISTRATION TRADE POLICY: A RATIONAL TRADE WAR?

The United States started raising tariffs on imports in 2018 in a series of policy actions. First, tariffs were increased on imports on steel and aluminum against all trading partners (invoked under section 232 of the Trade Expansion Act). Then tariffs were increased for imports from China in a wide range of sectors (invoked under section 301 of the Trade Act of 1974). From then until now, the United States and China have pursued continuing conflict over a wide range of products (Chad Bown of the Peterson Institute for International Affairs provides continuing updates). In response, various trading partners have raised tariffs on imports from the United States. These events could lead to further tariff increases with a global trade war as a possible outcome. Table 5-1 provides an overview of early tariff measures taken by the United States and its trading partners.

TABLE 5-1. Trade Measures Implemented by the United States and Its Trading Partners, 2018

WTO member	Date imposed	Description of measure	Imports covered (billions of US$)
Canada	July 1	Countermeasures on steel and aluminum products	12.8
China	April 2, 2018	Countermeasures on steel and aluminum products	3.0
	July 6	Reaction to US section 301 of the 1974 Trade Act (first batch, part 1)	31.9
	August 23	Reaction to US section 301 of the 1974 Trade Act (first batch, part 2)	13.3
	September 24	Reaction to US section 301 of the 1974 Trade Act (second batch)	57.7
European Union	June 22	Countermeasures on steel and aluminim products	6.5
Mexico	June 5	Countermeasures on steel and aluminum products	3.6
Russian Federation	July 6	Countermeasures on steel and aluminum products	0.4
Turkey	June 21	Countermeasures on steel and aluminum products	1.8
United States	March 23	National Security Issue (section 232 of the Trade Expansion Act), steel and aluminum	41.2
	July 6	Section 301 of the 1974 Trade Act, against China's unfair trade practices (first Batch, part 1)	31.9
	August 23	Section 301 of the 1974 Trade Act, against China's unfair trade practices (first batch, part 2)	13.1
	September 24	Section 301 of the 1974 Trade Act, against China's unfair trade practices (second batch)	187.8
Total			405.0

Source: Calculated from notifications and WTO Integrated Data Base, https://i-tip.wto.org/goods/default.aspx?language=en.

The government of the United States has motivated the tariff increases in at least three different ways. First, as part of the policy to "Make America Great Again" it aims to bring manufacturing jobs back to the United States, and views imposing tariffs on manufacturing imports as an appropriate tool to do so. Second, the government believes that tariff rates should be reciprocal, meaning that tariff rates at the tariff line level imposed by the United States should be at the same level as tariffs faced by the United States. Third and related, the imbalance between tariffs imposed and tariffs faced is considered an important driver of the US trade deficit. Raising import tariffs on imports in general and on Chinese imports in particular would help reduce the trade deficit in general and the bilateral trade deficit with China in particular. Other factors also play a role in the tariffs imposed on imports from China: the poor protection of intellectual property rights in China, alleged enforced technology transfer of foreign companies investing in China, and the heavy involvement of the Chinese government in its economy through (implicit) subsidization of state-owned companies (SOEs). As a matter of fact, these other factors are the official reasons for the tariffs imposed on China based on section 301 of the 1974 Trade Act.

Most economists dismiss these three main arguments for the tariff increases. Most of the reduction in the manufacturing share of employment can be explained by structural change (lower productivity growth in services combined with a low substitution elasticity between manufacturing and services). Kehoe, Ruhl, and Steinberg (2018) find that only 15 percent of the reduction in the manufacturing share of employment between 1992 and 2012 can be explained by the presence of trade deficits in this period, whereas most of the decline is explained by differential productivity growth. Bekkers (2019) shows in simulations with a dynamic computable general equilibrium (CGE) model that over a twenty-year period tariff increases in a global trade war scenario would not compensate for the decline in US manufacturing as a result of structural change.[6]

Many analysts have pointed out that trade policy is not an appropriate tool to reduce trade imbalances, since these are driven macroeconomic on (public) savings and investment (Obstfeld 2018). Griswold (2019) explains that "reciprocal tariffs"—that is, tariffs imposed by the United States equal to those it faces at the tariff line level—would be at odds with the most favored nation (MFN) principle and would raise the administrative burden of tariff policy considerably. From our perspective, it is striking that such reciprocal tariffs would not be the outcome of a Nash equilibrium in tariffs.

Additional US tariff measures are under discussion in 2019. The US government is considering raising tariffs on imports of cars and car parts (about $300 billion) to 25 percent with the same legal justification as for the steel and aluminum tariffs: national security under section 232 of the Trade Expansion Act. Such tariffs would in turn provoke retaliation. In April 2019 the United States is considering raising tariffs on imports with a value of $11 billion on various products from the European Union as retaliation for the WTO-inconsistent subsidies to Airbus provided by the European Union. This will likely trigger retaliation by the EU on US imports (on import value of $12 billion) because of WTO-inconsistent subsidies to Boeing.

Overall then, although there are many examples of trade wars in the historical record, the theory of rational trade wars would seem to have very little to say about them. The same seems to be true of current trade conflicts. Suppose we approach this a different way: Can the theory of rational trade wars rationalize observed tariff structures between countries? In the next section we briefly review the computational literature on rational trade wars.

COUNTERFACTUAL ANALYSIS OF TRADE WARS

Different models are used for counterfactual analysis of trade wars. The expected effect of the tariff increases in 2018 have been analyzed with three different types of models. First, traditionally computable general equilibrium (CGE) models have been the tool for counterfactual analysis of trade policies and are still widely applied by international institutions and academics. Francois and Baughman (2018), for example, analyze the expected effects of the 232 steel and aluminum tariffs on the US economy, using a short-run approach with sticky wages. Devarajan and others (2018) explore the expected effects of the tariff war between the United States and China on developing countries and the best response of these countries. Bekkers and Teh (2019) project the expected medium-run effects of a global tariff war based on the estimates of the difference between cooperative and noncooperative tariffs as estimated by Nicita, Olarreaga and Silva (2018).

Second, dynamic stochastic general equilibrium (DSGE) models have been used mainly by international institutions and central banks to analyze the macroeconomic effects of tariff increases. The International Monetary Fund (2018), for example, explores five different scenarios in its World Economic Outlook, showing that the GDP of countries in North America would be particularly affected by US car tariffs and retaliation.[7] Third, so-called new quantitative trade (NQT) models have been employed for counterfactual analysis of the potential effects of a trade war. Felbermayr, Steininger, and Yalcin (2017), for example, analyze various potential US trade policy scenarios.

All three types of models are microfounded models handling international trade through the Armington assumption.[8] The DSGE models are dynamic, featuring forward-looking savings and investment behavior, monetary policy, and financial frictions. Most of these features are absent actual social economic accounts, thus capturing intermediate linkages as in the data. The main difference between CGE models and NQT models is that the former include more behavioral parameters taken from the literature, whereas in the NQT-models many choice nests are Cobb-Douglas. CGE models include capital accumulation in a recursive dynamic way. An important difference between DSGE models and CGE and NQT models is the size of the Armington elasticities, which are much lower in the former than in the latter. The three model structures conduct counterfactual analyses of a trade war in a similar way. Tariff-change scenarios are designed based on either actual or expected changes in trade policy and implemented in the models to calculate the counterfactual effects of these scenarios for trade, GDP, other macroeconomic variables and sectoral output and trade effects.

Table 5-2 summarizes the numerical estimations of noncooperative Nash tariffs in the literature. These studies, however, differ widely on model specifications with varying degrees of complexity and data requirements (from $2 \times 2 \times 2$ Heckscher-Ohlin-Samuelson models to complex global multisector multifactor CGE models). The diverse features and parameter values employed in these quantitative trade models, as well as different data years and parties involved in the trade war, can partially explain the wide range of calculated Nash tariffs: from 0 to 160 percent, with a simple mean of around 40 percent. Country size is also important, with larger countries usually having larger Nash tariffs (e.g., the United States against smaller countries).

Tariffs of around 50 percent are usually mentioned as the result of the trade war following the Smoot-Hawley Tariff Act of 1930. The current

TABLE 5-2. Studies Estimating Nash Tariffs

Study	*Parties involved*	*Time period*	*Calculated Nash tariff (%)*	*Simple mean*
Hamilton and Whalley (1983)	2 countries	Analytical	5 to 78	42
Whalley (1985)	2 countries	Analytical	4 to 79	42
Markusen and Wigle (1989)	US and Canada	1977	US: 18; Canada: 6	12
Lee and Roland-Holst (1999)	US and Japan	1985	US: 50; Japan: 40	45
Perroni and Whalley (2000)	7 OECD countries	1986	64 to 161	113
Ossa (2011)	7 global regions	2004	10 to 29	20
Whalley, Yu, and Zhang (2012)	China and RoW	2005	0 to 33	17
Ossa (2014)	7 global regions	2007	55 to 77	66
Balistreri and Hillberry (2017)	US, Mexico, and China	2011	US/Mexico: 12 /6; US/China: 11/–5	6
He and others (2017)	US, EU, China, and RoW[a]	2013	68 to 104	87
Bouët and Laborde (2018)	US, Mexico, and China	2011	US/Mexico: 14/9, US/China: 7/3, US/Mexico/ China: 10/10/3	8
Bekkers and others (2019)	US and RoW	2014	10 to 34	22

[a] He and others (2017) model each country separately with the RoW (i.e., US-RoW, EU-RoW, China-RoW).

Note: RoW = rest of the world.

(ongoing) US-China tariff escalation has so far resulted in tariffs of around 12 percent (in trade-weighted terms). At least for the current case, then, these estimates of Nash equilibrium tariffs seem quite high, though the actual tariffs could easily get much larger. The large range of estimated Nash tariffs hinders the practical political and empirical use of these estimates (unless a comprehensive assessment of these studies narrows the tariff range to comply with common best-practice modeling standards).

WHAT WENT WRONG? AUDITING RATIONAL TRADE WAR THEORY

Counterfactual methods, as an application of standard trade theory, have proven their value in the positive analysis of trade policy. The same is true of econometric studies of trade flows based on those theories. So, what goes wrong when we turn to the analysis of optimal policies (nonstrategic or strategic)? In this section, we consider two sorts of problems: those deriving from the complexity of the policy environment, and those deriving from the lack of a clear objective function for the policymaker.

We have already quoted Murray Kemp on the complexity behind the apparent simplicity of the standard 2-good × 2-country optimal tariff. Things get even trickier when we turn to the case of many goods.[9] Formally characterizing the n-good optimal tariff schedule is not much more difficult than the 2-good case.[10] Unfortunately, actually calculating such a thing is problematic. First, it is a standard result that, with many goods, the tariff structure is not unique, but depends on which good is taken as the *numeraire* (Horwell and Pearce 1970). Perhaps most important, although the formulas for optimal tariffs look straightforward and easy to interpret, they rely on information about cross elasticities that, as a practical matter, policymakers simply do not possess.[11] It is important to recall here Kemp's reminder that these elasticities depend on the equilibrium (i.e., they are not usually constants). Much current theoretical work in fact adopts assumptions that ensure that this problem does not arise (e.g., quasilinear preferences and a production structure featuring specific factors in all sectors except the *numeraire* sector, which is a freely traded Ricardian sector). This is a perfectly reasonable practice when developing a model for illustrative purposes, but when it comes to empirical and policy analysis, this is a much harder claim to accept.[12]

These problems get worse when we turn to strategic analysis. Now, even abstracting from the nonuniqueness problem, the elasticity information will depend on the Nash equilibrium. But note that both governments (in the two-country case) must have global elasticity information about both countries so that they can identify the equilibrium tariff vectors. Of course, it is also the case that there are many, even many large, countries. Most countries work with a single tariff schedule applied to major trading partners (this is the upshot of the generalized MFN treatment that is one of the core commitments of WTO members).[13] Unless the underlying economy supports representation of that multicountry game as an aggregative game (Acemoglu and Jensen 2013; Camacho, Kamihigashi, and Sağlam 2018), the optimal policy would involve multiple tariff rates and the constrained optimal single-schedule tariff would be, understating considerably, very difficult to calculate.

The other major problem has to do with the objective function of the government. *Optimal* tariff theory requires such an objective function to give meaning to "optimal." In all textbook presentations of the theory, and most research on the subject, this objective is something called "national welfare," and that's fine for textbooks. In those presentations, confusion is eliminated by assuming that there is an unambiguous representative agent. As often as not, we simply assume that there is a well-behaved (Bergson-Samuelson) social welfare function.[14] An alternative is to assume that the structure of the economy is such that there is a positive representative agent. This usually involves assuming some version of Gorman polar form preferences (commonly identical homothetic or quasilinear). If we also assume that the government has a utilitarian social welfare function, so there are no distributional preferences, we also get a normative representative agent and our analysis proceeds without problem. Unfortunately, these assumptions are spectacularly unrealistic, and under any other assumptions the social welfare function requires ongoing redistribution to support welfare maximization.

When we move away from positive representative agents to economies characterized by even minimally realistic taste heterogeneity among households, things get worse rapidly. Interestingly, this was seen as a key issue in the modern analysis of optimal tariffs and rational trade wars.[15] The problem from a positive perspective is that demand is sensitive to income distribution, so calculation of optimal tariffs requires information about income distribution (and household preferences). That is, as Kemp already noted for the 2×2 case, there is an infinity of optimal tariffs depending on the income distribution. From a normative perspective, as we just noted, redistributive policy is necessary to underwrite the existence of a coherent social welfare function. What is a problem for welfare analysis is the foundation of political-economic analysis. The usual motivation for political economic analysis is a loosely empirical claim that the existing tariff structure of an economy cannot be rationalized by optimization of social welfare. This, in turn, implies that the income distribution does not reflect any welfare optimization. However, when we turn to optimal tariff theory, once we leave the world of identical Gorman polar form preferences, the determination of the tariff structure by political action is exceptionally unlikely to yield aggregate policy preferences with any particular properties. That is, political economy takes the problems associated with heterogeneous preferences and magnifies them by providing an additional source of distortion in aggregate preferences. To make much analytical progress, then, requires a set of fairly strong (i.e., wildly counterfactual) assumptions.

Where taste and endowment heterogeneity means that we might not have a very good sense of what the objective function is for the single country whose tariff vector we want to evaluate for its consistency with the optimum, this is considerably more important in the case of Nash equilibrium tariffs. That is, not only must the analyst be confident that she knows the nature of a government's objective function, but more important, each of the governments (in the two-country case) must know the objective function of the other government. If that is not the case, and even if the government knows its own objective function, neither can solve the (already quite complicated) overall system for the Nash equilibrium.[16] As in the single-country case, these problems are made worse by the fact that the government objective function includes more than simple welfare optimization (whatever that might mean).

The issues deriving from heterogeneity carry over to the analysis of politics as an input to the objective function of trade policymakers in trade wars. The assumptions necessary to illustrate the interaction of domestic politics with a broad commitment to social welfare (Grossman and Helpman 1995; Bagwell and Staiger 2002) are even more severe when we want to build game-theoretic interaction on top of the domestic political analysis. As in the previous point, all players need to know the objective functions of all the players (or at least the distribution over the types of players). Quick reality check: What do we think is the objective function of the Trump administration on trade policy? What was it during the administration of UK prime minister Theresa May?

While the game theoretic analysis has provided greater clarity in the interpretation of the modern theory of rational trade wars, it also raises difficulties that were not recognized in the earlier literature. We will note two: existence; and multiple equilibria. John Nash was not awarded the Nobel Prize for characterizing what we now call "Nash equilibrium," which is essentially a straightforward extension of rationality to a strategic environment, but for proving that such an equilibrium exists under quite general conditions. Technically, a Nash equilibrium is a fixed point of a set of mappings representing the optimizing behavior of all the players (Nash 1951). As long as the mappings derived from the underlying economy satisfy the conditions required by the appropriate fixed-point theorem, we can be sure that an equilibrium exists. Otherwise not. If an equilibrium cannot be shown to exist, not only is it not clear what we are talking about when we talk about Nash equilibrium tariff schedules, but any comparative static analysis would seem to lack clear foundations. Thus the question is whether we can be confident that, given an underlying economy, an equilibrium in tariff schedules exists.

Existence for the case of 2 countries × 2 goods is relatively straightforward. Wong (2004) presents a careful analysis of the 2-country × 2-good case. In this, as in the more general case, the key is the structure of the reaction function (surface), alternatively the curvature of the offer curve (surface), and the difficulty is that these are affected by tariffs.[17] This difficulty becomes all the more severe when there are many goods. As a result, all of the attempts to prove existence of a Nash equilibrium in tariffs for the many-goods case adopt quite special assumptions either on the space of strategies (Kuga 1973), preferences of the representative agent (Kim and Roush 1988), or the "beliefs" of the policy authority about the underlying economy (Otani 1980). None of these scholars' arguments increase our confidence that we can expect a Nash equilibrium in tariff schedules to exist generically.

Suppose we can be sure that an equilibrium exists, can we be sure that that equilibrium is unique? Debreu (1970) showed long ago that uniqueness was not necessary for analyzing the general equilibrium of an economy. However, the situation in game theory is very different. The whole point of an equilibrium is that it is a set of behaviors that is consistent— each player is playing her part in a self-enforcing solution to a strategic situation. If there are multiple equilibria, in which players' parts in those equilibria differ, not only does the model not predict a specific outcome, but the observed behavior is not even equilibrium behavior with strictly positive probability.[18] Contemporary game theoretic research approaches this issue via refinements and equilibrium selection. These turn on stories about how participants view deviations from predicted behavior off the equilibrium path (trembles, mistakes, incorrect or different theories of the strategic situation, signaling—see, e.g., Kreps 1989) and theories that attempt to provide more complete models of agent reasoning (Perea 2012; Brandenburger 2014). Because the applied literature on trade wars virtually always assumes a unique equilibrium, these issues do not arise. However, given the likelihood of multiple (or no) equilibria in even modestly general trade war games, thinking more systematically about what political leaders think they are doing is surely a high-payoff exercise.

Our review of the results from attempts to calculate optimal and Nash optimal tariffs, and recalling all of the caveats that surround such analysis, suggest that observed tariffs are far lower than what the models suggest. This is actually the opening wedge for a claim that this literature successfully accounts for observed behavior. Considering the Nash optimal tariff as the reversion point of a failed attempt to liberalize trade between national economies, there are a variety of ways of accounting for cooperation. The easiest simply assumes that countries are able to commit to binding agreements to liberalize trade and applies one or another of the cooperative solutions (Mayer 1981; Riezman 1982). The difficulty with this analysis, for all that the results appear more consonant with existing low levels of protection, is that there is no real account of implementation. In the face of the trade policies of Trump and May, it is very hard to keep a straight face and talk about binding trade agreements. An alternative is to consider repeated interaction and consider the variety of ways that open the door to cooperation. Unfortunately, all of this analysis is based on Nash equilibria in even more demanding environments than the one-shot analyses that yield the trade war equilibria. That is, all of the problems that we have discussed to this point apply to these analyses.

CONCLUSION: WHAT DO WE LEARN ABOUT TRUMP TRADE WARS FROM RATIONAL TRADE WARS?

We might start with the warning of David Kreps, who argues that:

> Any formal, mathematical theory is applied to a model of a given situation. This model will at best be an approximation to the situation.

It is therefore crucial to have a sense—intuitive if need be but better if buttressed by theory—of when the conclusions of the theory turn on features of the model about which the model-builder is fairly uncertain. In such cases one trusts the conclusions of the theory at great peril. (Kreps 1990, 123)

So (rational theory of trade) "War, what is it good for?" To quote Edwin Starr, in the Motown classic penned by Norman Whitfield and Barrett Strong: "absolutely nothing." Even if the idea of a (positive and normative) representative agent made sense, and even if some possible government were willing to act on the preferences of that agent, and even if that government possessed the knowledge of the economy necessary to calculate an optimal tariff for itself, and even if it possessed similar knowledge about its trading partners so that it could calculate its part of a Nash equilibrium (in confidence that all other governments were doing the same, and in confidence that they were all coordinated on the same Nash equilibrium, which is taken to exist), we would have to believe that all of these things applied, at least approximately, to some specific set of existing countries in some specific interaction. Without *all* of these things being true, the idea of an actually existing Nash equilibrium tariff schedule is literally nonsense. So, as a practical matter, the theory of rational trade wars cannot tell us about actually existing trade wars. Perhaps more important, the notion that it tells us anything about the trade policy of the Trump administration toward, say, China (or Europe, or its NAFTA partners) literally beggars belief.

Our discussion to this point has been pretty relentlessly negative. Does this mean that we believe that the collective efforts of first-rate economists who developed the theory of optimal tariffs and its extension to the theory of rational trade wars was a waste of quality effort? No. The purpose of some theory is to provide a first-order framework for understanding policy decisions and their effects, but it is the purpose of other theory to provide a meta-analytic framework for organizing our thoughts about more complex situations. The theory of economic policy of which the theory of optimal tariffs can be seen as a part (e.g., Johnson 1963; Bhagwati 1971; Corden 1997) is an example of the second sort of theory. Simple, low-dimensional, transparently "unrealistic" theory can help us quickly develop a first response to a complex situation because the various components have proved to be a robust framework for doing such a calculation. Our confidence in such a framework flows from confidence in its internal coherence and in its ability to represent precisely the causal relations that we suspect to be of first-order importance. Low-dimensional general equilibrium theory plays an essential role in this sort of theory. One of the easiest things to forget when doing policy analysis is the way general equilibrium effects can interfere with partial equilibrium intuition. Training ourselves in general equilibrium helps us guard against making this mistake. Similarly, we remind ourselves to think like economists about trade wars by using the theory of rational trade wars as a lens, or the back of an envelope, when we start our thinking about the issue. In any given case, one or another of the elements that we have simplified away will strike us as particularly important for further thought. And it is to such an area that we apply tools of detailed formal and statistical analysis.

In the case of the current trade policy of the Trump administration, the most difficult issue would seem to be figuring out what the president, and what for want of a better term we will call "advisers," are using for an objective function. Clearly not among them are: social welfare (however we might want to define that); reelection maximization as represented in standard political economy forces (to the extent that we can tell, the distribution of costs and benefits seems all wrong for that); and pursuit of geostrategic goals (the policies seem too collectively incoherent to reflect such goals). At this point, we seem to fall back on personal psychology, an area in which, as economists, we are manifestly unqualified.

A minimum necessary condition to have any hope of prosecuting a trade war rationally is that there be clarity on the objective. The helter-skelter nature of US trade policy under President Trump makes it difficult, if not impossible, to determine what the goal is. The president has urged US companies to pull back investment in, sourcing from, and sales to China. If that is the objective, then high and persistent tariffs may make some sense. But in the next breath the president expresses optimism that the two sides will reach a deal in which China opens more markets and lowers trade and investment barriers—in which case there will be much more exchange between the two, including outward investment by US companies. The phase 1 deal agreed between China and the United States at the end of 2019 is mostly mercantilist, centered on Chinese promises to significantly increase imports from the United States. It may be that this was the main goal of the president. It is certainly not the goal of US businesses, who are looking for structural reforms in China.

To finish on a positive note: nothing in this chapter should be seen as a criticism of the positive analysis of trade policy and its effects. The tools, theoretical, computational, and econometric, with which we evaluate the effects of trade policy on national income, the distribution of national income, growth, and other outcomes, remain useful. To develop our analysis with direct application to the current situation, we could do what the mercantilists did and seek to provide practical advice based on our understanding of the politics of the situation and the psychology of Donald Trump. Alternatively, we could follow the example of analysts like Harry Johnson, who used a variety of simple models, along with practical information about the current situation, to build up an account of the incentives in that situation and the appropriate responses. Both approaches involve story-telling, and the validity of those stories rests very strongly on the facts of the matter that flesh out the story, but only the latter approach reveals the analytical structure of the story.

NOTES

The project to which this chapter contributes has received funding from the European Union's Horizon 2020 research and innovation program under grant agreement no 770680.

1. To return to analogy with heart attacks and earthquakes, we believe it is the case that we can study the effects of a trade war on such things as national income and its distribution. That is, the tools we have developed for positive analysis do not fail simply because our normative analysis fails.

2. We distinguish between "modern" and "contemporary" theory of rational trade wars primarily on two related grounds: explicit attention to the contents of the objective function of the state; and the explicit use of game theoretic tools. The modern theory is concerned with the former and, mostly, was applied before the game theory revolution of the 1980s; the contemporary theory treats the objective function as unproblematic and uses game theoretic tools extensively. Our paper "Rational Trade Wars and Stupid Trade Disputes" (Bekker and others 2019b) provides a detailed survey of these, as well as earlier, bodies of research on trade wars.

3. Later analyses argue that quota wars tend asymptotically to autarky, so both countries must lose from a trade war pursued with quotas (Rodriguez

1974; Tower 1975). However, Falvey (1985) argues that the tendency to autarky is produced by an unrealistically strong assumption on the distribution of quota rents.

4. It should be clear that there was no notion whatever of welfare maximization at this time. Thus the objective function of optimal tariff theory is clearly inappropriate for this period.

5. For the long view, see Davis and Engerman (2006).

6. In the global trade war scenario, tariffs would rise by about 32 percent on average based on the estimates of the difference between cooperative and noncooperative tariffs in Nicita, Olarreaga, and Silva (2018). In this scenario, US tariffs would increase by about 60 percent on average.

7. Most central banks have open economy DSGE models, which can be employed to study the repercussions of trade war scenarios. Two such studies have been conducted by Dizioli and Van Roye (2018) and Bolt, Mavromatis, and Van Wijnbergen (2019).

8. New quantitative trade models often use the Eaton and Kortum specification. However, as shown in the literature in reduced form Eaton and Kortum and Armington are equivalent. See for example, Arkolakis, Costinot, and Rodríguez-Clare (2012) or Bekkers and Francois (2016).

9. According the US Census Bureau website (https://www.census.gov/econ/overview/mt0100.html), there are "more than 18,000 import commodity codes." For our purposes, we need not get into the question of whether goods are homogeneous within each of these codes, as they would need to be for a single tariff per trading partner to be applied on a tariff line.

10. The first to present the n-good case was Graaff (1949), but it is also clearly presented in many advanced textbooks (e.g., Kemp 1969; Dixit and Norman 1980; Woodland 1982).

11. If we take 18,000 as the number of goods, the trade policy authority would need 18,000 direct elasticities and something like $(18,000 \times 18,000) - 18,000 = 323,982,000$ cross elasticities. It should be clear that these data do not exist.

12. Graaf's (1949, 54) warning that "to neglect [cross-elasticities] is to commit the unjustifiable act of carrying over into general equilibrium analysis assumptions appropriate to partial equilibrium analysis only" is particularly important in this context. Of course, computational analysis just generates these elasticities mechanically.

13. There are, of course, a variety of details. However, neither special and differential treatment nor administered protection seems to be an essential part of the strategic component of trade policy that the Nash equilibrium tariff schedule seeks to characterize.

14. From here any reference to a "social welfare function" should be understood to refer to a Bergson-Samuelson social welfare function.

15. The modern period in trade policy analysis is coextensive with the development of "the new welfare economics," and many of the same researchers were actively involved in both literatures (e.g., Kaldor, Scitovsky, Samuelson, Baldwin, Johnson). This is not surprising given that the new welfare economics grew out of attempts to answer Lionel Robbins's (1938) question about the validity of welfare claims, illustrated by the case of gains from trade.

16. The issue here is not uncertainty about one's opponent. As long as the types of governments (i.e., their objective functions and any other behavioral information relevant to calculating equilibrium strategies) and the distribution of those types is known, identifying optimal strategies is a well-understood problem. The issue here is that it may not be possible to know the type-space. Neither is it the point that governments are not rational (though that is something of an open question); it is that governments do not possess the knowledge or capacity to act rationally in the sense required here. Since we presume that both governments know this, it is far from clear how we are to interpret behavior that appears consistent with any theory of strategically rational behavior. Thus, if we want to understand the behavior of, say, the Trump (or Carter, or Reagan, or Bush, or Clinton, or Bush, or Obama) administration's trade policy it is not clear what the theory of Nash trade wars does for us. Given substantial differences in core constituency, ideology, context, and other factors, the problem is even worse if we want to account for continuities, or discontinuities, across these administrations. We can, and should and do, calculate or "estimate" such equilibria based on more-or-less explicit assumptions permitting such work, but when we do, as we do in our related work, we should be as clear as possible how we are filling in these huge gaps and what that means for our conclusions.

17. This is why Johnson (1953–54) ultimately focuses on constant elasticity offer curves, and many analyses since Johnson have done the same. Wong (2004, Lemma 1) shows that, if both offer curves are convex, a Nash equilibrium in tariffs exists. Unfortunately, this condition is far from generic even in the 2×2 case. Thus, Wong's analysis focuses on homothetic (Theorem 1) and quasi-linear (Theorem 2) preferences of the countries' representative agents.

18. That is, with multiple equilibria, one possibility is that agents randomize over the strategies that they play in some equilibrium (they play a "mixed strategy").

REFERENCES

Acemoglu, Daron, and Martin Kaae Jensen. 2013. "Aggregate Comparative Statics." *Games and Economic Behavior* 81: 27–49.

Arkolakis, Costas, Arnaud Costinot, and Andrés Rodríguez-Clare. 2012. "New Trade Models, Same Old Gains?" *American Economic Review* 102: 94–130.

Bagwell, Kyle, and Robert W. Staiger. 2002. *The Economics of the World Trading System*. MIT Press.

Balistreri, Edward J., and Russell H. Hillberry. 2017. "21st Century Trade Wars." Twentieth Global Trade Analysis (GTAP) Conference, Purdue University.

Bekkers, Eddy. 2019. "Challenges to the Trade System: The Potential Impact of Changes in Future Trade Policy." *Journal of Policy Modeling* 41 (3): 489–506.

Bekkers, Eddy, and Joseph Francois. 2016. "Incorporating Modern Trade Theory into CGE Models." *GTAP Resource* No. 5093.

Bekkers, Eddy, and Robert Teh. 2019. "Potential Economic Effects of a Global Trade Conflict—Projecting the Medium-Run Effects with the WTO Global Trade Model." Working Paper. Geneva: World Trade Organization.

Bekkers, Eddy, and others. 2019a. "Trade Wars and Trade Disputes: The Role of Equity and Political Support." Working Paper. Bern: World Trade Institute.

Bekkers, Eddy, and others. 2019b. "Rational Trade Wars and Stupid Trade Disputes." Working Paper. Bern: World Trade Institute.

Bhagwati, Jagdish N. 1971. "The Generalized Theory of Distortions and Welfare." In *Trade, Balance of Payments and Growth*, edited by J. N. Bhagwati and others, 69–90. Amsterdam: North-Holland.

Bolt, Wilko, Kostas Mavromatis, and Sweder van Wijnbergen. 2019. "The Global Macroeconomics of a Trade War: The Eagle Model on the US-China Trade Conflict." CEPR Discussion Paper No. DP13495, January.

Bouët, Antoine, and David Laborde. 2018. "U.S/ Trade Wars in the Twenty-First Century with Emerging Countries: Make America and Its Partners Lose Again." *World Economy* 41 (9): 2276–2319.

Brandenburger, Adam. 2014. *The Language of Game Theory: Putting Epistemics into the Mathematics of Games*. Singapore: World Scientific Publishing.

Camacho, Carmen, Takashi Kamihigashi, and Çağrı Sağlam. 2018. "Robust Comparative Statics for Non-Monotone Shocks in Large Aggregative Games." *Journal of Economic Theory* 174 (March): 288–99.

Cooper, Richard N. 1972. "Trade Policy Is Foreign Policy." *Foreign Policy* 9 (Winter): 18–36.

Corden, W. Max. 1997. *Trade Policy and Economic Welfare*. Oxford University Press.

Davis, Lance E., and Stanley L. Engerman. 2006. *Naval Blockades in Peace and War: An Economic History since 1750*. Cambridge University Press.

Debreu, Gerard. 1970. "Economies with a Finite Set of Equilibria." *Econometrica* 38 (3): 387–92.

Devarajan, Shantayanan, and others. 2018. "Traders' Dilemma: Developing Countries' Response to Trade Disputes." Policy Research Working Paper. Washington, D.C.: World Bank.

Dixit, Avinash K., and Victor D. Norman. 1980. *Theory of International Trade: A Dual, General Equilibrium Approach.* Cambridge University Press.

Dizioli, Allan Gloe and Björn Van Roye (2018). "Macroeconomic Implications of Increasing Protectionism." *ECB Economic Bulletin*, 6/2018.

Eichengreen, Barry. 1992. *Golden Fetters: The Gold Standard and the Great Depression, 1919–1939.* Oxford University Press.

Falvey, Rodney E. 1985. "Quotas and Retaliation: A Re-Examination." *Economics Letters* 17 (4): 373–77.

Felbermayr, Gabriel, Marina Steininger, and Erdal Yalcin. 2017. "Quantifying Trump: The Costs of a Protectionist US" *CESifo Forum* 18 (4): 28–36.

Findlay, Ronald, and Kevin H. O'Rourke. 2007. *Power and Plenty: Trade, War, and the World Economy in the Second Millennium.* Princeton University Press.

Francois, Joseph, and Laura Baughman. 2018. "Does Import Protection Save Jobs? The Estimated Impacts of Proposed Tariffs on Imports of US Steel and Aluminum." www.tradepartnership.com.

Gaddis, John Lewis. 2005. *Strategies of Containment: A Critical Appraisal of American National Security Policy during the Cold War.* Oxford University Press.

Graaff, Johannes de V. 1949. "On Optimum Tariff Structures." *Review of Economic Studies* 17 (1): 47–59.

Griswold, Daniel. 2019. "Mirror, Mirror, on the Wall: The Danger of Imposing 'Reciprocal' Tariff Rates." Working Paper. Arlington, VA: Mercatus Center, George Mason University.

Grossman, Gene M., and Elhanan Helpman. 1995. "Trade Wars and Trade Talks." *Journal of Political Economy* 103 (4): 675–708.

Hamilton, Bob, and John Whalley. 1983. "Optimal Tariff Calculations in Alternative Trade Models and Some Possible Implications for Current World Trading Arrangements." *Journal of International Economics* 15 (3): 323–48.

He, Chuantian, and others. 2017. "The Armington Assumption and the Size of Optimal Tariffs." *Economic Modelling* 66 (November): 214–22.

Heckscher, Eli F. 1922. *The Continental System: An Economic Interpretation.* Oxford: Clarendon Press.

Hirschman, Albert O. 1945. *National Power and the Structure of Foreign Trade.* University of California Press.

Hoffman, Philip T. 2015. *Why Did Europe Conquer the World?* Princeton University Press.

Hogan, Michael J. 1987. *The Marshall Plan: America, Britain, and the Reconstruction of Western Europe, 1947–1952.* Cambridge University Press.

Horwell, David J., and Ivor F. Pearce. 1970. "A Look at the Structure of Optimal Tariff Rates." *International Economic Review* 11 (1): 147–61.

International Monetary Fund (IMF). 2018. *World Economic Outlook, October 2018. Challenges to Steady Growth.* Washington, D.C.: IMF.

Irwin, Douglas A. 2017. *Clashing over Commerce: A History of US Trade Policy.* University of Chicago Press.

Johnson, Harry G. 1953. "Optimum Tariffs and Retaliation." *Review of Economic Studies* 21 (2): 142–53.

———. 1963. "Optimal Trade Intervention in the Presence of Domestic Distortions." In *Trade, Growth, and the Balance of Payments*, edited by R. E. Baldwin and others, 3–34. Chicago: Rand McNally.

Kehoe, Timothy, Kim Ruhl, and Joseph Steinberg. 2018. "Global Imbalances and Structural Change in the United States." *Journal of Political Economy* 126 (2): 761–96.

Kemp, Murray C. 1969. *The Pure Theory of International Trade and Investment.* Englewood Cliffs, N.J.: Prentice-Hall.

Kim, K. H., and F. W. Roush. 1988. "Strategic Tariff Equilibrium and Optimal Tariffs." *Mathematical Social Sciences* 15 (2): 105–34.

Kindleberger, Charles Poor. 1986. *The World in Depression, 1929–1939.* University of California Press.

Kreps, David M. 1989. "Out-of-Equilibrium Beliefs and Out-of-Equilibrium Behavior." In *The Economics of Missing Markets, Information, and Games*, edited by F. Hahn, 7–45. Oxford University Press.

———. 1990. *Game Theory and Economic Modelling.* Oxford University Press.

Kuga, Kiyoshi. 1973. "Tariff Retaliation and Policy Equilibrium." *Journal of International Economics* 3 (4): 351–66.

Lee, Hiro, and David Roland-Holst. 1999. "Cooperation or Confrontation in US–Japan Trade? Some General Equilibrium Estimates." *Journal of the Japanese and International Economies* 13 (2): 119–39.

Mann, Michael. 1986. *The Sources of Social Power.* Vol. 1: *A History of Power from the Beginning to A.D. 1760.* Cambridge University Press.

Markusen, James R., and Randall M. Wigle. 1989. "Nash Equilibrium Tariffs for the United States and Canada: The Roles of Country Size, Scale Economies, and Capital Mobility." *Journal of Political Economy* 97 (2): 368–86.

Mayer, Wolfgang. 1981. "Theoretical Considerations on Negotiated Tariff Adjustments." *Oxford Economic Papers* 33 (1): 135–53.

Milward, Alan S. 1977. *War, Economy, and Society, 1939–1945*. University of California Press.

———. 1984. *The Reconstruction of Western Europe, 1945–51*. University of California Press.

Nash, John. 1951. "Non-Cooperative Games." *Annals of Mathematics* 54 (2): 286–95.

Nelson, Douglas R. 1989. "The Domestic Political Preconditions of US Trade Policy: Liberal Structure and Protectionist Dynamics." *Journal of Public Policy* 9 (1): 83–108.

Nicita, Alessandro, Marcelo Olarreaga, and Peri Silva. 2018. "Cooperation in WTO's Tariff Waters?" *Journal of Political Economy* 126 (3): 1302–38.

Obstfeld, Maurice. 2018. "Targeting Specific Trade Deficits Is a Game of Whack-a-Mole" *Financial Times*, April 22.

Ormrod, David. 2003. *The Rise of Commercial Empires: England and the Netherlands in the Age of Mercantilism, 1650–1770*. Cambridge University Press.

Osborne, Martin J. 2004. *An Introduction to Game Theory*. Oxford University Press.

Otani, Yoshihiko. 1980. "Strategic Equilibrium of Tariffs and General Equilibrium." *Econometrica* 48 (3): 643–62.

Parker, Geoffrey. 1996. *The Military Revolution: Military Innovation and the Rise of the West, 1500–1800*. Cambridge University Press.

Perea, Andres. 2012. *Epistemic Game Theory: Reasoning and Choice*. Cambridge University Press.

Perroni, Carlo, and John Whalley. 2000. "The New Regionalism: Trade Liberalization or Insurance?" *Canadian Journal of Economics/Revue canadienne d'économique* 33 (1): 1–24.

Riezman, Raymond. 1982. "Tariff Retaliation from a Strategic Viewpoint." *Southern Economic Journal* 48 (3): 583–93.

Robbins, Lionel. 1938. "Interpersonal Comparisons of Utility: A Comment." *Economic Journal* 48 (192): 635–41.

Rodriguez, Carlos Alfredo. 1974. "The Non-Equivalence of Tariffs and Quotas under Retaliation." *Journal of International Economics* 4 (3): 295–98.

Scitovsky, Tibor. 1942. "A Reconsideration of the Theory of Tariffs." *Review of Economic Studies* 9 (2): 89–110.

Tower, Edward. 1975. "The Optimum Quota and Retaliation." *Review of Economic Studies* 42 (4): 623–30.

Viner, Jacob. 1948. "Power versus Plenty as Objectives of Foreign Policy in the Seventeenth and Eighteenth Centuries." *World Politics* 1(1): 1–29.

Whalley, John. 1985. "Optimal Tariffs, Retaliation and Trade Wars." In *Trade Liberalization among Major World Trading Areas*, 231–49. MIT Press.

Whalley, John, Jun Yu, and Shunming Zhang. 2012. "Trade Retaliation in a Monetary-Trade Model." *Global Economy Journal* 12 (1): 1–29.

Wong, Siu-kee. 2004. "Existence of Trading Nash Equilibrium in Tariff Retaliation Models." *Mathematical Social Sciences* 47 (3): 367–87.

Woodland, Alan D. 1982. *International Trade and Resource Allocation.* Amsterdam: North-Holland.

6

"WE CAN ALSO DO STUPID"

THE EU RESPONSE TO "AMERICA FIRST" PROTECTIONISM

SIMON EVENETT

The title of this chapter was part of a warning by European Commission President Jean-Claude Juncker delivered on March 3, 2018, one week before President Donald Trump issued a proclamation imposing tariffs on imported steel and aluminum. The full quote is: "So now we will also impose import tariffs. This is basically a stupid process, the fact that we have to do this. But we have to do it. We will now impose tariffs on motorcycles, Harley Davidson, on blue jeans, Levis, on Bourbon. We can also do stupid. We also have to be this stupid."[1]

After Trump campaigned on a platform of America First, it was inevitable that questions would arise whether, once installed in the White House, he would follow through with this confrontational approach to international trade relations.[2] After all, albeit with a different style, President Barack Obama had been critical of trade deals signed by his predecessors but, upon assuming office, adopted a less critical tone toward America's trading partners. In retrospect, Trump's emphasis in 2017 on getting his Cabinet nominated and confirmed, attempting unsuccessfully to repeal Obama's health care legislation (widely known as Obamacare), and enacting wide-ranging tax reforms, left some observers with the impression that, like his predecessors, Trump's protectionist instincts were no more than a campaign ploy.

In fact, the Trump administration used 2017 to plant the seeds of the protectionism that was to come in 2018 by initiating a number of investigations and reviews. The bitter fruit that resulted has since been causing indigestion in capitals around the world, in particular in governments that have traditionally supported a rules-based multilateral trading system. Coming on top of a World Trade Organization (WTO) weakened by the failure to complete the Doha Round of multilateral trade negotiations, fears arose that a meaningful pillar of the postwar economic order is under serious threat. Since the implementation of tariff hikes on US exports, China is arguably a bigger target of American ire than the European Union. Still, President Trump and his officials have bitterly criticized the goods trade imbalance between the EU and the United States and the 10 percent import tariff on cars imported into the EU, as well as characterizing the EU as having much more protectionist policies. To such critics, the EU's fine words about multilateralism are just that—rhetoric belied by experience on the ground.[3] The EU has both a direct stake, and an indirect systemic stake, in current US trade policy.

There was no shortage of advice to European policymakers on how best to react to America First protectionism. Jean, Martin, and Sapir (2018) recommend a response that blends "firm and credible" retaliation with the offer of multilateral or plurilateral talks on macroeconomic imbalances, enhanced WTO dispute settlement, stronger rules on subsidies and intellectual property rights, as well as new rules on state-owned enterprises, environmental protection and global warming, and tax evasion and optimization. For Pisani-Ferry (2018) the current transatlantic tensions, which relate to defense as well as to trade policy, mark a pivotal moment for the EU. Having thrived under the umbrella of postwar US institutions, the EU must define its "strategic stance *vis-à-vis* a more distant and possibly hostile United States, and *vis-à-vis* rising powers that have no reason to be kind to it. It must stand for its values." Demertzis (2018) advocates that the EU match US threats and tariffs, in order to demonstrate to the Americans the lose-lose nature of protectionism. In contrast, Beattie (2018a) argues that "matching Mr. Trump tariff for tariff will at some point become counterproductive. If the United States no longer wishes to anchor the world economy, it may be better for other governments to get on and supplant it rather than using trade restrictions to try to force it back to its former role." Later he poured cold water on the prospects of the European Commission concluding the trade talks called for by Presidents Juncker and Trump in July 2018 on terms acceptable to the European Union (Beattie 2018b). Dadush and Wolff (2019) see a broader "trade crisis," of which America First policies are one (admittedly important) component. They advance a plan A whose goal is to preserve the multilateral trading system. In their view this would involve the EU revisiting the "red lines" in sensitive areas, such as agriculture (a step they argue would facilitate bilateral talks with the United States as well), and macroeconomic reforms in EU member states running large current account surpluses. Should plan A fail and the multilateral trading system fragment into blocs, then a plan B would be needed, in which separate bilateral negotiations with China and the United States would be envisaged.

The purpose of this chapter is to characterize and evaluate how the European Commission, acting on behalf of the European Union, has reacted to the provocative trade policy actions taken by the Trump administration during 2018 and 2019. These matters are of interest not only for what they reveal about how the EU attempts to defend its commercial interests when under pressure, but also because (at this time of writing in 2020) further American protectionism cannot be ruled out. The world trading system— still put on a pedestal as an example of well-functioning global governance by many scholars[4]—looks very different now than two years ago. That alone says something about the robustness of the current arrangements and, by implication, about the need to reform them.

I begin this chapter by characterizing the four pillars of the America First trade policy of the Trump administration. As that policy has been implemented, many of the United States' trading partners, including the European Union, have responded using the classic playbook for dealing with American trade discrimination. I reprise that playbook here, its apparent logic and, more important, the weaknesses in that logic. As the playbook had evidently failed by mid-2018, a closer look at the actions taken by the European Commission is warranted. These actions inform my assessment of the European Commission's approach under President Juncker.

THE FOUR PILLARS OF THE AMERICA FIRST TRADE POLICY OF THE UNITED STATES

In addition to annual trade policy agenda documents (released in March of each year), the Trump administration issued a National Security Strategy in December 2017 that had a substantial trade policy component. While some may be tempted to divine the "real" strategy underlying the Trump administration's America First trade policy from these documents, on the principle that "actions speak louder than words," another approach is to focus on the trade policy steps taken since Trump was inaugurated in January 2017.

Those steps can be assembled into four groups—each constituting a different pillar of the America First strategy (see table 6-1). Reflecting the different types of trade policy, there is a multilateral pillar, a preferential trade pillar, a bilateral pillar specifically focusing on trade relations with China, and a unilateral pillar. In addition to the usual drumroll of trade remedy cases, the last pillar includes unilateral acts based on investigations into whether different types of imports constitute a national security threat to the United States, the latter being, it seems, a favored tool of the Trump administration.[5]

In the multilateral pillar, the Trump administration has continued the Obama administration's practice of criticizing the operation of the WTO's Dispute Settlement Understanding and vetoing the appointment of new members of the Appellate Body.[6] Again, like the Obama administration, Trump officials have raised concerns at the WTO about the extent and manner of Chinese state intervention.

Clear differences with its predecessor can, however, be found in the Trump administration's policy toward regional trade agreements (RTAs). In addition to ordering a review of all existing RTAs, the Trump administration sought amendments to both the US-Korea RTA and the North American Free Trade Agreement. The United States has withdrawn from one megaregional trade agreement and ceased negotiating another. The Trump administration has also been critical of G-20 initiatives, in particular as they relate to reducing excess capacity in the steel sector (see USTR 2019a, 23). The Trump administration also successfully opposed the renewal of the G-20 pledge on protectionism, which was dropped from the communiqué of the G-20 leaders' summit in December 2018.

Trump administration officials reserve particular criticism for China. This is not the place to state and evaluate each of those criticisms, many of

TABLE 6-1. The Four Pillars of America First Trade Policy and the European Union's Principal Response

	Pillar			
	Multilateral	*Regional trade agreements*	*Bilateral/China*	*Unilateral/"national security"*
Matters of interest to the United States or relevant forums	WTO reform, in particular of the Dispute Settlement Understanding	Withdrawal from Trans-Pacific Partnership; the Trans-Atlantic Trade and Investment Partnership negotiations put on ice	Section 301 investigation of Chinese policies toward intellectual property and related matters	Section 232 investigation of steel and aluminium imports
	G-20 Global Forum on Steel Excess Capacity	Renegotiation of the North American Free Trade Agreement		Section 232 investigation of auto-mobiles and automotive parts
	G-20 trade work programme, including protectionist pledge (up for renewal in December 2018)	Renegotiation of the US–Korea Free Trade Agreement		Section 232 investigation of uranium imports

(continued)

TABLE 6-1. (continued)

	Pillar			
	Multilateral	*Regional trade agreements*	*Bilateral/China*	*Unilateral/"national security"*
Principal European Union response	Proposed reforms to the WTO, specifically: • New rules on subsidies and state-related businesses • Strengthened notification and monitoring provisions • Two-step process to reform the WTO dispute settlement understanding		Develop a trilateral approach with Japan and the United States that involves information exchange about third parties' policies and development of new multilateral trade rules to level the commercial playing field.	• With respect to steel and aluminium tariffs, having failed to obtain an exemption, a WTO case was brought, safeguard duties placed to limit trade deflection, and phased-in retaliatory tariffs adopted. • A joint US-EU initiative launched on July 25, 2018, with, among others, the goal of removing trade barriers on industrial goods other than cars. As part of this accord neither side is supposed to levy new tariffs on the other, with possible implications for the ongoing section 232 investigation into car imports. • Public threats of retaliatory tariffs on €18–20 billion of US exports to the EU if the US implements imports tariffs on EU cars.

which were also articulated by Obama administration officials. What matters was the change in approach, with the Trump administration prepared to invoke wide-ranging tariffs on Chinese exports unless China undertakes fundamental changes in its industrial and other policies. During 2018 and again in May 2019, Trump threatened to put tariffs on all of China's exports to the United States, covering some half a trillion dollars of trade. By July 2019, however, only $278 billion of American imports from China were subject to tariffs.[7] A "phase one" deal was signed by Beijing and Washington, D.C., in January 2020, bringing to a halt tariff increases but doing little to reduce those already imposed.

The final pillar—the unilateral pillar—is frequently framed by US officials as relating to the threat posed by international trade to the national security of the United States.[8] The Trump administration has to date launched four investigations under section 232 of the Trade Expansion Act of 1962. By far the most significant in terms of potential trade affected, which at this time of writing has not yet resulted in tariffs being imposed,[9] relates to the apparent threat that imports of cars and car parts pose to US national security. The European Union exported, for example, €37 billion of cars and car parts to the United States in 2018 (Eurostat 2019). Still, the tensions inflamed by the imposition of US tariffs on national security grounds on steel and aluminum imports were substantial.[10]

The commercial interests of the European Union are implicated in each of these four pillars. Even the Chinese pillar affects European interests since European firms have invested in both China and the United States and may be adversely affected by tariffs imposed on imports into either nation. Disruption to supply chains and to the associated corporate strategies built on them are another legitimate concern. Moreover, US actions threaten the principles and the operation of the system of world trade rules which European officials have stated repeatedly that they value. Given there is much at stake, how then have European officials traditionally reacted to high-profile acts of US trade discrimination?

REPRISING THE PLAYBOOK FOR AMERICAN PROTECTIONISM

When the United States previously resorted to blatant protectionism, such as when President George W. Bush announced the imposition of higher tariffs on imported steel in the form of safeguard measures on March 5,

2002, many of America's trading partners have followed what might be termed a playbook. Former European commissioner for trade Karel De Gucht explained the essence of this approach as follows: "You retaliate on sensitive products. The approach is always to achieve the maximum result with the minimum effort. You retaliate to hurt somebody" (*Financial Times* 2018b).

Recognizing that imposing tariffs on imports from the United States harms European buyers, the goal then is to select products for retaliation that have the greatest impact on US political decisionmaking at the least possible cost to European interests. With respect to the latter, this shifts the calculus in favor of retaliating on products for which ready alternatives to US suppliers exist.

With respect to the former, however, the key point is that retaliation is driven by the desire to alter the political economy of trade policymaking in the country that has undertaken protectionism, with the ultimate goal of rescinding that protectionism as soon as possible. It is for this reason that, in the context of protectionism imposed by the United States, high-profile exports from states represented by senior members of the United States Congress are frequently targeted. High-profile exports from electorally significant states may also be chosen.[11] This is in addition to making direct representations to the most senior members of the committees overseeing trade policy in Congress.

The list of American exports targeted for retaliation by the European Commission (after US tariffs on steel and aluminum came into effect for European exporters on June 1, 2018) appear to have followed this playbook. Orange juice from Florida, a state of some electoral importance, was targeted. As was bourbon whiskey from Kentucky, which is represented in the Senate by the majority leader, Mitch McConnell. Cranberries and Harley-Davidson motorcycles, which are made in Wisconsin (among other locations), were targeted too. A congressional district in Wisconsin was represented at the time by the Paul Ryan, who was then speaker of the US House of Representatives.

It is not clear that following the playbook has been successful. Press reports point to criticism from congressional officials of the Trump administration's trade policy,[12] which is a necessary condition for the playbook to work, and some contend that the July 2018 meeting between Presidents Trump and Juncker went better as a result. However, as of July 2020, US steel and aluminum tariffs had not been reversed; nor was the European Union permanently exempted from them. Consequently, it makes sense to revisit the logic underlying the playbook.

Recall that the goal of surgical retaliation is to alter the "political economy" of trade policy decisionmaking in the United States. For the playbook to be successful, enough affected US exporters have to persuade US policymakers to remove the offending protectionism so that their access to the EU market is restored. Several things can go wrong here—as the saying goes, there is many a slip between cup and lip.

First, US protectionism may be part of a larger package of policy changes that benefit the US exporters affected by EU retaliation. Recall that Congress passed, at the prompting of the Trump administration, a generous package of tax cuts in 2018. Consequently, the US exporters that are targeted by the EU may feel that, on net, they have gained from the Trump administration's policies. Moreover, congressional representatives may rebuff US exporters' concerns, arguing that overall they are better off with the package of policies, of which protectionism is only one part.[13]

Second, if a US exporter believes the European retaliation is going to last "too long" or get out of hand, then, if sales to the EU market are critical, one response is to set up or expand production in the EU. The EU may benefit from such "tariff jumping" foreign direct investment, but for the playbook to work the affected US exporters have to remain in the United States and fight the Trump administration's protectionism. This is not just a theoretical conjecture. Recall that, after Harley-Davidson was targeted for retaliation by the European Commission, it announced that it would supply much more of the EU market from production facilities in Europe.

Third, a US firm exporting a product targeted by the EU for retaliation can choose how it supplies the EU market. For example, a US firm may have production facilities in the United States and in Mexico. Such a firm could switch production for the EU market from the United States to a Mexican plant so as to avoid paying the duties in the EU. Here switching production substitutes for expending political capital by lobbying elected US representatives.

Fourth, the relative size of switching costs for exporters matters. If a US firm finds it more expensive to supply the EU market after retaliation, and if the cost of switching exports to a new overseas destination are low, then it may be preferable to do that than to lobby US elected representatives.

Fifth, to the extent that the playbook seeks to influence US administration decisions, it does so indirectly by influencing the views of US elected representatives. If the US president of the day feels that he or she can ignore the critical representatives and senators, then the playbook is unlikely to work. In this regard, it is worth recalling two further structural factors: comparatively speaking, the US economy is less dependent on exports than most (so fewer elected representatives will see defending exports as central to their constituents' well-being); and the support that elected representatives give a US president depends on factors other than trade policy (and those other factors may dominate in the calculus of any elected member of Congress.)

In sum, there are plenty of reasons why following the traditional playbook will not result in a reversal of high-profile acts of US protectionism. Simply put, the playbook is contingent on too many factors falling into place for it to be reliable. Economists have traditionally been nervous about supporting retaliatory measures on welfare grounds, and the concerns raised here ought to add to that disquiet. The uncertain gains from following the playbook have to be weighed against the certain losses to European buyers' welfare from raising tariffs on US exports.

Having written this, one should acknowledge that EU retaliation against American protectionism may also serve the domestic political purpose of not being seen to be pushed around by a foreign power. The merits of such virtue signaling can be questioned, not least because alternatives to retaliation do not appear to be given much consideration during policy deliberation. Indeed, one major trading partner of the United States did turn its cheek when hit by US tariffs on imported steel and aluminum in 2018, suggesting that the political "logic" of retaliation is far from apparent to everyone.

THE EUROPEAN COMMISSION'S REACTION TO AMERICA FIRST PROTECTIONISM

In characterizing the European Commission's approach to the Trump administration's trade policy, it may be tempting to discuss its reaction to actions guided by each of the four pillars of the America First policy. Ultimately that is the approach taken here, however it is important to acknowledge the potential links across the pillars. For example, the European Commission joining forces with the United States (and Japan) to advance the level-playing-field agenda (which ostensibly has Chinese policies in its sights) may be difficult to sustain support for if the United States is concurrently imposing tariffs on EU exports.

Moreover, trying to find common ground with the United States on improvements to the WTO's Dispute Settlement Understanding cannot be made easier if both parties are bringing cases against each other to Geneva and alleging rule violations by the other. Last, negotiating away trade barriers with the Trump administration, perhaps as part of a broader package to normalize trade relations, may seem counterintuitive given it was the same US administration that walked away from the Transatlantic Trade and Investment Partnership (TTIP) negotiations. Such complications will be difficult to ignore, will undoubtedly be raised by some in intra-EU deliberations, and ought to influence how the EU approach to handling transatlantic trade tensions is evaluated in the round.

In describing the EU approach, it helps to keep the key decisions made in Beijing, Brussels, and Washington in mind.[14] It is now apparent that 2017 was the quiet before the storm. Inevitably, it takes time for senior US officials to be vetted, nominated, and confirmed by the Senate. Moreover, the Trump administration pursued nontrade policy priorities in 2017, such as the unsuccessful repeal of Obamacare and the successful enactment of a large tax reform bill in December 2017.

Still, the groundwork for the tariffs imposed in 2018 and 2019 was laid in 2017, with investigations launched in April and August 2017.[15] Since no high-profile trade barriers were erected by the United States in 2017, it was possible for some to claim then that President Trump had pulled his (trade-related) punches. A more plausible explanation is that investigations take time and that for the Trump administration in 2017 obtaining a landmark legislative achievement was a bigger priority.

During the first year of the Trump administration its officials took the opportunity to articulate a number of themes that were to recur—namely, the perceived link between economic prosperity and national security; the alleged link between foreign trade distortions and associated US bilateral trade deficits; the deficiencies of the World Trade Organization's agreements and procedures and their adverse impact on the interests and legitimate objectives of the United States; and the apparent incompatibility between the Chinese economic development model and extant multilateral trade rules. However lacking in merit these claims and links are, no one can plausibly claim surprise in hearing them for the first time in 2018. In sum, arguments were articulated and means established (investigations) in 2017, laying the groundwork for the trade tensions that arrived in 2018.

Trade relations between the European Union and the United States entered a new, more adversarial phase following the imposition of tariffs by the Trump administration in 2018. Across-the-board safeguard duties were imposed on imported solar panels and washing machines on January 22. More important, on March 1, the United States announced that an additional tariff of 25 percent on all imported steel would be imposed along with a 10 percent tariff on imported aluminum, although on March 22, imports from the European Union were temporarily exempted. That temporary exemption was further extended on April 30 but ended on June 1. On June 22, the European Union retaliated by imposing tariffs on $3.2 billion of American exports.

Looking at the four pillars, it is possible to discern differences in the reactions of the European Commission. The de facto abandonment of the TTIP negotiations by the Trump administration did not require much of a reaction from the European Commission, except expressions of disappointment.

The Level-Playing-Field Agenda

With respect to the pillars relating to China and to multilateral forums, the European Commission has sought to engage in dialogue and develop proposals with the United States. In the case of China, this engagement also included Japan and led to the elaboration of a series of scoping papers published in May 2018. A statement released by the three parties on May 23, 2019, following a meeting in Paris, referred to "progress made in discussions on text-based work on increasing transparency, identifying harmful subsidies that merit stricter treatment and ensuring that appropriate benchmarks can be used" and included an instruction to officials to finalize such a text (EC 2019a). It is not yet known if any trilateral proposals have been put to the Chinese government or what the process is for taking them forward.[16] The trilateral group, as it is called, has continued to meet and issue statements, but rather than negotiate China has demurred.

WTO Reform

With respect to the WTO, the European Commission developed a range of proposals that were leaked in July 2018 (EC 2018b).[17] These proposals were organized around three themes: new and upgraded rules especially as they relate to subsidies, state-linked firms, and services as well modalities for negotiations; notification and monitoring obligations; and WTO dispute settlement. The European Commission tabled proposals to modernize the WTO in September 2018 (EC 2018c) and to reform the Appellate Body in November 2018 (WTO 2018). Subsequently, in January 2020, working with sixteen other WTO members, the European Commission proposed the creation of a Multi-Party Interim Appeal Arrangement that would for the time being substitute for the Appelate Body (EC 2020). In this regard it is worth noting that on more than one occasion President Trump has stated that he might withdraw the United States from the WTO unless it is reformed.[18]

Reaction to Unilateral US Acts

The unilateral pillar, especially as it relates to the national security–related investigations undertaken by the United States, is the area where the European Commission's position has evolved the most over time. Initially, the Trump administration temporarily exempted EU steel and aluminum exports from duties, which the European Commission sought to make permanent. Failing that, beginning in March 2018, the EC made it clear it would bring a WTO case against the United States, impose retaliatory duties on US imports in line with the EC's reading of WTO rules, and initiate a safeguard action on steel imports to ensure that shipments no longer sold in US markets were not redirected to Europe.

Coupled with this three-prong strategy was the insistence, initially at least, that the EU would not negotiate with the United States on this matter until the threat of tariffs was withdrawn. In a number of press reports it has been suggested that US officials saw the threat of tariffs as a means of gaining negotiating leverage and that trading partners were expected to offer or to accept curbs on steel and aluminum exports to the United States or otherwise lift trade barriers facing US exports. If this account of the US approach is correct, then the preconditions were in place for a dialogue of the deaf across the Atlantic.

Once the expectation arose that the EU exemption from steel and aluminum tariffs would not be extended beyond June 1, 2018, conflicting signals were sent by the governments of France and Germany to the United States in late April and early May 2018. While EU leaders were able to agree at a meeting in Sofia, Bulgaria, that discussions (rather than negotiations) with the United States on the bilateral economic relationship could begin only after the threat of US tariffs was dropped, the appearance of divisions among the member states, while hardly a new phenomenon, could not have enhanced the position of the European Commission in its discussions with American counterparts.

The announcement toward the end of May 2018 that the United States would investigate whether cars and car parts threatened its national security did not go unnoticed, in particular in Germany, which is a major exporter of those products. The willingness of officials in Berlin to countenance a deal with the United States apparently without the withdrawal of the threat of steel- and aluminum-related tariffs likely influenced the events that followed.

The ultimate imposition on June 1, 2018, of tariffs on EU steel and aluminum exports to the United States served as a reminder that the threats to EU commercial interests were no longer hypothetical. Soon thereafter, the EU imposed tariffs on an amount of US exports equivalent to 44 percent of the value of EU exports harmed by the new US tariffs on steel and aluminum.[19] Moreover, it was reported that, in a submission to the US Department of Commerce, the European Commission warned that global retaliation to any US tariffs on cars and car parts could affect up to $294 billion of US exports (*Financial Times* 2018d). The intended audience for this submission may have included other affected US trading partners as well as decisionmakers in Washington.

The Juncker-Trump Meeting in July 2018 and Reaction

A shift in the EU's approach to handling trade tensions with the United States became apparent after Presidents Juncker and Trump met in Washington on July 25, 2018. Before the meeting it was reported that, consistent with its view that any deals must benefit all participants, the EU would offer to negotiate a plurilateral deal to lower trade barriers by the world's major car exporters. In addition, a review of EU barriers to US exports was to be offered, as well as joint approaches to Chinese trade practices (*New York Times* 2018).

It appears the meeting of July 25, 2018, did not go according to plan. Suggestions to negotiate a plurilateral deal among car exporters were not embraced, presumably by the American side. Instead, according to a joint statement issued after the meeting, four steps were agreed.[20] First, it was agreed "to work together toward zero tariffs, zero non-tariff barriers, and zero subsidies on non-auto industrial goods. We will also work to reduce barriers and increase trade in services, chemicals, pharmaceuticals, medical products, as well as soybeans." Notice the phrase "work together" can have a different meaning than "negotiate." Perhaps the more important point is that the scope of this barrier-reduction exercise goes beyond (and seems to exclude) cars and inevitably invited comparisons to the lapsed TTIP negotiations.

Second, greater cooperation on energy policy was envisaged, with specific reference to EU interest in importing more liquid natural gas from the United States. Third, a dialogue on regulatory standards and their effects on trade would be launched. Fourth, the EU and the United States agreed to work with like-minded trading partners to reform the WTO and to address third-party trade distortions (more code for Chinese trading practices).

Last, the following cryptic phrase was included in the statement: "While we are working on this, we will not go against the spirit of this agreement, unless either party terminates the negotiations." This has been interpreted principally by European observers to mean that the United States will not impose new tariffs on EU exports while discussions are ongoing.[21]

Subsequently, this meeting was seen as declaring a truce in transatlantic trade tensions. An Executive Working Group, jointly chaired by the European commissioner for trade and the US trade representative, was established to take this initiative forward. Reaction within the EU to this deal was, however, mixed. German and Dutch government representatives welcomed the deal. Meanwhile, the French government sought clarifications about its content, especially as it relates to sensitive agricultural trade policies and environmental and health standards. The criticism was made both in Paris and by a leading member of the European Parliament that the European Commission was unable to secure the elimination of the US tariffs on steel and aluminum first (*Financial Times* 2018e).

Others pointed out that full-fledged trade negotiations would require a separate mandate from the EU member states and that the EU was not going to engage in managed trade of soybeans and liquid natural gas. Yet it transpires that the European Union has imported much more soybeans from the United States since the July 25, 2018 meeting. In a memorandum to EU member state representatives on January 30, 2019, European Commission officials noted:

There has been a significant increase in US exports since the start of the 2018/19 marketing year on 1 July 2018. Over the first 31 weeks of the marketing year, up to 27 January 2019, the EU imported 6.1 million tonnes of soybeans from the US, representing an increase of 114% compared to the same period in 2017–18. Given this strong trade performance, the US presently has a 77% share of all EU imports of soybeans (compared to 39% in the same period in 2017–8). (EC 2019b, 4)

How this feat was pulled off and which trading partners lost market share was not reported. Furthermore, the European Commission initiated a process by which the use of US soybeans to produce biofuels in the European Union will be permitted.

After the initial reaction to the meeting of the two presidents, attention switched to which items would be included in the subsequent negotiating agenda. Representatives of both parties diverged from the presidents' joint statement in important respects. Commissioner Cecilia Malmström suggested including cars in the negotiations to eliminate tariffs on industrial goods. US officials suggested including agricultural trade reform in the talks.

Negotiating Mandates

The United States has made clear its objectives for the subsequent talks with the European Union. In its annual strategy statement of 2019, the USTR states, "Despite this significant trade volume, US exporters in key sectors have been challenged by multiple tariff and non-tariff barriers for decades, leading to chronic US trade imbalances with the EU" (USTR 2019a, 29). The USTR published detailed objectives for the negotiation of a trade agreement with the European Union on January 11, 2019. These objectives are far-reaching; they cover twenty-four areas of public policy and give little sense of prioritization (USTR 2019b).

On agricultural trade reform, the United States is seeking "comprehensive market access for US agricultural goods in the EU by reducing or eliminating tariffs" as well as reforms to European sanitary and phytosanitary rules. The United States is also seeking access to EU government procurement markets while seeking to exclude from the negotiations its own Buy American policies. Another US negotiating objective is to preserve exceptions on national security grounds (USTR 2019b).

The European Council gave the European Commission a mandate to negotiate with the United States on the elimination of tariffs on industrial goods only on April 9, 2019. Negotiations on agricultural products were specifically excluded. Moreover, the Council made specific reference to "sensitivities" that it felt should be taken into account during negotiations (EC 2019c). Another decision by the European Council allowed for negotiations over conformity assessment.

In contrast to the US document on negotiating objectives, the corresponding EU documents are sparse, to say the least. The impression that both parties to this negotiation are not aligned on its agenda is hard to dispel. That impression is reinforced by statements in the report to EU member state representatives mentioned earlier (which was finalized after the US negotiating objectives were published but before the European Council approved the Commission's negotiating mandate). The European Commission's report argued:

> It should be kept in mind that the two Presidents agreed in this joint agenda to focus on a limited range of areas where results could be realistically achieved quickly and without entering areas of significant sensitivity for either side. This is why for example the joint agenda does not include agriculture—which is a sensitivity for the EU side—or public procurement—which is a sensitivity for the US. In this sense, cooperation under the joint agenda should not be compared with the wide-ranging and comprehensive scope of a typical modern EU trade agreement. (EC 2019b, 2)

This statement begs the question, What, specifically, is the joint agenda?[22] One way to reconcile this statement from the European Commission with the published negotiating objectives of the United States is that the latter document is for domestic consumption and that there is an understanding that the agenda is narrower and arguably less ambitious. Such a reconciliation beggars belief.

European Commission officials have also made clear that the "removal of restrictions on exports of steel and aluminum is a precondition for the conclusion of negotiations" (EC 2019b) and that they would refuse to negotiate further with the United States should it impose tariffs on imported cars and car parts on national security grounds.[23] When asked to give an assessment of the status of EU-US talks in June 2019, Commissioner Malmström made specific reference to progress on trade in soybeans and liquefied natural gas. She conceded that officials were still at the exploration stage on conformity assessment and that negotiations on an agreement to free up trade in industrial goods had not started yet. Tellingly she observed, "And here there is a discrepancy on mandates," especially as it relates to agricultural trade and government procurement. She noted that "there is no way EU member states will engage on agriculture" (*Inside US Trade* 2019a).

Pressure to include agricultural trade matters in the negotiation has come from influential members of Congress. Senator Charles Grassley, chairman of the Senate Finance Committee, which oversees trade matters, has consistently argued for the inclusion of agriculture in the negotiating agenda. He has argued that doing so creates more room for beneficial trade-offs. He has also put the matter more negatively and is reported as stating in April 2019, "I don't think you can go ahead unless there's an agreement on what you're going to debate. So, the talks won't proceed" (*Inside US Trade* 2019b).[24] Senator Grassley was also opposed to the suggestion, made by the United States Trade Representative, that the negotiation proceed in stages.

A year after the Juncker-Trump meeting, the European Commission issued a report on the state of the negotiations between the United States and the European Union (EC 2019e). This document is revealing as much for what it does not discuss as what it does. Seven pages were devoted to regulatory cooperation and three more to developments in two specific sectors (soya beans and energy). Only half a page was devoted to the talks to liberalize trade in industrial products, essentially restating that a mandate had been given by the European Council in April 2019. No information was provided on the subject matter, organization, or outcomes of the negotiations.

Greater Impetus to the Negotiation of Selected Regional Trade Agreements (RTAs)

In addition to taking the steps described in the previous section, the European Commission has placed greater emphasis on completing and starting new RTA negotiations with trading partners other than the United States. The logic appears to be to demonstrate that, while others may turn inward, the European Union wants to open up further, at least on a reciprocal basis. On May 22, 2018, the European Council agreed to start separate RTA negotiations with Australia and New Zealand. On July 17, 2018, the European Union and Japan signed a strategic partnership agreement, which came into force on February 1, 2019. A "political agreement" with the four members of the Mercosur group was reached on June 28, 2019, on the margins of the G-20 leaders' summit in Osaka, Japan.[25] The EU signed a free trade agreement and an investment protection agreement with Vietnam on June 30, 2019. Existing RTAs with Chile and Mexico are being "modernized." As of July 2020, the negotiations with Chile were deemed "on hold." The seventh round of negotiations between the European Commission and Mexico took place on May 25, 2020.

Other Developments in 2019

Two other developments further complicated EU trade relations with the United States during 2019. The first is the long-standing sore that relates to subsidies to wide-body aircraft producers Boeing and Airbus. Following a WTO ruling in its favor, the USTR proposed on April 12, 2019, that additional import tariffs up to 100 percent would be imposed on imports from the EU worth $21 billion (USTR 2019c). Moreover, on July 1, 2019, USTR proposed adding eighty-nine more products to this retaliatory list, bringing the total value of EU exports at risk up to $25 billion. In fact, in October 2019 the United States imposed additional duties on $7.5 billion of imports from European Union member states.[26]

The second development was the decision by the USTR, on the direction of President Trump, to start an investigation under section 301 of the Trade Act of 1974 of the newly enacted French Digital Services Tax. This announcement was made on July 10, 2019. The associated Federal Register notice notes, "The tax applies only to companies with annual revenues from the covered services of at least €750 million globally and €25 million in France" and that "Available evidence, including statements by French officials, suggest that France expects the tax to target certain large, US-based tech giants" (USTR 2019d). This particular investigation was supposed to determine whether the French measure constitutes de facto discrimination against American companies, whether the retroactive application of the tax was fair, and whether the new French tax diverged "from norms reflected in the US tax system and the international tax system in several respects." The investigation was concluded on December 10, 2019, with a finding that the French tax constituted an unreasonable or discriminatory burden on US business. On July 16, 2020, the United States imposed 25 percent tariffs on a range of French products, further exacerbating translatlantic trade tensions (Federal Register 2020).

ASSESSING THE EU'S APPROACH TO MANAGING TRADE
TENSIONS WITH THE UNITED STATES

The following questions can be used to evaluate the European Commission's approach:

1. Did the approach result in the removal of America First–related US tariffs or the removal of the threat of the imposition of such tariffs?

2. Has the approach resulted in other outcomes (such as reforms to the WTO or changes in government policy) that are likely to reduce trade tensions globally?

3. Was the approach consistent over time?

4. Was the approach coherent or well founded in logic or evidence?

5. Was the approach consistent with the multilateral trade principles the EU seeks to uphold?

6. Was the approach optimal? Were there no preferable alternatives?

The first two questions relate to outcomes. The third, fourth, and fifth questions relate to the choice of means rather than results. The sixth question relates to alternative means. I evaluate each one in turn in the following sections.

Removal of Tariffs and the Threat of New Tariffs

As of this writing in July 2020, the European Commission's approach has not resulted in the removal of the tariffs imposed by the United States on imported steel and aluminum on national security grounds. Moreover, until the United States confirms to the contrary, the threat of tariffs on imported cars remains, notwithstanding the talks initiated following the meeting of Presidents Juncker and Trump in July 2018. This is a rather negative evaluation of the European Commission's approach, but it may be too soon to predict the outcome. After all, when President George W. Bush imposed tariffs on imported steel in March 2002, these were followed by threats of retaliation by the European Union. When the United States lost the associated WTO dispute, the EU threatened retaliation again, and the Bush administration withdrew the tariffs soon after in December 2003. Those steel tariffs, which were supposed to last for three years, were removed after only twenty months.[27]

Even if one is prepared to grant that it is too soon to come to a judgment, the disagreements between Brussels and Washington over the scope of the negotiating mandate for liberalizing industrial goods trade cast doubt on developing a path that results eventually in the steel and aluminum tariffs being removed. Of course, one could try to argue that in the absence of the European Commission's approach matters would have been worse, but what evidence is there to support that conjecture? By setting up a bilateral negotiating initiative with counterparts in the Trump administration, perhaps one could credit the European Commission for stalling higher US tariffs on imported cars and any retaliation that would bring forth from the EU. Maybe the best that can be said for the European Commission's approach is that it is a holding operation.

Systemic Payoff

With respect to any systemic payoff in the form of lower trade tensions, it is hard to point to any benefits that have followed from the European Commission's approach. As of this writing, there are no reforms to WTO rules or procedures to credit to the European Commission. Neither is it evident that the European Commission joining forces with Japan and the United States has resulted in first-order changes in the Chinese government's behavior. Moreover, it is not apparent that the United States has moderated its criticisms of China as a result of cooperating with the EU and Japan. Likewise, there has been no moderation of US criticism of the WTO's dispute settlement procedures. In sum, the best one can say about the European Commission's approach is that the steps it took in 2018 and 2019 to reduce systemic trade tensions have laid the foundation for future improvements.[28]

Consistency over Time

With respect to consistency over time, the European Commission's approach fails this standard. The initial EU approach sought to deny the United States negotiating leverage by arguing that Brussels would not negotiate under the threat of tariff increases. Since the perceived American leverage depended on their tariff increase, demanding that the United States abandon the latter before talks began was not going to succeed. Plus, as Secretary Ross pointed out, if China could negotiate under the shadow of threatened tariff increases, then why couldn't the European Union? Worse, as the likelihood that steel and aluminum tariffs would be imposed on EU exports grew, combined with the additional threat of tariffs on car and car part exports, it is not surprising that some member states felt that there was enough at stake to merit a different approach and made direct overtures to Washington. That the European Union has not presented a united front is hardly lost on decisionmakers in the US capital and may well encourage the latter to hold out even longer for concessions from the European Union in return for abandoning any tariffs on cars and car parts. Given their extensive experience, perhaps American policymakers have a playbook for dealing with the European Union on trade policy matters?

Coherence

With respect to logical coherence and compelling supporting evidence, I raised concerns earlier in this chapter about the effectiveness of imposing retaliatory tariffs as a way to induce the Trump administration to reverse the imposition of tariffs on imported steel and aluminum. Reinforcing the doubts about the effectiveness of the standard EU playbook is the limited scale of US exports subject immediately to EU retaliatory tariffs. If the playbook were followed with conviction, unless there is a lack of suitable targets (which itself would be revealing), WTO rules notwithstanding, surely as many US exports should be hit as soon as possible?[29] This is not an argument for mass retaliation. Rather it is to question the value of token retaliation and to encourage reflection on what factors are holding back the scale of EU retaliation.[30]

Adherence to Multilateral Trade Principles

With respect to adherence to multilateral trade principles, the justification for the European Commission's retaliation against the US imposition of tariffs on imported steel and aluminum was that the latter act constituted de facto a safeguard action. The United States disagrees and argues that the latter act follows from an investigation of the implications for national security of the said imports. For those persuaded by this particular American argument, the European Union's retaliatory tariffs violate WTO rules and leave the EU open to the charge that it is, paradoxically, breaking its WTO obligations so as to defend the rules-based world trading system. Whatever the legal merits of the EU's case, the optics are unfortunate and should surely have shifted the decisionmaking calculus further away from retaliating in the first place.

Another concern is that the European Union's increased imports of US soybeans since July 2018, the proposed new rule to allow US soybeans to be converted into biofuel in the EU, and the apparent granting of a country-specific quota for American beef might be regarded as rewards to the United States for violating accepted multilateral trade principles. Moreover, the vast shifts in soybean sourcing to the United States smacks of the kind of managed trade that the European Commission publicly eschews.

Optimality

With respect to the optimality of the European Commission's approach, one way to test this is to ask, "compared to what alternative?" Here it is worth contrasting the approach taken by the government of Japan with that of the European Commission. On a per capita basis, both Japan and the European Union exported approximately the same amounts of steel and aluminum to the United States in 2017. Both are large exporters of cars and car parts to the United States. In short, both jurisdictions have significant stakes in how potential trade flows are affected, after normalizing for their difference in size. Both too have a stake in the successful operation of the multilateral trading system, and both are on record expressing concerns about the Chinese government's practices and its associated economic development model.

Japan's response to America First trade policy has four aspects to it. First, as noted earlier, Japan and the EU joined forces with the United States to develop proposals for a level commercial playing field. Second, although Japan has yet to file a WTO dispute settlement case against the United States concerning the latter's tariffs on steel and aluminum, news reports in June 2018 cite Japanese government officials stating they want to cooperate with the EU on the case it has brought against these tariffs.[31] Third, Japan also notified the WTO on May 18, 2018, of its right to suspend equivalent concessions on exports from the United States. Crucially, however, to date Japan has not chosen to impose retaliatory tariffs on the United States. For sure, the United States has not exempted Japan from these tariffs despite lobbying by Prime Minister Shinzo Abe, actions and outcomes that in many respects parallel that of the European Union. However, by not retaliating, Japan has avoided the associated welfare losses and avoided the accusation that it has broken WTO rules in order to defend them.

Fourth, Japan and the United States have initiated negotiations toward a regional trade agreement. The Trump administration is pursuing this negotiation under its Trade Promotion Authority. Pursuant to that, negotiating objectives were published in December 2018 and confirmed the traditional US practice of seeking negotiations on a wide range of matters implicating goods trade, services trade, digital trade, investment, intellectual property, and state-owned enterprises. However, the United States Trade Representatives indicated that it may pursue the negotiation with Japan in stages rather than have a comprehensive negotiation (Congressional Research Service 2019). President Trump and Prime Minister Abe declared on September 25, 2019, that an agreement to liberalize tariffs on selected agricultural and industrial products had been reached. The United States began implementing those tariff reductions on January 1, 2020.

Another difference in approach between Japan and the European Commission is that on July 17, 2018, the EC imposed a preliminary safeguard measure of 25 percent duties on imported steel, justified in part by concerns about trade deflection. The additional 25 percent steel tariffs applied in the United States may make it commercially unattractive for some steel producers to sell there, and those shipments may be diverted to EU markets, depressing prices there and threatening steel producers in the European Union. A careful reading of the relevant Commission Implementing Regulation[32] reveals that much of the evidence mustered applies to the era before the section 232–related tariffs were imposed by the United States in 2018. Only steel imports from members of the European Economic Area were exempted. While the harm to European steel buyers was arguably limited by the adoption of a tariff rate quota, rather than an across-the-board tariff on all affected steel imports, this action contributes to the "multilateralization" of the problem created by the original US tariff increase. Despite being a major steel producer, to date Japan has not chosen to follow suit, thus avoiding further welfare losses associated with restricting imports.[33]

In sum, a comparison between Japan's and the European Commission's approach is instructive. Both nations failed to win exemptions from US steel and aluminum tariffs. Japan, however, has shown greater restraint in erecting tariff barriers in response to America First protectionism, whether in direct retaliation or on account of potential trade deflection. Whether such Japanese restraint endures, especially if the United States imposes tariffs on imported cars and car parts, remains to be seen. At the moment, however, on several grounds Japan's approach has the edge over the response of the European Union.

CONCLUDING REMARKS AND IMPLICATIONS
FOR THE NEXT EUROPEAN COMMISSION

President Juncker reacted to the threat of US steel and aluminum tariffs in March 2018 by stating, "We can also do stupid." So how stupid was the European Commission's response to the flagrant US protectionism of 2018? To be sure, the years 2018 and 2019 have been an extraordinary time for senior trade policymakers. Still, outbreaks of US protectionism are not new (even if the scale of recent interventions is unusually large), the United States' political system is relatively more transparent than many other nations', and by initiating investigations in 2017 the Trump administration gave notice that it might act aggressively in 2018.

Arguably, the European Commission's response has fallen short. Perhaps the best evidence to support this comes from the Commission itself. Specifically, there was a marked shift in approach in July 2018 when the European Commission conceded that it would negotiate with the United States under the threat of new tariffs (on cars and car parts) and with steel and aluminum tariffs still in place. If the strategy of the US government was to gain negotiating leverage by raising tariffs or threatening to do so, then it has worked insofar as discussions are envisaged concerning reducing barriers to American exports. Of course, whether those discussions amount to anything is another matter (and reasons for doubt are presented in this chapter).

The contrast between Japan's response to America First protectionism and that of the European Union is instructive. After failing to win exemptions for Japanese steel, the government in Tokyo decided against erecting trade barriers against the United States or against other steel producers. In so doing, the harm to Japanese buyers from higher trade barriers has been avoided. European importers have not been so fortunate. Indeed, there is a whiff of opportunism in the July 2018 decision by the European Commission to impose a preliminary safeguard on imported steel. Fears of trade deflection following US protectionism could become the favored argument of European interests seeking to erect more barriers to imports. Had the United States followed through and imposed 25 percent tariffs on all imports from China, then such fears would have be fanned in Europe.

This chapter also examines the logic of retaliation against foreign protectionism. When the contemporary realities of US politics and the full range of options available to firms are taken into account, the logic of the traditional EU playbook for dealing with high-profile acts of US protectionism was found wanting. It is important to remember that the purpose of retaliation is to alter the political economy of trade policymaking in the nation that erected the offending trade barrier. Circumstances change, so European trade policymakers should be cautious about assuming that a playbook that may have "worked" in the past will continue to do so.

Looking forward, what did the Juncker Commission bequeath to its successor? Rather than induce a reversal of US tariff increases on imported European steel and aluminum, the best that can be said for the approach taken during the Juncker Commission is that it stalled for nearly two years the imposition of American tariff increases on cars and car parts. In doing so, pressures from European Union member states to retaliate further against American protectionism have been contained, at least for now.

But how long can this approach last? That trade officials in Brussels and Washington are so far apart in defining the negotiating agenda for bilateral trade talks, and that so little progress has been made since Presidents Juncker and Trump met, calls into question the durability of the current approach of the European Commission. Getting a bilateral negotiation up and running may have been an effective short-run *tactic* to stall pressures for further protectionism on both sides of the Atlantic, but to date little in terms of *strategy* to reverse American tariff increases or, more generally, to alter American trade policy can be divined from the approach of the Juncker Commission.

When subsequent developments in 2019 are taken into account, further doubts arise about the length of time that the European Commission can hold the line. The determination of the Trump administration to impose duties on $7.5 billion of EU exports on account of the Airbus-Boeing dispute raised hackles among affected European interests and among the EU member states. Moreover, USTR's investigation into the new French digital services tax set up a clash in 2020. Plus, the US presidential election cycle (which is in full swing at this writing) is not known for its enlightening effect on American trade policymaking.

The potential upside of the nascent US-EU negotiation on industrial goods and the other elements of the work program following the Juncker-Trump meeting of July 2018 are unlikely to be enough to contain the trade tensions raised by these developments. Consequently, the European Commission will have to revise its approach to the America First trade policy;

the fragile construct arranged by the Juncker Commission being likely to buckle under pressure.

That revision should give serious consideration to which objectives can be realistically accomplished by the European Commission given the political dynamics on both sides of the Atlantic. Evidently, the standard playbook won't do. But the deeper question is whether, even with its heft, the European Union can induce first-order changes in the trade policy of the United States. And, should the United States continue to turn inward, it does not follow that the European Union should follow, consciously or unconsciously, with repeated attempts to retaliate against American trade discrimination. There will, of course, be self-serving advocates of retaliation by the European Union, but those advocates should be forced to spell out the logic and evidence linking their proposed trade restrictions to more enlightened trade policy in the United States.

And that is not all. In light of the recriminations over responsibility for the coronavirus, there is still the risk that the United States will impose high tariffs on all imports from China, a risk that is higher if President Trump is re-elected. While the partial Phase 1 deal concluded at the end of 2019 reduced the prospect of this happening, it could still come to pass. If so, fears that some of the half-trillion dollars of affected Chinese exports will be deflected into EU markets will be articulated. Were that to provide certain European interests with a pretext for widespread application of safeguards on European imports, transatlantic trade tensions could morph into a far more serious conflict between the European Union and many of its trading partners. Alas, there is scope for European Union trade policy to become a lot more stupid.

NOTES

I thank, without implicating, Per Altenberg, Bernard Hoekman, Sébastien Jean, Patrick Low, Piotr Lukaszuk, and Edwin Vermulst for comments on earlier versions of this chapter. An initial version of the arguments here was published in December 2018 in the Japan Institute of International Affairs journal *Kokusai Mondai*. The project to which this chapter contributes has received funding from the European Union's Horizon 2020 research and innovation program under grant agreement No 770680.

1. *Euronews*, "Juncker Responds to Trump's Trade Tariffs: We Can Also Do Stupid," March 3, 2018, www.euronews.com/2018/03/03/juncker-responds -to-trump-s-trade-tariffs-we-can-also-do-stupid-.

2. See, for example, President Trump's speech on trade policy in Monessen, Pennsylvania, on June 28, 2016, http://time.com/4386335/donald-trump-trade-speech-transcript/.

3. Social media interventions aside, on my review of the press conducted for this chapter, of all the US officials quoted, the secretary of commerce has made the most negative comments about EU commercial policy. For example, in a May 17, 2018, article in *Inside US Trade*, Secretary Ross is reported as saying: "The United States is one of the least-protectionist major countries, and we have deficits to show for it. China and Europe are highly protectionist and their positive trade balances with us reflect it. . . . [China and Europe] eloquently espouse free-trade rhetoric, but—in practice—are far more protectionist than the United States. Our trade policy's main objective is to make their real-world behavior match their free-trade speeches" (*Inside US Trade* 2018a).

4. In my view far too many scholars have let their normative preference for the current rules-based trading system blind them to the system's evident and growing deficiencies (in the negotiating function, monitoring and deliberation functions, and increasingly the dispute settlement function).

5. In another piece of evidence of the contemporary legacy of the trade policy of the Reagan administration, a study by the Congressional Research Service noted that the last time a US president undertook a section 232 investigation into the threat posed by imports was in 1986. At that time, the Commerce Department found that imports of metal cutting and metal-forming machine tools threatened to impair the national security of the United States (Fefer and others 2018).

6. See, for example, the trenchant critique on p. 6 of USTR (2019a) as well as remarks on pp. 25–27.

7. For an overview of the trade barriers imposed during the Sino-US trade war, see chap. 3 of Evenett and Fritz (2019).

8. Secretary Ross, in an interview on CNBC on May 24, 2018, stated, "Economic security is military security. And without economic security, you cannot have military security" (*Financial Times* 2018a).

9. President Trump postponed making a decision to impose tariffs on imported cars and car parts on May 17, 2019. USTR was given until November 13, 2019, to negotiate an arrangement for these goods with relevant trading partners, including the European Union. This November 2019 deadline passed with no import tariffs being imposed.

10. In a speech at Georgetown University in Washington, D.C. on March 7, 2019, Commissioner Malmström made clear: "Europe was seriously offended by the imposition of steel and aluminium tariffs last summer under section 232. We do not consider that our exports are a security threat to the United States. We are friends and allies, not a threat. And now we are carefully watching the president's decision on car and car parts" (Malmström 2019).

11. Bear in mind the vagaries of the US Electoral College and the tendency of some states to be "swing" states.

12. See *Financial Times* (2018c) and *Wall Street Journal* (2018).

13. This point, among others, was made in the May 26, 2018 edition of *The Economist*, whose cover was devoted to relations between President Trump and the US business community (*Economist* 2018).

14. In this regard, the timeline presented (and frequently updated) by Bown and Kolb (2019) is valuable.

15. Other investigations were launched in May 2018 (into whether cars and car parts imports represented a threat to the national security of the United States) and in July 2018 (into whether uranium imports represented a threat to national security as well.)

16. The EU does conduct a High-level Economic and Trade Dialogue with China. According to the European Commission, the seventh meeting of that dialogue, which took place on June 25, 2018, involved an agreement "to set up a working group to concretely co-operate on reform to help the WTO meet new challenges and to further develop rules in key areas relevant for the global level playing field, such as industrial subsidies" (EC 2018a). Chinese reports on this meeting make no mention of the global level playing field or subsidies.

17. For an evaluation of these proposals see Evenett (2018).

18. On the matter of WTO reform it is should also be noted that the European Union is a member of the Ottawa Group, led by Canada, that is seeking to identify proposals that a broad base of governments can support.

19. The balance, 56 percent, would be hit by EU tariffs should the EC's WTO case against the United States prevail, or after three years, whichever comes sooner.

20. See "Joint U.S.-EU Statement following President Juncker's Visit to the White House," https://eeas.europa.eu/delegations/united-states-america/48861/joint-us-eu-statement-following-president-junckers-visit-white-house_en.

21. See, e.g., "Trump Says No New Tariffs against EU after Parties Agree to Trade Negotiations," https://www.politico.eu/article/donald-trump-jean-claude-juncker-announces-trade-negotiations-with-eu/.

22. As a result of a legal requirement in the United States relating to securing Trade Promotion Authority for an upcoming trade negotiation, the United States and the European Commission did not engage in a "scoping exercise" before publication of the United States' negotiating objectives.

23. In November 2108, Economy Minister Margarete Schramböck of Austria was reported as saying, "Agricultural products are not part of that mandate so they are not the object of the negotiation. We expect the Americans to move because the Europeans have already moved. We have shown that the quota for non-hormone treated beef and veal—there's been a lot of movement on that." The implication is that a country-specific import quota had been established for

the United States, or was planned. Whether the United States is prepared to forgo all of its negotiating objectives on agriculture for this quota remains to be seen. At the time this statement was made, Austria held the presidency of the European Union. See *Inside US Trade* (2018b).

24. Senator Grassley also observed, "As long as [USTR Robert] Lighthizer has put out a statement and a basis for negotiation that disagrees with Europe because it [has] agriculture in it, then I think it's a moot question until Europe comes around" (*Inside US Trade* 2019b).

25. In a statement, Commissioner Malmström put the RTA with Mercosur in the following context: "Over the past few years the EU has consolidated its position as the global leader in open and sustainable trade. Agreements with 15 countries have entered into force since 2014, notably with Canada and Japan. This agreement adds four more countries to our impressive roster of trade allies" (EC 2019d).

26. In a revealing remark on June 9, 2019, Commissioner Malmström said, "We haven't really started those talks" (about a possible resolution to the threat of US tariffs on cars and car parts) (*Inside US Trade* 2019a).

27. There again, given the Appellate Body deadlock, resolution of the US section 232 measures through the WTO within twenty months appears unlikely, if not impossible. I thank Edwin Vermulst for making this point to me.

28. Again, one might fall back on the argument that it is too soon to judge the European Commission's approach.

29. Put differently, to the extent that WTO rules on immediate retaliation against safeguard measures limit the size of US exports affected, then this further weakens the effectiveness of the EU playbook. In turn this begs the question whether the EU can simultaneously support the multilateral trading system and deploy an effective playbook that induces changes in American trade policy.

30. After all, some of the factors limiting EU retaliation may make a lot of sense.

31. On June 8, 2018, Japan asked to join the consultations between the European Union and the United States over the former's WTO dispute settlement case concerning the steel and aluminum tariffs imposed by the Trump administration.

32. Commission Implementing Regulation (EU) 2018/1013 of July 17, 2018, imposing provisional safeguard measures with regard to imports of certain steel products. Available in the *Official Journal* at https://eur-lex.europa.eu/eli/reg_impl/2018/1013/oj.

33. According to the World Steel Association, in 2017 Japanese steel plants produced 104.7 million tons of crude steel (World Steel Association 2018). The largest EU producer of steel, Germany, produced 43.4 million tons of crude steel in 2017.

REFERENCES

Beattie, Alan. 2018a. "How Best to Respond to Trump's Trade Attacks? Just Do Nothing." *Financial Times*, July 16.

———. 2018b. "The Dangers for Brussels of Talking Trade with Trump." *Financial Times*, September 4.

Bown, Chad P., and Melina Kolb. 2019. "Trump's Trade War Timeline: An Up-to-Date Guide." *Trade & Investment Policy Watch* (blog), June 15, https://www.piie.com/blogs/trade-investment-policy-watch/trump-trade-war-china-date-guide.

Congressional Research Service. 2019. "US-Japan Trade Agreement Negotiations." *In Focus*, June 5.

Dadush, Uri, and Guntram Wolff. 2019. "The European Union's Response to the Trade Crisis." Bruegel Policy Contribution 5. Brussels, March 14. https://www.bruegel.org/2019/03/the-european-unions-response-to-the-trade-crisis/.

Demertzis, Maria. 2018. "The EU Should Not Sing to Trump's Tune on Trade" (blog). Bruegel. Brussels, May 17, https://www.bruegel.org/2018/05/the-eu-should-not-sing-to-trumps-tune-on-trade/.

European Commission (EC). 2018a. "EU and China Discuss Economic and Trade Relations at the 7th High-Level Economic and Trade Dialogue." June 15.

———. 2018b. "WTO-EU's Proposals on WTO Modernisation. Brussels, July 5.

———. 2018c. "WTO Modernisation: Introduction to Future EU Proposals. Brussels, September 18.

———. 2019a. "Joint Statement of the Trilateral Meeting of the Trade Ministers of the United States, European Union, and Japan." Paris, May 23.

———. 2019b. "EU-US Relations: Interim Report on the Work of the Executive Working Group." Note for the TPC/INTA, January 30.

———. 2019c. Council of the European Union. COUNCIL DECISION Authorising the Opening of Negotiations with the United States of America for an Agreement on the Elimination of Tariffs for Industrial Goods. 6052/19, April 9.

———. 2019d. "EU and Mercosur Reach Agreement on Trade." Press Release, June 28.

———. 2019e. "Progress Report on the Implementation of the EU-U.S. Joint Statement of 25 July 2018," July.

———. 2020. "Trade: EU and 16 WTO Members Agree to Work Together on an Interim Appeal Arbitration Agreement." Press Release, January 24.

Economist. 2018. "The Affair: Why Corporate America Loves Donald Trump." May 26.

Eurostat. 2019. "International Trade in Cars." April.

Evenett, Simon J. 2018. "Triage? Assessing the EU's Modernisation Proposals for the WTO." *Intereconomics: Review of Economic Policy* 53 (5): 253–56.

Evenett, Simon J., and Johannes Fritz. 2019. *Jaw not War: Prioritising WTO Reform Options*. 24th Global Trade Alert Report. *Vox*, June 13. https://voxeu .org/article/jaw-jaw-not-war-war-prioritising-wto-reform-options.

Federal Register (2020). *Notice of Action in the Section 301 Investigation of France's Digital Services Tax*. Docket No. USTR–2019–0009. July 16.

Fefer, Rachel F., and others. 2018. "Section 232 Investigations: Overview and Issues for Congress." Washington, D.C.: Congressional Research Service, August 21.

Financial Times. 2018a "Trump Stirs Global Anger with Car Tariff Threat." May 25.

———. 2018b. "EU Proves Reluctant Playmate in Trump's Game of Chicken on Trade." June 25.

———. 2018c. "US to Announce $12bn in Farm Aid to Ease Tariff Impact." July 24.

———. 2018d. "EU Warns of $300bn Hit to US over Car Import Tariffs." July 1.

———. 2018e. "Germany Welcomes 'Breakthrough' US-EU Trade Accord." July 26.

Inside US Trade. 2018a. "Ross Says WTO Rules Prevent 'Reciprocal' Trade with EU, China." May 17. https://insidetrade.com/daily-news/ross-says-wto -rules-prevent-%E2%80%98reciprocal%E2%80%99-trade-eu-china.

———. 2018b. "EU Hopes to Have Negotiating Mandate for US Talks by Early 2019." November 16. https://insidetrade.com/daily-news/eu-hopes -have-negotiating-mandate-us-talks-early-2019.

———.2019a. "EU Trade Chief: Auto Talks with US Have Yet to Begin; E-commerce Goal May Be 'Optimistic.'" June 11. https://insidetrade .com/share/166642.

———. 2019b. "Grassley: Without Ag in US-EU Talks, Valuable 'Trade-offs' Left Out." April 19. https://insidetrade.com/daily-news/grassley-without -ag-us-eu-talks-valuable-%E2%80%98trade-offs%E2%80%99-left -out.

Jean, Sébastien, Philippe Martin, and André Sapir. 2018. "International Trade under Attack: What Strategy for Europe." Bruegel Policy Contribution 12. Brussels, August 2018.

Malmström, Cecilia. 2019. "The Next Transatlantic Project." John D. Greenwald Memorial Lecture. Georgetown University, March 7.

New York Times. 2018. "E.U. to Offer Trade Proposals in Bid to Ease Tensions." July 24.

Pisani-Ferry, Jean. 2018. "Is Europe America's Friend or Foe?" Opinion. Bruegel Newsletter. Brussels, July 30. https://www.bruegel.org/2018/07/is -europe-americas-friend-or-foe/.

United States Trade Representative (USTR). 2019a. "2019 Trade Policy Agenda and 2018 Annual Report of the President of the United States on the Trade Agreements Program." Washington, D.C.

———. 2019b. "United States-European Union Negotiations: Summary of Specific Negotiating Objectives." January. Washington, D.C.

———. 2019c. "Notice of Hearing and Request for Public Comments: Enforcement of US WTO Rights in Large Civil Aircraft Dispute." Washington, D.C., July 5.

———. 2019d. "Initiation of a Section 301 Investigation of France's Digital Services Tax." Washington, D.C., July 10.

Wall Street Journal. 2018. "US, Europe Call a Truce on Trade—Trump, Juncker Agree to Hold Off on Further Tariffs as They Work to Take Down Barriers." July 26.

World Steel Association. 2018. *World Steel in Figures 2018.* Brussels.

World Trade Organization (WTO). 2018. "Communication from the European Union, China, Canada, India, Norway, New Zealand, Switzerland, Australia, Republic of Korea, Iceland, Singapore and Mexico." WT/GC/W/752. Geneva, November 26.

7

BURNING DOWN THE HOUSE?

THE APPELLATE BODY AT THE CENTER OF THE WTO CRISIS

BERNARD HOEKMAN AND PETROS C. MAVROIDIS

Following months of refusal by the United States to agree to new appointments to the World Trade Organization's Appellate Body (AB) as the terms of appointees expired, in mid-December 2019 the number of sitting AB members dropped to one. Since appeals require at least three AB members, the WTO appeals function became essentially defunct.[1] The progressive reduction in membership of the AB—from seven to six to five to four to three and then to one—has led to a blame game. The US delegation to the World Trade Organization (WTO) has repeatedly expressed the view that its actions reflect its desire to ensure that the AB performs the institutional role of dispute settlement assigned to it in the agreement negotiated in the Uruguay Round—the Dispute Settlement Understanding (DSU). The United States argues that the AB has not abided by its terms of reference, that the AB has in various ways acted as if it were a principal instead of an agent, as it is required to do by Article 3.2 of the DSU, and that only drastic action could bring it back to order.

Although the United States is the prime mover in creating the Appellate Body crisis, others have played along. The rest of the WTO membership has not been willing to address the situation head-on by pushing for majority decisions in this respect, as it can do under Article IX.1 of the Agreement Establishing the WTO.[2] Instead, several WTO members have submitted proposals to anticipate a situation in which the AB becomes defunct. The European Union, for example, has taken the lead in suggesting that WTO members consider an ad hoc (transitional) appeals system: using Article 25 of the DSU as legal scaffolding, two disputing parties would consent to the establishment of a body that would act as an appeals board.[3] Such "plan B" proposals are stopgaps at best. For parties to a dispute to agree to adopt a panel report "as is" (i.e., abstain from appeal) or to make recourse to arbitration along the lines suggested by the EU, the consent of the defendant is necessary. But the whole purpose of the DSU was to move to negative consensus.[4]

The dispute on the WTO dispute settlement mechanism has led the WTO membership into no-man's land. Unfortunately, none of the proposals put forward to date as a response to the demise of the AB addresses the real issue raised by the United States: its call for measures to ensure that the appeals mechanism operates as intended when the WTO entered into force in 1995. Notwithstanding speculation that some in the United States would prefer to go back to the GATT system of dispute settlement in which the establishment of a panel and adoption of reports by panels could be blocked, the United States has made clear it is not questioning the premise of binding and automatic dispute settlement.

Clear differences in view exist between WTO members on whether the AB has sidestepped or exceeded its mandate. To assess whether and where the AB has done so it is necessary to have a common understanding of what the original intent was. In this chapter, we ask what the framers wished to achieve through the establishment of the AB, and the eventual mandate of the AB, through the lens of the relevant negotiating documents. We investigate what the negotiating record tells us about the intended function of the AB. Our premise is that unless we have established this picture, it will be hard to take positions on current views of the membership regarding the AB and what should be understood by the US position that the AB needs to "go back to 1995."

We take at face value the purpose of the AB that is reflected in the rather uninformative Article 3.7 of the DSU. Art. 3.7 states:

The aim of the dispute settlement mechanism is to secure a positive solution to a dispute. A solution mutually acceptable to the parties to a dispute and consistent with the covered agreements is clearly to be preferred. In the absence of a mutually agreed solution, the first objective of the dispute settlement mechanism is usually to secure the withdrawal of the measures concerned if these are found to be inconsistent with the provisions of any of the covered agreements. The provision of compensation should be resorted to only if the immediate withdrawal of the measure is impracticable and as a temporary measure pending the withdrawal of the measure which is inconsistent with a covered agreement. The last resort which this Understanding provides to the Member invoking the dispute settlement procedures is the possibility of suspending the application of concessions or other obligations under the covered agreements on a discriminatory basis vis-à-vis the other Member, subject to authorization by the DSB of such measures.

We juxtapose the US critique of the operation of the AB against this provision, which reflects what was negotiated and agreed by the Uruguay Round negotiators. Our aim is to take seriously the desire expressed by the United States to "go back to 1995"—that is, that the AB do no more and no less than what was agreed in the Uruguay Round. We do not ask whether the AB has helped achieve compliance with the WTO, or more generally assess its contribution. Nor do we express a view whether the United States chose the appropriate means to advance its dispute settlement agenda.[5] We take as given the situation with respect to the AB as it has emerged, whether this is the result of US intransigence or nonchalance or a preference for second-best solutions by the rest of the WTO membership.

We also do not enter into a comprehensive discussion of why and how the AB, too often referred to as the crown jewel of the trading system in the academic literature, turned from venerable to vulnerable like a modern Cinderella. Any such discussion would necessarily entail considering the selection process for AB members, the quality of the chosen individuals, the role of the WTO Secretariat, and so forth. It is AB 1.0 that we are after, the original design as determined in 1995.[6] Our approach is to review the legitimacy of the US complaints against the intended function of the AB—the original mandate—as revealed not only by the text of Article 3.7 of the DSU but by the negotiating record.

We start with a brief discussion of the AB powers and mandate as reflected in the current DSU provisions, followed by a discussion of the negotiating record. We then provide a taxonomy of the major players and their respective negotiating positions, and demonstrate that the negotiation of the AB was not a priority issue for any of them. The establishment of an appeals board was proposed just twelve months before the end of substantive negotiations. Against this background, we then discuss the United States' complaints about the AB.

THE URUGUAY ROUND AB NEGOTIATIONS

The AB was designed to provide the last word in a system of compulsory third-party adjudication under the aegis of the WTO. The text of the DSU—the statute administering dispute adjudication at the WTO—comprises eleven provisions (articles) dedicated to the work of panels (Articles 6–16). Only one provision deals exclusively with the AB (Article 17). Two others concern both panels and the AB (Articles 18, 19).

The negotiating record explains this imbalance in the text. When the Uruguay Round was launched in 1986, no one had thought of a two-instance adjudication process. The AB, or an appeals board to be more precise, only was proposed at the end of 1989, relatively close to the end of the substantive negotiations in the Uruguay round. The negotiating record, to which we refer in what follows, leaves no doubt in this respect. We kick off our discussion with the current statutory provisions concerning the function of the AB, before we travel back in time to discuss how we ended up where we now are.

The AB and Its Statutory Role in
WTO Dispute Settlement

As mentioned, the DSU has only one provision dedicated to the AB, Article 17. Most of the text in this provision deals with matters of peripheral importance, such as the deadlines for issuing reports, the confidentiality of its proceedings, and so forth. Only one paragraph (para. 13), deals with the function of the AB: "The Appellate Body may uphold, modify or reverse the legal findings and conclusions of the panel."

Unsurprisingly, the absence of an initial, elaborate legislative design resulted in some glaring omissions. The most obvious omission is a provision regarding the standard of review for the AB. Article 11 of the DSU addresses this issue only insofar as panels are concerned. It was thus left to case law to fill the gaps (standing case law, for example, makes it clear that Article 11 of the DSU applies to the AB also), as well as through "secondary" law. Article 17.9 of the DSU mandates the AB to adopt its own Working Procedures, and address matters not covered in the DSU.

Being part and parcel of the WTO dispute adjudication process, the AB has to adjust its workings within the statutory parameters reserved to the functioning of WTO adjudication. In this respect, the key provision is Article 3.7 of the DSU, which establishes a hierarchy of objectives that adjudication at the WTO level must serve, namely:

- The prime objective of WTO adjudication is to secure a mutually acceptable solution (MAS) between the parties to the dispute.
- If reaching a MAS proves an impossibility, it is the withdrawal of the challenged measure that is privileged, assuming, of course, that it has been found to be inconsistent with the WTO law.
- The WTO regime has a clearly expressed statutory preference for property over liability rules:[7] compensation of the injured party, if this is accorded, is temporary, until withdrawal of the illegal measures has been secured.
- Finally, suspension of concessions is the last resort to which the winning party can have recourse to in order to enforce a ruling.

This provision does not say much about the role of the judge. Moreover, one can question its internal coherence: if the prime objective is to secure a MAS, why not privilege mediation, a technique supremely adjusted to the specificities of resolving disputes amicably, instead of relegating it to a second-order option? Or, why not introduce the possibility for *ex aequo et bono* litigation, whereby recourse is made to the "fairness" of adjudicators, instead of a legalistic approach, which is ill-suited to compromises?

We do not address these questions here. The law and economics literature has been struggling to make an operational distinction between good- and bad-faith disputes, which could help determine which provisions need to be renegotiated. It has not gotten far. Few would disagree with the statement that the GATT (and the WTO's subsequent agreements) are incomplete contracts, in the sense that the adjudicator might, on occasion, need to go beyond the text in order to meaningfully interpret the various provisions embedded therein. For reasons first expounded by Baldwin (1970), what is at issue are unavoidably incomplete agreements. Horn, Maggi, and Staiger (2010) have developed a framework that recognizes this context, in which they regard the role of the judge as akin to completing the contract. What matters in this framework is that judges (i.e., the AB) are agents and have no choice but to embark in this exercise, but must do so without altering the will of the principals, the WTO members. The proverbial phrase reflecting this concept is embedded in Article 3.2 of the DSU, which asks adjudicators to respect the balance of rights and obligations struck by the framers.

The problem is that the framers, who negotiated the balance, might on occasion have an incentive to disrespect it. No one has expressed this point better than Tibor Scitovsky. As noted by John Leddy, Scitovsky, writing before the advent of the GATT, thought of trade integration in the following terms: "Because of the real or presumed benefits which national governments may anticipate from trade restrictions, and because of the supervening demands of special interest groups, an international free-trade system has a natural tendency to disintegrate and must be enforced by some kind of international convention" (Leddy 1958, referring to Scitovsky 1942).

The GATT (and now the WTO) in other words, is mostly not a coordination game—that is, a situation where the problem is to agree on a solution that is in the self-interest of all parties to implement.[8] There are incentives for defection—that is, nonimplementation of what was negotiated. Because the WTO is self-enforcing, such defection will be met by retaliation (withdrawal of concessions). Litigation serves the purpose of sustaining the negotiated deal, allowing parties to challenge perceived violations and to ensure that retaliation is both legitimate and proportional. Litigation is therefore an important part of the system. A problem is that it may—and perhaps often does—occur for "bad" reasons from a cosmopolitan perspective, although theory has not managed to come up with a framework that distinguishes wheat from chaff in this regard.[9] Good- and bad-faith litigation represent the two ends of the spectrum. It is against this background that trading partners met in the Uruguay Round aiming to improve the GATT dispute settlement procedures. Wisely, they did not distinguish between the two extremes. Litigation is litigation is litigation, and the same remedies apply irrespective of the good- or bad-faith nature of a dispute.

The DSU Negotiators: Doves, Hawks, and the Categories in Between

The GATT did not contain elaborate dispute settlement procedures. Two provisions (Articles XXII and XXIII) covered the whole area. Over the years, a series of initiatives were undertaken aiming to address actual, not potential, issues. This GATT "pragmatism" instilled confidence in the trading community about the capacity of the GATT to adjudicate disputes. Various GATT decisions added to the original statutory language. What they all have in common is that they crystallized existing practice into regulatory language.[10]

For many, this way of doing things was quite appealing. They were happy to live in a world where only incremental changes would occur, as they believed that was all an increasingly heterogeneous membership could accept. The European Union definitely belonged to this camp (Ehlermann 2015). For some, especially the United States, this was all too little, too late. Disappointed by the impossibility to enforce dispute settlement outcomes in the realm of farm trade (the European Union routinely blocked panel rulings that were adverse to its interests), and the lack of progress in integrating services trade and protection of intellectual property rights into the GATT framework, the US administration took justice into its hands. "Section 301," "Special 301," and "Super 301" became commonly used terms to mean roughly the same thing: the US administration would enforce its "rights" unilaterally—that is, without observing GATT Articles XXII and XXIII.[11] The Uruguay Round negotiation on dispute settlement was the multilateral reaction to US unilateralism. The underlying challenge was to define and agree on a dispute settlement system that would persuade the United States to give up the "nuclear option" of unilateral enforcement and antisystemic behavior.[12]

We can classify the negotiators into four distinct types or groups:

1. The hawk: the United States. From day one, the US administration left no one in doubt that it wanted a drastic overhaul, an authentic root-and-branch reform of dispute adjudication. The foundations of its position were strict deadlines for panels to complete their work and the removal of the possibility to block establishment of panels and adoption of their reports.

2. The doves: led by Japan and Korea, who did not want to undo what had been achieved under the GATT. To them, past practice worked wonders, and consensus was necessary at every step of the way to provide the regime with the necessary legitimacy. Brazil, India, and many developing countries were closer to this line of thinking than to any other.[13]

3. The hawkish doves: countries like Australia and Canada, which, unlike the United States, could not enforce the contract unilaterally (at least not against the big players with whom they had often raised disputes in the past). These countries were prepared to support the US quest for change, even though they did not see eye to eye with the US delegation on all issues, and certainly lacked its gung-ho attitude. They would follow (at least up to a certain point) but would not lead;

4. The dovey hawk: the European Union, which enjoyed enough bargaining power to behave unilaterally but had abstained from doing so in the past. In this, as in many other areas, the EU became the "honest broker," the proverbial intermediary who held the pen during the drafting stage, helped iron out differences, and secured the eventual compromise.

It is no exaggeration to suggest that the holy grail of the DSU negotiations was how to combat US unilateralism. As we have already suggested, and numerous accounts have made it clear, the key question for negotiators was what kind of changes in the GATT would persuade the United States to abandon unilateralism.[14] The road to change was not a straight one. Some trading nations were opposed to change. Indeed, in the beginning, the US delegation was quite isolated. Eventually, it was the countries opposing change—the doves—that were left isolated and ultimately decided to jump on the US bandwagon.

Negotiating Group (NG) 13 was the group in which changes in dispute adjudication were negotiated. It was staffed with some of the most experienced trade experts. The chair was Julio Lacarte-Muro, from Uruguay, ever-present in the GATT since its original negotiation and later a member of the first AB. He was occasionally replaced by Ambassador Julius Katz, a seasoned US delegate. NG13 included several other experienced and respected figures from national administrations.[15]

The United States: Gung-Ho for Change

The original US proposal rested on three pillars:

- It identified stalling as the key issue that needed to be addressed. Disputes would not be resolved expeditiously, and sometimes not at all.

- It further expressed its skepticism regarding the quality of panelists chosen to serve on panels. This is a time when the GATT counted few lawyers on its staff, and its Legal Affairs Division was *in statu nascendi*.[16]

- The US delegation was quite cautious only in its first submission. It did not propose that the GATT should do away with the consensus rule for voting immediately. The first time, it signaled the issues and left a root-and-branch reform for later.[17]

The US position evolved rapidly. Within two months, in the next document it submitted to NG13,[18] the US called for binding arbitration, fixed time limits for the duration of consultations, automatic establishment of panels (that is, negative consensus), and, as per the "Leutwiler report,"[19] the establishment of a roster of nongovernmental panelists. This last proposal was motivated by the premise that governmental panelists might be prone to listen to their own government when deciding on specific matters raised in a dispute. Along with the proposal for automatic establishment of the panel, these were the two more far-reaching proposals. Whereas the United States could invoke the Leutwiler report with respect to the use of exclusively nongovernmental panelists, the proposal for automatic establishment of panels was its own.

The US delegation was prepared to negotiate three distinct options on the adoption of panel reports:

- Consensus minus two—that is, panel reports would be adopted by the GATT membership, but the parties to the dispute would have no vote on the issue.

- Panels issuing binding reports—that is, negative consensus would extend to the adoption of reports.

- Alternatively, in the absence of consensus, the adoption of reports would be considered in the GATT Council or before the relevant committee (on antidumping, safeguards, and other issues).

Expedited procedures were a priority item for the United States. In various documents, the US delegation repeated that the phrase "not unduly obstruct the process" used on occasion by both Japan and the European Union to delineate unacceptable policies, was unclear and inadequate. Clear deadlines, automaticity in the establishment of panels, and moving toward negative consensus were key features that were nonnegotiable for the United States.[20] But the US delegation was willing to compromise elsewhere. Eventually, for example, when it realized that it was isolated on this score, it stopped pressing for exclusive recourse to nongovernmental panelists.[21] It became clear to all that the consensus view was to continue with the GATT practice of predominantly governmental panelists, with only occasionally resorting to non-governmental panelists. The establishment of an appeals mechanism was not a feature of US proposals, either: it did not propose an AB as a compensatory mechanism for its proposal in favor of negative consensus.

Japan, Korea, and Other Doves: No Change Required

Japan and Korea led the chorus of countries that suggested there was little need to tinker with the GATT regime. More than anything else, they were unwilling to undo the need for consensus for panel reports to be adopted. Japan was prepared to see some changes in the regime, but it was all in favor of trading nations keeping control of the process. For example, Japan wanted each party to a dispute to have the right to nominate one arbitrator and entrust the director-general with the nomination of the umpire. It preferred all panelists to be governmental.[22] Japan understood the process to be predominantly conciliatory, and not adjudicatory, and believed that the nominated panelists should commit to working toward this objective.[23] Korea largely agreed with Japan, but if all participants agreed, it would not oppose binding arbitration.[24] Korea nevertheless, maintained that, absent an agreed amendment to this effect, arbitration should be nonbinding, that mediation should become the dominant mode for resolving disputes, that the right to a panel should be acknowledged, and that panel proceedings should not exceed nine months.[25]

Korea and Japan received some support from developed countries like Switzerland[26] and the European Union,[27] as well as from a few developing countries, like Brazil. The latter emphasized the role of developing countries and insisted on conciliation as the key element for dispute adjudication in the GATT.[28] In a similar vein, Mexico emphasized that consensus should be a requirement for adoption of panel reports.[29] These voices became the minority opinion quite early on in the negotiating process. The doves, including Japan and Korea, did not include any mention of an appeals board (an AB) in their proposals.

Australia, Canada, and the Hawkish Doves: Yes to Change (in Principle)

Various countries in this group submitted comparable proposals, largely echoing the essential elements of the US submissions. Australia favored strict time limits for each phase of the dispute adjudication, supported explicit acknowledgment of the right to a panel, and endorsed the "consensus minus two" formula.[30] The Nordics (Finland, Norway, and Sweden) were willing to support recourse to binding arbitration and right to a panel.[31]

Canada placed the accent on most favored nation status (MFN) in the context of adjudication. To this effect, it declared its willingness to support introduction of binding arbitration, under the condition that third parties' rights were protected. Canada wanted to avoid a situation whereby litigating parties would end up reaching solutions that would not observe MFN and was eager to enhance transparency through which third parties could secure their rights. It also endorsed the right to a panel and supported the idea of putting together a roster of qualified panelists but did not require that they be limited to nongovernmental persons.[32] In a subsequent joint proposal that Canada tabled with Argentina, Hong Kong, China, Hungary, Mexico, and Uruguay, it reaffirmed its support for the right to a panel and advocated an enhanced role for the GATT director-general and the chair of the Dispute Settlement Council in adjudication. The proposal did not define what exactly the enhanced role would comprise, but it was clear that those who had signed the proposal thought of it as yet another move toward third-party adjudication and less interference in the process by the litigating parties.[33] An appeals board was not proposed by any of these countries during the initial stages of the negotiation.

The European Union: Reluctant Supporter of Change

The European Union changed its attitude over time, as it did in other areas of the Uruguay Round as well. As mentioned, initially it sided with the doves, but subsequently its position evolved to move closer to the US position, even though not wholeheartedly so (Ehlermann 2015). The EU declared its willingness to support recourse to binding arbitration, but suggested this be limited to a few cases, which, it submitted, negotiators would need to define. It was prepared to support the acknowledgment of the right to a panel, but in its view the adoption of panel reports would require consensus. Finally, in the EU view, recourse to governmental panelists remained preferable.[34]

The EU delegation did not change its opinion overnight. Eventually, it did not object to the changes proposed by the US delegates, especially since the quid pro quo would entail that Section 301 would be limited to an instrument of diplomatic protection. In the interim it submitted proposals that aimed to sugar-coat the position of doves, or at best, implied meeting the United States half way. The most imaginative proposal was to dissociate the question of GATT-conformity of challenged measures from the question of remedies in case of a finding that the challenged measures were GATT-inconsistent: whereas the former could be adopted by negative consensus, the latter should be approved if there was a consensus to this effect. If consensus proved impossible, the GATT Council was simply to take note of the reports.[35]

The EU suggestion was opposed by other parties. The most persuasive argument against it was that by dissociating findings on conformity from remedies, it would lead to authentic interpretations of the GATT. In fact, those disagreeing with the EU feared that a hierarchy of the various types of findings would be introduced. Findings of conformity would suffer from less legitimacy in the eyes of the membership. If the ensuing remedy were also agreed by the losing member, then these findings would, ipso facto, be more legitimate. Consensus on remedies would thus confer findings on conformity with an accretive legitimacy effect. It would transform them to something akin to authentic interpretations, a privilege bestowed on the WTO membership only. A similar outcome would be worse than the binding precedents that the European Union and others wished to avoid.[36] Since the EU delegation was not a strong supporter of negative consensus, it should come as no surprise that it did not favor tinkering with the GATT rules. In its adjudication model, there was no place for an appeals board.

The GATT Secretariat: Honest Broker

The GATT Secretariat played an important role throughout the process. It did not exercise initiative, but whenever requested, it provided excellent papers, which revealed the status quo of the GATT dispute adjudication system, and, as a result, informed negotiators accurately about the pros and the cons of the regime. This information helped nudge the negotiators in one or another direction. Among the various documents produced, we single out the following:

- One remarkable document in which the Secretariat explained the status of all disputes formally raised before the GATT since 1947, providing a "single window" for negotiators permitting them, among other things, to check the identity of parties, the subject matter of disputes, the rate of adoption of panel reports, and the final resolution of disputes.[37]

- Several papers explaining the changing nature of disputes, focusing on the more recent and ongoing disputes.[38] These pointed to the falling rate of adoption of panel reports, and provided a basis for deliberation on why this was the case—for example, whether this reflected the subject matter of disputes, the identity of the players, increasing homogeneity of the players, or a combination of these reasons.

- Other papers by the Secretariat dealing with specific topics, including:

  o Nonviolation complaints (NVCs), including a focus on the compensation that was agreed as an interim solution pending resolution of disputes.[39]

  o The types of complaints that had been brought forward and the rationale for maintaining the option of diplomatic resolution of disputes in the statutes (as it reduced the potential for a situation where one party is victor and one a loser, helping to preserve the prestige of all involved in a dispute).[40]

  o The role of developing countries in dispute settlement was discussed extensively in a paper evaluating the usefulness of the 1966 procedures intended to support the participation of developing countries in dispute adjudication. The Secretariat paper notes that these procedures were invoked only four times, even though there were 107 complaints up to 1988, twenty of which were raised by developing countries.[41] This paper cast doubt on the meaningfulness of replicating similar procedures in the future and continued working on special and differential treatment in more general terms.[42] It revealed that little use had been made of provisions aimed to help developing countries, and that usefulness of such processes might need rethinking. Either the procedures would have to be modified, or the whole idea of a two-tier process would have to be rethought from the beginning.

○ The Secretariat also prepared documents that served as overviews and summaries of proposals submitted during the negotiation of the Uruguay round. These made clear, for example, that there was increasing adherence to the view that the selection of panelists be entrusted to the director-general when the parties could not agree.[43]

Thus, despite not having a right of initiative, the Secretariat managed through its papers to steer the discussion toward the major issues that had plagued dispute adjudication, while highlighting the many positive aspects of prior experience.

The Negotiation of the AB

At the end of 1988, the GATT Secretariat circulated a draft DSU, a document reflecting the status of negotiations up to that point. There was no mention of an appeals board and no party objected to the draft.[44] Matters did not change until the end of 1989. The first three years of the Uruguay Round negotiation record therefore reflects no discussion at all of an appeals board. This suggests an appeals mechanism was not a priority issue for any of the negotiating partners.

Canada Shoots First

An originally unidentified country first tabled a proposal for a body entrusted with the task of performing appellate review in December 1989,[45] only two years before the end of substantive negotiations on the DSU (by the time the Dunkel Draft was circulated in December 1991 the DSU negotiations had been concluded).

It was Canada that proposed the establishment of an appeals board (Steger 2015).[46] It thought of it as a sort of fast-track procedure that should be completed within thirty days. Fast track, in Canada's eyes, would discourage routine recourse to appeals after a panel report was issued. Canada left the composition of an appeals board open, stating no preference in favor of either a standing tribunal or a roster with potential members. The various negotiating documents reveal that no one opposed the Canadian proposal. Many of the submitted papers sought to streamline and improve the original proposal for an appeals board, but no one outright rejected the idea. The US delegation felt that it was a right price to pay (a bit of delay in proceedings) in order to secure the advent of its priority items (right to a panel; negative consensus; strict time-limits). Japan and Korea thought of an appeals board as an additional layer of legitimacy, extra time to reconcile before impartial judges. Australia, the European Union, and developing countries tagged along as well. An appeals board could, in principle at least, be seen either as an additional push toward a rules-oriented regime or another bite from the conciliation pie.

Steger (2015), citing various sources including negotiators, has argued that the advent of the AB was the quid pro quo for parties losing the right to block adoption of reports. This is definitely a plausible explanation for all but the United States, which had argued for negative consensus irrespective of an appeals board.

Negotiating Article 17 of the DSU

There are few negotiating documents on what became Article 17. Most were prepared by the GATT Secretariat. The most salient features of the negotiation were:

- The expressed will to avoid delaying resolution of disputes because of the advent of an appeals board argued that recourse to this body should not be encouraged and that statutory deadlines should be fixed.[47] The European Union emerged as the broker in this respect, playing an active role in the discussion of deadlines, which, when combined with the panel process, replicated to some extent those in US Section 301.[48]
- The United States preferred a fixed pool of experts.[49] Originally, the idea was to put together a small body of three judges, with four more acting as alternates.[50] Canada's original proposal

to leave it open, potentially, to a larger roster of members (and the ensuing ad hoc composition) was soon abandoned.

- The United States believed that the GATT Council was not an appropriate forum in which to discuss legal interpretations, noting that it saw a role for such discussion only in extraordinary circumstances. It was more comfortable with an appeals board consisting of a pool of judges entrusted with this competence.[51] In a subsequent Secretariat document, we find the language "uphold, modify, reverse," which captures the current scope of the AB review as we now know it. When making a ruling, the appeals board should limit itself to issues of law.[52]

The Dunkel Draft and the Shift from NG13 to the Legal Drafting Group

The Dunkel draft (December 1991) signals for all practical purposes the negotiation of substantive elements of the AB. It made clear that it would be limited to a review of legal issues, and that it could uphold, reverse, or modify panels' rulings. The sixty-day deadline within which, in principle, the AB should reach its decision was also decided at this stage, as was the acknowledgment that the AB would require technical support to aid its work. What remained an open issue was the membership. While it was clear that only three would decide any given case, whether the total membership would be three or five members and four alternates remained to be seen.[53]

In the remaining two years of the Uruguay Round (1991–1993) negotiations on the AB moved from NG13 to a new group, the Legal Drafting Group. This group convened under the leadership of Deputy Director-General M. G. Mathur, an old GATT hand with vast experience on institutional matters. The main objective of this group was to review the legal conformity and internal consistency of the Dunkel Draft. It started work on January 23, 1992.[54] Top lawyers and trade experts participated in the group.[55] From day one, Mathur made it clear to all that the discussions in the group could not lead to changes in the balance of rights and obligations established through the negotiations that had been concluded.[56] The mandate was to improve the expression in the various provisions that had been agreed, without altering their scope. At that time, the WTO was still referred to as the MTO (Multilateral Trade Organization). Besides linguistic scrubbing, the idea was to ensure that dispute settlement would be coherent throughout all agreements coming under the aegis of the MTO, and not confined to GATT use only.[57] The Secretariat emerged as a key player in this process, as it was entrusted with streamlining the final text of the DSU, based, of course, on instructions that it would receive from delegates to this group.[58] The group held a few formal, but also various informal meetings in order to complete its work.[59] Before issuing the final text, Mathur circulated a text comparing the work of the group with the text as embedded in the Dunkel Draft.[60] Following one last reading, it was sealed and approved. The AB had found its place in the world trading system.

US COMPLAINTS AGAINST THE AB IN LIGHT OF THE FINAL URUGUAY ROUND TEXT

The purpose of what follows is not to provide an elaborate legal assessment of the merits of US complaints regarding the operation of the Appellate Board. Instead, the aim is to juxtapose the US complaints against the agreed text and function of the AB. We discuss the US complaints as formulated in various informal papers and in interventions before the Dispute Settlement Body (DSB). We do not consider arguments that the US (or other delegations) has advanced before the ongoing DSU Review.

The United States has advanced three complaints:

- The AB has undone the balance of rights and obligations by outlawing zeroing in antidumping investigations. It should have been led to the opposite conclusion, since, according to Article 17.6 of the Agreement on Antidumping, zeroing is a "permissible" interpretation of dumping margin. Nevertheless, by practically reading out this provision as well, the AB has outlawed zeroing, which the US domestic authorities practice.[61]

- The AB has mischaracterized factual as legal issues, and, as a result, it has expanded its jurisdictional scope against the letter and the spirit of the DSU.

- Finally, the AB has not respected the statutory deadlines for issuing its reports.

On occasion, the US delegation has also complained about aspects of AB activities. One of these is the use of Rule 15 of the AB Working Procedures. According to this provision, an outgoing member of the AB can still serve in a division, if the member was appointed to the division before his or her term expired. This argument seems to have subsided, and we do not discuss it here. Another dimension of US skepticism concerns the precedential value of AB reports. The argument is that consistency is not a value in and of itself, since one can be consistently wrong. Since mistakes can occur, why repeat them? Two remarks are in order on this question. First, the US delegation has not made this a key point of contention. Indeed, the United States, when a complainant, consistently refers to prior case law in its pleadings. Second, and more substantively, if the role of the AB is limited to interpretations of law, some precedential value of its findings is unavoidable. Indeed, understanding the law irrespective of the underlying facts is almost synonymous with the term "precedent." So, either the role of the AB has to be rethought (raising the fundamental question of what value a second panel can bring), or the WTO membership has to accept "precedential" value.

To avoid misunderstanding, we note that this does not imply that precedents must be followed without considering their usefulness. Indeed, the role of Supreme Courts in common law systems is, among other things, to rethink the usefulness of precedents and modify them, if warranted. In the absence of a Supreme Court, the AB should be in position to change its mind, provided it justifies the reasons for doing so. A similar construction makes sense, and would take care of the heart of the concerns expressed by the United States. To paraphrase Lord Keynes, when confronted with new information, reasonable people change their minds.

Zeroing in Light of the Antidumping Standard of Review

Zeroing refers to the practice of not considering negative dumping margins when calculating the dumping margin in an antidumping investigation. The result is potentially to increase the calculated dumping margins significantly. Between 2002 and 2014, eighteen disputes were brought against the United States contesting the use of zeroing. As Mavroidis and Prusa (2018) and others have noted, case law on this is incoherent: the AB has consistently outlawed zeroing, whereas panels, in defiance of the AB ruling expressed in Mexico-Stainless Steel (DS344, April 8, 2013) that they should observe relevant AB findings—another feature of AB behavior to which the United States objects—have on various occasions ruled otherwise.

To understand the merits of the US claim, the following elements are salient:

- the absence of explicit regulation of zeroing in the Agreement on Antidumping;
- the obligation of investigating authorities to perform a fair assessment of dumping margins (Article 2.4 of the Agreement on Antidumping);
- the obligation of panels to perform an objective assessment of matters before them (DSU Article 11);
- the additional obligation of panels to accept permissible interpretations by investigating authorities, per Article 17.6 of the Agreement on Antidumping.

The main US criticism is that the AB only paid lip service to Article 17.6. This criticism is well founded. Panels and the AB have routinely repeated a statement to the effect that the Article 17.6 standard of review is not at odds with the generic standard of review, and, as a result, have not seriously engaged with Article 17.6. Mavroidis and Prusa (2018) argue that in all likelihood little would have changed with respect to zeroing case law had the AB approached the interpretative issue from the angle of Article 17.6. It is unfortunate that it did not do so.[62]

Treatment of Issues of Facts and Law

The US claim is that the AB has occasionally treated issues of fact as issues of law. It cites the treatment of municipal law as a paradigmatic illustration. To review the legitimacy of the US claim, the following elements seem pertinent to us:

- the obligation of panels to perform an objective assessment of the matter before them (Article 11 of the DSU);
- the mention in Article 1.1 of DSU that disputes can arise under the covered agreements (domestic law does not fall under the covered agreements);
- case law, which has consistently suggested that domestic law can be reviewed by panels as an issue of fact. The AB has never distanced itself from this jurisprudence.

Respecting Time Limits

The US claim here concerns disrespect of statutory deadlines solely by the AB, even though empirical evidence suggests that panels are the major offenders on this front. Article 17.5 of the DSU states that the AB should complete its work within sixty days of the filing of a notice of appeal. In exceptional cases, this deadline could be extended to ninety days (with the agreement of the parties).

Johannesson and Mavroidis (2017) document that the AB has by and large adhered to the statutory deadlines, although in the 2017–2019 period, observance of the deadlines became less frequent (Hoekman, Mavroidis, and Saluste 2021), largely because the AB began to operate in diminished capacity as a result of the US decision not to renew members whose term was expiring. In a sense, it is US-inflicted damage.

CONCLUDING REMARKS

US grievances started when the AB confirmed that zeroing was illegal. They reached their zenith when the AB closed the door to zeroing even in instances where recourse was made to the exceptional method—that is, the weighted average to transaction comparison methodology (Mavroidis and Prusa 2018). The US authorities obtained some solace when panels decided to deviate from the AB ruling in this respect, but the United States never got what it wanted: the AB did not flinch. This probably explains why US criticism is directed toward the AB, and not toward panels, even though panels have on occasion committed some of the sins the United States accuses the AB of. Indeed, one might wonder whether the United States would have mounted its criticism with the same tenacity, and whether it would have stopped new appointments to the AB, had the AB agreed with the panels that found that zeroing was WTO-consistent.

We do not side with those whose view is that all is good as far as the AB is concerned. There is room for improvement in both the quality of the output and the institution itself (Hoekman and Mavroidis 2020). But we do not believe that the AB's stance on zeroing should be the reason for its downfall. WTO members should not throw the baby out with the bathwater, even if the AB has disappointed on a few occasions.

The negotiating record and the final WTO text help to clarify what the AB "as conceived and agreed in 1995" needs to do to address the specific matters raised by the United States. The DSU does not define issues of fact and issues of law, but the distinction between the two should be crystal clear, especially to experienced judges. The same is true regarding the power of AB rulings and the extent to which they should be considered to set precedent. The situation is also clear with respect to time limits, as we explain in the preceding section.

The situation is more ambiguous on zeroing, as the text permits greater discretion. Undeniably, panels and the AB have only paid lip service to the wording of Article 17.6 of the Antidumping Agreement. It seems that they have reduced the term "permissible interpretation by investigating authorities" (Art. 17.6 Antidumping Agreement) to redundancy. The question is whether zeroing is a permissible interpretation of the dumping margin. Mavroidis and Prusa (2018) responded in the negative. This does not imply that US criticism is futile. The AB could have done many things better. In our view, any constructive criticism is to be welcomed. What is unsupportable is the manner in which the United States voiced its opinion. Using the WTO working practice of consensus to block all new AB appointments is no doubt an effective mechanism to force WTO members to consider the US claims, but destroying the village to save it is not the mindset that should prevail. The United States should work with the WTO membership to resolve the situation.

Given the long-standing preference of all WTO members not to resort to voting in the WTO (notwithstanding this being provided for by the Uruguay Round negotiators), the pragmatic path forward is to take the United States at its word. Taking seriously the US position that it does not desire to go "back to the GATT"—that it is not questioning the two-stage dispute settlement process agreed in the Uruguay Round—requires bringing WTO dispute resolution "back to 1995." If the matter is to ensure the AB does what it was tasked to do in 1995, as reflected in both the DSU text and the negotiating record, then there is no reason the WTO membership should oppose this. Doing so would constitute a monumental failure of collective leadership. A collective (re)commitment to this effect, including agreement to put in place procedures to hold the AB accountable for operating within this mandate, would not imply reopening the DSU. Failure by the United States to accept such a commitment would be an act of destruction. The WTO DSU is the only extant compulsory third-party adjudication regime in international relations. Undoing it might lead to a domino effect, a perilous prospect by any reasonable benchmark. Insofar as the US stance results in an understanding that some things that were taken for granted need to be revisited, it may provide a (welcome) wake-up call for the world trading community to improve the operation of the WTO.

In 2002, a former AB member, Claus-Dieter Ehlermann, referring to the WTO dispute adjudication system, prophetically stated: "It seems to me wise not to take its existence for granted, and to be guaranteed forever, but to contribute to its consolidation and further development" (Ehlermann 2002). His ominous prophecy seemed a remote possibility in 2002, and yet fifteen years later it all but materialized. Many former AB members are eloquent in their praise of their collective contribution to the world trade regime. Lacarte-Muro (2015) and Ganesan (2015) think the AB has made a clear contribution to the rule of law. But past AB members disagree on various aspects of its function. This is something we all should keep in mind. The covered agreements, for reasons that have been explained in the economics literature, are "incomplete" and sometimes "highly incomplete" contracts (e.g., Horn, Maggi, and Staiger 2010). Those called to interpret them must be entrusted with some margin of discretion. The risk of doing so is not a mere theoretical possibility. Indeed, the AB members do not necessarily speak with one voice. They enjoy some discretion almost by construction, but they do not necessarily agree on how to use this discretion.

The Vienna Convention on the Law of Treaties, the agreed means to interpret the covered agreements, is not a mathematical formula. It cannot guarantee that interpreters will not overstep their mandate, even though it does circumscribe their function in aggregate terms. The major weakness is that it does not include a weighing of the various elements it contains: How much more should a judge defer to context than to plain text, for example? Zhang (2015) understands it as a move away from diplomatic resolution of disputes to a quasijudicial approach. And yet Matsushita (2015, 550) insists on underlining the primary responsibility of the membership:

> Negotiators at the Uruguay Round negotiations did not wish to create an independent court of international trade with decision-making power distinct and separate from that of the WTO members. . . . Negotiating parties wanted the WTO to be a member-run organization where the membership has the ultimate power to decide everything.

AB members' understanding of whether they can use extra-WTO law to resolve disputes is also not harmonious. Bacchus (2015, 515) sees no problem at all embarking on extra-WTO law to resolve disputes brought before the AB:

> There is nothing in the WTO treaty to suggest that the applicable law available to panels and the Appellate Body in fulfilling their responsibilities to the members of the WTO is limited to the covered agreements. When necessary to do their job, WTO jurists can range far and wide in other international law. But it seems clear that the substantive jurisdiction of WTO jurists is limited to claims under the covered agreements.

But this is precisely what the United States has taken issue with. This expansive view does not bode well in the view of some stakeholders. Paul Luyten (2015, 84), never an AB member but a very experienced high official of both the GATT and the European Union, spoke for those who disagree:

> It seems to me that a tendency toward legalization of the trading system has led lawyers to sometimes partly take over from negotiators, filling gaps, reinterpreting, and, at the limit, even restructuring agreements under the guise of interpretation.

Criticism is unavoidable. It simply cannot be, as Olavo Baptista (2015), another former AB member wrote, that the source of the pushback against the AB simply reflects sour grapes by those who lost their argument before the AB. The question is how to respond to criticism. Whether the extent of criticism can be reduced is also important, but preventive action along the lines of the different "plan B" proposals put forward by the EU and other WTO members to put in place a voluntary ad hoc appeals mechanism that mirrors as much as possible the structure of the AB are in our view insufficient. This is not only because they imply an unwillingness to address the criticism, but because pursuit of plan B is likely to impede the prospects of broader WTO reform and the negotiation of new agreements. Much needs to be done to update the WTO rulebook and WTO working practices (Bertelsmann Stiftung 2018; Hoekman 2019). Continued deadlock on the AB will impede the pursuit of this broader agenda.

Our discussion in this chapter suggests "going back to 1995" should not be particularly difficult or fraught. The principles proposed by Ambassador David Walker of New Zealand to address US concerns about the operation of the AB (WTO 2019b) illustrate that such agreement is feasible. They include ensuring that appeals are completed within ninety days; that

AB members do not serve beyond their terms; that precedent (case law) is not binding; that facts cannot be the subject of appeal; that the AB may not issue advisory opinions; and that AB findings cannot add obligations or take away rights provided by the WTO agreements. All of these are fully consistent with—and indeed often echo—what is in the DSU. While action on Ambassador Walker's report proved impossible before the demise of the AB in early December 2019, his consultations clearly demonstrated that many WTO members were willing to revisit Article 17 DSU (which leaves the elaboration of its working procedures to the AB to determine) as well as other procedural provisions in the DSU. Assuming a modicum of good faith and good will—which is not always in abundant supply—reaching an understanding to address US concerns regarding procedural and administrative matters should be feasible since it does not require reopening or revising the DSU.

More difficult is to address the fundamental challenge: removing the burden on the WTO dispute settlement function to adjudicate matters where the WTO agreements are unclear or simply missing. It is here where the main focus of attention should be, as it requires unlocking the legislative function of the WTO. Doing so calls for broader WTO reforms that go beyond the dispute settlement system.[63]

NOTES

We are grateful to Rodd Izadnia, Gabrielle Marceau, Ernst-Ulrich Petersmann, Neeraj R.S., and Debra Steger for helpful discussions and comments on prior drafts. The project leading to this chapter received funding from the European Union's Horizon 2020 research and innovation program under grant agreement No 770680 (RESPECT).

1. The AB is supposed to have a full complement of seven members according to the WTO Dispute Settlement Understanding (DSU).

2. Art. IX(1) states that, except as otherwise provided, where a decision cannot be arrived at by consensus, the matter at issue shall be decided by voting, with each member of the WTO having one vote, and decisions of the Ministerial Conference and the General Council taken by a majority of the votes cast, unless otherwise provided in the WTO Agreement itself or the relevant multilateral trade agreements.

3. In January 2020, Australia, Brazil, Chile, China, Colombia, Costa Rica, Guatemala, South Korea, Mexico, New Zealand, Panama, Singapore, Switzerland, and Uruguay agreed they would join the EU, Canada, and Norway in participating in this initiative. "EU, China, and 15 Others Agree Tem-

porary Fix to WTO Crisis," Reuters, January 24, 2020. For a description of what is envisioned, see European Commission, "Joint Statement by the European Union and Canada on an Interim Appeal Arbitration Arrangement," July 25, 2019, https://trade.ec.europa.eu/doclib/press/index.cfm?id=2053.

4. We understand, of course, that the EU proposal is to allow for ad hoc recourse to Article 25. If the European Union wished to formalize its proposal it would have to propose an amendment, which would require consensus before it could be enacted.

5. For example, one could ask whether it would have been more appropriate for the United States to seek alliances in the realm of the ongoing DSU Review to "instrumentalize" its criticism of the AB. This raises important considerations associated with WTO working practices, notably consensus, which would affect the salience of any such effort. We leave this question aside in this chapter.

6. In Hoekman and Mavroidis (2020) we discuss what could be done to improve the quality of adjudicators and reduce the need for appellate review, given a presumption that WTO members would be willing to consider reforms that go further than "going back to 1995."

7. By "property rules," we understand the specific performance of contractually agreed arrangements. "Liability rules" refer to the possibility for a party bound by contractual obligations to "buy its way out of the contract"; see Kaplow and Shavell (1996), and Shavell (2003), for a lengthier explanation, and for how these rules affect litigation behavior.

8. The 2013 Agreement on Trade Facilitation is an exception, given that it defines the outcome of a comprehensive discussion to define what constitutes good practice in the area of border management and clearance. It may be that future plurilateral initiatives continue down this route—for example, toward a potential agreement on investment facilitation.

9. Speaking of chaff, Grossman and Helpman (1994) have advanced a framework demonstrating the conditions why, in equilibrium, governments might use trade instruments to expose some and shield others from international competition. Similar behavior could, of course, lead to litigation.

10. There are two excellent accounts of the GATT dispute settlement. See Davey (1987) on the evolution of the regime over the years. Hudec (1993) provides a very persuasive argument that GATT pragmatism helped transform dispute settlement of the GATT to an (almost) de facto compulsory adjudication regime, and paved the way to the Montreal rules (1989) and eventually negative consensus.

11. Various contributions in Bhagwati and Patrick (1991) underline this point. Mavroidis (2016), based on the negotiating record, shows how a more effective dispute settlement system was the quid pro quo for the US administration to do away with unilateral measures.

12. It is an open—and important—question whether the current pursuit of aggressive unilateralism by the Trump administration will generate similar dynamics.

13. Unavoidably, as with any taxonomy, some marginal players could be classified under neighboring categories.

14. Mavroidis (2016) provides a comprehensive review of the literature on this question, as well as the negotiating record.

15. See, for example, the list of delegates in GATT Doc. MTN.GNG/NG13/INF/1 of September 21, 1987.

16. Lindén (2016), Petersmann (2016), and Roessler (2016) discuss the advent of the first GATT Legal Office.

17. Initial US negotiating position in GATT Doc. MTN.GNG/NG13/W/3 of April 22, 1987.

18. GATT Doc. MTN.GNG/NG13/W/6 of June 25, 1987.

19. The then director-general of the GATT, Arthur Dunkel, had invited Fritz Leutwiler to head a group of seven luminaries, and prepare a report on the way forward for the GATT; see https://docs.wto.org/gattdocs/q/GG/GATTFOCUS/33.pdf. The final report was published as "Trade Policies for a Better Future: the 'Leutwiler Report,' the GATT, and the Uruguay Round" (Dordrecht, the Netherlands: Martinus Nijhoff, 1987).

20. GATT Doc. MTN.GNG/NG13/4 of November 18, 1987.

21. GATT Doc. MTN.GNG/NG13/8, of July 5, 1988.

22. GATT Doc. MTN.GNG/NG13/W/9 of September 18, 1987.

23. GATT Doc. MTN.GNG/NG13/3 of October 12, 1987.

24. GATT Doc. MTN.GNG/NG13/3 of October 12, 1987.

25. GATT Doc. MTN.GNG/NG13/W/19 of November 20, 1987.

26. GATT Doc. MTN.GNG/NG13/3 of October 10, 1987.

27. GATT Doc. MTN.GNG/NG13/5 of December 7, 1987.

28. GATT Doc. MTN.GNG/NG13/W/24 of March 7, 1988.

29. GATT Doc. MTN.GNG/NG13/7, of May 11, 1988.

30. GATT Doc. MTN.GNG/NG13/W/11 of September 24, 1987.

31. GATT Doc. MTN.GNG/NG13/3 of October 10, 1987.

32. GATT Doc. MTN.GNG/NG13/W/13 of September 24, 1987.

33. GATT Doc. MTN.GNG/NG13/W/16 of November 11, 1987.

34. GATT Doc. MTN.GNG/NG13/W/12 of September 24, 1987.

35. GATT Doc. MTN.GNG/NG13/W/22, of March 2, 1988.

36. GATT Doc. MTN.GNG/NG13/6, of March 31, 1988.

37. GATT Doc. MTN.GNG/NG13/W/4, of June 10, 1987.

38. GATT Doc. MTN.GNG/NG13/W/28, of July 5, 1988.

39. GATT Docs. MTN.GNG/NG13/W/32, of July 14, 1989; MTN.GNG/NG13/15 of July 26, 1989; MTN.GNG/NG13/16 of November 13, 1989.

40. GATT Doc. MTN.GNG/NG13/W/20, of February 22, 1988.

41. GATT Doc. MTN.GNG/NG13/W/27, of June 30, 1988.

42. GATT Docs. MTN.GNG/NG13/9, of September 21, 1988; MTN. GNG/NG13/W/14, of June 2, 1989.

43. GATT Doc. MTN.GNG/NG13/W/2, of July 15, 1987.

44. GATT Docs. MTN.GNG/NG13/W/29, of August 8, 1988, and MTN. GNG/NG13/10, of October 4, 1988.

45. GATT Doc. MTN.GNG/NG13/17, of December 15, 1989.

46. Debra Steger was the Canadian negotiator in charge of the DSU negotiation, as well as the first director of the Legal Service of the AB.

47. GATT Doc. MTN.GNG/NG13/18, of April 5, 1990.

48. GATT Docs. MTN.GNG/NG13/19, of May 28, 1990; GATT Doc. MTN.GNG/NG13/W/44, of July 19, 1990.

49. GATT Doc. MTN.GNG/NG13/W/40, of June 4, 1990.

50. GATT Doc. MTN.GNG/NG13/W/43, of July 18, 1990.

51. GATT Doc. MTN.GNG/NG13/W/40, of June 4, 1990.

52. GATT Doc. MTN.GNG/NG13/W/43, of July 18, 1990.

53. GATT Doc. MTN.GNG/NG13/W/45, of September 21, 1990.

54. GATT Doc. GATT/AIR/3285, of January 16, 1992.

55. GATT Doc. MTN.TNC/LD/INF/1, of January 23, 1992.

56. GATT Doc. MTN.TNC/LD/1, of January 30, 1992.

57. GATT Doc. MTN.TNC/LD/4, of March 13, 1992.

58. GATT Doc. MTN.TNC/LD/6, of May 22, 1992.

59. See, for example, GATT/AIR/3380, of November 30, 1992, and GATT/AIR/5546, of January 28, 1994.

60. GATT Doc. MTN/FA/Corr. 5 of March 11, 1994.

61. See Prusa and Vermulst (2009) for a discussion of the WTO law in this area, the associated types of disputes that have arisen, and how zeroing works to inflate calculated dumping margins in investigations.

62. In April 2019, a panel concluded unanimously that zeroing was legal when recourse to the exceptional methodology (weighted average to transaction) was being made. See United States—Anti-Dumping Measures Applying Differential Pricing Methodology to Softwood Lumber from Canada (DS534).

63. See, e.g., McDougal (2018) and Hoekman and Mavroidis (2020).

REFERENCES

Bacchus, James. 2015. "Not in Clinical Isolation," in *A History of Law and Lawyers in the GATT/WTO*, edited by Gabrielle Marceau, 507–16. Cambridge University Press.

Baldwin, Robert E. 1970. *Non-Tariff Distortions of International Trade.* Brookings.

Bertelsmann Stiftung. 2018. *Revitalizing Multilateral Governance at the World Trade Organization.* Report of the High-Level Board of Experts on the Future of Global Trade Governance. Gütersloh, Germany.

Bhagwati, Jagdish, and Hugh Patrick, eds. 1991. *Aggressive Unilateralism, America's 301 Trade Policy and the World Trading System.* University of Michigan Press.

Davey, William J. 1987. "Dispute Settlement in GATT." *Fordham International Law Journal* 11 (1/2): 51–99.

Ehlermann, Claus-Dieter. 2015. "Revisiting the Appellate Body: The First Six Years." In *A History of Law and Lawyers in the GATT/WTO*, edited by Gabrielle Marceau, 482–506. Cambridge University Press.

Ganesan, A. V. 2015. "The Appellate Body in Its Formative Years: A Personal Perspective." In *A History of Law and Lawyers in the GATT/WTO*, edited by Gabrielle Marceau, 517–46, Cambridge University Press.

Grossman, Gene M., and Elhanan Helpman. 1994. "Protection for Sale." *American Economic Review* 84 (4): 833–50.

Hoekman, Bernard. 2019. "Urgent and Important: Improving WTO Performance by Revisiting Working Practices." *Journal of World Trade* 53 (3): 373–94.

Hoekman, Bernard, and Petros C. Mavroidis. 2020. "Preventing the Bad from Getting Worse: The End of the World (Trade Organization) as We Know It?" EUI Working Paper RSCAS 2020/06. Florence: European University Institute.

Hoekman, Bernard, Petros C. Mavroidis, and Maarja Saluste. 2021. "The WTO Dispute Settlement 1995–2020: A Data Set and Its Descriptive Statistics." *Journal of World Trade*, forthcoming.

Horn, Henrik, Giovanni Maggi, and Robert W. Staiger. 2010. "Trade Agreements as Endogenously Incomplete Contracts." *American Economic Review* 100 (1): 394–419.

Hudec, Robert E. 1993. *Enforcing International Trade Law.* London: Buttersworth.

Johannesson, Louise, and Petros C. Mavroidis. 2017. "The WTO Dispute Settlement System 1995–2016: A Data Set and Its Descriptive Statistics. *Journal of World Trade* 51 (3): 357–408.

Kaplow, Louis, and Steven Shavell. 1996. "Property Rules vs. Liability Rules: An Economic Analysis." *Harvard Law Review* 109: 713–90.

Lacarte-Muro, Julio. 2015. "Launching the Appellate Body." In *A History of Law and Lawyers in the GATT/WTO*, edited by Gabrielle Marceau, 476–81. Cambridge University Press.

Leddy, John. 1958. "GATT—A Cohesive Influence in the Free World." *American Journal of Agricultural Economics* 40 (2): 228–37.

Lindén, Åke. 2016. "The First Years of the GATT Legal Service." In *A History of Law and Lawyers in the GATT/WTO*, edited by Gabrielle Marceau, 135–40. Cambridge University Press.

Luyten, Paul. 2015. "We Were Young Together: At the GATT, 1956–58." In *A History of Law and Lawyers in the GATT/WTO*, edited by Gabrielle Marceau, 79–84. Cambridge University Press.

Matsushita, Mitsuo. 2015. "Reflections on the Functioning of the Appellate Body." In *A History of Law and Lawyers in the GATT/WTO*, edited by Gabrielle Marceau, 547–58. Cambridge University Press.

Mavroidis, Petros C. 2016. "Mind over Matter." In *Handbook on Commercial Policy*, edited by Kyle Bagwell and Robert W. Staiger, 333–78. Handbooks in Economics. Amsterdam: Elsevier.

Mavroidis, Petros C., and Thomas J. Prusa. 2018. "Die Another Day: Zeroing in on Targeted Dumping—Did the AB Hit the Mark in US-Washing Machines?" *World Trade Review* 17 (2): 239–264.

McDougal, Robert. 2018. "Crisis in the WTO: Restoring the WTO Dispute Settlement Function." CIGI Papers 194. Waterloo, Ontario, Canada: Center for International Governance Innovation.

Olavo Baptista, Luiz. 2015. "A Country Boy Goes to Geneva." In *A History of Law and Lawyers in the GATT/WTO*, edited by Gabrielle Marceau, 559–69. Cambridge University Press.

Petersmann, Ernst-Ulrich. 2016. "The Establishment of the GATT Office of Legal Affairs and the Limits of 'Public Reason' in the GATT/WTO Dispute Settlement System." In *A History of Law and Lawyers in the GATT/WTO*, edited by Gabrielle Marceau, 182–207. Cambridge University Press.

Prusa, Thomas, and Edwin Vermulst. 2009. "A One-Two Punch on Zeroing: US–Zeroing (EC) and US–Zeroing (Japan): United States—Laws, Regulations and Methodology for Calculating Dumping Margins (Zeroing) and United States—Measures Relating to Zeroing and Sunset Reviews." *World Trade Review* 8 (1): 187–241.

Roessler, Frieder. 2016. "The Role of Law in International Trade Relations and the Establishment of the Legal Affairs Division of the GATT." In *A History of Law and Lawyers in the GATT/WTO*, edited by Gabrielle Marceau, 171–74. Cambridge University Press.

Scitovsky, Tibor. 1942. "A Reconsideration of the Theory of Tariffs." *Review of Economic Studies* 9: 89–110.

Shavell, Steven. 2003. *Foundations of Economic Analysis of Law*. Harvard University Press.

Steger, Debra P. 2015. "The Founding of the Appellate Body." In *A History of Law and Lawyers in the GATT/WTO*, edited by Gabrielle Marceau, 447–65. Cambridge University Press.

Van den Bossche, Peter. 2006. "From Afterthought to Centerpiece: The WTO Appellate Body and Its Rise to Prominence in the World Trading System." In *The WTO at Ten: The Contribution of the Dispute Settlement System*, edited by Giorgio Sacerdoti, Alan Yanovich, and Jan Bohannes, 289–312. Cambridge University Press.

World Trade Organization (WTO). 2019. "Informal Process on Matters Related to the Functioning of the Appellate Body—Report by the Facilitator, H. E. Dr. David Walker." JOB/GC/222, October 15.

Zhang, Yuejiao. 2015. "Contribution of the WTO Appellate Body to Treaty Interpretation." In *A History of Law and Lawyers in the GATT/WTO*, edited by Gabrielle Marceau, 570–98. Cambridge University Press.

PART II

CHALLENGES FOR MULTILATERAL COOPERATION

8

THE AGRICULTURAL CHALLENGE IN THE TWENTY-FIRST CENTURY

ANNE O. KRUEGER

Patrick Messerlin has been a key contributor to understanding the costs of protectionist measures and the benefits of an integrated international economy. He has also been, in my judgment, exceptionally brave, taking on "sacred cows" at a time when the opinion of policymakers was firmly set in inappropriate directions and when the likelihood that opinion might change seemed small. I congratulate the organizers for recognizing Patrick, and Patrick for all that he has accomplished.

My focus is on world trade in agriculture. If some forecasts are right, the future problems of global agriculture will be associated with demand rising more rapidly than supply. Assuming those forecasts are right, the (relatively little) discipline over agriculture so far achieved under the World Trade Organization (WTO), and even that which would have been augmented under the Doha Round, is fighting the last war. WTO disciplines (including those proposed under Doha), while welcome, are based on the premise that there is a secular trend of falling world prices of agricultural commodities, and that distortions arise because of overproduction. If, instead, distortions start to take the form of export restrictions on the part of agricultural exporters, distortions may be quite different in the future, although protection by high-cost producers might still be part of the problem.[1]

BACKGROUND

Although the liberalization of trade in manufactured goods was a triumph for the GATT/WTO over its first sixty years of life, the fate of trade in agricultural products was disappointing. Until the Uruguay Round, there was virtually no GATT/WTO discipline over trade in agricultural products. Many countries that were natural importers invoked "food security" as a basis for protection. Even some countries that should have had a comparative advantage in a number of agricultural commodities discriminated so much in favor of manufactures that they became importers![2]

At the founding of the GATT after World War II, agricultural production was well below prewar levels in Europe and Japan, and it was natural that incentives would be given to restore productive capacity. And, in the case of the United States, because programs had begun during the Great Depression with the intention of protecting agriculture, it insisted on grandfathering these into the initial agreement. Meanwhile, many other countries invoked "food security" or "foreign exchange shortage" (especially in the case of developing countries) as a rationale for maintaining domestic prices well above world levels through import prohibitions, high tariffs, or quantitative restrictions on imports of agricultural commodities.

Agricultural production increased rapidly as disruptions from World War II were overcome. Although tariff barriers on manufactures were falling as a result of multilateral tariff negotiations, distortions resulting from protection for agricultural commodities and the search for food security increased the global misallocation of agricultural resources. Once agricultural production was above prewar levels in Europe, the Common Agricultural Policy (CAP) protected European farm prices and, for an extended period, resulted not only in increased protection but also in subsidization of exports for some agricultural commodities.[3] The Japanese, and later the South Koreans, built high walls of protection against imports for many agricultural commodities, with tariff equivalents for rice and some meat products of several hundred percent.[4]

Although the United States maintained its program of price supports and other assistance for agriculture, it was a net exporter of agricultural commodities. If any one of the three groups—the Europeans, the Americans, or the East Asians—had removed their farm programs unilaterally, adjustment costs would have been far greater than if they could have found a coordinated approach. To a degree, each used the others' protection as a rationale for maintaining its own. Agricultural protection was crying out for a multilateral solution.

Most developing countries, meanwhile, were attempting to provide incentives for increasing domestic production of manufactures, using tariffs and quantitative restrictions on their imports (on agricultural commodities, on consumer goods, and even on farm inputs), with overvalued exchange rates, which penalized agricultural exporters.[5] There were also high prices for domestically produced manufactured inputs for agriculture and imported consumer goods for farmers and imports in many poor countries.

For the world as a whole, there appeared to be a secular trend toward falling relative prices of agricultural commodities, and the global problem, or "challenge" if you prefer, appeared to be to reduce distortions in agriculture primarily by reducing incentives for production in developed countries at above world prices. Yet, increasing agricultural productivity in some developing countries by enough to meet upward shifts in their demand from rising per capita income and growing populations appeared to be a virtually insurmountable challenge.

THE URUGUAY ROUND

Until the Uruguay Round, launched in 1986, it had proved impossible to agree on any multilateral discipline over production and trade in agricultural commodities. In part this was because of the domestic priorities individual countries and groups of countries gave to their farm objectives. But in part the problem was that, unlike manufactures, agriculture was protected by a large number of policy instruments, so even estimating the level of protection was challenging. Different countries adopted differing combinations of import tariffs and quantitative restrictions, domestic price and income supports, subsidized credits for farmers, and export subsidies to try and achieve their objectives. Moreover, again unlike for manufactures, there was widespread belief that developing countries as a group had a comparative advantage in production of agricultural commodities and were harmed by the "overproduction" in developed countries. Whereas industrial countries had collectively agreed to reduce tariffs on manufactures (in which they generally did have a comparative advantage) and could lead the negotiations, they were reluctant to alter their farm policies; and developing countries had, until Uruguay, been free riders on the tariff cuts (almost entirely on manufactures) negotiated among the industrial countries and did not consider taking leadership or even urging reducing agricultural protection.[6]

By the mid-1980s, technical research had suggested that the measure "producer subsidy equivalent" (PSE) could be used to render comparable the production levels in different countries despite their very different combinations of border and domestic measures to support agriculture.[7] At about the same time, budgetary burdens, particularly in the European Union, led to pressure to modify farm support programs.[8]

The Uruguay Round achieved the first serious GATT/WTO discipline over agriculture, although there was disappointment that the ceilings negotiated in the round were not more binding.[9] It was agreed that agricultural programs could be categorized in one of three pillars: a green box, into which policies toward agriculture that were judged to have virtually no (trade-distorting) effect on output of individual commodities were placed; a blue box for "moderately distorting" measures; and an "amber" box, which contains the trade-distorting measures.[10]

The green box was to contain policies such as land set-aside programs for environmental purposes, research and development support, and subsidies not linked to production levels. Only the amber box commodities were subject to ceilings, as it was thought that blue box measures would be a step toward reducing distortions.[11] Countries were to list in the amber box all the measures which increased incentives to produce individual commodities above those that would have existed at world prices.

However, the actual indicator to be employed to measure distortions was not the PSE, but rather the aggregate measure of support (AMS).[12] The AMS was to be calculated for each major commodity as the percentage of the various price-distorting measures (including tariffs, subsidies without ceilings on land use or production, and administered prices at above world levels) of the reference price. The reference price was the 1986–1988 price, rather than the prevailing world price. Hence, in years when world prices were above those of the reference period, the AMS overstated the distortion, since the divergence between domestic prices and world prices was smaller than the AMS, while in years of low world prices, the AMS understated the distortions.

Countries were to notify the WTO of their measures annually, and the Committee on Agriculture was to meet regularly, evaluate whether policies were appropriately categorized, and estimate the resulting magnitudes. There were negotiated AMS targets for each country in the Uruguay Round. AMS included limits for major individual commodities (such as wheat) and overall totals (the total aggregate measure of support, or TAMS) over all commodities. The AMS and related measures were negotiated for each country and included in the Uruguay Round agreement.[13] The Uruguay Round also required an average tariff cut of 36 percent, the conversion of import quotas into tariffs, and a number of other measures to reduce agricultural protection. All of these were, in principle, designed to reduce total protection to agriculture, primarily in industrial countries. But by the time the ceilings and categories were negotiated, the actual reductions were far less than the aggregate measures suggested.

POST–URUGUAY ROUND AGRICULTURAL SUPPORT TRENDS

Figures 8-1a through 8-1c provide an indication of what happened from 1986 to 2018, both to the PSEs and the TAMS, for the EU, Japan, and the United States, respectively. The data are in the respective national currencies. Relative to the levels in the latter part of the 1990s, by both measures support has fallen. Part of this drop reflected higher world prices. But the divergence between the PSEs and the TAMS increased as countries shifted from direct price supports to other means of assisting agriculture. For Japan and the United States the value of the PSE and TAMS both fell substantially in the 1990s. The measures were as close together as they were because high world prices resulted in less support for farmers.

There was, and is, considerable variation in PSEs among farm commodities and among countries. In the United States, for example, average PSEs (as a percentage of gross farm receipts) in 2002–2004 were 33 for rice, 57 for sugar, and 40 for milk, but 4 for poultry, pork, beef and veal, with an overall PSE of 18. Japan's PSEs for rice, wheat and oilseeds were 83, 85, and 57, respectively, with an overall average of 56.[14] PSEs do not include general support for agriculture, but only those measures that affect the incentives

FIGURE 8-1A. European Union: Producer Subsidy Equivalents (PSEs) and Total Aggregate Measure of Support (TAMS), 1966–2017

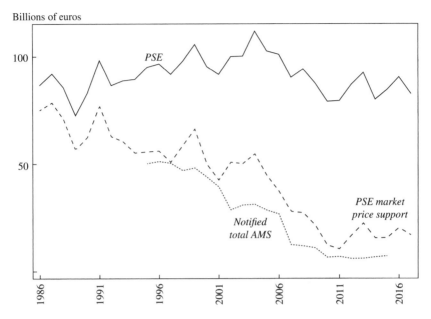

Billions of euros

Source: PSEs are from the OECD and AMS are from WTO.

FIGURE 8-1B. Japan: Producer Subsidy Equivalents (PSEs) and Aggregate Measure of Support (AMS)

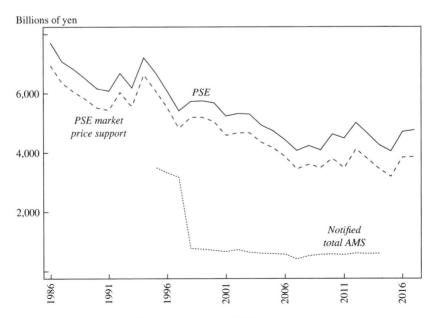

Billions of yen

Source: PSEs are from the OECD and AMS are from WTO.

FIGURE 8-1C. United States: Producer Subsidy Equivalents (PSEs) and Aggregate Measure of Support (AMS)

Billions of US dollars

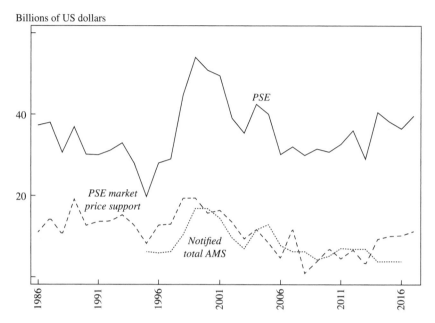

Source: PSEs are from the OECD and AMS are from WTO.

to produce particular crops. Thus the PSE does not include measures that provide price supports for a crop if they also restrict acreage so that production cannot be increased. When there is a food subsidy, such as in the US Food Stamp Program (now called SNAP [Supplemental Nutritional Assistance Program]), that does not count as part of the PSE but does count in the TAMS. Measures that are not commodity-specific include items such as water subsidies not tied to individual crops, research, and land set-asides for environmental reasons. To simplify exposition, the PSE is the metric reported in the remainder of this chapter because it is a better measure of distortions than the AMS.[15]

Figure 8-2 gives indicators of the magnitudes of the PSEs as a percentage of farm receipts since 1986–1988 for the OECD member countries. For the OECD as a whole, the PSE fell from around 30 percent in the 1990s to below 20 percent after 2010. Declines are also observed for the United States, the European Union, and Japan. This drop primarily reflects two phenomena: a decline in applied import tariffs—by 6 percentage points

FIGURE 8-2. **Producer Subsidy Equivalent (PSE) Indicators, 1986–2018**

PSE share of gross farm receipts (%)

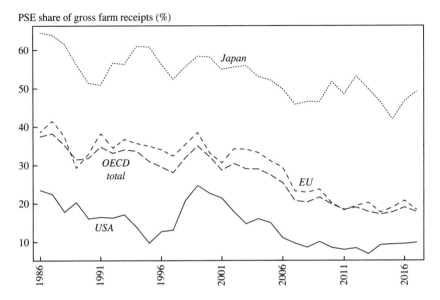

Source: OECD (2019).

since 2000 (OECD 2019) and a shift in support away from direct price supports (with no acreage limits) to other programs and price supports with
acreage limits. It is by no means assured that PSEs would remain so low if
world prices of agricultural goods were to fall. As noted previously, higher
farm prices imply that PSEs will fall even without any government action.
Overall agricultural prices have increased over the period, although with
significant volatility. Between 2010 and 2014–2015, for example, many agricultural commodity prices fell substantially, before recovering in 2016–2017.
At this writing in 2020, they stand around 20 percent below 2010–2013
levels.

Prices of agricultural commodities peaked in 2007–2008. As a result, in
most countries farm incomes were at all-time highs: in the United States,
the average farm family income had already risen above average urban
family income by 2002, and rose further above it when farm prices peaked.[16]
Since then, PSEs as a share of gross farm receipts fell by 10 percentage
points in the EU, the United States, and the OECD as a whole (figure 8-2).
One reason for this is that, overall, in the period since the Doha Round
was launched, average world food prices rose.

Farmers, however, experienced more of a roller coaster than the PSEs indicate. Farm prices fell during the Great Recession, then rose about 20 percent by 2011, and another 15 percent by 2015–2016. Thereafter, however, they fell, and the index stood at only 94 in 2019. As if that were not enough, the prices of farm inputs (e.g., feed, seed, and fertilizer), which had moved at about the same rate as prices received until 2014, began falling. The index, which stood at 115 in 2014 (on a 2011 base), fell to 93 in 2019 (OECD 2019). The pain of falling output prices was magnified by the continuing rise in input prices. Once the WTO had established the PSE limits, governments shifted some of their support from those covered in the PSEs to others. Consequently, while government payments to farmers rose, the PSEs changed very little.

US real farm income peaked in 2013 at $123.4 billion and fell to $63.1 billion in 2018.[17] The most recent American farm bill, which is up for renewal about every five years, was passed in 2018.[18] A major expenditure under the farm program, SNAP, was reduced from its earlier levels in the last two acts. Other than that, and shifting away from payments counted in PSE measures, the Farm Bill was not significantly changed in the two versions that passed after the Great Recession in 2014 and 2018. In Europe as well, PSEs were lower than they had been before the PSE limits, but were partially offset by policies outside the PSE restrictions.

For present purposes, two points are relevant. First and most important, the Uruguay Round established a framework for WTO discipline over support to agriculture. Second, the Uruguay framework was based on the assumption that the problem was that incentives for more production were greater than they would have been had commodity prices cleared in an efficient world market. Fortunately (or otherwise), prices of agricultural commodities rose sharply as the Uruguay Round constraints were gradually coming into effect (starting in 1995). The result was that many countries had to do little or nothing to meet their commitments under the round, since farm prices and incomes were generally sufficiently high that intervention costs were below the limits set forth in the final agreement.

When countries needed to act to meet their Uruguay Round constraints, there was some reduction in support, but in many cases there was a shift away from supports for commodity prices (and acreage under production) to direct income support. The OECD estimates, for example, that Switzerland's PSE for farmers fell from 77 percent of its total support to

55 percent, while its total support fell from over 90 percent to around 70 percent in the fifteen years following the Uruguay Round. But the most salient facts are that discipline had begun, and that countries were largely in compliance with it.[19]

When world prices of agricultural commodities fell early in the 2000s, most countries' programs were within the limits set under the Uruguay Round—both because of the 1986–1988 base and because countries had shifted from reliance on direct price supports to income supports with acreage limitations or other exemptions. Farm incomes were therefore effectively protected at the same time that the limits on distortive measures negotiated in the Uruguay Round were observed. Nonetheless, there could not be any question but that industrial countries were still subsidizing their farmers heavily. For the OECD as a whole, PSEs as a percentage of gross farm receipts were 40 percent in 1986 and around 30 percent in 2001 when the Doha Round was launched. For the European Union, the corresponding figures were 45 percent and 35 percent, while those for the United States were 25 percent.

THE DOHA ROUND

The Uruguay Round ceilings are, of course, still in effect, as there has been no closure to the Doha Round. During the initial years of Doha negotiations, strengthened disciplines were negotiated and tentatively agreed on for agriculture. If these measures had become part of a final Doha Round agreement, they would have further constrained distortive agricultural policies.[20] As Orden, Josling, and Blandford (2011b, 420) concluded: "a Doha agreement built on the December 2008 draft modalities would achieve real progress on the path toward substantial progressive reductions envisioned in the 1994 Agreement on Agriculture. A Doha agreement . . . would impose some meaningful constraints, especially for developed countries."

There can be little doubt that acceptance of these measures would improve the efficiency of world agriculture. Whatever the secular trend in world prices of agricultural commodities, there are bound to be periods of low prices, and constraints on the degree to which there can be incentives for additional production would serve to reduce the variance in world prices of agricultural commodities. Thus, an upward secular trend could reverse at a future date, just as the secular downward trend of much of the past fifty years has perhaps now been reversed. Hence the ceilings negotiated in Doha would represent progress.

This would be especially true if meaningful bounds on support for commodities such as ethanol and cotton could be included in the agreement. Despite the progress that would be represented should the 2008 undertakings be enacted, there are special problems with a few key commodities, and those result in considerable distortions in the global economy.

Perhaps the most serious from a global viewpoint is ethanol—it is estimated that 17 percent of the global maize crop is now destined for production of biofuels (OECD/FAO 2019). Originally mandated by the US Congress as an environmental measure consistent with renewable energy resources, the Renewable Fuel Standard (RFS) was established by the Energy Policy Act of 2005 and expanded in 2007. The RFS requires that transportation fuels contain an increasing volume of renewable fuels over time. The mandate was 4 billion gallons of renewable fuel in 2006. As of 2019, the Environmental Protection Agency (EPA) had increased the mandate to 19.9 billion gallons (Bracmort 2019).[21] One result of the mandate, together with subsidies for maize production—totaling roughly $90 billion between 1995 and 2010 (not including ethanol subsidies and the mandates) (Foley 2013)—is that the United States has become the leading global producer of ethanol, accounting for 50 percent of world output, and the second largest producer of biodiesel (19 percent of world output) (OECD/FAO 2018).

The environmental impact of the RFS is questionable. The advanced biofuel component of the RFS, which would yield greater greenhouse gas emission reductions and generate fuel from nonfood biomass, has missed the statutory targets by a large margin. The initially assumed environmental benefits of ethanol from maize production are small at best because of the energy, fertilizer, and other inputs used in growing corn and in ethanol production (Foley 2013). If the mandated increases in the ethanol content of gasoline were not adjusted by the EPA, much of the US maize crop would have to go to ethanol. As it stands, about 40 percent of the US maize crop is used for biofuel production,[22] and sizable acreage has been diverted from soybeans and other crops or been brought into production. The sharp upward shift in demand for corn for ethanol is estimated to have accounted for 25 percent or more of the increase in world grain prices in the late 2000s. Reducing the use of corn for fuel would reduce upward price pressures, lower demand for scarce natural resource inputs, including land, and expand food output.

The magnitude of subsidies for ethanol production in the United States has been reduced since Congress removed a 54 cents per gallon specific tariff on imports of ethanol, as well as tax credits to refiners of 46 cents per gallon in 2011. The increased requirements for ethanol production were deemed sufficient protection, and there was little protest from the industry. Redressing the ethanol situation will be difficult (since large investments have been made in ethanol plants), but it will become even more so as time passes. The impact on food supply and prices and the lack of benefits makes a clear case for removal of support policies for ethanol, but the refiners and corn growers are strongly resistant.

Another high-cost program is the US cotton price support program. It was expanded markedly in the late 1990s and resulted in a large increase in US production, much of which was exported. The result was a sharp drop in world cotton prices, with pronounced impacts on some small countries for whom cotton was the major export and a large part of small farmers' incomes. West African cotton-exporting countries were especially hard hit because many small farmers relied on cotton for most, or even all, of their income. The four African exporters consider that a sharp change in the cotton program, or compensation for their reduced export prices, is essential for them. Brazil pursued a WTO dispute case and eventually won some compensation. Negotiating a significantly lower cap on the PSE for cotton would result in a higher world price for cotton, with benefits for efficient use of agricultural resources and for the exporting countries.[23]

LOOKING TO THE FUTURE

Completion of the Doha Round, including the elements of what emerged in 2008 to strengthen agricultural disciplines, would have represented a significant step toward more efficient world agriculture. Even if it had been completed, much would be left for future negotiations. The EU, Japan, and the United States continue to have costly and inefficient farm support programs. Moreover, PSEs have been increasing in emerging economies, roughly doubling, from 5 to 10 percent, in the past decade.

As already seen, the disciplines negotiated in the Doha Round would have further constrained countries' use of distortive measures in years of falling prices. But while the Doha Round has languished, it is quite possible that the distortions in world agricultural production may be changing. During the period of peak prices in 2007–2008, a number of exporting

TABLE 8-1. **Partial List of Restrictions on Agricultural Exports, 2008–2011**

Country	Restriction	Date imposed
India	Cap on cotton exports	August 16, 2011
India	Extension of ban on edible oil exports	August 16, 2011
India	Partial removal of export duty on basmati rice	July 4, 2011
Kyrgyz Rep.	Temporary export taxes on agricultural products	July 1, 2011
Serbia	Temporary export restrictions on wheat and flour	April 1, 2011
Moldova	Export ban on wheat	February 2, 2011
Ethiopia	Ban on export of raw cotton	November 15, 2010
Ukraine	Export quotas on agricultural products	October 4, 2010
India	Extension on ban of pulses exports	August 19, 2010
India	Ban on cotton exports replaced by licensing	May 21, 2010
Argentina	Reference prices for designated exports	March 5, 2010
Argentina	Export registration requirements	November 1, 2009
Indonesia	Export tax on cacao beans	April 1, 2010
Argentina	De facto ban on bovine meat exports	February 1, 2020
Kazakhstan	Temporary ban on rice and milk exports	December 1, 2008
Egypt	Repeat ban on rice exports	September 24, 2010

Source: Simon Evenett, provided through correspondence from the Global Trade Alert database, November 2011.

countries (including, in particular, Argentina, Russia, and Ukraine) imposed quantitative restrictions or outright prohibition on the export of key commodities. Table 8-1 lists some of the export restrictions applied to agricultural commodities over the ten quarters starting from the end of 2008. The list is almost certainly not comprehensive and only includes measures that were listed in sources accessible to Global Trade Alert compilers. The motive for imposition of restrictions was to keep domestic prices below world prices.

Under present arrangements, such measures do not violate WTO disciplines. While there are limits on distortive border and domestic measures that encourage agricultural production, there are no constraints on export prohibitions or restrictions.[24] But there are many forecasts of shortages and hence rising prices of agricultural commodities over the next half century, with rising populations and real income growth. If that is correct (and it seems to be the view of the majority of agricultural economists and the agricultural policy community), the danger of increased distortions to agricultural production almost certainly arises more from the risks of export limitations and the reactions that they are likely to evoke. Not only will world prices rise further at times when export restrictions or prohibitions are imposed, but countries importing agricultural commodities will become concerned about their long-term food security and resort to protective measures to induce more domestic production.

The agricultural agreements already negotiated in Doha are desirable not only because the future trajectory of supply and demand is not certain, but also because even if the past trend toward lower prices is reversed, there are bound to be price fluctuations and therefore periods of low prices—as well as periods of high prices.

To increase the efficiency of world agriculture and to prevent (or restrict) the emergence of a new set of distortive policies guarding against high prices rather than low ones, discipline over export restrictions is also needed.

It is easy to see the dangers. Export restrictions or prohibitions on the part of countries with a comparative advantage would not only distort world agriculture, but would also intensify any trend toward higher prices for agricultural commodities. If exporters impose restrictions during periods of high prices, it is very likely that importing countries will respond at least partially by increasing protection for their own domestic agriculture. This might be done in retaliation, or in the name of food security. And, if prices of agricultural commodities are expected to continue to increase (or even to be maintained at very high levels), policymakers in importing countries could also argue that higher domestic production would be, or would shortly become, economic.[25] If that were to happen, distortions in world agriculture would increase. Moreover, it is likely that the average prices of farm commodities would rise even more than they would with an efficient allocation of resources, while the fluctuations in world prices of agricultural commodities would intensify (as, perhaps, would fluctuations in individual

FIGURE 8-3. Top Five Users of Agricultural Export Restrictions, 2009–2018

Number of implemented export restrictions

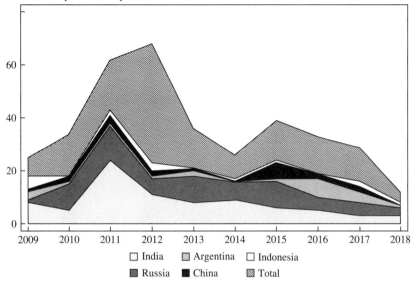

Source: Global Trade Alert.

countries as exporters lost their markets and importers were increasingly affected by domestic supply variations).

Since 2010–2012, the use of export restrictions fell as world prices dropped (figure 8-3). There is no assurance, however, that a similar pattern in the use of export restrictions will not reemerge if prices spike again. Several countries imposed restrictions on exports of certain agricultural products in the first half of 2020 in the context of the COVID-19 pandemic. Although the use of such measures was relatively limited compared to 2007–08 (a total of thirty-two countries imposed forty-nine export restrictions between January and July 2020, and many of these were rescinded during this period), it illustrated again the willingness of countries to impose export restrictions.[26] If some countries that normally export impose quantitative restrictions or prohibitions on exports of key commodities at times of high prices or in response to supply shocks, the fluctuations in world prices of agricultural commodities would intensify. World prices of traded agricultural commodities whose exports are restricted will rise more during periods of high prices than they otherwise would. That, in turn, would almost certainly induce reactions from countries that, in an efficient allocation of resources, would be net importers of agricultural commodities.

Domestic prices in "natural" exporters would be lower because of restrictions on exports, and hence there would be less production and more consumption, and smaller exports. Moreover, farmers in "natural" exporting countries would experience lower prices, and therefore incomes, both in times of high prices (because domestic prices would be below world prices) and in times of low prices (because the "natural" importers would be producing more but consuming less because of higher prices, and thus importing less). Hence, at a time of increasing upward pressure on prices of agricultural commodities (as is assumed here), production would shift from former exporters (the lower-cost producers) to former importers (the higher-cost producers). If, as is believed, it is desirable to increase agricultural output efficiently, the net effect would be in exactly the opposite direction. One of the few achievements of the Doha Round was a 2015 agreement to ban agricultural export subsidies. Complementing this with an equivalent agreement to ban export restrictions would be very desirable.

CONCLUSION

Completion of the Doha Round would improve the world agricultural economy. It would, nonetheless, leave numerous challenges. High on the list is the difficulty that will arise if the trend for world agricultural prices over the past half century is reversed and a secular upward trend replaces it. Although the future trajectory of agricultural prices cannot be forecast with certainty, most careful assessments project increases. If prices rise, the Uruguay Round disciplines over agriculture and their intensification under it would still be useful, but the WTO will be lacking disciplines over the additional distortions that might arise in times of rising prices. For that purpose, an agreement to refrain from export restraints when prices rise would be needed.

Such an agreement would benefit agricultural exporting countries and would result in lower average world prices than would be the case if exporters (importers) move toward export restrictions (higher levels of protection against imports). If the world's problem is, as would seem likely, rising world prices, there is a strong reason for bringing export restrictions under discipline now before future runups in prices induce more such measures. If the future holds higher prices for agricultural commodities, it will also be highly desirable to find disciplines that balance trade-offs between environmental concerns and the supply of agricultural products much more effectively than has happened to date. This could take the form of a discipline, such as that governing phytosanitary concerns, that requires scientific evidence of the supposed benefits of environmental measures and use of the least-cost way of achieving the desired environmental outcome.

The prospect that some distortions in world agriculture could be removed through two large preferential trading arrangements, the Trans-Pacific Partnership (TPP) and the Transatlantic Trade and Investment Partnership (TTIP), has not materialized. The former did constrain some highly protectionist countries, including Japan and South Korea. Thus the Comprehensive and Progressive Agreement for Trans-Pacific Partnership (CPTPP), the successor to the TPP which was rejected by the Trump Administration, will entail a reduction in agricultural protection in East Asia. But it will not do so in the United States since the United States withdrew from the TPP and put the TTIP negotiations with the EU on hold. Even if agreements spanning the EU and United States were concluded, it seems evident that some of the distortions to agriculture (such as ethanol and cotton) would probably not be greatly reduced, as too many producers of cotton (in Africa especially) and producers and consumers of maize are not part of the negotiations. The need for global disciplines remains.

A major change in the global agricultural economy came about in 2018 when the United States initiated its trade war with China. The United States imposed tariffs on a number of Chinese goods, and the Chinese retaliated in part by purchasing soybeans, corn, and other grains from other suppliers. Part of the recorded drop in US farm prices in 2018 and early 2019 was attributable to the shift in those Chinese purchases from the United States to Brazil and other countries. Although the US administration committed $28 billion to US farmers, there were important political protests against the resulting decline in farm prices. As of mid-2020, many of the American tariffs and the measures the Chinese took in response are still in place and it remains to be seen if the January 2020 agreement between the United States and China, under which China undertook to boost imports of American agricultural products, will be implemented. The outlook for tariff removal is not clear.[27]

It would clearly be desirable to revive multilateral efforts to bolster disciplines on agricultural policies. Even if all that is feasible is what was on the table in 2008, there would be gains. For agriculture, increased discipline would benefit the global economy. The opportunity cost of not completing the Doha Round is not only that existing disciplines on domestic support have not been tightened. Issues of equal importance, such as the need for discipline over agriculture in times of high prices, require urgent attention.

NOTES

After I wrote a first draft of this chapter early in this decade for the conference in honor of Patrick Messerlin, farm prices rose and then began falling again after 2014–2015. Little has changed by way of policy. I am more heavily indebted to David Orden, Lars Brink, and Tim Josling than is usually the case with an acknowledgment. They provided support not only by providing data but also in navigating the complexities of the Uruguay Round. I am also grateful to Simon Evenett for sharing his Global Trade Alert (GTA) results, to Matteo Fiorini for updating the GTA and agricultural support data through 2018, and to Farouq Ghandour for research assistance. The responsibility for any errors of fact or interpretation in the chapter is solely mine.

1. Challenges that may arise for global efficiency of agricultural production because of future environmental considerations are not dealt with in this chapter. A brief discussion of the impact ethanol subsidization has had on agricultural production and food prices is provided to give an illustration of the sorts of problems that might arise.

2. See Krueger (1992) for estimates for some countries in the mid-1980s.

3. It will be recalled that the variable levy under the CAP maintained high prices for producers and in some years resulted in production in excess of domestic consumption, resulting in exports that were subsidized.

4. See Anderson and Hayami (1986) for a discussion.

5. Nominal exchange rates were kept fixed for long periods despite inflation rates much above those in the developed countries, and hence overvaluation was rife. The rationale for this was that it would make imported capital goods cheap and thus enable more investment. The difficulty was that, with overvalued exchange rates the incentives for exports were weakened, foreign exchange earnings rose less rapidly than demand for foreign exchange, or even stagnated, and hence exchange controls tightened and imports of capital goods could not increase as had been expected.

6. It is not entirely clear that all developing countries have identical interests in agriculture. Some are net importers of food products, and others are net exporters; some have comparative advantage in tropical commodities, and some in temperate. But it was considered that developing countries as a group had an interest in reducing high levels of protection for agriculture in advanced countries.

7. The acronym PSE is used to denote both "producer subsidy equivalent" and "producer support estimate."

8. By that time, the European Union historically had difficulties with mounting inventories of supported agricultural commodities. Perhaps the support program that most vividly typified the problem was that for butter. The "butter mountain" became a standard jibe at the CAP. But the variable levy (which took import proceeds and distributed them to farmers for "double protection" and the export subsidies of the CAP) led to widespread pressure for program modification.

9. The aggregate measure of support, the metric actually used by the WTO, is somewhat different than the PSE proposed by the OECD. See later discussion of the differences between the two measures.

10. The volume from Orden, Josling, and Blandford (2011b) is invaluable in analyzing the agricultural provisions of the outcome of the Uruguay Round.

11. This meant, however, that Japan, for example, could reduce its reported AMS by maintaining high levels of border protection for rice, while eliminating its administered price which had been well above world levels.

12. Orden, Josling, and Blandford (2011b), especially the chapter by Brink (2011), provide extensive discussion.

13. See Brink (2011) for a detailed exposition.

14. Estimates are from Elliott (2006, 29, table 2.4).

15. Even PSEs suffer from the property that the same legislated farm support program can result in differing levels of distortion in different years depending on world prices and the type of protection accorded in domestic programs. A guaranteed minimum price, for example, would confer no protection (or distortion according to the PSE measure) in a year when world prices were above the guaranteed minimum. Such a guarantee, however, could nonetheless influence incentives for producing the crop by reducing uncertainty.

16. It is estimated that a typical farmer in US corn-producing states was earning between $750,000 and $1.4 million annually by 2011 (Mufson 2011).

17. USDA forecast and numbers as reported in US Department of Agriculture, NASS highlights, on July 1, 2019, at www.nass.usda.gov.

18. The interested reader can learn more in the volume by Smith, Glauber, and Goodwin (2018).

19. From appendix tables in OECD (2009).

20. See appendix B of Orden, Josling, and Blandford (2011a) for an abridged text of the agreement.

21. The statutory goal to be achieved in 2022 is 36 billion gallons, a target that will not be achieved (Bracmort 2019). No more than 15 billion of the 36 billion gallons may be corn-based.

22. See data from the Alternative Fuels Data Center at https://afdc.energy .gov/data/10339 and the US Department of Agriculture at https://www.ers

.usda.gov/data-products/us-bioenergy-statistics/us-bioenergy-statistics/#Supply
%20and%20Disappearance.

23. Glauber (2018) discusses changes in US cotton support policy and advocates shifting away from the changes imposed in the 2014 Farm Bill that removed direct and countercyclical payments.

24. Of course, under Doha, subsidization of agricultural exports was to cease, but that again is a measure protecting against glut.

25. Martin and Anderson (2012) have estimated that, in the 2006–2008 agricultural price surge, 45 percent of the increase in the price of rice and 30 percent of the change in the price of wheat can be explained by changes in border protection rates. Many importers had lowered their border protection as export restraints were imposed elsewhere (in response to rising prices) to ease the upward pressure on domestic prices, which exacerbated the impact on world prices of export restrictions.

26. See EUI, Global Trade Alert and World Bank, Tracking Pandemic-Era Trade Policies in Food and Medical Products, https://www.globaltradealert.org /reports/54.

27. The "phase 1" deal concluded by China and the United States in January 2020 retained the 25 percent tariffs imposed on $250 billion of Chinese exports but cut US tariffs on an additional $120 billion of Chinese exports imposed in September 2019 by 50 percent, to 7.5 percent, and suspended the US threat to impose punitive tariffs on those exports not already targeted by the United States. The main feature of the agreement was a promise by China to increase imports from the United States within two years by $200 billion more than the country had imported in 2017. See "Economic and Trade Agreement between the Government of the United States and the Government of the People's Republic of China, January 15, 2020," https://ustr.gov/sites /default/files/files/agreements/phase%20one%20agreement/Economic_And _Trade_Agreement_Between_The_United_States_And_China_Text.pdf.

REFERENCES

Anderson, Kym, and Yujiro Hayami. 1986. *The Political Economy of Agricultural Protection: East Asia in International Perspective*. Sydney: Allen and Unwin.

Bracmort, Kelsi. 2019. "The Renewable Fuel Standard (RFS): An Overview." Congressional Research Service R43325. January 23.

Brink, Lars. 2011. "The WTO Disciplines on Domestic Support." In *WTO Disciplines on Agricultural Support: Seeking a Fair Basis for Trade*, edited by David Orden, Timothy Josling, and David Blandford, 23–58. Cambridge University Press.

Elliott, Kimberley Ann. 2006. *Delivering on Doha*. Washington, D.C.: Center for Global Development.

Foley, Jonathan. 2013. "It's Time to Rethink America's Corn System." *Scientific American*, March 5.

Glauber, Joseph. 2018. "Unraveling Reforms? Cotton in the 2018 Farm Bill." Washington, D.C.: American Enterprise Institute, January.

Krueger, Anne O. 1992. *The Political Economy of Agricultural Pricing Policy: A Synthesis of the Political Economy in Developing Countries*. Johns Hopkins University Press.

Martin, Will, and Kym Anderson. 2012. "Export Restrictions and Price Insulation during Commodity Price Booms." *American Journal of Agricultural Economics* 94 (2): 422–27.

Mufson, Steven. 2011. "Ethanol Subsidy Fight Not Over." *New York Times*, June 16.

Orden, David, Timothy Josling and David Blandford. 2011a. "The Difficult Task of Disciplining Domestic Support," in David Orden, Timothy Josling and David Blandford (eds.). *WTO Disciplines on Agricultural Support: Seeking a Fair Basis for Trade*. Cambridge University Press, pp. 391–432.

———, eds. 2011b. *WTO Disciplines on Agricultural Support: Seeking a Fair Basis for Trade*. Cambridge University Press.

Organization for Economic Cooperation and Development (OECD). 2009. *Agricultural Policies in OECD Countries: Monitoring and Evaluation*. Paris.

———. 2019. *Agricultural Policy Monitoring and Evaluation 2019*. Paris.

OECD/Food and Agriculture Organization of the United Nations. 2019. "Biofuels." In *OECD-FAO Agricultural Outlook 2019–2028*. Paris: OECD Publishing.

Smith, Vincent H., Joseph W. Glauber, and Barry K. Goodwin. 2018. *Agricultural Policy in Disarray*. Washington, D.C.: American Enterprise Institute.

9

SUBSIDIES, SPILLOVERS, AND MULTILATERAL COOPERATION

BERNARD HOEKMAN AND DOUGLAS NELSON

I t has become almost a cliché that we live in a supply chain world. Nevertheless, it is true, and this fact has changed the relative importance (salience) of different types of trade and external policies. The organization of global value chains (GVCs) is very sensitive to transaction costs. Policies that raise (reduce) operating costs will lower (increase) the competitiveness of activities in specific locations and influence the allocation of investment. Participation in GVCs is conditional on low barriers to trade and efficient national regulatory systems that minimize delays in border clearance and uncertainty with respect to the ability to enforce contracts, meet production quality standards, and protect intellectual property. Policy design and international cooperation in a GVC world are more complicated than they are in a world where goods are produced with domestic factors and inputs and supply chains are national. For example, production subsidies in one country (location) may have the effect of assisting production and exports in another. International specialization, in conjunction with the associated flows of foreign direct investment (FDI), attenuates the incentives to use traditional trade policy instruments (Blanchard 2015; Gawande, Hoekman, and Cui 2015).

While tariffs and related border policies become less effective as an instrument of industrial policy in a GVC world, governments continue to have incentives to support domestic firms and local employment, and firms continue to have incentives to lobby governments for assistance. Subsidies and subsidy-like interventions have dominated the post-2008 trade policy landscape. These types of instruments are used to target specific domestic economic activities deemed desirable from an economic growth and development perspective. This is nothing new. The motivations and pressures to assist domestic economic activity have not changed simply because the structure of international production has changed over the past twenty-some years. What has changed—notwithstanding the pursuit by President Donald Trump ("Tariff Man") of an aggressive unilateralist trade policy—is the decline in the relative weight of traditional border protectionism in the trade policy of most governments.

Analogous to tariffs and similar at-the-border protectionist instruments, domestic policies that support local economic activity may create negative international spillovers. Such interdependencies become more prevalent—and more complex—in a GVC world. Important questions for policy are to determine the magnitude of the negative spillovers created by industrial policies and whether and how to redesign multilateral rules to discipline the use of measures that result in negative externalities for trading partners and the trading system. All governments pursue policies that affect the operation of markets. What has increased the political salience of industrial development policies as a perceived source of negative spillovers for other countries is the rapid growth of China and views that large-scale subsidization of Chinese firms, especially state-owned enterprises (SOEs), is one reason for China's success.

A distinct feature of concerns about the implications of the rising share of China and other emerging economies in world production and trade is the role and prevalence of SOEs in these economies. An estimated 22 percent of the world's largest 100 firms are effectively under state control (OECD 2016). In 2018, Chinese firms accounted for 22 percent of the list of 500 largest firms globally compiled by *Forbes* magazine.[1] The five largest Chinese companies on the list—20 percent of the top twenty-five global companies—are all SOEs. Many SOEs operate in GVC-intensive sectors, both upstream such as energy and downstream such as transport, and often are active in cross-border mergers and acquisitions (outward FDI). Concerns about the potential for SOEs to distort competition reflect views that SOEs are effectively subsidized (through soft loans, guarantees, and preferential access to factor inputs other than directed credits, such as energy and land) and may indirectly subsidize downstream firms in both home and foreign markets through below-market pricing for their goods and services. In addition, SOEs may benefit from protection from foreign competition (e.g., reflected in FDI restrictions, joint venture requirements, preferential access to public procurement markets).[2]

The United States, the European Union, and other World Trade Organization (WTO) members also argue that China has put in place incentives for foreign firms to invest in China rather than serve the market through exports, and that the Chinese government supports Chinese firms operating in international markets. The resulting trade tensions have led to the use of countervailing duties against Chinese exports and discussions among the EU, Japan, and the United States to identify gaps in WTO disciplines and ways to strengthen rules for subsidies, SOEs, and technology transfer policies. The trilateral discussions focus on suggestions to expand the existing list of prohibited subsidies in the WTO and to define SOEs as "public bodies" to allow action against products that have used inputs provided by an SOE (e.g., intermediate inputs, credit). A general aim is to broaden the definition of what constitutes an actionable subsidy—for example, open-ended financial guarantees, support for insolvent or failing companies with no credible restructuring plan, and preferential pricing for inputs such as raw materials and components.[3]

A basic problem in the design of international rules for subsidies and related industrial policies is to strike a balance between the legitimate role of governments to support economic development goals and to address market failures on the one hand, and the negative spillovers that domestic policies may create on the other. This chapter reflects on these issues. We argue that elements of the current rules embedded in the WTO are no longer fit for purpose. We also make a case that the solution involves a shift in approach to recognize that there are legitimate reasons for governments to use subsidies. There is a strong case for WTO members to launch a process to identify and evaluate the use of competition-distorting policies, and to provide a forum in which to discuss the impacts and spillover effects of specific policies on investment decisions and trade. A precondition for determining whether new disciplines are needed, or old ones should be adapted, is information and analysis: empirical research on the magnitude and incidence of negative international spillovers that are created by prevailing policies. Whatever the normative case for stronger multilateral rules on industrial policies, greater transparency (information on applied policies) and more assessments of impacts are needed to inform both domestic policy processes and the design of international cooperation (rulemaking).

We start with a brief summary of post-2008 trends in the use of subsidies. We then review potential rationales for government intervention in a GVC-driven world economy. The next sections discuss gaps in the existing rules and then the implications for the design of international cooperation aimed at reducing international spillovers and containing subsidy-related trade conflicts.

USE OF TRADE-RELATED POLICIES SINCE 2008

Data on nontariff policies are notoriously patchy. Most WTO notification requirements are only partially complied with. Incomplete and out-of-date information applies even for measures that are subject to explicit commitments in the WTO such as export subsidies for agricultural products, impeding analysis of the effects of policies and the effectiveness of trade disciplines—see, for example, Hoekman and Messerlin (2006). The trend seems to be that WTO members are reporting fewer measures and with greater delays. The percentage of members that did not submit notifications on subsidies rose from 27 percent in 1995 to 44 percent in 2013 (WTO 2014). Since then, matters have not improved much. As of the end of 2018, 78 WTO members (out of a total of 164) had not made the subsidy notifications that were due in 2017, 63 members had not made the notifications due in 2015, and 56 members had still to deliver the notifications due in 2013.[4]

The lack of comprehensive notifications to the WTO by members puts much of the burden of policy data collection on third parties. A very useful source of data on the use of trade-related policy instruments is the Global Trade Alert (GTA).[5] GTA data start in 2009 and are therefore skewed by the fact that policies responded to the financial crisis; we cannot compare post-2009 trends to the "baseline" use of different types of policies before the crisis, but it provides valuable information on the relative intensity of use of different policies. Figures 9-1 to 9-3 summarize the data on all measures reported in the GTA database.

FIGURE 9-1. New Trade-Related Policy Measures, All Countries, 2009–2018

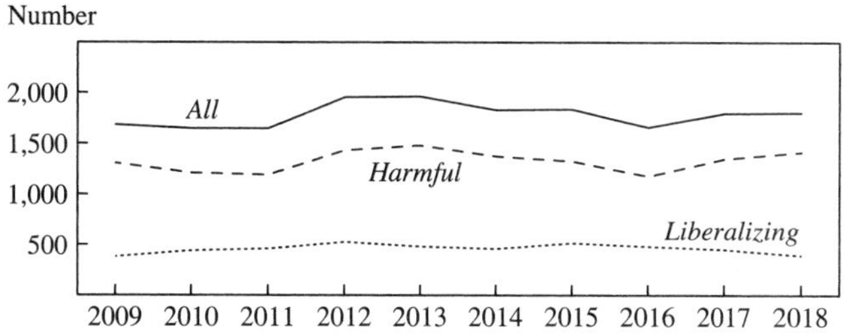

Number

Source: Global Trade Alert website, www.globaltradealert.org.

As of end-2018, some 18,000 trade-related measures were included in the database, ranging from tariffs and quotas to antidumping and investment measures (policies affecting the ability of or cost for foreign firms to establish or maintain a commercial presence in a country). Of these, three-quarters were trade distorting and one-quarter reflected actions to liberalize trade. Figure 9-1 shows that the number of trade-distorting measures imposed each year between 2009 and 2018 was relatively stable, averaging some 1,350 measures per year. Governments were more active in removing trade barriers (implementing liberalization) in the years after the crisis. Since 2016, the trend in the number of liberalization measures was declining. Tariffs and contingent protection ("trade remedies" or "temporary barriers to trade") accounted for 16.5 and 13.4 percent, respectively, of all measures classified as harmful by the GTA team that were implemented between 2009 and 2018.[6] By far the largest share of trade-distorting measures took the form of subsidies to production or measures to support exports (figure 9-2).

GTA distinguishes among several subsidy categories, including state aid or production support and export support measures (including tax rebates and concessions). The most frequently observed firm-specific state aid measures are public sector loans or loan guarantees and tax or social insurance relief. Taken together, subsidies accounted for 52 percent of all trade-related measures implemented between 2009 and the end of 2018 (some 6,900 measures).[7] The G-7 group of industrialized countries accounts for the greatest share of subsidies granted, while large emerging markets tend to implement more trade-related investment and price control measures (Evenett 2019).

FIGURE 9-2. Use of Policy Instruments, Total 2009–2018

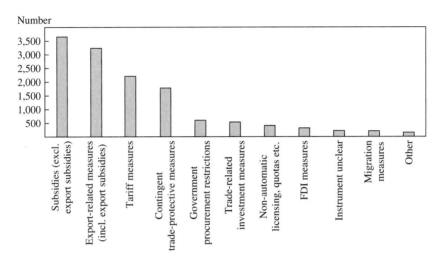

Source: Global Trade Alert website, www.globaltradalert.org.

Subsidies account for a much smaller share of the total measures imposed by low-income developing countries. Insofar as subsidies are observed, they tend to target exports, suggesting a policy focus on promoting exports as opposed to protectionism (Hoekman 2016a).[8]

Figure 9-3 breaks down the use of measures according to whether they target goods, services, or investment. For measures targeting trade in goods, the GTA database reveals that governments use tariffs actively, but this reflects a mix of protectionism and liberalization. Over the 2009–2018 period, the countries included in the dataset implemented more liberalizing actions than protectionist ones: more tariffs were lowered than were increased (see first panel of figure 9-3). A similar pattern applies for quantitative restrictions and nonautomatic licensing requirements: the number of instances of removal of such measures slightly exceeds the total number of measures imposed over the decade. In contrast, trade defense measures tend to persist. The same applies to subsidy instruments.

Because it is difficult to subject services trade to import tariffs or temporary trade restrictions like antidumping (except indirectly), it is not surprising that subsidies and other "nonborder" measures are used relatively more intensively for services. For the sample as a whole, subsidies account for almost all measures pertaining to services (second panel of figure 9-3).[9]

FIGURE 9-3. Measures Affecting Goods, Services, and Investment, 2009–2018

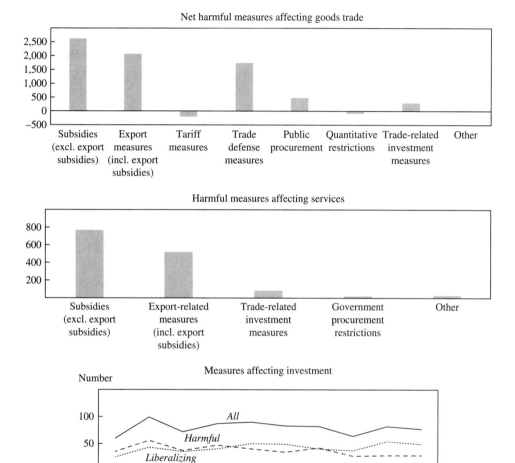

Source: Global Trade alert website, www.globaltradealert.org.

Investment measures are the third most frequently observed measure affecting trade in services. The GTA data indicate that high-income countries make the most intensive use of subsidies, whereas lower-income countries rely relatively more on investment measures. Overall, countries appear to pursue a policy of encouraging FDI—since 2012, the number of liberalizing measures has been greater than the number of harmful measures (third panel of figure 9-3). Investment measures taken by lower-income developing

FIGURE 9-4. **New Harmful Measures Imposed, by Country, 2009–2018**

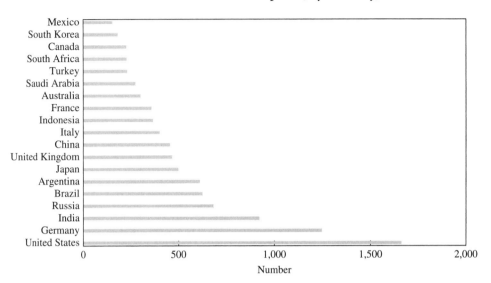

Source: Adapted from Evenett and Fritz (2019, fig. 9.1).

countries tend to be weighted more toward reducing discrimination against foreign firms; in member countries of the Organization for Economic Co-operation and Development (OECD) and upper-middle-income nations there is a rough balance between liberalizing and more discrimination. Evenett and Fritz (2018) note that in 2018 the number of restrictive investment measures, most in the form of local content requirements, increased significantly.

The United States is the "market leader" measured by the number of new trade-distorting measures implemented during the 2009–2018 period, followed by Germany and India (figure 9-4). In the case of the United States and India, most of these are related to traditional border protection (tariffs, trade defense measures), while in the case of Germany export support measures play a big role (export credit, trade finance-related policies).[10] China is generally a major focus of targeted measures. In many G-20 countries, a high share of total imports from China are subject to trade barriers or affected by discriminatory policies (figure 9-5). As noted by Bown (chapter 2 in this volume), China is the number one target, reflecting efforts to manage Chinese competition and perceptions that "China Inc." (Wu 2016) engages in unfair competition and trade-distorting practices.

FIGURE 9-5. **Share of Chinese Exports Subject to Discriminatory Trade Policies**

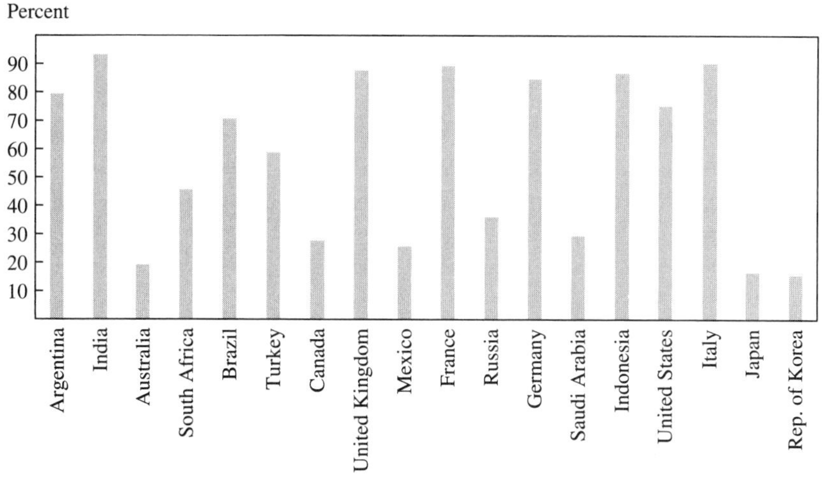

Percent

Source: Evenett and Fritz (2019, table 7.1).

Note: Data on the share of trade affected by a given intervention are adjusted by the number of days that the intervention has been in force. Data encompass the 2009–2018 period.

MOTIVATIONS FOR SUBSIDIES

Subsidies may be motivated by economic or noneconomic goals. Economic goals include offsetting market failures (to improve the efficiency of re-source allocation), inducing investment, shifting profits or rents, or redistrib-uting income to disadvantaged communities or politically well-connected individuals or groups. A basic efficiency rationale for tax and subsidy schemes is to bring marginal private costs or benefits into alignment with marginal social costs or benefits. The need for this arises when externalities (market failures) cause social and private costs and benefits to diverge, with the result that private agents have no incentive to take into account the costs or benefits of their actions on others in the economy. For a more efficient allocation of resources to result from intervention, market failure must be diagnosed cor-rectly and the policy must address the reasons for it.

Any policy that has differential effects on sectors or activities will act as a tax or subsidy. Some policies that are sector-specific may have an econo-mywide objective. Examples include subsidies to sectors such as health, ed-ucation, transportation, and communications. Conversely, policies that are economywide in scope may effectively be industry-specific—for example, the pursuit of an environmental objective where the effect of a measure is primarily on an activity that is associated with specific sectors.

Many of the subsidy measures pursued by governments come under the heading of industrial policy. The traditional rationale for supporting an industry or productive activity has not changed for centuries. The premise of "infant industry support" is that the candidate industry is a positive net present value (NPV) industry, but the normal operation of the market will not support the establishment of the industry. A limited period of policy intervention can then create conditions conducive to the industry's establishment. Two tests need to be satisfied for an activity to have positive NPV: the Mill test, which requires *private* positive NPV, and the Bastable test, which requires *social* positive NPV—that is, the costs of protection to society and any social benefits not captured in prices need to be taken into account when calculating profits. Any activity that passes the positive NPV test taking into account both social and private costs must be profitable, raising the classic question: Why doesn't the market invest in it? In other words, what is the market failure? Proponents of industrial policy are rarely explicit about the source of market failure, but the details of the market failure are essential to identify the optimal form and level of intervention. The usual claims are that there are capital market failures and dynamic externalities (e.g., links of some kind). These are arguments for *temporary* intervention. Baldwin (1969) pointed out that any market failure must be correctable within a finite period of intervention.

Thinking about the rationale for industrial policy has moved from an approach based largely on product market interventions (production subsidies, state ownership, tariff protection) to market-failure-correcting taxes and subsidies operating mainly on factor markets (R&D incentives, training subsidies, investment allowances, easier access to finance) and a focus on "interventions that help build systems, create networks, develop institutions and align strategic priorities" (Warwick 2013, 47).[11] Aghion, Boulanger, and Cohen (2011) make a strong case for growth-enhancing sectoral policies that are competition- and innovation-friendly and that aim at internalizing knowledge spillovers. They note that long-standing arguments for industrial policy continue to be valid—such as credit constraints that result in inadequate capital being allocated to high-growth-potential activities given that high-tech firms and startups often have limited assets and thus limited collateral to use to get loans. They also argue that the potential for capture and "white elephants" is reduced if industrial policy intervention and state aid are decentralized and target firms located in different regions, as well as sectors where there is more intrasector competition, as this enhances the probability that sectoral state aid will have a positive effect on export and innovation performance. In principle, such a policy should not differentiate between firms on the basis of their nationality.

Standard economic frameworks for considering the rationale for government intervention continue to apply in a GVC world. Horizontal measures—a supportive business environment; investment in skills (education) and infrastructure; rule of law and protection of property; safeguarding competition—arguably become even more important. In a world of extensive value chain trade, firms must face a stable economic, legal, and political environment. At the same time there may be need for *specific* intervention to deal with coordination failures and information asymmetries. Interventions that expand the ability of a country to contribute to GVCs may not only have positive local spillover effects but also improve the competitiveness of a GVC as a whole. Interventions may be associated with positive as well as negative cross-border spillovers (Van Biesebroeck 2010; Blanchard 2015).[12] The direction and size (distribution) of spillover effects will depend on links between countries *within* a GVC and links *across* chains—reflecting activities that may use the same type of inputs or demand similar products (Baldwin and Venables 2015).

Developed countries are primarily seeking to dominate frontier sectors. This effort will generally involve access to highly skilled labor and protection of intellectual property. In old-time development theory ("big push") the emphasis was on locational externalities in production. In a GVC context, locational externalities have more to do with creating environments that attract and retain skilled workers to support the skill-intensive part of value chains (Moretti 2012). Thus, subsidies to education (especially in sciences, engineering, and technology) and to R&D and liberal immigration rules (especially for students and skilled workers) may play a role. Developing countries, by contrast, are seeking to connect with GVCs and "move up" the value chain through policies that support employment and upgrading their position in the value chain. Some of this will depend on efficient communication and on transport and logistics services and networks.

Policies that support (subsidize) local production of intermediate inputs can help attract value-chain-motivated FDI, with the impact on GVC participation depending on the range of available input production capabilities in the host country (Baldwin and Venables 2015). Reliable and low transaction costs for access to inputs and getting processed and final products into export markets are critical in a GVC world. While investment incentives are potentially an instrument governments can use to offset specific locational or operating disadvantages, trade policy is important as well. Kimmitt and Slaughter (2015), for example, note that the small number of trade agreements negotiated by the United States led the car manufacturer Audi to set up a plant in Mexico instead of Tennessee, in part because Mexico offered a location that had duty-free access to some forty countries with which it had trade agreements.

A key finding of research on strategic use of trade policy in the 1980s and 1990s is that governments can easily get policy wrong and reduce welfare. This applies equally to policy in a GVC world. For example, Blonigen (2016) examines the impact of policies to support local steel production on the export competitiveness of downstream manufacturing sectors that are significant users of steel. He finds that a one standard deviation increase in the use of export subsidies and nontariff barriers leads to a 3.6 percent decline in export competitiveness for an average downstream manufacturing sector. But this negative effect can be as high as a 50 percent decline for sectors that use steel as an input most intensively. Conversely, policies that target downstream activities may harm upstream suppliers, especially if the former have market (monopsony) power (Van Biesebroeck and Sturgeon 2013).

Cross-Border Spillovers

Abstracting from the important question of the domestic welfare effects of government policies, from a global perspective what matters is the sign and size of associated international spillovers. These may be dynamic as well as static if national policies have longer term anticompetitive effects on global markets. The extent of spillovers and their incidence is an empirical question that calls for analysis. Such analysis is pertinent for all countries and should consider the policies of all major countries.

An interesting implication of the differentiation in interests created by GVCs is that negative policy spillovers are likely to be between similar countries. Developed countries will have the same interest in frontier sectors and pursue policies with the same goals. While these will be negative for other high-income countries, by strengthening value chains these policies may benefit developing countries that participate in them. Developing countries at similar levels of development will have similar interests and pursue policies with the same goals. These may generate negative spillovers for similarly situated developing countries, but the industrial policy competition will benefit (parts of) GVCs located in developed countries. This pattern of interests has implications for the institutions used to manage spillovers and the rule structures involved in their management.

Investment incentive competition between jurisdictions can lower overall welfare. Ossa (2017) provides an illustration, analyzing the effects of investment-related tax and subsidy incentives at the state level in the United States. US states "spend" some $80 billion a year on tax incentives and subsidies to investment, reflecting a vigorous competition to attract investment. Ossa finds that this competition increases state-level welfare (by attracting firms, increasing employment, and raising wages) but generates beggar-thy-neighbor effects. Although there are potentially large gains at the state level from subsidizing investment, subsidies distort resource allocation by making intermediate inputs too cheap and generating excessive entry. There is a significant cost to the United States as a whole—if states were to cooperate and refrain from competing for investment, real US manufacturing income would be 3.9 percent higher.

Most assessments of the potential spillover effects on developing countries of foreign policies have tended to focus on measures implemented by the European Union and the United States. With the rise of large emerging economies as major actors, such assessments need to include these countries as well. Figure 9-6 plots the post-2009 trend in the share of products exported by a group of low-income countries that benefit from subsidies in Brazil, China, and India.[13] The share is substantial, ranging from 10 to 25 percent. It is also volatile for Brazil and India, as these interventions presumably in part reflect responses to macroeconomic conditions (the aftermath of the 2008 financial crisis). The overall share of potentially affected exports of the selected low-income countries was 65 percent higher in 2018 for Brazil and India than it was in 2008 (before the crisis). Insofar as the rise in the spillover incidence of subsidies reflects a fiscal response to the macro shock, there seems to be a ratchet effect as well. This may be because other policy objectives are in play or because governments have difficulty removing subsidies once implemented.

The basic point is that greater consideration should be given to monitoring and assessing the use and incidence of trade-distorting measures

FIGURE 9-6. Potential Negative Spillover Effects of Subsidies on Low-Income Exports

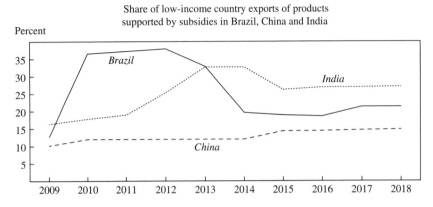

Share of low-income country exports of products supported by subsidies in Brazil, China and India

Source: Global Trade Alert database, www.globaltradealert.org/data_extraction.

and their possible negative spillover effects. Such efforts need to consider implications for—and operation of—GVCs as these involve firms and plants in many countries.

GAPS IN WTO RULES

Many policies can act to promote an economic activity. Any measure by a government to disadvantage one activity relative to another will have the effect of advantaging the latter. It is therefore necessary to recognize that if one seeks to discipline policies that give rise to negative international spillovers, the focus of attention must be on effects rather than narrowly defined policy instruments. In the WTO context, the focus is on discrimination—domestic policies (subsidies, taxes, administrative or regulatory measures) that skew incentives for domestic agents to source locally. Often the instruments used to do this are tax-related and frequently take the form of tax exemptions or rebates that are conditional on local content.

Article III of the GATT requires that domestic policies satisfy the national treatment principle: this implies that behind-the-border regulatory measures must apply equally to domestic and foreign goods. A violation of this principle constitutes a de facto illegal subsidy. This broad notion of subsidy includes financial support: measures that impose a direct burden on the budget, are specific to an activity (as opposed to benefiting economic activity more generally), and convey a benefit to those they target. The focus of WTO rules is on potential trade effects—that is, adverse effects on foreign products. A distinction is made between specific and general subsidies. Only the former are actionable. Specific subsidies include direct financial support for exports and local content requirements and other policies that reduce incentives to import.

Historically, the center of attention for WTO members has been agriculture, reflecting the extensive support provided by many high-income countries to this sector. The Uruguay Round significantly reduced the ability of members to use agricultural subsidies and encouraged governments to decouple support from production. More recently (in 2015), WTO members agreed to a ban on agricultural export subsidies. In comparison with the early 2000s, there has been a remarkable reduction in trade-distorting production support in high-income countries, illustrating the value and feasibility of cooperation to reduce the negative spillovers created by subsidies.[14] Welfare considerations enter only implicitly into WTO rulemaking. Thus the preference for income support (assistance decoupled from production) and carving out such support through a "green box" of permitted subsidies was not because of recognition of *national* welfare implications, but because of the presumed lack of trade distortions associated with such support.

The main WTO instrument regulating use of subsidies and actions by members to offset the competitive (trade) effects of foreign subsidies is the Agreement on Subsidies and Countervailing Measures (SCM Agreement). This pertains only to goods—there are no disciplines on subsidies for services in the General Agreement on Trade in Services (GATS). The SCM Agreement has a twofold objective: first, to prevent the use of subsidies by members to circumvent negotiated market access (tariff) concessions; second, to regulate countervailing duties (CVDs) used to offset the adverse effects of foreign subsidization of goods on domestic producers.[15] Export subsidies are prohibited, but the WTO does not regulate domestic subsidies per se (Horlick and Clarke 2010). Subsidies other than export subsidies can be used but can lead to the imposition of countervailing duties in destination markets.[16] The WTO rules are not concerned with why a government has implemented a subsidy—for example, whether it can be justified by a market failure.[17] Another important dimension of the rules is that remedies are retrospective—there is no scope to claim private damages.

As noted earlier, rising concerns about subsidies are correlated with the increasing weight of SOEs in the world economy. SOEs may be a source of subsidies for downstream firms and industries they supply as well as a potential source of concern for competition on markets in themselves. The WTO is not concerned whether a country has SOEs but focuses on whether SOEs engaging in trade (state trading enterprises—STEs) operate on a commercial basis and prohibits discrimination by STEs. GATT Article XVII (on STEs) only requires firms granted exclusive or special trade privileges to abide by the nondiscrimination rules. Recent preferential trade agreements have gone further than the WTO in agreeing to disciplines on SOEs and offer insight into what participating countries presumably would like to see incorporated into the WTO.[18]

The WTO disciplines were crafted in the 1980s, before the rise of GVCs, the growth of China, and the emergence of the digital economy.[19] WTO subsidy-related rules are premised on trade-comprising goods that are produced in one country and consumed in another, and implicitly assume that most of the value-added embodied in a product is generated by domestic factors of production. This is not the case today, making it less clear who benefits from a subsidy. Is the benefit associated with a GVC as a whole and the impact reflected in the price of the final good? Or is the impact on specific segments of a GVC? Who captures the benefit? In any assessment of such questions the first order of business is to identify and define the spillovers that are of concern.

The exclusive focus on trade effects in WTO rules is arguably a downside of the status quo. One reason is that the rules do not cover investment incentives and related policies that are not conditional on local sourcing—that is, policies that conform to the national treatment principle. Another weakness is that what constitutes a subsidy is unclear. The major example that has arisen in the WTO case law is whether an SOE is a "public body." Another gap is the treatment of input subsidies. For example, the tax regime can be used to lower domestic prices of inputs used for domestic or export production. Yet another issue concerns the incentives for firms to petition for action to offset the effects of subsidies. Firms may not be willing to claim injury or adverse effects if they consider the overall balance of all the policies they benefit from, including in both the target country of a complaint and in third countries that contribute to or are part of their operations. Of course, from an economic perspective this is not a problem.

The prospective nature of WTO remedies and absence of compensation for (private) damages is likely to further reduce the incentives for large firms (multinationals) to petition for cases to be initiated in the WTO by their governments or to be willing (or even able) to document that they have been injured. Indeed, it may not be clear in practice which country a multinational "belongs to" and thus which government to petition. The government-to-government nature of the WTO is in this respect another potentially constraining feature of the extant system that needs to be taken into account in reassessing its salience.

Policy cooperation is harder to design in a GVC world, given that the distributional effects and the efficiency (efficacy) of interventions are more difficult to determine ex ante and the potentially greater scope or need for targeted interventions to address coordination failures that may affect local participation in GVC activities. In the GATT the focus is on the domestic industry—as long as a sufficiently large share of the industry is in agreement that they are being injured by a foreign subsidy, action can be initiated. It has always been recognized that taking action—imposing a CVD—will be detrimental to consumers and downstream users. But in a GVC world a CVD may have no effect on the firms that bring an antisubsidy case for import protection. GVCs embody complex relationships between the links in the chain or nodes of the network to ensure reliability of supply, quality, interconnection, and so on. Domestic input suppliers may not benefit from CVDs on imported inputs that are processed locally and reexported. The CVD is unlikely to induce a lead firm to switch its sourcing to the local firms that bring a case—instead the firm may simply move the affected part of the chain elsewhere if the CVD raises costs too much. Moreover, firms that participate in the value chain(s) will oppose CVD petitions. As noted by Hoekman and Messerlin (2000) the political economy of trade policy reflects the balance of interests of firms depending on where they are located in the supply chain: users of inputs have incentives to lobby for measures that reduce their input costs. From an FDI-attraction perspective, permitting firms to launch CVD actions is likely to run counter to investment-promotion objectives and have detrimental impacts on the reputation of a country as a platform for GVC-based activity.

Incentives to attract investment are not covered by WTO rules. The focus of WTO subsidy rules is on whether interventions are export subsidies or cause adverse effects for exporters in third markets or domestic import-competing producers. But if the main goal and effect of GVC participation-related policies is to attract or retain FDI, the issue becomes one of investment diversion and global efficiency—cooperation aimed at preventing inefficient competition between jurisdictions that simply generates rent transfers to investors rather than addressing a market failure.

An implication of the centrality of FDI and more generally the importance of investment for GVC-related policy interventions is that discrimination may not be a motivating factor in policy, in which case national treatment is less of a constraint on government action. Investors will operate plants that generate local employment, independent of nationality of ownership. The spillovers that may arise are therefore somewhat different from those generated by the mercantilist motivation for many WTO rules—a concern about the effects of policy on exporters. If the issue is investment incentives, effects are not (only) on exporters but on locations for investment—that is, the potential problem is investment diversion. Nondiscriminatory investment policies may be distorting by attracting investment to less efficient locations at the cost of other jurisdictions, generating nontrade spillovers the WTO cannot address because the rules do not cover such policies.

Negotiating disciplines on investment policies is likely to be a very difficult exercise. One reason is politics: investment incentives are a favored tool of local governments. Another is the complexity of determining the distributional effects of interventions, which will center in part on identifying the counterfactual: what would have happened in the absence of a policy mix that led to an investment going to one location instead of somewhere else? In the WTO working group on investment (one of the so-called Singapore issues), it became clear early on that many (most?) governments were not willing to discuss investment incentives or subsidies, removing much of the potential rationale for a multilateral agreement (Hoekman and Saggi 2000). Moreover, the high import content of many GVCs means investment subsidies will benefit some foreign interests as well as local ones, reducing incentives to negotiate disciplines. Account also needs to be taken of the role played by services as inputs. If services benefit from government support, indirect subsidies may dominate the net treatment of final products. On average, services account for one-third or more of the value of goods (WTO 2019).

BOLSTERING DISCIPLINES FOR SUBSIDIES AND SOEs: PATHWAYS FORWARD

In considering how to update multilateral rules on subsidies and SOEs, more attention should be given to the aims and effects of subsidies and to enabling the use of subsidy instruments to address market failures. A basic need is to determine to what extent "gaps" in existing rules can lead to systemic negative spillovers. Coherence calls for such an effort to cut across existing GATT-GATS-sectoral silos and adopt a perspective that is informed more by competition than by a narrow legal focus on discrimination (national treatment), specificity, and (re)defining the definition of an actionable subsidy. There are lessons to be learned from the EU experience in this regard, where disciplines on state aid and SOEs are linked to competition policy and center on evaluating and limiting the potential distortions to competition that arise from government intervention.

A key input into any deliberation on rules of the road should be better data on the policies used by central and subcentral levels of government around the world—not just China. The Global Trade Alert data discussed earlier suggest there is a lot of action, but what matters is which of the many measures move the needle most. What creates large spillovers? What does not? What types of intervention harm global welfare? Answering these questions requires a shift in mindset—away from closed-door discussions between like-minded countries (such as the trilateral talks among the EU, Japan, and the United States) toward an open process of deliberation based on evidence and analysis of effects. Such a process should encompass relevant entities in and outside governments that are concerned with implementing and monitoring subsidy programs. Tax and subsidy-related policy instruments fall under the purview of finance and economy ministries and executing agencies—generally sectoral ministries and regional and municipal public bodies. An implication is that forums to identify, measure, assess, and address the cross-border effects of tax and subsidy measures should go beyond trade ministries and those charged with implementing trade policy.

In contrast to other areas of trade-related policy such as trade facilitation, intellectual property protection, sanitary and phytosanitary measures, and product safety standards, there is no epistemic community (Haas 1992) focused on subsidies.[20] Many government agencies and international organizations are involved in the design and implementation of such policy instruments, with many professionals (primarily lawyers and economists) working on subsidy-related matters, but there is no international forum that brings these "stakeholders" together. Relevant players include national ministries of finance, national competition agencies (and in the EU, the Directorate-General for Competition in the European Commission), specialized agencies (e.g., the Australian Productivity Commission), and international organizations, notably the International Monetary Fund (IMF) and the OECD, but also sectoral organizations. Mobilizing an epistemic community that connects these "silos" to focus on measuring support and determining the spillover effects of subsidies could do much to prepare the ground for deeper cooperation. This could start with identifying what types of data are already being collected, and what more is needed, and foster the information sharing necessary to build trust. Considering the use of indicators can help legitimize the overall program, as was done for agriculture by the OECD (with the producer support estimates).

Such efforts will need an institutional anchor. The WTO is the obvious candidate, but this implies the membership being able to agree to give such a mandate to the organization. Given the difficulty of achieving the necessary consensus, it may be more feasible to consider alternative forums such as the G-20 (working through the Trade and Investment Working Group)[21] and the International Competition Network (ICN), an informal grouping of agencies that cooperate in areas of competition policy.[22]

To some extent, the major players in the global trading system have already taken initiatives that cut across silos in government and leverage the analytical capacity and knowledge base of international organizations to address subsidy-related concerns. A prominent example is the G-20 Global Forum on Steel Excess Capacity,[23] an initiative established at the 2016 G-20 summit in China. The mandate of this forum, facilitated by the OECD, included producing and sharing reliable statistics on production, capacity, and excess capacity among major steel producers, and identifying measures to reduce global production, including assessing the role of subsidies in generating overcapacity. The forum provided a platform for the exchange of data on steel capacity, subsidies, and other support measures, thus improving the information base and the transparency of the relevant policies implemented by major steel producing countries. The forum reported to G-20 ministers annually during the period 2017–2019 and met at least three times a year.[24]

Some of the elements for making progress are already embodied in different WTO agreements. These include the so-called green box approach used in the Agreement on Agriculture, which exempts subsidies that cause minimal distortion, understood to include programs such as direct income supports for farmers that are decoupled from production levels or prices, environmental protection, and regional development programs. The agreement also allows developing countries additional flexibility in providing domestic support.[25] The various de minimis provisions included in these WTO agreements for developing countries are a way of recognizing that the spillover effects created by subsidies used by low-income countries are likely to be small from a systemic perspective. The green box approach in the Agreement on Agriculture and the provisional inclusion of Article 8 on non-actionable subsidies in the SCM Agreement (a provision that expired in 1999) illustrate the possibility of balancing stronger disciplines on subsidies with a recognition that some types of subsidies are unlikely to affect trade. Going beyond this to recognize that some subsidies may have an important function in addressing market failures and launching a concerted effort to improve information on tax and subsidy policies targeting investment in industrial and service sector activities arguably are necessary conditions for making progress in additional rulemaking.

Many WTO members have emphasized the need for better information on subsidies. The recent focus in the WTO by the United States, the European Union, and others on the problem created by inadequate notification has made clear this is a problem. However, the suggested remedies— addressing the notification deficit by imposing stronger penalties for late or incomplete reporting by members—is unlikely to do much to improve matters. It would be more effective to create positive incentives for greater transparency by governments (Wolfe 2017, 2018). Sharing experiences on the payoffs from a national governance perspective of compiling better information; provision of technical assistance and identification of good practices; using web-scraping techniques to collect data on policies from government websites and public reporting by companies and the specialized press (a source of information used by the GTA); and leveraging extant data collection efforts by ministries of finance would do much to fill the gaps. Given the incentive problems associated with reliance on firms to report perceived problem policies and document their effects, options that rely on other actors—including other international organizations—are more likely to be effective.

A successful example of the type of approach needed is the long-standing effort that commenced in the late 1970s to measure the extent and effects of policies supporting the agricultural sector (see Legg and Blandford 2019; Wolfe 2020). This resulted in the development of summary indicators such as the producer support estimate (PSE) that have become core elements of monitoring policy in this sector and focal points for policymakers in their reflections on the magnitude and incidence of a broad array of policy measures used to support agriculture. More recent examples that are directly pertinent to the issue of industrial subsidies include the Global Steel Forum mentioned earlier and the OECD's detailed firm-level sector-specific study of the magnitude and incidence of subsidies along the aluminum supply chain (OECD 2019c).[26]

Data are necessary but not sufficient. Analysis of effects is just as important. Ideally, such analysis would be provided by the WTO secretariat and provide a basis for discussion among members. The Trade Policy Review (TPR) Mechanism provides a possible framework on which to build, as it is intended to inform periodic deliberations in the WTO on country-specific policies (WTO members with the largest shares of world trade are discussed more frequently, every two years), as well as discussion about developments in the trading system more generally. The latter topic was addressed in the GATT years and was resuscitated after the 2008 financial crisis as a means of monitoring the use of policy responses by WTO members. A central feature of the TPR process is peer review—it is left for members to engage with each other on the basis of the factual report prepared by the secretariat. There is relatively active participation in the TPR process (Karlas and Parízek 2019b). Such review would benefit from more analysis by the secretariat of the effects of policies, something that is precluded at present.

A core challenge in defining possible rules is to agree on what in principle constitutes desirable (globally welfare-enhancing) policies and what types of subsidies are more likely to generate undesirable spillover effects, based on empirical analysis and evidence. In thinking about moving forward, there may be lessons from the EU in ensuring a level playing field for firms in its integrated market. In the EU, subsidies are covered by EU competition policy disciplines. For state aid to be declared illegal: (i) state resources (a subsidy or tax expenditure) must lead to (ii) a selective advantage for a firm or activity that (iii) distorts competition and (iv) affects trade between member states. These criteria apply to undertakings to which member states have granted special or exclusive rights—that is, SOEs. EU member states must comply with transparency obligations for state aid allocations over €500,000, including the name of the beneficiary and the amount of aid granted.[27] This data compilation effort is complemented by evaluation of selected large state aid schemes to assess their impact and guide possible improvements in the design of programs as well as the subsidy rules.

A central feature of the EU approach to regulating subsidies is that measures falling under a General Block Exemption Regulation (GBER) are deemed to raise few or no concerns about distorting competition on the EU market. These include regional aid (including for ports and airports), aid for small and medium-sized enterprises (SMEs), and aid for R&D and innovation, broadband infrastructures, energy and the environment, employment and training, natural disasters, and sports and culture. Agreeing to a set of subsidies that are deemed not to cause spillover concerns along the lines of what is done by the EU could help differentiate between subsidies that are not considered to have harmful trade spillover effects and those that may have such consequences and should be actionable.[28] Following a 2012 reform, EU member states are no longer required to notify the Commission about state aid they expect to provide if the measures fall under the GBER, leaving the Commission to focus on measures that are deemed of greater risk of distorting competition. In 2017, most new aid measures fell under the GBER. The quid pro quo for no longer having to provide advance notification is stronger controls at the member state level, greater transparency, and better evaluation of the impact of state aid.

Approaches Informed by Competition Policy

A major feature of the "WTO approach" to subsidies (and more generally to trade policies) is hard law, mercantilism (a focus on exports and market access), and reliance on self-interested firms to complain to governments and request CVDs or to raise the matter in the WTO. To effectively address the interface challenges posed by subsidies and related industrial policies, this focus arguably is too narrow. A policy approach that is geared more to competition considerations (competitive neutrality, contestability of markets) than to foreign market access is called for. This approach can draw on some of the basic concepts used in the EU, including agreement that some types of policies are prima facie "OK" (the block exemption or green box approach discussed earlier) and use of competitive neutrality principles to address concerns that state aid and SOEs may distort the operation of markets. Moving in this direction does not require a supranational body; a more competition-centric approach can be applied in an intergovernmental setting like the WTO.

The design and enforcement of competition law and policy is distinct from trade law and policy in relying to a much greater extent on economic analysis. Recognizing the need to balance the potential market failure motivations for subsidies against the potential spillover effects on competition often will call for theoretically grounded empirical analysis. Simple heuristics or rules may be too blunt. Complementing "black letter" law approaches with a "law and economics" approach as in the implementation of competition policy could help WTO members avoid a head-on confrontation between countries with different economic systems—such as the "China Inc." problem (Wu 2016). An example is provided by current claims that Chinese SOEs engage in essentially predatory behavior by using their privileged status and access to capital and other resources to undercut the international competition. We know what conditions have to apply for such a strategy to be profitable—there must be high entry barriers or large dynamic economies of scale and learning that prevent firms from (re)entering markets. The economics literature has found that SOEs are on average less productive and profitable (Kowalski and others 2013; OECD 2016; Harrison and others 2019). Presumably insofar as there are significant subsidies allocated to SOEs these will not be permanent, as this would be a recipe for recurring losses. In the long run these cannot be sustained. These types of considerations should enter into discussions on possible rules to address the potential negative effects of SOEs operating on global markets. We note again that EU competition rules apply to SOEs. The EU does not care about ownership, but about behavior. The same should apply in the WTO setting: we should care about constraining potential long-term anticompetitive effects. This cannot be done using the current rulebook.

Another design element that arguably needs reconsideration concerns the entities that are expected (required) to challenge perceived anticompetitive practices. There may be a need to shift the burden away from firms and their trade interests and toward national or global welfare. There is a case for creating a mechanism through which matters of "systemic" import can be brought on behalf of the trading system. In the EU, the European Commission may act as an agent to defend the interests of the majority of the principals (member states) if one member takes actions that impede the operation of the single market. Given the sovereignty concerns of all WTO members and enormous heterogeneity across the 164 members, there is no prospect of the WTO secretariat playing such a role, even on a limited scale. More feasible may be to agree on the creation of processes to identify large spillovers that are of systemic concern. Bolstering the Trade Policy Review process is one possibility. Another is to relax the constraints imposed on the WTO secretariat to act as an agent of transparency (Mavroidis and Wolfe 2015). Yet another would be to establish an "ombudsman" body that is mandated to undertake and publish analytical assessments of the policies that have systemic impacts (Hoekman and Mavroidis 2000).

These possibilities may seem like a bridge too far, especially in an environment where geoeconomic tensions are high, but the same was true when the TPR Mechanism was first proposed in the Uruguay Round and when the Food and Agriculture Organization and the OECD commenced analytical work to measure the magnitude of support provided to agriculture. Incremental steps allowing learning by doing should be feasible with a minimum of good will—or a modicum of credible threats to dissolve multilateral cooperation.

CONCLUSION

The global economy has become much more integrated in recent decades as a result of the political decision by China to adapt an outward-oriented development strategy, extensive trade and investment liberalization by numerous countries, and technological advances. The rise of global value chains is both a response to and driver of global integration. It has changed the policy mix used by many WTO members—not just China. Tariffs—notwithstanding Tariff Man Trump—are no longer an important policy tool. The emphasis today is on subsidies broadly construed. Policy cooperation has become more complex than in the 1980s, the last time WTO rules were reconsidered, when trade involved less vertical specialization and less of the unbundling of production activities across many locations that prevails today.

The current trade conflicts and tensions illustrate the need to revisit the rules. This should start with bolstering transparency through a collective effort to collect and compile information on subsidies (going beyond reliance on notifications by countries) and to launch a process of dialogue and deliberation in the WTO to define a negotiating agenda. Better data on applied policies is important to help countries determine whether there are serious, systemic spillovers. Analysis centered on spillovers is needed to inform deliberation on addressing lacunae in the rules. Filling the information gap will require a shift in prioritization of the transparency and monitoring efforts of international organizations, not just the WTO, and a concerted effort to map the nontariff measures that are used by governments to affect and target investment and economic activities in their jurisdictions.

When it comes to rulemaking efforts, the basic question should be: What generates major systemic spillovers? Determining the answer implies also identifying policies that are (or should be) of less concern. The green box approach is already an element of the WTO rules for agricultural policies. Extending this by building on the example of block exemptions coupled with notification would seem to be a reasonable path to pursue. This will also permit differentiation across WTO members—for example, by agreeing to de minimis provisions for specific sets of countries or facilitating the process of requesting and obtaining waivers. The foregoing discussion of the changing incentives and incidence of subsidy-type policies in a GVC world suggests there is cause to revisit the salience of "national treatment" and the WTO focus on "discrimination" as the key tests for adverse effects.

Making progress in updating the rules of the game for subsidies and associated sources of potential cross-border spillovers such as the behavior of SOEs requires deliberation that includes all the major trading powers—those capable of generating negative externalities that are of systemic importance. Preparing the ground is a complex undertaking, as it requires recognition that subsidies may promote efficiency by helping to address market failures and overcome collective action problems—such as dealing with climate change. A law *and* economics approach is called for, akin to what has gradually emerged in the area of competition law (Hoekman and Nelson 2020). Designing such an approach requires deliberation between—and support of—the various actors in and outside government that are involved in the design and implementation of subsidies and responsible for ensuring that markets are competitive.

NOTES

We are grateful to Simon Evenett, Matteo Fiorini, and Johannes Fritz for help with data and to Mary Lovely, Robert Wolfe, and participants in the 2019 World Trade Forum (Bern), the September 2019 conference on "A New Global Economic Order" (UIBE, Beijing), a July 2019 EUI workshop on revitalizing multilateral trade cooperation, and the 2019 Joint Murphy Institute–EUI conference on the future of trade governance for helpful comments and suggestions.

1. See *Fortune Global 500*, http://fortune.com/global500/list/filtered?hqcountry=China.

2. Chinese SOEs have a lower cost of capital (reflected in lower interest rates on their debt) and privatized SOEs continue to benefit from government support relative to private enterprises (Harrison and others 2019; Wood 2019).

More generally, the evidence suggests that SOEs are less profitable and less productive than private firms in their respective sectors (see, e.g., Kowalski and others 2013 for a broad sample of countries).

3. See, e.g., Joint Statement on Trilateral Meeting of the Trade Ministers of the United States, Japan, and the European Union, January 9, 2019, https:// ustr.gov/about-us/policy-offices/press-office/press-releases/2019/january /joint-statement-trilateral-meeting.

4. See World Trade Organization, "Subsidies Committee Members Express Concerns on Lack of Notifications," https://www.wto.org/english/news _e/news18_e/scm_26oct18_e.htm. Collins-Williams and Wolfe (2010) and Karlas and Parízek (2019a) discuss the state of play in the WTO in this area.

5. The GTA website is at www.globaltradealert.org/.

6. Because the GTA data are only available starting in 2009, we do not know what the baseline use was of the different instruments. Virtually all governments engage in FDI promotion and offer incentives of varying kinds to attract FDI, often at the level of local governments (provinces, regions, municipalities). The same is true of import tariffs. Conversely, the use of "temporary trade restrictions" such as antidumping is more concentrated in a limited number of countries.

7. Note again that the focus here is on a simple count of measures, not on the value of the support granted or their effects. Given that state aid and subsidies often are substantial in value, the implied share of subsidies vs. other policies may be a downward-biased measure of the economic significance of such instruments.

8. The WTO prohibits export subsidies, except in the case of agriculture, subject to specific commitments laid out in the Agreement on Agriculture, and in the case of developing countries with a per capita income of less than $1,000. The observed pattern of export subsidy use post-2008 may in part reflect the greater leeway for low-income countries to use export subsidies.

9. In interpreting these data it should be recognized that services account for only a small share of total measures covered by the GTA database. The main focus of trade policy is on goods.

10. Dawar (2019, 2020) discusses the (very limited) data available needed to form a judgment about whether and to what extent export credit measures go beyond what is permitted under the OECD Export Credit Arrangement, noting that a major difficulty in this regard is that the arrangement permits OECD export support agencies to "meet the competition" from nonsignatory export credit and development finance entities, and the fact that the WTO rules in this area embody a carve-out for countries that have signed the OECD arrangement.

11. This observation is increasingly perceived not to apply to China, given recent growth trends in the size and market share of SOEs in the economy.

12. McGuire (2014) documents how some countries have used selective government intervention to help national firms accumulate the necessary expertise and experience to build a niche in specific segments of the international global aerospace value chain, based in part on collaboration with global players in the industry.

13. The affected countries are Afghanistan, Benin, Burkina Faso, Burundi, Central African Republic, Chad, Comoros, DPR Korea, DR Congo, Eritrea, Ethiopia, Gambia, Guinea, Haiti, Liberia, Madagascar, Malawi, Mali, Mozambique, Nepal, Niger, Rwanda, Senegal, Sierra Leone, Somalia, Syria, Tajikistan, Tanzania, Togo, Uganda, Yemen, and Zimbabwe.

14. In the 2016–19 period the decoupling trend appeared to have stalled (OECD 2019a).

15. Adverse effects include injury to a domestic industry, nullification or impairment of tariff concessions, and serious prejudice to the country's interests. Serious prejudice is defined to exist if the total ad valorem subsidization of a product exceeds 5 percent, if subsidies are used to cover operating losses of a firm or industry, or debt relief is granted for government-held liabilities. Serious prejudice may arise if the subsidy reduces exports of WTO members, results in significant price undercutting, or increases the world market share of the subsidizing country in a primary product. The focus of WTO disciplines in cases of prejudice is on the amount of the assistance given, not on the extent to which a subsidy harms trading partners.

16. De minimis provisions allow developing countries to use subsidies subject to certain thresholds. If the subsidy is less than 2 percent of the per unit value of products exported, developing countries are exempt from CVDs (for less-development countries the threshold is 3 percent). De minimis also applies if the import market share of a developing country is below 4 percent and the aggregate share of all developing countries is below 9 percent of total imports. The SCM Agreement exempts nations with per capita incomes below 1,000 from the WTO prohibition on the use of export subsidies and precludes CVDs on associated exports if global market share is less than 3.5 percent for a product. De minimis provisions are also included in the WTO Agreement on Agriculture, permitting support of up to 10 percent of output in developing countries.

17. In the Uruguay Round a third category, nonactionable subsidies, was included in the SCM Agreement spanning environmental, R&D, and regional subsidies. This provision was time bound and lapsed at the end of 1999 because consensus could not be obtained to extend it. As a result, countries are left with GATT Article XX, the general exceptions article, under which a WTO member can argue that a measure is necessary to restrict goods made with prison labor or, inter alia, to protect human, animal, or plant life or health or conserve exhaustible natural resources. Article XX was drafted in the 1940s

and does not adequately cover many of the market failures that may justify policy interventions.

18. Disciplines on SOEs are included in recent preferential trade agreements (PTAs) such as the Comprehensive and Progressive Agreement for Trans-Pacific Partnership (CPTPP) and the United States-Mexico-Canada Agreement (USMCA), and the relevant provisions are enforceable through dispute settlement procedures. These disciplines require that SOEs make purchases and sales on the basis of commercial considerations; specify that subsidies granted to SOEs, both direct fiscal transfers and indirect subsidies, are actionable; and that signatories may not discriminate in favor of SOEs (i.e., they must apply the national treatment principle). The agreements also include provisions requiring signatories to list their SOEs and publish data on measures used to assist them.

19. This and the following paragraphs draw on Hoekman (2016a).

20. See Hoekman (2016b) for a discussion of the epistemic community that underpinned the eventual successful negotiation of the 2013 WTO Agreement on Trade Facilitation.

21. The G-20 Trade and Investment Working Group (TIWG) was created in 2015 as a forum to prepare the ground for trade initiatives by G-20 members. It includes the main international organizations—the IMF, OECD, World Bank, International Trade Center, United Nations Conference on Trade and Development (UNCTAD), and the WTO. The TIWG provides a forum for coordination of the activities of the organizations in areas defined by G-20 members. Activities of the TIWG have centered on the importance of reducing trade costs for global value chains, policies to address adjustment costs of globalization, and investment facilitation. Work orchestrated by the TIWG helped prepare the ground for the launch of plurilateral discussions on e-commerce and investment facilitation in the WTO.

22. The ICN was formed in 2001 by national competition agencies in part as a consequence of the effort to launch negotiations on competition policy in the WTO in the early 2000s. See Kovacic and Hollman (2011).

23. See, e.g., Ministerial Report, "Global Forum on Steel Excess Capacity," www.g20.utoronto.ca/2018/global-forum-on-steel-excess-capacity-180920 .pdf; and Ministry of Economy, Trade and Industry, News Release, https:// www.meti.go.jp/english/press/2019/1026_001.html. For an economic analysis of subsidies and excess capacity, see Blonigen and Wilson (2010).

24. The forum allowed participants to identify the underlying causes of steel overcapacity and define concrete actions to address them. See European Commission, "European Commission Welcomes Continuation of Global Forum on Steel Excess Capacity Work," https://trade.ec.europa.eu/doclib /press/index.cfm?id=2077.

25. See World Trade Organization, "Domestic Support in Agriculture: The Boxes," https://www.wto.org/english/tratop_e/agric_e/agboxes_e.htm.

26. See OECD (2019b) for a short summary of information on government support and approaches used to collect such data.

27. An annual State Aid Scoreboard (http://ec.europa.eu/competition/state _aid/scoreboard/index_en.html) collects data reported by member states. It covers all existing aid measures to industries, services, agriculture, and fisheries except aid to railways and services of general economic interest. In 2017, member states spent €116.2 billion, or 0.76 percent of total EU gross domestic product, on state aid. Over 90 percent of total state aid was allocated to horizontal objectives of common interest, such as environmental protection, research, development and innovation, and regional development.

28. The EU treaty includes a public services exception (Art. 106 of the Treaty on the Functioning of the European Union, TFEU), which specifies that undertakings "entrusted with the operation of services of general economic interest or having the character of a revenue-producing monopoly" are subject to the competition rules of the treaty "insofar as the application of such rules does not obstruct the performance . . . of the particular tasks assigned to them." TFEU Article 107(3) lists measures that may be considered compatible with the internal market: "(a) aid to promote the economic development of areas where the standard of living is abnormally low or where there is serious underemployment. . . . (b) aid to [. . .] remedy a serious disturbance in the economy of a Member State; (c) aid to facilitate the development of certain economic activities or of certain economic areas, where such aid does not adversely affect trading conditions to an extent contrary to the common interest; (d) aid to promote culture and heritage conservation where such aid does not affect trading conditions and competition in the Union to an extent that is contrary to the common interest; (e) such other categories of aid as may be specified by decision of the Council on a proposal from the Commission."

REFERENCES

Aghion, P., J. Boulanger, and E. Cohen. 2011. "Rethinking Industrial Policy." Bruegel Policy Brief 2011/04. Brussels, June.

Baldwin, R., and A. Venables. 2015. "Trade Policy and Industrialization When Backward and Forward Linkages Matter." *Research in Economics* 69 (2): 123–31.

Blanchard, E. 2015. "A Shifting Mandate: International Ownership, Global Fragmentation, and a Case for Deeper Liberalization under the WTO." *World Trade Review* 14 (1): 87–99.

Blonigen, B. 2016. "Industrial Policy and Downstream Export Performance." *Economic Journal* 126 (595): 1635–59.

Blonigen, B., and W. Wilson, 2010. "Foreign Subsidization and Excess Capacity." *Journal of International Economics* 80 (2): 200–11.

Collins-Williams, T., and R. Wolfe. 2010. "Transparency as a Trade Policy Tool: The WTO's Cloudy Windows." *World Trade Review* 9 (4): 564–65.

Dawar, K. 2019. "EU Export Credit Agencies: Assessing Compliance with EU Objectives and Obligations." RESPECT Working Paper. http://respect .eui.eu/wp-content/uploads/sites/6/2019/12/Final-K-Dawar-Horizon 2020-Work-Package-4.2.pdf.

———. 2020. "Official Export Credit Support: Competition and Compliance Issues." *Journal of World Trade.* 54 (3): 373–95.

Evenett, S. 2019. "Protectionism, State Discrimination, and International Business since the Onset of the Global Financial Crisis." *Journal of International Business Policy* 2 (1): 9–36.

Evenett, S., and J. Fritz. 2018. *Brazen Unilateralism: The US-China Tariff War in Perspective.* 23rd Global Trade Alert Report. London: CEPR.

Gawande, K., B. Hoekman, and Y. Cui. 2015. "Global Supply Chains and Trade Policy Responses to the 2008 Financial Crisis." *World Bank Economic Review* 29 (1): 102–28.

Gereffi, G. 2014. "A GVC Perspective on Industrial Policy and Development." *Duke Journal of Comparative and International Law* 24: 433–58.

Harrison, A., and others. 2019. "Can a Tiger Change Its Stripes? Reform of Chinese State-Owned Enterprises in the Penumbra of the State." NBER Working Paper 25475. Cambridge, Mass.: National Bureau of Economic Research.

Haas, P. 1992. "Introduction: Epistemic Communities and International Policy Coordination." *International Organization* 46 (1): 1–35.

Hoekman, B. 2016a. "Subsidies, Spillovers and WTO Rules in a Value Chain World." *Global Policy.* DOI: 10.1111/1758-5899.12327.

———. 2016b. "The Bali Trade Facilitation Agreement and Rulemaking in the WTO: Milestone, Mistake or Mirage?" In *The World Trade System: Trends and Challenges,* edited by J. Bhagwati, P. Krishna, and A. Panagariya. MIT Press.

Hoekman, B., and P. C. Mavroidis. 2000. "WTO Dispute Settlement, Transparency and Surveillance." *World Economy* 23 (2): 527–42.

Hoekman, B., and P. Messerlin. 2000. "Liberalizing Trade in Services: Reciprocal Negotiations and Regulatory Reform." In *GATS 2000—New Directions in Services Trade Liberalization,* edited by P. Sauvé and R. Stern. Brookings.

———. 2006. "Assessing the Impacts of Export Subsidies." In *Agricultural Trade Reform and the Doha Development Agenda,* edited by K. Anderson and W. Martin. Basingstoke, UK and Washington, D.C.: Palgrave Macmillan and World Bank.

Hoekman, B., and D. Nelson. 2020. "Rethinking International Subsidy Rules." EUI Working Paper RSCAS 2020/20.

Hoekman, B., and K. Saggi. 2000. "Assessing the Case for Extending WTO Disciplines on Investment-Related Policies." *Journal of Economic Integration* 15 (4): 629–53.

Horlick, G., and P. Clarke. 2010. "WTO Subsidy Disciplines during and after the Crisis." *Journal of International Economic Law* 13 (3): 859–74.

Karlas, J., and M. Parízek. 2019a. "Supply of Policy Information in the World Trade Organization: Cross-National Compliance with One-Time and Regular Notification Obligations, 1995–2014." *World Trade Review.* https://doi.org/10.1017/S1474745618000393.

———. 2019b. "The Process Performance of the WTO Trade Policy Review Mechanism: Peer-Reviewing Reconsidered." *Global Policy.* https://doi.org/10.1111/1758-5899.12672.

Kimmitt, R., and M. Slaughter. 2015. "How to Make Sure Volvo Is Starting a Trend: An Underappreciated Benefit of Liberalizing Trade: More Foreign Investment in the US." *Wall Street Journal*, April 9.

Kovacic, W., and H. Hollman. 2011. "The International Competition Network: Its Past, Current, and Future Role." *Minnesota Journal of International Law* 20: 274–323.

Kowalski, P., and others. "State-Owned Enterprises: Trade Effects and Policy Implications." OECD Trade Policy Paper 147. Paris: OECD.

Legg, W., and D. Blandford. 2019. "The Role of International Organizations in Agricultural Policy Analysis." In *Global Challenges for Future Food and Agricultural Policies*, edited by D. Blandford and K. Hassapoyanneseds, 307–32. Singapore: World Scientific.

Lucas, D. 2014. "Evaluating the Cost of Government Credit Support: The OECD Context." *Economic Policy* 29 (79): 553–97.

Mavroidis, P. C., and R. Wolfe. 2015. "From Sunshine to a Common Agent: The Evolving Understanding of Transparency in the WTO." *Brown Journal of World Affairs* 21 (2): 117–29.

McGuire, S. 2014. "Global Value Chains and State Support in the Aircraft Industry." *Business and Politics* 16 (4): 615–39.

Moretti, E. 2012. *The New Geography of Jobs.* Boston: Mariner Books.

Organization for Economic Cooperation and Development (OECD). 2016. *State-Owned Enterprises as Global Competitors: A Challenge or an Opportunity?* Paris.

———. 2017. "Support to Fisheries: Levels and Impacts," OECD Food, Agriculture and Fisheries Paper 103. Paris.

———. 2019a. *Agricultural Policy Monitoring and Evaluation 2019.* Paris.

———. 2019b. "Levelling the Playing Field: Measuring and Addressing Trade-Distorting Government Support." OECD Global Forum on Trade. https://www.oecd.org/trade/events/documents/oecd-gft-2019-summary -record.pdf.

———. 2019c. "Measuring Distortions in International Markets: The Aluminium Value Chain." OECD Trade Policy Paper 218. Paris.

Ossa, R. 2017. "A Quantitative Analysis of Subsidy Competition in the US." https://pdfs.semanticscholar.org/b97e/272a372e27e344c0604ec31f00a4 182004c2.pdf.

Shaffer, G., R. Wolfe, and V. Le. 2015. "Can Informal Law Discipline Subsidies?" *Journal of International Economic Law* 18 (4): 711–41.

Van Biesebroeck, J. 2010. "Bidding for Investment Projects: Smart Public Policy or Corporate Welfare?" *Canadian Public Policy:Analyse de politiques*, Vol. XXXVI, Supplement/numéro special, S1-S17.

Van Biesebroeck, J., and T. Sturgeon. 2010. "Effects of the 2008–09 Crisis on the Automotive Industry in Developing Countries: A Global Value Chain Perspective." In *Global Value Chains in a Post-Crisis World: A Development Perspective*, edited by O. Cattaneo, G. Gereffi, and C. Staritz, 209–44. Washington, D.C.: World Bank.

Warwick, K. 2013. "Beyond Industrial Policy: Emerging Issues and New Trends." OECD Science, Technology and Industry Policy Papers 2. Paris.

Wolfe, R. 2017. "Sunshine over Shanghai: Can the WTO Illuminate the Murky World of Chinese SOEs?" *World Trade Review* 16 (4): 713–32.

———. 2018. "Is World Trade Organization Information Good Enough? How a Systematic Reflection by Members on Transparency Could Promote Institutional Learning." https://www.bertelsmann-stiftung.de/en /publications/publication/did/is-world-trade-organization-information -good-enough/.

———. 2020. "Yours Is Bigger Than Mine! How an Index Like the PSE Helps in Understanding the Comparative Incidence of Subsidies." Mimeo.

Wood, A. 2019. "China: Long-Term Development Issues and Options, Past and Present." TMCD Working Paper 079. University of Oxford.

World Trade Organization (WTO). 2014. *Director-General's Overview of Developments in the International Trading Environment.* WT/TPR/OV/17/ Corr.1.

———. 2019. *World Trade Report 2019: The Future of Services Trade.* Geneva.

Wu, M. 2016. "The 'China, Inc.' Challenge to Global Trade Governance." *Harvard International Law Journal* 57 (2): 261–324.

10

DISENTANGLING DATA FLOWS

INSIDE AND OUTSIDE THE MULTINATIONAL COMPANY

ERIK VAN DER MAREL

n today's world, the flows of data between countries are a force of global-ization in addition to the flows of goods, services, people, and finance. Although the notion of data flows is relatively new, many companies use some kind of data in their production process that adds value to their ac-tivities in the so-called digital economy. Economic activities in the digital economy span a wide range of goods and services production, from digital products to online services and e-commerce to pure cross-border data flows and traditional telecom services and software. The common feature of all these activities is that value is embodied in data used in companies' production processes, either as inputs or as outputs. Indeed, cross-border data flows have become an essential component of globalization, enabling firms to become more productive (Manyika and others 2016).

Where exactly are data used and produced inside an economy? Where are these data flowing between countries? And who has a comparative ad-vantage in data? This chapter uses various data sets to address these and other issues related to data flows. To date not much is known about data flows, and research on the subject is still nascent. Bauer, Erixon, and Lee-Makiyama (2013), Bauer and others (2014), and Christensen and others (2013) have investigated the role of domestic regulation on data flows. Ferracane, Lee-Makiyama, and van der Marel (2018); Ferracane and van der Marel (2019), and Ferracane, Kren, and van der Marel (2019) find that requirements to localize personal data have a significant impact on firm-level productivity and on services trade. These studies find that although regulatory barriers regarding the localization of data are burdensome, this is not necessarily the case for rules regarding the handling of domestic data. Other studies focus on so-called data-enabled trade in services (Meltzer 2014) and the specific links between data and e-commerce (Martens 2013).

The existing research does not analyze where data are produced and employed and how companies are likely to use data internally as part of their multinational activities. This chapter investigates the role of data produced and used by goods and services industries, and where these goods and services are traded across countries around the world. Detailed input-output information is used to trace at a disaggregated level how much value of data input goes into each downstream industry sector covering six-digit goods and services inside the US economy. This investigation reveals, unsurprisingly, that data are used intensively in sectors such as telecommunications and data processing services. It also reveals that data are used intensively for management purposes inside multinational companies. These findings motivate the analysis here of patterns of trade in management and other data-intensive services using the most recent available data on international trade in services.

Since gross trade values tell only one side of the story, I also undertake some preliminary calculations to guesstimate the amount of value added that is produced and exported by these management and other data-intensive services for a typical European country, in this case France. The simple computations demonstrate that although management services themselves represent only a small share of the entire value added exported in services, they nonetheless can be of equal importance to other services such as finance. Finally, I try to uncover the determinants of national comparative advantage in data-intensive management services.

The chapter is organized as follows. The next section sets out a framework describing the use (input) of data upstream and the production (output) of data downstream in the economy. Next I calculate the so-called data intensities of sectors by analyzing the extent to which data are used as an input in the production of downstream industries. The following section matches these data-intensive industries with trade data in an attempt to determine which countries are the main traders of data. Finally, because the results indicate that a large amount of data flows inside multinational companies, I conclude with a brief discussion of policy implications.

WHERE ARE DATA LOCATED?

Data are widely used in all sectors. As products and services have become increasingly digitized, so have their production processes. The way data should be viewed in the production function is still open to much debate. On the one hand, data may serve as an output embodied in a digital product or online service. On the other hand, data can also be used as an input for many sectors as part of the production, development, and delivery of an offline good or service. Even though in the case of online services the data are directly provided by companies, many other goods and services in the digital economy are nondigital, at least at first sight. But even these nondigital goods and services are highly dependent on data, which help to develop the components used in production processes. Without the data, these goods and services would have less economic value. One example is logistics and delivery input services, which could not be efficiently supplied without storage, documentation, and software data (Kommerskollegium 2015). For this reason this chapter treats data as either an input or an output within the wider economy of goods industries and service sectors, as outlined in figure 10-1.

Figure 10-1 presents schematically where data are located within the wider economy. It is a simple representation of where sectors that produce and use data for their business practices are placed. Figure 10-1 shows that data are located both upstream and downstream, affecting both input goods and services as well as final output goods and services in the digital economy. The size of the boxes indicates the importance of data in the overall economy. Data can be seen as an input in both upstream and downstream industries, and are therefore placed behind the three squares that represent the entire goods and services economy (both upstream and downstream). Once the data are embodied in a good or service, value is created. Only then do the data become a productive item in a company's value chain and part of the digital economy.

FIGURE 10-1. **Data Use in the Wider Economy**

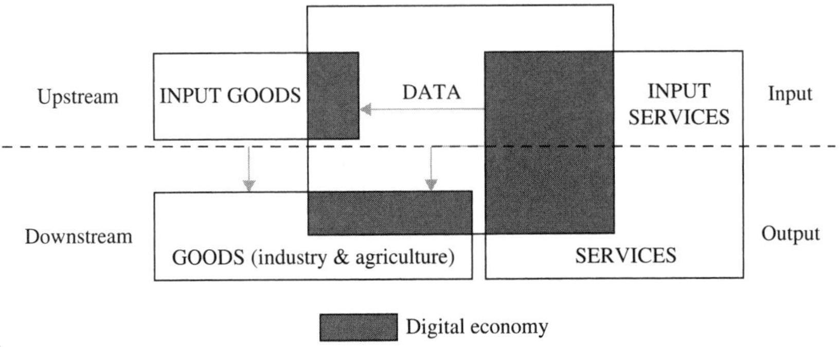

Source: Author.

As the figure shows, data can be used as an input in other input goods in the upstream part of the economy. As these intermediate input goods are processed downstream, eventually the data are embodied in final goods. Examples of this are intermediate inputs covered by the World Trade Organization's International Technology Agreement (ITA). The ITA agreement identifies industries that produce final goods or intermediate inputs. For instance, Miroudot, Rouzet, and Spinelli (2013) show that around 56.3 percent of the electrical machinery and apparatus industry (ISIC 31) produce intermediate inputs as defined by the United Nations' Harmonized System (HS) classification of trade. Other intermediate inputs covered by the ITA agreement include radio, television, and communication equipment and other non-metallic mineral products. The authors estimate that around 41 percent of the products covered by the ITA agreement are intermediate inputs.

Although some intermediate inputs that use data are further processed by downstream industries, data are also used directly in goods that downstream industries produce. In large part these are the final goods represented in the ITA agreement. For instance, a majority of the products produced in the machinery and equipment industry are actually final (downstream) goods. Similarly, many final goods covered by the ITA agreement can be found in the medical, precision, and optical instruments industry. Miroudot, Rouzet, and Spinelli (2013) estimate that around 60 percent of the items covered by the ITA agreement are final products.

Significant amounts of data are also used in services. Examples include data used in the telecom services sector and in the computer and information services sector. Many of these services are used as production inputs by downstream goods industries. Services that use a lot of data and are located upstream in the economy include telecoms, data processing services, financial services (including insurance), information technology (IT) consulting, data storage and system integration services, and marketing research services. These services are often used in the production processes of downstream companies, which in turn produce final goods and services. For a typical developed country, approximately 60 percent of all services sectors use intermediate services to produce final services.

In addition, upstream services can also be consumed as part of a final output service. For instance, in addition to being used as an input in the production chain, a substantial share of telecom services are also used by final consumers. These include personal services such as educational services, which also use a large amount of data in their production and delivery. Many other services sectors in the digital economy have emerged over the past decade. These include online services, web portals, search engines, internet or over-the-top (OTT) services, e-commerce, and software services. These are often consumed by users directly, but can also be used in the production processes of other downstream goods and services firms.

The common ground shared by all of the goods and services producers in figure 10-1 is their use of data to add value in the wider economy. In other words, data are a productive element in the production processes of all companies that produce goods and services.

WHO ARE THE PRODUCERS AND USERS OF DATA?

As noted, users of data include producers of goods, services, and agricultural products. Not all companies use an equal amount of data, however, and there is large variation in the use of data across sectors. This section investigates which sectors are the main producers and users of data in the wider economy. This part of the analysis relies on the Bureau of Economic Analysis (BEA) Input-Output Use data tables, which provide detailed information about different sectors' use of input value from other sectors, including data and data services. I select a small subset of sectors whose main activity is producing and developing data as core sectors that provide data as a final output. In order to get a precise picture, I selected all of these sectors from the six-digit level, the most detailed level provided by the BEA. All of the categories are services, so they exclude goods covered under the

TABLE 10-1. **Sectors Covering Producers in the Digital Economy**

Six-digit code[a]	Sector description
511200	Software publishers
517110	Wired telecommunications carriers
517210	Wireless telecommunications carriers (except satellite)
518200	Data processing, hosting, and related services
519130	Internet publishing and broadcasting and Web search portals
541511	Custom computer programming services
541512	Computer systems design services
541513	Other computer-related services, including facilities management

Source: US Department of Commerce, Bureau of Economic Analysis (BEA).

[a] The six-digit codes are the classification codes used in the BEA's input-output tables.

ITA. As discussed in the next section, manufacturing and agricultural goods are mainly users, not producers, of data.

Table 10-1 shows eight key sectors that are the main producers of data in the digital economy. As such, they provide inputs (or final output) to other downstream users or final output industries. These digital sectors are software publishers, internet publishers, web search portals, and telecommunications carriers. Of course there are more sectors that develop data in the domestic economy, but in these core data sectors the majority of tasks are dedicated to developing and therefore producing data. For example, software publishers are companies engaged in the design, development, and publishing of computer software with the use of data. The primary business goal of these companies is to carry out operations necessary for the production and distribution of software. This sector includes producers of games, operating systems software, programming languages, compiler software, and other software products.[1]

The telecommunications sector is divided into two segments, wired and wireless. The former conducts activities related to the operation and provision of access to transmission facilities or other infrastructure. These transmission facilities and infrastructure are owned by telecom companies for sending voice, data, text, sounds, and video using wired telecom networks. In addition, the telecom companies operate and use the network to provide a wide range of services such as wired telephone services, VoIP services, audio and video programming distribution, and wired broadband internet services. This category also includes online access service providers using their own wired telecom infrastructures. The wireless telecom category entails activities that are related to operating and maintaining switching and transmission facilities in order to provide communications services over the airwaves. After obtaining so-called spectrum licenses, companies can provide services using the spectrum, which include phone services, paging services, wireless internet access, and wireless video services.

Data processing and hosting, internet publishing and broadcasting, and web search portals cover a wide variety of data-related services. Companies in the data processing, hosting, and related services sector provide infrastructure for web hosting, streaming services and application hosting, and application services. They also include operations to produce complete processing and specialized reports from data supplied by clients and the delivery of automated (including electronic) data processing and data entry services. Internet publishing and broadcasting (including web search portals) are separated into those activities that publish and broadcast content exclusively on the internet; web search portals are websites that use a search engine to generate and maintain extensive databases of internet addresses and content in easily searchable format. The internet publishing and broadcasting companies provide text, audio, and video content through the internet only. Web search portals can also provide services such as e-mail, auctions, news, and connections to other websites.

The last category into which the last three sectoral activities fall cover all tasks that require expertise in the field of information technology; they (a) write, modify, test, and support software; (b) plan and design computer systems that integrate hardware, software, and communication technologies; (c) provide onsite management and operations of clients' computer systems and data processing facilities; and (d) offer other technical computer-related services. Other services related to software analysis include webpage design, programming, computer-aided design, engineering, and manufacturing (CAD, CAE, CAM), systems integration design services, local area network (LAN) computer system integration design, and data processing facilities management and operation services.

WHO ARE THE USERS?

Using the BEA's input-output tables, it is possible to identify the users and how much each user uses the data-related services as defined in table 10-1. National input-output tables are a good indicator of how much one unit of input from each of these data services is used by every downstream goods and services industry sector in an economy. Although ideally the input-output information of all countries would be analyzed, this is not possible because most national tables are too aggregated in their classifications and use different classification schemes. I select the US national input-output tables from the BEA for this exercise for two main reasons. These tables provide the most detailed worldwide data, including the disaggregated data sectors described earlier. Also, the tables' industry classification fits perfectly with the NAICS sector descriptions, which can easily be matched with trade data in the next section.[2]

To perform the calculations, I select the six-digit input use table at producers' price value from the Economic Accounts of the BEA, which provides input use figures for 389 industry groups, including services and goods sectors as well as agriculture and mining. These detailed industry groups are further sorted according to seventy-one three-digit combined industry groups and also into fifteen aggregated two-digit industry groups. The value of data use as a share of their total input use from the data-producing sectors in table 10-1 is calculated for each six-digit disaggregated industry sector. Then, in order to aggregate these detailed sector classifications into higher group sectors (either three-digit or two-digit) an unweighted average is computed. Figure 10-2 summarizes the results by two-digit sector and shows the main users of the services provided by data producers.

Unsurprisingly, the sectors that use data most intensively are the same sectors that also produce data services. Figure 10-2 shows that telecom and data processing services, internet publishing and web portals, together with publishing services (including software) and motion picture services are large users of data. In other words, those who produce data are also the ones that use data. On average this amounts to a data input usage of almost 12 percent of the value of total input use of all services and goods. However, a more surprising result shown in figure 10-2 is that the highest share of data, about 14 percent, appears to be used for management purposes inside companies. This share of data usage for management services inside companies is 2 percent higher than the share used by data services sectors themselves. It indicates that data play a crucial role in the process and development of firms' management strategies and execution by their affiliates and other establishments.[3]

Another important user of data is the administrative services sector, which includes office administrative services, employment services, and

FIGURE 10-2. Share of Data Services Input Use by Sector, 2012 (in total input)

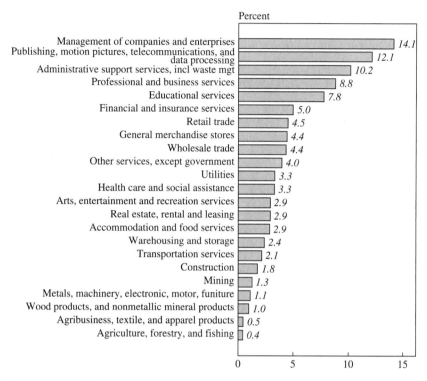

Source: Author's calculations, using US Department of Commerce Bureau of Economic Analysis (BEA).

business support services. These services are essential to operating a firm but are most often outsourced to external services suppliers and therefore do not constitute an important factor in the management decisions of companies. The share of data input usage in total input usage of this sector averages almost 10 percent. Next are business and professional services, which use around 9 percent of the data services inputs in total input usage. These types of services differ from office administrative services in the sense that they cover professional services. Examples are legal services, computer systems design and related services, and accounting, engineering, and management consultancy services, as well as market research and research and development services. These services are also usually provided by outside suppliers.

A second somewhat surprising result is that educational services is also a big user of data, even bigger than the financial and insurance sector. The education sector absorbs close to a share of 8 percent of data services inputs into total input usage, whereas the financial sector's share of data usage is 5 percent. This is unexpected in the sense that the policy literature has emphasized the critical role of data in the development of the financial services sector. Figure 10-2 suggests that data likely play an equally important role in the development of the education sector. Included in the category of educational services are colleges, universities, and professional schools, business schools and computer and management training, and elementary schools and junior colleges.

The next categories that use data somewhat intensively are real estate, rental and leasing activities, wholesale trade, retail trade, arts and recreational services, warehousing and storage services, general merchandise stores, and utilities. Most of these services use data as an input that varies more or less between 2 and 4.5 percent. On the whole, all these sectors that report high data usage are services. The first goods sector listed in figure 10-2, apart from mining, is the metals, machinery, and electronics sector, which uses on average only 1.1 percent. Some disaggregated industry sectors, however, are rather data-intense, such as support activities for printing (NAICS 323120) with a usage of 7.6 percent, and optical instrument and lens manufacturing (NAICS 333314) with an input intensity of 4.2, but these are rare. Across all detailed manufacturing sectors, the average data input usage is 1 percent (see table 10A-1 in the appendix). Table 10A-2 lists the twenty disaggregated six-digit sector categories that use data most.

WHERE IN THE WORLD ARE DATA AND DATA SERVICES FLOWING?

Since most of the highest data intensities are found in services, I use the World Bank's new Trade in Services (TIS) database to explore which sectors hold the biggest shares of trade in data-intensive services. This database is the most advanced source of information on services trade around the world, bringing together data from various other databases. Using mirror techniques, the TIS database collects information on bilateral trade flows from the Organization for Economic Cooperation and Development, Eurostat, the United Nations, and the International Monetary Fund. As such, it provides a consolidated and reconciled version of multiple sources of bilateral data in trade in services, and forms currently the best effort at doing so (see Saez and others 2015 for further insights).

As Meltzer (2014) points out, a lot of the services trade in the world takes place across the Atlantic. This is visible in table 10-2, which uses the TIS data and reports trade data in gross values for European Union, the United States, and the rest of the world (ROW). Table 10-2 sorts out the various sector classifications for which there are trade data available for the data-intensive services sectors given in figure 10-2. Note that services trade data are not available for all sectors mentioned in figure 10-2. As a result, table 10-2 is restricted to services sectors only, which can be justified by the fact that goods industries use only a small share of data in their input structure (as discussed in the previous section). Moreover, although the TIS database does report flows of personal services such as educational services and arts, entertainment, and recreation services, it is extremely hard for statisticians to collect trade data for these services. Therefore some data in these services sectors may be missing.

Table 10-2 indeed shows that most of the trade in data-intensive services sectors is captured by the EU and the US, but there are large differences. In fact, the United States holds a smaller trade share of these sectors. For instance, the highest US share in world trade is publishing, motion pictures, telecoms, and data processing, which is in line with what we could expect, since the United States is home to one of the world's largest multinationals in this field. Yet this US share is less than the 40.2 global share held by the EU. Other sectors in which the United States holds a large world trade share are administrative services, business services, and financial services. But here too these figures are also lower than those of the EU. Therefore, an additional robustness check is performed in table 10-2, comparing the mean share of all three regions with aggregate services trade data (figures provided by the World Bank's World Development Indicators). Table 10-2 shows, however, that differences between these two sources are relatively small, and hence the low trade shares of the US relative to the EU seem to be consistent across the two databases. Taken together, the figures point to the fact that, on average, a much larger share of sectors using data most intensively is captured by the EU.

An interesting case in point is the trade share capture in management services between related enterprises. Table 10-2 shows that the EU has a much bigger trade share than the US in this sector as well. This category of trade in management services between related enterprises is the closest

TABLE 10-2. Trade Shares for the European Union, the United States, and Rest of the World, 2012

Percent

IO two–digit code[a]	Industry description	European Union	United States	Rest of world
51	Publishing, motion pictures, telecommuications, and data processing	40.2	29.6	30.2
55	Management of companies and enterprises	66.6	12.0	21.3
56	Administrative support services, incl. waste management	35.5	25.8	38.7
54	Professional and business services	30.1	22.7	47.2
61	Educational services	76.8	4.5	18.7
52	Financial and insurance services	39.1	25.4	35.5
42	Wholesale trade / distribution	43.1	2.5	54.4
62	Health care and social assistance	57.0	7.5	35.5
71	Arts, entertainment, and recreation services	49.9	5.8	44.3
72	Accommodation and food services	16.8	19.3	63.9
48	Transportation services	29.9	10.7	59.5
23	Construction	25.3	3.5	71.2
	Mean	42.5	14.1	43.4
	Mean WDI	39.8	13.2	47.0

Source: World Bank, Trade in Services database; World Bank Development Indicators (WDI). EU figures are based on extra-EU trade with the world.

[a] The two-digit codes are the classification codes used in the BEA's input-output tables.

to the BEA's input-output classification of management of companies and enterprises (as in figure 10-2) and can therefore offer some insight into the trading patterns in this data-intensive sector. This category includes services flowing from the parent to the affiliate enterprise company, and vice versa, that relate to the planning, organization, and control of these enterprises—that is, management services. These are flows of services activities inside multinational companies and are, on average, very data-intensive, as the previous section noted.[4]

What kinds of tasks constitute management services? Further insight on this question comes from the US Bureau of Labor Statistics (BLS), which gives a more precise picture of what occupations this services sector includes. The Occupational Employment Statistics database of the BLS is part of the US Department of Labor and records the share of occupations for each six-digit NAICS category that matches exactly with the management services sector category in figure 10-2. It therefore provides a clearer picture of which specific services tasks are actually traded inside the sector of management services. Among the major tasks grouped together in this sector, they relate to (in percentage terms of total amount of occupations) business and financial operations (21.8 percent), management occupations (20 percent), computer occupations (10.5 percent), and administrative support services (25.8 percent), which together constitute almost 80 percent of all occupations in this sector. Interestingly, one can see that these activities are closely related to the business services activities recorded in table 10-2 but in this case are traded within related companies. On a more detailed level, these in-house business activities include bookkeeping, accounting and auditing clerks, financial managers, first-line supervisors and managers of office and administrative support workers. They also cover general and occupational managers, business operations specialists, market research analysts and marketing specialists, management analysis, and even human resources activities.

Table 10-3 provides an overview of which countries are the biggest traders in this field, both importers and exporters. The table lists the countries that together represent around 95 percent of the total trade in management services between related enterprises worldwide. Most are developed countries, but some emerging countries are also listed, such as China, Russia, and Brazil. The largest traders in this services sector are the Netherlands, Great Britain, and Belgium, with 13.6, 11.1, and 10.7 percent shares, respectively, in the world. For smaller countries such as the Netherlands and

TABLE 10-3. **Services Transactions between Related (Affiliated) Enterprises**

Country	Exports (millions of US dollars)		Imports (millions of US dollars)		Total trade as share of GDP
	Value	Share of world	Value	Share of world	
Netherlands	16,969.37	13.63	20,178.80	17.09	4.51
United Kingdom	13,860.95	11.13	7,290.15	6.17	0.81
Belgium	13,369.63	10.74	10,713.95	9.07	4.83
France	11,261.27	9.05	5,672.39	4.80	0.63
US	98,76.69	7.93	7,041.60	5.96	0.10
Italy	7,943.12	6.38	4,378.47	3.71	0.59
Germany	7,198.22	5.78	7,279.68	6.17	0.41
Spain	7,076.68	5.68	7,582.89	6.42	1.08
Sweden	6,868.67	5.52	4,872.56	4.13	2.16
Korea	4,007.30	3.22	6,212.30	5.26	0.84
Switzerland	3,475.28	2.79	8,790.26	7.44	1.84
Austria	3,337.91	2.68	2,587.59	2.19	1.45
Denmark	1,876.88	1.51	2,000.81	1.69	1.20
Israel	1,644.09	1.32	1,641.64	1.39	1.28
Hungary	1,412.25	1.13	1,998.83	1.69	2.69
China	1,160.84	0.93	772.34	0.65	0.02
Ireland	1,152.47	0.93	5,948.62	5.04	3.20
Czech Republic	1,086.40	0.87	1,354.40	1.15	1.18
Finland	1,037.09	0.83	1,593.23	1.35	1.03
Poland	810.96	0.65	1,098.22	0.93	0.38
Singapore	748.76	0.60	1,132.01	0.96	0.66
Russia	737.15	0.59	289.78	0.25	0.05
Japan	705.94	0.57	358.33	0.30	0.02
Brazil	664.46	0.53	957.07	0.81	0.07
Luxembourg	650.00	0.52	764.97	0.65	2.51
Total	118,932.37	95.53	112,510.89	95.29	–

Source: World Bank, Trade in Services database.

Belgium, the total trade shares (including imports) are more sizable and represent, respectively, 4 and 5 percent of their national gross domestic product (GDP). Other countries for which the services trade between related affiliates forms a significant part of their domestic economies are also relatively small, such as Ireland, Hungary, and Luxembourg.

Among the larger countries, France, Italy, and Spain have shares of services trade in affiliated enterprises that are also large relative to their economic size, particularly in comparison with other large economies such as the United States and Germany. These latter two countries (especially the US) show low shares relative to their economies, although their nominal figures nonetheless remain strong. One potential explanation for the higher average share of the European countries is the world distribution of outward foreign direct investment (FDI) stocks: whereas the EU holds a stake of around 40 percent, the US has a relatively smaller share of outward stock in the world of around 24 percent (UNCTAD 2014). This may well be reflected in the United States' lower share in services within multinationals worldwide. Yet both smaller and bigger countries capture a large share of world flows in management services within companies. This points to the fact that other factors apart from the structural determinants such as market size play a role in facilitating the data-intensive flows of these services. One obvious candidate is the digital infrastructure that helps companies to transmit data-intensive services.

WHERE ARE THE DATA FLOWING?

Although the ranking in table 10-3 is dominated by European countries and the US, some non-transatlantic countries are also included in the list. For example, Korea holds a larger share of management services than some European countries. Moreover, other emerging countries such as China, Russia, Brazil, and Israel also appear to capture a sizable share of imports and exports in management services between affiliated enterprises, despite the fact that the share of GDP is still comparatively low. On the whole, it therefore looks as if smaller countries are in a better position to hold world shares of trade in this type of services. On the other hand, smaller countries generally show higher relative shares of services trade given that a large majority of their economic activities is in services. The same is true for other data-intensive services such as business and administrative services. Seeing the specialization pattern in this light, services between related enterprises are just a part of the overall services sector and therefore can find a natural place in smaller economies.

Still, the two largest services economies, namely the EU and the US, do take up together a substantial share of all existing bilateral trade flows worldwide in data-intensive services, including management services between related enterprises. Figure 10-3 shows the transatlantic bilateral relationship of both imports and exports expressed as a share of the total

FIGURE 10-3. Shares of Trade in Services: Transatlantic and Rest of the World (RoW), 2012

Bilateral share of world

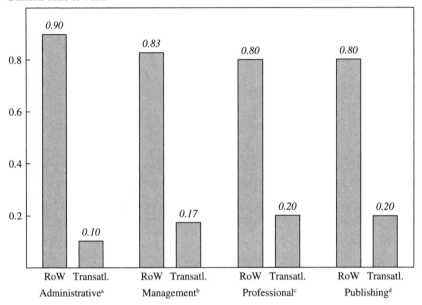

Source: World Bank, Trade in Services database.

[a] "Administrative" comprises administrative support services, including waste management.
[b] "Management" encompasses management of companies and enterprises.
[c] "Professional" includes professional and business services.
[d] "Publishing" covers publishing, media, telecommunications, and data processing activities.

amount of trade held by all other bilateral trade relations in services around the world. Figure 10-3 only shows the most data-intensive sectors as defined in figure 10-2, namely administrative support services (including waste management), management of companies and enterprises; professional and business services; and finally publishing, motion pictures, telecoms, and data processing. Both the US and the EU capture around 20 percent of the global trade in both professional and business services and publishing, motion pictures, telecom, and data processing services. This share is likely to be larger than between any other two bilateral trading partners worldwide and confirms Meltzer's (2015) point that much of the services trade that is enabled by ICT and data takes place between the two Atlantic economies. For management services between related affiliates, the transatlantic parties embody around 17 percent of total world trade in this sector. Next is administrative services, at 10 percent.

On a larger scale, most of the bilateral trade in data-intensive sectors take place between OECD member countries. This is visible in figure 10A-1 in the appendix, which shows the bilateral trade shares within the OECD and for the rest of the world for each of the four data-intensive sectors. In this figure, the OECD captures the highest share in management services between related (affiliated) enterprises of around 86 percent. The shares of both administrative services and business services are 83 percent and 81 percent respectively in the OECD economies. The only sector that seems to be more widespread among the emerging economies is publishing, motion pictures, telecoms, and data processing services, with a share held by the rest of the world of 23 percent. Still, the large majority of trade in this sector takes place inside the OECD. One strong determinant of higher trade shares in data-intensive services is FDI. Particularly for management services in related enterprises, the amount of outward FDI as part of GDP appears to be strongly associated with total trade in this sector. This can be seen in figure 10A-2 in the appendix.

WHERE IS THE VALUE ADDED IN DATA?

As stated by the OECD (2013), the trade numbers presented in the previous figures are based on gross terms and therefore do not account for the real value added of exports. This is because gross trade includes double-counting of trade flows and does not measure exports of domestically produced goods and services only. Countries often produce services at home that are used as an input in other downstream goods (and services) production and then (indirectly) exported. Counting in gross terms therefore understates the importance of services, including data services. For this reason, the OECD has developed a new data set measuring the exact value-added of goods and services produced and then exported, directly or indirectly. Overall, this means that on the basis of value added in the US for instance, the significance of services increases to almost 50 percent, with particular importance for US downstream sectors such as wood and paper, transport equipment, and food products. In the EU this share is currently above 50 percent where value-added services are an important ingredient in transport equipment and food products in addition to electrical equipment and textiles and apparel.

FIGURE 10-4. Value-Added Share of Management Services among Other Services for France, 2009

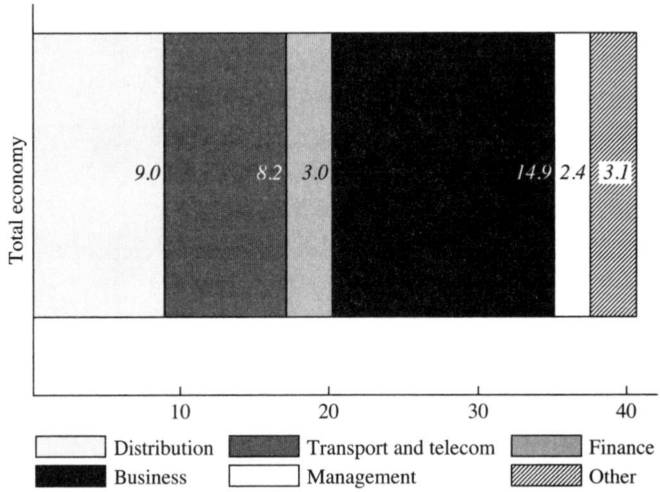

Source: Author's calculations using OECD, Trade in Value Added database and World Bank, Trade in Services database.

However, how much actual value added to data-intensive services flows into the wider direct and downstream economy? To take stock of most of the important data-intensive services as defined in the previous analysis, figure 10-4 presents a breakdown of the value added in services (of which data-intensive services are a part) for a typical European country, in this case France. Based on gross trade figures from the World Bank's TIS database and using value-added figures from the OECD's Trade in Value Added (TiVA) database, a rough estimate can be calculated that reflects the share of management services between affiliates as part of the overall business services sector. The estimate is obtained through a simple back-of-the-envelope calculation of the ratio of value added to gross values in the same service category. Admittedly, this is a crude measure, but it is only a first step in providing an approximation of the importance of management services. Note that the TiVA database sums the data for other sectors together, such as transport and telecom services, which are not separated from each other in figure 10-4. The TiVA database also includes other sectors such as distribution and financial services.

Figure 10-4 shows that, for France, the total economy takes up a value-added share of services of more than 40 percent, which is close to the

OECD's average of 48 percent. Within this services sector one can see that business services use the largest share of value-added services, around 15 percent. The distribution, transport, and telecom sectors are other large services sectors that produce and export value added output. Note that telecom and business services (which also includes administrative support and professional services) are considered data-intensive sectors. Management services between related affiliates have a share of 2.4 percent, which is more or less comparable to the amount of value added produced by the financial services sector in France. As such, this sector forms a nonnegligible part of the value-added production in the French economy, and together with all other services sectors that are data-intensive, shows the importance of data in reaping value added from these sectors. Of course, the importance of each sector is different in different economies. Yet, in most developed countries, data-dependent sectors such as business services, telecoms, finance, and management are important contributors to their economies.

In sum, both the producers of data services and the users of data services are situated everywhere around the globe, as are flows of data. Both the EU and the US, and especially the developed OECD countries, capture a large market share of trade in services that produce or use data—the so-called data-intensive and digital services. In fact, the both the US and the EU countries capture the majority of these very data-intensive services trade. Together the transatlantic economy shares are around 20 percent of the total data trade that flows between their individual markets. Surprisingly, the data tell us that a second important services sector that uses a lot of data in its production processes is management services between related enterprises—that is, transactions between related affiliates—a fact that has been somewhat overlooked in the literature. In this category, both small and large countries are large traders of data-intensive services, although the importance of these services tends to increase adversely with the size of the economy.

WHO HAS COMPARATIVE ADVANTAGE IN DATA-INTENSIVE SECTORS?

The fact that the economic importance of services, including data-intensive services, is greater for smaller countries does not necessarily mean that they have a comparative advantage in these digital services. Comparative advantage is defined as the relative productivity premium that countries have in producing and trading in a particular sector because they can provide the institutions, endowments, and investment climate that industries can capitalize on to increase the efficiency of their production processes. In other words, there is a "match" between the input components a country can provide and what an industry or sector needs. This can come in many forms. Some sectors need a strong rule of law because their sectors are sensitive to hold-up problems and therefore require strong contract enforcement mechanisms; other sectors are dependent on the availability of high-skilled or technological labor; and other sectors are likely to operate in countries with flexible labor markets because their methods of production require easy employment adjustments. These determinants of comparative advantage also have bearing for data-intensive sectors.

For these data-intensive sectors, table 10-4 uses a common measure called revealed comparative advantage (RCA) to show who has a comparative advantage between the EU and the US and the rest of the world in these sectors.[5] Although this index is subject to some criticism, it is useful in identifying the relative productivity and trade specialization patterns of countries in a certain sector.[6] Table 10-4 tells us that the EU has a strong comparative advantage in some data-intensive sectors such as management of companies and enterprises, educational services, and wholesale and retail trade. In addition, the EU holds a comparative advantage in the category covering telecoms and data processing services, but the US appears to have an even stronger comparative advantage in these sectors. Similarly, for professional and business services, administrative support services, and financial services the US appears to have a stronger position in export productivity differences between sectors, though in some of these sectors the EU also has a comparative advantage.

WHO IS BEST PLACED TO HAVE COMPARATIVE ADVANTAGE IN DATA?

The RCA indicator does not yet provide the countrywide factors that influence the performance of data-intensive industries and sectors and their difference in productivity across countries. In other words, the figures in table 10-4 do not say anything about what actually determines why countries trade more or less of a service that is data-intensive. As noted earlier, a good match between what a country can provide in endowment structure and the needs of a specific sector defines the source of comparative ad-

TABLE 10-4. **Revealed Comparative Advantage of Data-Intensive Sectors, 2012**

Two-digit code[a]	Industry description	European Union	United States	Rest of world
51	Publishing, motion pictures, telecommunications, and data processing	1.2	1.7	0.6
55	Management of companies and enterprises	1.9	0.6	0.3
56	Administrative support services, incl. waste management	1.0	1.3	0.6
54	Professional and business services	1.1	1.3	0.9
61	Educational services	2.2	0.3	0.4
52	Financial and insurance services	1.0	1.4	0.6
42	Wholesale trade	1.3	0.1	1.0
62	Health care and social assistance	1.9	0.3	0.4
71	Arts, entertainment, and recreation services	1.6	0.4	0.9
72	Accommodation and food services	0.8	1.1	1.2
48	Transportation services	0.9	0.5	0.9
23	Construction	0.9	0.2	1.4

Source: Author's calculations, using World Bank, Trade in Services database.

[a] The two-digit codes are the classification codes used in the BEA's input-output tables.

vantage. If a sector is skill-intensive it will most likely place its production facility in a country that can provide a skilled labor force. Likewise, if an industry is prone to many hold-up problems in the supply chain, companies in this sector are likely to choose a country with strong rule of law so that contracts can be enforced.[7] Countries differ in their ability to provide these factors and institutions. As for sectors that use lots of data, some use more data than others, as figure 10-2 shows, because of the way they produce a good or service. Therefore companies that produce data-intensive services are more likely to settle where the "digital infrastructure" is best so that data can be used efficiently.

FIGURE 10-5. Correlation between Network Readiness and Exports in Management Services, 2012

Per capita exports affiliate services

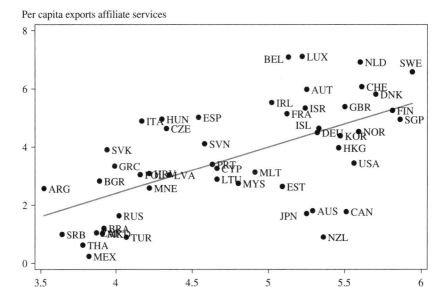

Network Readiness Index

Source: Author's calculations using data from World Economic Forum (2012); and World Bank Trade in Services database

The World Economic Forum (WEF) Network Readiness Index is one indicator of a location's digital infrastructure. The index measures the extent to which an economy is prepared to apply the benefits of information and communications technologies (ICTs) to promote economic growth and well-being. Included in this measure are factors such as the amount of broadband and the number of internet subscriptions in a country, whether a country has the latest technologies available, whether firms absorb technology, and whether multinational corporations bring new technologies into the domestic economy. These subindicators of the NRI all signify in one way or another whether data can move efficiently within a country. This information will affect the productivity term of data-intensive industries: a good match between a country's digital infrastructure and the level of trade required by data-intensive services sectors can give them a comparative advantage. Figure 10-5 indeed shows that, for instance, countries with a higher index value of network readiness are better able to export management services between affiliates, which is as we have seen a data-intensive sector. This correlation also holds for the other data-intensive sectors.

As figure 10-5 shows, countries that are lower on the horizontal axis, which measures network readiness, such as Venezuela and Iran, also show lower export levels of affiliated management services within enterprises, which is measured on the vertical axis. On the other hand, countries that ranked high in table 10-3 (and higher on the vertical axis in figure 10-5) such as Sweden, Spain, and the Netherlands are situated on the right-hand side of the Network Readiness Index, indicating high levels of exports in management services between enterprises. Some countries are doing better than others. For instance, Japan, which has a high network readiness score, is below the fitted values line, which means that one would expect it to have a higher level of exports in affiliate services. This is for instance confirmed by the fact that Germany and Austria, which have an equal level of data infrastructure (i.e., network readiness) as Japan, show much higher affiliated services exports and are therefore placed above the (average) fitted values line.

To formally test whether countries with a better digital infrastructure truly export more data-intensive services (including management services) a small empirical estimation can be applied. This estimation uses an econometric strategy to test for the assertion that the Network Readiness Index is indeed a robust factor in determining the level of trade in data-intensive services. Equation 1 uses this countrywide indicator to proxy for the quality of data infrastructure while plugging in the data intensities by sector. These two indicators are then interacted with each other and used as a dependent variable in a regression:

$$X_{oi} = DI_i * NRI_o + DI_i * COU_o + \delta_i + \gamma_o + \varepsilon_{oi} \qquad (1)$$

where X_{oi} stands for the exports of country o in each sector i sourced from the Trade in Services database from the World Bank (Saez and others 2015). The first term on the right-hand side of equation 1 is the interaction variable of interest, which represents the source of comparative advantage regarding data usage and data infrastructure (NRI). This interaction variable interacts the data intensities of all sectors (both data-intensive and non-data-intensive) with the Network Readiness Index. The third term is also an interaction term using data intensities, but controls for various other

TABLE 10-5. **Regression Output for Data-Intensity (Share) and Countrywide Factors**

	1 EXP	2 EXP	3 EXP	4 EXP	5 EXP
Data share * NRI[a]	5.596*** (1.720)	4.546** (1.932)	5.249*** (1.949)	−3.319 (6.716)	−4.414 (6.626)
Data share * HC[b]		3.063 (4.331)	−0.786 (4.294)	0.205 (4.165)	0.507 (4.164)
Data share * K[c]			2.830*** (1.042)	3.273*** (1.060)	2.987*** (1.131)
Data share * Rulaw[d]				7.227 (5.306)	7.354 (5.570)
Data share * GDP pc[e]					1.488 (4.974)
Observations	1,279	1,133	1,007	1,007	983
R-squared	0.759	0.764	0.763	0.763	0.763

Source: Author's calculations using data from World Economic Forum (2012); US Department of Commerce, Bureau of Economic Affairs (BEA); and World Bank Trade in Services database. Robust standard errors are in parentheses clustered by country.
*** $p < 0.01$, ** $p < 0.05$, * $p < 0.1$.

[a] NRI = Network Readiness Index (World Economic Forum)

[b] HC = Human capital

[c] K = Physical capital

[d] Rulaw = Rule of law (Rulaw) is a proxy for domestic institutions.

[e] GDP pc = Gross Domestic Product per capita

determinants of comparative advantage found in the literature with which data intensity might correlate. These include a better quality of education and the quality of domestic institutions. Once these are added to the regression the true marginal importance of the NRI as a determinant is revealed. I also control for all other issues that may be found collinear at the level of exporter, γ_o, and sector, δ_i, which are the so-called fixed effects. Last, the term ε_{oi} stands for the error term satisfying the usual assumptions. The year 2012 is chosen for all the variables, and services sectors are used only to avoid data inconsistencies. Data for data-intensities (DI) are based on the ones presented in figure 10-2. Data for all other variables are sourced from standard data databases.

The results of the regression are presented in table 10-5. Column 1 shows the data intensity share of all sectors interacted with the Network Readiness Index. Not only is the coefficient positive and very significant; the coefficient size is also quite large. The large coefficient size indicates that there is a large effect of this source of comparative advantage on a country's trade patterns in data-intensive services sectors. Hence, countries that indeed provide a better digital infrastructure also have high levels of data-intensive exports. Column 2 adds a separate entry to the interaction term where data intensity is multiplied with a measure of human capital (HC), using quality of education indicators described by the World Economic Forum (2013). It shows that this interaction variable becomes positive but insignificant, and that the original term with the network readiness component remains robustly positive and significant.

This remains true when I add a separate entry (column 3) to the countrywide variable—the availability of capital (K)—although this term also becomes positive and significant. It indicates that next to the network readiness measure, the amount of capital a country has is probably also a factor that influences trade in data-intensive services. Finally, I include two additional factors that may influence the significance of the previous variables. These are the quality of institutions (rule of law) from the World Bank's Governance Database and GDP per capita from the World Development Indicators. The NRI interaction term loses its significance and the outcome of this variable becomes negative. The switch of sign and significance indicates that there are some collinearity issues in the regression. The reason for this is that both GDP per capita and the quality of rule of law are highly collinear with each other and with the NRI indicator. On the other hand, the interaction term with the quantity of capital stock remains significant and robust.

CONCLUSION AND POLICY IMPLICATIONS

This chapter attempts to disentangle flows of data by documenting the sectors and activities in the economy where most data are produced and used, analyzing which countries capture most of the trade in data-intensive services, and assessing factors that determine a country's success in exporting data-intensive services. Unsurprisingly, most data are used in telecom services, sound recording services, data processing and hosting services, and web portal services. These are also to a large extent the producers of data services. Most developed countries hold a large share of trade in these sectors, although emerging countries also capture a sizable part of global trade in data-intensive services sectors, especially the bigger ones, such as China.

One surprising result of this study is that such large quantities of data are not only used in the aforementioned services sectors, but also in services that flow between affiliates of the same enterprise, so-called management services. These are services that relate to the supervision, control, and organization of related subsidiaries and affiliates within the same enterprise. Many tasks within these services between affiliates consist of financial planning services, management monitoring, bookkeeping services, and various other business and administrative support services. This category of services may have been overlooked in the existing literature, but using detailed input-output tables shows that this sector has had a higher data share in recent years than the data-producing industries such as telecom and data processing services. Moreover, trade in these data-intensive services is substantial for developed and emerging economies. Given that services supply chains are likely to grow with the progressive application of internet technologies, this type of trade within multinationals is likely to increase further.

These dynamics have implications for policy. Current policy initiatives around the world regarding the flow of data aim to secure the transfer of so-called personal data. An example is the EU's General Data Protection Regulation (GDPR), which provides a regulatory framework for the protection of personal data and the privacy of individual EU citizens. It also addresses the cross-border transfer of personal data outside the EU and European Economic Area (EEA) and establishes certain conditions that firms need to meet to move personal data outside the EU or the EEA. If these are not met, data must be kept within these two areas, unless the EU establishes so-called adequacy status to a particular country (this is based on a determination by the EU that the country has equally protective rules regarding personal data). Other countries apply different standards and approaches to data privacy. In the countries of the Association of Petroleum Exporting Countries (APEC), for example, Cross-Border Privacy Rules (CBPRs) apply. These are based on an accountability approach and are legally enforceable. They also give rise to compliance costs for firms but are claimed to be more business-friendly.

Many firms active in the data-intensive sector are dealing with data that consumers provide during transactions such as bank account transfers and travel arrangements booked online. Yet these types of data are only part of the story. As noted, many services use a lot of data, much of which flows inside firms. Although these data will include personal information about client firms used to develop marketing strategies or information about employees used for human resources purposes, many services exchanged between affiliates of multinationals will have less direct links with personal information. The amount of personal information in data flows across borders is not known. One analysis claims that a substantial share of data flowing around the globe is in fact personal (MIT 2015). One reason is that many of the services tasks undertaken by affiliates deal with finance, accounting, and the overall control (management) of enterprises. Personal data are likely to be embedded in some way in many of these activities.

Personal data inside the firm are regulated in many countries. The finding here that many data-intensive services are associated with management services exchanged between affiliates will put a natural policy emphasis on the way data are treated inside a multinational firm. Current frameworks dealing with intrafirm data include Binding Corporate Rules (BCRs), which are legally enforceable within a corporate group and require a uniform level of regulation for all affiliates across the countries in which the multinational firm operates. The EU GDPR specifies that if no adequacy (equivalence) decision applies to a given partner country, firms can use these BCRs to transfer data across borders, although this will be associated with certain additional costs as these rules and clauses can be burdensome.

To the extent that this type of regulatory framework seems appropriate for exchange of data between affiliates, it would not apply to inter- or intraindustry data flows between nonaffiliated firms. For that purpose, some countries have implemented or proposed regulatory policies for the transfer of data to third parties. Examples include consent requirements, the Safe Harbor Framework between the EU and the US, and standard contractual clauses. The APEC cross-border privacy rules also allow for a compliance program for data transmissions to third parties, but as a private standard. A final policy proposal that deals with intracompany and third-party data flows is to award a "privacy seal" to companies that prove they are capable of abiding by a certain set of rules. Such certification would allow data to flow between trusted importers and exporters. Some countries such as the UK are organizing this policy on a sector-specific basis. This may be an efficient way of dealing with the matter for data-intensive services, as most of these services fall in the same sector category, namely business services.

A better approach to dealing with data policies, and in particular strict requirements conditional data transfers, would be at the multilateral level. For basic economic reasons this would allow countries (and firms) to profit from rules that are applied in a nondiscriminatory manner or in a way that the costs of the rules are equally shared by the trading partners. Therefore, a 2019 joint statement on e-commerce at the WTO by a group of more than seventy-six members was a very welcome step forward. At the 2019 World Economic Forum in Davos, these members agreed to start negotiations to put in place global rules on electronic commerce. A multilateral agreement on data localization policies and associated regulatory requirements would be very beneficial given the increasing prevalence of such policies (Ferracane, Lee-Makiyama, and van der Marel 2018).

APPENDIX

TABLE 10A-1. **Summary Data Use Statistics, Averages of Six-Digit Sectors**

| Sector | Data intensity | | | | |
	Mean	Maximum	Minimum	IQR	Standard deviation
Manufacturing	0.010	0.076	0.000	0.010	0.009
Distribution	0.044	0.069	0.000	0.021	0.017
Transport	0.022	0.047	0.002	0.024	0.017
Finance	0.040	0.105	0.002	0.063	0.037
Business	0.105	0.429	0.005	0.084	0.079
Personal	0.037	0.167	0.000	0.014	0.032

Source: Author's calculations, using US Department of Commerce Bureau of Economic Analysis (BEA).

Note: IQR = interquartile range.

TABLE 10A-2. **Top Twenty Users of Data by Six-digit Sectors**

Six-digit code[a]	Data intensity	Industry description
517A00	0.429	Satellite, telecommunications resellers, and all other telecom
517210	0.255	Wireless telecommunications carriers
519130	0.225	Internet publishing and broadcasting and Web search portals
517110	0.206	Wired telecommunications carriers
812900	0.167	Other personal services
611B00	0.161	Other educational services
511200	0.153	Software publishers
561500	0.153	Travel arrangement and reservation services
518200	0.152	Data processing, hosting, and related services
561600	0.143	Investigation and security services
550000	0.141	Management of companies and enterprises
5419A0	0.138	Other professional, scientific, and technical services
561400	0.134	Business support services
541100	0.132	Legal services
54151A	0.131	Other computer related services, including facilities management
541200	0.118	Accounting, tax preparation, bookkeeping, and payroll services
561100	0.114	Office administrative services
541610	0.113	Management consulting services
561300	0.111	Employment services
5416A0	0.108	Environmental and other technical consulting services

Source: US Department of Commerce, Bureau of Economic Affairs (BEA).

[a] The six-digit codes are the classification codes used in the BEA's input-output tables.

FIGURE 10A-1. **Bilateral Share of Trade in Services for OECD and the Rest of the World (RoW), 2012**

Bilateral share of world

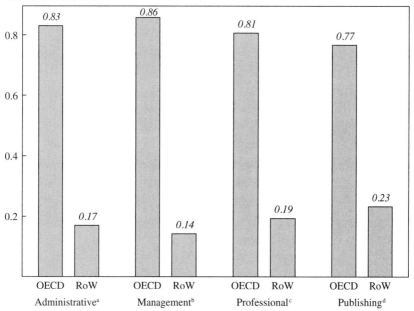

Source: World Bank, Trade in Services database.

[a] "Administrative" comprises administrative support services, including waste management.

[b] "Management" encompasses management of companies and enterprises.

[c] "Professional" includes professional and business services.

[d] "Publishing" covers publishing, media, telecommunications, and data processing activities.

FIGURE 10A-2. **Correlation between Foreign Direct Investment and Trade (Imports and Exports) in Management Services, 2012**

Log of trade in management services in GDP

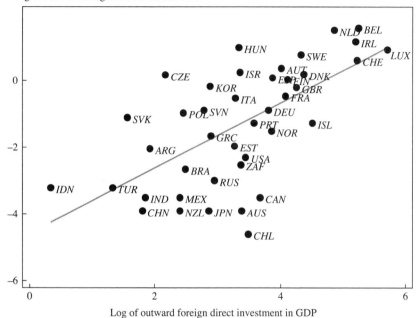

Log of outward foreign direct investment in GDP

Source: Author's calculations from World Economic Forum data (2012); World Bank, Trade in Services database; and World Bank World Development Indicators.

NOTES

1. The explanations that follow describe each six-digit sector listed in table 10-1 and follow closely the US Census explanations of the NAICS classification system.

2. Note that using US input-output tables to calculate any kind of intensity (capital, labor, or institutional, e.g.) and extrapolate to other countries is a common exercise in the empirical trade literature.

3. The BEA's input-output tables are classified according to the NAICS classification system, NAICS 55000. This category comprises two types of establishments: (1) those that hold shares or securities of companies and enterprises with a view to influencing management decisions or owning a controlling interest; and (2) those that administer, oversee, and manage affiliates of the company or enterprise. The latter establishments have a strategic or organizational planning and decisionmaking role in the company or enterprise and may also hold shares or securities of the company or enterprise. The purpose of this output sector is to consolidate the performance of essential in-house activities to realize economies of scale through management and organizational decisions that lower the long-term average expenditures by the company by spreading fixed costs over many units of output.

4. The *Manual on Statistics of International Trade in Services 2010* (MSITS2010) states that trade in services transactions between related enterprises are recorded separately from unrelated enterprises. In the Extended Balance of Payments Services Classification (EBOPS2010), this category of transactions between related enterprises is recorded under the three-digit code 285. The category of trade in services between related enterprises therefore provides information on the value of services flowing between affiliated companies or enterprises in which a direct investment has taken place and includes payments from the parent company to the affiliate establishment, and vice versa, related to the management of establishments, subsidiaries, associates, or the parent company. This category captures all types of services transactions and is not recorded for each services sector separately. Contracts involving outsourcing to unrelated specialist companies previously supplied are not included. These latter types of services are usually recorded in the appropriate sector classification within EBOPS according to the type of service.

5. The RCA index compares the share of a sector's exports in a country's total exports with the share of exports of all countries in the same sector in total world exports. The higher the ratio, which can range from zero to infinity, the more competitive the country is in the sector. The RCA index is calculated as follows: $RCA_{ik} = (x_{ik}/X_i) / (x_{wk}/X_w)$ where x_{ik} is country i's exports of

sector k, Xi is total exports of country i, xwk is world exports of sector k, and Xw is total world exports.

6. One criticism is that this measure is not insensitive to policies that alter the patterns of trade, which will then be included in the comparative advantage indicator. It would not therefore be a neutral indicator. For example, policy variables such as regulation could affect comparative advantage, although other policies such as subsidies could increase the export volumes rather than exploit productivity differences. See Siggel (2006).

7. See Chor (2012) and van der Marel and Shepherd (2013) for further insights on comparative advantage.

REFERENCES

Bauer, M., F. Erixon, and H. Lee-Makiyama. 2013. "The Economic Importance of Getting Data Protection Right: Protecting Privacy, Transmitting Data, Moving Commerce." Brussels: European Centre for International Political Economy.

Bauer, M., and others. 2014. "The Costs of Data Localization: A Friendly Fire on Economic Recovery." ECIPE Occasional Paper 3/2014. Brussels: European Centre for International Political Economy.

Chor, D. 2011. "Unpacking Sources of Comparative Advantage: A Quantitative Approach." *Journal of International Economics* 82 (2): 152–67.

Christensen, L., and others. 2013. "The Impact of the Data Protection Regulation in the EU." Intertic Policy Paper, http://citeseerx.ist.psu.edu/viewdoc/download?doi=10.1.1.657.138&rep=rep1&type=pdf.

Ferracane, M. F., J. Kren, and E. van der Marel. 2019. "Do Data Policy Restrictions Impact the Productivity Performance of Firms and Industries?" EUI Working Paper RSCAS 2019/28. Florence: European University Institute.

Ferracane, M. F., H. Lee-Makiyama, and E. van der Marel. 2018. "Digital Trade Restrictiveness Index." Brussels: European Centre for International Political Economy.

Ferracane, M. F., and E. van der Marel. 2019. "Do Data Flows Restrictions Inhibit Trade in Services?" EUI Working Paper RSCAS 2019/29. Florence: European University Institute.

Kommerskollegium. 2015. *No Transfer, No Production: A Report on Cross-Border Data Transfers, Global Value Chain, and the Production of Goods.* Stockholm: Kommerskollegium.

Manyika, J., and others. 2016. "Digital Globalization: The New Era of Global Flows." McKinsey Global Institute. Washington, D.C.: McKinsey.

Martens, B. 2013. "What Does Economic Research Tell Us about Cross-Border E-commerce in the EU Digital Single Market?" JRC-IPTS Working Papers on Digital Economy 2013-05. Seville, Spain: Institute of Prospective Technologies Studies, Joint Research Centre.

Melzer, J. 2014. "The Importance of the Internet and Transatlantic Data Flows for US and EU Trade and Investment." Global Economy and Development Working Paper 79. Brookings.

Miroudot, S., D. Rouzet, and F. Spinelli. 2013. "Trade Policy Implications of Global Value Chains: Case Studies." OECD Trade Policy Paper 161. Paris: OECD Publishing.

Massachusetts Institute of Technology (MIT). 2015. "A Business Report on Big Data Gets Personal." *MIT Technology Review*. MIT.

Organization for Economic Cooperation and Development (OECD). 2013. "OECD-WTO Database on Trade in Value-Added: First Estimates." Paris: OECD Publishing.

———. 2014. "FDI in Figures: International Investment Stumbles into 2014 after Ending 2013 Flat." Paris: OECD Publishing.

Saez, S. D., and others. 2015. *Valuing Services in Trade: A Toolkit for Competitiveness Diagnostics*. Washington, D.C.: World Bank.

Siggel, E. 2006. "International Competitiveness and Comparative Advantage: A Survey and Proposal for Measurement." *Journal of Industry, Competition and Trade* 6 (2): 137–59.

Van der Marel, E., and B. Shepherd. 2013. "International Tradability Indices for Services." Policy Research Paper 6712. Washington, D.C.: World Bank.

World Economic Forum. 2012. *The Global Information Technology Report 2012: Living in a Hyper-Connected World*. Geneva.

———. 2013. *The Human Capital Report*. Geneva.

11

WHAT CAN BE DONE TO BLUNT POTENTIAL CONFLICT BETWEEN CLIMATE CHANGE AND TRADE POLICIES?

PATRICK LOW

A growing literature considers how climate change policy and the multilateral trade regime will interact as policy-imposed carbon constraints begin to bite harder than they have so far.[1] This literature is not matched, however, by comparable engagement on the issue among governments. Under the United Nations Framework Convention on Climate Change (UNFCCC) in Durban, South Africa, in December 2011, the relationship between trade policy and climate change was only addressed in side events. Moreover, one strand of the discussions on which agreement proved elusive was not so much what should be done, but where—whether under UNFCCC auspices or in the World Trade Organization (WTO). That suggests constructive engagement has some way to go.

Subsequent annual meetings of the UNFCCC's Conference of the Parties (COP), held in Doha (2012), Warsaw (2013), Lima (2014), Paris (2015), Marrakesh (2016), Bonn (2017), Katowice (2018), and Madrid (2019) made no progress in shaping agreed rules for managing the interface between climate

change policy and trade measures. In fact, the issue was not even addressed.[2]
The twenty-first COP meeting (COP21) held in Paris in December 2015
established a post–Kyoto Protocol agreement for addressing climate change.
Subsequent COPs have sought in different ways to improve, consolidate,
and give effect to the Paris commitments. The shift in emphasis toward
self-determined emissions targets in the COP21 approach to mitigation
may raise the risk of disputes over the use of trade restrictions or taxes as
part of nationally determined strategies. Yet it is precisely the move toward
"best-endeavors," or unilaterally determined targets, that could lessen
enthusiasm for constructing explicit understandings on permissible trade
policy actions to support mitigation.

   In short, the greater the reliance on nationally determined actions on
climate change, the greater the scope for a clash of regimes. An Australian
Productivity Commission study of carbon emission reduction policies in
nine major economies identified hundreds of variations in adopted approaches (Australian Government Productivity Commission 2011). This is
hardly surprising in the absence of coordination and is likely to be even
more true in the face of more far-reaching action aimed at mitigating climate change. A classic scenario is where the costs imposed on a particular
industry through carbon constraint measures in one jurisdiction lead to the
migration of that industry to a carbon-constraint-free jurisdiction elsewhere
(carbon leakage). The affected industry then complains that its competitiveness has been undermined in the name of a climate change policy that
will do nothing to reduce global warming. An obvious reaction of a carbon-
constraining government to prevent this outcome is to deploy trade (or
trade-related) policy to neutralize the negative competitiveness effects.
Notwithstanding research suggesting that minimal carbon leakage will result from unilateral emissions cuts at the national level (Mattoo and others
2009), there is a risk that the WTO could become a flash point of policy
clashes in the absence of international precommitments on climate policies.
In the absence of adequate accommodation, both climate change policy and
trade policy will be adversely affected.

   In a more optimistic frame of mind, Patrick Messerlin provides an interesting perspective on the risk of regime clash (Messerlin 2012). He argues that the climate and trade communities share a common interest in
dealing with an international public good. The climate community has no
interest in seeing protectionist trade polices used to slow down climate

change mitigation efforts. The trade policy community has no interest either in seeing protectionist policies reduce opportunities for socially desirable gains from trade opening. The two communities could make common cause against governments that accommodate protectionist interests. Whether or not such a coalition develops as climate change policies bite harder than they do at present, the fact remains that governments are going to have to negotiate some aspects of trade policy behavior as well as climate change policy.

The areas in which trade policy may interact with climate change policy are several (Low, Marceau, and Reinaud 2011). They include tax policies, subsidies, antidumping and countervailing duties, regulations (standards and labeling), trade-related investment measures (TRIMS), and trade-related aspects of intellectual property rights (TRIPS). This is not an exhaustive list. This chapter focuses on the first two—tax policies at the border and subsidies. Within these two areas, other aspects of trade policy may still be relevant. Instead of adjusting taxes at the border, for example, a standard or regulation may apply to imported products. The standard could be cost-augmenting and expressed as a tax equivalent, but it would likely be WTO-consistent if the same standard were applied and administered in a way that imparted no competitive advantage on like domestic products.

Likewise, subsidies may attract a countervailing or an antidumping duty or a legal dispute if they are considered illegal. A TRIPS angle could also enter the picture if something were done to accommodate subsidy practices associated with research and development expenditures. Despite the interconnectedness of these various policy areas, however, the approach taken here is to focus primarily on the tax and subsidy elements of the interface between climate change and trade policies. The salience of focusing on border taxes has increased given the 2019 decision of the new European Commission under the leadership of Ursula von der Leyen to pursue a European Green Deal as a priority in the years 2020–2024. The introduction of a carbon border tax is to be a key component of the new policy (von der Leyen 2019).

The next section deals with the tax aspects. I then take up subsidy issues and the policy reactions that follow in cases where prior agreement has not been secured on the permissible use of subsidies.

INTERNATIONAL TAX POLICY IN THE SHADOW OF
NATIONAL CLIMATE CHANGE POLICY

The focus here is on developing tax policy that addresses carbon leakage and the loss of competitiveness. Potential difficulties arise from differing degrees of effort to mitigate climate change at the national level, combined with the absence of an international agreement on the appropriate distribution of responsibility for tackling global warming. The extent to which the tension arises depends in part on the policy chosen.

A Carbon Tax

If a uniform carbon tax were agreed to internationally, managing the potential competitiveness consequences of carbon reduction policies could in principle be relatively straightforward. A complication would arise, however, if carbon taxes were treated analogously to value-added taxes in international trade. Since a carbon tax is an indirect tax on products and not a direct tax on the factors of production, it would presumably be treated as a "destination principle" tax subject to a border tax adjustment. In other words, a carbon tax would not be paid on exports but levied by the importing country at rates equal to those charged domestically. But this approach is somewhat arbitrary because the incidence of any tax will depend on the competitive conditions in the market. Seemingly, the assumptions associated with direct and indirect taxes originate in the fact that, historically, direct taxes were property taxes that could not be readily shifted to consumers, whereas indirect taxes were the "sin" taxes on alcohol and tobacco that were usually paid by consumers (Hufbauer 1996).

A carbon tax would not be as straightforward as a value-added tax to adjust at the border because there would likely be many different effective rates, depending on the carbon intensity of production, even if the tax itself were uniform. Setting a carbon tax would not only be a matter of distinguishing between clean and dirty industries or products and setting the tax accordingly. For the incentive effects of a carbon tax to operate effectively, there would need to be differences in tax incidence within product categories. By contrast, value-added taxes tend to apply at a standard rate on the value of products. Moreover, they are paid on the value of arm's length transactions—a comparatively straightforward tax base. In light of these complexities, one might consider a departure from the standard practice in trade policy of adjusting indirect taxes at the border. If a carbon tax were uniform across countries, why not simply treat it as a direct tax and rule out any border tax adjustments? This would have the incentive effect of inducing firms to improve production techniques or technologies in order to pay less tax and be more competitive. The absence of border tax adjustments might add a further stimulus to that incentive by removing any possibility of manipulating border adjustments to afford protection to a domestic industry. But this approach would call for a high, possibly unattainable, level of cooperation.

If an agreement could be reached on a global carbon tax, however, and border adjustments were disallowed, much of the debate on the interface between trade and climate change could be rendered moot, at least on the aspect of the interface. If the carbon tax were indeed global, however, equity issues would surely arise. In the spirit of the principle of "common but differentiated responsibilities" enshrined in the Kyoto Protocol (1997), transfers of one sort or another might be appropriate if all countries were to adopt a uniform carbon tax. Alternatively, a threshold could be established below which the aggregate carbon emissions of a country were sufficiently minor to justify an exemption from the carbon tax. Carbon taxes would become payable once the threshold had been reached.

Forging an international agreement on a carbon tax would be a significant challenge, in part because of the way taxes are regarded in political discourse. Nordhaus (2008) has pointed out that some of the opposition to taxes may be because "goods" rather than "bads" are typically taxed—that is, the reason for taxing incomes is because they provide a convenient tax base, not because income is a negative externality. By contrast, opposition to taxing negative externalities such as carbon emissions should logically not encounter the same degree of opposition.

A shift of the tax burden away from "goods" and onto "bads" should not be sector-specific. In other words, those paying the carbon tax should not be exempted from taxes on income or profits that would otherwise apply, since doing so would reduce the incentive effects of a carbon tax designed to reduce carbon emissions. Selective tax breaks might also run afoul of WTO rules if they were regarded as specific subsidies.

Another concern relating to a carbon tax is that business would be reluctant to brook the size of transfers implied by such a tax (McKibbin and Wilcoxen 2002). This problem could arise if firms were required to pay more in taxes than they would spend on emissions. In contrast to a permit system that sets an upper limit on emissions and renders emissions below that threshold free, a tax would apply to all emissions. The degree to which this could be a problem would depend on how severe the emissions constraint is and how high the tax. McKibbin and Wilcoxen argue that this consideration explains why Pigouvian taxes such as a carbon tax have rarely been used as an environmental policy. They go on to devise a hybrid scheme involving the best elements of both policies that avoids large fiscal transfers.

A further criticism of taxes is that they do not provide a "quantitative steer," since it is impossible to tell with accuracy beforehand what the effects of a given tax rate will be on emissions levels. Permits, on the other hand, set absolute limits on the amount of permitted pollution. As Nordhaus (2008) points out, however, so much uncertainty exists about the optimal level of abatement that this particular advantage of quantitative limitations is attenuated.

Moreover, as Stern (2007) observes, in a world of uncertainty there is no valid prima facie assumption about the superiority of permits or taxes in contributing to the general welfare. When policy changes have been required to fix policy that led to an inappropriate level of taxes or permits, the consensus has been that taxes are welfare-superior in the short term and permits in the long term. This is because of the relative slopes of the cost and benefit curves associated with mitigation actions over time.[3]

Cap and Trade

Despite the economic arguments in favor of taxes over permits that have been strongly advocated by Nordhaus (2008), Cooper (1998), and most recently, a group of almost 3,500 US economists (*Wall Street Journal* 2019), permits are a prominent feature of climate mitigation efforts in a growing number of jurisdictions. Permits are usually tradable, thus combining administrative decisions with the market mechanism in a cap-and-trade scheme. The European Union leads the field with its Emissions Trading System (ETS), introduced in 2005. The Kyoto Protocol embraced cap and trade by setting quantitative limits on the emissions of some industrialized countries (so-called Annex B countries) and allowing the permits to be traded. According to Chichilnisky and Sheeran (2009), cap and trade was a compromise between those that favored regulation and those that believed the market held the secret to efficient climate change mitigation.

Another selling point of cap and trade was that in an efficient market the initial distribution of permits did not matter, so it was an instrument that could be deployed for international financial transfers. Low emitters would be given permits they could not use, and they would then be able to sell them in the market to those that did need them. The environmental consequences of such an arrangement would depend crucially on what the revenue from unused permits would be used for.

The ETS is the best place to look for experience with how cap and trade has functioned. Early results have been modest, perhaps intentionally so, because it was felt experimentation with the mechanism was necessary and its public acceptance would be easier if it did not lead immediately to significant carbon constraints. Problems with the ETS have included tax fraud (involving cases where VAT rules were ignored or averted in transactions involving imported goods between different EU member states), the theft of Certified Emission Reduction certificates, the failure to retire permits from circulation that had already been used, and the practice of some utilities of raising prices under the guise of having to meet carbon constraint costs that were not actually incurred. In general, these are problems that can be fixed through regulatory improvements.

Structural features of the market are harder to manage, such as the fact that supply is relatively fixed, through government fiat, while demand fluctuates, creating considerable price volatility from time to time. Another consideration is whether, if the market is internationalized, sovereign wealth funds will have the market muscle to manipulate prices.

When the ETS was introduced, permits were given away, which kept production costs down, reduced innovation incentives, and slowed the pace of adoption of cleaner technologies. Some have also argued that the Clean Development Mechanism—a mechanism for earning carbon credits through climate-friendly development projects in other countries—may have inhibited innovation, since it relaxes the incentive to reduce emissions domestically.

The EU has tried to address the ineffectiveness of the ETS in reducing emissions over the years, first by auctioning rather than freely allocating permits and later by "backloading" the supply of permits. Starting in 2019, a market stability reserve was introduced to provide a long-term solution to the surplus of emissions allowances. Apart from managing the surplus, the new arrangement is intended to increase the system's resilience in the face of major exogenous shocks and rely on predefined rules that eliminate the exercise of discretion on the part of member states and the European Commission.

These weaknesses in the EU ETS have reduced the competitiveness that could have led to pressure on trade policy interventions to reduce carbon leakage. In addition, constrained sectors have tended to be those in which less trade takes place and there is less susceptibility to international competition. What will happen when schemes like the EU ETS, along with climate change policies in other countries, begin to have more significant competitiveness implications across borders? In the absence of concerted action among governments, it is then that potential regime clashes could occur.

Border Tax Adjustments

The previous discussion suggests that the choice between carbon taxes and cap-and-trade arrangements does not depend primarily on any advantage associated with managing border tax adjustments. It does not really matter in that context whether charges on carbon constraints take the form of taxes or quotas. In either case, border tax adjustments would likely prove complicated and contentious. The advantage of the tax, however, is that it could be made uniform across countries and sectors,[4] thereby taking away the logic for making such adjustments provided taxes were collected at origin. The latter requirement would circumvent any need to make border adjustments to take account of variations in the incidence of the tax within sectors arising from differences in technology and production techniques among jurisdictions. Cap-and-trade arrangements, on the other hand, rely on administered emission allocations across sectors and therefore impinge more directly on competitiveness issues for which border adjustments would be required.

The already copious literature on border tax adjustments has been framed largely in terms of cap and trade, primarily because it is the most common form of emissions reduction policies. Some have argued that border tax adjustments on emissions would infringe WTO rules, and others have argued the contrary. The issue turns primarily on the definition of likeness and on whether charges or constraints on inputs to the production process that are not physically incorporated in the product can be adjusted at the border.

A further complication relates to the difficulties of calculating the carbon content of imports and the attendant risk of overadjustments that are inconsistent with WTO rules. If a justification cannot be found for border adjustments through regular WTO rules, it might be possible to invoke the public policy exception of GATT Article XX for environmental reasons.

These issues are not explored further here.[5] Suffice it to say that a uniform carbon tax charged at origin would obviate the need for border tax adjustments on competitiveness grounds. The only way a cap-and-trade scheme would be comparable in this sense is if some way were found to issue emissions permits uniformly across all emitters—hardly a realistic prospect. If governments start to rely on border tax adjustments, it is difficult to see how legal and political complications could be avoided, particularly if there has been no prior negotiation on the issue. One only has to look at the commotion caused by the unilateral decision by the EU to include air transport in the ETS a few years ago to see why difficulties would be likely to arise. Finally, an important point to note about border tax adjustments motivated by competitiveness concerns is that they only partially do the job, for the simple reason that they cannot address competitiveness issues in third markets.

A Possible Alternative

If a uniform carbon tax cannot be instituted internationally, even among the major carbon source countries, an alternative approach to avoiding border tax adjustments may warrant consideration.[6] This approach would involve a trade-off that would effectively separate environmental objectives from competitiveness considerations, while ensuring that carbon leakage is no longer an issue. Twenty countries (counting the EU as one) account for around 80 percent of global greenhouse gas (GHG) emissions. Suppose those twenty countries were to agree to binding, internationally justiciable emissions reduction commitments at the national level. This negotiation would be undertaken against the background of the principle of common but differentiated responsibility enunciated in the Kyoto Protocol.

Once the emissions ceilings were agreed, it would be for governments to decide in which sectors they wished to reduce emissions. If, as a consequence of a particular sectoral choice, an industry decided to migrate to an unconstrained jurisdiction—potentially resulting in industry-level carbon leakage—it would be for that jurisdiction to make compensating adjustments elsewhere in order to meet its emissions reduction obligations.

If governments eschewed an across-the-board approach to constraining carbon, opting instead for a variant of industrial policy, they would have to accept that their choice of where to intervene would effectively become part of the calculus of comparative advantage. They could no longer behave as if their choices needed to be mirrored by their trading partners. If governments succeeded in negotiating their emissions reductions and accepted that, in exchange for the adoption by all major emitters of binding emissions ceilings, there would be no recourse to border tax adjustments, one potential problem would still remain.

Firms or industries within sectors subject to carbon constraints might try to claw back some of their competitiveness, at least in the domestic market, by filing antidumping or countervailing duty action, or they might ask for safeguards.[7] Avoidance of such an outcome would require buy-in from industry, or governments would have to find ways of forestalling such a reaction. This would not be easy, which brings me back to the argument that a uniform carbon tax would still be the superior approach, assuming it could ever be agreed.

WHAT ABOUT SUBSIDIES?

Only the most committed free marketeer would claim that subsidies have no place in public policy. For most analysts the challenge is to distinguish between good and bad subsidies. A textbook approach to this is straightforward, since it only requires that subsidies be deployed when market imperfections—such as the existence of externalities, increasing returns to scale or information asymmetries—drive a wedge between public and private welfare. But that is where simplicity ends, because the existence of these market imperfections is difficult to pin down with precision. Even if there is agreement that an externality or some other market failure is present, it is another matter to agree on its magnitude and therefore on the appropriate degree of intervention to address it. Moreover, subsidies may also be deployed for noneconomic reasons, such as to address a socially unacceptable distribution of income.[8]

Subsidies that purport to be in the public interest can have severely distorting consequences, let alone those that serve narrow interests at the expense of national welfare. Examples abound of bad subsidies, including ones that are touted as solutions for the shortcomings of markets. In order to avoid a lengthy discussion, the focus here is on only one kind of subsidy—support to research and development (R&D) expenditures in the name of developing technologies that will assist in combating climate change.

One of two assumptions is necessary to respond to the assertion that this kind of subsidy is unnecessary where private capital, supported by a system of intellectual property rights, is sufficient to the task of supplying climate-friendly technologies. The first is that the urgency of the need for such technologies, and the risks associated with R&D investments in this field, are too great for private capital to respond adequately. The second is that subsidies are needed, if not at the R&D stage, then at least to hasten the diffusion and lower the costs of such technologies. These arguments might make the case for subsidies, but they do not address the reality that many climate-change-related subsidies can be shown to be inefficient, distorting, and excessive.[9]

Let us assume that all the health warnings against the abuse of subsidies are heeded and the case can still be made for R&D subsidies to support climate-related innovation. The question then is whether the trade rules would allow such subsidies to be deployed, or would they result in trade frictions that ultimately undermine the use of subsidies designed to hasten technological solutions to climate change?

Subsidies can take many forms if they are broadly enough defined. They can constitute taxes that confer an advantage within a market if some products or producers in that market are exempted from paying the tax. The same applies to regulatory interventions if they are designed in a particular fashion. Even the absence of regulation might in some circumstances be argued to amount to a subsidy (Trachtman 1993). Subsidies also operate through the financial system in the form of preferential interest rates or loans. Subsidies to R&D can be more or less direct, and therefore more or less transparent and more or less distorting. They could operate in factor markets or in product markets.[10]

The WTO Rules on Subsidies: Legal Uncertainty

The multiplicity of ways in which subsidies can be designed and the elasticity of the definition of what constitutes a subsidy pose a challenge for international rulemaking. Although the WTO has opted for a relatively narrow definition, socially desirable subsidies may still be successfully challenged on competitiveness grounds. Indeed, Green (2006) suggests that many of the policies used today to foster the green economy could be challenged under the Agreement on Subsidies and Countervailing Measures (SCM Agreement). To the extent that this is so, climate change policies operate with a degree of uncertainty that could frustrate socially sound approaches to the climate externality and presage regime clash.

A growing literature demonstrates the extent of that uncertainty, which unsurprisingly goes beyond the specifics of subsidies related to climate change policies (e.g., Sykes 2003; Trebilcock and Howse 2005). The discussion that follows only seeks to illustrate that interpretive differences remain unresolved, and that the economic logic of possible legal interpretations demonstrates that economics and law are not always well aligned.

The SCM Agreement distinguishes between actionable and prohibited subsidies. The latter are defined as subsidies contingent upon exports, and the requirement to use domestic rather than foreign inputs in production. A disagreement some years ago between China and the United States over Chinese measures affecting the production of wind turbines, for example, illustrates how climate change policies and industrial policies can become intertwined. The United States alleged that China was subsidizing the use of domestic inputs rather than imported ones—a prohibited subsidy under the SCM Agreement. China responded that its support for the wind turbine industry was to foster investment in wind power technology (ICTSD 2011).

Had Articles 8 and 9 of the SCM Agreement not expired (see below), they may have shed some light on the question of whether China's measures were WTO-consistent. Jurisprudence from the Appellate Body suggests that the public policy provisions of Article XX could perhaps be interpreted to justify environment-related subsides (Howse 2010; Low 2011). Regardless of the direction in which the legal analysis goes, these two representations of Chinese measures on wind turbines illustrate the tension between climate change policy and competitiveness concerns. In the event, China announced the discontinuation of the program, and so no formal action from the US side went forward.

Other key elements in the SCM Agreement relate to the definition of a subsidy. A subsidy is deemed to exist if it entails a financial contribution and confers a benefit. The subsidy must also be specific and cause adverse effects in order to be actionable. Each of these elements is potentially subject to competing legal interpretations and can be the source of policy uncertainty and conflict.

On the issue of the existence of a financial contribution, for example, Eliason and Howse (2009) argue that emissions permits might be considered a subsidy on the grounds that they constitute government-granted access to an exhaustible natural resource. A benefit would be conferred if permits were grandfathered (given away free). Stiglitz (2008) has argued that the failure of the United States to ratify the Kyoto Protocol constitutes a subsidy to US industry. These sorts of arguments do not find favor among all analysts.

When it comes to benefits, Sykes (2003) has pointed out that a true economic analysis of a benefit that might result from a subsidy requires clarification of the basis on which the assessment is made. Other government policies may have affected the conditions of competition in the market such that the subsidy in question does not confer a benefit. Rather, it may serve to rectify a situation in which the recipient was previously disadvantaged. The characterization of the market in which a subsidy is granted is therefore crucial in the determination of whether a benefit has been conferred.

Specificity is also a concept that carries complications. Writing in 1982, I argued that the specificity criterion was a good rule of thumb from an economic perspective (Low 1982). The rationale for the argument was that the more specific the subsidy is, the sharper will be its distorting effect on relative prices. More recent literature is less sanguine on this point, arguing that there is no reason to assume from a welfare perspective that a subsidy aimed at a particular industry rather than of more general application will be less applicable in the face of a market failure (Sykes 2003). The situation is made more complicated by the fact that the SCM Agreement covers both de jure and de facto specificity.

Reducing Uncertainty?

Howse (2010) has summarized four approaches through which the specifics of climate change policy might be exempted from the current situation of legal uncertainty with respect to the use of subsidies. The first involves the use of Article XX of GATT, which contains the public policy exceptions to GATT rules that would otherwise prohibit certain actions. This is an approach favored by Green (2006), and arguably the *Brazil–Retreaded Tyres* case (Gray 2008) points in the direction of allowing a broad interpretation of the permissibility of applying trade policies in pursuit of environmental objectives. On the other hand, as governments become increasingly concerned about the growing use of subsidies for putatively environmental ends, such an interpretation of Article XX could become more contentious. This may lead to a use of unilateral contingency protection measures such as countervailing duties, which would do little to reduce uncertainty.

Second, a proposal that has attracted fairly widespread support, at least among those who are concerned about climate change, is to resurrect Articles 8 and 9 of the SCM Agreement. In the Uruguay Round SCM text, Article 8 and Article 9 dealt with nonactionable subsidies. Under carefully specified conditions, Article 8 allows for subsidies to offset some firm costs of environmental regulation.[11] This, and other Article 8 exceptions for R&D and for regional development, were agreed for a trial period of five years; the default on the decision was that members would have to agree explicitly to the continuation of these exemptions from antisubsidy action. In the event, no decision was made to extend the provisions. Reviving them could certainly contribute to softening the tension between environmental policy and competitiveness.

Howse's third proposal is for a negotiation-based approach. This refers to the Doha mandate to negotiate down (i.e., reduce) obstacles to trade in environmentally friendly goods and services. The mandate refers to both tariffs and nontariff barriers (NTBs), but the negotiators have focused only on tariffs. They have been unable to agree on the definition of environmentally friendly products, which does not auger well for an expansion of the discussion to include NTBs. On the other hand, as Howse points out, if that were to be done, we would have a forum for discussing fossil fuel subsidies and subsidies to biofuels that many argue harm the environment. But whether the WTO would be the best forum for such a negotiation is a moot point.

Finally, the fourth suggestion is for the climate change community to come to closure on how to handle environmental subsidies and for the WTO to agree on a waiver that would protect subsidies permitted in the context of UNFCCC negotiations from legal action under WTO provisions.

Emerging Tension between Climate Change Policy and Contingency Protection Actions

We are beginning to witness a number of actions against alleged subsidies that are at least putatively designed to foster R&D aimed at developing more climate-friendly technologies. I referred earlier to the disagreement on wind turbine subsidies between the United States and China. Other cases have emerged over the years.

An added wrinkle in this context is that if a subsidy associated with R&D is successfully deployed and lowers the price of a traded good, it may not only face a countervailing duty, but could also be challenged through an antidumping petition. This is because the definition of dumping is broad and only requires evidence of a lower price in international trade than the "normal" domestic price. Since such price differentiation between segmented markets is commonplace (and can be explained by a variety of factors), finding a dumping margin can be quite straightforward. This leaves the injury test in antidumping investigations as the major filter through which an antidumping petition could be rejected.

Are There Ways of Separating the Environmental and Competitiveness Aspects of Subsidies?

One way of softening the clash between environment and competitiveness might be to find ways of "exhausting" the subsidy in the marketplace from a competitiveness standpoint without undermining the R&D effort. Consider two situations—one in which the subsidy goes to a university department and the other where it goes to a firm. If a patentable technology advancement emerges from a laboratory in a university, the government might claim ownership of the discovery and make it free. The R&D would then have been rewarded without affecting competition in the market

This might not be the case if the university researchers were permitted to claim ownership of any patentable invention they were responsible for. If the scientists decided to use the patent and establish their own business, the R&D subsidy would not be exhausted. On the other hand, it would be if the scientists sold the patent at an appropriate price to an investor who then went into business.

If R&D subsidies were paid directly to firms, the government would have to step in and claim the patent once a successful invention had been discovered in order to exhaust the subsidy in the marketplace. This action would presumably be a disincentive to firms considering whether to accept government subsidies for undertaking research. It could also have an adverse effect on firms' willingness to reveal inventions if doing so caused them to lose their research subsidies. Exhaustion may therefore require that the firm that develops the invention be paid at least something for surrendering a patent to government so that the invention is made available for general use.

It is important to note that, in effect, a subsidy will never be exhausted even if the discovery is sold at the market value. This is because the marketplace cannot be insulated from the fact that without the subsidy the invention would simply not exist, regardless of who paid what for it (Grossman and

Mavroidis 2003, 2005). Notwithstanding this observation, the near-exhaustion of a patent through some purchasing or regulatory arrangement would surely blunt the tension between environmental policy and competitiveness

CONCLUSIONS

This chapter examines the actual and potential interaction between climate change policy and trade policy, stressing two areas in particular where regime conflict could occur in the absence of precommitment among governments. It is unclear how tensions between the climate change regime and the WTO are going to be avoided unless governments negotiate on the areas vulnerable to such a clash.

I note several areas in which these difficulties could occur but focus on two: border adjustment measures and subsidies. There is little doubt that an appropriately administered uniform carbon tax set at a level that internalizes the social costs of greenhouse gas emissions would on the whole be the most economically efficient approach to addressing potential regime conflict that arises from tensions between climate change policy and competitiveness.

I discuss the arguments for and against this approach and note that, apart from its other efficiency properties and potential flexibility in designing tax incidence at the national level, a uniform carbon tax would embody all the desired incentives for reducing carbon emissions without running into the political economy challenges of a cap-and-trade system. On the other hand, political resistance to carbon taxes is strong.

If cap and trade is to continue being the dominant mode for climate change policy, and carbon constraint obligations are going to be set in quantitative terms, I believe that internationally binding emissions limitation commitments, combined with the freedom for governments to choose where to apply carbon constraints, would lessen the need for border adjustment measures. This arrangement would probably need to be backed up with constraints on the use of contingency protection measures.

On the subsidies front, the challenge of distinguishing between good and bad subsidies is formidable in practical terms. WTO rules are not able to do this, and even if they were, socially desirable subsidies still might not be immune from contingency protection measures. Several options have been put forward for softening the potential for conflict in this area. Solutions are most likely to emerge through an approach that effectively ring-fences genuine R&D subsidies from neutralization through retaliatory policies of one kind or another. But none of these solutions stand much chance of working in the absence of negotiations. This brings us back to Patrick Messerlin's argument (Messerlin 2012) that the best way to engage governments in such a negotiation is for the climate change and the trade communities to articulate and make common cause around their shared interest in avoiding damage to the climate or damage to trade.

NOTES

1. In spite of the development of carbon constraint policies across many nations in recent years, at both the national and subnational levels, most of the action still constitutes promises about future action. Existing arrangements such as the EU Emissions Trading Scheme have yet to achieve significant emissions reductions.

2. The interface between trade and environment has, however, been addressed in relation to the positive synergy between open trade in environmentally friendly goods and services and environmental quality—clearly an issue relevant to climate change.

3. In the short term the abatement cost curve is steeper than the benefit curve, and the relationship is reversed in the longer term. This accounts for the difference in welfare costs measured along the price and quantity axes.

4. As already noted, an exemption could be made for countries with emissions levels below a certain threshold. This should not for the most part raise major competitiveness issues.

5. For a full discussion see, for instance, Pauwelyn (2007), UNEP and WTO (2009), Condon (2009), and Low, Marceau, and Reinaud (2011).

6. This approach was also mooted in Low, Marceau, and Reinaud (2011)

7. I am indebted to Patrick Messerlin for this point.

8. For a more thorough but nevertheless brief discussion of these issues, see Low (2001).

9. See, for example, the work of the International Institute for Sustainable Development (IISD 2008, 2010).

10. For a useful taxonomy of subsidy policies and review of what governments are actually doing in the name of reducing carbon emissions, see Australian Government Productivity Commission (2011).

11. Article 9 deals with the possibility of consultations and authorized remedies upon invocation by WTO members of Article 8.

REFERENCES

Australian Government Productivity Commission. 2011. *Carbon Emission Policies in Key Economies.* Melbourne, Australia: Productivity Commission Research Report. May.

Bradsher, Keith. 2011. "200 Chinese Subsidies Violate Rules, U.S. Says." *New York Times*, October 8.

Chichilnisky, G., and K. A. Sheeran. 2009. *Saving Kyoto.* London: New Holland.

Condon, B. J. 2009. "Climate Change and Unresolved Issues in WTO Law." *Journal of International Economic Law* 12 (4): 895–926.

Eliason, A., and R. Howse. 2009. "Domestic and International Strategies to Address Climate Change." In *International Trade Regulation and the Mitigation of Climate Change*, edited by T. Cottier, O. Nartova, and S. Z. Bigigdeli. Cambridge University Press.

Gray, Kevin R. 2008. "Brazil: Measures Affecting Imports of Retreaded Tyres." *American Journal of International Law* 102(3): 610–16.

Green. A. 2006. "Trade Rules and Climate Change Subsidies." *World Trade Review* 5 (3): 377–414.

Grossman, G. M., and P. C. Mavroidis. 2003. "US—Imposition of CVDs on Certain Hot-Rolled Lead and Bismuth Carbon Steel Products Originating in the UK: Here Today, Gone Tomorrow? Privatization and the Injury Caused by Non-recurring Subsidies." In *The WTO Case Law of 2001*, edited by H. Horn and P. C. Mavroidis. Cambridge University Press.

———. 2005. "United States—Countervailing Measures Concerning Certain Products from the EC (WT/DS212/AB/R): Recurring Misunderstanding of Non-recurring Subsidies." In *The WTO Case Law of 2002*, edited by H. Horn and P. C. Mavroidis. Cambridge University Press.

Howse, R. 2010. "Climate Mitigation Subsidies and the WTO Legal Framework: A Policy Analysis." International Institute for Sustainable Development, https://www.iisd.org/pdf/2009/bali_2_copenhagen_subsidies_legal.pdf.

Hufbauer, G. 1996. "Fundamental Tax Reform and Border Tax Adjustments." *Policy Analyses in International Economics 43*. Washington, D.C.: Institute for International Economics. January.

International Institute for Sustainable Development. 2008. "Biofuels at What Cost?" www.iisd.org/gsi/biofuel-subsidies/biofuels-what-cost.

———. 2010. "Untold Billions: Fossil-Fuel Subsidies, Their Impacts and the Path to Reform." www.iisd.org/gsi/untold-billions-fossil-fuel-subsidies-their-impacts-and-path-reform.

———. 2011. "China to End Challenged Subsidies in Wind Power Case." *Bridges Trade BioRes* 11 (11).

Kyoto Protocol. 1997. http://unfccc.int/resource/docs/convkp/kpeng.html.

Low, P. 1982. "The Definition of Export Subsidies in GATT." *Journal of World Trade Law* 6 (5): 375–90.

———. 2001. "The Treatment of Subsidies in the WTO Framework." In *European Competition Law Annual 1999: Selected Issues in the Field of State Aids*, edited by Claus Dieter Ehlermann and Michelle Everson. Oxford, UK: Hart.

Low, P., G. Marceau, and J. Reinaud. 2011. "The Interface between the Trade and Climate Change Regimes: Scoping the Issues." Staff Working Paper ERSD-2011-1. Geneva: World Trade Organization.

Mattoo, A., and others. 2009. "Reconciling Climate Change and Trade Policy." Working Paper 1750. Washington, D.C.: Petersen Institute for International Economics.

McKibbin W. J., and P. J. Wilcoxen. 2002. "The Role of Economics in Climate Change Policy." *Journal of Economic Perspectives* 16 (2): 107–129.

Messerlin, P. 2012. "Climate Change and Trade Policy: From Mutual Destruction to Mutual Support." *World Trade Review* 11 (1): 53–80.

Nordhaus, W. 2008. *A Question of Balance: Weighing the Options on Global Warming Policies.* Yale University Press.

Pauwelyn, J. 2007. "U.S. Federal Climate Policy and Competitiveness Concerns: The Limits and Options of International Trade Law." Nicholas Institute for Environmental Policy Solutions, Duke University.

Reuters. 2010. "Japan Starts WTO Dispute with Canada on Clean Power." September 13.

Stern, N. 2007. *The Economics of Climate Change: The Stern Review.* Cambridge University Press.

Stiglitz, J. E. 2008. "A New Agenda for Global Warming." In *The Economists' Voice: Top Economists Take on Today's Problems*, edited by J. E. Stiglitz, A. S. Edlin, and J. B. DeLong. Columbia University Press.

Sykes, A. 2003. "The Economics of WTO Rules on Subsidies and Countervailing Measures." Olin Law and Economics Working Paper 186. University of Chicago Law School.

Trachtman, J. 1993. "International Regulatory Competition, Externalization and Jurisdiction." *Harvard International Law Journal* 34 (1): 47–104.

Trebilcock, M., and R. Howse. 2005. *The Regulation of International Trade.* 3rd ed. London: Routledge.

United Nations Environment Programme (UNEP) and World Trade Organization (WTO). 2009. *Trade and Climate Change: A Report by the United*

Nations Environment Programme and the World Trade Organization. Geneva: WTO.

von der Leyen, U. 2019. "A Union That Strives for More." Political Guidelines for the Next European Commission, 2019–2024. https://ec.europa.eu /commission/sites/beta-political/files/political-guidelines-next-commi ssion_en.pdf.

Wall Street Journal. 2019. "Economists' Statement on Carbon Dividends." January 17. https://www.clcouncil.org/economists-statement/.

World Trade Organization. 1994. *Agreement on Subsidies and Countervailing Measures.* www.wto.org/english/docs_e/legal_e/24-scm.pdf.

12

REGIONAL TRADE AGREEMENTS AND TRADE COSTS IN SERVICES

SÉBASTIEN MIROUDOT AND BEN SHEPHERD

There are several motives for negotiating regional trade agreements (RTAs) and not all of them are based on economic considerations (WTO 2011).[1] However, it seems straightforward that when signing an RTA, countries' aim is to reduce trade barriers among themselves. Preambles of trade agreements usually emphasize the promotion of trade and the removal of trade distortions as objectives that motivate the disciplines of the agreement. We should therefore expect RTAs to decrease trade costs between their parties, and empirical work in the case of goods tends to support this idea (see, e.g., Pomfret and Sourdin 2009; Chauffour and Maur 2011; and WTO 2011 for a review).

Regional trade agreements covering services have not proliferated as much as those covering goods, but about half of RTAs in force cover services. There were 149 agreements notified to the WTO under the General Agreement on Trade in Services (GATS) at the end 2018; 294 were notified under the General Agreement on Tariffs and Trade (GATT). The number of RTAs notified each year decreased for several years after 2010, and subsequently began accelerating after that. This is true both for goods agreements and services agreements. Hence the focus in our empirical work on 1999–2011, which was the period of rapid expansion of services RTAs.

Recently signed RTAs are generally characterized as having characteristics of "deep integration" because they go beyond traditional market access concerns and deal with a broad range of trade-related issues. They also deal more with "behind-the-border" policies and address domestic regulations that have an impact on trade. Services is somehow a "borderline" area. Part of services commitments in RTAs is, strictly speaking, about "market access." But as barriers to trade in services are mainly behind-the-border, services also illustrate the so-called deep integration disciplines in recent RTAs.

Moreover, there is a consensus in the literature that services RTAs are WTO-plus. Several studies comparing market access and national treatment commitments in GATS and commitments in RTAs have found unequivocally that the latter cover many more subsectors than the former (Marchetti and Roy 2008; Fink and Molinuevo 2008; Miroudot, Sauvage, and Sudreau 2010)[2]. But commitments are legal bindings and do not always correspond to the actual trade regime, which might be more liberal (or less liberal). The extent to which services RTAs have led to trade liberalization and actually reduced trade costs becomes an empirical question.

Building on Miroudot, Sauvage, and Shepherd (2012), where we developed theory-consistent estimates of bilateral trade costs for a large number of countries over the period 1999–2009 (and which we extend to 2011 here), we further analyze the relationship between regional integration and the evolution of trade costs in services industries. The next section explains how we measure trade costs in services and describes the database of services commitments in RTAs that we use in the analysis. The following two sections provide stylized facts on trade costs within and outside regional trade agreements and discuss why services RTAs seem to have a limited impact on trade costs in services.

EMPIRICAL DATA ON TRADE COSTS AND SERVICES TRADE LIBERALIZATION AT THE REGIONAL LEVEL

Starting from the standard, theory-consistent gravity model of Anderson and van Wincoop (2003), Novy (2011) develops a comprehensive measure of bilateral trade costs.[3] Equation 1 presents that measure in ad valorem equivalent terms as τ_{ijkt}, where k indexes sectors and t indexes time. It is the geometric average of bilateral trade costs for exports from country i to country j and from country j to country i, expressed relative to domestic trade costs in each country ($\frac{t_{ij}}{t_{ii}}$ and $\frac{t_{ji}}{t_{jj}}$ respectively). To calculate it, all that is required are data on domestic production relative to nominal exports in both countries ($\frac{x_{ii}}{x_{ij}}$ and $\frac{x_{jj}}{x_{ji}}$ respectively). The parameter σ is the elasticity of substitution among varieties in a sector, assuming the Anderson and Van Wincoop–based derivation of Novy's measure of trade costs.

$$\tau_{ijkt} = \frac{t_{ijkt} \cdot t_{jikt}^2}{t_{iikt} \cdot t_{jjkt}} - 1 = \left(\frac{x_{iikt} \cdot x_{jjkt}}{x_{ijkt} \cdot x_{jikt}} \right)^{\frac{1}{2(\sigma-1)}} \tag{1}$$

Intuitively, Novy's measure captures the fact that if a country's trade costs fall more than those of its trading partners, then a part of its production that was previously consumed domestically will instead be shipped overseas. Trade costs are thus closely related to the extent to which a country trades with itself rather than other countries, and data on this kind of relative openness can be used to track the level of trade costs and their variation over time. Importantly, this measure of trade costs is "top down" rather than "bottom up." By this we mean that it infers the ratio of inter- to intranational trade costs based on observed patterns of production and trade around the world, rather than building up an estimate of trade costs based on data covering particular types of impediments to trade. It thus takes account of all factors that influence trade costs, and is not subject to the kind of omitted variables bias that calls into question the results of previous attempts to measure trade costs in services by analyzing the results of gravity model estimates (e.g., Walsh 2006).

Bilateral Trade Costs in Services: A Database Covering Sixty-one Countries over the Period 2000–2011

We use the above approach to calculate new trade cost measures for sixty-one countries and nine broadly defined industries (including four for services) over the period 2000–2011. Our measure of trade costs captures the costs associated with "pure" cross-border services trade under Modes 1, 2, and 4 of the General Agreement on Trade in Services (GATS). We do not extend the analysis to sales by foreign affiliates (GATS Mode 3) due to lack of data.[4] For sectoral output and exports, we rely on the information provided in the OECD Inter-Country Input-Output tables that are constructed for the OECD-WTO Trade in Value Added (TiVA) database.[5] These data are

FIGURE 12-1. Average Trade Costs in Services Sectors, Tariff Equivalent, 2000–2011

Average trade costs (tariff equivalent)

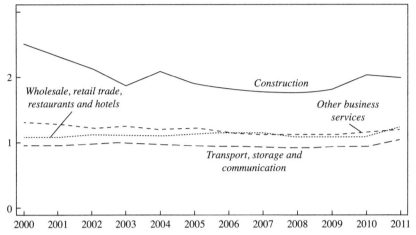

Source: Authors' calculations.

already harmonized and made comparable across countries. They are sourced from national accounts but reconciled with trade statistics in a global accounting framework. For data on trade in goods, we rely on the OECD's International Trade by Commodity Statistics (ITCS) database, which provides data on bilateral trade flows directly in the ISIC Revision 3 format. Things are more complicated for services, where the coverage of official statistics is generally weak and data are not always available at the bilateral level by industry. We also rely on the work done by the OECD and the WTO in the context of the TiVA database, using a set of harmonized data from the OECD's Trade in Services by Partner Country database (TISP), Eurostat's balance of payments statistics, and the UN's Service Trade database. This data set includes various estimates, and all data are converted from the Extended Balance of Payments Services (EBOPS) classification to ISIC Revision 3 using a concordance.[6] In line with Novy (2011), we assume $\sigma = 8$ throughout, but our results are robust to alternative assumptions.

By way of introduction to the trade costs data, figure 12-1 presents average figures for the period 2000–2011. The data are disaggregated by sector, and trade-weighted tariff equivalents are calculated.

Trade costs are very high for the construction industry (keeping in mind that only cross-border flows corresponding to short-term construction projects are accounted for in balance of payments statistics), while a convergence is observed for other services industries, with still significantly high trade costs around 100 percent when expressed as a tariff equivalent. Trade costs declined between 2000 and 2008, but services trade costs began rising again after the crisis.

Services Commitments in Sixty-six Regional Trade Agreements

To assess the impact of RTAs on trade costs, we use a database developed at the OECD that covers all services agreements to which an OECD economy, China, or India is a party (Miroudot, Sauvage, and Sudreau 2010). This accounts for sixty-six of the eighty-eight agreements notified to WTO under GATS Article V (as of August 2011).[7] The database reports market access and national treatment commitments in the 155 subsectors of the GATS Services Sectoral Classification List (referred to as W/120). Horizontal restrictions—those that apply to all subsectors—are also taken into account and reported for all subsectors. The information is provided for each signatory of the RTA by mode of supply.

Commitments are "full" (no limitation), "partial" (some limitations listed), or "unbound" (no commitment). In addition, "partial" commitments are broken down into nine different types of trade-restrictive measures, four for market access and five for national treatment. This classification of nonconforming measures is detailed in table 12-1. The database includes similar analysis for commitments in GATS and can be used to assess to what extent RTAs are WTO-plus and provide for additional commitments.

As this database is of a qualitative nature, we compute indexes that capture the extent to which services RTAs are more preferential than the GATS. The methodology is the following. An initial score of 100 is assigned to each agreement, country, subsector, and mode of supply regardless of its degree of commitment (including the GATS). Then, depending on whether the subsector is full, unbound, or subject to some restrictions (partial), some points are deducted from this amount. The precise number of points granted to each restriction relies on a few assumptions:

- Market access matters relatively more than national treatment.
- Unbound is worse than partial, which is in turn worse than full.
- Quantitative restrictions such as quotas and licensing requirements are more trade restrictive than discrimination on subsidies or prohibitions on partnerships, for instance.

TABLE 12-1. **Typology of Limitations in Partial Market Access and National Treatment Commitments in Regional Trade Agreements**

Market access	Type of restriction	Mode of supply	Examples
MA1	Scope of subsector limited (in comparison with the W/120 classification)[a]	All	Commitment limited to a list of activities Commitment in subsector x but not including y
MA2	Restrictions on foreign ownership or on the type of legal entity	Mode 3	Foreign equity limits Only joint ventures allowed Restrictions on mergers and acquisitions for foreign firms
MA3	Quantitative restrictions on the service or services	Modes 1, 2, 3	Limitations on the number of service suppliers (e.g., quota or economic need test) Limitations on the total value of transactions or assets Limitations on the quantity of service output
MA4	Market access restrictions on the movement of people	Mode 4	Limitations on the number of natural persons Nationality requirements for suppliers of services
National treatment			
NT1	Nationality and residency requirements for boards of directors and managers; discriminatory licensing requirements	Modes 1, 3	Nationality and residency requirements for boards of directors and managers Discriminatory licensing requirements
NT2	National treatment restrictions on the movement of people	Mode 4	Discriminatory qualification or licensing requirements
NT3	Discriminatory measures with regard to subsidies or taxes	Modes 1, 2, 3	Eligibility for subsidies reserved for nationals Tax imposed on nonresidents
NT4	Restrictions on ownership of property and land	Modes 1, 2, 3	Foreigners not allowed to acquire direct ownership of land Nonresidents excluded from the acquisition of real estate

TABLE 12-1. *(continued)*

Market access	Type of restriction	Mode of supply	Examples
NT5	Other discriminatory measures	Modes 1, 2, 3	Discriminatory measures with respect to competition Prohibition on the hiring of local professionals Local content requirements Technology transfer and training requirements

Source: Authors.

[a] W/120 = General Agreement on Trade in Services, services sectoral classification list.

There is some inherent subjectivity in ranking and weighting the importance of trade-restrictive measures, and it is beyond the scope of this chapter to discuss how those calculations can be done. Table 12-2 summarizes our own subjective assessment and details the scores for each mode of supply (the points that are lost out of a total of 100 when the subsector is unbound or partial). We note that no commitment at all (unbound) does not give a score of zero for a given subsector and mode of supply but 20 (out of 100). "Unbound" means that there is no commitment in the RTA to provide market access and national treatment, but this should not be understood to mean that trade is banned. It could be the case that no restrictive measure is actually in place in the country.

Since we work with data on cross-border trade in services, we assign Mode 1 a much larger weight (70 percent) than the other modes (10 percent for each). Yet we choose not to give a zero weight to Modes 3 and 4 to account for the potential complementarities that may exist between modes of supply. Mode 2 is also part of cross-border trade but is economically less important and rather difficult to restrict. We are now left with a score ranging between 0 and 100 for each agreement, country, and subsector. The next step is to compute for each RTA the difference between the agreement's score and the GATS score. This difference therefore takes on values from –100 to 100. Because an agreement that is worse than GATS (i.e., GATS minus) is de facto ineffective, we replace all negative values with zeros, which means there is no preferential treatment. The higher the value

TABLE 12-2. Scores Used to Calculate the Regional Trade Agreement Indexes

Mode of supply	Market access						National treatment						
	Unbound	MA1	MA2	MA3	MA4	Full	Unbound	NT1	NT2	NT3	NT4	NT5	Full
Mode 1	50	15	0	20	0	0	30	15	0	2.5	2.5	2.5	0
Mode 2	50	20	0	0	0	0	30	0	0	5	5	5	0
Mode 3	50	15	20	5	0	0	30	15	0	2.5	2.5	2.5	0
Mode 4	50	15	0	0	20	0	30	0	15	0	0	0	0

Source: Authors' calculations.

of the index, the more preferential the RTA for a given country and subsector.

Last, we convert W/120 subsectors into ISIC Revision 3 sectors using the UN's Provisional Central Product Classification as an intermediate correspondence. Since W/120 subsectors and ISIC Revision 3 sectors do not match one-to-one, we average the RTA index when needed using equal weights. Eventually, we get an index of the preferential content of RTAs for each party to an agreement that is compatible with our trade costs data at the sector level.

TRADE COSTS AND REGIONAL TRADE AGREEMENTS: STYLIZED FACTS

Our data set provides bilateral trade costs at the industry level. To compare the average trade costs within and outside RTAs, we use a trade-weighted average across countries. Trade costs for goods within RTAs are the average bilateral trade costs in manufacturing industries of countries that are party to an RTA covering goods. Trade costs for services are measured within RTAs that have provisions on services (a smaller subset of the RTAs covering goods). In addition, we keep only pairs of countries for which we have consistent data over time (between 2000 and 2011). Figure 12-2 highlights the important difference between goods trade and services trade in RTAs. Trade costs for goods are significantly lower within RTAs. The difference tends to narrow over time, but trade costs in 2011 were still 22 percent lower in RTAs. Trade costs were on average higher for services than for goods. Tariff equivalents, whether within or outside RTAs, are always between 100 and 125 percent. Moreover, there was no major difference between trade costs measured within RTAs and between countries that were not part of a services trade agreement. In 2011, trade costs for services were on average 10 percent lower within RTAs. Goods RTAs are therefore associated with a difference in trade costs of about twice as much as services RTAs.

The increase in trade costs over the period (both for goods and services) is partly a composition effect. The group of countries with an RTA at the end of the period have a relatively higher level of trade costs. One could explain this by the fact that countries initially signed RTAs with their main trading partners, which are closer geographically as well as culturally and institutionally. It is therefore not surprising to see a decrease in the discrepancy

FIGURE 12-2. **Trade Costs Within and Outside Regional Trade Agreements (RTAs): Goods and Services, 2000–2011**

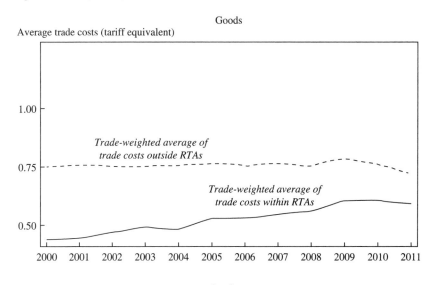

Goods

Average trade costs (tariff equivalent)

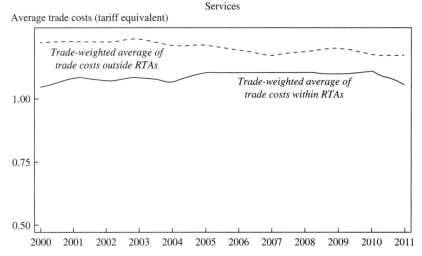

Services

Average trade costs (tariff equivalent)

Source: Authors' calculations.

between trade costs within and outside RTAs. But the results for services suggest that services agreements are of a different nature than goods agreements.

To further assess to what extent figure 12-2 reflects the composition of the group of countries having signed an RTA or the evolution of trade costs

FIGURE 12-3. Trade Costs Five Years before and after the Entry into Force of a Regional Trade Agreement

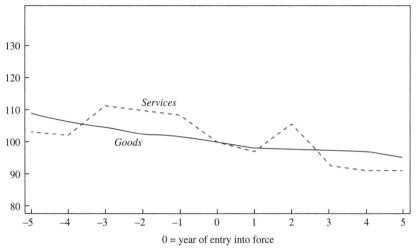

Average bilateral trade costs
(entry into force = 100)

0 = year of entry into force

Source: Authors' calculations.

within these RTAs, figure 12-3 gives an average bilateral trade cost before and after the entry into force of the RTA. We set to $t = 0$ the year of entry into force of each agreement, and we report the average trade costs (over all the RTAs) up to five years before and after this date. As trade costs are to some extent cyclical and vary over time, pulling different years together introduces some volatility, but the results suggest that for both goods and services RTAs contribute to a decrease in trade costs. Of course, these descriptive data do not say anything about causality, but suggest more of a composition effect.

Last, in figure 12-4 we present results for the European Union. We have separately calculated average bilateral trade costs among EU members and in EU RTAs (i.e., between EU members and countries with which the EU has signed an RTA). We also include in the figure the average trade costs for non-EU RTAs (i.e., other RTAs to which EU countries are not a party). One reason for focusing on the EU is that EU countries have among themselves the deepest level of integration for services industries. There are more than 500 European Commission (EC) regulations dealing with services in the EU, and the objective of creating an effective internal market

FIGURE 12-4. Trade Costs within and outside Regional Trade
Agreements (RTAs): European Union, 2000–2011

Average trade costs (tariff equivalent)

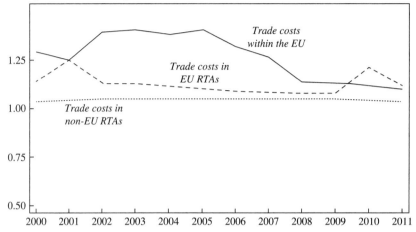

Source: Authors' calculations.

in services has been a priority since the adoption of the Single Market Act
in 1992 (Messerlin 2012). Moreover, a large share of observations in our data
set are for EU countries, and it is interesting to see how including or excluding EU countries in the analysis affects the results.

The surprise in figure 12-4 is that, after 2002, we measure higher trade
costs among EU countries than in the RTAs signed by the EU or in other
non-EU RTAs, although there is some convergence toward the end of the
sample period. We investigate in more detail in the next section what could
drive these results, but figure 12-4 is not at odds with the gravity literature
that finds that an EU dummy variable usually has a negative sign (indicating that EU countries trade a lower volume of services than is predicted by
the gravity model). Whether or not one believes the data, there is the question of why services RTAs are not clearly associated with lower trade costs.

WHY ARE SERVICES TRADE COSTS NOT LOWER
WITHIN REGIONAL TRADE AGREEMENTS?

Anybody working in the area of services trade knows that cross-border trade
statistics at a disaggregated level (by partner country or by industry) are
problematic. To begin with, the coverage of balance of payments trade data

is not comprehensive. While total trade in services is available for most economies, trade by partner country or by industry is missing for a significant number of reporters. In addition, for countries that do provide the disaggregated data, there is still a large share of unallocated trade (Miroudot and Lanz 2008; Spinelli and Miroudot 2015). For example, in the OECD TISP database, adding all the bilateral-by-industry data gives a figure that represents, on average, 70 percent of the total trade reported by countries. Almost one-third of trade in services is not allocated to specific partners or industries.

In addition to unallocated trade, one can question what the balance of payments measures precisely. With the development of the internet and new technologies, many services transactions are difficult to account for. Measuring trade in services is more challenging than before, and one should not underestimate the impact of these issues on the results of our study and any measure of trade costs based on actual trade data. But the quality of the data cannot by itself explain the trend observed over time, since the there is no sign of a systematic bias that would minimize international trade in services over years only for countries within an RTA (and not for pairs of countries not belonging to any RTA). Issues related to statistics affect all economies within or outside RTAs. The only case where we should seriously investigate the role of statistical issues is the EU. Because of the European integration process, there is less information available on intra-EU trade than on extra-EU trade.

More important, it seems to us, is the question of whether covering only cross-border trade in services has an impact on our assessment of regionalism. Cross-border trade in services includes Mode 1 and to some extent Mode 2 and Mode 4 trade in services. But with some rare exceptions, Mode 3 trade in services is not part of the cross-border trade statistics.[8] To the extent that RTAs encourage Mode 3 over cross-border trade (in particular when they include an investment chapter that also liberalizes foreign direct investment), a substitution between cross-border trade and sales through commercial presence could explain why we do not see a significant impact of RTAs on cross-border trade costs.

Unfortunately, data on sales of foreign affiliates are even less available than cross-border trade in services data. We can however apply a methodology similar to the one we apply to cross-border trade to measure the bilateral "investment costs," or more exactly, the cost of selling through a foreign affiliate, the foreign affiliate sales (FAS) cost. Building on Head and Ries

FIGURE 12-5. Foreign Affiliate Sales (FAS) Costs within and outside the European Union, 2001–2006

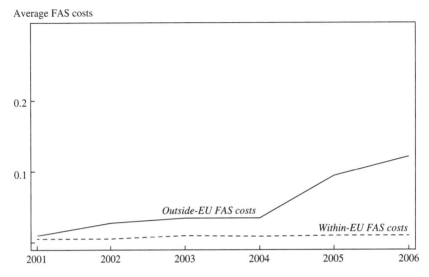

Source: Authors' calculations.

(2008), Gormsen (2011) has developed a measure of the cost of barriers to foreign direct investment (FDI). We can apply a similar methodology to sales of foreign affiliates, as the formula is at the end a derivation of the gravity equation and the gravity equation applies to FAS as well (see Bergstrand and Egger 2007; Kleinert and Toubal 2010).

We calculate the bilateral FAS cost as: $\tau_{ij} = \sqrt{\dfrac{Sales_{ij}\,Sales_{ji}}{Sales_{ii}\,Sales_{jj}}}$ where sales from i in j and j in i are bilateral FAS, while the sales of i in i (and j in j) are the domestic sales (calculated as the national turnover minus the sales of foreign affiliates).

Deriving the equation from a theory-consistent FAS gravity model, there should be a parameter similar to σ in the Anderson and van Wincoop (2003) model or γ in the Chaney (2008) model. Here we take a very simple approach to comparing FAS costs over time in the context of EU integration, so we abstract from this issue that could be explored in future research.

Due to constraints on the availability of such data, we calculate these bilateral FAS costs for fifty-four countries over the period 2001–2006. Figure 12-5 presents the average FAS cost intra- and extra-EU. Since there are very few non-EU countries in the data set, one should not overinterpret the results, and generally speaking FAS statistics are quite fragmentary. But the point is that for EU countries for which we have relatively better FAS data, there is no indication that FAS costs diminished within the EU in the first half of the 2000s. However, FAS costs are found to be lower within the EU, and the discrepancy between intra- and extra-EU FAS costs increases over time. This increase is likely to reflect the greater availability of data over time, and because of the gaps in the data there are more and more non-EU pairs after 2004.

We can thus offer a more nuanced picture regarding the impact of RTAs. In the case of the EU, there seems to be an impact on the cost of providing services through Mode 3. But we have insufficient data to check whether this is specific to the EU and the deep integration achieved through the single market or whether a similar trend would be observed in all RTAs that cover Mode 3 or have a substantive investment chapter.

Services Reforms: Do They Benefit Domestic and Foreign Producers in a Similar Way?

In our analysis, we define trade costs as the costs foreign suppliers pay that domestic producers do not. Equation 1 relates "domestic trade costs" to international trade costs. Because the measure is relative, a reform that would have the same (or a proportional) impact on domestic and foreign suppliers would not affect trade cost estimates. Another way of interpreting figure 12-2 is that any services trade liberalization (resulting from an RTA or not) lowers trade costs for all suppliers and so does not change the ratio between foreign and domestic costs.

This would be the case, first, if RTAs had no impact on the actual trade regime. Schedules of commitments in services are legal bindings. Countries make market access and national treatment commitments, but often these commitments just reflect the current state of regulations. At the multilateral level, the literature already points out that countries have locked in their current regime and not used GATS to liberalize trade (Hoekman 1996; Adlung and Roy 2005). It is even less likely that they would use RTAs to open up new services sectors. Reforming the telecommunications sector or changing regulations for maritime transport will generally not be the outcome of a bilateral trade agreement. The political economy of services trade negotiations, involving a trade ministry that is usually not in a position to commit to reforming key product markets, could explain why RTAs are about legal bindings and not actual trade reforms (VanGrasstek

2010). Such bindings could nonetheless have a positive impact on trade by reducing the uncertainty around the trade regime and by bounding the level of restrictiveness the partner country could introduce in the future.

Another assumption is that, when they do change the trade regime, RTAs have no impact on measures that discriminate against foreign suppliers. The concept of preferences is not easy to tackle in the context of services trade (Sauvé and Mattoo 2011; Sauvé and Shingal 2011). Some measures do not typically discriminate between domestic and foreign suppliers. For example, market regulations introducing rules on prices, providing access to networks, or increasing the powers of a competition authority will benefit domestic and foreign services suppliers equally. In order to create a market that is more competitive for domestic suppliers only, foreign suppliers would have to be excluded from this market. Also, by introducing measures such as licenses or taxes, it would be technically feasible to discriminate between domestic and foreign producers, but in practice this has not happened. In the end, discriminatory measures are limited to foreign equity restrictions, labor market tests for the entry of natural persons, and the recognition of qualifications. But even in these areas, not all countries introduce discriminatory measures.

The trend in services reforms is also to increase competition, including by allowing foreign producers to enter the domestic market and compete. Countries that have reformed their telecommunications or energy sectors, for example, have generally encouraged the entry of foreign firms to increase productivity and lower prices for consumers. In the presence of an incumbent firm that previously benefited from a domestic monopoly, foreign competition is important for the market to become competitive. Because most services reforms are not discriminatory, negotiators of RTAs have few opportunities to offer genuine preferences to partner countries.

Is Services Trade Liberalization de Facto MFN Treatment?

For the same reasons stated previously, there is no clear evidence that discrimination among foreign producers is the objective or outcome of services RTAs. Unlike tariffs on goods, which are easy to apply, there is no easy way to grant preferences to services providers in specific countries—in effect, most favored nation (MFN) treatment. Market access barriers and barriers to competition apply in the same way to all foreign suppliers. In the case of the recognition of qualifications or visa policies, some advantage may be given to a privileged partner country. For example, a mutual recognition agreement can be signed or a quota can be granted to temporary services providers of a given nationality. But in practice, there are very few instances where countries discriminate in this way.

Once again, one should keep in mind that services are usually regulated in domestic laws that are designed for domestic purposes by the ministries in charge of specific services sectors. Such laws are not used for commercial diplomacy and do not include legal instruments that allow trade negotiators to grant preferences to specific countries. This is why services RTAs are most of the time about "preferential bindings" rather than actual preferences.

Another reason is that rules of origin for services are quite liberal in the case of legal persons (Fink and Nikomborirak 2007; Miroudot, Sauvage, and Sudreau 2010). GATS Article V(6) requires that foreign services suppliers established in a country and engaged in "substantive business operations" benefit from the treatment granted in RTAs signed by that country. For example, EU companies established in the United States benefit from NAFTA/USMCA provisions and have the same treatment as US companies exporting services to Mexico or Canada. The "substantive business operations" criterion is not normally subject to specific tests or requirements.[9] This could explain why countries are not willing to introduce discriminatory barriers to cross-border trade in services. Such barriers could be circumvented by the establishment of companies in countries that would provide the most preferential treatment.

This being said, we observe in our data set differences in trade costs by partner country. Figure 12-6 highlights differences based on the architecture of RTAs and the way of scheduling commitments. Trade costs tend to be lower between countries that have signed a NAFTA-inspired RTA where there is a negative list of commitments and where services and investment (including investment in services) are dealt with in two separate chapters.[10] GATS-inspired RTAs that follow the GATS approach for scheduling commitments (a positive list of subsectors where market access and national treatment commitments are made by mode of supply, followed by a list of limitations) have higher trade costs on average, even higher than for pairs of countries with no RTA.

However, figure 12-6 should not be interpreted as showing a causal relationship between the way of scheduling commitments and the level of trade costs. The results are essentially based on the composition of each

FIGURE 12-6. Trade Costs by Type of Scheduling, 2000–2011

Trade-weighted average of trade costs

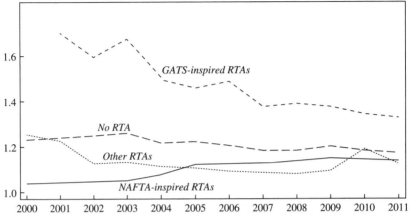

Source: Authors' calculations.

group of countries whose trade costs are being measured. Trade costs are the lowest (at the end of the 2000–2011 period) in the group of "other RTAs" that includes economic integration agreements, such as the EC Treaty, the European Economic Area (EEA) agreement, the agreement of the European Free Trade Association (EFTA), and the Australia–New Zealand Closer Economic Partnership Trade Agreement (ANZCEPTA). By definition, parties to these agreements are geographically and culturally closer, hence their lower bilateral trade costs. NAFTA-inspired agreements were originally signed between close countries (initially Canada, Mexico, and the United States), and over the period trade costs are found to be higher when the NAFTA template is used by other countries. GATS-inspired agreements include many North-South and South-South RTAs signed between countries that are geographically or culturally more distant and where services trade is less developed.

CONCLUSION

This chapter investigates whether services RTAs have an impact on bilateral trade costs. In the case of services, there is no clear evidence that trade costs are much lower within RTAs than outside. This is not a surprising result when one looks more closely at how services trade liberalization takes place and what the role of services chapters in RTAs is. Services agreements are about preferential bindings but generally do not include preferential treatment of the parties to the agreement. As such, services RTAs are to some extent paradoxical. They signal a preference for specific partner countries, but they do not provide them with preferential treatment, unlike RTAs for goods. From an economic perspective, this is all the better, as preferences lead to trade distortions.

Do our results mean that RTAs have no economic impact and do not affect trade costs? Further research on this question is required, including the specification of a full econometric model explaining observed trade costs, including membership in an RTA. Preliminary findings based on graphical analysis and descriptive statistics suggest, however, that RTAs might lower trade costs, although not to a striking degree, but the costs are lower not only for the parties to the agreement but also for other parties. This could be explained by the liberal rules of origin that extend the benefits of market access and national treatment commitments beyond parties, or more simply by the unilateral and de facto MFN nature of services trade liberalization. Most reforms in services sectors are driven by domestic concerns and adopted independently of any trade negotiation. RTAs bind these reforms, and their provisions reflect the more recent state of the law and new regimes that are more favorable for foreign suppliers. Our results are consistent with this interpretation of services RTAs.

APPENDIX: LIST OF SERVICES AGREEMENTS COVERED IN THE DATA SET

ASEAN-Australia-New Zealand Free Trade Agreement (FTA)
ASEAN-China FTA
ASEAN-Korea FTA
Australia-Chile FTA
Australia-New Zealand Closer Economic Relations (CER)
Dominican Republic-Central American FTA (CAFTA-DR)
Canada-Chile FTA
Canada-Peru FTA
Chile-Colombia FTA
Chile-Costa Rica FTA
Chile-El Salvador FTA
Chile-Mexico FTA
China-Chile FTA
China-New Zealand FTA

China-Pakistan FTA

China-Peru FTA

China-Singapore FTA

Costa Rica-Mexico FTA

European Economic Area (EEA)

European Free Trade Association (EFTA)-Chile FTA

EFTA-Korea FTA

EFTA-Mexico FTA

EFTA-Singapore FTA

El Salvador-Mexico FTA

European Union (EU)-Albania Stabilization and Association
    Agreement (SAA)

EU-Caribbean Forum (CARIFORUM) States Economic Partnership
    Agreement (EPA)

EU-Chile Association Agreement (AA)

EU-Croatia SAA

EU-FYROM SAA

EU-Korea FTA

EU-Mexico EPA

EU-Montenegro SAA

Guatemala-Mexico FTA

Honduras-Mexico FTA

India-Korea Comprehensive Economic Partnership Agreement (CEPA)

India-Singapore Comprehensive Economic Cooperation
    Agreement (CECA)

Japan-Brunei Darussalam EPA

Japan-Chile EPA

Japan-Indonesia EPA

Japan-Malaysia EPA

Japan-Mexico EPA

Japan-Philippines EPA

Japan-Singapore EPA

Japan-Switzerland EPA

Japan-Thailand EPA

Japan-Vietnam, EPA

Korea-Chile FTA

Korea-Singapore FTA

Mainland and Hong Kong CEPA

Mainland and Macao CEPA

Mexico-Nicaragua FTA

North American Free Trade Agreement (NAFTA)

New Zealand-Hong Kong, China CEP
New Zealand-Singapore CEP
Panama-Chile FTA
Singapore-Australia FTA
Thailand-Australia FTA
Trans-Pacific Strategic Economic Partnership (SEP)
US-Australia FTA
US-Bahrain FTA
US-Chile FTA
US-Jordan FTA
US-Morocco FTA
US-Oman FTA
US-Peru TPA
US-Singapore FTA

NOTES

The authors are writing in a strictly personal capacity. The views expressed are theirs only, and do not reflect in any way those of the OECD Secretariat or the member countries of the OECD. The authors are grateful to the Groupe d'Economie Mondiale at Sciences Po for supporting this research, and to Patrick A. Messerlin for many helpful discussions and comments. The analysis of services commitments in regional trade agreements was carried out with the help of Jehan Sauvage and Marie Sudreau.

1. A note on terminology: we refer to "regional trade agreements" rather than "preferential trade agreements" or "free trade agreements," because the expression seems to us more neutral. Of course, it could be pointed out that most agreements are "bilateral" rather than "regional." But trade agreements in the case of services are not always "preferential" and never lead to "free trade." Switching to PTAs or FTAs does not improve the accuracy of the terminology.

2. Some studies have also uncovered the phenomenon of GATS-minus commitments. See Adlung and Miroudot (2012).

3. In fact, Novy (2011) shows that basically the same measure can be derived from a wide variety of theoretical models of international trade, including those of Chaney (2008) and Eaton and Kortum (2002). The interpretation of some parameters changes depending on the model used, but the overall approach remains very similar. Novy's approach builds on Head and Ries (2001).

4. Later in the chapter we report results for sales of foreign affiliates based on a small sample of countries for which data are available. We also indicate how bilateral "Mode 3 trade costs" could be calculated with an approach similar to Novy (2011).

5. We have both gross output and exports at the industry level in this set of I-O tables, the two variables needed to calculate domestic trade.

6. See Spinelli and Miroudot (2015) for detailed information on the creation of these services trade statistics.

7. The full list of RTAs included is given in Appendix 12-1.

8. For example, in the case of construction services, balance of payments data cover to some extent short-term contracts where there is commercial presence in the sense of GATS but no establishment (the foreign company operates in the territory of the partner country on the basis of a local office and remains a nonresident entity whose revenues are regarded as an international transaction recorded in the balance of payments). Construction services data sometimes include the cost of construction materials, which are goods, further complicating the issue of accurately measuring the services trade involved.

9. An exception is found in the agreements signed by China with Hong Kong and Macao (see Emch 2006).

10. See Houde, Kolse-Patil, and Miroudot (2007) for a more detailed comparison of NAFTA-inspired and GATS-inspired regional trade agreements.

REFERENCES

Adlung, R., and S. Miroudot. 2012. Poison in the Wine? Tracing GATS-Minus Commitments in Regional Trade Agreements. *Journal of World Trade* 46 (5): 1045–82.

Adlung, R., and M. Roy. 2005. Turning Hills into Mountains? Current Commitments under the General Agreement on Trade in Services and Prospects for Change. *Journal of World Trade* 39 (6): 1161–94.

Anderson, J. E., and E. van Wincoop. 2003. Gravity with Gravitas: A Solution to the Border Puzzle. *American Economic Review* 93 (1): 170–92.

Bergstrand, J., and P. Egger. 2007. A Knowledge-and-Physical-Capital Model of International Trade Flows, Foreign Direct Investment, and Multinational Enterprises. *Journal of International Economics* 73 (2): 278–308.

Chaney, T. 2008. "Distorted Gravity: The Intensive and Extensive Margins of International Trade." *American Economic Review* 98 (4): 1707–21.

Chauffour, J.-P., and J.-C Maur, eds. 2011. *Preferential Trade Agreement Policies for Development. A Handbook.* Washington, D.C.: World Bank.

Eaton, J., and S. Kortum. 2002. "Technology, Geography, and Trade." *Econometrica* 70 (5): 1741–79.

Emch, A. 2006. "Services Regionalism in the WTO: China's Trade Agreements with Hong Kong and Macao in Light of Article V(6) of GATS." *Legal Issues of Economic Integration* 4 (33): 351–78.

Fink, C., and M. Molinuevo. 2008. "East Asian Preferential Trade Agreements in Services: Liberalisation Content and WTO Rules. *World Trade Review* 7 (4): 641–73.

Fink, C., and D. Nikomborirak. 2007. "Rules of Origin in Services: A Case Study of Five ASEAN Countries." Policy Research Working Paper 4130. Washington, D.C.: World Bank.

Gormsen, C. 2011. "The Declining Barriers to Foreign Direct Investment and How to See Them." Mimeo, January.

Head, K., and J. Ries. 2001. "Increasing Returns versus National Product Differentiation as an Explanation for the Pattern of U.S.-Canada Trade." *American Economic Review* 91 (4): 858–76.

———. 2008. "FDI as an Outcome of the Market for Corporate Control: Theory and Evidence. *Journal of International Economics* 74 (1): 2–20.

Hoekman, B. 1996. "Assessing the General Agreement on Trade in Services." In *The Uruguay Round and the Developing Countries*, edited by W. Martin and L. A. Winters, 88–124. Cambridge University Press.

Houde, M.-F., A. Kolse-Patil, and S. Miroudot. 2007. "The Interaction between Investment and Services Chapters in Selected Regional Trade Agreements. OECD Trade Policy Working Paper 55. Paris: OECD Publishing.

Kleinert, J., and R. Toubal. 2010. "Gravity for FDI." *Review of International Economics* 18 (1): 1–13.

Marchetti, J. A., and M. Roy. 2008. "Services Liberalization in the WTO and in PTAs. In *Opening Markets for Trade in Services. Countries and Sectors in Bilateral and WTO Negotiations*, edited by J. A. Marchetti and M. Roy, 61–112. Cambridge University Press.

Messerlin, P. A. 2012. "The European Community Trade Policy." In *The Oxford Handbook of International Commercial Policy*, edited by M. E. Kreinin and M. G. Plummer. Oxford University Press.

Miroudot, S., and R. Lanz. 2008. "Measuring Bilateral Trade in Services: A Note on the Data Collected and Estimated for the Services Trade Restrictiveness Index." Tech. Rep. TAD/TC/SXM(2008)2. Paris: OECD.

Miroudot, S., J. Sauvage, and B. Shepherd. 2012. "Trade Costs and Productivity in Services Sectors. *Economics Letters* 114 (1): 36–38.

Miroudot, S., J. Sauvage, and M. Sudreau. 2010. "Multilateralising Regionalism: How Preferential Are Services Commitments in Regional Trade Agreements?" OECD Trade Policy Working Paper 106. Paris: OECD Publishing.

Novy, D. 2011. "Gravity Redux: Measuring International Trade Costs with Panel Data." CESifo Working Paper 3616. Munich: CESifo Group.

Pomfret, R., and P. Sourdin. 2009. "Have Asian Trade Agreements Reduced Trade Costs? *Journal of Asian Economics* 20 (3): 255–68.

Sauvé, P., and A. Mattoo. 2011. "Services." In *Preferential Trade Agreement Policies for Development. A Handbook* Edited by J.-P. Chauffour and J.-C. Maur, eds., 235–74. Washington, D.C.: World Bank.

Sauvé, P., and A. Shingal. 2011. "Reflections on the Preferential Liberalization of Services Trade." *Journal of World Trade* 45 (5): 953–63.

Spinelli, F., and S. Miroudot. 2015. "Estimating Bilateral Trade in Services by Industry—The EBTSI Data Set." Tech. Rep. Paris: OECD. October.

VanGrasstek, C. 2010. "The Political Economy of Services in Regional Trade Agreements." OECD Trade Policy Working Paper 112. Paris: OECD Publishing.

Walsh, K. 2006. "Trade in Services: Does Gravity Hold? A Gravity Model Approach to Estimating Barriers to Services Trade. Discussion Paper Series 183. Institute for International Integration Studies, Trinity College Dublin.

World Trade Organization (WTO). 2011. "The WTO and Preferential Trade Agreements: From Co-existence to Coherence." World Trade Report 2011 Geneva: World Trade Organization.

PART III

ECONOMIC DEVELOPMENT AND THE TRADING SYSTEM

13

FROM GLOBAL VALUE CHAINS TO GLOBAL DEVELOPMENT CHAINS

CHANGING PARADIGMS

OLIVIER CATTANEO AND SÉBASTIEN MIROUDOT

International trade is not new. Greeks and Phoenicians were already known to trade a variety of goods and services across the Mediterranean Sea in ancient times. The same can be said about international production; raw materials available in one country have always been traded to others not endowed with the same resources. Vertical specialization—that is, the unbundling of production into different stages performed in different places—was already common in thirteenth-century England with "cottage workers" (Jones and Kierzkowski 2005).

What is new is first and foremost the scale of the phenomenon. As noted by Baldwin (2006, 2012), there was a first "unbundling" in the second half of the nineteenth century (1850–1914) and from the 1960s onward, corresponding to the separation of production and consumption. Trade liberalization and technological advances have reduced trade costs to such an extent that most goods (and an increasing number of services) produced in one country can be shipped to others for final consumption without being at a price disadvantage. Concentrating production in one location is cost-efficient because of scale economies, and low trade costs ensure that goods can be cheaply delivered despite the distance from the location of production.

In what can be described as a "second unbundling," production itself is split among countries. Starting in the mid-1980s, more and more firms began fragmenting their production processes, taking advantage of lower costs of production and access to specific inputs and skills in different countries. The second unbundling is explained both by the reduction in trade costs and by lower "coordination" or "transaction" costs. Organizing production in a global value chain involving several countries is costly because intermediate goods and services have to be moved across space but also because activities performed in different places have to be coordinated. This coordination is expensive, but technological advances (e.g., the internet) and progress in management methods have reduced the cost in the past three decades, enabling firms to increase the fragmentation of production. By splitting production among several locations, firms pay more for "services links" and coordination activities but can still benefit from location-specific advantages (knowledge assets, skills, and technological spillovers, as well as lower labor costs).

There are two dimensions to the second unbundling. Production activities are geographically and organizationally separated, through off-shoring (moving some stages of production abroad) and outsourcing (the strategy of firms to focus on their core competencies and have independent suppliers carry out activities that were previously performed in-house). Offshoring describes the relocation of activities across countries while outsourcing is the redefinition of firms' boundaries. As figure 13-1 shows, firms that retain in-house production do not have a strategy of off-shoring or outsourcing. Firms that move some stages of production abroad but keep the activity within the firm are conducting vertical foreign direct investment (a form of offshoring), while firms that use independent suppliers to provide the product are performing offshore outsourcing (or just domestic outsourcing if the supplier remains domestic). Vertical FDI creates intrafirm trade while offshore outsourcing leads to vertical arm's-length trade. Vertical trade (between affiliated companies or at arm's length) explains most of the growth in world trade (Yi 2003). While diffi-

FIGURE 13-1. New Sourcing Strategies

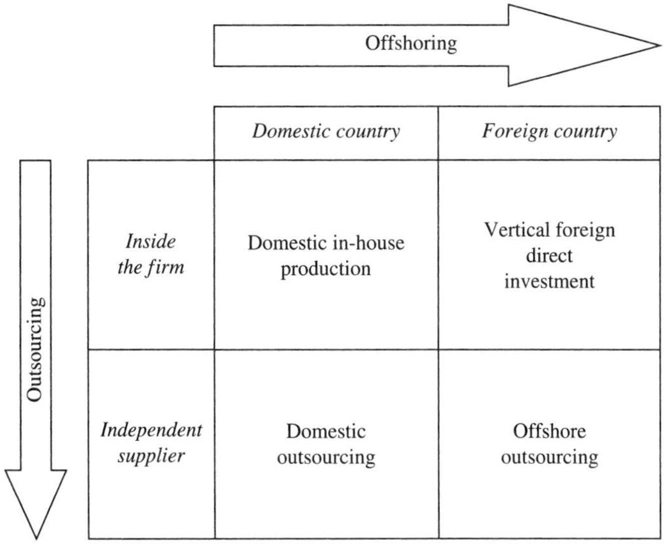

Source: Antràs and Helpman (2004).

cult to measure, intrafirm trade has also increased in recent decades (Lanz and Miroudot 2011).

What the recent literature on "firm heterogeneity" highlights is that different types of firms make different choices and co-exist in the same market (Bernard and others 2007). Firms start to export when their productivity reaches a certain cutoff level (Melitz 2003), and the most productive tend to vertically integrate (Antràs and Helpman 2004). The least productive firms exit the market, and there is thus an intra-industry reallocation of resources. Above the productivity cutoff, several types of firms with different outsourcing and offshoring strategies co-exist. Multinational enterprises are not the only users of global production networks; there are also firms without any foreign affiliates that participate in global value chains, including small and medium-sized enterprises (SMEs).

Analysis of Global Value Chains

A value chain includes the full range of activities that firms undertake, starting from the conception of a product to its end use by consumers (Gereffi and Fernandez-Stark 2016). These activities, such as design, production, marketing, and support, are increasingly spread over different countries and have reshaped international trade.

As explained by Bair (2005), the origin of the analysis of global value chains can be traced back to the 1970s when the concept of a "commodity chain" was introduced by Hopkins and Wallerstein (1977). The idea was to trace all the sets of inputs and transformations that lead to an "ultimate consumable" and to describe a linked set of processes that culminate in this item. The concept of a "global commodity chain" was later introduced in the work of Gereffi (1994). Figure 13-2 shows the example of the apparel commodity chain, from the raw materials (such as cotton, wool, or synthetic fibers) to the final products (garments).

In the 2000s, there was a shift in terminology from the "global commodity chain" to the "global value chain," the latter coming from the analysis of trade and industrial organization as a value-added chain in the international business literature (Porter 1985). The concept of a value chain is not hugely different from that of the commodity chain, but it is more ambitious in the sense that it tries to capture the determinants of the organization of global industries (Bair 2005). Gereffi, Humphrey, and Sturgeon (2005) provide a theoretical framework for the value chain analysis and describe five types of global value chain governance: market, modular, relational, captive, and hierarchy.

A third and more recent strand of research emphasizes the concept of "network" rather than "chain" (Coe and Hess 2007). This change in the metaphor highlights the complexity of the interactions among global producers: "Economic processes must be conceptualized in terms of a complex circuitry with a multiplicity of linkages and feedback loops rather than just 'simple' circuits or, even worse, linear flows" (Hudson 2004, 462).

The analysis of global value chains is therefore a relatively new field at the crossroads of business, sociology, and economic research. In the area of trade, the global value chain (GVC) approach builds on the concepts of "production sharing" (Yeats 1997), "international fragmentation" (Jones and Kierzkowski 2001), "vertical specialization" (Hummels, Ishii, and Yi 2001), "global sourcing" (Antràs and Helpman 2004), "second unbundling" (Baldwin 2006), and "trade in tasks" (Grossman and Rossi-Hansberg 2008). This literature has shed light on the motivations of firms to offshore and fragment production processes, as well as the gains expected from the international division of labor.

FIGURE 13-2. The Apparel Commodity Chain

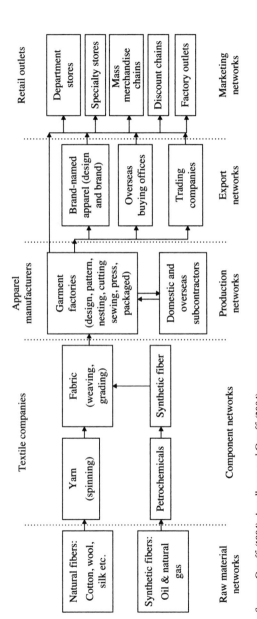

Source: Gereffi (1994); Appelbaum and Gereffi (2004).

Twenty-first Century or Back to the Past?

In discussions of the impact of global value chains on trade theory and trade policy, there are always skeptics who say that the global value chain is merely a repackaging of things that trade economists have known for a long time. To some extent, this is true: the fragmentation of production has always existed, and it piqued the interest of some analysts before the beginning of the "second unbundling" in the 1980s.

For example, intra-industry trade was the focus of Grubel and Lloyd's (1975) attempt to explain international trade with differentiated products. But one should also recall that initially intra-industry trade was regarded as a statistical artifact (Jones and Kierzkowski 2005). To explain intra-industry trade in intermediate inputs, the theory of "trade in middle products" was proposed by Sanyal and Jones (1982). With respect to investment, Agmon (1979) was already asking whether foreign direct investment (FDI) and intra-industry trade were substitutes or complements. Finally, input-output analysis, which is at the heart of new empirical work on the measurement of trade in value-added terms (OECD and WTO 2012), comes from the work of Leontief, who was already considering multiregional flows (Leontief and Strout 1963).

One can even look further in the past to Ohlin (1933). To echo Paul Krugman (1982), who asked whether all was in Ohlin, Ohlin made the case for the fragmentation of production and the role of firms in international trade. Ohlin wrote, for example, that "production is in many cases divided not into two stages—raw materials and finished goods—but into many." In addition, he provided a theory on the location of activities: "The localisation of producers' buying markets (e.g., the manufacturing of paper) . . . depends upon the localisation of consumers' markets for the finished products and upon the localisation of 'half material' production (pulp)." One can even find the concept of firm heterogeneity in his work: "It should be noted also that a commodity may be produced by several different processes, and that the best location for a firm using one of them may be different from that for firms using another." The following excerpt is also very close to the conclusions that can be found in the empirical work of Bernard and others (2007) and the theoretical work of Melitz (2003): "International trade is between firms, not between nations. Certain firms export while others do not; some export only to a few special foreign markets, others to a number of them. Some firms are able to hold a part of the home market against foreign competition, others succumb."

Needed: A New Paradigm for Trade and Development Policies

Turning to the economic development challenge: What are the implications of the observed changes in international trade and production for the potential role of trade in economic development? How did governments adjust their trade and development policies to these new global business practices?

In their reviews of fifty years of trade and development policies, Krueger (1997) and Winters (2000) observed a number of changes, including the radical move from an "import substitution" model to an "outer-oriented" trade regime. Table 13-1 summarizes these policy trends and evolutions. In the 1950s, it was thought that import substitution would lead to industrialization, and domestic markets were protected to allow infant industries to reach a critical stage of development before being exposed to competition. In practice, however, an alternative strategy based on promoting trade, rather than curtailing it, proved more successful with the early success (in the 1960s) of the so-called Asian tigers. At the same time, some analytical efforts were made to evidence the negative side effects of import substitution strategies, including arbitrariness, poor specialization choices, economic distortions, and rents. With a view to achieving higher growth rates, some countries chose to open their economies and remove selected trade barriers. Outward orientation became the prevailing trade regime, although the debate still rages today, in particular after the 2008 global economic crisis stressed the risks associated with the increasing interdependence of world economies (Haddad and Shepherd 2011).

Trade-focused development policies have changed accordingly. Import substitution policies justified the introduction of "special and differential treatment" in favor of developing countries, including the authorization to adopt unilateral trade preferences (i.e., tariffs below the most favored nation rate): developing countries could have preferential access to developed countries' markets or, put differently, they could maintain higher tariffs than their richer counterparts. These unilateral preferences, in turn, were criticized, in particular when they were associated with strict rules of origin or disparate conditions that created discrimination among developing

TABLE 13-1. A Stylized History of Postwar Thinking on Trade Policy as Development Policy, 1950s–1990s

Decade	Macro policy	Resource allocation
1950s	Import substitution • Commodity pessimism and industrialization • Infant economy protection • Special and differential treatment • Regionalism	Welfare economics of trade • Second best
1960s and 1970s	Export promotion	General theory of distortions • Infant industry arguments Costs of protection Effective protection
1980s	Outward orientation • Getting prices right • Fallacy of composition • Costs of adjustment	Political economy of protection • Rent seeking
1990s	Endogenous growth • Theory and evidence • Governance Economic geography	Trade and technology Poverty/income distribution

Source: Winters (2000).

countries, or confined developing countries to the production of low-value-added goods. These criticisms, combined with the progressive erosion of preferences that resulted from the successful lowering of average tariffs on most goods, led to the replacement of unilateral trade preferences by reciprocal trade preferences (e.g., in the context of regional trade and partnership agreements) and the creation of a form of aid dedicated to trade adjustment and capacity building. The launch of the so-called Aid for Trade Initiative in 2005, led by the World Trade Organization (WTO), aimed to enable developing countries to benefit from further trade liberalization in partner countries by building their capacity to trade: indeed, market access is not sufficient to create new export opportunities if the country lacks basic infrastructure, production capacities, human resources, transport and logistics, telecommunications, and other functions that it needs to be competitive, respond to international demand, and participate in global trade flows.

Thus trade and development policies have evolved over time. The move to reciprocity and aid for trade (AFT) has put more emphasis on trade capacities than on market access and traditional barriers to trade. As such, it paves the way for further adaptation of trade and development policies to the reality of trade and business strategies: building capacities not only helps domestic firms become more competitive and better linked to global markets; it also makes the country more attractive to foreign investors and international business in search of input providers and opportunities to delocalize production and services.

At the same time, in practice, AFT often seems to be more of the same for the same, reflecting old aid and trade policy paradigms. First, it appears that the bulk of AFT is old aid repackaged. A meta-evaluation of AFT projects has thus revealed that objectives assigned to AFT projects are often only remotely—if at all—related to trade (OECD 2011; Messerlin and others 2011). This is typically the case for infrastructure projects that once were excluded from AFT accounts.

Second, benefactors of old preferences often became AFT recipients. For example, a number of projects have targeted the textile industry that faced the phasing out of quotas under the Multi-Fiber Agreement, which was in effect from 1974 to 2004. This could be interpreted either as a success of AFT as an adjustment tool, or a vector of the prolongation of existing rents.

Third, one could argue that aid unilateralism has replaced preference unilateralism. The geography of bilateral AFT still reflects old preferences. In addition, donors have continued to promote access to selected products in their own markets—in the spirit of unilateral preferences—rather than access to third markets. For example, a number of AFT projects have promoted standards and rules (e.g., for geographical indications and for patents) that are country- or region-specific: this has prolonged the dependence of developing countries on traditional markets and hindered diversification efforts. The shift in demand from OECD to emerging markets could challenge this strategy, resulting in a lower return on investment in standards.

Fourth, one can ask whether policies moved from picking the winners of import substitution to picking the winners of outward orientation. Export promotion strategies sometimes have the flavor of industrial policies, picking sectors with a high export potential and replicating success stories. There is thus a vast economic literature on export discovery and survival.

In sum, the appearance of change hides an important inertia in trade and development policies that widens the gap between the reality of trade and business strategies and policy interventions aimed at facilitating developing countries' participation in global trade. The following section suggests a new fundamental change in trade and development policies to fill this gap and further improve the effectiveness of AFT and trade and development strategies more generally.

Preliminary Reflections on the Concept of Global Development Chains

The need for a new trade and development policy paradigm has become more obvious since the economic crisis of 2008–2009, which accelerated preexisting trends in international trade, such as the shift in demand from the OECD countries to emerging markets and the consolidation of global value chains. A number of state intervention mechanisms have been challenged: developed countries could not massively resort to protectionism as they did in the 1930s owing to existing regional and international trade commitments (i.e., rules contained in plurilateral and multilateral trade agreements, such as the WTO) and an increased dependence on backward and forward links within GVCs; developing countries became collateral damage of a crisis born in the collapse of the US housing and subprime mortgage markets through their participation in GVCs. Developed and developing countries appeared more interdependent than ever, and old trade policy intervention mechanisms were revealed to be obsolete. A change in paradigm is needed, both from the perspective of the developed countries to restore or increase the effectiveness of trade and development policies, and from the perspective of developing countries to fully harness the benefits of trade, aid, and other forms of transfers that foster socioeconomic upgrading.

The concept of global development chains captures those recent changes in practice. Trade and socioeconomic upgrading (or development) now take place within global value chains: pull the links apart (e.g., through the adoption of new barriers to trade) and the whole system collapses; tighten the links (e.g., through increased trade flows or capacity-building efforts) and the whole system becomes stronger. The concept of global development chains not only reinforces the idea of intertwined and interdependent economies, thereby introducing a more balanced relationship between donor and recipient countries of development aid; it also recognizes the role of the private sector in trade and development. The debt and budget crises faced by many donor countries also argue in favor of development schemes that do not fully rely on public contributions and that reconsider the respective roles of the public and private sectors in socioeconomic upgrading.

Adapting trade and development policies to the reality of business and global economic relations will require four major changes in paradigm that are captured in the concept of global development chains and are further detailed and explained in the following sections.

CHANGES IN THE RELEVANT STRATEGIC FRAMEWORK: FROM COUNTRIES TO FIRMS AND GLOBAL VALUE CHAINS

The first and most important change introduced by global value chains is the need for policies to look beyond individual countries and be global from the start. Both import substitution and export promotion strategies assume that capacity should first be developed within a given country and that only then can "home-grown" companies compete in international markets. The new paradigm of global development chains suggests that this happens first by linking global buyers with suppliers to develop capacity and that access to imports is more important than exports when trying to move up the value chain.

From Single-Country Strategies to Global Value Chains

Most of development thinking so far has focused on the development of capacity within a closed economy not yet connected to the rest of the world. The old paradigm looks like the diagram in figure 13-3. Through import substitution or some kind of industrial policy, domestic firms have to grow and become productive. Once they have the capacity to compete in international markets, efforts should be made to put in place trade facilitation and export promotion policies to sell domestic products to consumers in developed countries. This old paradigm assumes that there is a sequencing issue and that the link to world markets only happens at the end of the process, when the local industry is "ready." Aid for trade and open markets policies are regarded only as tools to reach consumers in developed countries.

The strategies illustrated in figure 13-3 can be more or less protectionist. The infant industry argument would suggest putting prohibitive trade barriers in place to ensure that domestic consumers only buy the products of the local industry. Once nurtured by high tariffs, domestic companies can then compete internationally (when they have reached the required

FIGURE 13-3. The Old Paradigm

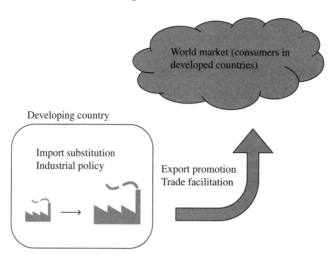

productivity). A more protrade liberalization version of figure 13-3 consists of letting foreign products compete with the local industry, to give enough incentives to domestic firms to increase their productivity and possibly learn from foreign competitors. But the focus of the trade agenda will be on the export side to promote domestic products and reduce trade costs with partners in the developed world.

What is missing in figure 13-3 are imports of intermediate products and the fact that the "local industry" can contribute not by reproducing the full production process domestically, but rather by specializing in one stage. This will allow it to quickly become efficient using local capacities and to "upgrade" (move up the value chain to other activities) by connecting with global buyers and suppliers. The new paradigm is represented in figure 13-4. Efficient sourcing (the import side) is as important as the reduction in trade costs on the export side. World markets are not only consumers in developed countries waiting for products from the developing world; world markets provide inputs to be processed, as well as capital, services, and technology. The local capacity depends on these flows of production factors and knowledge, which are even more important with the digital transformation of economies.

Within the country, policies should focus on infrastructure and efficient services to ensure that the "mechanics of development" work (Lucas 1988). Figure 13-4 also emphasizes that access to consumers includes consumers

FIGURE 13-4. The New Paradigm

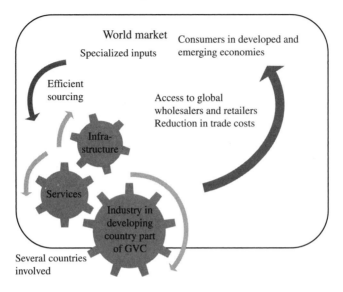

in the developed world and in emerging economies. Moreover, this access is not direct. An important role is played by wholesalers and retailers because the global value chain does not end when the final product is produced. It has to be shipped, marketed, and sold in a retail network. This part of the chain is as important as the rest (including the value added that is generated), and the role of "intermediaries" in international trade is increasingly highlighted in economic research (Bernard, Grazzi, and Tomasi 2011). And once again, these important actors in international trade and production are private firms, not states.

The Length of GVCs (Domestic and Intercountry)

The new reality of business in global value chains can be illustrated by looking at input-output data and calculating indicators of the fragmentation of production. Figure 13-5 below provides an index from the input-output literature that can be understood as the "length" of GVCs. The higher the value, the higher the number of production stages involved. And the data allow a distinction between the domestic part of the value chain (involving domestic companies) and the international part (involving companies in other countries). Figure 13-5 illustrates that, in most manufacturing industries and a growing number of services industries, value chains are long and complex, and often highly internationalized.

FIGURE 13-5. The Length of Global Value Chains, Domestic and Intercountry, by Industry

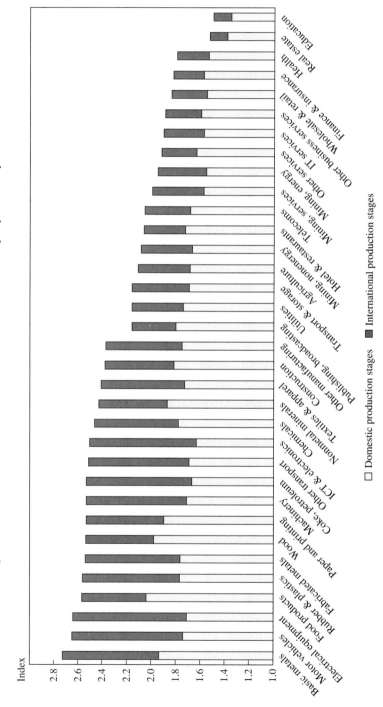

Index

□ Domestic production stages ■ International production stages

Basic metals
Motor vehicles
Electrical equipment
Food products
Rubber & plastics
Fabricated metals
Wood
Paper and printing
Machinery
Coke, petroleum
Other transport
ICT & electronics
Chemicals
Nonmineral minerals
Textiles & apparel
Construction
Other manufacturing
Publishing, broadcasting
Utilities
Transport & storage
Agriculture
Mining, nonenergy
Hotel & restaurants
Telecoms
Mining, services
Mining, energy
Other services
IT services
Other business services
Wholesale & retail
Finance & insurance
Health
Real estate
Education

Source: Authors' calculations, based on the methodology described in Miroudot and De Backer (2013). Data are for 2015.

The "Servicification" of Manufacturing

Another empirical fact that supports the new paradigm presented on figure 13-4 is the real role of services in international trade when looking at trade on a value-added rather than a gross basis. Although international trade in services is generally regarded as accounting for only about 25 percent of total trade (Loungani and others 2017), the reality is a bit different, because most services that are traded are embodied in goods. A more accurate calculation of the share of gross exports representing value added in the services sector is that about 49 percent of world trade is services trade (Miroudot and Cadestin 2017).

Services are the "links" that permit the functioning of value chains. The logistics chain involves transportation services, communication services, storage, and packaging services. Trade has to be financed, and goods and people insured, so there are important financial services involved. Moving and training people relies on a variety of social services. Business services cover a broad range of consulting, accounting, and advertising services needed by firms. An empirical study conducted by the Swedish National Board of Trade identifies about forty different types of services that are involved when a manufacturing firm internationalizes its production (figure 13-6). These services are also key for development and for the insertion of developing countries in GVCs.

In addition, manufacturing firms increasingly sell and export services to their customers. By becoming service providers, these firms add value, create loyalty, and generate a more stable income flow along the product life cycle. This phenomenon, described as the "servicification of manufacturing" in the business and management literature (Vandermerwe and Rada 1988), blurs the lines between goods and services and implies that developing countries do not have to choose between goods and services in their exports. They need both to participate in global value chains.

From the Old to the New Paradigm: Policy Implications

It should be recognized that both trade and development policies have long been entrenched at countries' borders: traditional trade policy instruments are applied by customs authorities, and traditional development aid is dispensed at the country level, according to Poverty Reduction Strategy Papers (PRSPs) and other studies that are country-focused. As early as the

FIGURE 13-6. The "Servicification" of Manufacturing

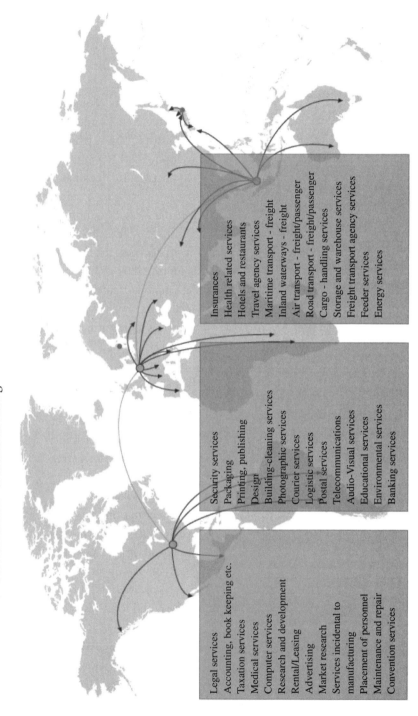

Legal services
Accounting, book keeping etc.
Taxation services
Medical services
Computer services
Research and development
Rental/Leasing
Advertising
Market research
Services incidental to
manufacturing
Placement of personnel
Maintenance and repair
Convention services

Security services
Packaging
Printing, publishing
Design
Building-cleaning services
Photographic services
Courier services
Logistic services
Postal services
Telecommunications
Audio-Visual services
Educational services
Environmental services
Banking services

Insurances
Health related services
Hotels and restaurants
Travel agency services
Maritime transport - freight
Inland waterways - freight
Air transport - freight/passenger
Road transport - freight/passenger
Cargo - handling services
Storage and warehouse services
Freight transport agency services
Feeder services
Energy services

Source: Swedish National Board of Trade (2010).

1960s, trade policies started to adjust and negotiations targeted "beyond-the-border" obstacles to trade: a series of plurilateral "codes" were adopted during the Tokyo Round of multilateral trade negotiations (1974–1979), and the Uruguay Round (1986–1994) extended the scope of the negotiations to include more disciplines on beyond-the-border regulations—for example, in the domain of services. The Doha Development Agenda that was launched in 2001 for the first time included truly cross-border disciplines, such as trade facilitation (e.g., freedom of transit). Progress in development policies has been slower, although the development of Regional Economic Communities (RECs) introduced new perspectives for regional aid coordination and projects.

The Aid for Trade Initiative helped shift the focus from obstacles at the border and market access to beyond-the-border obstacles and capacity constraints. However, the move from supply to demand-driven trade and development strategies has not been fully achieved: in the same way that industrial policies aimed to pick national champions that would ultimately become exporters, AFT projects often pick sectors with high export potential (on the basis of success stories in countries with similar endowments or levels of development) and supplement capacity building with export promotion efforts. After trying to remedy market failures affecting export discoveries, governments then measure their success and review the key determinants of export survival.

Within GVCs, imports are just as important as exports; a country cannot become a major exporter unless it first becomes a major importer and is well connected to world markets both upstream and downstream in its production. Participation in GVCs secures the demand for certain goods and services and is a key determinant of export survival. Discovery and diversification can also take place in GVCs depending on the type of GVC and the lead firm. As a result, instead of focusing on export promotion, trade and development policies should focus on encouraging foreign direct investment (FDI), fixing the domestic business environment, and removing obstacles to imports. In addition to building capacities and infrastructure, AFT can promote trade facilitation, transport, and logistics.

For example, in the food sector, an old-type supply-driven AFT project could consist in developing green bean production in an African country, replicating successful experiences in comparable countries, and hoping for the same success. A new-type demand-driven policy would facilitate the establishment of international retailers: those retailers would first import products that meet their standards until local producers could upgrade and meet those same standards. Then the retailer would source most of its products locally and eventually select a few products that have a high potential for export and distribute them in other countries where the retailer is already established (see Mattoo and Payton, 2007 for the example of ShopRite in Zambia). The same model can be applied to international manufacturers, with a first phase of establishment and production for the local market, and a second phase of exporting products with high potential to places where the manufacturer distributes its products. In both cases, only the private sector bears the cost of discovery and runs the risk of export survival.

Until recently, socioeconomic development and upgrading had been discussed in the context of old-type trade and development strategies based on import substitution and export orientation (Fold and Larsen 2008). With the emergence of global production in many sectors, upgrading has been increasingly linked to GVCs (Kaplinsky and Morris 2001). This helped shift the focus from the country to the firm level. For example, Humphrey and Schmitz (2002) proposed an influential fourfold upgrading classification:

- functional upgrading, whereby an improvement in the position of firms would result from increasing the range of functions performed and moving from lower-value activities with high competition (e.g., manufacturing) into higher-value activities (e.g., design, branding, marketing, and logistics);
- process upgrading, which yields efficiency gains by reorganizing the production system and introducing new technologies;
- product upgrading, with higher unit value prices as products become more sophisticated;
- interchain upgrading, with capabilities that were acquired in one chain leading to competitive benefits in another.

Upgrading also includes social and development dimensions, since the positioning on higher-value activities could result in an increase in the value of trade captured by the country, and could be associated with the diffusion of higher standards, safer and greener production methods, and knowledge-intensive activities. However, it appears that upgrading opportunities vary with the core competencies of the lead firm (e.g., buyer-led versus retailer-led GVC; see Gereffi 1994, 1999; Bair and Gereffi 2001) and the type of network structure: captive, relational, or modular (Gereffi,

FIGURE 13-7. Three Phases of Development in the Global Value Chain

Phase 1: Predation

Developing countries are limited to the exportation of raw materials and importation of processed goods and services.

Phase 2: Segmentation

– Developing countries benefit from the delocalization of certain production activities, mostly to serve local markets.

– Innovation is imported.

"Bottom of the pyramid"; "Just enough"

Phase 3: Consolidation

– Local innovation in developing countries leads to the exportation of processed goods and services to other developing and developed countries.

– Multinational companies conduct reverse innovation (see General Electric).

– There is more content development but fewer developing country beneficiaries.

Humphrey, and Sturgeon 2005). In turn, different types of policy measures are needed to accompany upgrading efforts and prevent noncompetitive practices within GVCs. Figure 13-7 shows how the maturity of GVCs is linked with their development content: not all GVCs have the potential to become global development chains. Some lead firms tap into the resources of poorer countries without transferring any knowledge or technology or offering real upgrading prospects. Three phases of development are distinguished: a predation phase in which developing countries are limited to the exportation of raw materials and importation of processed goods and services; a segmentation phase in which developing countries benefit from the delocalization of certain production activities, mostly to serve local markets; and a consolidation phase in which local innovation leads to the export of processed goods and services to other developing and developed countries. While the last phase has the highest development content, it is also more selective: the consolidation of GVCs corresponds to a diminution in the number of participants in GVCs, and hence threatens to leave more developing countries outside major trade flows and upgrading paths.

Staritz, Gereffi, and Cattaneo (2011) have also analyzed changes in upgrading prospects within GVCs when end markets shift to the South. In line with the theory of maturation of GVCs presented in figure 13-7, lead

FIGURE 13-8. China's Imports of Gabonese Logs and Selected Wood Products, 1970–2007 (thousand cubic meters)

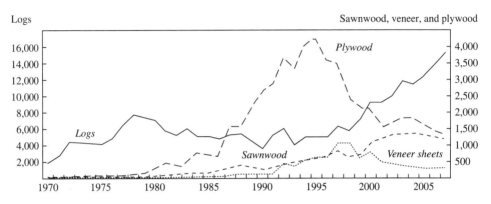

Source: Kaplinsky, Terheggen, and Tijaja (2010), based on ForeSTAT data.

firms and end markets shape the development path of upstream participating countries. Figure 13-8 shows the example of the timber value chain between Gabon in China: between 1985 and 1995, China's imports of processed wood (plywood) grew steadily, until China could acquire the technology to build its own transformation industries; thereafter, China mostly imported logs (unprocessed wood), causing the crisis of the transformation industry in Gabon. Chinese lead firms in this industry are thus in a predation phase. Kaplinsky, Terheggen, and Tijaja (2010) show that Chinese importers are mostly interested in quantities and price, paying little attention to labor standards and sustainable harvesting. Thus, socioeconomic upgrading is limited in this phase, corresponding instead to a loss in capacities and downgrading.

CHANGES IN THE RELEVANT ECONOMIC FRAMEWORK: FROM INDUSTRIES TO TASKS AND BUSINESS FUNCTIONS

The second change necessitated by the introduction of global value chains is related to the relevant unit of analysis. Most development strategies are presented as "industrial policies" by which the state sponsors the birth of new industries. Economists discuss whether the initial growth of such industries should be sheltered from foreign competition or, instead, oriented toward exports and international markets. From our point of view, the main mistake is not in thinking that governments can effectively identify and promote successful industries, but in already assuming that new industries should be created to compete with existing value chains. Today, the specialization of countries is not in industries but in specific tasks and activities in the value chain—what the management literature has described as "business functions." There is a functional specialization in trade that makes what countries do more important than what they export (Timmer, Miroudot, and de Vries 2019). Industries already exist, and new entrants on international markets should find their place in the network of suppliers of inputs and final goods and services producers. They are very unlikely to recreate domestically complex supply chains that are now split among countries to maximize productivity.

FROM INDUSTRIES TO TASKS AND BUSINESS FUNCTIONS: WHAT "SLICING UP" THE VALUE CHAIN MEANS

The value chain analysis starts with the identification of steps in the production process, steps that can be performed in-house or that can be offshored and outsourced. Porter (1985) was among the first to propose a decomposition of the value chain according to different types of activities (figure 13-9). Primary activities include inbound logistics, operations, outbound logistics, marketing and sales, and some after-sale services. These primary activities are supported by more horizontal corporate activities: firm infrastructure, human resources management, technology development, and procurement.

The (international) fragmentation of production first took place among the primary activities. Assembly and manufacturing were outsourced and offshored, most often to nearby countries. More recently, as international trade and transaction costs have declined, more services activities, such as human resources, research and development, and customer service are outsourced or offshored to more remote countries (emerging economies).

What is important to understand from figure 13-9 is that "business functions" are offshored or outsourced, not firms or industries. The fragmentation of production is within the value chain. If a single firm is in charge of all activities and some of those activities are offshored or outsourced, this firm still exists in the domestic economy and there is specialization in specific parts of the production process. The outcome is very different from competition between two producers, where one gains market share and the other may "disappear."

FIGURE 13-9. The Value Chain: Outsourcing and Offshoring

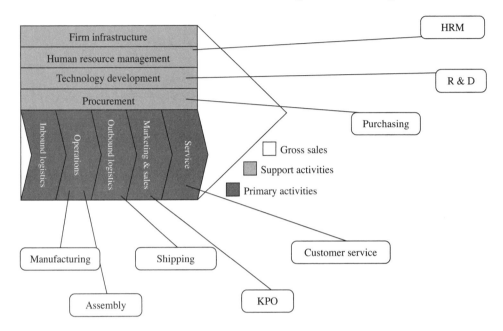

Source: Porter (1985); OECD (2011). Boxes indicate the outsourced and offshored activities.

An encouraging corollary is that developing economies do not have to build capacity in all business functions before exporting. Becoming part of a value chain implies a specialization in only one step of the production process. The entry cost is thus lower than with import-substitution strategies; joining a GVC is faster and easier (Baldwin 2012).

The trade literature has also introduced a smaller unit of specialization based on specific workers' activities: the tasks they perform. When tasks are outsourced their offshoring becomes "trade in tasks" (Grossman and Rossi-Hansberg 2006). Some evidence on changes in the task intensity of output can be found, but as emphasized by Lanz, Miroudot, and Nordås (2012), there is no clear evidence that the fragmentation of production goes to the task level. Firms generally prefer "multitasked" workers: "Toyotism" rather than "Fordism" remains the dominant production model.

The important point is that production isn't treated as if it happens inside a "black box" but is analyzed as consisting of four layers (Baldwin and Evenett 2012): tasks, occupations, stages, and products. It is at the level of "stages" that most of the unbundling and internationalization of produc-

FIGURE 13-10. **Upgrading within Value Chains**

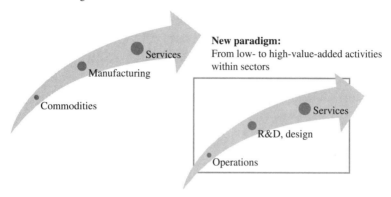

Old paradigm:
From low- to high-value-added sectors

New paradigm:
From low- to high-value-added activities within sectors

Services

Manufacturing

Commodities

Services

R&D, design

Operations

tion takes place. And this explains why globalization is seen as more "granular" in the context of GVCs.

New Upgrading and Development Paths

The shift from industry to tasks allows the definition of far more precise development strategies. Socioeconomic development is not only about moving from low- to high-value-added sectors—for example, from agriculture to manufacturing and services; it is about identifying, within each sector, high-value-added activities to specialize in (figure 13-10). Specialization according to comparative advantage takes place within GVCs, and the competitiveness of the whole chain depends on the best repartition of tasks within the chain. Thus GVCs offer a new path for diversification that is more incremental than stochastic discoveries.

In turn, the upgrading and diversification dynamics that take place in GVCs could play against the further segmentation of global production. Indeed, the most recent trend is toward the consolidation of GVCs—the bundling of tasks along GVCs to limit the number of partners involved. For example, going forward, a country that is currently specialized in apparel production might not be able to remain part of major GVCs unless it also develops a capacity to offer design, logistics, marketing, and other services to the lead firm. Those countries able to upgrade and diversify their tasks will remain in the chain, and others will be excluded. Thus it is not enough to build capacity in only one segment of the production chain, and

FIGURE 13-11. Value-Adding Activities in the Apparel Global Value Chain

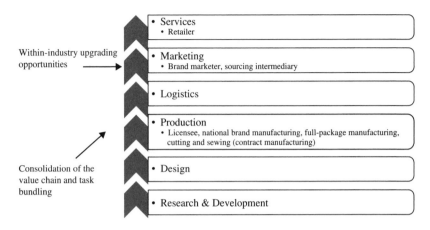

Source: Adapted from Frederick (2010).

countries should adopt development strategies that promote task bundling in a context of GVC consolidation. It is not about reverting to industry-level strategies, but bundling tasks at key levels of the production chain to increase the local value added (figure 13-11).

CHANGES IN THE RELEVANT ECONOMIC ASSETS: FROM ENDOWMENTS AND STOCKS TO FLOWS

As emphasized by Henderson and others (2002), "In order to understand the dynamics of development in a given place . . . we must comprehend how places are being transformed by flows of capital, labor, knowledge, power, etc." The idea that flows matter more than stocks and endowments was quite a shift, given that trade theory still largely viewed capital and labor endowments as the source of comparative advantage. According to the new thinking, policies should focus on how to link to global production networks and attract flows of capital, labor, and knowledge, implying that policies should look beyond borders and traditional actors such as states.

Flows Are More Important Than Stocks and Endowments

In an open economy, productivity does not depend only on local factors of production. The economics literature has identified several links between international flows of capital, labor, and knowledge (including data) and the productivity in a given location. First, in the world of GVCs, production factors are not immobile. Capital moves easily from one location to another. Recent theories emphasize that capital does not go where it is scarce and consequently more remunerated, but that another driving force is the export specialization of the economy in capital-intensive sectors (Jin 2012). This explains why capital flows more often to advanced economies than it does to developing countries—a paradox first identified by Lucas (1990). This link between export specialization and capital flows is important for understanding how productivity and local capacity are developed through connections to global value chains. With respect to labor, despite important restrictions on the movement of people, there is evidence that the migration of high-skill workers has a positive impact on productivity (see, e.g., Grossman and Stadelmann 2012). In the context of GVCs, people often move as "intracorporate transferees," and there are fewer barriers to this temporary movement of persons.

Second, technology can be traded and imported (Keller 2004). R&D flows can be seen as "services" or "intangible assets" and directly improve the productivity of domestic firms. Technology can also be directly transferred through foreign direct investment when foreign companies create affiliates and transfer their technology internally. Movements of people also carry the know-how and technology of workers who share their knowledge with domestic firms. Last, technology is embodied in foreign inputs. Trade in intermediate inputs can explain international links that are key to growth and development (Jones 2011).

In addition, there are technological spillovers or indirect transfers of technology. The literature emphasizes forward and backward links when firms are engaged in vertical trade or vertical FDI (Havranek and Irsova 2011). Companies increase their productivity by using foreign inputs, but contacts with customers and buyers are also important. Their feedback and help to improve products and services also increase productivity. Last, pro-competitive effects from foreign firms and foreign products also stimulate productivity growth in the domestic economy.

It is beyond the scope of this chapter to review all the literature on the productivity impact of international flows of capital, labor, and knowledge. There are sometimes mixed results, and the experience may be different from one country to another, depending on its "absorptive capacity." But there are two important conclusions from this literature. First, productivity does not increase when producers are isolated from the rest of the world.

An important source of productivity growth is through the connectedness with the rest of the world, and even more the digitalization of economies. Second, the interaction between different types of flows matters. As illustrated with capital flows, they cannot be understood if one does not look at international trade. Similarly, FDI spillovers are higher when trade is liberalized (a result from the meta-analysis carried out by Havranek and Irsova 2011). Flows matter more than endowments and stocks, but the combination of different flows is the driver of productivity gains.

Global Development Chains in Action

As we have already noted, upgrading and development prospects that accompany flows and transfers of all kinds within GVCs may vary with the origin, nature, and maturity of the lead firm. In the three-phase typology of figure 13-7, at the predation phase, knowledge and technology transfers from the lead firm to subcontractors are almost nonexistent; they increase progressively, along with capacity-building efforts, with the maturity of the GVC and its lead firm. Once a certain level of maturity is reached, GVCs become a major channel of transfers of all kinds, with the potential to remedy initial capacity issues. Thus, through GVCs, the private sector has become a major contributor to trade capacity building in developing countries, along with the public sector through the AFT Initiative.

In 2011, the World Bank analyzed those global development chains in action by collecting case stories relating international business's contribution to trade capacity-building efforts in developing countries (World Bank 2011). Those efforts were classified in four categories:

1. Human Capacity Building

The transmission of knowledge within GVCs is important, whether the lead company is established abroad or just sources out some activities to foreign contractors. Insofar as the workforce is deficient in specific skills needed, foreign companies often establish training programs. While benefiting the company in the short run, such programs can contribute to sustainable long-term benefits for the recipients who can apply their newly acquired skills in numerous ways, resulting in positive spillover effects for the country (e.g., alumni of multinational corporations often count among the most successful local entrepreneurs and exporters). For example, over

2.4 million Chinese farmers participated in the Cargill rural development program that aims to enhance local farmers' productivity.

2. Productive Capacity Bolstering

The efficiency of each link in the GVC affects the competitiveness of the whole chain and its lead firm. With a view to reducing operating costs and improving business operation all along the value chain, multinational corporations proceed to transfer technology, know-how, capital, and other assets to local affiliates and contractors. For example, GE opened a technology and innovation center in India, which exports goods and services worth over US$1 billion. Syngenta disseminated crop advice using mobile technology in India. Danone helped with the development of milk co-operatives in Ukraine. During the crisis, 41 percent of Kohl's suppliers benefited from the group's supply chain finance program.

3. Value Chain Performance Enhancement

Beyond capacity building, promoting the sustainable inclusion of small producers in global value chains is fundamental to fighting poverty. If small-scale producers can link to the chain while at the same time obtaining assistance to help with needed certification for higher-value-added production, they will be able to take much better advantage of market access opportunities. For example, Kraft Foods' participation in the Africa cashew initiative aims to reinforce market links; the Nespresso AAA sustainable quality program aims to improve production quality standards; Dow's safer operations and emergency preparedness program in China aims to increase safety standards; Unilever's SustainabiliTea project aims to promote sustainable farming.

4. Trade Facilitation and Business Environment Improvement

Finally, it is important to facilitate the flows between the different links of the GVC. A number of projects pertain to trade facilitation, such as the Global Express Association's work to improve risk assessment at customs in Latin America. Trade facilitation could also be interpreted in a broader sense to include the removal of nontrade barriers, such as the fight against road insecurity (Total's road safety project in Africa) or corruption (Diageo's business coalition against corruption in Cameroon).

Dynamic Effects of Global Development Chains

Transfers and capacity-building efforts that take place within GVCs have both direct and indirect or dynamic effects. While benefiting the company at the origin of the transfers, the capacity-building efforts to improve infrastructure or the business environment can be expected to have positive spillover effects on the local economy at large. It is also easier to evaluate the impact of private sector–led projects since the company aims to increase its benefits and therefore needs a return on "investment."

Potential spillover effects are most obvious in the case of hard capacities, such as infrastructure: for example, the German Technical Cooperation Agency (GTZ) analyzed the economic, environmental, and social impact of BASF investments in the region of Nanjing, China, and observed positive spillover effects for the local population, including through the use of new transport and power facilities (Kurz and Schmidkonz 2005). Such spillover effects also exist for soft capacities, such as knowledge: for example, the partnership between the United Nations Industrial Development Organization (UNIDO) and Hewlett-Packard (HP) has created over 17,000 jobs and trained more than 42,000 students to convert their business plans into commercial ventures. Sometimes investment programs also include development projects not directly linked to the investment itself that benefit the local community at large: for example, Barrick launched an initiative in Argentina to help farmers in mining regions where it invested to develop a sustainable sun-dried tomato business—thereby also raising the available income of households by offering job opportunities to the wives of their mine employees (World Bank 2011). In its SAGCOT project in Tanzania, the World Economic Forum and its partners adopted a holistic approach to foreign investment, with the objective of adding 420,000 jobs and US$1.2 billion in annual farming income, and lifting 2 million out of poverty (World Bank 2011).

The evaluation of AFT has long been a challenge for the donor community (see e.g., OECD 2010). Global development chains offer new perspectives for evaluation, since private sector capacity-building efforts need to generate commercial benefits. The case stories described earlier provide good examples of impact evaluation, with precise data on the number of jobs created, income generated, productivity gains, exports, and other information. Those who do trade are best able to measure the impact of trade capacity-building efforts. Those measurements can pertain to the international business's benefits and productivity gains, as well as the benefits to local contractors: for example, it is estimated that the PepsiCo Educampo project in Mexico led to an 80 percent increase in local farmers' productivity and a 300 percent increase in income (World Bank 2011).

A New Role for Trade and Development Policies

Global development chains call for a new role for trade and development policies, including AFT (OECD 2012). If GVCs are a major source of trade and socioeconomic upgrading opportunities, trade and development policies can help developing countries to participate in such chains, facilitate the transfers that take place within the chains, and promote forward and backward links. Similarly, if the consolidation of GVCs represents a major risk of exclusion for some developing countries, trade and development policies can aim to maintain those countries in GVCs by helping them improve productivity through the upgrading and task development required by lead firms.

Policies aimed at facilitating transfers within GVCs will differ depending on the type of transfer, from capital to technology to knowledge. In general terms, policies should be about improving business environment and the legal and regulatory framework for investment. Trade and private sector development (PSD) policies tend to be more closely aligned when trade policies tackle beyond-the-border issues. For example, it quickly became evident during the Uruguay Round of multilateral trade negotiations that "trade-related intellectual property rights" (TRIPS) covered most aspects of intellectual property protection: in the context of GVC development, the protection of intellectual property rights is essential to technology transfers. Other aspects include competition law, investment protection, and labor law.

In addition, global development chains can become a laboratory for successful trade and development projects owing to the "obligation of result" of the private sector. Collected case stories show significant (and measured) results, somewhat limited, however, to the level of ambition of the lead firms: for example, a foreign company can only train a limited number of engineers; revealed needs can create incentives for further training and capacity building by public authorities. A better coordination of public and private efforts can help scale up successful initiatives in the private sector.

CHANGES IN THE RELEVANT BARRIERS AND IMPETUS:
FROM PUBLIC TO PRIVATE

While most development thinking is state-centric, becoming part of a value chain is done by private actors. This is the fourth important change related to the emergence of global value chains. Firms, not governments, conduct international trade; firms organize the flows of capital, labor, and knowledge. The role of development policies is very different when states are no longer in charge of starting new economic activities but have to help domestic companies connect to global production networks. While governments must still ensure that they provide the right business-enabling environment, this might not be enough to reach suppliers, buyers, and consumers around the world. New types of policies have to be designed that facilitate the insertion of local actors into global networks.

Public versus Private Barriers in Access to World Markets

By moving from border to beyond-the-border barriers, trade policy has adjusted somewhat to the change in the relevant strategic framework, from countries to GVCs and firms. For example, in the area of competition law, the market of reference is not necessarily the domestic market of a single country: it could extend beyond the borders to include multiple trade partners (e.g., the European Union). Figure 13-12 shows the evolution of trade barriers over time, from the border to beyond the border, and from the public to the private sphere: private anticompetitive behaviors can affect the terms of trade as much as official quotas and taxes. Governments therefore moved into the regulation of such behaviors, creating standards, norms, and other rules that can become nontariff barriers to trade in the absence of regional or multilateral harmonization.

With the prevalence of GVCs, trade barriers have made a further step into the private sphere at the same time that they became truly borderless. For example, private standards have replaced public ones: while these standards are voluntary, lack of compliance can prevent companies from participating in GVCs. These standards might be adopted at the level of a profession, a consortium of firms, or a single lead firm—sometimes also under the umbrella of corporate social responsibility (CSR). For example, in the medical tourism sector, most countries have their own certification and accreditation rules for hospitals; however, an accreditation by the Joint Commission International (JCI) is often necessary to attract foreign pa-

FIGURE 13-12. The Evolution of Trade Barriers

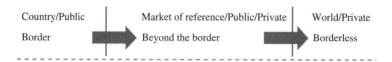

tients. The Global Food Safety Initiative (GFSI) provides another example of the importance of private standards and certification in the food industry (see next section). ISO standards are private, although widely used and recognized, including in public administrations.

In addition, some lead firms have enough leverage not only to impose their own standards (quality, labor conditions, sustainability, and the like), but also to challenge the normal functioning of the market. Depending on the type of network structure prevailing in a GVC—captive, relational, modular—the lead could become a price maker and the developing country providers could be confined to the role of price takers (Gereffi, Humphrey, and Sturgeon 2005). A farming contract, for instance, guarantees an income for smallholder farmers in developing countries, but also limits the potential benefits from major peaks in farm commodity prices. Some vertical agreements within GVCs might therefore present challenges from a competition law perspective. Land grabbing and the capture of scarce natural resources by foreign groups also raises concerns and objections.

Promoting the Convergence of the Public and Private Agendas

Trade and development policies need, once again, to adjust to the recent trends and changes in paradigm of business practice. GVCs provide both an opportunity and a risk for development: an opportunity because of the important transfers of all kinds that take place within GVCs and capacity-building efforts that are properly evaluated and could be scaled up to foster socioeconomic upgrading and development; a risk because of the consolidation phenomenon that threatens to reverse the process of worldwide division of labor, the predatory attitude of some lead firms in low-maturity GVCs, and the appearance of new forms of allegiance that threaten the normal functioning of markets. In other words, there is a case both for further recognizing and encouraging the role of the private sector and GVCs in trade capacity building, and for ensuring that GVCs promote fair, balanced, equitable, and sustainable development. The first step is for development partners and the private sector to agree on common objectives and the means to achieve them.

The G-20's Action Plan on Food Price Volatility and Agriculture, released in 2011, is a good illustration of the possible convergence of public and private agendas. The collection of over fifty case stories on private sector trade capacity-building efforts in the food and agriculture sector set the scene for the private sector in action. Fairly quickly, the negotiations over the G-20 Action Plan developed a number of consensual principles, objectives, and priorities for action among the participants, which included international organizations, a CEO task force, and G-20 members. Their final recommendations revealed a high degree of convergence.

The final consensus reached by the G-20, the international organizations and the private sector should inspire future actions and partnerships in other sectors. In a number of places, the Action Plan calls for explicit public-private partnerships. For instance, the Action Plan encourages multilateral and regional development banks to continue supporting country-owned development strategies and further strengthen their engagement with the private sector. From its inception, the Action Plan was conceived as a multistakeholder initiative on topics ranging from increasing production and productivity to promoting sustainable sourcing and production, improving business environments, strengthening markets and supply chains, and improving food safety and risk management.

Preventing Abuses of Dominant Positions within GVCs

The ability of public and private sectors to agree on common objectives and priorities for action should not minimize the difficulty of the task and the diversity of incentives and goals among lead firms and GVCs. The main objective of private firms remains profit, whereas the main driver of public actions should be the public good. Thus relationships within GVCs can be unbalanced and not always in the interests of the developing countries if, for instance, a lead firm abuses its dominant position. GVCs can be the scene of emergence of new barriers to trade that are more difficult to identify and remove.

Vertical agreements and anticompetitive behaviors within GVCs are frequent, and not all countries have sophisticated enough competition laws or enforcement mechanisms to monitor or remedy them. Similarly, lack of transparency in procurement rules can be unfair to small business. With regard to investment, a number of initiatives were launched to agree on "responsible investment principles." For example, the Extractive Industries Transparency Initiative (EITI) is a coalition of governments, companies, civil society groups, investors, and international organizations that promotes transparency and good governance in the extraction of natural resources and the use of its revenues; in the agricultural sector, the United Nations Conference on Trade and Development (UNCTAD), the Food and Agriculture Organization (FAO), the International Fund for Agricultural Development (IFAD), and the World Bank have jointly developed a set of Principles for Responsible Agricultural Investment (PRAI) that respects rights, livelihoods, and resources; and the UN Global Compact asks companies to embrace, support, and enact, within their sphere of influence, a set of core values in the areas of human rights, labor standards, the environment, and anticorruption.

Most of those initiatives are nonbinding sets of principles and recommendations (i.e., soft law). Thus the challenge of regulating new barriers to trade in GVCs remains. Paradoxically, the so-called Singapore issues (trade facilitation, competition, transparency in government procurement, and investment) that were once in the Doha Development Agenda and withdrawn (with the exception of trade facilitation) from the negotiations mandate in 2003, would have been the most relevant set of rules for dealing with new barriers to trade that are inherent in business relationships within GVCs.

A New Distribution of Public and Private Roles

Notwithstanding those risks, the potential of global development chains is important, and it appears more than ever useful to combine public and private forces to build trade capacity in developing countries. Progress could be easily made on a joint trade capacity-building agenda given the importance of already existing efforts. Some projects already coordinate or combine public and private actions. A more systematic and organized dialogue could be established with a view to:

- *Sharing information about initiatives pertaining to trade capacity building.* This effort would respond to the lack of awareness in governments of what the private sector is doing, and vice versa. Concretely, it would consist in the designation of contact points and regular online posting of case stories presenting initiatives undertaken jointly by the public sector, the private sector, and nongovernmental organizations (NGOs).

- *Fostering leadership and operational-level dialogue among public and private sector actors as well as NGOs to identify and agree on shared priorities for action.* Each actor might have access to different types of information or data that would help others better identify the problems and solutions. For instance, the private sector is best positioned to identify obstacles to the efficient functioning of markets (such as trade costs). Each could also bring its experience to the table to identify best practices and success stories that could be reproduced on a larger scale. Each also has specific responsibilities (e.g., the governments to adopt trade and investment enabling rules; multinational corporations to disseminate technologies and expertise).

- *Identifying opportunities for public-private-civil society collaboration to advance progress on agreed priorities, particularly to enable scaling up of effective models and leveraging of public sector funds to catalyze increased private sector investment.* Projects could be joint or merely better coordinated with each other.

- *Monitoring and assessing the impact of existing public and private sector or NGO trade capacity-building initiatives to share lessons and define best practices.*

All these objectives should be pursued with due regard to the priorities set by the recipient country or region in its development programs. Donors, the private sector, and NGOs should cooperate with local governments and actors, in particular smaller businesses and communities, to assist with their development plans and respond to their needs. Such cooperation should not exclude the active participation and assistance of international public and private actors in the elaboration of those development plans.

Figures 13-13 and 13-14 illustrate a change in paradigm in the provision of AFT to take into account the reality of the markets and the way trade takes place within GVCs. In the first scenario, the donor supports capacity building in the certification of rubber in Cambodia: the institutional change is valuable, but the post-project evaluation underlines the questions of the producers' capacities, the connection with international markets, and the financial sustainability of the newly created institutions (AFD 2009). This type of project is typical of the old paradigm, where AFT is supply-driven and used to raise the standards in developing countries,

FIGURE 13-13. Standards under the Old Aid for Trade Paradigm: Rubber Certification in Cambodia

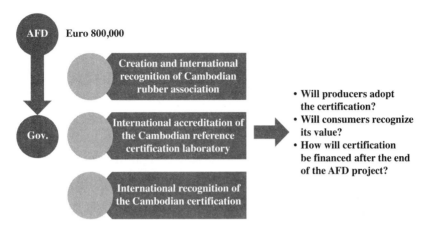

FIGURE 13-14. Standards under the New Paradigm of Aid for Trade: The Global Food Safety Initiative

Source: Authors, based on information from the Global Food Safety Initiative.

focused on institutional capacities, without sufficient connections with the private sector (upstream and downstream) and the markets. In the second scenario, the private sector is in the driver's seat, with global capacity-building programs that target small and less-developed businesses (SLDBs) around the world. Once certified following the guidelines of the Global Food Safety Initiative (GFSI), the products are recognized everywhere. This type of project is typical of the new paradigm, where capacity building is demand-driven, and participants in the initiative not only benefit from the capacity-building efforts made by a consortium of 650 stakeholders in seventy countries, but also get access to a market of over €2 trillion of sales (GFSI 2012). Of course, this type of project also raises questions pertaining to competition and relationships within GVCs, as noted earlier, but it is an example of coordination and results-oriented trade capacity-building efforts that could inspire other private and public interventions in developing countries.

CONCLUSION: ADAPTING AID FOR TRADE

Globalization and the prevalence of GVCs point at new development paths. Tasks that were previously executed in developed countries can now be outsourced to developing countries, creating local jobs and value added, encouraging knowledge and technology transfers, and other advancements. The more mature GVCs have become a major channel for socioeconomic upgrading in developing countries. However, in the consolidation phase of GVCs the number of beneficiaries of transfers will shrink, and only those developing countries that are able to offer the appropriate "bundle of tasks" will remain in the game; others will be excluded from major trade flows. Moreover, relationships within GVCs might raise competition and other issues pertaining to the privatization of standards that have not yet been tackled by public policy.

It is time for trade and development policies to adjust to these new business practices to maximize the opportunities and minimize the risks associated with the successive waves of fragmentation and consolidation of global production. Maximizing the opportunities means facilitating all kinds of transfers (including capital, knowledge, and technology) from lead firms to small producers in developing countries, promoting foreign investment, and securing socioeconomic upgrades through the capture of higher-value-added segments of production. Minimizing the risks means defining the rules for responsible investment and due respect of competition within GVCs, as well as supporting adjustment to the changing needs of those who conduct trade (e.g., by diversifying tasks in order to remain in the game when global production enters the consolidation phase).

Accordingly, trade development strategies should change. Old references have become obsolete: the relevant strategic framework has shifted from countries to firms and GVCs; the relevant economic framework has shifted from industries to tasks and business functions; the relevant economic assets have become flows rather than stocks and endowments; and the relevant barriers to trade and the impetus have shifted from public to private. These changes will need to operate in a context that is particularly difficult for aid policies in general, owing to the budget and debt crises faced by traditional donors. At the same time, crises might prompt changes that bring greater efficiency and facilitate monitoring and evaluation of AFT projects.

The successful transformation of global value chains into global development chains will take time and eventually happen with the maturity of international business, or it will require more cooperation between the public and private sectors. Joining forces in trade capacity building should help increase the efficiency and accountability of public aid, as well as the scaling up of successful private sector initiatives, and prevent behaviors that would adversely affect socioeconomic upgrading prospects in developing countries. Global development chains are responsible global value chains with a higher value for trade.

REFERENCES

Agence Française de Développement (AFD). 2009. "Projet d'appui à la certification et à la commercialisation du caoutchouc au Cambodge." *Fiche de Performance des Projets Post-évalués.* Paris: AFD.

Agmon, T. 1979. "Direct Investment and Intra-Industry Trade: Substitutes or Complements." In *On the Economics of Intra-Industry Trade*, edited by H. Giersch, 3–38. Tübingen, Germany: JCB Mohr.

Antràs, P., and E. Helpman. 2004. "Global Sourcing." *Journal of Political Economy* 112 (3): 552–80.

Appelbaum, R. P., and G. Gereffi. 1994. "Power and Profits in the Apparel Commodity Chain." In *Global Production: the Apparel Industry in the Pacific Rim*, edited by Bonacich and others, 42–64. Temple University Press.

Bair, J. 2005. "Global Capitalism and Commodity Chains: Looking Back, Going Forward." *Competition and Change* 9 (2): 153–80.

Bair, J., and G. Gereffi. 2001. "Local Clusters in Global Value Chains: The Causes and Consequences of Export Dynamism in Torreon's Blue Jeans Industry." *World Development* 29 (11): 1885–1903.

Baldwin, R. 2006. "Globalisation: The Great Unbundling(s)." Contribution to the project Globalisation Challenges for Europe and Finland, organised by the Secretariat of the Economic Council. https://julkaisut .valtioneuvosto.fi/handle/10024/80508.

———. 2012. "Global Supply Chains: Why They Emerged, Why They Matter, and Where They Are Going. CEPR Discussion Paper 9103. London: Centre for Economic Policy Research. August.

Baldwin, R., and S. Evenett. 2012. "Value Creation and Trade in 21st Century Manufacturing: What Policies for UK Manufacturing?" In *The UK in a Global World: How Can the UK Focus on Steps in Global Value Chains That Really Add Value?*, edited by David Greenaway, 71–128. London: Centre for Economic Policy Research.

Bernard, A., and others. 2007. "Firms in International Trade." *Journal of Economic Perspectives* 21 (3): 105–30.

Bernard, A., M. Grazzi, and C. Tomasi. 2011. "Intermediaries in International Trade: Direct versus Indirect Modes of Export." NBER Working Paper 17711. Cambridge, Mass.: National Bureau of Economic Research, December.

Cattaneo, O., G. Gereffi, and C. Staritz, eds. 2010. *Global Value Chains in a Postcrisis World: A Development Perspective.* Washington, D.C.: World Bank.

Coe, N. M., P. Dicken, and M. Hess. 2008. "Global Production Networks: Realizing the Potential." *Journal of Economic Geography* 8 (3): 271–95.

Coe, N. M., and M. Hess. 2007. "Global Production Networks: Debates and Challenges." Paper prepared for the GPERG workshop, University of Manchester.

Dietzenbacher, E., and I. Romero. 2007. "Production Chains in an Interregional Framework: Identification by Means of Average Propagations Lengths." *International Regional Science Review* 30 (4): 362–83.

Fold, Niels, and Marianne Nylandsted Larsen. 2008. "Key Concepts and Core Issues in Global Value Chain Analysis." In *Globalization and Restructuring of African Commodity Flows*, edited by Niels Fold and Marianne Nylandsted Larsen, 26–43. Uppsala: Nordiska Afrikainstitutet.

Frederick, S. 2010. "Development and Application of a Value Chain Research Approach to Understand and Evaluate Internal and External Factors and Relationships Affecting Economic Competitiveness in the Textile Value Chain." PhD dissertation, North Carolina State University.

Gereffi, G. 1994. "The Organization of Buyer-Driven Global Commodity Chains: How US Retailers Shape Overseas Production Networks." In *Commodity Chains and Global Capitalism*, edited by G. Gereffi and M. Korzeniewicz, 95–122. Westport, Conn.: Praeger.

———. 1999. "International Trade and Industrial Upgrading in the Apparel Commodity Chain." *Journal of International Economics* 48 (1): 37–70.

Gereffi, G., and K. Fernandez-Stark 2010. "The Offshore Services Value Chain: Developing Countries and the Crisis." In *Global Value Chains in a Post-crisis World. A Development Perspective*, edited by O. Cattaneo, G. Gereffi, and C. Staritz, 335–72. Washington, D.C.: World Bank.

———. 2016. *Global Value Chains Analysis: A Primer.* 2nd ed. Duke Center on Globalization, Governance and Competitiveness. Duke University.

Gereffi, G., J. Humphrey, and T. Sturgeon. 2005. "The Governance of Global Value Chains." *Review of International Political Economy* 12 (1): 78–104.

Global Food Safety Initiative (GFSI). 2012. *GFSI Guidance Document.* 6th ed., Issue 3, Version 6.2. Paris: GFSI.

Grossman, G., and E. Rossi-Hansberg. 2006. "The Rise of Offshoring: It's Not Wine for Cloth Anymore." In *The New Economic Geography: Effects and Policy Implications*, 59–102. Jackson Hole Conference Volume. Federal Reserve of Kansas City.

———. 2008. "Trading Tasks: A Simple Theory of Offshoring." *American Economic Review* 98 (5): 1978–97.

Grossmann, V., and D. Stadelmann. 2012. "Wage Effects of High Skilled Migration: International Evidence." IZA Discussion Paper 6611. Bonn, Germany: Institute for the Study of Labor. May.

Grubel, H., and P. Lloyd. 1975. *Intra-Industry Trade: The Theory and Measurement of International Trade with Differentiated Products.* London: Macmillan.

Haddad, M., and B. Shepherd. 2011. *Managing Openness: Trade and Outward-Oriented Growth after the Crisis.* Washington, D.C.: World Bank.

Havranek, T., and Z. Irsova. 2011. "Estimating Vertical Spillovers from FDI: Why Results Vary and What the True Effect Is." *Journal of International Economics* 85 (2): 234–44.

Henderson, J., and others. 2002. "Global Production Networks and the Analysis of Economic Development." *Review of International Political Economy* 9 (3): 436–64.

Hopkins, T., and I. Wallerstein. 1977. "Patterns of Development of the Modern World-System." *Review* 1 (2): 111–45.

Hudson, R. 2004. "Conceptualizing Economies and Their Geographies: Spaces, Flows and Circuits." *Progress in Human Geography* 28: 447–71.

Hummels, D., J. Ishii, and K. M. Yi. 2001. "The Nature and Growth of Vertical Specialization in World Trade." *Journal of International Economics* 54 (1): 75–96.

Humphrey, J., and H. Schmitz. 2002. "How Does Insertion in Global Value Chains Affect Upgrading in Industrial Clusters?" *Regional Studies* 36 (9): 1017–27.

Jefferson, G. 2008. "How Has China's Economic Emergence Contributed to the Field of Economics?" *Comparative Economic Studies* 50 (2): 167–209.

Jin, K. 2012. "Industrial Structure and Capital Flows." *American Economic Review* 102 (5): 2111–46.

Jones, C. 2011. "Intermediate Goods and Weak Links in the Theory of Economic Development," *American Economic Journal: Macroeconomics* 3 (April): 1–28.

Jones, R., and H. Kierzkowski. 1990. "The Role of Services in Production and International Trade: A Theoretical Framework." In *The Political Economy of International Trade*, edited by R. Jones and A. Krueger, 31–48. Oxford: Basil Blackwell.

———. 2001. "A Framework for Fragmentation." In *Fragmentation: New Production Patterns in the World Economy*, edited by S. Arndt and H. Kierzkowski, 17–34. Oxford University Press.

———. 2005. "International Fragmentation and the New Economic Geography." *North American Journal of Economics and Finance* 16 (1): 1–10.

Kaplinsky, R. 2010. "The Role of Standards in Global Value Chains." Policy Research Working Paper 5396. Washington, D.C.: World Bank.

Kaplinsky, R., and M. Morris. 2001. *A Handbook for Value Chain Research* http:// asiandrivers.open.ac.uk/documents/Value_chain_Handbook_RKMM _Nov_2001.pdf.

Kaplinsky, R., A. Terheggen, and J. Tijaja, 2010, "What Happens When the Market Shifts to China? The Gabon Timber and Thai Cassava Value Chains." In *Global Value Chains in a Postcrisis World. A Development Perspective*, edited by O. Cattaneo, G. Gereffi, and C. Staritz, 303–44. Washington, D.C.: World Bank.

Keller, W. 2004. "International Technology Diffusion." *Journal of Economic Literature* 42 (3): 752–82.

Krueger, A. O. 1997. "Trade Policy and Economic Development: How We Learn." *American Economic Review* 87 (1): 1–22.

Krugman, P. 2002. "Was It All in Ohlin?" In *Bertil Ohlin: A Centennial Celebration (1899–1999)*, edited by R. Findlay, L. Jonung, and M. Lundhal, 389–406. MIT Press. Kurz, S., and C. Schmidkonz. 2005. *The Impact of Direct Investment of BASF in Nanjing, China on the Sustainable Develop-*

ment of the Region. Bonn, Germany: German Technical Cooperation Agency (GTZ).

Lanz, R., and S. Miroudot. 2011. "Intra-firm Trade: Patterns, Determinants and Policy Implications." OECD Trade Policy Working Paper 114. Paris: OECD Publishing.

Lanz, R., S. Miroudot, and H. Nordås. 2012. "Offshoring of Tasks: Taylorism versus Toyotism." *World Economy*. DOI: 10.1111/twec.12024.

Leontief, W., and A. Strout. 1963. "Multiregional Input-Output Analysis." In *Structural Interdependence and Economic Development*, edited by T. Barna, 119–50. New York: St. Martin's.

Loungani, P., and others. "World Trade in Services: Evidence from a New Dataset." IMF Working Paper WP/17/77. Washington, D.C.: International Monetary Fund.

Lucas, R. 1988. "On the Mechanics of Economic Development." *Journal of Monetary Economy* 22 (1): 3–42.

———. 1990. "Why Doesn't Capital Flow from Rich to Poor Countries?" *American Economic Review* 80 (2): 92–96.

Mattoo, A., and L. Payton. 2007. *Services Trade and Development: The Experience of Zambia*. Washington, D.C.: World Bank.

Melitz, M. J. 2003. "The Impact of Trade on Intra-Industry Reallocations and Aggregate Industry Productivity." *Econometrica* 71 (6): 1695–1725.

Messerlin, P., and others. 2011. "Lessons from a Meta-Evaluation of Aid for Trade" Paris: Groupe d'Economie Mondiale.

Miroudot, S., and K. de Backer. 2013. "Mapping Global Value Chains." OECD Trade Policy Papers 159. Paris: OECD Publishing.

Miroudot, S., and C. Cadestin. 2017. "Services In Global Value Chains: From Inputs to Value-Creating Activities." OECD Trade Policy Paper 197. Paris: OECD Publishing.

Miroudot, S., R. Lanz, and A. Ragoussis. 2009. "Trade in Intermediate Goods and Services." OECD Trade Policy Working Paper 93. Paris: OECD Publishing.

Miroudot, S., and A. Ragoussis. 2009. "Vertical Trade, Trade Costs and FDI." OECD Trade Policy Working Paper 89. Paris: OECD Publishing.

National Board of Trade. 2010. "At Your Service. The Importance of Services for Manufacturing Companies and Possible Trade Policy Implications." *Kommerskollegium* 2010:2. www.kommerskollegium.se/globalassets/.

Ohlin, B. 1933. *Interregional and International Trade*. Harvard University Press.

Organization for Economic Cooperation and Development (OECD). 2011. *Strengthening Accountability in Aid for Trade*. Paris: OECD Publishing.

————. 2012. *Managing Aid to Achieve Trade and Development Results: An Analysis of Trade-Related Targets*. COM/DCD/TAD(2012)12/FINAL. Paris: OECD.

Organization for Economic Cooperation and Development and World Trade Organization. 2012. *Trade in Value-Added: Concepts, Methodologies and Challenges*. Paris and Geneva: OECD and WTO.

Porter, M. E. 1985. *The Competitive Advantage: Creating and Sustaining Superior Performance*. New York: Free Press.

Sanyal, K., and R. Jones. 1982. "The Theory of Trade in Middle Products." *American Economic Review* 72 (1): 16–31.

Staritz, C., G. Gereffi, and O. Cattaneo. 2011. "Shifting End Markets and Upgrading Prospects in Global Value Chains." *International Journal of Technological Learning, Innovation and Development* 4 (1/2/3): 1–12.

Timmer, M. P., S. Miroudot, and G. J. de Vries. 2019. "Functional Specialisation in Trade." *Journal of Economic Geography* 19 (1): 1–30.

Vandermerwe, S., and J. Rada. 1988. "Servitization of Business: Adding Value by Adding Services." *European Management Journal* 6 (4): 314–24.

Winters, L. A. 2000. "Trade Policy as Development Policy: Building on Fifty Years' Experience." Paper prepared for the Tenth United Nations Conference on Trade and Development. Bangkok.

World Bank. 2011. *The Role of International Business in Aid for Trade: Building Capacity for Trade in Developing Countries*. Washington, D.C.

Yeats, Alexander. 1997. "Just How Big is Global Production Sharing?" World Bank Policy Research Paper No. 1871. Washington, D.C.

Yi, K. M. 2003. "Can Vertical Specialization Explain the Growth of World Trade?" *Journal of Political Economy* 111 (1): 52–102.

14

THE AID FOR TRADE INITIATIVE

A WTO ATTEMPT AT COHERENCE

JEAN-JACQUES HALLAERT

C ollaboration with the Bretton Woods Institutions "with a view to achieving greater coherence in global economic policymaking" (i.e., coherence) is one of the five formal functions of the World Trade Organization (WTO).[1] But achieving coherence is not easy. It often involves high transaction costs for little result (Winters 2007). The Aid for Trade Initiative is arguably the strongest WTO attempt at coherence: coherence among trade policy, aid policy, and development policy.

This history of the Aid for Trade Initiative discusses how coherence has been understood and implemented, and how it has evolved. Developing countries' experience with the Uruguay Round of trade negotiations led them to request that promises of technical and financial assistance in implementing a multilateral agreement be met with more than just lip service. The WTO could not ignore this request but could not respond to it either and therefore entered into a collaboration with other organizations and agencies that led to the Aid for Trade Initiative. I discuss the choices made in shaping the initiative, their implications, and the impact of the stalled Doha Round negotiations. In its Aid for Trade Work Programme for 2012–2013, the WTO implicitly acknowledged that little coherence in policymaking had been achieved but did not attempt to change the situation, limiting itself to calling donors to consider the trade dimension of their new development priorities. More recently, the Trade Facilitation Agreement (TFA) offers the initiative an opportunity to address its challenges by focusing on clearly trade-related projects. But this opportunity may not be seized.

THE LEGACY: WHEN THE URUGUAY ROUND HAUNTS THE DOHA ROUND

Traditionally, developing countries have been suspicious of the contribution of trade to development. This suspicion was at the root of the opt-out strategy they followed in the General Agreement on Tariffs and Trade (GATT) round of trade negotiations. For two main reasons, developing countries were more active in the Doha Round negotiations than in previous rounds.

First, when the Doha Round negotiations started in 2001, trade appeared to be a possible engine for growth and poverty reduction. The success of small export-oriented East Asian countries was followed by the success of large countries like China.

Second, the Uruguay Round had demonstrated that opting out was no longer cost-free. As long as the multilateral trade negotiations were limited to tariffs, the opt-out strategy had no visible cost. Thanks to the unconditional most-favored-nation clause, a developing country could benefit from other countries' tariff cuts even if it did not reduce its own tariffs. There were hidden costs, though. Opting out of GATT rules and relying on preferential market access in practice limited developing countries' bargaining power in the negotiations but did little to foster their exports and even hampered their export diversification. Since developing countries lost the capacity to negotiate tariff cuts on the goods they exported, it is not surprising that the negotiated tariff cuts did not cover agricultural goods and left largely untouched the high protection for labor-intensive products such as shoes, textiles, and apparel. In the Uruguay Round, when trade rules were extended to cover textiles and agriculture, developing countries gained a strong incentive to be involved in the negotiations because they were in part about market access for their main exports.

Moreover, starting with the Uruguay Round, opting out no longer meant being exempted from commitments. Because the Uruguay Round created a new international organization—the WTO—to replace the temporary GATT, all members had to accept all the provisions of the agreement. This principle, which also governed the Doha Round negotiations, implied that developing countries would adhere to legally binding commitments on issues such as sanitary and phytosanitary standards (SPS), technical barriers to trade (TBT), trade-related aspects of intellectual property rights (TRIPS), and customs valuation.[2] These commitments required substantial and costly policy and administrative reforms. The possibility that the WTO could negotiate, and that those negotiations could lead to new commitments on issues such as labor or environmental standards or the "Singapore issues" (competition, investment, government procurement, and trade facilitation), further increased developing countries' incentives to be active in the negotiations. They initially adopted a defensive posture. For example, the Like Minded Group, a coalition of developing countries, organized itself at the 1996 Ministerial Conference in Singapore to prevent labor standards from becoming part of the WTO negotiations. This coalition also tried to block the launch of a new round from 1998 to 2001 (Jones 2010).

When the Doha Round was eventually launched in 2001, developing countries expressed concerns about the potential adjustment and implementation costs of the agreement under negotiation. They forcefully requested both technical and financial support. Their concerns were largely the result of their experience with the Uruguay Round.

The benefits they had expected the Uruguay Round to provide for their exports of agricultural goods and textiles and apparel did not materialize. The "dirty tariffication" of agricultural nontariff barriers[3] and the special agricultural safeguards, combined with other protectionist devices such as quotas and tariff escalation, large subsidies, and SPS, had in effect limited their access to rich countries' markets. The phasing out of the Multi-Fiber Arrangement (MFA) quotas that had distorted trade in textiles and apparel for decades was in practice delayed to 2005, and only a few countries were able to seize the opportunities of the liberalization. Therefore, in the Doha Round, developing countries requested support to build the trade capacity they need to turn the trade opportunities of a Doha Round agreement into trade flows.

In contrast, the implementation costs of the Uruguay Round agreement were visible. The agreements on SPS, TRIPS, and customs valuation were costly and difficult to implement, diverting limited resources and capacities from other projects that were arguably more important for development (Finger and Schuler 2000). As a result, most developing countries did not, or could not, comply with their obligations. In 2000, according to Stiglitz and Charlton (2005), 90 of the 109 WTO developing country members were in violation of SPS, TRIPS, or customs valuation agreements. This experience prompted their calls for financial and technical assistance so that countries could implement both the Uruguay Round commitments and the expected Doha Round commitments.

Developing countries also requested support to mitigate the perceived adjustment costs from an agreement. Mauritius, which was expected to be significantly affected by the end of the textiles quotas and by the erosion of preferences on sugar, suggested the creation of a compensation mechanism to address the impact of preference erosion. Net food-importing developing countries expressed concerns about the impact of a price increase following the negotiated elimination of agricultural subsidies.

Finally, developing countries requested that support take the form of *actual* assistance, not *promises* of assistance. This was another legacy of the Uruguay Round. As summarized by Finger (2007), developing countries' experience was that "the Uruguay Round agreements imposed bound commitments to implement, but provide only unbound promises of assistance." The Uruguay Round agreement included:

- *A promise to enable developing countries to turn the trade opportunities of the agreement into trade.* In the Decision on Measures in Favour of Least-Developed Countries (LDCs), ministers agreed that LDCs "shall be accorded substantially increased technical assistance in the development, strengthening and diversification of their production and export bases including those of services, as well as in trade promotion, to enable them to maximize the benefits from liberalized access to markets."[4]

- *A promise to implement the agreements.* The agreements on TBT,[5] on the application of SPS measures,[6] on customs valuations,[7] and on TRIPS[8] all have articles indicating that developing countries *should* receive assistance.

- *A promise to help developing countries cope with the adjustment costs.* In the Decision on Measures Concerning the Possible Negative Effects of the Reform Programme on Least-Developed and Net Food-Importing Developing Countries, ministers agreed "to give full consideration in the context of their aid programmes to requests for the provision of technical and financial assistance to least-developed and net food-importing developing countries to improve their agricultural productivity and infrastructure."[9]

Because they were unfunded, nonbinding, and unenforceable, these promises were, however, soon forgotten.

In sum, developing countries' requests for financial and technical assistance in the Doha Round were both a legacy of the Uruguay Round and the result of the expansion of the WTO to behind-the-border issues. The novelty is that developing countries made forceful requests that the promises of technical assistance be fulfilled.

PROMOTING COHERENCE BETWEEN AID, TRADE, AND DEVELOPMENT: TOO MUCH FOR THE WTO SECRETARIAT ALONE

Developing countries' requests for assistance in the Doha Round negotiations could not be ignored, for three main reasons.

First, following the failure in 1999 of the WTO Ministerial Conference in Seattle to launch the Millennium Round of trade negotiations, the WTO emphasized the development dimension of trade to garner enough support for a new round, called the Doha Development Agenda (DDA) or the Development Round. Technical and financial support was an important component of the development dimension, and the Ministerial Declaration that launched the Doha Round states: "We have established *firm commitments* on technical cooperation and capacity building in various paragraphs in this Ministerial Declaration. We . . . reaffirm . . . the important role of sustainably financed technical assistance and capacity-building programmes."[10]

Second, developing countries had demonstrated their readiness to block an agreement if they perceived that their interests and concerns were not sufficiently taken into account. The Like Minded Group had made the resolution of the Uruguay Round implementation issues a condition for the launch of a new round (Jones 2010). In 1999 at the WTO Ministerial Conference in Seattle, developing countries opposed the launch of a round that would discuss labor standards. In 2003, the WTO Ministerial Conference in Cancún collapsed in part because developing countries felt that the draft texts did not reflect their priorities.

Third, developing countries agreed that trade facilitation would be part of the Doha Round negotiations only in 2004 and on the condition that aid would be provided. The "modalities for the negotiations on trade facilitation" (WTO 2004) include commitments to provide developing countries with support as early as the negotiation phase: "It is recognized that the provision of technical assistance and support for capacity-building is vital for developing and least-developed countries to enable them to fully participate in and benefit from the negotiations. Members, in particular developed countries, therefore commit themselves to adequately ensure such support and assistance during the negotiations."[11] More important, the implementation of the agreement was, from the start, explicitly conditional on the country capacities to do so and thus on the availability of support to build this capacity: "It is understood, . . . that in cases where required support and assistance . . . is not forthcoming, and where a developing or least-developed Member continues to lack the necessary capacity, implementation will not be required" (WTO 2004). As a result, the Trade Facilitation Agreement concluded in December 2013 dramatically changed the approach to special and differential treatment: instead of providing exemptions and transition periods, it explicitly links the implementation of the agreement by developing countries to the provision of adequate assistance in building the necessary capacity.[12]

In this context, "providing something to developing countries had become of paramount importance politically—in most eyes it had become the *sine qua non* for completing the Round" (Winters 2007). But what should be provided and how?

The WTO could not itself respond to the requests for financial support. It is not an aid agency, and both the link between trade and development and the management of adjustment costs belong on the agenda of other international institutions. Answering developing countries' calls therefore required cooperating with other organizations and the development community; it required coherence.

Other organizations and donors stood ready to help. In an example of coherence, in 2004 the International Monetary Fund (IMF) established the Trade Integration Mechanism (TIM) to "mitigate concerns that implementation of the WTO agreements might give rise to temporary balance of payments shortfall" (IMF 2004). The IMF established the TIM to facilitate the Doha Round negotiations, despite its assessment that preference erosion or fiscal revenue losses from tariff cuts would be a problem only for a few countries. The IMF assessment of losses from preference erosion was presented in a communication to the WTO (IMF 2003). Later, in response to the Hong Kong Ministerial declaration calling for more analysis of the scope of the tariff dependency problem, the IMF published estimates of fiscal revenue losses from various tariff-cutting formulas considered in the negotiations (Elborgh-Woytek and others 2006). In the absence of a Doha Round agreement, only three countries requested and obtained support under the TIM (Bangladesh, the Dominican Republic, and Madagascar). In all cases, the assistance was intended to mitigate the impact of the end of the MFA quotas.

The development community was also ready to embrace the calls to supplement its usual activities with efforts to promote trade as an engine for development. Donors have long financed projects that have an impact on trade, but, with a few exceptions, this impact was less an objective than a side effect. In the early 2000s, the situation had changed. Donors were facing calls to scale up aid to reach the Millennium Development Goals (MDGs), as well as growing evidence that aid alone might not boost growth (Easterly 2001, 2003; Calì and te Velde 2011) and could even make matters worse (Rajan and Subramanian 2005). Thus they were looking for ways to go beyond the double-gap model (Chenery and Strout 1966) emphasizing that money alone is not the answer and aid effectiveness is crucial, arguments that led to the principles of the Paris Declaration on Aid Effectiveness in 2005 (OECD 2005).

Against this background, the aid to support trade projects appealed to donors. Aid for trade could be branded as an effort to reach the MDGs.[13] Moreover, aid for trade had the potential to be very effective. The aid and growth literature and the trade and growth literature were both providing new empirical evidence on ways to increase the impact of aid and trade on economic growth and poverty reduction. Moreover, they were providing intellectual support to the need to achieve coherence among trade policy, aid policy, and development policy.

In the early 2000s, there was mounting evidence that aid does more for economic growth and poverty reduction in a good policy environment and that effectiveness depends on "complementary policies."[14] The importance of complementary policies was echoed in the trade and growth literature. Complementary policies had long been recognized by trade economists as a factor that determines the impact of a trade reform on both trade and growth. However, their role had been challenging to show empirically in cross-country analyses. In the first half of the 2000s, developments in econometric techniques allowed this to be done (Hallaert 2006). Chang, Kaltani, and Loayza (2005) showed that the positive impact of trade on growth is larger if it is accompanied by improvements in education and infrastructure, a deeper financial sector, and institutional and regulatory reforms. Bolaky and Freund (2004) found that the impact of trade liberalization is greater if it is accompanied by regulatory reform. These findings prompted trade economists to emphasize more vigorously the role of complementary policies and the role aid could play in improving the ability of developing countries to use trade for growth and poverty reduction (Hallaert 2010; Hoekman 2007; Hoekman and Olarreaga 2007; Hoekman and Prowse 2005; Prowse 2005; Winters, McCulloch, and McKay 2004).

By 2005, the political economy was ripe for the launch of an aid-for-trade initiative. Several high-profile reports were published that year detailing the rationale for an initiative that would focus on alleviating the constraints that prevent developing countries from benefiting from trade opportunities and making trade a tool to reach the growth needed to achieve the MDGs: the UN Millennium Task Force on Trade report of which Patrick Messerlin was a lead author (United Nations Millennium Project 2005); a report supported by the UK Department for International Development (Zedillo and others 2005); the report of the Commission for Africa (2005) and a report commissioned by Sweden on developing countries and the WTO (Page and Kleen 2005).

The intellectual advocacy was accompanied by political commitments. In May 2005, the Group of 8 (G-8) heads of government committed "to increase our help to developing countries to build the physical, human and institutional capacity to trade, including trade facilitation measures" and "called on the IFIs to submit proposals to the annual meetings for additional assistance to countries to develop their capacity to trade and ease adjustment in their economies" (G-8 2005). A few weeks earlier at the IMF-World Bank spring meetings, the Development Committee stressed the need for aid for trade and called "on the Bank and Fund to work with others to develop proposals to help developing countries adjust to and take advantage of the round, for consideration by our next meeting" (IMF and World Bank 2005a). At the annual meetings in September 2005, the IMF and World Bank staff's proposal to provide more aid for trade capacity building was endorsed (IMF and World Bank 2005b). Then, in December 2005 at the WTO Ministerial Conference in Hong Kong, the Aid for Trade Initiative was officially launched.

The Ministerial Declaration (WTO 2005) reflects the interests and objectives of both the WTO ("Aid for Trade should aim to help developing countries, particularly LDCs, to build the supply-side capacity and trade-related infrastructure that they need to assist them to implement and benefit from WTO Agreements and more broadly to expand their trade") and donors ("Aid for Trade cannot be a substitute for the development benefits that will result from a successful conclusion to the DDA, particularly on market access. However, it can be a valuable complement to the DDA").

HOW TO DELIVER AID FOR TRADE?
A COHERENCE CHALLENGE

The first challenge for coherence was how to deliver aid for trade. The Integrated Framework for Trade-Related Technical Assistance to Least-Developed Countries (IF) was an obvious channel through which to provide aid, to implement a multilateral trade agreement, and to deal with its implementation costs. The IF, an early attempt at policy coherence, is an initiative of six multilateral institutions (IMF, International Trade Center (ITC), UN Conference on Trade and Development (UNCTAD), UN Development Program (UNDP), World Bank, and WTO) that was set up in 1997 to help with the delivery of trade-related technical assistance in response to the needs identified by each LDC. Thus the Development Committee of the World Bank and the IMF argued that the IF should deliver aid for trade. In order to increase its firepower,[15] it was agreed at the 2005 IMF-World Bank annual meetings to provide the IF with $US200 million–400 million in additional resources (IMF and World Bank 2005b).

Others favored a different delivery mechanism. The lack of financial resources was not the only problem with the IF. It had disappointed many developing countries: it was not operational (in part because coordination issues had slowed down its action); it was plagued by high bureaucratic costs;

and it was limited to assistance to LDCs, whereas the requests for support in the Doha Round were made by developing countries. Therefore, many stakeholders favored another delivery mechanism that would be both sufficiently large and quickly operational. The EU, the OECD, the G-8, the WTO, and several bilateral donors supported the idea of an aid for trade initiative and donors pledged "more money than the IF had ever received" (Winters 2007).

This difference in views persisted at the WTO Ministerial in Hong Kong. Ministers launched the Aid for Trade Initiative but also indicated in their Declaration that they "continue to attach high priority to the effective implementation of the Integrated Framework (IF) and reiterate our endorsement of the IF as a viable instrument for LDCs' trade development, building on its principles of country ownership and partnership" (WTO 2005).

The Hong Kong Ministerial Declaration gave the WTO the mandate to shape the initiative, stressing the importance of collaborating with other institutions: "We invite the Director-General to create a task force that shall provide recommendations on how to operationalize Aid for Trade. The Task Force will provide recommendations . . . on how Aid for Trade might contribute most effectively to the development dimension of the DDA. We also invite the Director-General to consult with Members as well as with the IMF and World Bank, relevant international organisations and the regional development banks with a view to reporting . . . on appropriate mechanisms to secure additional financial resources for Aid for Trade" (WTO 2005).

The choice to give the WTO the lead in shaping, monitoring, and defining precisely the scope of the initiative was made by default. Although it was in the context of the Doha Round negotiations that developing countries' requests for support were most clearly expressed, the WTO has no expertise in delivering aid and no mandate to do so. But there was no other politically viable alternative. Developing countries feared that the IF would focus too much on market liberalization, while donors suspected that the UNDP would promote it too little (Winters 2007).

This choice had two major implications. First, the WTO put resource mobilization at the core of the initiative. Pascal Lamy, then head of the WTO, was clear: "Resource mobilization was really the focus of our efforts. . . . It must remain central" (WTO 2011a). The Hong Kong Declaration had instructed the WTO Director-General to do so because showing that financial resources are available was important to facilitate the

Doha Round negotiations. There was also an institutional motivation for the WTO to focus on resource mobilization—lobbying for more resources and monitoring the financial flows is all that the WTO Secretariat could do given the limits of its mandate.

The second implication was that donor coordination and coherence in policymaking could not be enforced, or even advocated, given the limit to the WTO mandate.[16] This problem was increased by the delivery mode that the task force recommended. The delivery mode was widely debated and involved virtually all donors (bilateral, multilateral, and regional) but also the Bretton Woods Institutions, the UN agencies, the Commonwealth Secretariat, and the OECD. The debate boiled down to the question of creating a dedicated fund or leaving aid for trade as part of regular official development assistance (ODA). Eventually, the latter was chosen.[17] This choice had the advantage of maximizing resource mobilization because it allows regular aid projects that are somewhat related to trade to be labeled as "aid for trade" and because some donors might have political or institutional difficulty funding a dedicated fund. It had the disadvantage that aid for trade is delivered in an uncoordinated manner leaving donors free to choose the projects they support, and do so on their terms. Therefore there is no coherence in the Aid for Trade Initiative, and collaboration between institutions and donors is largely limited to the preparation of the Global Review of Aid for Trade that takes place every two years.

"DEEPENING COHERENCE": FROM COHERENCE IN POLICYMAKING TO MAINTAINING AWARENESS OF THE ROLE OF TRADE IN DEVELOPMENT

The Aid for Trade Initiative succeeded in mobilizing a large amount of resources but, after five years, resource mobilization was at risk. Facing a fiscal crisis, many donors were cutting their development budgets. Moreover, because the Doha Round negotiations had stalled, the resources mobilized could not support the implementation of a multilateral agreement and instead were used to finance other projects, some of them only remotely related to trade. In this context—delivered on donors' terms through existing channels and without coordination—aid for trade was difficult to distinguish from other forms of aid. Its rationale was blurred, and many developing countries began to question the "additionality" of aid for trade (Hallaert 2013),[18] while for many donors, in the absence of a Doha Round agreement, trade capacity building was increasingly falling out of favor as new priorities emerged.

The WTO response was to expand the already broad scope of the initiative to cover donors' new priorities. In its Aid for Trade Work Programme for 2012–2013, titled "Deepening Coherence," the WTO claimed that donors' new priorities, such as gender empowerment, green growth, food security, energy, and climate change, could be part of aid for trade. It also gave a higher profile to topics—such as trade finance and the role of the private sector in development—that had always been part of the initiative but were attracting more attention (WTO 2011b).[19]

In the Work Programme, the WTO also called for donors to consider the trade dimension of their new priorities. Raising donors' and developing countries' awareness of the role trade can play in development is probably a major achievement of the Aid for Trade Initiative. As part of the 2009 monitoring exercise, the WTO and the OECD asked recipient countries to evaluate the role given to trade in their development strategy (OECD and WTO 2009). The answers suggest that awareness of trade as a development tool is extremely high, reaching levels unthinkable only two decades ago: 96 percent of developing countries claimed that they had mainstreamed trade in their development strategy. This is certainly an overestimate that reflects the bias of a monitoring exercise based on self-assessment; the assessment of outsiders is more nuanced. At the time that the OECD-WTO survey was conducted, UNCTAD (2009) wrote: "Mainstreaming trade into national development strategy is a major concern. . . . So far, only a minority of country-level plans includes trade-related policies and assistance among their priorities." A more recent UNDP study found that 85 percent of Poverty Reduction Strategy Papers (PRSPs) included a trade component, whereas only 25 percent had this in 2000 (UNDP 2011).[20] These more nuanced views are consistent with the IMF-World Bank joint assessments of the PRSPs.[21]

In the Work Programme, therefore, the WTO watered down significantly the meaning of coherence when applied to aid for trade. "Deepening coherence" was not about more or better coherence in policymaking but about lobbying donors to consider the trade dimension in their new objectives. In fact, coherence was conspicuous for its absence in the Work Programme. In paragraph 3, the WTO explains how aid for trade should work:

Operationalization of Aid for Trade lies in the hands of developing countries, regional economic communities (RECs) and their development partners. Mainstreaming of trade into national and regional development programmes helps ensure that demand for Aid for Trade is expressed in dialogues with development partners; demand against which Aid for Trade support can be aligned. Implementation of Aid for Trade programmes is multi-faceted, encompassing a diverse range of delivery mechanisms and development partner organizations including, *inter alia*, bilateral donors, international financial institutions (including the World Bank Group and regional development banks), RECs and multilateral agencies.

This paragraph acknowledges the diversity in delivery and in development partners, instead of stressing the need to ensure coherence in policymaking and aid delivery. Moreover, it does not mention any role for the WTO but repeats the utopian conception underlying the Paris Principles—that developing countries are expected to identify and prioritize their needs and sequence the implementation of projects. Donors would then benevolently align their support on these priorities. The burden of policy coherence was passed to the developing countries, a formidable task for countries that are often deemed to have insufficient capacities.

To some extent, in its Work Programme for 2012–2013 the WTO acknowledged the reality of aid for trade. The WTO Secretariat is not in an institutional position to push for coherence. Aid-for-trade resources are increasing, but they are delivered by donors on their terms without incentives for collaboration or coherence. Aid for trade is not any different from other form of ODA and suffers from the same flaws of lack of donor coordination and volatility.

WILL THE TRADE FACILITATION AGREEMENT BE A MISSED OPPORTUNITY TO REINVENT THE AID FOR TRADE INITIATIVE?

At the Ministerial in Bali in December 2013, the Doha Round delivered the first multilateral agreement since the creation of the WTO—the Trade Facilitation Agreement (WTO 2014a) which entered into force in February 2017. The TFA makes an explicit link between implementation by developing countries and the technical and financial assistance they receive.

Moreover, developing countries are required to implement many of their obligations under the agreement only when they believe they have the capacity to do so (Hoekman 2014a; Neufeld 2014).[22]

Aid for trade therefore has an important role to play in the TFA implementation, and the TFA provides a unique opportunity for the Aid for Trade Initiative to tackle its challenges. By focusing its activities on trade facilitation and, more broadly, on reducing trade costs, the initiative could become more efficient and restore its credibility (Hallaert 2013). Will the opportunity be seized?

At first glance, there are reasons for hope. The WTO Aid for Trade Work Programme 2014–2015 emphasized that the "Bali Package emerged as a central theme" of the initiative, and the theme of the Fifth Global Review of Aid for Trade held in the summer of 2015—reducing trade costs—was clearly the core rationale of Aid for Trade and of the TFA (OECD and WTO 2015). Moreover, initially donors appeared to respond. According to the OECD, disbursements to support trade facilitation projects increased in real terms by 22 percent in 2013, and commitments remained high by historical standards (they declined by 8 percent after a 34 percent increase in 2012).[23] Adding another incentive for donors to finance trade-related projects are the Sustainable Development Goals (SDGs) for 2015–2030 adopted at a UN Summit in September 2015; following in the steps of the MDGs, they consider trade to be a tool for development.

A closer look suggests, however, that the TFA is not an opportunity for the Aid for Trade Initiative, but business as usual.

For the development community, the focus remains unchanged: mobilizing resources and improving market access. The SDGs are broader in scope than the MDGs, reflecting the view that development policies need to consider issues of equity and inclusion as well as the environmental impact of human activity. Aid for trade is seen as a tool for achieving the SDGs, but its role is limited to the usual resource mobilization. The "Means of Implementation" (section 8.a) proposes to "increase Aid for Trade support for developing countries, particularly LDCs, including through the Enhanced Integrated Framework for Trade-Related Technical Assistance to Least Developed Countries." As in the MDGs, trade has a role to play (goals 17.10 to 17.12), and, as in the MDGs, the focus is on market access rather than reducing trade costs (Hoekman 2014b) notwithstanding the growing body of evidence that reducing trade costs will bring larger benefits than improving market access, and the recent empirical evidence that the role of imports for growth and development is as large as the role of exports (Hallaert 2015).

Against the background of a broadening of development goals and notwithstanding the institutional importance of the TFA, the incentives for the WTO to call for an expansion of the scope of the initiative are strengthened. In the Aid for Trade Work Programme 2014–2015, the WTO claims that the Bali Package "*add[s]* a significant, novel dimension to on-going work on Aid for Trade" (WTO 2014b, emphasis added). Similarly, Pascal Lamy, who as head of the WTO oversaw the birth and development of the Aid for Trade Initiative, has stressed the importance of helping "least developed countries [to] acquire the capacity to raise the quality of their production to the required level. This *adds* a large Aid for Trade area, *besides* existing support programs for production capacity, infrastructure, trade facilitation or trade finance" (Lamy 2015, emphasis added). Clearly, reducing trade costs had not become the focus of the Aid for Trade Initiative, but just another expansion of its scope.

The Aid for Trade Work Programme 2016–2017 focused on "Promoting Connectivity' by reducing trade costs" (WTO 2016). Reducing trade costs was meant to be much broader than trade facilitation as an "increased focus [was put] on services trade and upgrading infrastructure." The 2017 *Aid for Trade at a Glance Report* (published on the occasion of the Sixth Global Review) noted that "trade facilitation tops the aid-for-trade priorities of both developing countries and their development partners, *albeit in a broader conception that also includes physical connectivity, such as transport corridors, and digital connectivity too*" (OECD and WTO 2017, emphasis added).

Finally, the Aid for Trade Work Programme 2018–2019 is broad in scope:

> The new Work Programme will seek to further develop analysis on how trade can contribute to economic diversification and empowerment, with a focus on eliminating extreme poverty, particularly through the effective participation of women and youth, and how Aid for Trade can contribute to that objective by addressing supply-side capacity and trade-related infrastructure constraints, including for Micro, Small and Medium-sized Enterprises (MSMEs) notably for

those MSMEs in rural areas. Other issues to be developed during
the Work Programme will include industrialization and structural
transformation, digital connectivity and skills, as well as sustainable
development and access to energy. (WTO 2018)

Though very broad, the Work Programme does not mention trade facilitation and has only two references to trade costs: one to highlight their link
with poverty and the other to emphasize their gender dimension.

Despite efforts to remain in line with donors' priorities, the growth of
aid-for-trade disbursements slowed dramatically: after growing in real terms
by 11 percent a year on average over the period 2008–2012, disbursements
grew by only 5 percent per year on average from 2012 through 2015 and
then by 2 percent from 2016 to 2018. Disbursements for trade facilitation
accounts for only about 1 percent of total aid-for-trade disbursements. They
had increased in the run-up to the TFA agreement (by 22 percent in both
2012 and 2013) but experienced a decline of 6.4 percent per year on average
in the years 2014–2017. The entry into force of the TFA appears to have
reversed the trend: preliminary data for 2018 report a 62 percent increase.
This rebound may have come at the expense of other projects since total
aid-for-trade disbursements slightly declined in 2018.

The financial cost of implementing the TFA is small and thus does not
require a large increase in aid-for-trade resources. The OECD estimates
that the initial investment cost ranges between US$5 million–25 million
per country and that the annual operating costs do not exceed US$3.5 mil-
lion (OECD 2014). The World Bank estimates range from US$7 million–
11 million (Jackson and McLinden 2013).

Nonetheless, in another sign that developing countries are skeptical
about the additionality and delivery of aid for trade, they express concerns
that support may not be available to implement the TFA. These concerns
were so strong that in July 2014, in a show of coherence, nine international
organizations (ITC, OECD, UNCTAD, UN Economic Commission for
Europe (UNECE), UN Economic Commission for Latin America and the
Caribbean (ECLAC), UN Economic Commission for Asia and the Pacific
(ESCAP), UN Economic and Social Commission for Western Asia
(ESCWA), World Bank, and World Customs Organization (WCO)) issued
a joint statement stressing their commitment to provide coordinated assis-
tance, and the WTO announced the launch of the Trade Facilitation
Agreement Facility (TFAF) financed on a voluntary basis by WTO mem-

bers (WTO 2014c). Its purpose is to address possible aid-for-trade delivery failure.[24] As such, it responds to the credibility issue of the initiative, but because it is limited in scope it is only a partial response. The Aid for Trade Initiative needs to do more and should seize the opportunity of the TFA to reinvent itself.

CONCLUSION: HAS THE AID FOR TRADE INITIATIVE PASSED THE TEST OF COHERENCE?

The Aid for Trade Initiative increased donors' and developing countries' awareness of the role trade can play in development. It has also been instrumental in increasing aid to build trade capacities and in donor financing to the productive sector.

However, the Aid for Trade Initiative failed to bring coherence to policymaking. The WTO Secretariat is not in a position to promote coherence in aid for trade. It has no expertise in aid delivery or in development policies, and perhaps more important, cannot institutionally steer the initiative. Its role is largely limited to calling for more resources and to monitoring aid flows. Thus the initiative is headless and, in the absence of a Doha Round agreement, without a precise goal. The consequence is that donors deliver aid for trade the same as any other form of aid—on their own terms and in an uncoordinated way. Experience has demonstrated that complementary policies and sequencing are crucial for the success of trade reforms; thus the failure to achieve coherence reduces the effectiveness of aid for trade.

In this context, and with the Doha Round ending without an agreement, aid for trade has become less of a priority for donors. In its Aid for Trade Work Programme 2012–2013, the WTO implicitly acknowledged this reality. Unable to promote coherence in policymaking, it redefines coherence as coherence "in objectives" by calling for donors to consider the trade dimension of their new priorities.

The Trade Facilitation Agreement has the potential to transform the Aid for Trade Initiative and to increase policy coherence. However, the TFA risks being a missed opportunity for the initiative. The WTO considers trade facilitation, and more generally reducing trade costs, as merely an expansion of the scope of the initiative rather than an opportunity to focus its activities. Similarly, for the development community, the TFA does not lead to a revisiting of "business as usual." The role of trade in the post-2015 development agenda remains the same as it was in the MDGs: improving market access. Despite its large benefits and low cost, reducing trade costs is largely ignored.

NOTES

I would like to thank Patrick Messerlin for suggesting this analysis and for his comments on a previous version.

1. Article III(5) of the Agreement establishing the WTO, www.wto.org /english/docs_e/legal_e/04-wto_e.htm. For more details, see the "Declaration on the Contribution of the World Trade Organization to Achieving Greater Coherence in Global Economic Policymaking," http://www.wto.org/english /docs_e/legal_e/32-dchor_e.htm.

2. Rules on customs valuation are a good example of how rules evolved. Previously, developing countries could opt out of the Tokyo Round code on customs valuation (and most of them did), but the Uruguay Round's agreement on customs valuation is legally binding on *all* WTO members.

3. As part of the Uruguay Round, some members agreed to replace their nontariff barriers on agriculture with ad valorem tariffs. Estimating the ad valorem equivalent of nontariff measures is difficult. The tariffication was usually done in a way that the tariff equivalent was high and arguably has not reduced protection.

4. World Trade Organization, Uruguay Round Agreement, "Decision on Measures in Favour of Least-Developed Countries," www.wto.org/english/docs _e/legal_e/31-dlldc_e.htm. It is noteworthy that the decision includes assistance to strengthen and diversify the production base. This is outside the WTO mandate and will be an aid-for-trade objective.

5. World Trade Organization, Uruguay Round Agreement, "Agreement on Technical Barriers to Trade," Article 12(7), www.wto.org/english/docs_e /legal_e/17-tbt_e.htm.

6. World Trade Organization, Uruguay Round Agreement, "Agreement on the Application of Sanitary and Phytosanitary Measures," Article 9, www .wto.org/english/docs_e/legal_e/15sps_01_e.htm.

7. World Trade Organization, Uruguay Round Agreement, "Agreement on Implementation of Article VII of the General Agreement on Tariffs and Trade 1994, Article 20, www.wto.org/english/docs_e/legal_e/20-val_01_e.htm.

8. World Trade Organization, Uruguay Round Agreement, "Trade-Related Aspects of Intellectual Property Rights," Article 67, www.wto.org /english/docs_e/legal_e/27-trips_01_e.htm.

9. World Trade Organization, Uruguay Round Agreement, "Decision on Measures Concerning the Possible Negative Effects of the Reform Programme on Least-Developed and Net Food-Importing Developing Countries," www .wto.org/english/docs_e/legal_e/35-dag_e.htm.

10. World Trade Organization, Ministerial Declaration, November 20, 2001, paragraph 41, emphasis added, www.wto.org/english/thewto_e/minist_e/min01_e/mindecl_e.htm.

11. World Trade Organization, Doha Development Agenda, August 1, 2004, Annex D, paragraph 5, www.wto.org/english/tratop_e/dda_e/draft_text_gc_dg_31july04_e.htm#annexd.

12. See Articles 14 to 20 of the Trade Facilitation Agreement (WTO 2014a).

13. Millennium Development Goal 8 addresses both trade and aid. Its target 12 is to "develop further an open, rule-based, predictable, non-discriminatory trading and financial system" that works for developing countries. Its targets 13 and 14 address the special needs of LDCs, landlocked developing countries, and small island developing states. "Proportion of ODA provided to help build trade capacity" is listed under MDG 8, indicator 41. The relation between aid for trade and the MDGs was made explicit in the recommendations of the WTO Task Force on Aid for Trade. The task force indicates that an objective of aid for trade is "to enable developing countries, particularly LDCs, to use trade more effectively to promote growth, development and poverty reduction and to achieve their development objectives, including the Millennium Development Goals" (WTO 2006a).

14. For a review, see De Lombaerde and Mavrotas (2009), as well as Calì and te Velde (2011).

15. In early 2004, the IF had received only US$21.1 million from donors for the Diagnostic Trade Integration Studies and for technical assistance (Winters 2007). On the eve of the WTO Ministerial Conference in Hong Kong, the IF had given out a maximum of only US$1 million in aid to each country (Beattie 2005).

16. It seems that the WTO initially hoped to be able to do so. Finger (2007) reports that, in a chatroom discussion (on October 16, 2006), WTO DG Pascal Lamy explained that while the WTO makes only a modest contribution to capacity building, it seeks to contribute coherence and clarity to others' efforts.

17. For details, see Hoekman (2007) and Luke, Monge-Roffarello, and Varma (2009).

18. Additionality is a major concern of developing countries; they fear that aid for trade will divert aid from other sectors. Reflecting this concern, Kofi Annan, the United Nations secretary-general, indicated at the WTO Ministerial in Cancùn that "developing countries need aid for trade, and such aid must not come at the expense of aid for development" (WTO 2003). The additionality of aid for trade is explicit in both the Hong Kong Declaration (WTO 2005) and the task force recommendations (WTO 2006a).

19. Trade finance was a high-profile issue during the "great trade collapse" of 2008–2009. In November 2008, Pascal Lamy claimed in his report to the WTO General Council that the World Bank support for trade finance was

"aid for trade in action." The Aid for Trade Initiative provided the WTO with extra leverage to promote its trade finance agenda (Hallaert 2011). As for the role of the private sector in development, the Fourth High Level Forum on Aid Effectiveness held in 2011 emphasized that the private sector is essential to move from "aid effectiveness" to "development effectiveness." In this context, the role of the private sector was given particular attention at the Third Global Review of Aid for Trade.

20. Inclusion of a trade component is obviously a softer criterion than the WTO-OECD criterion of "mainstreaming trade in development strategy" or UNCTAD's "priority."

21. See the "Joint Staff Advisory Notes" and the "Progress Reports" published on the IMF website. For an evaluation of the (lack of) mainstreaming of trade in development strategies when the initiative was launched, see WTO (2006b).

22. Developing countries notify the WTO of the provisions they will implement when the agreement enters into force or, in the case of LDCs, within one year after entry into force (category A); the provisions they will implement after a transitional period following the entry into force of the agreement (category B); and the provisions they will implement on a date after a transitional period following the entry into force of the agreement and that require the acquisition of assistance and support for capacity building (category C). Category C is thus of relevance for AFT. As of September 3, 2020, ninety-four WTO members had made notifications under category C.

23. The OECD's Creditor Reporting System can be accessed at www.oecd.org/dac/aft/aid-for-tradestatisticalqueries.htm. Aid to trade facilitation is reported under code 33120.

24. The TFAF provides two types of grants to developing countries that have been unable to access support for their TFA commitments through regular channels. Project preparation grants (up to US$30,000) are available to members requiring additional support to successfully apply for assistance to implement their category C provisions. Project implementation grants (up to US$30,000) are available for implementation of applicants' specific category C provisions of the TFA. For details, see the website of the Trade Facilitation Agreement Facility at https://www.tfafacility.org/.

REFERENCES

Beattie, A. 2005. "Experts Say No Need for Freer Trade Aid Fund." *Financial Times*, September 20.

Bolaky, B., and C. Freund. 2004. *Trade, Regulations, and Growth*. Policy Research Paper 3255. Washington, D.C.: World Bank.

Calì, M., and D. W. te Velde. 2011. "Does Aid for Trade Really Improve Trade Performance?" *World Development* 39 (5): 725–40.

Chang, R., L. Kaltani, and N. Loayza. 2005. *Openness Can Be Good for Growth: The Role of Policy Complementarities.* NBER Working Paper 11787. Cambridge, Mass.: National Bureau of Economic Research.

Chenery, H. B., and A. M. Strout. 1966. "Foreign Assistance and Economic Development." *American Economic Review* 56 (4): 679–733.

Commission for Africa. 2005. *Our Common Interest.* Report of the Commission for Africa. London. http://www.commissionforafrica.info/wp-content /uploads/2005-report/11-03-05_cr_report.pdf.

De Lombaerde, P., and G. Mavrotas. 2009. "Aid for Trade, Aid Effectiveness and Regional Absorption Capacity." In *Aid for Trade: Global and Regional Perspectives*, edited by P. De Lombaerde and L. Puri. The Netherlands: Springer.

Elborgh-Woytek, K., and others. 2006. *Fiscal Implications of Multilateral Tariff Cuts.* IMF Working Paper 06/203. Washington, D.C.: International Monetary Fund.

Easterly, W. 2001. *The Elusive Quest for Growth: Economists' Adventures and Misadventures in the Tropics.* MIT Press.

———. 2003. "Can Foreign Aid Buy Growth?" *Journal of Economic Perspectives* 17 (3): 23–48.

Finger, J. Michael. 2007. "Implementation and Imbalance: Dealing with Hangover from the Uruguay Round." *Oxford Review of Economic Policy* 23 (3): 440–60.

Finger, M., and P. Schuler. 2000. "Implementation of Uruguay Round Commitments: The Development Challenge." *World Economy* 23 (4): 511–25.

G-8. 2005. *Africa.* Gleneagles, Scotland. data.unaids.org/topics/universalaccess /postg8_gleneagles_africa_en.pdf.

Hallaert, J.-J. 2006. "A History of Empirical Literature on the Relationship between Trade and Growth." *Mondes en Développement* 135 (3): 63–77.

———. 2010. *Increasing the Impact of Trade Expansion on Growth: Lessons from Trade Reforms for the Design of Aid for Trade.* Trade Policy Working Paper No. 100. Paris: OECD Publishing.

———. 2011. "Why Boosting the Availability of Trade Finance Became a Priority during the 2008–2009 Crisis." In *Trade Finance during the Great Trade Collapse*, edited by J.-P. Chauffour and M. Malouche. Washington, D.C.: World Bank.

———. 2013. "The Future of Aid for Trade: Challenges and Options." *World Trade Review* 12 (4): 653–68.

———. 2015. "Importing Growth: The Critical Role of Imports in a Trade-Led Growth Strategy." *Journal of World Trade* 49 (1): 49–72.

Hoekman, B. 2007. "Development and Trade Agreements: Beyond Market Access." In *Global Trade and Poor Nations—The Poverty Impacts and Policy Implications of Liberalization*, edited by B. Hoekman and M. Olarreaga. Brookings.

———. 2014a. *The Bali Trade Facilitation Agreement and Rulemaking in the WTO: Milestone, Mistake or Mirage?* RSCAS Working Paper 2014-102. Florence: European University Institute.

———. 2014b. *Lowering Trade Costs: A Key Goal in the Post-2015 Sustainable Development Agenda*. Global Governance Programme. Policy Brief 2014/03. Florence: European University Institute.

Hoekman, B., and M. Olarreaga. 2007. "The Challenges to Reducing Poverty through Trade Reform: Overview." In *Global Trade and Poor Nations—The Poverty Impacts and Policy Implications of Liberalization*, edited by B. Hoekman and M. Olarreaga. Brookings.

Hoekman, B., and S. Prowse. 2005. *Economic Policy Responses to Preference Erosion: From Trade as Aid to Aid for Trade*. Policy Research Paper 3721. Washington, D.C.: World Bank.

International Monetary Fund. 2003. *Financing of Losses from Preference Erosion, Note on Issue Raised by Developing Countries in the Doha Round*. Communication to the WTO from the International Monetary Fund, WT/TF/COH/14. Washington, D.C.

———. 2004. *Fund Support for Trade-Related Balance of Payments Adjustment*. Washington, D.C. www.imf.org/external/np/pdr/tim/2004/eng/022704.pdf.

International Monetary Fund and World Bank. 2005a. *Development Committee Communiqué*. Washington, D.C. April 17. https:/.devcommittee.org /sites/dc/files/download/Communiques/DCCommuniqueSpring2005 .pdf.

———. 2005b. *The Doha Development Round and Aid for Trade*. Washington, D.C. September 19. www.imf.org/external/np/pp/eng/2005/091905.pdf.

Jackson, Selina, and Gerard McLinden. 2013. "WTO Trade Facilitation Agreement: A Development Opportunity." *The Trade Post* (blog), October 7. http://blogs.worldbank.org/trade/wto-trade-facilitation-agreement -development-opportunity.

Jones, K. 2010. *The Doha Blues—Institutional Crisis and Reform in the WTO*. Oxford University Press.

Lamy, Pascal. 2015. "The New World of Trade—The Third Jan Tumlir Lecture." Jan Tumlir Policy Essay 2015/1. Brussels: ECIPE.

Luke, David, Luca Monge-Roffarello, and Sabrina Varma. 2009. "Perspectives on Aid for Trade." In *Aid for Trade: Global and Regional Perspectives*, edited by P. De Lombaerde and L. Puri. The Netherlands: Springer.

Neufeld, Nora. 2014. *The Long and Winding Road: How WTO Members Finally Reached a Trade Facilitation Agreement*. Staff Working Paper ERSD-2014-06. Geneva: World Trade Organization.

Organization for Economic Cooperation and Development (OECD). 2005. Paris Declaration on Aid Effectiveness. Paris. www.oecd.org/dataoecd /11/41/34428351.pdf.

———. 2014. *OECD Trade Facilitation Indicators: An Overview of Available Tools*. Paris.

OECD and WTO. 2009. *Aid for Trade at a Glance 2009: Maintaining Momentum*. Paris and Geneva.

———. 2015. *Aid for Trade at a Glance 2015: Reducing Trade Costs for Inclusive, Sustainable Growth*. Paris and Geneva.

———. 2017. *Aid for Trade at a Glance 2017: Promoting Trade, Inclusiveness and Connectivity for Sustainable Development*. Paris and Geneva.

Page, S., and P. Kleen. 2005. *Special and Differential Treatment of Developing Countries in the World Trade Organization*. Global Development Studies 2. Stockholm, Sweden: Ministry of Foreign Affairs.

Prowse, S. 2005. "Aid for Trade" Increasing Support for Trade Adjustment and Integration—a Proposal. www.ycsg.yale.edu/focus/researchPapers.html.

Rajan, R., and A. Subramanian. 2005. "What Undermines Aid's Impact on Growth?" NBER Working Paper 11657. Cambridge, Mass.: National Bureau of Economic Research.

Stiglitz, J. E., and A. Charlton. 2005. *Fair Trade for All—How Trade Can Promote Development*. Oxford University Press.

United Nations Conference on Trade and Development (UNCTAD). 2009. "Aid for Trade and Development." In *Aid for Trade: Global and Regional Perspectives*, edited by P. De Lombaerde and L. Puri. The Netherlands: Springer.

United Nations Development Program (UNDP). 2011. *Trade and Human Development. A Practical Guide to Mainstreaming Trade*. New York: UNDP.

United Nations Millennium Project Task Force on Trade. 2005. *Trade for Development*. New York: United Nations.

Winters, L. A. 2007. "Coherence and the WTO." *Oxford Review of Economic Policy* 23 (3): 461–80.

Winters, L. A., N. McCulloch, and A. McKay. 2004. "Trade Liberalization and Poverty: The Evidence So Far." *Journal of Economic Literature* 42 (1): 72–115.

World Trade Organization (WTO). 2003. United Nations—Message of the UN Secretary-General, Mr. Kofi Annan. WT/MIN(03)/12. Geneva.

———. 2004. Doha Work Programme—Decision Adopted by the General Council on 1 August 2004. WT/L/579. Geneva.

———. 2005. Doha Work Program—Ministerial Declaration. WT/MIN(05)/DEC. Geneva.

———. 2006a. Recommendations of the Task Force on Aid for Trade. WT/AFT/1. Geneva.

———. 2006b. Summary of Contributions from Inter-Governmental Organizations: Aid for Trade Task Force. WT/AFT/W/17. Geneva.

———. 2011a. "Lamy Hails "Encouraging" Third Global Review of Aid for Trade." Geneva. www.wto.org/english/news_e/sppl_e/sppl201_e.htm.

———. 2011b. Aid-for-Trade Work Programme 2012–2013: "Deepening Coherence." WT/COMTD/AFT/W/30. Geneva.

———. 2014a. Agreement on Trade Facilitation. WT/L/931. Geneva.

———. 2014b. Aid-for-Trade Work Programme 2014–2015: "Reducing Trade Costs for Inclusive, Sustainable Growth." WT/COMTD/AFT/W/51. Geneva.

———. 2014c. "Azevêdo Launches New WTO Trade Facilitation Agreement Facility to Deliver Support to LDCs and Developing Countries." https://www.wto.org/english/news_e/news14_e/fac_22jul14_e.htm.

———. 2016. Aid-for-Trade Work Programme 2016–2017: "Promoting Connectivity." WT/COMTD/AFT/W/60. Geneva.

———. 2018. Aid-for-Trade Work Programme 2018–2019. "Supporting Economic Diversification and Empowerment for Inclusive, Sustainable Development through Aid for Trade." WT/COMTD/AFT/W/75. Geneva.

Zedillo, E., and others. 2005. *Strengthening the Global Trade Architecture for Economic Development: An Agenda for Action.* Policy Brief. New Haven, Conn.: Yale Centre for the Study of Globalization. www.ycsg.yale.edu/focus/gta/GTA_policy_brief.doc.

15

BANANAS, SUBJECT OF THE LONGEST TRANSATLANTIC DISPUTE IN THE WORLD TRADING SYSTEM

A POSTMORTEM

JAIME DE MELO

On a rarement vendu sous l'étiquette 'L'Europe Sociale' davantage de mensonges, de privilèges et d'injustices

PATRICK MESSERLIN, "MOURIR POUR LA BANANE," *LE FIGARO*, SEPTEMBER 19, 1997

Le coeur du conflit, exemplaire, reste que la production latino-américaine de la banane, outre des atouts physiques indéniables, trouve l'essentiel de sa compétitivité dans le niveau scandaleusement bas des salaires versés aux paysans, alors qu'aux Antilles les salaires versés sont au niveau du SC européen

MICHEL ROCARD, "POUR QUE VIVE LA BANANE," *LE FIGARO* NOVEMBER 10, 1997

After rice, wheat, and maize, bananas are the world's fourth most important food crop. It is a staple food and a key export commodity for many low-income countries. Bananas were also the topic of the longest-running dispute in the post–World War II multilateral trading system. It started in 1991 when a most favored nation (MFN) supplier, Costa Rica, expressed concern that the European Union's new banana regime triggered by the Single Market Act would discriminate against Central American MFN suppliers. The ensuing unresolved disputes and claims (eight disputes and five claims, according to W/T/L/784) took eighteen years to be brought to rest when, in December 2009, an agreement was reached calling for a progressive lowering of the (specific) import tariff on MFN bananas from €176 per ton to €114 per ton by 2017.

The banana case is interesting in several respects. First, since bananas are a homogeneous product, it is a perfect textbook case of the economic effects of a tariff-rate quota (TRQ) regime as taught in the classroom. Second, from the point of view of dispute settlement, although the functioning of the TRQ regime was not transparent, the decision to move from a TRQ regime to a tariff-only (TO) regime was, in principle, easy to adjudicate since it was not hostage to litigation over interpretations of "like products" or technical barriers to trade. Third, the vagueness in the panel decisions, in the compromises among the parties, and in the rules for tariffication all contributed to delays in reaching a denouement. Fourth, it is an interesting case of how the world's two largest trading partners at the time, the European Union and the United States, came to fight over a product that was not produced on either continent. Finally, straddling equally the periods covered by the General Agreement on Tariffs and Trade (GATT) and World Trade Organization (WTO), the narrative of the dispute is a good example of the application of GATT rules of progression and of the progressively greater reliance on rules in resolving disputes.

In addition to a good illustration of the ascendency of rules in trade conflicts between powerful and less powerful countries, the "banana split" in transatlantic trade relations is an interesting case study of how particularistic interests prevailed in the trade policy decisionmaking of the EU and the US. As indicated by the above excerpts from an exchange in the press between Patrick Messerlin and Michel Rocard (who had been France's prime minister at the time the TRQ regime was under elaboration), the debate was spirited. Not engaging in the debate would have been uncharacteristic of Patrick Messerlin, who always stated his views with clarity and conviction.[1] It is therefore a pleasure to revisit this case now that the conflict has been resolved.

THE CONTOURS OF THE INTERNAL AND EXTERNAL CONFLICTS ON THE EU'S BANANA TRADE REGIME

I describe briefly the history of the conflict that proved so resistant to mediation within the EU, in transatlantic relations, and within the multilateral trading system (important dates and outcomes are summarized in table 15-1).[2] I start with some background, and then turn to the elaboration of the EU's banana trade regime that was required by the formation of the Single European Market (SEM) in 1993.

Background

In the late 1980s, 75 percent of the world's banana exports originated in Latin America (Ecuador, Costa Rica, and Colombia, followed by Honduras, Mexico, Nicaragua, Panama, and Venezuela)—all developing countries and henceforth referred to here as the MFN suppliers. The EU consumed 40 percent of the world's bananas, with one-third coming in equal proportion from MFN suppliers, EU overseas territories (Canary islands, Martinique, Guadeloupe), and former British and French colonies—the African, Caribbean, and Pacific (ACP) countries. The level of self-sufficiency in bananas in the EU was thus much lower than for most other agricultural products, including most fruits.

As for the Banana Trade Regime (BTR) in the EU, before the creation of the Single European Market, it was segmented, as Spain and France had overseas territories growing bananas (Martinique, Guadeloupe, and the Canaries) and, along with Britain, had colonial ties with the ACP countries enshrined in the 1975 Lomé Convention. Bananas from the African and Caribbean states were "beneficiaries" of the Lomé Convention. The legally binding article 1 of the banana protocol under that convention stated: "In respect of its banana exports to the markets of the Community, no ACP state will be placed, as regards to its traditional markets and its advantages on those markets, in a less favorable situation than in the past or at present."

When the SEM was put in place, cost disparities among suppliers were substantial: the costs of high-cost producers (EU territories and the Windward Islands) were more than double those of Latin American suppliers.[3]

Before the start of the dispute, the banana market in the EU was segmented into three parts. The largest and most dynamic was the German market (fueled by German reunification), where bananas were imported freely. In the middle was the Hanseatic market (Benelux, Denmark, Sweden), which applied the 20 percent common external tariff (€75 per ton, the level that was bound in the Dillon Round of multilateral trade negotiations, 1959–1962). At the other extreme, France, Britain, and Spain had closed markets: all of Spain's bananas came from the Canary Islands, half of those consumed in France came from the Caribbean (Martinique and Guadeloupe), and the rest from Cameroon and Côte d'Ivoire. Three-quarters of bananas consumed in Britain came from the Caribbean, with over half from the Windward Islands (Dominica, Santa Lucia, Saint Vincent, and the Grenadines).

The trade in bananas from the EU overseas territories and the Caribbean was dominated by two firms, Geest (British) and Fyffes (Irish). The MFN bananas were marketed by Chiquita, Dole, and Del Monte. Chiquita, which sourced its bananas in Latin America, had almost two-thirds of the world market and accounted for 90 percent of the German market, which was the most open (with zero tariffs).

Moving to an SEM created two problems, an internal one and an external one. Within the EU, where bananas circulate freely, if a tariff-only (TO) rate at approximately the common external tariff (CET) rate had been adopted, then the commitment under article 1 of the Lomé Convention would have been undermined and the EU producers would have been shut out. The solution that was adopted was to create a system of quotas that restricted entry of all non-ACP bananas to a level that would maintain the marginal EU producers in the market. The result was that the Germans then had to pay higher prices.[4]

Externally, the problem was that the Lomé Convention contradicted the principle of nondiscrimination (GATT Article I). However, three qualifications under the GATT allowed countries to discriminate against third parties: (1) the "enabling clause" or "special and differential treatment" (SDT) adopted in 1979 in the GATT; (2) when creating a free trade agreement (FTA) or a customs union (CU) (Article XXIV); (3)

TABLE 15-1. Import and Retail Prices of Bananas: United States and France, 1990–2002

Real US$ per kilo

	United States		France	
Year	Import	Retail	Import	Retail
1990	0.66	1.19	1.19	1.41
1993	0.48	1.02	0.79	1.11
1998	0.46	1.01	0.73	1.72
2000	0.38	0.98	0.43	1.26
2001	0.50	0.96	0.51	1.40
2002	0.45	0.95	0.44	1.32

Source: Melo (2015, table 1); FAO (2003, table 6).

countries can agree to waive any rule—that is, to permit discrimination (Article XXV). Since the Latin American MFN exporters were developing countries, SDT was excluded, and since option 2 did not apply, this left only option 3 as the justification for article I of the Lomé Convention. Indeed, throughout the conflict, no country objected to granting a waiver from article I.

At the time of the conflict, the most important issue was the extent of rents and who was going to get them, since there was no open market for quota licenses and these licenses were distributed by the EU to the major operators. At the time, the price differential between the US internal price where bananas entered duty-free and the EU internal price was fairly constant (Vanzetti, Fernandez, and Chau 2004, figure 3). Since the SEM in 1993 meant that imported goods could be reexported to other member states, a comparison of prices in a tariff-free market like the United States where the (homogeneous) bananas entered duty-free and any market in the EU (France in table 15-1) gives an estimate of the rents up for capture. As shown in table 15-1, the price was between 40 percent and 60 percent. Taking the lower figure, this amounts to $400 or €300 per ton at the $/€ exchange rate ($1.3 = €1 in 2004). Since the same quality bananas were sold in both markets and shipment costs were ostensibly the same, with a market of about 4,000 tons per year, rents (including tariff revenues and rents to suppliers and marketers) were at least €1.2 billion per year.[5]

Patching up the Common Organization of the Market
for Bananas (COMB) Trade Regime

Because of the combination of a favorable climate, topography, soil, and labor regulations in the Canary Islands, Guadeloupe, and Martinique patterned on those in continental Europe, the creation of an open SEM would have had disastrous consequences for the banana industries in the French, former British Caribbean, and other EU territories. Representatives of these states and territories argued that climatic conditions prevented them from diversifying into other products and that the abolition of the prevailing BTR would lead to their economic ruin while politicians in EU countries with overseas banana production would face "political suicide" if they abolished the BTR. Five years of negotiations in the Commission of the European Community led to the Common Organization of the Market for Bananas (COMB), a hard-fought compromise that replaced the BTR. This new regime was compatible with the requirements of the SEM and the obligation to maintain market share for ACP producers under the Lomé Convention. This compromise was entirely at the expense of MFN producers and the US sellers of MFN bananas in the EC.

Borrell (1999) and others have argued that, on paper at least, the EU had several options that would have largely dominated the COMB. Besides establishing a single unified market, the most significant change resulting from the COMB was a new quota allocation scheme that would in effect result in the subsidies to inefficient ACP and EU suppliers being paid by MFN banana traders in the EU market (i.e., the US multinationals) in part because of the pressure on expenditures associated with the Common Agricultural Policy (CAP).[6] Using a series of studies, Borrell (1999) estimated that a tariff of 17 percent would have sufficed. However, this option would not have been possible because EU budgetary law prohibits tariff revenues from being earmarked for product-specific subsidies. Therefore the money for the subsidies for producers would have to be raised by EU finance ministers, who in the 1990s wanted to contain any rising costs in the Common Agricultural Policy. Regarding compensation to ACP states, the WTO panels repeatedly confirmed that the "Lomé waiver" would have been GATT-compatible. Yet the COMB was designed so that the burden of adjustment fell on banana traders using MFN suppliers.

The outcome under the COMB was exactly the opposite of the one predicted by the models of "interest group" politics. As predicted by these models, by maintaining a high price, the COMB passed the costs of protection to consumers. However, one would have expected the MFN suppliers and operators to have obtained some of the rents. Initially, however, that did not happen (see tables 15-2 and 15-3) because all licenses were awarded to EU marketers, an arrangement that amounted to a winner-take-all outcome: EU traders and EU and ACP growers got all the benefits, while growers and traders of dollar bananas got nothing.

THE CONFLICT

Assembling the COMB was a long process that lasted five years because a "qualified" majority was necessary in the EU since a "blocking minority" coalition of Hanseatic countries could have prevented the adoption of a new protectionist Banana Trade Regime. This explains why warnings surfaced at the GATT before the adoption of the COMB. I start with a description of the conflict at the GATT, then turn to its evolution when the GATT was replaced by the WTO (for details of the chronology of the main events see Melo (2015, table II).

. . . at the GATT

The conflict started when a group of banana producers expressed their concerns to the GATT council in 1991 about the anticipated new BTR, which they believed would be unfavorable to them ("Bananas I"). They hoped that these consultations would influence the design of the BTR before the conclusion of the Uruguay Round. When consultations failed, five GATT members requested that a panel against the EU's COMB be put in place in July 1993 ("Bananas II"). They argued that the COMB was incompatible with the GATT on three grounds, the most important being the allocation of quota licenses to companies (not to countries) that had traditionally traded EU and ACP bananas in the EU market. The ensuing Banana Framework Agreement (BFA) helped assuage Colombia, the largest MFN supplier that had no licenses accorded to it under the COMB, but not Guatemala, which did not receive any licenses and hence refused to sign the BFA.

Because the EU was failing to react to the panel decisions and Chiquita had not succeeded in obtaining any licenses, Chiquita used political tactics to persuade the Office of the US Trade Representative to file a GATT

Section 301 investigation against the EU.[7] This was the first turning point since, regardless of the outcome at the GATT/WTO, the United States had a credible threat to impose sanctions on EU imports, especially given the "carousel" method of selecting imports subject to sanctions on a rotation basis.

The last significant decision under the GATT was the waiver obtained by the EU in the last hours of the Uruguay Round negotiations in December 1994, a waiver that allowed the continuation of the BFA until 2000, when the new Lomé IV Convention had to be approved.

... at the WTO

Thanks to the waiver granted at the conclusion of the Uruguay Round, the EU had until 2000 to make its banana policy GATT-compatible. Except for Ecuador, the important dollar suppliers were GATT members. Yet until the change from "consensus to accept" to "consensus to reject" with the creation of the WTO, it was still possible for EU policymakers or EU courts to reject GATT decisions and to ignore the GATT panel rulings, as evidenced by the decision of the European Court of Justice in 1994, which rejected the GATT panel ruling. This changed with implementation of the dispute settlement process at the WTO. Also, Ecuador, by far the dominant MFN supplier, had now joined the WTO. With the complaints now lodged under the Dispute Settlement Understanding (DSU), panel findings were acquiring traction.

In May 1997, a WTO panel ruled that the EU BFA violated GATT rules in three respects, a ruling that was upheld by the Appellate Body in September 1997 ("Bananas III"). An important decision in the ruling indicating the move toward rule-based resolution of trade conflicts was the interpretation of the wording in the waiver from Article I. The wording referred to "preferential treatment in general" and not to "preferential tariff treatment," but the panel concluded that the wording did not allow the EU to interpret its meaning as it wished—that is, to decide how quotas would be allocated.[8] The panel also found that BFA countries were allowed to manage their own export certification system and that non-BFA countries were not.

Importantly, the panel ruled against the 30 percent allocation of the MFN quota (857,000 tons) given to historical importers of the EU and traditional ACP bananas (the allocation under category B in table 15-2). This allocation was between 50,000 and 100,000 tons greater than the best-ever export volume before 1991. In sum, the decision required the EU to pro-

TABLE 15-2. Transition from a Tariff-Rate Quota to a Tariff-Only Regime for Bananas

Event/Date		Quota type	Quantity (tons)[f]	Tariff rate (€ per ton)[g]	Tariff type	ACP tariff preference
1993	COMB	ACP[a]	857 KT	0		
		A[b]	1.3 MT	100 ECUs		
		B[c]	600 KT	100 ECUs		
		C[d]	70	100 ECUs		
		Out-of-quota (MFN)		850 ECUs		
		Out-of-quota ACP & European[e]		750 ECUs		
EU/US April 2001	Phase 1 Step 1 (July 2001)	A	2.2 MT	75	Bound	75
		B	353 KT	75	Aut.[i]	75
		C	850 KT	300	Aut.	300
		Out-of-quota		680	Aut.	300
EU/US April 2001	Phase 1 Step 2 (Jan. 2002)	A	2.2 MT	75	Bound	75
		B	453 KT	75	Aut.	75
		C	750 KT	n.a.[h]		n.a.
		Out-of-quota		680	Aut.	300

Source: Melo (2015, table 3). Elaboration based on Messerlin (2001), Badinger, Breuss, and Mahlberg (2001, tables 1 and 2), and Vanzetti, Fernandez, and Chau (2004, table 1).

Notes: One Ecu was approximately equivalent to one Euro. During the period, all bananas were sold in-quota because the out-of-quota tariff was prohibitive. Quota B was created in 1995 to reflect the enlargement of the EU to include Austria, Finland, and Sweden. Quotas A and B are managed as if they formed a single quota and are often referred to as quota A/B. Tariffs under quota A are bound; tariffs under quotas B and C are not bound.
[a] Traditional ACPs (Cape Verde, Cameroon, Côte d'Ivoire, Belize, Dominica, Jamaica, Suriname, Somalia, Windward Islands (Dominica, Santa Lucia, Saint Vincent, Grenadines).
[b] Category A: Licenses for established operators of MFN and nontraditional suppliers in EC (65 percent of quota). Licenses are transferable within the category.
[c] Category B: Licenses for established European companies in EC (30 percent of quota). Licenses are transferable within the category.
[d] Category C: New operators (post-1992) (3.5 percent of quota). Licenses cannot be sold.
[e] Nontraditional ACPs: (Dominican Republic and Ghana) plus European producers (French overseas departments, Balearic Islands, and Crete).
[f] KT = 1,000 kilos; MT = million tons.
[g] One euro was approximately equivalent to one European Currency Unit (ECU).
[h] n.a. = not available.
[i] Aut. = autonomous.

vide the same treatment to ACP and non-ACP suppliers in its quota allocations, implying that it would not be allowed to cross-subsidize ACP bananas via the quota allocation mechanism. This meant that if the EU was
to give quotas to the ACP legally on a basis other than in proportion to
market share in its BTR, it would need a waiver to Article XIII. This, in
turn, would require three-quarters support at the WTO (50 percent at
the GATT).

A new banana regime announced by the EU in January 1999 failed once
more to be WTO-compatible, and the WTO granted the application of
compensatory sanctions to Ecuador and to the US ("Bananas IV," Melo
2012, table 2, entry number 7). Most important, the panel granted Ecuador sanctions that could be applied on imports of services in recognition
that sanctions on goods would not be sufficiently punitive. Even though in
the end these sanctions were never applied (it would have been difficult to
estimate damages in services), this was a landmark in the conflict and, more
broadly, for those who wished to see the World Trading System become
more rule-oriented.

During the dispute settlement procedures under "Bananas IV," the panel
heard representations from third parties that included the Caribbean states.
Among these, the Windward Islands were high-cost producers depending
heavily on exports of bananas at the prevailing prices in the EU. The prosperity created by the tariff-rate quota led to bananas being called "green
gold" in these vulnerable islands. The Caribbean Banana Exporting Association that represented 7 percent of the EU market rejected financial aid
that would, according to them, amount to "subsidy idleness." They wanted
to be "traders not beggars." They argued that moving to a tariff-only (TO)
regime would require at least a ten-year adjustment period to prevent the
total collapse of the Windward Islands.[9] With the adverse panel finding, it
had become clear that the BTR would not be able to serve as development
assistance to the ACP through cross-subsidization by MFN producers and
traders.

Faced with the prospect of these sanctions, the EU consulted with the
US and with Colombia and Costa Rica, the major MFN exporters who had
what they considered fair quota shares under the BTA. It was clear from
Bananas IV that a TO regime would be WTO-compatible and easier than
the alternative that required a waiver to Article XIII on the rules about
quota allocation. While the EU would have envisioned moving to a TO
regime, the ACP and Ecuador were satisfied with their quota shares based

on a post-1993 reference period, and the US also preferred to maintain a TRQ, though one based on the pre-1991 period when Chiquita had a much larger share. The US also made it clear that it would not lift sanctions unless the new BTR was found to be WTO-compatible. The EU also found out that the two options for license allocation (first-come, first-serve or by auction) other than the use of a historical reference period (if the US and Ecuador disagreed on the reference period) had no support among the banana operators.

The EU was then in a difficult position. On one side it was faced with the desire by operators to keep the opacity of a TRQ where "obfuscation" (the description by Magee, Brock, and Young 1978) would allow them to keep rents unnoticed, and on the other side it was being held hostage by MFN suppliers who would not grant the waiver on Article 1 necessary for the approval of the Cotonou Agreement, which was to replace Lomé IV. With the prospect of a new round at Doha in sight, the EC finally reached an agreement with the US, then after further negotiations with Ecuador. Licenses were to be allocated on a historical basis (1994–1996) with a license reduction of 100,000 tons to the ACP. The EC also promised to implement a tariff-only regime by January 1, 2006, in return for the promise by Ecuador and the US to suspend sanctions (Melo 2012, table 2, entry number 8).[10] Table 15-2 shows the two steps that the EU was proposing to carry out during phase I between July 2001 and 2006 (the next steps were not specified).

At the Doha Ministerial where the agreement was formalized (Melo 2012, table 2, entry number 9), the Decision specified that "any rebinding of the EC tariff on bananas under the relevant GATT Article XVIII procedures should result in at least maintaining total market access for MFN banana suppliers and its willingness to accept a multilateral control on the implementation of this commitment."

Article XVIII stipulates that the country undertaking tariffication should consult with supplying countries and that if no agreement can be found, the latter may seek arbitration at the WTO. That the maintenance of market access for dollar banana exporters was a central aspect of the transition was further clarified in the decision's annex, which stated that "if the rebinding would not result in at least maintaining total market access for MFN suppliers, the EC shall rectify the matter. . . . If the EC failed to rectify the matter, this waiver shall cease to apply to bananas upon entry into force of the new EC tariff regime."

Note that market access was purposely left vague: Was it in volume or in value terms? What was the choice of base years for calculations?" And most important, was it applicable to all MFN suppliers rather than to individual MFN suppliers?[11]

Between 1993 and 2001 the major change was the allocation of 49 percent of quotas in category A away from established operators to Colombia, Costa Rica, Nicaragua, and Venezuela under the BFA (Melo 2015, table 2, entry number 4).

In the following years, the EU inched toward the TO regime, but the negotiations lasted another eight years, essentially doubling the time required to resolve the conflict. This was partly because of the incompatibility of guaranteeing market access to MFN and ACP suppliers in an unchanging market with changing preferences, which would elicit supply response and hence changing market shares. It was also partly because of the typical vagueness in the diplomatic language and in the tariffication procedures.[12]

In July 2004, the European Commission notified the WTO of its intention to enter Article XXVIII negotiations (required to rebind the EU tariff on bananas).[13] A succession of consultations and panel decisions followed, starting in late 2004. On one end, MFN suppliers said that the EU tariff should be the MFN tariff of €75 per ton and, at the other end, an ACP Council of Ministers indicated that they considered €275 per ton to be the lowest acceptable level for the tariff. In December, outgoing commissioner Pascal Lamy announced €230 per ton as an initial negotiation position for the EU, although in October Germany had publicly voiced its desire to see the tariff rebound at a low level. This figure was announced by the EU in January 2005. Following other adverse panel rulings, the EU lowered the proposed tariff to €178 per ton at the end of 2005, a level that continued to be unacceptable to the MFN suppliers.

Exasperation with the EU's lack of compliance at the Hong Kong Ministerial, resulting in further disputes filed by the US and MFN suppliers, led to yet another panel ruling that the duty-free quota for ACP violated Articles I and XIII on nondiscriminatory allocation of quotas. A facilitator was assigned to help with confidential negotiations that finally led to the December 15, 2009, comprehensive agreement. Not only was EU trade in bananas to be fully WTO-compatible at the substantially lower tariff of €117 by 2017 (allowing a nearly ten-year period to find alternative compensation for the Windward suppliers), but all other pending disputes (eight) and claims (five) at the WTO were finally settled after eighteen years of litigation.

THE POLITICAL ECONOMY

This prolonged dispute had two components, the transatlantic trade conflict between the EU and the US, and the WTO dispute with the MFN suppliers. I examine both next, arguing that the transatlantic dispute was largely explained by domestic politics in the EU and the US, while the dispute with the MFN suppliers that lasted for another eight years following the 2001 Doha agreement could have been resolved earlier if the WTO panels had been more willing to accept economic analyses.

EU Decisionmaking and US Domestic Politics

Since the implementation of the SEM did not result in a move toward a significantly more protectionist stance, why did it happen with the adoption of the COMB?[14] As argued by Cadot and Webber (2002) and others (see, e.g., Barfield 2003), three traits of agricultural and trade policymaking in the EU contributed to the outcome. First, the lead Directorate-General (DG) for agricultural trade was DG agriculture (under scrutiny for CAP expenses). Unlike DG trade, which is required to balance domestic political exigencies with external political obligations, DG agriculture gives greatest priority to domestic agricultural interests. Second, the absence of an EU cabinet contributed to sectoral policymaking that was also reflected in intergovernmental relations (e.g., German chancellor Helmut Kohl deferring to French leadership on bananas to avoid a Franco-German trade conflict). Since inter-DG conflicts on bananas could not be resolved within the college of commissioners, DG agriculture alone was left to resolve the conflict. This was made possible by the practice of issue linkage or package making.

The constituency for bananas was concentrated in the Mediterranean with British and Irish trading companies that coalesced with Mediterranean growers. As there was no banana constituency in the Hanseatic states, they were compensated with victories on other agricultural policy issues in the council at the time. Realizing that it would never get its way in Europe (i.e., it would not get licenses to sell to the Hanseatic states), Chiquita decided that it would have to "go to Washington" to get the regulation changed (Cadot and Webber 2002, 16, and Melo 2012, table 2, entry number 4).[15] In Washington, that course of action was becoming increasingly likely to succeed, especially if one had a big "war chest" as in the case of bananas and otherwise costly lobbying could be avoided.[16]

Again three characteristics of trade policymaking, this time in the United States, increased the likelihood of conflict. First, the Congress was reasserting its constitutional prerogatives over foreign trade policy as the executive was finding it increasingly hard to get "fast-track authority." Second, the 1988 Trade Act with its controversial revised Section 301, which made the administration more accountable to the interests of the private sector, greatly reduced the leeway for the executive branch to protect consumer interests. Revised 301 institutionalized the growing practice of giving the decision on unfair foreign trade practices to the head of the USTR (where firms had direct access). Third was the "buying of electoral outcomes" by private sector donations; the 1990s saw a sharp increase in electoral campaign contributions. Cadot and Webber (2002, table 1) report that, during Bill Clinton's presidency, Chiquita contributed $6 billion and Dole $660 million. Traditional old-fashioned trade politics on both sides of the Atlantic were playing out, but particularistic interests were increasingly preventing Brussels and Washington from formulating more moderate positions.

Resolution of the transatlantic dispute in April 2001 was helped by Chiquita's bankruptcy, a new US administration, and the upcoming Doha negotiations.

The Dispute over Market Access for MFN Suppliers

As was made clear at the Doha Ministerial, the EU would only benefit from the waiver needed to give preferential access to ACP countries if the rebinding of the tariff maintained the market shares of the MFN suppliers. At the same time, the EU had to maintain market access to ACP countries (to honor its legal commitment to maintain market access under the Banana protocol). To move to the TO regime, the European Commission relied on the price-gap conversion method, proposing a "tariff-equivalent" to the TRQ of €230 per ton in January 2005 (Melo 2012, table 2, entry number 10). The assumption was that this tariff rate, calculated as the difference between a suitably defined internal price index and a suitably defined external price index—a cost, insurance, and freight (CIF)-landed price—would maintain the internal price unchanged and leave the market unaffected. The EC however, acknowledged that there would be a supply response by ACP producers under a higher preferential margin (three times higher than previously).

All sides expended energy interpreting a mechanical application of the price-gap (PG) methodology to compute the tariff equivalent of the TRQ regime (Melo 2015). For the bananas under dispute (so-called dessert or Cavendish bananas sold in boxes of seventeen kilograms each), being homogeneous, country i will sell in the EU if unit production costs (say per box), c_i, augmented by all additional transaction costs (unit transport costs to the EU, θ_i; unit packing costs, φ_i; tariffs (for MFN suppliers only), τ; and rents accruing to supplier i, λ_i) do not exceed the unit market price in the EU, P^{EU}:

$$c_i + \theta_i + \varphi_i + \lambda_i + \tau \le P^{EU}$$
$$EP + \lambda_i + \tau = IP \Rightarrow PG = IP - EP$$

If this condition is not met, then supplier i will not sell in the EU. Since all bananas can be considered of the same quality, the same condition prevails in the US except that the "cost less than price" condition is expressed as a unit price in the US, P^{US}. This condition also allows the expression to calculate the tariff-equivalent of the TRQ by the price-gap (PG) method (Melo 2015, table 4). The condition shows that if we have reasonably accurate estimates of unit production costs (freight and packaging costs are relatively easy to obtain), it is straightforward to use this expression to compute rents. Likewise, if there had been a market for licenses, the computation of the PG would have been less controversial.

A graphical analysis assuming that bananas from different origins are perfect substitutes can be used to analyze equilibrium in the market under the quotas applying to the three distinct groups of suppliers (MFNs, ACPs, and the EU) to the EU. Tariffication should lead to a reduction in the equilibrium price in the EU market, and market access could improve for MFN countries since quantities consumed would increase, although this is not necessarily so because the tariffication also elicits a supply response from ACP producers and redistributes supply between MFN and ACP producers in a way that can penalize the former (see Melo 2015, figure 1).

ESTIMATING THE TARIFF EQUIVALENT TO THE TRQ

I apply three different approaches ("triangulation") to estimate the tariff equivalent of the TRQ (Melo 2015). All three lead to similar results that I summarize here. The first is the PG conversion method chosen by the European Commission. The PG method ignores the supply response, which had to be important given that the many estimates were around three times the MFN bound rate of €75 per ton. In its choice of a "conversion method," the EC felt that a PG conversion would be less controversial than a simulation analysis. The EU chose to justify its proposed TO rate of €230 by using the PG method, which it applied to the twenty-five EU members in order to account for the new members using an average over the period 2000–2002. Though straightforward in principle, the application turned out to be complicated and controversial, leading to a wide range of estimates, depending on the author's selection of time-series (FAO time series or World Bank "pink sheets"), who was the sponsor of the study, and the accompanying modifications that were made to series to obtain a suitable tariff equivalent of the TRQ regime. The wide range of price-gap estimates and blatant inconsistencies are summarized in Melo (2015, table 4).

The large discrepancies in the estimates generated by price-gap analysis raise questions about the methodology, the choice of prices, and the possibility of fruit quality effects. An alternative then is to "let the data speak" and exploit all the data on banana trade over a long time period straddling the period of the COMB. This gives an estimate of the determinants of banana trade and helps isolate the effects of the COMB. Application of the popular gravity model of trade over the period 1988–2003, in which dummy variables are used to detect the effects of the TRQ, provides such estimates. Results of this second method give a range of very plausible estimates for all coefficients, including the tariff equivalent of the quota regime (Melo 2015, table 5). The combined effect of the quota and in-quota tariff is estimated at €158 + €75 = €233.

These two sets of estimates do not take into account supply response under the new tariff regime, so they cannot be used to determine what TO regime would allow MFN suppliers to retain their market share. A transparent and minimalist model that calibrates demand and supply elasticities and transport costs provides plausible estimates (see Melo 2015, table 6). These estimates also point out what information would have been needed to progress more rapidly in the negotiations. The model also lays bare the arbitrariness in the discussion due to suppliers' desire to maintain confidentiality about cost data.

Three cases were simulated:

Case 1: Individual countries receive *nontransferable quotas* (more representative of the situation prevailing before 2001).

Case 2: Quotas are transferable within categories (more representative of the situation post-2001, when quotas became transferable within MFN and ACP categories).

Case 3: Fully transferable quotas across all categories. Then rents are equalized as they would be under a tariff-only regime.

The estimated rents implied by these data applied to the demand-supply model indicate an average rent of €125 per ton for MFN producers and €67 for ACP producers. If the landed price in the EU were €500, the corresponding rents would be €53 for MFNs and €5 for ACPs, implying that the ACPs would not be in business. The modeling approach is useful because it helps narrow the discussion.

Recall that, at the time, the conflict was about the TO scheme that would maintain supplies for all MFN producers. Crucial to this task is the supply response that, for equal supply elasticities, will depend on the assumed estimate of rents across countries. Three options for the sharing of rents across suppliers allows one to bracket the range of likely supply response estimates. On the assumption that the cost data are accurate, results in table 15-3 show that if rents were not equalized within categories, a tariff of €150 would have maintained the aggregate share of MFN suppliers at the 2004 level; the EU proposal would have led to a loss of market share of 5 percentage points. However, most of the adjustment would be by Ecuador, the low-cost producer, a reason for the fears expressed at the time by other MFN suppliers (e.g., Costa Rica). Starting from a situation where rents are equalized within MFN and ACP groups, a tariff of €150 per ton would have maintained the shares of all MFN suppliers. Now the pattern of adjustment across suppliers is different because the cost advantage of the high-rent suppliers (e.g., Ecuador for the MFNs) is diminished relative to others (e.g., Costa Rica).

Taken together, the results of the simulations reported in table 15-3 confirm that a low tariff would favor MFN producers at the expense of ACP producers and that no single tariff would have maintained the status quo

TABLE 15-3. Alternative Tariff-Only Simulation Scenarios

Rents equalized within quota categories

Tariff	Tariff rate (€ per ton)	EU price (€ per box)	MFN share	CR	ECUA
				(% change)	
Base (quotas)	75	10.4	0.77	0.0	0.0
EU proposal	230	10.5	0.72	–13.5	4.5
	150	9.6	0.77	–2.0	23.0
	75	8.9	0.81	11.0	43.0

Rents equalized across quota categories

Tariff	Tariff rate (€ per ton)	EU price (€ per box)	MFN share	CR	ECUA
				(% change)	
Base (quotas)	75	10.4	0.77	0.0	0.0
EU proposal	230	10.7	0.70	–9.00.0	0.014.0
	150	9.8	0.76	5.00.0	0.08.3
	75	8.9	0.81	18.6	31.0

Source: Melo (2015, table 7).

Note: In all simulations, $\varepsilon_p = 1.0$, $\varepsilon_s = 1.0$.

among the main banana producers. This "basic result," which is robust to a wide range of changes in ingredients in this minimalist model, was not recognized in the debate. Indeed, in the eight-year debate that ultimately led to the December 2009 agreement, model results were rarely used and, when used, their underpinnings were never spelled out. In sum, like the PG calculations, the models were descriptive rather than informative.

CONCLUSIONS

The banana conflict was the longest-running trade conflict in the current world trading system. Its resolution confirmed that tariffication of quota regimes is difficult to carry out, as it was with the negotiations on agriculture during the Uruguay Round. In the end, the prolonged period of negotiations corresponded to the amount of time that the high-cost Windward producers said would be necessary to adjust, since at the hearings by the Bananas IV panel in 1999, the producers' association requested at least a ten-year adjustment period; an eight-year period of adjustment that was finally agreed upon in 2009. This outcome also resembles the outcome on the removal of other quota regimes such as the Mulfi-Fiber Arrangement, which took place over a ten-year period.

For the transatlantic component of the dispute, the substantial vested interests over annual rents of around $2 billion by a handful of powerful banana traders on each side of the Atlantic, along with the decisionmaking processes in the EU and in the US, explains why it occurred, even though no bananas were grown on either continent. Regardless of the evolution of the trading system from the GATT to the WTO, this dispute could have been solved by threats.

For the MFN suppliers however, absent the transition to a more rule-oriented system, the stalemate that characterized the conflict under the GATT would likely have continued. Its resolution would have been difficult if MFN suppliers had not held the EU hostage on the renewal of the Lomé Convention at the Doha Ministerial. The EU then would have had to find a way to maintain a TRQ that allowed the cross-subsidization of ACP (especially small Caribbean) producers by MFN producers, even though the preferential access under negotiation was already losing its significance.

The economics of the dispute were straightforward, and even though the rents were cleverly hidden, it would have been relatively easy to recognize early on that any tariffication would have altered market shares and led to negotiations for a tariff-only regime in the range of €100–150 per ton. As shown by a triangulation of estimation methods (even with available information), this range could have been easily established by an independent panel mandated by the WTO.

NOTES

I thank the FERDI for support and encouragement to write this chapter. It draws on and summarizes Melo (2015).

1. In the exchange, Michel Rocard cited Nobel Prize winner Maurice Allais as espousing his views about the "scandalously low" salaries in the Caribbean. Throughout the chapter I refer to the European countries as the EU even though it was initially the EC.

2. This section is taken from Melo (2015, section 2).

3. Throughout, the conflict was about Cavendish or dessert bananas. These are homogeneous and are always packed in boxes of seventeen kilograms. During the conflict, the per-ton costs of bananas—free on rail (FOR) or free

on truck (FOT)—of the low-cost suppliers were between $150 and $200 per ton; the costs of the Windward Islands suppliers were $500 per ton and in Martinique $700 per ton (Vanzetti, Fernandez, and Chau 2004; Borrell 1999). Chiquita sourced its bananas from MFN suppliers; Dole, the second largest seller in the EU market, sourced largely from ACP producers.

4. The Treaty of Rome almost collapsed when West Germany, which had no colonies, insisted on being exempt from applying the 20 percent bound tariff on bananas negotiated under the Dillon Round. This was possible before the SEM since Article 113 allowed countries to have their own quotas and in effect their own trade policies. Thus the Benelux and other North European countries applied the CET, while Germany imported bananas at zero tariff under a special protocol of the Treaty of Rome that permitted unrestricted imports of bananas. Interestingly, Germany (supported by Belgium and the Netherlands) lost a case challenging the banana trade regime adopted in July 1993 (see table 15-2) denying the direct effect of GATT provisions. When the GATT was replaced by the WTO with its enhanced dispute settlement power, WTO decisions could no longer be rejected, as they could under the GATT.

5. Several studies have calculated the rents accruing to license holders and the associated welfare costs to EU consumers of both the old BTR and the one adopted under the Common Organization of the Market for Bananas (COMB). Borrell (1999) estimated an annual welfare loss of $2 billion per year associated with the COMB (an increase of 20 percent relative to the old regime) compared to free trade. Messerlin (2001) estimated a loss of 582 million European Currency Units (ECUs) for 1990. Badinger, Breuss, and Mahlberg (2001) give estimates by categories of countries comparing the costs of the COMB with those in the previous BTR regime based on trend projections.

6. Under the COMB, banana suppliers were put into three quota categories, with quotas going directly to established banana traders in the EC (see table 15-3). ACP suppliers were exempt from the tariff on their quota allocations. Traders of ACP bananas had to purchase the higher-priced ACP bananas in order to sell their bananas in the EU market.

7. Of course, in spite of the large campaign contributions by the banana traders to both Democrat and Republican parties, the USTR denied any link between his decision and campaign contributions. In the late 1990s, Chiquita became the third largest contributor to political campaigns (Cadot and Webber 2002).

8. Article XIII on the allocation of quotas stipulates that they should be applied on a proportional basis to all members with a "substantial interest"— defined as at least a 10 percent market share. The panel found that quota allocations had been fair only for Colombia (21 percent) and Costa Rica (23 percent)

but not for other suppliers with substantial interests. The EU was also found to be unfair in its allocations to countries with "nonsubstantial" interests.

9. This position was reflected in the report submitted by NERA Economic Consulting on behalf of Oxford Policy Management to DFID (see their TO equivalent estimates in table 3 below).

10. This agreement was to be formalized at the Doha Ministerial: it formally linked the EU's pledge to move to a TO regime by 2006 with obtaining waivers from GATT Articles I (MFN) and XIII (how to apply nondiscriminatory QRs) requested by the EU to cover special treatment for ACP countries under the Cotonou Agreement as part of a transitional arrangement extending to 2007. Read (2004) clearly explains the issues surrounding the waivers. He also points out that if the EC did not reach agreement with the MFN suppliers on market access, and it wanted to rebind its TRQ at a level above €75 per ton, it would have to compensate the MFN suppliers. Even though the MFN suppliers could withdraw "substantially equivalent concessions," it is unlikely to have led to a desirable outcome because the MFN countries would have had to impose such high tariffs on EU imports that they would have been substantially hurting themselves in the process. Furthermore, since Article XVIII on rebinding does not provide derogation from Article I, compensatory concessions would have had to be applied to all countries.

11. The WTO summed up the decision as follows: "The Doha Ministerial decision essentially transformed a bilateral agreement into a binding multilateral commitment. In accordance with the terms of the April agreement, the US and Ecuador supported the EU's waiver request" (WTO, WT/MIN(01)/15).

12. As shown in the bottom part of table 15-2, a succession of MFN tariff rates to replace the TRQ were found to be WTO-incompatible, principally because MFN suppliers were not going to preserve previous market access. FAO (2004, table 4) shows the huge variation in claims by the various stakeholders when they submitted their estimate of the TO: at one end, MFN suppliers wanted a tariff of less than €75 per ton and at the other over €300 for EU banana importers.

13. If the EU intended to set the new tariff at €75 per ton, no rebinding would be necessary and Article XXVIII negotiations would not be called for. Anything higher would involve a rebinding and must accordingly follow Article XVIII procedures. These are: (i) providing of information by the EU on the method used to calculate the new tariff level and, following the announcement of its intentions, (ii) allowing any interested party to request arbitration should a negotiated solution fail to be reached.

14. This section draws on Cadot and Webber's (2002) excellent review of the politics behind the EU-US transatlantic dispute.

15. Cadot and Webber note that Geest, the large British banana importer, had participated in British banana policy since the 1950s. The European Court of Justice rejected an attempt by the German government (supported by Belgium and the Netherlands) to have consumer interests prevail.

16. Contributing directly to electoral funding is less costly and less uncertain in terms of resources than expending resources on legal spending to change domestic legislation. Also, there were at most three contestants, which also reduces spending for a given probability of success. (In a Cournot model where n symmetric contestants vie for a rent of amount R with equal probability of success, per-contestant expenditure will be given by $X = R(n-1)/n$.)

REFERENCES

Badinger, H., F. Breuss, and B. Mahlberg. 2001. "Welfare Implications of the EU's Common Organization of the Market in Bananas for EU member States." *Journal of Common Market Studies* 40 (3): 515–26.

Barfield, S. 2003. "Multilateral Agreement on an EU Banana Trade Regime—a Political Compromise." Mimeo.

Borrell, B. 1999. "Bananas: Straightening Out Bent Ideas on Trade as Aid." Canberra, Australia: Center for International Economics.

Borrell, B., and M. Bauer. 2004. "EU Banana Drama: Not Over Yet." Canberra, Australia: Center for International Economics.

Borrell, B., and K. Hanslow. 2004. "Banana Supply Elasticities." Canberra, Australia: Center for International Economics.

Cadot, O., and Douglas Webber. 2002. "Banana Splits: Policy Process, Particularistic Interests, Political Capture, and Money in Transatlantic Trade Politics." *Business and Politics* 4 (1): 5–39.

Commission of the European Community. 2004. "Communication from the Community on the Modification of the European Community Import Regime for Bananas." Brussels.

Food and Agriculture Organization (FAO). 2003. "The World Banana Economy: 1985–2002." Rome.

———. 2004. "Bananas: Is There a Tariff-Only Equivalent to the EU Tariff Rate Quota Regime? Insights from Economic Analysis." Trade Policy Technical Notes 3. Rome.

Feenstra, R. 2003. *Advanced Theory of International Trade: Theory and Evidence.* Princeton University Press.

Guyomard, H., C. Laroche, and C. Le Mouël. 1999. "An Economic Assessment of the Common Market Organization for Bananas in the European Union." *Agricultural Economics* 20 (2): 105–20.

McCorriston, S. 2000. "Market Structure Issues and the Evaluation of the Reform of the EU Banana Regime." *World Economy* 23 (7): 923–37.

Magee, S., W. Brock, and L. Young. 1978. *Black Hole Tariffs and Endogenous Policy Theory: Political Economy in General Equilibrium*. Cambridge University Press.

Melo, J. de. 2012. "Bananas, the GATT, the WTO and US and EU Domestic Politics." FERDIWP Working Paper 54. Clermont-Ferrand, France. https://ferdi.fr/dl/df-siD4wkjANUc8dDEWa5k6UMkG/ferdi-p54 -bananas-the-gatt-the-wto-and-us-and-eu-domestic-politics.pdf.

———. 2015. "Bananas, the GATT, the WTO and US and EU Domestic Politics." *Journal of Economic Studies* 42 (3): 377–99.

Melo, J. de, and J. M. Grether. 2005. "Assessing the EU's Banana's Conversion Proposal." Mimeo, University of Geneva.

Messerlin, P. 2001. *Measuring the Cost of Protection in Europe: European Commercial Policy in the 2000s*. Washington, D.C.: Institute for International Economics.

NERA Economic Consulting & Oxford Policy Management. 2004. *Addressing the Impact of Preference Erosion in Bananas on Caribbean Countries*. Report for the UK Department for International Development.

Raboy, D. 2004. "Calculating the Tariff Equivalent to the Current EU Banana Regime." Mimeo, NOVA Communtiy College; Walter Reed National Medical Center/Bolling Air Force Base, Central Texas College.

Read, R. 2004. "Establishing a Flat Tariff on Bananas." Mimeo, Brussels.

Swedish Ministry of Agriculture. 2004. "A Tariff Only Regime for Bananas— Why the Tariff Rate Should Be Set at a Low Level." Mimeo.

United Conference on Trade and Development (UNCTAD). 2003. "Major Developments and Recent Trends in International Banana Marketing Structures." Mimeo.

Vanzetti, D., S. Fernandez, and V. Chau. 2004. "Banana Split: How EU Policies Divide Global Producers." Mimeo, UNCTAD.

16

UNILATERAL LIBERALIZATION WITHIN THE GATT/WTO SYSTEM

JOSEPH MICHAEL FINGER

The past is never dead. It's not even past.

WILLIAM FAULKNER

The motivational framework for the conference honoring Patrick Messerlin that this paper was originally prepared for contrasted trade policy reforms in the 1980s and early 1990s with further, more recent, reform
efforts. Whereas the action in the 1980s and early 1990s was mostly unilateral, with some countries "using" trade agreements/GATT as a mechanism to lock in/motivate reforms, more recently effort has been put into
reforming through the mechanism of trade agreements (i.e., on a quid pro
quo basis). This raises the question whether attempts to liberalize through
reciprocal negotiations have been successful. Several participants at the conference noted that the WTO has not been a driver of liberalization and
also questioned the extent to which regional agreements have done much

better in generating significant liberalization. The framework then suggests that more attention should be given to unilateral reform, giving rise to something along the lines of "21st-Century Trade Policy: Back to the Past?," which indeed became the title of this volume.

The theme is certainly suggestive, and my aim in this essay is to build on it in a particular way. I elaborate the point that "unilateral reforms"— reforms *not* made by negotiation and acceptance of an international agreement—can be reasonably interpreted as part of the World Trade Organization (WTO) system. More broadly, I call attention to national decision processes related to trade policy, and to how the reformers that drive national liberalization use the WTO rules and procedures to advance "unilateral" liberalization. A liberal international trading system is one in which GATT/WTO principles of governance are incorporated into national management of trade policy. It is not one in which international rules are policed by a supranational authority. I draw on recent research on Latin American trade reforms to illustrate these points.

"UNILATERAL" DOES NOT MEAN SEPARATE
FROM THE GATT/WTO SYSTEM

Much of contemporary analysis has been in the frame of thought that Kyle Bagwell and Robert Staiger label "the political economy of trade reform." One key premise of this approach, they point out, is that "most trade-policy decisions that governments face today arise in the context of a variety of international commitments that must be considered; hence, the study of commercial policy in international trade has in effect become the study of trade agreements, in which the GATT/WTO plays a central role" (Bagwell and Staiger 2010, 224).[1]

Regarding the Latin American liberalization experiences my colleagues and I have studied over the past decade,[2] this statement is both descriptively incorrect and analytically misleading. Liberalization was not fashioned through the process of reciprocal bargaining, but through national processes in which reform leaders were able to change the domestic political economy of trade policy so that it supported liberalization. How these reform leaders used international negotiations to support the reform process is an important part of the story.

The same applies to the application by Latin American governments of GATT/WTO rules on antidumping and other trade remedies. These governments were not bargaining over the content of the rules. When the reforms were put in place, all except Mexico were GATT-contracting parties and hence had already accepted (and sometimes ignored) the international law obligations of those rules. They were using the rules—as they existed—as part of the *national politics* of closing down the plethora of ad hoc mechanisms that had accumulated and to restructure domestic policy-making institutions to ensure that the philosophies and interests that supported the ongoing reforms would have a voice in the management of pressures for protection that might arise in the future.[3] How reform leaders used international rules to support the reform process is another important part of the story.

A principal conclusion from the Latin American studies is that trade policy reform has been at its core a national decision. To think simply of the WTO as a forum in which members "decide" to reduce trade restrictions or as a set of rules specifying what a member can and cannot do overlooks a good deal of what makes the WTO system work.

VOICES FROM THE PAST

Another indication that the past is not yet past relates to two points, taken from two of my intellectual heroes of a prior generation. One of these is from Bela Balassa, who, in his path-breaking study of trade policy in developing countries, observed that "the existing system of protection in many developing countries can be described as the historical result of actions taken at different times and for different reasons. These actions have been in response to the particular circumstances of the situation, and have often been conditioned by the demands of special interest groups" (Balassa 1971, xv).

Starting from that observation, "reform" is not a matter of substituting one textbook strategy for another—for example, export-oriented development for an import substitution strategy. To presume that what is in place is a coherent strategy is to give away a major part of the case against it. As Balassa pointed out, policies in place often have no overall purpose or logic. Achieving coherence—meaning, simply, discipline with respect to *any* overall strategy—is perhaps a greater challenge than choosing one strategy over another. The history of Argentina's trade policies shows that Raul Prebisch's "*dependencia*" theory came after Juan Perón's economic "policies" were in place, not before. In the institutionalist perspective that I am finding more and more valuable, one of the old truths is that *academic scribblers draw more from madmen in authority than vice versa.*

Had Balassa allowed the policy situations he sought to reform to call themselves "coherent strategies," he would have been giving up a key part of his argument.[4]

The other point I take from Robert E. Hudec. In much of his work, Hudec framed the GATT/WTO agreements as commitment by participants to apply only approved methods of trade control, and to subject these controls to a long-term process of discipline through reciprocal negotiations.[5] In the language of mathematical programming, Hudec's view might be thought of as the logical "dual" to the more familiar view of the GATT/WTO system as a process of negotiating trade disciplines.

How the GATT/WTO system supported the domestic politics of eliminating the plethora of restrictions that Latin American countries had accumulated was an important part of trade reform there. Most of these countries had in place instruments for a protection seeker to choose among, often administered by different ministries or subministries. Adopting GATT-sanctioned trade remedies facilitated the closing down of these instruments; taking them on one-by-one would have been impossible.

"LOCKING IN" IS ABOUT DOMESTIC INSTITUTIONS

Hudec's perspective leads to one of the important conclusions of our studies in Latin America: for a country to use the modern value-chain economy as a vehicle for development, WTO rules and other policy disciplines must have operational content in *national* institutions. It would take years, for example, for a company that had been overcharged by customs to get recourse under the WTO tariff bindings, and thus would be of no commercial value either to the exporting company or to the importing company. Likewise for misuse of other trade controls—those the GATT/WTO system allows and those it does not.

The case of Argentina brings out the negative side of this point; it demonstrates that accepting GATT/WTO legal obligations does not lock them in as national policy.[6] Argentina, in becoming a charter WTO member in 1995, accepted all of the obligations of the Uruguay Round agreements. Furthermore, under the Argentine constitution, such treaties are self-enacting, automatically becoming part of the Argentine legal system.[7] Even so, these international law obligations did not prevent the administrations of Presidents Néstor Kirchner and Cristina Kirchner from imposing a highly restrictive trade regime, primarily through a return to "off-the-books" restrictions applied through processes not sanctioned by the GATT/WTO system. They are the sort of ad hoc measures that Balassa warned against, many having no formal existence in Argentine law or regulation and no identifiable fingerprint in Argentine administrative records.

Baracat and others (2013) document such practices as far back as 2003. One example is that shipments of books were not released from customs until Argentine book companies presented the government with business plans showing how they would modify their product lines so that all books written or edited in Argentina could and would be printed in Argentina. A common element in the actions was that the eventual release of imports depended on reaching agreement with the government on commitments to countertrade, to substitute in the future domestic products for previously imported ones, and sometimes to make investments in domestic facilities.[8]

Not until 2012 did a WTO member (the EU, joined by several other members) enter a complaint under the WTO dispute settlement process. The informality of Argentine practices and procedures complicated the WTO judicial process. As there was no journal record of the Argentine restrictions, the eventual Panel and Appellate Body investigations had to draw on information from news reports, and sometimes government press releases, for evidence. Part of Argentina's response to the legal challenge was that the investigation presented no evidence from Argentine law or regulation that the practices in question existed.

The Panel and the Appellate Body reports were adopted in January 2015—finding against Argentina. The WTO dispute settlement web page says that the EU and Argentina agreed that until December 31, 2015 would be a "reasonable period of time" for Argentina to bring its practices into conformity.[9] If by then Argentina had not satisfied the complaining members that it had brought its practices into conformity, the dispute settlement process would take up the determination of appropriate retaliation. In sum, illegal import practices in place at least since 2003 were still in place as of August 2015 and would not be subject to WTO-authorized action until well into 2016.

PERU: ENTERING THE GLOBAL ECONOMY WITH CONFIDENCE

When Lester Maddox was governor of the US state of Georgia (1967–1971) someone asked him for his views on prison reform. Governor Maddox replied, "If we are going to have better prisons, the first thing we will need is a better class of prisoner." Alberto Fujimori was president of Peru from 1990 to 2000. When asked for his views on trade policy reform, President Fujimori replied, "If we are going to have better trade policy, the first thing we will need is a better class of trader." Those statements dramatize an important point: exposure of domestic business people to the competition and opportunities of international markets will lead to economic advancement only if the local business community is up to it.

Alberto Fujimori became president of Peru in the context of one of the most severe economic and political crises in the country's history. Fujimori was not elected on a liberal platform, but during the election campaign of 1990, candidate Mario Vargas Llosa's liberal message was no longer regarded as a rationalization for big business and became, instead, a legitimate argument in favor of the national interest. Fujimori's lack of political ties or debts, his practical way of perceiving things, and the situation of emergency led him into the liberal path (Webb Camminati, and León Thorne [2006] elaborate).

President Fujimori drew extensively on the Asian example to build the political momentum for reform. As president, he paid close attention to the relationships with the Pacific Basin economies. On his initiative the government used participation in Asia-Pacific Economic Cooperation (APEC) meetings to provide Peruvian business leaders opportunities to network with Asian business leaders. He took Peruvian business people to the meetings, hoping they would come away thinking as boldly and as optimistically as the Asians they met.

Alejandro Toledo, who in 2001 replaced Fujimori as president (Valentín Paniagua served seven months as president of the transition government after Fujimori fled Peru in 2000), continued to pursue the reforms. One astute Peruvian said to me, "Toledo had not many alternatives. It was either push the correct/publicly acclaimed green button or the disaster red button."

Alan García, in his first term as president, from 1985 to 1990, had supported protectionist policies. Peruvian reforms had taken hold by the time he was elected a second time, in 2006. This time he voiced optimism about Peru's future in the global economy. He expressed an eagerness to "climb up on the wave of growth" and a confidence to "ride the tiger," to deal with the United States in the legalistic terms that characterize US dealings on international trade, and to come out the better for it. Translated into English, the title of Garcia's 2011 memoir is "Against Economic Fear: Believe in Peru."

Taking on this Asian approach to world markets was a departure for Peru from the restraint often observed in the Latin American business community. When reform began, Peru was a member of the Community of Andean Nations (CAN), whose economics included a plan for a negotiated agreement on which members would produce which products for the entire community, thus providing guarantees against competition from outside the CAN, or even from other CAN producers. (The plan—either to reduce intra-CAN restrictions or to divide the market—was minimally implemented.) The original plan for Mercosur provided for a similar division of the market that Argentine and Brazilian producers would negotiate, but that part of the plan was thrown out by Argentina's minister of the economy, Domingo Cavallo, during the reforms of the early 1990s (Botto and Bianculli 2009, 107).

A similar point was made by Eleanor Hadley, an economist at the US Tariff Commission when I met her some years back. Hadley had been the only economist and the only woman on General Douglas MacArthur's civilian staff when he commanded the US occupation of Japan after World War II. According to her, the staff's economic plan for Japan was in large part about agriculture. Recognizing, however, that Japan lacked sufficient fuel and minerals to be self-sufficient, the plan called for Japan to have an industry that would exchange simple manufactures with other Asian countries for the needed materials. When the plan was presented to the Japanese business community, the community objected strenuously. They saw themselves as capable of competing in any market in the world and were insulted to be presumed competent only in the poor (at the time) markets of Asia.

In Peru, reform leaders drew on the Asian example for a general sense of what to do, but perhaps more important, to buoy Peruvian self-confidence that they could succeed as part of the global economy. Their approach also provided a means to communicate to the public what the reforms—and their results—would be.

TRADE NEGOTIATIONS TO BUILD DOMESTIC
MOMENTUM FOR REFORM

Another way in which Peruvian leaders built enthusiasm for integrating Peru into the global economy was to initiate trade talks with the United States. With passage of the Andean Trade Preference Act (ATPA) in 1991, the United States unilaterally offered Andean countries limited preferential access to the US market in exchange for cooperation on the US effort to suppress the drug trade. Peruvian participation was initiated in 1991, but the economic benefits were minor. In 2001, when Peruvian participation was up for renegotiation, Peruvian leaders saw an opportunity. The US initiative for a Free Trade Area of the Americas (FTAA) was going nowhere, and the US trade representative, Robert Zoellick, responded favorably when Peru suggested the negotiation of a free trade agreement between the United States and Peru.

Entering into negotiations with the United States attracted attention in Peruvian politics far beyond Peruvian participation in WTO negotiations. As one Peruvian observed to me, large countries such as the United States, India, and Brazil can use leadership in WTO negotiations as part of the management of their domestic politics of trade policy, but their doing so takes away the same opportunity for smaller countries.

Peru has maintained this source of momentum by negotiating trade agreements with a number of additional countries, including Canada, Chile, China, Costa Rica, Japan, Korea, Mexico, Panama, and Singapore, as well as the European Free Trade Association and the European Union.

The influence of these negotiations on the *content* of Peru's reforms is taken up next.

A NEW TRADE MINISTRY ORIENTED TOWARD THE WORLD

Within this environment Peruvian reform leaders were able to introduce major changes in the institutions for managing trade policy. One of these was to close the existing trade ministry and replace it with a new one, the Ministerio de Comercio Exterior y Turismo (MINCETUR). The old ministry's identity and orientation had been reflected in the CAN—a reluctance to take on the challenges and opportunities of world markets, and an acceptance of collaboration among businesses as a form of economic organization. MINCETUR drew its orientation from the then ongoing negotiations with the United States. Its associations are with the parts of Peruvian society that are interested in and confident about Peru's place in the world.[10]

USING *ONLY* GATT/WTO-APPROVED METHODS
OF TRADE POLICY MANAGEMENT

An important and early part of trade policy reform was the installation of GATT/WTO-sanctioned trade remedies (safeguards, antidumping, countervailing duties) as the mechanisms through which the government would formalize management of domestic pressures for protection. Effective administration of the new laws and procedures would require more than technical expertise; it would also require independence from political power. Moreover, the culture of decisionmaking would have to change from one in which decisions were based on long-standing relationships to one in which decisions were based on the facts of economic potential.

To this end, in 1992 the Fujimori government created by law the Instituto Nacional de Defensa de la Competencia y de la Protección de la Propiedad Intelectual, Indecopi (National Institute for the Defense of Competition and the Protection of Intellectual Property). Indecopi's overall responsibility is to maintain a competitive market economy in Peru. Organizationally, it is a collection of autonomous commissions that provide the functional and regulatory frameworks for competition policy, intellectual property, small business development, and other parts of the infrastructure of a market economy. One of its commissions, the Antidumping and Countervailing Measures Commission, is responsible for antidumping and countervailing duty investigations and for the imposition of remedies. This commission is also the investigating authority for safeguard cases, the final decision on such cases being made by a multisector commission consisting of several ministers.[11]

Through Indecopi, the government of Peru has introduced the procedural standards of the WTO into domestic decisionmaking. Indecopi recognizes the rights and participation of interested parties; investigations and decisions follow previously specified procedures and criteria. Because trade remedies and competition policy are regulated through one umbrella agency, the conflict that Patrick Messerlin has identified in the EU—import protection reinforcing the position of concentrated industries—has not arisen as a problem (see, e.g. Messerlin 2001; Messerlin 1990; Bourgeois and Messerlin 1998; Hindley and Messerlin 1996).

MAINTAINING A LIBERAL RULE-OF-LAW SYSTEM IN PERU

Peru has been one of the most successful countries at confining protectionist pressures within formal trade remedy mechanisms and in maintaining discipline over new restrictions. The 2015 WTO Director General's Report on trade measures (WTO 2015, the press release for which was titled "Increasing Stockpile of Trade-Restrictive Measures 'a Cause for Concern'") reports no new restrictions by Peru. To the contrary, it lists a number of Peruvian liberalizations: elimination of import tariffs on 1,089 tariff lines, elimination of import clearance duties, and termination of two antidumping measures.

A critical part of how Peru has sustained its reforms is how leaders there have insisted that all pressures for protection be channeled through Indecopi. All the new controls that Peru has imposed since its 1990s reforms have been Indecopi-administered antidumping or countervailing measures. (Global Trade Alert data; Baracat and others [2015] provide details). As of June 30, 2014, Peru had in place no countervailing duties and only 13 antidumping measures in force, as compared with 242 antidumping and 52 countervailing measures in the United States, 208 antidumping and 2 countervailing measures in India, 125 antidumping and 6 countervailing measures in China, and 117 antidumping and 14 countervailing measures in the EU (WTO 2014a. 2014b).

Leaders interviewed by Baracat and others (2015) indicated that there had been pressures for off-the-books actions, some of them from powerful Peruvian interests. Saying "No. Go to Indecopi" has been in significant part an exercise in political courage by high officials.[12]

Again the records of Peru and Argentina provide a striking contrast. Argentina created agencies and instruments similar to those created in Peru, but this did not prevent the governments of Presidents Néstor Kirchner and Cristina Kirchner from reintroducing a protectionist regime through the application of informal measures. Using WTO-approved instruments of trade control is not the same as using *only* WTO-approved instruments.[13]

TWO VISIONS OF A LIBERAL INTERNATIONAL TRADING SYSTEM

Consider these alternative visions of a liberal international economic order:

- Vision One, in which authority over the instruments of trade control is ceded to a supranational authority, examples being trade among the fifty states of the United States or among the twenty-eight member states of the European Union.

- Vision Two, in which no national government imposes more than minimal restrictions on the freedom of its citizens to engage in economic transactions with citizens of other countries.

Consider as well these alternative views of how a liberal international trading system will continue to advance:

> The challenge of deepening global trade liberalization had become much less of a traditional mercantilist undertaking and more a task of providing a global public good, with all the sovereignty issues and free-rider complications that such an endeavor entails." (Zedillo 2007, 2)

> The most likely way a global polity will be created is gradually and bottom-up, by the work of millions of entrepreneurs, financiers, and Facebook friends who partner up across borders. . . . Leaders cannot abandon aspects of national sovereignty that their peoples treasure, but they can facilitate the transition to cooperation when the need is clear." (Hufbauer and Suominen 2010, 4)

The first is from Ernesto Zedillo, former president of Mexico, who has chaired the United Kingdom Department for International Development's (DFID) Global Trade and Financial Architecture Project and co-chaired the International Task Force on Global Public Goods.[14] The second is from Gary C. Hufbauer and Kati Suominen's book on globalization. Zedillo, in a review, criticized Hufbauer and Suominen for "their vague as well as naïve proposition that changes to the governance of the global economy will happen bottom up within the system" (Zedillo 2011, 558).

Vision Two and the Hufbauer-Suominen interpretation of how the liberal system is advanced see international cooperation not as a creator and enforcer of international law and rules, but as a means through which reform leaders can change the political economy of trade policy within their countries. The GATT/WTO system's governance principles bring participation of interested parties and rule of law into the national determination of trade policies. Indeed, it is the mercantilist perspective—exports being the gains from trade and imports the costs—that creates the illusion of trade liberalization creating economic free riders, and removing trade restrictions as a sacrifice of sovereignty to foreigners rather than a sacrifice of the liberty of citizens to choose whom they deal with.

For many (perhaps most) of the WTO's members the increasing incorporation of Hudec's principle—that *only* approved methods of trade control should be used—into national trade politics will continue to offer better support for integrating their economies productively into the international economy than will reciprocal exchanges with other countries or the creation of supranational authority over trade policies. The Western European model of policy formation by creating a supranational authority does not describe the economic histories of many of WTO's members.

Robert Wolfe has pointed out that the death of the Doha Round does not mean that the WTO is dead. To think simply of the WTO as a negotiation to determine what a member can and cannot do overlooks a good deal of what makes the WTO system work. Wolfe reminds us that the 1995 Agreement Establishing the World Trade Organization specifies its first function as facilitating the application and furthering the objectives of the WTO agreements (Wolfe 2015, 22). Peru's experience shows that much of this is accomplished through domestic institutions rather than through WTO policing.

The spread of the value-chain economy makes Vision Two—that no national government should impose more than minimal restrictions on the freedom of its citizens to engage in economic transactions with citizens of other countries—the more promising vision.

NOTES

1. A broader social science explanation for this presumption might include the attractiveness or romance of studying international negotiations and the availability of Nash-Dixit bargaining models. Peter Bauer (another voice from the past) sometimes reminded development economists that "The poor are a gold mine!" Today he might say, "The WTO is a gold mine!"

Harry Johnson divided economists into three categories: those who write theory papers, those who write policy papers, and those who administer policy—i.e., work for the government. To these three I would add a fourth: those who staff funding agencies—to whose perceptions in the end we all succumb.

2. Finger and Nogués (2006) covered Argentina, Brazil, Chile, Colombia, Costa Rica, Mexico, and Peru. A follow-up study, Baracat and others (2015), covered Peru and Argentina.

3. More generally, several Latin American governments attempted to move governance away from *cortoplacismo* (short-termism) toward a greater degree of *previsibilidad* (predictability): in other words, stability of expectations

about the rules of the game and about agreed procedures for changing them (Lowenthal 2011). Among regional leaders, Alejandro Foxley, Chile's former minister of economy and of foreign affairs, explained such a vision in his address to the Conference "Gobernabilidad y Desarrollo 2009" ("Governance and Development") in Asunción, Paraguay in 2009 (www.hacienda.gov.py/web -hacienda/pub003.pdf).

4. A lesson from developing country experience may be that developing country (and developed country) governance cannot avoid corruption or capture of import substitution policy instruments. Free trade—as textbook economics—might be imperfect, but it avoids this governance problem. This interpretation speaks against the value of "policy space" as a policy argument. Balassa might interpret it as an argument for freedom to create the sort of mess he found prevalent in the 1970s, when he began his work. Winston Churchill might assert that free trade is the worst trade policy, except for the others that have been tried. (Since writing this I have found a similar expression in Martin Wolf's book on globalization, though he generalizes to "the market economy (Wolf 2004, xii).

5. e.g., in Hudec 2011, p. 119–120. Kennedy and Southwick (2002) provide a bibliography of Hudec's work.

6. I am not arguing with this example that members do not comply with WTO rules. Other evidence shows that they usually do. The case of Argentina does suggest, however, that the explanation for this compliance lies deeper than the simple weight of international law.

7. The GATT/WTO agreements are not self-enacting in all member states. For example, under the US constitutional structure, "accepting" a new trade agreement involves Congress changing US law and regulations—such as those for applying technical standards or antidumping measures—to make them consistent with the new agreement (though the congressional act is usually explicit that if there remain differences, US law takes precedence). One should not presume that everybody else does just what the United States does; other countries' constitutional structures do things differently. Jackson, Louis, and Matsushita (1984) examine the differences.

8. Baracat and others (2015) analyze these as the output of the "informal sector of government"; the WTO Panel and Appellate Body reports on the Argentina cases label them "unwritten measures."

9. World Trade Organization, "DS438: Argentina–Measures Affecting the Importation of Goods," https://www.wto.org/english/tratop_e/dispu_e /cases_e/ds438_e.htm.

10. For an informative glimpse of Peru in the world, watch "Peru Visits Peru" at https://www.youtube.com/watch?v=qo_2vq8Gm_A&feature=iv&src _vid=fAqFJP4N4ME&annotation_id=annotation_141552 (or simply do a YouTube or web search for "Peru, Nebraska").

11. Webb, Camminati, and León Thorne (2006) describe Indecopi's structure and functioning as well as its antidumping and safeguard procedures.

12. Harberger (1993) also points out the importance of political courage in sustaining economic reforms.

13. Here is an example (paraphrased) from my own experience as the World Bank's initial tabulator of trade restrictions imposed against developing countries' exports. My telephone would ring, and the caller would ask, "Is this Dr. Finger?"

"Yes, might I help you?"

"Are you the Dr. Finger who knows how the developed countries restrict imports?"

"Yes, I am."

"Could you come and brief us on that? It never hurts to know another way to restrict imports."

14. This task force was initiated by the governments of France and Sweden. The governments of Germany, the United Kingdom, and Norway also provided funding.

REFERENCES

Bagwell, Kyle, and Robert W. Staiger. 2010. "The World Trade Organization: Theory and Practice." *Annual Review of Economics* 2: 223–56.

Balassa, Bela. 1971. *The Structure of Protection in Developing Countries*. Johns Hopkins University Press.

Baracat, Elías A., and others. 2013. *Sustaining Trade Reform: Institutional Lessons from Argentina and Peru*. Washington, D.C.: World Bank. https://openknowledge.worldbank.org/handle/10986/15794.

———. 2015. "Trade Reform and Institution Building: Peru and Argentina under the WTO." *World Trade Review* 14 (4): 579–615.

Botto, Mercedes, and Andrea Carla Bianculli. 2009. "The Case of Argentine Research in Building Regional Integration." In *The Politics of Trade: The Role of Research in Trade Policy and Negotiation*, edited by Diana Tussie, 83–120. Leiden: Martinus Nijhoff.

Bourgeois, Jacques, and Patrick Messerlin. 1998. "The European Community's Experience." In *Brookings Trade Forum 1998*, edited by Robert Z. Lawrence, 127–45. Brookings.

Curzon, Gerard. 1965. *Multilateral Commercial Diplomacy: The General Agreement on Tariffs and Trade and Its Impact on National Commercial Policies and Techniques*. London: Michael Joseph.

Faulkner, William. 1951. *Requiem for a Nun*. New York: Random House.

Finger, J. Michael. 2011. Review of *Dispute Settlement at the WTO: Developing Country Experience*, edited by Gregory C. Shaffer and Ricardo Meléndez-Ortiz. *Journal of World Trade* 45 (6): 1285–90.

Finger, J. Michael, and J. Nogués. 2006. *Safeguards and Antidumping in Latin America Trade Liberalization*. Washington, D.C.: World Bank and Palgrave Macmillan.

García Pérez, Alan. 2011. *Contra el temoreconómico. Creer en el Perú*. Lima: Planeta.

Harberger, Arnold C. 1993. "Secrets of Success: A Handful of Heroes." *American Economic Review* 83 (2): 343–50.

Hindley, Brian, and Patrick Messerlin. 1996. *Antidumping Industrial Policy: Legalized Protectionism in the WTO and What to Do about It*. Washington, D.C.: American Enterprise Institute.

Hudec, Robert E. 2011. *Developing Countries in the GATT Legal System*. Cambridge University Press.

Hufbauer, Gary Clyde, and Kati Suominen. 2010. *Globalization at Risk*. Yale University Press.

Jackson, John H., Jean-Víctor Louis, and Mitsuo Matsushita. 1984. *Implementing the Tokyo Round: National Constitutions and International Economic Rules*. University of Michigan Press.

Lowenthal, Abraham F. 2011. "Disaggregating Latin America: Diverse Trajectories, Emerging Clusters and Their Implications." *Brookings Research and Commentary*, November 1. www.brookings.edu/papers/2011/1101 _latin_america_lowenthal.aspx.

International Task Force on Global Public Goods. 2006. *Meeting Global Challenges: International Cooperation in the National Interest*. Final Report. Stockholm, Sweden.

Kennedy, Daniel L. M., and James D. Southwick. 2002. *The Political Economy of International Trade Law: Essays in Honor of Robert E. Hudec*. Cambridge University Press.

Koch, Karen. 1969. *International Trade Policy and the Law of GATT*. Indianapolis: Bobbs-Merrill.

Messerlin, Patrick A. 1990. "Anti-Dumping Regulations or Pro-Cartel Law." *World Economy* 13 (4): 465–92.

———. 2001. *Measuring the Costs of Protection in Europe*. Washington, D.C.: Institute for International Economics.

Regúnaga, Marcelo, and Agustín Tejeda Rodriguez. 2015. *Argentina's Agricultural Trade Policy and Sustainable Development*. Issue Paper 55. Geneva: International Centre for Trade and Sustainable Development.

Webb, Richard, Josefina Camminati, and Raúl León Thorne. 2006. "Anti-dumping Mechanisms and Safeguards in Peru." In *Safeguards and Anti-dumping in Latin American Liberalization: Fighting Fire with Fire*, edited by Michael Finger and Julio J. Nogués, 247–77. Washington, D.C.: World Bank and Palgrave Macmillan.

Wolf, Martin. 2004. *Why Globalization Works*. Yale University Press.

Wolfe, Robert. 2015. "First Diagnose, Then Treat: What Ails the Doha Round?" *World Trade Review* 14 (1): 7–28.

World Trade Organization. 2013. "Trade Policy Review Argentina." Record of the Meeting Addendum (This document contains the advance written questions, and replies provided by Argentina.) WT/TPR/M/277/Add.1 19, July.

———. 2014a. "Report (2014) of the Committee on Subsidies and Counter-vailing Measures." G/L/1077, October 28, 2014.

———. 2014b. "Report (2014) of the Committee on Anti-Dumping Prac-tices." G/L/1079, October 31.

———. 2015. "Report to the TPRB from the Director-General on Trade-Related Developments." WT/TPR/OV/W/9, July 3.

Zedillo, Ernesto. 2007. "Introduction," pp. 1–8 in In *Global Trade and Poor Nations: The Poverty Impact and Policy Implications of Liberalization*," edited by Bernard Hoekman and Marcelo Olarreaga, 1–8. Brookings.

———. 2011. Review of *Globalization at Risk*, by Gary Clyde Hufbauer and Kati Suominen." *World Trade Review* 10 (4): 557–59.

APPENDIX

SELECTED PUBLICATIONS BY PATRICK MESSERLIN

BOOKS AND MONOGRAPHS

1995 *La nouvelle organisation mondiale du commerce.* Collection IFRI-Repères. Paris: Dunod.

1996 *Antidumping Industrial Policy: Legalized Protectionism in the WTO and What to Do about It.* Washington, D.C.: American Enterprise Institute (with Brian Hindley).

1998 *Commerce international.* Collection Thémis. Presses Universitaires de France.

2001 *Measuring the Costs of Protection in the European Community.* Washington, D.C.: Peterson Institute for International Economics.

2002 *Harnessing Trade for Development and Growth in the Middle East.* New York: Council on Foreign Relations (with Bernard Hoekman).

2004 *The Audiovisual Services Sector in the GATS Negotiations. Washington, D.C.:* American Enterprise Institute (with Stephen Siwek and Emmanuel Cocq).

2005 *Trade for Development*, Report to the U.N. Secretary General Mr. Kofi Annan, Task Force of the Millennium Project. New York: United Nations (with Ernesto Zedillo and Julia Nielson).

2006 *Europe after the "No" Votes.* London: Institute for Economic Affairs.

2010 "The Law and Economics of Contingent Protection in the WTO" (with P. Mavroidis and J. Wauters).

2011 *The EU-Georgia Negotiations on a Deep and Comprehensive Free Trade Agreement.* Brussels: Center for European Policy Studies (with M. Emerson, G. Jandieri, and A. Le Vernoy).

2020 *North Korea and Economic Integration in East Asia.* London: Routledge (with Yeongseop Rhee).

EDITED VOLUMES

1990   *The Uruguay Round: Services in the World Economy.* Washington, D.C. and
       New York: World Bank and the UN Centre for Transnational Corpo-
       rations (with Karl Sauvant).

2010   *2020 European Agriculture: Challenges and Policies.* Washington, D.C.:
       German Marshall Fund (with Pierre Boulanger).

2018   *Potential Benefits of an Australia-EU Free Trade Agreement: Key Issues and
       Options.* University of Adelaide Press (with Jane Drake Brockman).

2019   *Cultural Practices and Policies in the Digital and Global Age.* Special issue
       of *Kritika Kultura* (with Hwy-Chang Moon).

2020   *Cultural Policy and Protectionism.* Special issue of *Global Policy* (with Hwy
       Chang Moon and Jimmyn Parc).

ARTICLES AND CONTRIBUTIONS TO BOOKS

1978   "De la théorie du dumping." *Revue économique* 29 (5): 789–818.

1980   "Libre-échange et protection transitoire." *Economie appliquée* 1: 161–89.

1981   "The Political Economy of Protectionism: The Bureaucratic Case." *Re-
       view of World Economics* 117 (3): 469–96.

1982   "Les déterminants de la demande de protection: le cas français." *Revue
       économique* 33 (6): 1001–23.

1986   "Export Credit: Mercantilism à la Française." *World Economy,* 9 (4):
       385–408.

1987   "Export Credit Subsidies." *Economic Policy* (April): 149–75 (with Jacques
       Mélitz).

1988   "Price, Quality, and Welfare Effects of European VERs on Japanese
       Autos." *European Economic Review,* 32 (7): 1527–46 (with Jaime de
       Melo).

1989   "The EC Antidumping Regulations: A First Economic Appraisal,
       1980–85." *Weltwirtschaftliches Archiv* 125 (3): 563–87.

1990   "Antidumping Regulation or Pro-Cartel Law? The EC Chemical Cases."
       World Economy 13 (4): 462–92.

1990   "Institutional Reform for Trade Liberalization." *World Economy* 13 (2):
       230–49 (with Sam Laird).

1991   "The EC Antidumping and Anticircumvention Regulations: The Case
       of Photocopiers. Nomura Research Institute of Tokyo (with Yoshiyuki
       Noguchi).

1993   "The EC and Central Europe: The Missed Rendezvous of 1992?" *Eco-
       nomics of Transition* 1 (1): 89–109.

1994 "Should Antidumping Rules Be Replaced by National or International Competition Rules?" *World Competition*, 18 (3): 37–54.

1995 "The Impact of Trade and Capital Movements on Labour: Evidence on the French Case." *OECD Economic Studies* 24: 89–124.

1996 "The US and EC Antidumping Policies." *Economic Journal* 105 (433): 163–78 (with Geoffrey Reed).

1996 "France and Trade Policy: Is the "French Exception" Passée?" *International Affairs* (April): 293–309.

1998 "The European Community's Experience." In *Brookings Trade Forum*, edited by Robert Z. Lawrence, 127–45 (with Jacques Bourgeois).

1998 "Antidumping Policies in Electronic Products." *Brookings Trade Forum*, edited by Robert Z. Lawrence, 147–71 (with Yoshiyuki Noguchi).

1998 "Has Article 90 ECT Prejudged the Status of Property Ownership?" In *State Trading in the 21st Century*, edited by T. Cottier and P. Mavroidis. University of Michigan Press (with Petros Mavroidis).

1999 "External Aspects of State Aids." *European Economy*. Reports and Studies, State Aid and Single Market (3): 161–95.

2000 "Liberalizing Trade in Services: Reciprocal Negotiations and Regulatory Reform." In *GATS 2000—New Directions in Services Trade Liberalization*, edited by Pierre Sauvé and Robert M. Stern. Washington, D.C.: Brookings Institution (with Bernard Hoekman).

2000 "Trade Facilitation: Technical Regulations and Customs Procedures." *World Economy* 23 (4): 577–93 (with Jamel Zarrouk).

2003 "Initial Conditions and Incentives for Arab Economic Integration: A Comparison with the European Community." In *Arab Economic Integration: Between Hope and Reality*, edited by A. Galal and B. Hoekman. Washington, D.C.: Brookings Institution (with Bernard Hoekman).

2004 "China in the World Trade Organization: Antidumping and Safeguards." *World Bank Economic Review*, 18 (1): 105–30.

2005 "Need for Coherence among the WTO's Escape Clauses." In *China's Participation in the WTO*, edited by H. Gao and D. Lewis. London: Cameron May.

2005 "Agricultural Liberalization in the Doha Round." *Global Economy Journal* 5 (4): 1–13.

2005 "Three Variations on 'The Future of the WTO.'" *Journal of International Economic Law* 8 (2): 299–309.

2005 "Trade, Drugs, and Health-Care Services. *The Lancet* 365: 1198–2000.

2006 "Enlarging the Vision for Trade Policy Space: Special and Differentiated Treatment and Infant Industry Issues." *World Economy* 29 (10): 1395–1408.

2006 "Assessing the Impacts of Export Subsidies." In *Agricultural Trade Reform and the Doha Development Agenda*, edited by Kym Anderson and Will Martin. Basingstoke, UK: Palgrave Macmillan (with Bernard Hoekman).

2006 "The Political Economy of Agriculture in the Doha Round." In *Economic Development and Multilateral Trade Cooperation*, edited by S. Evenett and B. Hoekman. Basingstoke, UK: Palgrave Macmillan.

2007 "Why Is It So Difficult? Trade liberalization under the Doha Agenda." *Oxford Review of Economic Policy* 23 (3): 347–66 (with Will Martin).

2008 "Redesigning the European Union's Trade Policy Strategy towards China." European Center for International Political Economy (with J. Wang).

2011 "The European Union Single Markets in Goods: Between Mutual Recognition and Harmonisation. *Australian Journal of International Affairs* 65, (4): 410–35.

2011 "Climate, Trade and Water: A 'Grand Coalition'?" *World Economy* 34 (11): 1883–1910.

2012 "Climate Change and Trade Policy: From Mutual Destruction to Mutual Support, *World Trade Review* 11 (1): 53–80.

2012 "The Influence of the EU in the World Trade System." In *The Oxford Handbook on the World Trade Organization*, edited by A. Narlikar, M. Daunton, and R. M. Stern. Oxford University Press.

2012 "The Much-Needed EU Pivoting to East-Asia." *Asia-Pacific Journal of EU Studies* 10 (2): 1–18.

2014 "United States Antidumping Measures on Certain Shrimps and Diamond Sawblades from China: Never Ending Zeroing in the WTO?" *World Trade Review* 13 (2): 267–79 (with Dukgeun Ahn).

2014 "The Effect of Screen Quotas and Subsidy Regime on Cultural Industry: A Case Study of French and Korean Film Industries. *Journal of International Business and Economy* 15 (2): 57–73 (with Jimmyn Parc).

2015 "TTIP: The Services Dimension." In *Rule-Makers or Rule-Takers? Exploring the Transatlantic Trade and Investment Partnership*, edited by D. Hamilton and J. Pelkmans, 341–70. London: Rowman and Littlefield.

2017 "The K-Pop Success: How Big and Why So Fast?" *Asian Journal of Social Sciences* 45 (4–5): 409–39 (with W. Shin).

2017 "The Real Impact of Subsidies on the Film Industry (1970s–Present): Lessons from France and Korea." *Pacific Affairs* 90 (1): 51–74 (with Jimmyn Parc).

2018 "In Search of an Effective Trade Policy for the Film Industry: Lessons from Korea." *Journal of World Trade* 52 (5): 745–64 (with Jimmyn Parc).

2019 "Building Consistent Policies on Subsidies in the Film Industry."
     Kritika Kultura 32 (1): 375–96.

2020 "Overcoming the Incoherent 'Grand Maneuver' in the French Film
     and TV Markets: Lessons from the Experiences in France and Korea."
     Global Policy 11 (S2): 31–39 (with Jimmyn Parc).

CONTRIBUTORS

Eddy Bekkers is research economist at the World Trade Organization focusing on quantitative trade modelling. Before he was a postdoctoral researcher at the World Trade Institute and assistant professor at the Johannes Kepler University in Linz. Bekkers holds a PhD from Erasmus University Rotterdam and masters in economics and econometrics from the University of Amsterdam. He conducts research on a wide range of topics in international trade: firm heterogeneity, gravity modeling, traded goods prices, food price pass through, trade conflicts, foreign affiliate sales and trade in services. He has published in peer-reviewed journals such as the *Economic Journal, European Economic Review, Canadian Journal of Economics, Review of International Economics*, and *World Economy*.

Chad P. Bown is the Reginald Jones Senior Fellow at the Peterson Institute for International Economics. His research examines international trade laws and institutions, trade negotiations, and trade disputes. With Soumaya Keynes, he cohosts *Trade Talks*, a weekly podcast on the economics of international trade policy. Bown previously served as senior economist for international trade and investment in the White House on the Council of Economic Advisers and most recently as a lead economist at the World Bank, conducting research and advising developing country governments on international trade policy for seven years. Bown was a tenured professor of economics at Brandeis University for twelve years and also spent a year as a visiting scholar in economic research at the World Trade Organization Secretariat in Geneva.

Olivier Cattaneo is head of the policy analysis and strategy unit at the Organization for Economic Co-operation and Development, Development Cooperation Directorate. He previously worked as a senior economist at the World Bank. He was responsible for trade policy at the Agence Française de Développement, has worked as an adviser and speechwriter to French ministers and members of Parliament, and as a trade expert in several international organizations. Cattaneo was a research associate with the Groupe d'Economie Mondiale de SciencesPo and has taught at various institutions, including Yale University where he was a World Fellow. A member of the New York Bar, he holds a PhD in international law from the Graduate Institute of International Studies in Geneva, and is a graduate of SciencesPo and Georgetown University.

Jaime de Melo is emeritus professor at the University of Geneva, academic advisor at the Geneva Business School, and senior fellow at the Fondation pour les Études et Recherches sur le Développement International (FERDI), a think tank whose primary, research-based purpose, is to influence the international discussion on major development issues. Before joining the faculty at the University of Geneva in 1993, Professor de Melo taught at Georgetown University, worked in the World Bank's research department, and consulted for the International Monetary Fund, the Organization for Economic Co-operation and Development, SECO, the International Growth Centre, the World Bank, and several governments. A founding member of the World Trade Institute, he has held several editorial positions and was editor-in-chief of the *World Bank Economic Review* from 2005 to 2010. His interests are in developing countries, particularly issues relating to trade policy, migration, and the environment.

Simon Evenett is professor of international trade and economic development at the University of St. Gallen and the coordinator of Global Trade Alert, the independent trade policy monitor. Over the past decade his research interests have focused on protectionism and how governments and firms seek to influence or respond to it. Professor Evenett obtained his PhD in economics from Yale University and a BA (Hons) from the University of Cambridge. He has taught at the Universities of Oxford and Michigan, was a (nonresident) senior fellow in the economic studies program at Brookings Institution, and has served twice as a World Bank official. Twice he has been the DLA Piper Distinguished Visiting Professor at

Johns Hopkins University. He regularly engages with private sector practitioners, government officials and other thought leaders.

Joseph Michael Finger was with the World Bank from 1980 to 2001, where he served as lead economist and chief of the Trade Policy Research Group, and was the World Bank's initial coordinator for the Integrated Framework for Trade-Related Technical Assistance to Least Developed Countries. He is known for his seminal work in several areas of international economics, including how the GATT/WTO system relates to development; development assistance within the WTO system; trade restrictions, such as safeguards and antidumping in Latin American trade liberalization; and the commercial value of intellectual property in poorer communities. Before his work at the World Bank, he held key positions at the US Treasury Department and UNCTAD. Mr. Finger held a PhD in economics from the University of North Carolina. He passed away in 2018.

Joseph Francois is managing director at the World Trade Institute and professor of international economics at the University of Bern. He is a CEPR Research Fellow and director of the European Trade Study Group. Previously he was professor of economics at Erasmus University Rotterdam, research economist for the World Trade Organization, and chief of research and acting director of economics for the US International Trade Commission. His current research interests include cross-border production chains and employment; globalization and inequality; trade in services; open economy growth and development; and trade and investment policy under imperfect competition, among others. He holds a PhD from the University of Maryland.

Jean-Jacques Hallaert is currently senior economist in the European department at the International Monetary Fund (IMF). From 2002 to 2008 he was in the IMF's Policy Development and Review department under the Trade Policy division. He has spent most of his career with international organizations, having served as a senior trade policy analyst working on Aid for Trade at the OECD's Trade and Agriculture Directorate, in between two substantial terms at the IMF. He previously was with the French Ministry of Finances in the Forecasting Directorate where he worked on macroeconomic analysis of Russia, Central and Eastern Europe as well as on the EU enlargement. He was a lecturer at SciencesPo, from which he also received his master's degree and PhD under the direction of Patrick Messerlin.

Bernard Hoekman is professor and director of global economics at the Robert Schuman Centre for Advanced Studies, European University Institute in Florence, Italy where he also serves as the dean for external relations. Previous positions include director of the International Trade Department (2008–2013) and research manager in the Development Research Group (2001–2008) at the World Bank. He was a member of the General Agreement on Tariffs and Trade Secretariat during the Uruguay Round of trade negotiations. A CEPR Research Fellow and a senior associate of the Economic Research Forum for the Arab countries, Iran and Turkey, he has been a member of several World Economic Forum Global Future Councils. A graduate of the Erasmus University Rotterdam, he holds a PhD in economics from the University of Michigan.

Anne O. Krueger is senior research professor of international economics at the Johns Hopkins University School of Advanced International Studies, and a senior fellow of the Center for International Development (of which she was founding Director) at Stanford University. She was first deputy managing director of the International Monetary Fund (2001–2006), served as vice president for economics and research at the World Bank (1982–1986) and has taught at Stanford and Duke Universities. She is distinguished fellow and past president of the American Economic Association and a senior research fellow of the National Bureau of Economic Research. She has published extensively on economic development, international trade and finance, and economic policy reform. Her most recent book is *International Trade: What everyone needs to know* (2020). She holds a BA from Oberlin College and a PhD from the University of Wisconsin.

Patrick Low is a consultant on trade and trade-related matters. From 1997 to 2013 he was the chief economist of the World Trade Organization, where he was responsible for overseeing the organization's research work and statistical services. Subsequently, he was vice president for research at the Fung Global Institute where he focused on the role of services in production and trade; he then taught on trade and climate change as adjunct professor at the

Hong Kong University Business School. In 2017 he directed the Asia Global Institute's inaugural AsiaGlobal Fellows Program. During the 1980s he worked in various capacities for the Secretariat of the General Agreement on Tariffs and Trade(GATT). He holds a PhD in economics from Sussex University and has written widely on trade policy issues.

Petros C. Mavroidis is the Edwin B. Parker Professor of Foreign and Comparative Law at Columbia Law School. He teaches the law of the World Trade Organization, where he was previously a member of the Legal Affairs division. He is also professor of law at the University of Neuchâtel, and a nonresident fellow at the European University Institute, Florence. His latest major publication is the book *The Regulation of International Trade*, a meticulous exploration of World Trade Organization agreements regulating trade in goods which won the 2017 Certificate of Merit in a Specialized Area of International Law from the Executive Council of the American Society of International Law. At Columbia Law he is a member of the Center on Global Governance.

Sébastien Miroudot is senior trade policy analyst in the Trade in Services division of the OECD Trade and Agriculture Directorate. Previously he was a research assistant at Groupe d'Economie Mondiale and taught in the master's degree programme at SciencesPo, Paris. In 2016–2017, he was visiting professor at the Graduate School of International Studies of Seoul National University. His research interests include trade in services, the relationship between trade and investment and the role of multinational enterprises in international trade. At the OECD his current work is on the measurement of trade in value-added terms and the trade policy implications of global value chains. He holds a PhD in international economics from SciencesPo.

Douglas Nelson is professor of economics at Tulane University. He is currently an external fellow of the Leverhulme Centre for Research on Globalisation and Economic Policy at the University of Nottingham. In addition to previous positions with the US Treasury and the World Bank, he has held regular faculty positions at Rutgers University, University of Texas-Dallas, and Syracuse University, and has held recent visiting positions at ETH-Zurich; University of Bayreuth; University of Bern; and the

European University Institute. His primary research interests are in the areas of political economy of trade policy, the empirical link between globalization and wages, and trade and trade policy under increasing returns to scale. He obtained his PhD from the University of North Carolina at Chapel Hill.

Hugo Rojas-Romagosa is a research economist at the World Bank. He worked as senior fellow researcher at the World Trade Institute in Bern (2018–2020), as a senior researcher at the CPB Netherlands Bureau for Economic Policy Analysis (2006–2018), and previously at the Central Bank of Costa Rica. He has consulted for national governments (Switzerland, United Kingdom) and many international organizations, including the World Bank, the IADB, UNCTAD, UNDP, ECLAC, OECD, the Vienna Institute for International Economic Studies, and INCAE Business School (Costa Rica). He obtained his PhD in economics from the Erasmus University Rotterdam. His research interests include international trade policy, quantitative trade analysis and CGE modeling, the effects of globalization on labor markets and income distribution, foreign direct investment, trade in value-added, and global supply chains.

Ben Shepherd is the principal of Developing Trade Consultants, an organization that aims to spur economic growth and development with evidence-based research and analysis. Prior to founding DTC in 2009, he was a postdoctoral research associate at Princeton University's Niehaus Center for Globalization and Governance. He has worked on a wide range of trade and development issues with organizations such as the World Bank, the OECD, the Asian Development Bank, the IDB, the United Nations, the World Trade Organization, and the Asia-Pacific Economic Cooperation. He specializes in providing policy-relevant research, as well as capacity-building seminars for researchers working in trade and development. His areas of expertise include trade policy, global value chains, trade facilitation and logistics, trade in services, and global trade modeling. He holds a PhD in economics from SciencesPo, Paris.

Erik van der Marel is a senior economist at the European Centre for International Political Economy (ECIPE) and associate professor at the Université Libre de Bruxelles (ULB). His expertise is in services trade, digital trade, and the free flow of data, including policy regulations in these areas. Prior to ECIPE, Professor van der Marel lectured at the London School of Economics. He received his PhD in economics from Sciences-Po Paris and his current work includes the development of the Digital Trade Restrictiveness Index (DTRI), which records digital trade policy restrictions for sixty-four countries. Van der Marel has also gained professional experience as a consultant economist at the World Bank since 2013, and as a guest lecturer at the World Trade Institute and the European University Institute.

Craig VanGrasstek has been a consultant since 1982, working in over four dozen countries on five continents. In addition to advising governments, corporations, and international organizations, he has taught politics at American University, trade at Harvard, and literature at Georgetown. His areas of expertise include the history and structure of the trading system; the policymaking process; and the relationships between trade, power, and development. VanGrasstek received his doctorate in politics from Princeton University, and holds degrees in international relations from Georgetown's School of Foreign Service and the University of Minnesota. He is the author of *The History and Future of the World Trade Organization* (2013), and *Trade and American Leadership: The Paradoxes of Power and Wealth from Alexander Hamilton to Donald Trump* (2019), among other publications.

L. Alan Winters is professor of economics and director of the UK Trade Policy Observatory in the University of Sussex. From 2008 to 2011 he was chief economist at the British government's Department for International Development, and from 2004 to 2007 he was director of the Development Research Group of the World Bank. Professor Winters was editor of *The World Trade Review* from 2009 to 2020. He has advised the OECD, the European Commission, UNCTAD, the World Trade Organization, and the IDB. Winters is a leading specialist on the empirical and policy analysis of international trade, including that of Europe and of developing countries and has published in areas such as regional trading arrangements, trade and poverty, nontariff barriers, European integration, transition economies' trade, international migration, agricultural protection and the world trading system.

Ernesto Zedillo is director of the Yale Center for the Study of Globalization; professor in the field of international economics and politics; professor of international and area studies; and professor adjunct of forestry and environmental studies at Yale University. He served as president of Mexico from 1994 to 2000. He is a member of The Elders, an independent group of global leaders using their collective experience and influence for peace, justice and human rights worldwide, as well as a member of the Group of 30. Zedillo is chairman of the Rockefeller Foundation Economic Council on Planetary Health, and an international member of the American Philosophical Society. He earned his bachelor's degree from the School of Economics of the National Polytechnic Institute in Mexico and his MA and PhD from Yale University.

INDEX

Figures and tables are indicated by f and t following the page number.